Theories
of Personality
and Psychopathology

Theories
of Personality
and Psychopathology

THIRD EDITION

edited by
Theodore Millon

Holt, Rinehart and Winston
New York Chicago San Francisco Philadelphia
Montreal Toronto London Sydney
Tokyo Mexico City Rio de Janeiro Madrid

Library of Congress Cataloging in Publication Data
Main entry under title:

Theories of personality and psychopathology.

  Rev. ed. of: Theories of psychopathology and
personality. 2nd ed. 1973.
  Includes bibliographies.
  1. Psychology, Pathological—Addresses, essays,
lectures. 2. Pesonality—Addresses, essays, lectures.
I. Millon, Theodore.
RC458.T47   1983   616.89   82–25843

ISBN 0-03-062629-3

CBS COLLEGE PUBLISHING
Holt, Rinehart and Winston
The Dryden Press
Saunders College Publishing

To the memory of my parents
Abner and Mollie Millon
who showed me how well
intelligence and compassion can blend

Preface

A full decade has passed since the publication of the second edition of this anthology. As with the first book, the second was extremely well-received, maintaining its prior popularity as a supplementary undergraduate text and its utility as a graduate reference work. A minor "classic," if you will, both editions have been securely ensconced on the shelves of tens of thousands of students and professionals, a success that owes most to the authors and the thoughtful essays they contributed.

Sufficient time has passed since the second edition to warrant a reappraisal of the major trends of the prior decade, and perhaps to identify several forerunners of current thought who failed to be included in earlier editions. Time enough has passed also to retire notions of the recent past whose viability can no longer be sustained. The opportunity arises as well to expand upon viewpoints which remain both durable and substantive.

Among the retirees are the two sections that were introduced anew in the second edition, namely theories categorized as "sociocultural" and "integrative." As noted in the preface to that edition, both perspectives were added somewhat reluctantly; my reservations appear now to have been justified. The popularity of the "community" approach has waned, in part a consequence of the almost inevitable downfall of academic movements prompted more by the values and aspirations of social idealism than by their intrinsic scientific or philosophic merit. No doubt to the chagrin of some, we have decided to delete the part devoted to sociocultural theories.

The "integrative" perspective, despite my personal preference for it as a frame of reference for a theory of man, has also failed to take hold as a coherent and systematic point of view. Although I cannot be other than pleased that barriers once rigidly separating divergent theories have been effectively broached, and that significant rapprochements among once competing orientations have begun in earnest, few synthesizers have had the courage or vision to bridge more than two alternative models. Hence, among the more popular movements of the day are those which admit of a connection between cognitive and behavioral treatment modalities; similar initiatives have also been pursued between such erstwhile opponents as those of psychoanalytic and behavioristic persuasions. Limited in scope though these ventures may be, they do represent steps in the right direction, and do ensure at the very least an increased receptivity to what former adversaries have had to say; it is hoped that they will lead also to a broadening of once insular perspectives. In order to reflect these delimited, yet nonetheless promising efforts at synthesis, a set of papers on integrative trends has been introduced as part of each of the four major orientations which embody the text. With the exception of the editor's final essay, these papers replace the section on integrative theories that comprised the last group of articles in the second edition.

A major shift in orientation that had hesitantly been introduced in the second edition is now vital to the present anthology. It relates to the increasingly pivotal, if not indispensable, role of personality as a construct relevant to psychopathology. This intertwining of subjects reflects only in part the fact that the present anthology was adopted in courses on personality almost as often as in those of abnormal psychology. More importantly, it signifies the ineradicable connection between personality and abnormal functioning, a relationship that had been slighted if not ignored in recent decades, but is being brought into increasingly sharp focus again both by clinicians and theorists. Nowhere is this resurrection more tangibly evident than in the decision to assign the "personality disorders" a key role in the multiaxial schema of the DSM III. Personality and its disorders have not only reemerged as fundamental to the understanding of other psychopathologies, but are now firmly rooted in their own right as a part of the official nosology. To mirror this renascence, as well as in recognition of the fact that most of the major theorists of psychopathology were, first and foremost, theorists of personality, we have retitled the anthology, *Theories of Personality and Psychopathology*; moreover, we have introduced contributions from both historic and modern personality pathology theorists such as Abraham, Reich, Kretschmer, Kohut, and Kernberg.

My historical researches have led me repeatedly to uncover concepts that clearly preceded ideas I thought originated afresh in my own formulations; such discoveries were made sometimes to my dismay, but more often to my gratification in that they signified that my observations and ideas were neither totally idiosyncratic nor, worse yet, illusory. Among many such precursors is Karl Jaspers, who argued as long ago as 1913 for the view that different theories of psychopathology are best ordered in terms of the methods they employ to gather their data. He wrote,

> I try to grasp each different view of the whole and give it a place according to its significance and limitations. . . . Every theory that aims at completeness will be taken as valid for that particular standpoint only. . . . In the end no more can be done than to order them according to the methods and categories by which they have been individually constructed.

It was with personally more significant forerunners in mind that I dedicated the first edition of this anthology to my parents. And it is with deep love and sadness now that I dedicate this third edition to their memory. *Zichrono l'vrocho*.

Coral Gables, Florida   Theodore Millon

Contents

Introduction   1

  1 On the Nature of Theory in Personality and Psychopathology   1
     Theodore Millon

PART I
Biophysical Theories   13

Orientation
  2 The Biological Approach to the Study of Personality   14
     Roger J. Williams

Etiology and Development
  3 The Physiogenic and Psychogenic in Schizophrenia   24
     Eugen P. Bleuler
  4 Genetic Theorizing and Schizophrenia   29
     Irving I. Gottesman and James Shields

Pathological Patterns
  5 Dementia Praecox and Manic-Depressive Disease   41
     Emil Kraepelin
  6 The Schizoid Temperament   46
     Ernst Kretschmer
  7 A Constitutional Typology   54
     William H. Sheldon

Therapeutic Approaches
  8 Diagnosis and Pattern of Reaction to Drug Treatment: Clinically Derived Formulations   69
     Donald F. Klein
  9 New Developments in Human Psychopharmacology   82
     H.M. Van Praag

Critical Evaluation
  10 The Myth of Mental Illness   92
     Thomas S. Szasz

Integrative Directions
  11 The Role of the Mental Factors in Psychiatry   99
     Adolf Meyer
  12 Schizotaxia, Schizotypy, Schizophrenia   103
     Paul E. Meehl

PART II
Intrapsychic Theories   117

Orientation
13   The Metapsychology of Instincts, Repression and the Unconscious   118
     Sigmund Freud

Etiology and Development
14   The Influence of Oral Erotism on Character-Formation   128
     Karl Abraham
15   Growth and Crises   134
     Erik H. Erikson

Pathological Patterns
16   Psychological Types   155
     Carl G. Jung
17   Some Circumscribed Character Forms   161
     Wilhelm Reich
18   Non-Productive Character Orientations   168
     Erich Fromm

Therapeutic Approaches
19   Borderline Personality Organization: Diagnosis and Treatment   174
     Otto Kernberg
20   The Psychoanalytic Treatment of Narcissistic Personality
     Disorders   183
     Heinz Kohut

Critical Evaluation
21   Logical Foundations of Psychoanalytic Theory   193
     Adolf Grünbaum

Integrative Directions
22   The Dynamics of Psychotherapy in the Light of Learning Theory   217
     Franz Alexander
23   Dynamic Psychotherapy and Behavior Therapy: Are They
     Irreconcilable?   225
     Judd Marmor

PART III
Phenomenological Theories   235

Orientation
24   Personal Construct Theory   236
     George A. Kelly

Etiology and Development
25   The Nature and Origin of Character   243
     Alfred Adler
26   The Development of Depression: A Cognitive Model   247
     Aaron T. Beck

Pathological Patterns
27 Meaninglessness: A Challenge to Psychologists 256
    Viktor E. Frankl
28 Existential Psychology 263
    Rollo May
29 Ontological Insecurity 271
    R.D. Laing

Therapeutic Approaches
30 Existential Analysis and Daseinsanalysis 283
    Ludwig Binswanger and Medard Boss
31 Persons or Science? A Philosophical Question 289
    Carl R. Rogers

Critical Evaluation
32 The Phenomenological Approach in Personality Theory:
    Some Critical Remarks 302
    M. Brewster Smith

Integrative Directions
33 From Orthodox Psychoanalysis to the Gestalt Approach 309
    Frederick S. Perls
34 The Practice of Rational-Emotive Therapy 314
    Albert Ellis

Part IV
Behavioral Theories 323

Orientation
35 Behavior Theory and the Models of Man 324
    Albert Bandura

Etiology and Development
36 Conditioned Emotional Reactions 336
    John B. Watson and Rosalie Rayner
37 Etiology of Human Neuroses 342
    Joseph Wolpe

Pathological Patterns
38 Behavioral Analysis: An Alternative to Diagnostic Classification 350
    Frederick H. Kanfer and George Saslow
39 What Is Psychotic Behavior? 361
    B.F. Skinner
40 Behavioral Approaches to Depression 372
    Charles B. Ferster

Therapeutic Approaches
41 Learning Theory and Behaviour Therapy 383
    H.J. Eysenck
42 Behavioral Psychotherapy: Theory and Practice 396
    Isaac M. Marks

Critical Evaluation

43   Critique and Reformulation of "Learning-Theory" Approaches to
Psychotherapy and Neuroses   407
Louis Breger and James L. McGaugh

Integrative Directions

44   New Conditions of Therapeutic Learning   427
John Dollard and Neal E. Miller
45   Multimodal Behavior Therapy: Treating the BASIC ID   433
Arnold A. Lazarus

Conclusion

46   An Integrative Theory of Personality and Psychopathology   441
Theodore Millon

Introduction

1 On the Nature of Theory in Personality and Psychopathology

Theodore Millon

Nature was not made to suit our need for a tidy and well-ordered universe. The complexity and intricacy of the natural world make it difficult not only to establish clearcut relationships among phenomena, but to find simple ways in which these phenomena can be classified or grouped. In our desire to discover the essential order of nature we are forced to select only a few of the infinite number of elements which could be chosen; in this selection we narrow our choice only to those aspects of nature which we believe best enable us to answer the questions we pose. The elements we have chosen may be labeled, transformed, and reassembled in a variety of ways. But we must keep in mind that these labels and transformations are not "realities." The definitions, concepts, and theories scientists create are only optional tools to guide their observation and interpretation of the natural world; it is necessary to recognize, therefore, that different concepts and theories may coexist as alternative approaches to the same basic problem. An illustration in the field of bridge design may serve to clarify this point (Hebb, 1958):

> The engineer who designs a bridge must think at different levels of complexity as he works. His overall plan is in terms of spans, piers, abutments; but when he turns to the design of a particular span, he starts to think in terms of lower-order units such as the I-beam. This latter unit, however, is still quite molar; an engineer is firmly convinced that an I-beam is just a special arrangement of certain molecules, the molecule in turn being a special arrangement of electrons, protons and so forth. Now note: At a microscopic level of analysis, a bridge is nothing but a complex constellation of atomic particles; and a steel I-beam is no more than a convenient fiction, a concession to the limitations of thought and the dullness of human conception.

Abridged from Chapter 2 of *Modern Psychopathology*, Philadelphia: W. B. Saunders Co., 1969.

At another level of analysis, of course, the I-beam is an elementary unit obviously real and no fiction. At this level electrons have a purely theoretical existence, which suggests that "reality" is meaningful as designating, not some ultimate mode of being about which there must be argument, but the mode of being which one takes for granted as the starting point of thought.

With this perspective in mind, let us look at the question, What is psychopathology? Clearly, mental disorders are expressed in a variety of ways; psychopathology is a complex phenomenon which can be approached at different levels and can be viewed from many angles. On a behavioral level, for example, disorders could be conceived of as a complicated pattern of responses to environmental stress. Phenomenologically, they could be seen as expressions of personal discomfort and anguish. Approached from a physiological viewpoint, they could be interpreted as sequences of complex neural and chemical activity. Intrapsychically, they could be organized into unconscious processes that defend against anxiety and conflict.

Given these diverse possibilities, we can readily understand why psychopathology may be approached and defined in terms of any of several levels we may wish to focus upon, and any of a variety of functions or processes we may wish to explain. Beyond this, each level or angle of approach lends itself to a number of specific theories and concepts, the usefulness of which must be gauged by their ability to help solve the particular problems and purposes for which they were created. That the subject matter of psychopathology is inherently diverse and complex is precisely the reason why we must not narrow our choice of approach to one level or one theory. Each has a legitimate and potentially fruitful contribution to make to our study. What should be clear, however, is that a theory is not "reality," that it is not an inevitable or predetermined representation of the objective world.

Theories are merely optional instruments utilized in the early stages of knowledge. They serve to organize experience in a logical manner, and function as explanatory propositions by which experiences may be analyzed or inferences about them may be drawn. Their ultimate goal is the establishment of new empirical laws.

Goals of Scientific Systems

Man acquired reliable and useful knowledge about his environment long before the advent of modern scientific thought. Information, skill and instrumentation were achieved without "science" and its methods of symbolic abstraction, research and analysis. If useful knowledge could be acquired by intelligent observation and common sense alone, what special values are derived by applying the complicated and rigorous procedures of the scientific method? Is rigor, clarity, precision and experimentation more than a compulsive and picayunish concern for details, more than the pursuit for the honorific title of "science"? Are the labors of coordinating knowledge and exploring unknown factors in a systematic fashion worth the time and effort involved? There is little question in our "age of science" that the answer would be yes! But why? What are the distinguishing virtues of scientific systems? What sets them apart from everyday common sense methods of acquiring knowledge? It is these questions to which we must turn next.

Since the number of ways we can observe, describe and organize the natural world is infinite, the terms and concepts we create to represent these activities are often confusing and obscure. For example, different words are used to describe the same behavior, and the same word is used for different behaviors. Some terms are narrow in focus, others are broad and many are difficult to define. Because of the variety of events that can be considered and the lack of precision in language, useful information gets scattered in hodgepodge fashion across the whole landscape of a scientific topic, and communication gets bogged down in terminological obscurities and semantic controversies.

One of the goals of scientific systems is to avoid this morass of confusion. Not all phenomena related to a subject are attended to at once. Certain elements are selected from the vast range of possibilities because they seem relevant to the solution of specific and important problems. To create a degree of consistency among scientists interested in a problem these elements are grouped or classified according to their similarities and differences and given specific labels which describe or define them. This process of classification is indispensable for systematizing observation and knowledge. But it is only a first step.

Classification of knowledge alone does not make a scientific system. The card catalog of a library or an accountant's ledger sheets are well organized classifications but hardly to be viewed as a system of science. The characteristic which distinguishes a scientific classification system from others is its attempt to group elements according to established or hypothesized explanatory propositions. These propositions are formed when certain properties which have been isolated and classified have been shown or have been hypothesized to be related to other classified properties or groupings. The groupings of a scientific system, therefore, are not mere collections of miscellaneous or random information, but a linked or unified pattern of known or presumed relationships. This pattern of relationships is the foundation of a scientific system.

Certain benefits derive from systematizing knowledge in this fashion. Given the countless ways of observing and analyzing a set of complex events, a system of explanatory propositions becomes a useful guide to the observer. Rather than shifting from one aspect of behavior to another, according to momentary impressions of importance, he is led to pursue in a logical and consistent manner only those aspects which are likely to be related.

In addition, a scientific system enables the perceptive scientist to generate hypotheses about relationships that have not been observed before. It enlarges the scope of knowledge by altering the observer to possible new relationships among phenomena, and then ties these new observations into a coherent body of knowledge. Thus, from a small number of basic explanatory propositions, a scientific system develops broad applicability and subsumes a wide range of phenomena.

This generality or comprehensiveness leads to another important advantage. Because of the scope of the system, different observers are given an opportunity to check or verify the validity of its explanatory propositions. Thus, hasty generalizations, erroneous speculations and personal biases are readily exposed by systematic scrutiny. This exposure assures that propositions are supported by *shared* evidence and that the range of their validity is clearly delimited.

Bringing these points together then, we can see that a scientific system attempts to coordinate and seek relationships among a general but clearly delimited class of phenomena. The means by which a scientific system accomplishes these ends will be our next topic of discussion.

Structure and Orientation of Scientific Theories

Scientific endeavor consists of two types of activities. The *first* is the informal and systematic observation of empirical events and objects. The *second* involves the creation of abstract linguistic or mathematical symbols invented by the theorist to represent relationships among observable events, or relationships which he believes exist but have not been observed. This second, or symbolic and theoretical activity of science, will be our focus in this chapter.

As noted earlier, scientific systems consist of explanatory propositions which create order or render intelligible otherwise unrelated phenomena. There are two kinds of propositions in a scientific system, empirical laws and theories. An *empirical law* is a statement representing a universally established relationship observed among a group of empirical phenomena. A *theory*, in contrast, is composed of invented abstractions in the form of models, concepts, rules and hypotheses which function as provisional exploratory tools to aid the scientist in his search for empirical laws. Theories are subject to frequent change; empirical laws are durable.

Before we can discuss intelligently current theories of psychopathology we must examine the structural form into which theories are cast.

Formal Structure of Theories

Four major components of theory may be distinguished for our purposes: (1) an abstract *model* which serves as an analog or a visualizable pattern representing the overall structure of the theory; (2) a *conceptual terminology* by which various classes of phenomena relevant to the theory are symbolized or labeled; (3) a set of *correspondence rules* which coordinate relationships among the theoretical terms in accordance with the model; and (4) *hypotheses* which specify the manner in which these relationships may be tested in the empirical world.

Models A model is an analogy which exploits certain aspects of a familiar or easily visualized system to guide the understanding of a less familiar or difficult subject. For example, theorists have utilized an electronic computer model to describe the processes and structure of psychopathology. Thus, human beings are likened to computers in that both receive complex information from the environment, integrate this information through devious circuits with prior information and emit relatively uncomplicated responses. More commonly, psychopathology has been organized in accordance with a biological disease model. In this format, psychopathology is conceived as if it stemmed from the intrusion of a foreign agent upon normal biological functioning; as in most physical ailments, symptoms are considered to be the organism's reaction to the intrusion.

Few theorists expect the models they adopt to represent accurately all of the features of psychopathology. Rather, the model is used merely as a way to visualize psychopathology "as if it worked like this."

Models pose a number of risks to the theorist. Certain features of a model which may have proved useful in its original setting are often assumed mistakenly to be appropriate elsewhere. Should such a model be adopted, the theorist will waste his time constructing erroneous hypotheses and pursuing unprofitable research. The adoption of the disease model in psychiatry, for example, has been viewed by many psychologists to have led to years of fruitless biochemical research. Similarly, the intrapsychic conflict model underlying psychoanalytic theory has been seen to have delayed the development of more effective psychotherapies. Unfortunately, there are no simple ways to tell beforehand whether a given model will prove to be fruitful or misguided. What should be kept clear in one's thinking is that the model adopted for a theory should not be confused with the theory itself.

Conceptual Terminology The elements of a theory are represented by a set of concepts, that is, a language by which members of a scientific group communicate about a subject. Concepts may be seen as serving two functions. *First,* they possess a value in that they facilitate the *manipulation of theoretical ideas.* Concepts are systematically linked to other concepts; it is through the interplay of these concepts that meaningful ideas are formulated and deductive statements are made in the form of propositions and hypotheses. *Second,* most concepts possess an *empirical significance,* that is, they are linked in some explicit way to the observable world; although some concepts may represent processes or events which are not observable, they may be defined or anchored to observables. It is this translatability into the empirical domain that allows the theoretician to test his propositions in the world of "reality."

Ideally, all concepts of a scientific theory should be empirically anchored, that is, correspond to properties in the observable world. This would minimize confusion regarding the objects and events to which a term applies. Moreover, concepts should be more precise than words used in ordinary language; although everyday conversational language has relevance to significant events in the real world, it gives rise to ambiguity and confusion because of the varied uses to which conventional words are often put. Scientific concepts should be defined "precisely" in order to assure that their meaning is clear and specific.

Empirical precision, in the fullest sense of the term, can be achieved only if every concept in a theory is defined by a single observable phenomenon, that is, a different concept or label would be used for every difference that can be observed in the empirical world. This ideal simply is not feasible for reasons which will become apparent shortly. Psychological concepts do differ, however, in the degree to which they satisfy this criterion. A discussion of three types of concepts— operational definitions, intervening variables and hypothetical constructs—will be of value in noting these distinctions and their consequences.

Operational Definitions Certain concepts are defined literally by observable events and possess no meaning other than these events; they have been termed *operational definitions.* To paraphrase Bridgman (1927), the founder of "operationism," an operational definition is a concept that is defined by the procedure employed to measure the particular empirical event it represents; thus, the meaning of a concept is synonymous with how man measures it, not with what he says about it. For example, the concept "learning" would involve nothing more than the set of operations by which it is measured. There would be a different concept for learning when it is measured by the number of errors a child makes on a task than when measured by the speed with which he completes the same task. The advantage of operational definitions is obvious; concepts are unambiguous, and propositions utilizing these concepts are translatable directly into the empirical phenomena they represent.

Useful as operational definitions may be, they present several problems. Theoretical concepts should be generalizable, that is, they should enable the theorist to include a variety of observations with his concept. Operational definitions are restrictive; they preclude predictions to new situations that are even slightly different from the original situation. Certainly, one of the primary goals of a theory is to integrate diverse observations with a minimum number of concepts; a strict operational approach would flood us with an infinite number of concepts and clutter thinking with irrelevant distinctions. The major value of operational definitions is cautionary; it alerts the theorist to the importance of conceptual precision and empirical relevance.

Intervening Variables Certain concepts cannot be measured by currently available techniques (e.g., the earth's core and biochemical processes in memory). Also, internal or organismic processes which connect observable phenomena may not themselves be observable and must be inferred or invented until such time as they can be observed. These unobservables, often referred to as mediating structures or processes, are necessary in all phases of theory construction. Two types of concepts, intervening variables and hypothetical constructs, deal with these mediating factors; their similarities and differences are worthy of note.

An *intervening variable* is a concept which represents a guess regarding an unobserved mediating process which may account for an observed event. Although they signify an unknown mediating process, intervening variables are defined by and entirely reducible to empirical events. For example, the concept "habit," formulated as an intervening variable, may be defined empirically by the number of trials an individual was given to learn a task, or by the demonstrated speed with which he performs it. Although the term "habit" implies a residue of experience within the individual which cannot be observed, its existence is inferred from a *variety of observables,* e.g., the number of opportunities to learn a task or the skill of performance.

There is a similarity between intervening variables and operational definitions in that both are defined by or anchored to empirical phenomena. But they differ in two important respects. First, a *variety* of empirical phenomena may be used to define an intervening variable; in this respect it is less precise than an operational definition. Second, although both intervening variables and operational definitions are anchored to observables, intervening variables always *imply* the existence of a mediating process whereas operational concepts need not.

Hypothetical Constructs   The difference between an intervening variable and a hypothetical construct is largely a matter of degree. *Hypothetical constructs* are admittedly speculative concepts which are formulated without explicit reference to observable phenomena. Their freedom from specific empirical referents distinguishes them from intervening variables. Because they are not defined or anchored to observable events, their use in theory often is questioned. Clarity gets muddled and deductions often are tautological when psychological data are "explained" in terms of a series of hypothetical constructs. For example, statements such as "the mechanisms of the ego are blocked in the anal-character when libidinous energies are dammed up by super-ego introjections" are, at best, puzzling. Postulating connections between one set of hypothetical constructs and another leads to facile but often meaningless "explanations." Such use results in imprecise formulations which are difficult to decipher because we cannot specify observables by which they can be anchored or evaluated.

Vagueness and surplus-meaning are both the weakness and strength of the hypothetical construct. A theory is a human artifact; not every concept of a theory should be linked to empirical events since the purpose of a theory is to extend the range of our knowledge. Moreover, unrealistic standards of empirical anchorage in the early stages of theory construction may discourage the kind of imaginative speculation necessary to decipher elusive and obscure phenomena. Vague and risky as hypothetical constructs may be, they often are necessary tools in the development of a productive theory.

Correspondence Rules   Even if all the terms of a theory were empirically anchored and precise, something further would have to be added to indicate how these terms are combined and related to one another. Without a set of rules by which its concepts are integrated, a theory lacks internal coherence and its function as a tool for explaining and predicting empirical events is hampered markedly. Many labels have been coined for this linkage or correspondence system; it has often been referred to as the *syntax* of a theory because of its similarity to the rules of grammar.

These rules serve as deductive procedures by which theoretical concepts are arranged or combined to provide new inferences or insights about empirical relations. They give a theory a coherent system of interlocking channels through which diverse facts may be related and derived. For example, the calculational rules of mathematics are frequently used in science as inferential principles which guide the manipulation of concepts and their subsequent derivation into empirical hypotheses. When formulated logically and explicitly, correspondence rules provide tremendous power for systematizing experience and generating research hypotheses.

Hypotheses   Correspondence rules in psychopathological theories are usually loose and imprecise, if formulated at all. As a consequence, hypotheses, that is, provisional explanations which are stated as predictions about empirical relationships, are rarely derived rigorously from the correspondence rules of a theory. In most undeveloped sciences, hypotheses are formulated as a result of perceptive observations and intuitive hunches.

Whether hypotheses are rigorously derived or intuitively conjectured, it is important that their final form be translatable into empirical terms. We must recall that the ultimate goal of a theory is the development of empirical laws.

Such laws develop not only through ingenious speculation or derivation, but also by factual *confirmation*. Unless a hypothesis can be translated into a specific empirical test, its validity cannot be confirmed.

Our discussion has presented a condensation of relatively conventional notions about the structure of theory as formulated by logicians and philosophers of science. Most students may be unacquainted with these terms and may have found them difficult to grasp or see in perspective. Greater clarity may be obtained by reference to Figure 1 which summarizes these notions and their interrelationships in pictorial fashion. Although the serious student would do well to obtain a thorough grounding in these fundamental elements of theory, a sophisticated understanding is not essential to follow the major ideas presented later in the text.

Criteria for Evaluating Theories

Theories arise typically from the perceptive observations and imaginative speculations of a creative scientist. This innovator is usually quite aware of the limits and deficiencies of his "invention" and is disposed in the early stages of his speculation to modify it as he develops new observations and insights. Unfortunately, after its utility has been proven in a modest and limited way, the theory frequently acquires a specious stature. Having clarified certain ambiguities and survived initial criticisms, it begins to accumulate a coterie of disciples. These less creative thinkers tend to accept the theory wholeheartedly and espouse its superior explanatory powers and terminology throughout the scientific marketplace. They hold to its propositions tenaciously and defend it blindly and unequivocally against opposition. In time, it becomes a rigid and sacred dogma and, as a result, authority replaces the test of utility and empirical validity. Intelligent men become religious disciples; their theory is a doctrine of "truth," not a guide to the unknown.

Should we avoid theories knowing their frequent fate? The answer, of course, is no! Man will interpret his experience through either implicit or formal theories, regardless of the dangers and assumptions involved. Rather than dismissing theories as inevitable "religious doctrines," we should formulate criteria by which we can evaluate their genuine utility. There are several grounds upon which theories may be evaluated.

Simplicity and Parsimony Many theories are shrouded in a dense cloak of words and concepts. Their structure is so opaque that assumptions may be concealed, principles may be difficult to extract, and consistent connections to the empirical world may be impossible to establish. In short, the structure of the theory is formulated more complexly than necessary.

The criteria of simplicity and parsimony require that a theory depend on a minimum number of assumptions and a minimum number of concepts. Alone, these criteria neither eliminate theoretical opaqueness nor verify the utility of a theory's propositions; they merely suggest that excess baggage be eliminated so that the central features of the theory can be seen more clearly. Theorists who prefer to formulate their ideas in a complex network of concepts and assumptions must carry the burden of proving the necessity of these components. Excess baggage invites only trouble and confusion.

Generality Ideally, the number and extent of facts and data to which a theory may be generalized should not be limited. So comprehensive a system is, of course, neither feasible nor possible. However, many theories are constructed in their early stages to cover only the limited data from which they were generated; this first formulation often restricts its long-range or potential applicability. It is preferable, therefore, that the format and concepts of a theory be broad enough in scope to be extended to new data, should an elaboration be justified. Implicit in the criterion of generality, therefore, is the suggestion that the value of a theory may be gauged by its ability to generate new observations *after* its initial formulation. Despite the importance of this feature, it is wise to recognize that a disparity will exist between the *potential* range of a theory's applicability and its *actual* range of empirical support. Failure to keep this disparity in mind can lead only to erroneous generalizations.

Empirical Precision The need to coordinate the concepts of a theory with observable data leads us to the criterion of empirical precision. The empirical criterion refers to the extent to which concepts can be anchored to assigned properties in the observable world; precision

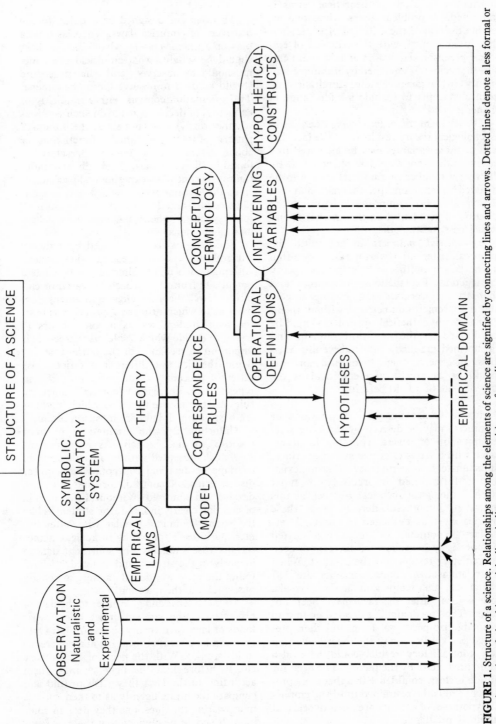

FIGURE 1. Structure of a science. Relationships among the elements of science are signified by connecting lines and arrows. Dotted lines denote a less formal or more imprecise relationship; straight lines indicate greater precision or formality.

refers to the number of empirical phenomena to which each of these theoretical terms is connected. A problem arises when one attempts to balance the criterion of generality, already mentioned, with the criterion of empirical precision. How does one maintain empirical specificity, and thereby minimize ambiguity in language, while simultaneously freeing concepts to include a wide range of phenomena?

The frequent use of *intervening variables* in psychological theory results from the fact that each of these variables may be anchored to a variety of different empirical phenomena. By allowing a number of empirical events to be included in one concept, theorists may approach an ideal compromise between the criterion of generality, on the one hand, and explicitness, on the other.

Hypothetical constructs do not fulfill the empirical criterion; nevertheless, they often are necessary in the early stages of theory construction. Explanations of complex and unobservable processes may be either impossible or extremely cumbersome without them. Ultimately, hypothetical constructs should be coordinated to the empirical domain and transformed gradually into intervening variables. In general, then, theoretical concepts should be as precise and empirical as the current state of a field permits.

Derivable Consequences Propositions or hypotheses may be derived by the systematic manipulation of several concepts in accordance with a series of correspondences rules. Unfortunately, these rules are either nonexistent or formulated imprecisely in most psychopathological theories. Because of this limitation, hypotheses derived from these theories must be evaluated carefully. After-the-fact "hypotheses" or "predictions" stated so imprecisely as to allow for different or even contradictory results must be avoided. When interrelationships among concepts are left ambiguous, the temptation arises to make "predictions" after the facts have been observed. The "prediction" is dressed up into an acceptable propositional form and then presented as a verification of the theory when, in fact, contradictory results could have also been "predicted" by the theory. The need for caution is clear: confidence in a theory's "predictions" must be restrained until the empirical hypotheses of a theory are unequivocal and genuinely predictive.

Orientation of Theories

Theories are designed as a guide to the discovery of empirical laws. Theories have a bias or *orientation* as to what kinds of laws should be sought, what empirical phenomena should be observed, and what procedure should be used to observe these phenomena. This orientation consists, either implicitly or explicitly, of decisions made on such issues as whether to: (1) seek laws about the "unique" pattern of each individual's functioning *or* about commonalities among characteristics found in all individuals; (2) obtain data under rigorously controlled experimental procedures *or* in the settings within which events naturally occur; and (3) observe biophysical *or* intrapsychic *or* phenomenological *or* behavioral phenomena.

The data and laws produced by a theory will reflect decisions on each of these issues. Although each of the alternatives noted is a potentially fruitful approach in search of empirical laws, theorists engage in intense debates as to which of these approaches is best; the poor student wastes needless hours in trying to decide which "side" is correct. It is important to recognize at the outset that different theories ask different questions, use different procedures, and focus on different types of data. There is no "correct" choice; no rules exist in nature to tell us which methods are best or which laws are most important.

Unfortunately, the orientations of most theories are not explicit. As a result, the student is presented with a fantastic array of overlapping data and concepts which appear disconnected and contradictory and leave him dazzled and confused. Without differences in orientation clearly in mind, the student is like the young Talmudic scholar who, after immersing himself for weeks in ancient manuscripts, rose suddenly one morning, danced joyously in the streets, and shouted, "I have found the most wonderful answer; somebody please tell me the question!"

To make sense and give order to the data of his science, the student must know what kinds of laws each theory seeks to find. Only then can he construct meaning and coherence in his studies. With the goals of each theory clearly before him, he may separate them according to the laws they wish to find and compare them intelligently as to their success in answering the questions they pose in common. It should be obvious that theories seeking biochemical laws cannot be compared to theories seeking behavioral laws. And theories seeking causal sequences between past and present events should not be compared to theories seeking correlations among present events, and so on.

The student might ask at this point why different kinds of theories are needed. Cannot one theory encompass all that need be known in psychopathology? For the time being, at least, the answer must be no! At this stage of our knowledge, theories must serve as instruments to answer particular rather than universal questions. The clinician in the consulting room needs a different kind of theory to facilitate his understanding of verbal therapeutic interaction from that needed by the psychopharmacologist, who seeks to discover the effects of biochemical properties.

Recapitulating then, theories differ not only in their models, concepts, and derivation rules, but also in their orientation. This orientation is composed essentially of decisions made on three basic issues: the idiographic *or* the nomothetic approach; the experimental *or* the naturalistic approach; and different approaches in the level of data observed and conceptualized. We shall discuss next each of these three sets of alternatives.

Idiographic and Nomothetic Approaches
Some theorists seek generalizations which will hold for many individuals, whereas others are interested in the pattern with which characteristics combine within single individuals.

Typically, scientists study a specific class of phenomena until some regularity or uniformity is found which characterizes all phenomena of that class. This method, known as the *nomothetic* orientation, overlooks minor or individual variations in its search for laws common to a specific class of phenomena. Many kinds of *nomothetic* laws will be found, however, to characterize a complex organism such as man. These laws may themselves be combined in many ways; the number of combinations possible may, in fact, be infinite. The pattern with which nomothetic laws combine in particular individuals has been referred to as the *idiographic* orientation. In contrast to the nomothetic theorist, who searches for laws common to people in general, the idiographic theorist attempts to combine these laws into distinctive patterns which reflect the "uniqueness" of individuality. Both approaches ultimately are needed for

scientific progress. Nevertheless, a vigorous debate has arisen in the literature as to which approach will be "most fruitful" to the study of psychopathology (Beck, 1953; Eysenck, 1954).

The issue of "fruitfulness" depends, of course, on one's personal predilections and the immediate goals one has in mind. In this regard, the nomothetic theorist usually is a basic laboratory scientist divorced from the pressing problems which the idiographic theorist faces in his typical activity of treating disturbed individuals. Away from the complexity of the whole person, the nomothetic theorist can pursue the search for basic general laws in a rigorous and systematic fashion. In contrast, the clinician, faced with the practical problems of distressed individuals, must find ways to "piece together" the unique set of experiences which have combined to create their problems. He cannot wait for the slow accumulation of group laws by nomothetic theorists because of his immediate needs and concerns. He must now discover laws which will enable him to make sense out of the pattern of experience of a particular individual.

Given the paucity of empirical laws in psychopathology, there need be no argument as to which approach is "most fruitful"; both are fully justified. What is unjustified are contentions that one approach alone is sufficient.

Experimental and Naturalistic Approaches
Scientists accept the principle of multiple determination, that is, that events do not result from random and isolated causes, but from an orderly and lawful sequence of complex influences. A problem facing the theorist concerns the settings and methods by which he will be able to trace the sequence and strands of these multiple determinants. Two solutions have been developed: (1) the classical experimental approach which stresses the manipulation and control of variables and seeks to establish the precise sequence of cause–effect relationships and (2) the naturalistic approach by which several variables are observed in their natural or real settings and then correlated in accord with the pattern of interaction.

In the experimental method, as borrowed from classical physics, the scientist selects certain variables which he considers basic and then manipulates them in a specially arranged setting that is less complex than the one in which they naturally function. This allows him to observe the precise consequences of one set of variables upon another. Its virtue is that the contaminating or obscuring effects of irrelevant variables are removed or under tight control. Hopefully, unequivocal conclusions may be drawn about causal effects or functional relationships.

Two objections have been raised against the experimental approach: controlled settings often are artificial, and the number and nature of variables which can be studied in this fashion are limited. These objections do not apply to the naturalistic approach. In this method the scientist analyzes a complex of naturally interacting variables without intervening controls or manipulations. Cronbach describes this approach in the following (1957):

> The method, for its part, can study what man has not learned to control or can never hope to control. Nature has been experimenting since the beginning of time, with a boldness and complexity far beyond the resources of science. The . . . mission is to observe and organize the data from Nature's experiments.

Proponents of the naturalistic approach point out that experimentally oriented scientists often control or eliminate factors which should not be excluded or ignored. What does one do, they ask, when crucial variables which must be explored cannot be manipulated experimentally? To abandon an investigation because variables cannot be controlled in a classical experiment design seems foolish and may not be necessary if these variables operate in real life settings. The distinguished psychologist, Raymond Cattell, commented on this problem in this statement (1965):

> The . . . laboratory method, with its isolation of the single process, has worked well in the older sciences, but where total organisms have to be studied, the theoretical possibility must be faced that one can sometimes hope to find a law only if the total organism is included in the observations and experiences—not just a bit of its behavior.
>
> The fact that he can study behavior in its natural setting means that he can deal with emotionally important matters and real personality learning. Neither our ethics, nor the self-protectiveness of people themselves, will stand for psychologists giving subjects major emo-

tional shocks or altering their whole personalities for a laboratory thesis.

An experimenter exactly following the classical experimental design, but who happened to be a moral imbecile, might with cold logic and force of habit set out to find the effect upon the personality of a mother of losing a child. Furthermore, he would need to "out-Herod Herod" by removing the child in half the cases, and continuing with the child in the other half of his "controlled experiment." Since life itself inevitably makes these tragic "experiments," a researcher . . . will simply compare mothers who have and have not suffered such bereavement and make his analysis of the result "balancing" for things he cannot manipulate.

There are two methods which utilize the naturalistic approach: one is essentially intuitive and qualitative; the other is objective and quantitative. The first approach uses the data of case histories, clinical observations, and interviews; data obtained with these methods are subject to the pitfalls of memory and to the observational and inferential skills of the clinician. Although brilliant insights often have been derived in this fashion, they tend to be loosely formulated and invariably nonquantitative. More systematic and quantitative are methods which apply the technique of correlational statistics. These procedures have been referred to as multivariate methods by Cattell, who wrote (1965):

> . . . the multivariate method is actually the same as in the clinical method, but it is quantitative and follows explicit calculations of laws and general conclusions. For the clinician appraises the total pattern by eye and tries to make generalizations from a good memory, whereas the multivariate experimenter actually measures all the variables and may then set an electronic computer to abstract the regularities which exist, instead of depending on human powers of memory and generalization.

In conclusion then, we may note that the experimental approach seeks to control contaminating influences and to establish precise causal connections between a limited number of variables. When complex interactions exist, or when crucial variables cannot be manipulated or controlled, the naturalistic approach may be fruitfully utilized. Both can contribute to the search for empirical laws in psychopathology.

Levels of Observation and Conceptualization A major source of confusion for students stems from their difficulty in recognizing the existence of different levels of scientific observation and conceptualization.

As indicated earlier, the basic scientist approaches his subject somewhat differently than the practitioner. No conflict need rise. Psychopathology can be studied from many vantage points; it can be observed and conceptualized in legitimately different ways by behaviorists, phenomenologists, psychodynamicists, and biochemists. No point of observation or conceptualization alone is sufficient to encompass all of the complex and multidimensional features of psychopathology. Processes may be described in terms of conditioned habits, reaction formations, cognitive expectancies, or neurochemical dysfunctions. These levels of conceptualization cannot be arranged in a hierarchy, with one level viewed as reducible to another. Nor can they be compared in terms of some "objective truth value." These alternative levels of approach merely are different; they make possible the observation and conceptualization of different types of data and lead, therefore, to different theories and different empirical laws.

Theories are best differentiated according to the kinds of data they elect to conceptualize. These choices are purely pragmatic, and questions of comparative utility should be asked only of theories which deal with the same kinds of data. Data are the basic ingredients for concepts and for the theories which coordinate these concepts. Irrelevant controversies and confusions are avoided if the conceptual level or the kinds of data to which they refer are specified clearly. When this is done properly, the student and researcher can determine whether two concepts are comparable, whether the same conceptual label refers to different data, whether different theories apply to the same data, and so on.

There are many ways in which the subject matter of psychopathology can be differentiated according to "data levels." What classification scheme of levels will serve our purposes best?

The major historical traditions in psychopathology suggest a particularly useful basis for us to follow, and one which corresponds closely to the major orientations in psychopathology today. These contemporary orientations not only reflect relatively distinct historical traditions, but, perhaps more importantly, also differ in the kinds of data they conceptualize. For example, followers in the tradition of psychiatric medicine focus upon the *biophysical* substrate of pathology; those within the psychodynamic tradition of psychiatry deal with unconscious *intrapsychic* processes; theorists within the clinical-personology tradition often are concerned with conscious *phenomenological* experience; and those in the academic-experimental tradition attend primarily to overt *behavioral* data. These levels—biophysical, intrapsychic, phenomenological and behavioral—reflect, therefore, both different sources of data and the major theoretical orientations in psychopathology.

Scientists who are preoccupied with only a small segment of the field often have little knowledge of the work of others. Intent on a narrow approach to the subject, they lose sight of perspective, and their respective contributions are scattered and disconnected. What is needed today is a synthesis in which divergent elements of knowledge are brought together to be seen as parts of an integrated whole. Until a psychological Newton or Einstein comes along, however, the student must do the next best thing: develop an attitude by which the various branches and levels of psychopathology are viewed as an interrelated, if not an integrated, unit. He must learn the language and orientation of each of the major approaches as if they were all parts of an indivisible piece. Until such time as a bridge is created to coordinate each theory and level of approach to the others, no one theory or approach should be viewed as all-embracing, or accepted to the exclusion of others. A multiplicity of viewpoints must prevail.

Any discussion of psychopathological theory should bring us to the question of defining psychopathology. It should be obvious from the foregoing that no single definition is possible. Psychopathology will be defined in terms of the theory one employs. An idiographically oriented theorist who emphasizes the importance of phenomenological experience will include uniqueness and self-discomfort in his definition of psychopathology; a biochemical theorist will formulate his definition in terms of biochemical dysfunctions, and so on. In brief, once a particular level and theory has been adopted, the definition of psychopathology follows logically and inevitably. Clearly, no single definition conveys the wide range of observations and orientations with which psychopathology may be explored.

Unfortunately, the observations, concepts, and propositions of the various theoretical approaches to psychopathology have not been collected within one cover. At present, no single journal covers all aspects of psychopathology either, nor is there a permanent professional organization which cuts across disciplinary lines on a regular basis. To fill this void is a monumental task and far beyond the scope of this book. At best, we hope to provide a brief panoramic view of these approaches and, hopefully, convey certain essential features.

In the following sections we will specify the major levels of theoretical analysis in greater detail. This will provide us with a picture of which data a theory has judged significant to its purposes and which it has de-emphasized. By arranging contemporary theories according to level of data observation and conceptualism, we shall be able to understand better the variety of definitions of psychopathology which have been developed. From this basis also, we should have a sound foundation for comparing the varied concepts and explanatory propositions which have been formulated regarding the development and modification of psychopathology.

REFERENCES

Beck, S. J. The science of personality: nomothetic or idiographic? *Psychol. Rev.*, 1953, *60*, 353–359.

Cattell, R. B. *The Scientific Analysis of Personality*, Baltimore: Penguin Books, 1965.

Cronbach, L. J. The two disciplines of scientific psychology, *Amer. Psychol.*, 1957, *12*, 671–684.

Eysenck, H. J. The science of personality: nomothetic, *Psychol. Rev.*, 1954, *61*, 339–342.

Hebb, D. O. Alice in Wonderland, or psychology among the biological sciences. In Harlow, H., and Woolsey, C. (editors). *Biological and Biochemical Basis of Behavior*, Wisconsin: University of Wisconsin Press, 1958.

PART I
Biophysical Theories

Introduction

Theories at this level assume that biophysical defects and deficiencies in anatomy, physiology, and biochemistry are the primary determinants of psychopathology. According to this view, biophysical data should serve as the basis for the conceptualization of psychopathology, and biophysical methods should be the primary instruments for therapy.

Ample evidence from medical science exists to justify this biophysical "disease" model. It may be illustrated in physical medicine by infections, genetic errors, obstructions, inflammations, or other insults to normal functioning which manifest themselves overtly as fevers, fatigue, headaches, and so on. Certainly, significant progress was made in physical medicine when it shifted its focus from surface symptomatology to the biophysical disruptions which underlie them. Extending this model to psychopathology, one sees that these theorists believe that biophysical defects or deficiencies ultimately will be found for such "surface" symptoms as bizarre behavior, feelings of anguish, or maladaptive interpersonal relations. The major difference they see between psychological and biophysical disorders is that the former, affecting the central nervous system, manifests itself primarily in behavioral and social symptoms, whereas the latter, affecting other organ systems, manifests itself in physical symptoms.

Orientation

❧ ━━❦━━ ❧

Although the history of the disease model may be traced first to the speculations of Hippocrates and later to the formulations of William Greisinger in mid-nineteenth century Germany, it was the writings of Emil Kraepelin and Eugen Bleuler at the turn of this century which provided the modern foundations of the biophysical perspective.

In the paper selected here to introduce this orientation, Roger Williams presents a persuasive argument favoring the role played by each individual's biological makeup. To Williams, the distinctive character of a person's morphology and chemistry is the most relevant factor in understanding development and behavior, the essentials comprising personality.

2 The Biological Approach to the Study of Personality

Roger J. Williams

The study of personality logically involves trying to answer three questions: First, of what is personality composed; e.g., if two people have differing personalities, in what specific ways do they or may they differ? Second, how do distinctive personalities arise? Third, how can improvement or modification of personality be brought about?

The first question, of what is personality composed, is a difficult and complicated one, and the answers to the second and third questions hinge upon the answer to it. Our discussion in this paper will be a contribution toward the answering of all these questions. Our approach is in a sense not new but it is largely unexplored and, we believe, rich in potentialities. It has the advantage that it can be used to supplement all other approaches; it does not require the rejection of older insights regardless of their origin or how time-honored they may be.

Certainly one of the earliest attempts to account for personality differences was made by the astrologers who recognized that people differed one from another and sought to explain these differences on the basis of the influence of the heavenly bodies. The

From a paper presented at the Berkeley Conference on "Personality Development in Childhood," University of California, May 5, 1960, by permission of the author.

hypothesis of the astrologers has not stood up well in scientific circles, but there are numerous citizens who still believe in horoscopes and many magazines and newspapers that publish them. The tenacious belief rests, I believe, on a fundamental failure of real scientists to come up with other reasons and explanations which satisfy.

In the beginning of the nineteenth century, Gall and Spurzheim developed phrenology which was destined to be in public vogue for a number of decades. This purported to be a science essentially concerned with the relation between personality traits and the contours of people's heads. Partly because it lacked scientific validity and partly because its implications were fatalistic and deterministic, the fundamental idea has largely been discarded.

In the middle portion of the nineteenth century the possible importance of heredity as a factor in the production of personality differences was brought to the fore by the investigations and writings of Darwin and his nephew Galton. Galton, the founder of eugenics, had none of our modern information as to how complicated heredity is; his emphasis on "good" and "bad" heredity (his own, of course, was "good") was misleading and his ideas of improving the race not only flew in the face of religious teachings but were so over-simplified that they came to be regarded as unsound scientifically. The eugenic view also had the disadvantage from the standpoint of public acceptance of being impregnated with determinism.

Before the end of the nineteenth century, Freudianism came into being and has subsequently received such wide acceptance that it has dominated decades. Fundamentally, Freudianism is a system of surmises of such a nature that they have not and cannot be tested by controlled experiments. These surmises appear to some minds to be plausible to such a high degree that they demand acceptance. On the other hand, to some minds, some of the surmises appear so implausible as to demand rejection. Controlled experiments are quite outside the routine thoughts and discussions of adherents of the Freudian school.

The surmises which form the basis of the Freudian doctrine include the essential idea that personalities are built during the lifetime of the individual and that the prime factors which enter are the environmental happenings beginning on the day of birth—possibly even before—and the thoughts that are developed as a result of these happenings. Therapeutic psychoanalysis is based upon the idea that if an individual can come to understand how the events of his earlier life have developed his present unfortunate attitudes, his personality difficulties tend to evaporate. Inherent in this approach is the idea that minds are much more complex than they superficially appear to be; they are like icebergs in that there is much more "out of sight" than there is in open view.

That the Freudian approach to personality has elements of strength is so obvious as not to require argument. It leaves room for the unknown and unexpected in human behavior (which is needed), it emphasizes the dynamic aspects of personality, and strongly encourages the belief that human beings are not powerless to change and modify their personalities and that parents have tremendous potentialities in developing the lives of their children. The wide acceptance of Freudian ideas bears out the thought that the public, including the physicians, are first people and second, if at all, scientists. Certainly a cold-blooded scientific approach would never have developed and fostered the Freudian concepts.

Freudian doctrine tacitly assumes that at the beginning of their lives individuals are substantially duplicates of one another. This doctrine is almost, if not wholly, universalized; that is, its pronouncements apply to everyone alike. Freud himself wrote, "I always find it uncanny when I can't understand someone in terms of myself."

To be sure, people develop later in life very diverse personalities, but the observed differences are, according to the Freudian school, essentially environmentally induced and the laws of development are the same for all. Freud and his followers sometimes make references to tendencies which are inherited by the human race as a whole but it is the consistent practice to disregard or minimize individual differences in heredity as a potential source of personality differences. Certainly Freudians as such have not fostered research in this area.

The neglect of hereditary factors among those who are concerned with personality disorders is so pronounced that the veteran physician, Walter C. Alvarez, has recently complained "in most of the present-day books on psychiatry, there is not even a short section on heredity. The book resembles a text on paleontology written for a fundamentalist college, with not one word on evolution!"[1] Of course, the dilemma of developing an environmentalist doctrine while paying some attention to heredity is a real one. If one begins to allow heredity to make inroads and demand attention, there is no telling where the process will end; the whole structure of environmentalistic Freudianism might come tumbling down.

On hard-nosed scientific ground one does not escape from determinism by adopting an environmentalist point of view, though many seem to think so. They resist considering the importance of heredity for this reason. Rigorous scientific thinking leads us to conclude that environmentalism is just as deterministic in its implications as is hereditarianism. People say, "If we don't like one environment we can move to another," but scientific reasoning if followed implicitly leads to the conclusion that we cannot move to a new environment unless there is some stimulus in the old or the new environment which *makes us* move.

This subject is much too large to discuss in detail in this paper, but as a prelude to further discussions I will briefly state my position. In the first place I have not the slightest doubt that heredity has a great deal to do with personality development. I do not resist this idea. I do not believe this recognition leads inevitably to determinism. I do not know how or why intelligence originated on earth; I do not understand how or why free will originated or just how it works. But there are many other questions to which scientific reasoning gives me no answer. I do not even know why positive electricity attracts negative or why every particle of matter in the physical universe exerts an attractive force on every other particle. I do accept the idea of free choice, with limitations imposed by laws, as a fundamental premise. With the acceptance, as a background for my thinking, of the exercise of intelligence and free choice as prime factors in life, I do not resist the recognition of hereditary influences. Their recognition does not pin me down to determinism.

Behavioristic psychology which at its inception was *completely* environmentalistic has bolstered the environmental approach of Freudianism. This school of psychology has as a fundamental basis the facts discovered by Pavlov using dogs and commonly designated as conditioned reflexes. The development of personality thus becomes a pyramiding conditioning process whereby the developing infant is continuously modified in his responses by the stimuli he or she received.

What was not quoted by the behavioristic school were correlative findings by Pavlov which are highly pertinent. Pavlov found as a result of extensive study of many dogs that they often exhibited innate tendencies to react very differently to the same stimulus. He recognized in his dogs four basic types: (1) excitable, (2) inhibitory, (3) equilibrated, and (4) active, as well as intermediate, types.[2] He recognized enormous differences in dogs with respect to their conditionability and was by no means inclined to focus his attention solely upon the behavior of *"the* dog." Scott and others have in more recent times found ample justification for Pavlov's concern over the fundamental differences between dogs of different breeds and between individual dogs within each breed. These differences, which can be studied under controlled conditions in dogs vastly easier than in human beings, are *not* the result of training.

It is beyond dispute, of course, that dogs, cats, rats, and monkeys, for example, show species differences with respect to their patterns of conditionability. Stimuli which are highly effective for one species may be of negligible importance for another. If hereditary factors make for inter-species differences, it is entirely reasonable to suppose that intra-species differences would exist for the same reason.

Before we proceed to the principal part of our discussion it should be pointed out that the pronouncements of men whose memories we may revere must be taken in their historical context. Freud, for example, developed most of his fundamental ideas before there was any knowledge of hormones, indeed before the term "hormone" was coined. He had at this time no knowledge of present-day biochemistry; the chemical factors involved in nutrition were almost wholly unknown; and he certainly had no knowledge of the close ties which exist between biochemistry and genetics. It can safely be assumed that if the youthful Sigmund Freud were reincarnated today, he would include these vast developments in endocrinology, biochemistry, and genetics in his purview, and that his thinking would follow quite different paths from those which it followed about the turn of the century.

A parallel case has existed in the field of medicine with respect to the monumental work of Louis Pasteur. Pasteur's thrilling contribution may be summarized in a single sentence: "Disease is caused by micro-organisms." To convince his contemporaries of this fact Pasteur had to overcome terrific resistance. Once established, however, the next generation not only accepted the idea but was strongly inclined to go even further and assert that disease is caused *exclusively* by micro-organisms. After Pasteur's death substantial evidence began to accumulate that disease could be caused by malnutrition. This idea in turn met with terrific resistance, possibly because this was considered a slur on Pasteur's memory. Actually, however, if the youthful Pasteur could have been reincarnated about 1900 he probably would have been one of the first to recognize the importance of malnutrition—an importance which many physicians even today do not fully recognize or welcome with open arms.

The parallel between the two cases may be discerned if we summarize Freud's contribution thus: "Personality disorders result from infantile conditioning." It appears that many followers of Freud tend to insert the word "exclusively" and to say "Personality disorders result exclusively from infantile conditioning." It seems an extremely doubtful compliment to Freud's memory to follow slavishly doctrines which he—if he were alive and in possession of present-day knowledge—would repudiate or radically modify.

A biological approach to personality should seek to bring from biology *everything* that can help to explain what personality is, how it originates, and how it can be modified and improved. Biology has much to contribute, particularly in an area of biology which has received relatively little attention; namely, that involving anatomical, physiological, biochemical (and psychological) individuality.

It seems indefensible to assume that people are built in separate compartments, one anatomical, one physiological, one biochemical, one psychological, and that these compartments are unrelated or only distantly related to each other. Each human being possesses and exhibits unity. Certainly anatomy is basic to physiology and biochemistry, and it may logically be presumed that it is also basic to psychology.

Let us look therefore in the field of anatomy for facts which are pertinent to our problem.

Anatomists, partly for reasons of simplicity, have been prone in centuries past to concentrate on a single picture of the human body. Obvious concessions are made, when necessary, in considering the male and the female of the species, and always anatomists have been aware that within these two groups there are variations and anomalies. Only within the past decade,[3] however, has comprehensive information been published which indicates how great these inter-individual variations are and how widespread they are in the general population.

It makes no difference where we look, whether at the skeletal system, the digestive tract, the muscular system, the circulatory system, the respiratory system, the endocrine system, the nervous system, or even at the microscopic anatomy of the blood, we find tremendous morphological variations within the so-called normal range.

For example, normal stomachs vary greatly in shape and about six-fold in size. Transverse colons vary widely in the positions at which they cross over in the abdomen and pelvic colon patterns vary widely. Arising from the aortic arch are two, three, four, and sometimes five and six branch arteries; the aorta itself varies greatly in size and hearts differ morphologically and physiologically so that their pumping capacities in healthy young men vary widely. The size of arteries

and the branching patterns are such that in each individual the various tissues and organs are supplied with blood unequally well, resulting in a distinctive pattern of blood supply for each.

Morphological differences in the respiratory systems of normal people are basic to the fact that each person exhibits a distinctive breathing pattern as shown in the spirograms of different individuals made under comparable conditions.

Each endocrine gland is subject to wide variation among "normal" individuals. Thyroid glands vary in weight about six-fold,[4] and the protein-bound iodine of the blood which measures the hormonal output varies to about the same degree.[5] Parathyroid glands also vary about six-fold in total weight in so-called "normal" individuals, and the number of lobes varies from 2−12.[4] The most prevalent number of lobes is 4, but some anatomists estimate that not over fifty per cent of the population have this number. The number of islets of Langerhans, which are responsible for insulin production, vary over a ten-fold range in diabetes-free individuals.[6] The thickness of the adrenal cortex, where the critical adrenal hormones arise, is said to vary from 0.5 mm to 5 mm (ten-fold).[7]

The morphology of the pituitary glands which produce about eight different hormones is so variable, when different healthy individuals are compared, as to allow for several-fold differences in the production of the individual hormones.[8,9,10] The male sex glands vary in weight from 10 to 45 grams in so-called "normal" males and much more than this if those with "sub-normal" sex development are included. The female sex glands vary in weight over a five-fold range and the number of primordial ova present at the birth of "normal" female infants varies over a thirteen-fold range.[4d] It is evident that all individuals possess distinctive endocrine systems and that the individual hormonal activities may vary over a several-fold range in individuals who have no recognized hormonal difficulty.

The nervous system is, of course, particularly interesting in connection with the personality problem, and the question arises whether substantial variations exist. The classification of the various kinds of sensory nerve endings, for example, is by no means complete nor satisfactory, and the precise functioning of many of the recognized types is unknown. Investigations involving "cold spots," "warm spots," and "pain spots" on the skin indicate that each individual exhibits a distinctive pattern of each. In a relatively recent study of pain spots in twenty-one healthy young adults, a high degree of variation was observed.[11] When subjected to carefully controlled test conditions the right hand of one young man "A" showed seven per cent of the area tested to be "highly sensitive," while in another, "B," the right hand showed one hundred per cent "highly sensitive" areas. On A's hand, forty-nine per cent of the area registered "no-pain" under standard pain producing test conditions. On B's hand, however, there was no area which registered "no pain."

It is evident that there is room for wide variations with respect to the numbers and distributions of sensory nerve endings in different individuals. That such differences exist is indicated by the extreme diversity in the reactions of individuals to many stimuli such as those involving seeing, hearing, and tasting. An entire lecture could be devoted to this subject alone.

The branching of the trunk nerves is as distinctive as that of the blood vessels.[3] Anson, for example, shows eight patterns of the branching of the facial nerve, each type representing, on the basis of examination of one hundred facial halves, from 5 to 22 per cent of the specimens. About 15 per cent of people do not have a direct pyramidal nerve tract in the spinal column; an unknown percentage have three splanchnic nerves as compared with the usual two; recurrent laryngeal nerves may be wholly unbranched or may have as many as six branches;[12] the termination of the spinal cord varies in different individuals over a range of three full vertebrae.[3]

Variations in brain anatomy have received little attention. Thirteen years ago, however, Lashley in a review wrote:[13] "The brain is extremely variable in every character that has been subjected to measurement. Its diversities of structure within the species are of the same general character as are the differences between related species or even between orders of animals. . . . Even the limited evidence at hand, however, shows that individuals start life with brains differing enormously in structure; unlike in number, size, and arrangement of neurons as well as in grosser features."

Unfortunately, partly due to the complexity of the problem, there is no information

whatever available as to how these enormous anatomical differences are related to the equally striking personality differences which are commonplace. Recently there has been published, primarily for the use of surgeons, an extensive study of differences in brain anatomy.[14]

Up to the present in our discussion we have paid attention only to certain facts of biology—those in the field of anatomy. Before we consider other areas—physiology, biochemistry, and psychology—it seems appropriate to note whether we have made any progress in uncovering facts that have important implications for personality development.

Consider the fact (I do regard it a fact and not a theory) that every individual person is endowed with a distinctive gastrointestinal tract, a distinctive circulatory system, a distinctive endocrine system, a distinctive nervous system, and a morphologically distinctive brain; furthermore that the differences involved in this distinctiveness are never trifling and often are enormous. Can it be that this fact is inconsequential in relation to the problem of personality differences?

I am willing to take the position that this fact is of the *utmost* importance. The material in the area of anatomy alone is sufficient to convince anyone who comes upon the problem with an open mind that here is an obvious frontier which should yield many insights. Those who have accepted the Freudian idea that personality disorders arise from infantile conditioning will surely be led to see that, *in addition*, the distinctive bodily equipment of each individual infant is potentially important.

The failure of psychologists—and of biologists, too—to deal seriously with innate individual differences in connection with many problems probably has deep roots.

McGill has said, "Experimental psychologists . . . ignore individual differences almost as an item of faith."[15] The same statement holds, in the main, for physiological psychologists, physiologists, and biochemists. Anatomists have adopted in the past (and some do even at present) the same attitude. Generally speaking, individual differences are flies in the ointment which need to be removed and disregarded. Every subject becomes vastly simpler and more "scientific" when this is done.

If one is pursuing knowledge about personality, however, neglect of innate individual differences is fatal. All of biology and all of psychology have suffered, in my opinion, from at least a mild case of "universalitis," an overruling desire to generalize immediately—oftentimes long before sufficient facts are gathered to give the generalization validity. This desire to generalize is of itself laudable, but the willingness to do so without an adequate background of information is unscientific and has devastating effects in the area of personality study.

The most treacherous type of premature generalization is the one that is not stated, but is merely accepted as obvious or axiomatic. Such a generalization is hidden, for example, in the famous line of Alexander Pope "The proper study of mankind is man." This common saying *assumes* the existence of a meaningful prototype, *man*, a universalized human being—an object of our primary concern. From the standpoint of the serious realistic study of personality, I object to this implied generalization. If we were to alter Pope's line to read "The proper study of mankind is men," we would have detracted from its poetic excellence but we would have added immeasurably to its validity in the area of personality study.

"Universalitis" is probably born of fundamental egotism. If one can makè sweeping generalizations, they are self-gratifying, they can be readily passed on to disciples, the atmosphere seems to clear, life becomes simple, and we approach being gods. It is more pleasant often to retain one's conceit than it is to be realistically humble and admit ignorance. "Universalitis" is thus a sign of immaturity. When personality study has grown up it will recognize realistically the tremendous diversity in personalities, the classification of which is extremely difficult and must be based upon far more data than we now have.

With these ideas as additional background for our thinking let us consider some of the other aspects of biology. Physiologically and biochemically, distinctiveness in gastrointestinal tracts is just as marked as is the distinctiveness in anatomy. The gastric juices of 5,000 individuals free from gastric disease were found to contain from 0—4,300 units of pepsin.[16] The range of hydrochloric acid in a smaller study of normal individuals was from 0.0 to 66.0 milliequivalents per liter.[17] No one can deny the probability that large variations also exist in the digestive juices which cannot be so readily investigated. Some "normal"

hearts beat more than twice as fast as others,[18] some have pumping capacities at least three times as large as others,[19] and the blood of each individual is distinctive. The discovery of the existence of "blood groups" was just the beginning of our knowledge of the individuality of the blood. Enzyme levels in the blood, which are a reflection of fundamental biochemical differences, vary from one well individual to another over substantial ranges, sometimes ten-fold or even thirty-fold or more.[20]

Our neuromuscular systems are far from assembly line products as can easily be demonstrated by a study of motor skills and by a large number of physiological tests. Our senses are by no means identical, as has been made clear by taste tests for PTC and many other substances,[21] by tests involving sense of smell (verbenas,[22] hydrocyanic acid[23]), sense of sight (peripheral vision, foveal size, flicker fusion, and related phenomena, eighteen types of color "blindness"), sense of balance, pitch discriminations and hearing acuities at different frequencies, etc., etc. From the tremendous variation in the action of specific drugs and chemicals on different individuals, we gain further evidence of fundamental differences in physiology and biochemistry.[24]

Thurston's pioneering work on primary mental abilities called attention to the fact that human minds have different facets, and that some individuals may be relatively well endowed with respect to arithmetical facility, for example, while being relatively deficient in word familiarity or spatial imagery. Others may be strong in the area of word familiarity but weak in rote memory or arithmetic. Guilford has more recently suggested that there are at least forty facets to human minds, involving a group of memory factors, four groups of thinking factors, the latter involving abilities relating to discovering, evaluating, and generating ideas.[25] All of this leaves room for a multitude of mental patterns (patterns of conditionability) which it seems reasonable to suppose must be related to the enormous variation in the anatomy of human brains. People even when confronted with the same facts, do not think alike, and this appears to have a sound anatomical as well as psychological basis.

. Those social anthropologists and other social scientists, who regard culture as the one factor which determines what an individual will be like, often say, or imply, that adult members of a society bear a very great resemblance to each other because of the similarities of their upbringing. In view of this common implication it may be well to ask whether inborn differentness and distinctiveness fades out as a result of the adjustment of the individuals to the culture to which they are exposed.

That this is not the case is indicated by the results of a game played anonymously with a group of 140 adults. They were given the following list of twenty desirable items, each of which was to be rated 0, 1, 2, 3, 4, or 5 depending on its satisfaction-giving value for the individual making the anonymous rating.

1. Animals, pets of all kinds
2. Babies, enjoyment of
3. Bargaining, buying and selling
4. Beauty, as seen through the eyes
5. Conversation, all kinds
6. Creative work
7. Exploring, travel
8. Food, eating of all kinds
9. Gardening
10. Medical care
11. Music, all kinds
12. Nature, enjoyment of
13. Odors, perfumes, etc.
14. Ownership of property
15. Reading, all kinds
16. Religious worship
17. Routine activities
18. Self adornment
19. Sex
20. Shows, all kinds

The results showed clearly that every individual was distinct and different from every other individual. No two patterns were alike even with respect to a half dozen items; no pattern had a faint resemblance to the average for the group. Furthermore, the distinctiveness of each was not based upon minor differences in ratings; every item on the list was rated 0 by some individuals; every item was rated 5 by some individuals. In fact every item received, by members of this group, every possible rating from 0 to 5!

At the risk of being naive, it appears that the whole story we have been unfolding hangs together. Individual infants are endowed with far-reaching anatomical distinctiveness; each has a distinctive endocrine system, a highly distinctive nervous system, a highly distinctive brain. The same distinctiveness carries over into the sensory and biochemical realms, and into their individual psychologies. It is not surprising therefore that each individual upon reaching adulthood exhibits a distinctive pattern of likes and dislikes not only with respect to trivialities but also with respect to what may be regarded the most important things in life.

That culture has a profound influence on our lives no one should deny. The serious question arises, however, as to the relative position that different factors occupy in producing distinctive personalities. To me it seems probable that one's distinctive endocrine system and one's distinctive brain morphology are more important factors than the toilet training one receives as an infant.

We cannot state as a demonstrated fact that differences in brain morphology or in endocrine systems have much to do with personality differences. On the other hand we have no rigorous scientific proof that toilet training has any substantial effect on personality development. We can only surmise. In one sense, personality study is in its very early infancy.

Another pertinent question—simple but important—awaits a clear answer: Are patterns of brain morphology inherited? On the basis of what is known about the inheritance of other morphological features including fingerprints and the branching of blood vessels in the chest, etc., it may be *inferred* that specific morphological features in the brain are handed down by inheritance, but we do not have definite proof.

A fact which makes the study of the inheritance of such morphological features difficult is that expressed by geneticists David and Snyder.[26] "It has become more and more widely recognized that single-gene differences which produce readily distinguishable discontinuities in phenotype variation are completely non-representative of the bulk of genetic variability in any species." Multiple gene effects are extremely common and in many cases, because of the complexity of the inheritance process, it is impossible to trace them in families or to know when and where such effects may be expected to arise. This complication is not the only one which exists; there is also the possibility (and certainty in some species) of maternal influence (cytoplasmic) which does not follow the rules of gene-centered genetics, and can thus throw one's calculations off.[27]

The complications of broad genetic study are so great that closely inbred animals, which, according to the simpler concepts of genetics, should be nearly identical in body make-up, are often relatively far from it. Even within relatively closely inbred groups of animals each has a distinctive pattern of organ weights, a distinctive excretion pattern, and at the same time a distinctive pattern of behavioral responses.

The technique of twin studies also has its pitfalls. Monozygotic twins have, according to the simpler concepts of Mendelian genetics, identical inheritance. Actually, however, because of cytoplasmic factors or other unknowns, they appear not to have. It is a common observation that so-called "identical" twins vary markedly in their resemblance to each other. Sometimes they have almost indistinguishable facial features and very similar temperaments. In other cases, however, they are readily distinguished one from another by facial features and/or by temperaments. Our study of excretion patterns suggests that these show in monozygotic twins a high degree of similarity but not an identity. Kallman states, "Discordance between them [monozygotic twins] is not, as is commonly assumed, a measure merely of postnatal or even prenatal development; it may also have a genetic component."[28]

Consideration of the available facts leads me to suppose, in the absence of completely definitive information, that differences in brain morphology, in endocrine patterns, in digestive, circulatory, muscular, and nervous systems, etc., have important roots in heredity. It is difficult to see how such differences as exist could arise independent of heredity. The exact mechanisms whereby all these differences are inherited will probably be obscure many decades hence.

The recognition of hereditary factors does not, by any means, exclude from consideration the dynamic aspects of personality development. Potentialities and conditionabilities are inherited, not fixed, characteristics. The widespread idea that personalities are developed from early childhood is fully in accord with an appreciation of the hereditary factors. Conditioning still takes place but the recognition of innate biological differences calls attention to distinct make-up that each new-born baby possesses. Conditioning does not take place starting with assembly-line babies, each one, according to

Watson, possessing exactly the same potentialities to develop into a "doctor, lawyer, artist, merchant, chief, and yes, even beggarman and thief."

We have two choices in personality study: one is to neglect hereditary factors as we have done in the past decades, in which case progress will come to a full stop; the other is to recognize the numerous individual differences to be observed in the various areas of biology and study them intensively and ascertain their pertinence.

If we adopt the latter course this means the cultivation of spontaneity in research and perhaps a de-emphasis on theory until some valuable data are collected. Hebb has recently called attention to the weakness of the "design of experiment" approach.[29] "It assumes that the thinking is done in advance of experimentation, since it demands that the whole program be laid out in advance; it tends also, in its own Procrustean way, to confirm or deny the ideas with which one began the experiment, but its elaborate mathematical machinery is virtually certain to exclude the kind of unexpected result that gives one new ideas. . . . We must not let our epistemological preconceptions stand in the way of getting research done. We had much better be naive and productive than sophisticated, hypercritical and sterile."

To tackle in one giant undertaking the problem of understanding, characterizing, and cataloguing all personalities from the biological or any other point of view seems hopeless. A strategy which seems far from hopeless, however, involves studying *one at a time* various personality characteristics to ascertain what biological roots they may have. The personality characteristics to be chosen for investigation should, obviously, be as definite as possible. They might include not only matters of temperament or emotion but also the ability to perform specified types of mental processes, or they might include personality problems of numerous types.

Studying even one particular personality characteristic to ascertain its biological roots is a large undertaking and might involve making scores, possibly hundreds, of measurements on every individual subjected to study. If one has some rational basis for selecting wisely the measurements to be made, the number of desirable measurements might be reduced. This fact would constitute an argument for selecting as the "personality problem" to be investigated, one for which the type of biological roots *might be* successfully guessed in advance. Such might include hyper- or hyposexuality, homosexuality, obesity, depression, alcoholism, insomnia, accident proneness, etc. When one after another of personality disorders have been studied from this standpoint, it seems very likely that the whole picture will begin to clear and that the study of specific personality characteristics and problems will become successively easier the farther it progresses. What I am considering is obviously a relatively long-range proposal.

Such a type of study as I am suggesting is not in line with the vast amount of experimentation which is currently fashionable. It is very common, for example, to develop a measurement and then apply it to large numbers of people. It is almost or totally unheard of to apply a large series of measurements to a relatively few individuals to determine their individual distinctive patterns. This must be done if we are to find the biological roots of personality characteristics, and psychologists should be warned that the major part of the work must be done in the area of biology, and the biological scientists concerned cannot be looked upon as minor contributors.

Digressing for a moment, it has been with this thought in mind that I have objected strenuously to the current widespread implication that "behavioral sciences" constitute a distinct group including psychology, sociology, and social anthropology and excluding the biological sciences. Hidden in this classification is the *assumption* that biological factors are of no importance in behavior and that conditioning is the whole story. It actually may well be, however, that anatomy, physiology, and biochemistry are, from the standpoint of the practical potentialities, the most important behavioral sciences at our disposal.

In connection with tracing the biological roots of personality characteristics or problems, a highly important part of the strategy is to recognize what I have elsewhere called "disconformities" in the various measurements that are made.[30] High or low values within the so-called "normal range," for example, are disconformities. Such values are abundant and may be highly meaningful, and more important (because of their wider occurrence) than "abnormalities," especially when, as is often the case, the adopted "norms" are selected arbitrarily and without any rational basis whatever.

One of the most encouraging aspects of this type of study is the potential application of high-speed computers to study biological disconformity patterns, and their pertinence to particular personality characteristics or personality problems. Techniques for studying patterns are in their infancy, but the possibilities are most alluring. It may spur our interest in these possibilities to know that, according to recent reports from the Soviet Medical Academy, an electronic diagnosing machine has been constructed. This utilizes, no doubt, some of the mathematical principles and techniques that would be useful in personality study.

Parenthetically, but very briefly, it may be stated that a study of disconformity patterns such as we have suggested is also urgent for reasons other than those involving personality study. These patterns constitute the basis for the complex patterns of innate susceptibilities which all individuals have for all types of diseases.

Space will not permit a discussion of the numerous ways in which my own discipline, biochemistry, impinges on personality problems.[31] The effects of various chemicals on personality behavior, the correlations between brain metabolism and behavior, the effects of various hormones on personality characteristics are all well recognized. What is not so well recognized is that each individual's body chemistry is distinctive and different, and that complex biochemical roots of personality characteristics are likely to be found when we look for them with due care and thoroughness.

Before I close this discussion, I want to stress a most important environmental factor which is capable of contributing enormously to healthy personality development.

The monumental work of Beadle and Tatum[32] demonstrated for the first time the vital connection between genes and enzymes, and, in effect, between heredity and biochemistry. Their work made clear the inevitable basis for individual body chemistry. As a direct consequence of this finding, it becomes inevitable that the nutritional needs of genetically distinctive individuals are quantitatively not the same. Carrying the idea still further it becomes inescapable that the brain cells of individual people do not have quantitatively identical nutritional needs.

It has been amply demonstrated that malnutrition of various kinds can induce personality disorders. This was observed in the starvation studies of Keys and associates,[33] in thiamin deficiency studies,[34] in amino acid deficiency studies,[35] and perhaps most notably in pellagra where unequivocal insanity may result from niacin deficiency and can be abolished promptly by administration of the missing vitamin. It has also been shown repeatedly that inadequacy of prenatal nutrition can cause all sorts of development difficulties and abnormalities in the growing fetus.

One of the most obvious environmental measures that can be taken to insure favorable personality development is to see, for example, that the nervous system of each distinctive individual, with his distinctive needs, receives prenatally and postnatally the best possible nourishment. Nourishment of brain cells like the nourishment of the other cells throughout the body can be maintained at many levels of excellence, and of course achieving the best is no small order.

Serious attention to nutrition which must involve the utilization of substantial manpower and a great deal of human ingenuity and persistence can, I believe, make tremendous contributions to our knowledge of personality states and personality disorders, and to the alleviation and prevention of personality difficulties.

In conclusion I would emphasize that the biological approach to personality, outstandingly important as I believe it to be, is not a substitute for all other valid approaches. Whatever we may know or may be able to accomplish by other approaches, if valid, is not lost. Consideration of the biological approach expands our horizon and gives us a much broader view. In my opinion the insight we may gain from this approach will be most valuable and productive. I should reiterate also what I have said before, that personality study is in its early infancy.

REFERENCES

1. Alvarez, Walter C., *Practical Leads to Puzzling Diagnoses*, J. B. Lippincott, Philadelphia, Pa., 1958, p. 181.
2. Maiorov, F. P., *History of Study on Conditioned Reflexes*, 2nd Rev. and Completed ed., U.S.S.R. Academy of Sciences, Moscow and Leningrad, 1954, p. 190. (In Russian.)
3. Anson, Barry J., *Atlas of Human Anatomy*, W. B. Saunders Co., Philadelphia, Pa. and London, England, 1951.
4(a). Grollman, Arthur, *Essentials of Endocrinology*, J. B. Lippincott Co., Philadelphia, Pa., 2nd ed., 1947, p. 155.
4(b). *Ibid.*, p. 247.
4(c). *Ibid.*, p. 460.
4(d). *Ibid.*, p. 497.
5. Williams, Roger J., *Biochemical Individuality*, John Wiley, New York, N.Y., 1956, p. 53.
6. Pincus, Gregory, and Thimann, Kenneth V., eds., *The Hormones*, Academic Press, Inc., New York, N.Y. 1948, Vol. 1, p. 303.
7. Goldzieher, Max A., *The Endocrine Glands*, D. Appleton-Century Co., New York, N.Y. and London, England, 1939, p. 589.
8. Rasmussen, A. T., *Am. J. Anat.*, 42, 1–27 (1928).
9. Rasmussen, A. T., *Endocrinology*, 12, 129–524 (1924).
10. Rasmussen, A. T., *Endocrinology*, 12, 129–150 (1928).
11. Tindall, George T., and Kunkle, E. Charles, *A.M.A. Archives of Neurology and Psychiatry*, 77, 605–610 (1957).
12. Rustad, William H., *Clin. Endocrinol. Metabolism*, 14, 87–96 (1954).
13. Lashley, K. S., *Psychological Reviews*, 54, 333–334 (1947).
14. Schattenbrand, Georges, and Bailey, Percival, *Introduction to Stereotaxis, with an Atlas of the Human Brain* (3 Vols.), Georg Thieme, Verlag, Stuttgart; Grune and Stratton, New York, N.Y., 1959.
15. McGill, W. J., *Amer. Psych. Ass'n. Symposium: Behavior Genetics and Differential Psychology*, New York, Sept. 4. 1957.
16. Osterberg, Arnold E., Vanzant, Frances R., Alvarez, Walter C., and Rivers, Andrew B., *Am. J. Digestive Diseases*, 3, 35–41 (1936).
17. Bernstein, Ralph E., *J. Lab. Clin. Med.*, 40, 707–717 (1952).
18. Heath, Clark W., et al., *What People Are*, Harvard University Press, Cambridge, Mass., 1945, p. 126.
19. King, C. C., et al., *J. Applied Physiol.*, 5, 99–110 (1952).
20. Williams, Roger J., *Biochemical Individuality*, John Wiley & Sons, New York, N.Y., 1956, pp. 69–79.
21. *Ibid.*, pp. 127–130.
22. Blakeslee, A. F., *Proc. Natl. Acad. Sci.*, 48, 298–299 (1918); *J. of Heredity*, 23, 106 (1932).
23. Kirk, R. L., and Stenhouse, N. S., *Nature*, 171, 698–699 (1953).
24. Williams, Roger J., *Biochemical Individuality*,

John Wiley & Sons, New York, N.Y. 1956, pp. 196–118.

25. Guilford, J. P., *Science, 122,* 875 (1955).
26. David, P. R., and Snyder, L. H., *Social Psychology at the Crossroads,* Harper and Bros., New York, N.Y., 1951, pp. 61–62.
27. Williams, Roger J., *J. of Heredity, 51,* 91–98 (1960).
28. Kallmann, F. J., *Am. J. Human Genetics, 6,* 157–162 (1954).
29. Harlow, Harry F., and Woolsey, Clinton N., eds., *Biological and Biochemical Bases of Behavior,* The University of Wisconsin Press, Madison, Wisconsin, 1958, p. 464.
30. Williams, Roger J., *Texas Reports Biol. and Med., 18,* 168–185 (1960).
31. Williams, Roger J., *Biochemical Individuality,* John Wiley & Sons, New York, N.Y., 1956, pp. 197–209.
32. Beadle, G. W., and Tatum, E. L., *Proc. Natl. Acad. Sci., 27,* 499–506 (1941).
33. Keys, Ancel, "Experimental Induction of Neuropsychoses by Starvation," in *Biology of Mental Health and Disease,* Paul B. Hoeber, Inc., New York, N.Y., 1952, pp. 515–525.
34. Wilder, Russell M., "Experimental Induction of Psychoneuroses through Restriction of Intake of Thiamine," in *Biology of Mental Health and Disease,* Paul B. Hoeber, Inc., New York, N.Y., 1952, pp. 531–538.
35. Rose, W. C., personal communication.

Etiology and Development

Few theorists would deny that constitution plays a role in psychopathology, but most would insist that these factors can be modified substantially by learning and experience. This moderate view states that constitution operates not as a fixed constant, but as a disposition subject to the circumstances of an individual's upbringing.

Eugen Bleuler attempts to formulate in the paper presented here a modest synthesis of the interaction of biological and experiential determinants. Despite his flirtation with psychological interpretations, Bleuler holds fast to his belief that overt behavioral features of schizophrenia are merely surface expressions of more basic physiological defects.

Irving Gottesman and James Shields, the most productive team of genetic researchers in contemporary psychiatry, summarize the implications of their work insofar as it supports the role of heredity in schizophrenia and suggests a probable mode of genetic transmission.

3 The Physiogenic and Psychogenic in Schizophrenia

Eugen P. Bleuler

Since Jung and myself following in Freud's footsteps pointed out, that a great part of the symptomatology of schizophrenia is to be regarded as psychic reaction, and Adolf Meyer at the same time based his well-known

From *Amer. J. Psychiat.,* 87:203–211, 1930, by permission of the American Psychiatric Association.

theory of the disease on psychic causes, some of us are often inclined to overlook that these psychic mechanisms, as they are known at the present time, do not explain the whole disease. They are only possible, if there is a certain predisposition of the brain and this disposition in schizophrenia seems to be a processive disease.

According to our conception, we can distinguish in schizophrenia, primary and secondary signs. Most of the symptoms described by Kraepelin, such as autism, delusions, illusions of memory, a part of the hallucinations, negativism, stereotypies, mannerisms and most of the catatonic signs, are secondary signs. For the explanation of all these phenomena we have to utilize the mechanisms which are also true for the normal psychology, working on the basis of the primary trouble. We consider as the main primary signs, both certain disorders in affectivity and in associations, which we have described upon other occasions. The disorder in the affectivity is the tendency of the feelings to work independently of each other, instead of working together, which becomes evident, for instance, in the ambivalence, in inadequate affective reactions, simultaneous crying and laughing, and many other observations which occur very frequently in schizophrenics. The associations, on the other hand, are no longer connected by a final aim and frequently deviate from the direction which is given in a normal person by the topic and by the aim of the central thoughts.

The purpose of this paper is to discuss for some forms and some signs in schizophrenia, what and how much can be explained by mere psychological considerations and, on the other hand, to show for what phenomena the psychological explanations are insufficient. There are even symptoms which seem to indicate that there must be physiological lesions.

The psychic mechanism is seen most clearly in paranoid forms. A working man, for instance, would like to earn more, and to be more than he actually is, but he does not get on. Even for a healthy person it is by no means pleasant to think that he himself is to blame for his failures. Everybody first looks elsewhere for the causes of his lack of success. The workman who makes impossible demands, must necessarily come into opposition or into actual conflict with his foreman and fellow-workers. This suggests to him, that these persons grudge him promotion or have given a post to one of their friends, which should have been given to him. Such a suspicion, it is true, can arise in the mind of a healthy person; but when there are primary lesions, when the affects exercise a greater influence on the process of thought than usual, the counter-concepts are suppressed and suspicion becomes more easily conviction. Hence, delusions of persecution occur in

many cases. The sick person finds direct fulfillment of his wishes in his delusions. According to the popular saying, even a healthy person believes in what he wishes; but the sick person knows it and actually *is* the founder of a religion.

Some delusions of grandeur ensue, when the thinking process has become so disintegrated or, in general, so illogical that the patient no longer notices the grossest contradictions to reality. This frequently occurs after long years of delusions of persecution. Then he is emperor, Pope, Christ, or even God himself; not only is he going to make inventions, but he actually *has* made them. Here, we can distinctly see how the psychic development of the delusions depends on the progress of the primary lesion.

Perhaps a patient will come to you and first complain of all sorts of paresthesias (neurasthenic state). After a year, possibly he may come again with the same sensations, but now, in spite of all the physician's proofs to the contrary, he draws the conclusion that he is suffering from some grave bodily disease, possibly syphilis, although he has never been infected (hypochondriacal stage). Again, after a long interval, the patient is seen to be in an excited state, inimically disposed towards his surroundings; he knows now that he has enemies who are causing him unpleasurable sensations, by all sorts of machinations; the paresthesias have become proprioceptive hallucinations. He is now in the paranoid stage and decidedly psychotic. The more seriously disturbed thinking process has drawn quite impossible inferences from the unpleasurable sensations.

In a somewhat different way, the disturbances in thinking are manifested in the case of a woman disappointed in love, who suddenly eliminates the bitter reality, and, in her hallucinations *is* engaged, married, and not infrequently a child is born. Such dream states, in contrast with mere hysterical (mere psychogenic) ones, may last for months at a time. In principle, therefore, they would be a purely psychogenic syndrome. Its schizophrenic basis, however, is clearly shown in several peculiarities; on the basis of them, as a rule, diagnosis can be made rapidly. (Lack of connection and sequence in the patient's stream of talk and in his behavior, etc.)

Psychic reactions on the basis of a morbid disposition, which are at once comprehensible, are the exalted or anxious *excitations to unpleasant events,* and also autism, the withdrawal from the unsatisfying real world into an imaginary one, which offers more to the patient. The mechanism is, therefore, similar to that in neuroses but nearly all of these signify a direct "flight into illness," and this is rare in schizophrenic reactions; such reactions stray from the right path and their schizophrenic coloring is possible only if a morbid predisposition is present; and in schizophrenia this predisposition is very clearly seen in disturbances in thought and in feeling. It is not his "complexes" as such which *cause* schizophrenia, but they *shape* the morbid picture. The fundamental disturbances, those of the thinking process and those of affectivity, develop quite independently of disagreeable experiences, from which not one of us is spared. Thus all the difficulties of the European War did not cause any increase in the number of cases of schizophrenia.

For us the alteration of the thinking-process, or, elementarily expressed, of the association, is of special importance, and, as a matter of fact, nearly all the psychogenic symptoms can be derived from it. As far as we can recognize this alteration, it is a dynamic one. Thus, we also see something similar even in those cases in which the power of the train of thought is normally weakened, as in dreams and lack of attention, and in so called mindwandering. In schizophrenia, it is the highest control which fails where it would be necessary to act, and this again must be referred to a disturbance of the connections of all the individual functions; *for this highest control (Oberleitung) is not a special function of our soul, but the outcome, the integrated summarizing of all the individual functions.*

With this dismemberment of the connections, it is comprehensible that the logical function of thinking is disturbed by affective needs, as it is clearly evident in the example of manic forms.

Although similar association disturbances may also occur under normal circumstances, the schizophrenic thinking seems to be of direct physical origin: It shows itself in no way dependent on psychic influences, but solely on the seriousness of a fundamental process. When the disturbance is particularly severe, in acute mental aberration, catatonia and dyskinesis, it is accompanied as a rule by other symptoms, which we are rightly accustomed to regard as bodily: Raised or lowered temperature, albumen in urine, metabolic disturbances, gnashing of teeth, "Flockenlesen,"

fainting fits or cramps, not infrequently followed by temporary paresis of the limbs or the language, pupillary disturbances, greatly increased idiomuscular reactions, vasomotor disturbances, edema, somnolence, disturbances of the chemistry of the body, especially of the liver-functions, abnormal protein content in the spinal fluid. In many cases, too, the brain-trouble is demonstrated from the psychic side by the fact that the confusions and delirium have absolutely the character of the "exogene" as Bonhoeffer designates it. Many cases of stupor, with their general prostration of the elementary psychic functions, conception and train of thought, often point clearly to brain-pressure, and, on autopsy, tense edema of the pia or brain-swelling is found. In the various forms of such deliria, the fundamental similarity of certain symptoms or of the whole picture to other physiogenic conditions, intoxication, fever psychoses, epileptic absences, meningitis, encephalitis cannot be denied, and in all such cases, we also find in the autopsy histological alterations of the brain tissue, which show some uniformity. But in all chronic cases, too, decreases in the amount of ganglion cells and certain changes in the glia, furnish a proof that we are in presence of a brain lesion, of course not in the sense that the histological finding is the direct foundation of the primary psychic symptoms; it is merely an *indicator* of the existence of brain lesions, which, on the one hand, express themselves as psychic, and on the other hand as anatomical. Chronic histological findings always correspond with the clinical chronic picture, and acute changes, with acute ones. Organic symptoms are also the hyperkinesis and akinesis, which are likewise found in various diseases of the basal ganglia.

In contrast to encephalitis, affectivity in schizophrenia is not destroyed, but is, in some way, hampered in expression. Affective impulses which are in no way psychically perceptible, can be demonstrated in the psychogalvanic experiment, and the affects can again appear if a catatonic patient becomes senile, or if he is analyzed according to Freud's methods. Yet, we always obtain the impression that the affectivity is also primarily altered, but by no means in the sense of a simple destruction of all feelings as it was formerly believed.

In the case of hallucinations, we have already mentioned the excitatory states of the proprioceptive apparatus; but there are still other hallucinations which are to be attributed to a physiologic excitation of the nervous system; viz., the various kinds of a photopsia, the sensations of threads, the majority of animal visions, musical hallucinations. With respect to the latter category, it must be added that also purely psychogenic animal visions appear, but in every case, these are animals with sexual significance which are evolved from erotic complexes. Music is also heard in states of ectasy which can be wholly, or in part, psychogenic and hysteriform.

Although we may register theoretically the majority of symptoms with great certitude, as physical or psychic, conditions in the clinical picture are often very complicated. There are catatonic spells of a purely physical, and others of a purely psychogenic nature, but when a certain psychogenic dulling of the consciousness is present, the spell may be brought about by something in connection with this disposition, which spell must then, naturally, have the commingled signs of both origins. Or a physiogenic spell increases the disintegration of the association so that the complex-tendencies, which are constantly present, can now manifest themselves by means of symptoms. The cause of the spell is physical, but the psychic symptomatology reveals the hidden complexes. Thus, it is the whole disease, and most distinctly with its acute exacerbations.

A girl is disappointed in love and has a catatonic episode. It is supposed that the disappointment is the cause of the episode, but it is only *one* of the causes; perhaps the girl has formerly experienced other equally great disappointments and has overcome them without any ill results. That the present disappointment has such results arises from the fact, that a physical process was already on the way, and when we are able to look more closely, we may find that the so-called falling in love was already a symptom and not the cause of the episode. We consequently see in these cases, too, a complete recovery, and in others, at least a disappearance of delirium, catalepsy or dyskinesis, *without any improvement in the situation.* The more serious the predisposing physical change, the less easily can the psychic causes produce an episode, or, better said, can make it manifest and vice versa. Hence, the physical and psychic symptoms and shades can mingle in all sorts of circumstances.

In *hallucinations,* we see yet other kinds of co-operation of both factors. The lack of

control by the dissociation of the individual functions certainly causes the tendency to hear voices; the content, however, is determined by the complexes. Thus, in all states, the voices are the expression and confirmation of the delusions, whilst in acute delirium, it is true, they often follow in their own laws. We have seen above how the paresthesias are transformed by the disturbance to logic and the need of justifying oneself, into bodily hallucinations, as a consequence of inimical machinations, but a fairly large portion of these same bodily hallucinations are psychogenic in later states.

In this way, the whole illness with its alterations, becomes intelligible. On the whole, schizophrenia seems to be a physical disease with a lingering *course,* which, however, can exacerbate irregularly from some reason unknown to us into sudden episodes and then get better again. We then see the physiogenic catatonia and delirium of exogenous character. In principle, they are capable of involution, and, so to speak, all of them really do involute, but some almost to their previous state, whilst others leave behind a more or less pronounced schizophrenic condition, the "secondary dementia" of the older school of psychiatrists. The episodes, with their changing issue, can repeat themselves, and then their psychic residues are often summarized in time into the same grave picture as, in other cases, the first episode has caused, but the same picture can develop quite imperceptibly without an acute attack. Actual chronic states seldom improve to a recovery; chronic catatonic states never.

Theoretically, reactions have to be sharply separated from the episodes, although both forms of exacerbation are in practice not always easily distinguishable from each other, and are prone to mix, but if they are really only psychogenic, they can heal to the earlier state; real deterioration is in connection with the physiogenic process. The prognosis of the psychogenic-physiogenic mixing is dependent on it, however important each of the two components may be in the picture, and then on the unfortunately incalculable capacity for involution of the physiogenic part.

Other not infrequent exacerbations are caused by the manic and the melancholic affective states, which may have quite different significances: a considerable part of these is a symptom of a manic-depressive psychosis, which mixes with the schizophrenia. Another, belongs to schizophrenia itself, and in addition, there must be other mood-swings whose genesis is not yet exactly known. The affective states, as such, heal. The prognosis, however, becomes less favorable if the physical process exacerbates with the manic or depressive state.

The manifest disease can remain at a standstill in every phase and everything that we can perhaps bring into relation with the acute cell-modifications can involute. I believe, however, that in most cases the standstill of the brain-process permits a considerable psychic recovery, because it is less a deficiency than an intoxication, or the continuance of the process which gives the symptoms their gravity. Such standstills and involutions are often practically identical to a recovery, and many formerly pronounced sick people are considered to be well, although in such cases the psychiatrist, as a rule, can still discover traces of the illness on closer inspection. *Improvements up to what is practically a recovery do not, therefore, contradict the diagnosis of a schizophrenia.* More for doctrinaire than for real reasons an attempt has been made to include in schizophrenia merely incurable forms. This, however, is contrary to experience. All attempts to separate deteriorating forms from non-deteriorating ones have failed. With its symptoms, as at present known, it cannot be subdivided, although I myself expect that this will be done some day. Out of three apparently like cases, one can deteriorate in a few months; the second only after several years by a new episode; the third not at all.

In acute stages, as already hinted, the purely psychogenic ones pass away without causing any injury. The acute physiogenic episodes are indeed capable of involution, and all of them involute to a certain degree, but in the majority of cases, leave slight, or serious chronic defects behind them. On these, some are purely psychic residues: a patient, for instance, who has a suicidal tendency motivated by schizophrenic depression, although he is no longer depressed, and could easily come to terms with life, now continues to try to commit suicide with the same persistence, but for no reason. Or, if in an acutely delirious state, he tore and soiled his clothing, and cannot refrain from doing so afterwards, nobody knows why. A girl who mixed up various languages and ideas in an incomprehensible confusion, keeps up the tendency by mere force of habit, and for other reasons; e.g.,

because she is unconsciously afraid to take up life's task again. Other "secondary" states are more closely connected with the expired, but not quite involuted, physical process.

Although a certain number of patients become deteriorated with every treatment, and others improve even in apparently severe cases, the treatment will decide in more than one-third of schizophrenic cases whether they can become social men again or not. Hence, one hospital has many, another, only few cases of improvement. Proper treatment, however, is possible only if it is known, who is accessible to our measures and at what period. Hitherto, we have not been able to influence the physical process, however many alkaloids and gland extracts we give the patients. In acute cases, we shall, therefore, confine ourselves to expectant treatment, but we shall not trouble the patient with proceedings till the physical process takes a turn for the better; only then shall we try to bring him back to reality. If he is left to himself, there is great danger that he will withdraw autistically into himself and lose touch with the world. Whether, in the course of a serious illness, an exacerbation occurs is quite independent of our treatment, but the fact that a certain patient breaks windows, soils and tears his clothes, cries, fights, *is not determined directly by the process of the disease; it belongs to the psychogenic superstructure, and it is a reaction of his complexes to inner, and particularly to outer experiences.* It is, therefore, possible to influence the patient in his symptoms. He should be made interested in some occupation, or, in grave cases, be so trained that, without his illness being improved, he gives up his bad manners and behaves better. A great deal can be accomplished with skill and patience. With many schizophrenics, not only negativistic ones, however, it is often impossible to get the necessary touch in the ordinary way; a semi-narcosis of 8 or 12 days, with somnifene or another narcotic, may bring about a complete change.

If, however, we do not wish to have all our trouble for nothing, and make the patient rebel against our measures, the right moment must be chosen for these. We must know, above all, when an acute process has so far improved that a good result is possible. Then it may happen that a patient who seemed to be quite deteriorated and was violent and noisy, can be given back to his parents, and behaves himself like a normal person from one minute to the other. We must notice when the patients have real needs to return home. Many patients have a secret animosity towards one or another members of the family; if, at this time, they are sent home, matters will go badly. Hence, we must wait till this attitude has been changed or dismiss them to another place. As the patients themselves are frequently unaware of such conditions, it is a great advantage for the physician to know all the signs that Freud has taught us to observe, which betray the concealed feelings of the patient with greater certainty than their words.

Ladies and gentlemen, no doubt a great many of the facts about which I have just spoken will be known to you: the more, therefore, may I hope for an understanding of those about which I was able only to hint. I hope, however, I have shown you how the exact knowledge of the connections of the symptoms can give us the proper directions for treating our patients and how theoretical science has also a practical utility in this matter.

4 Genetic Theorizing and Schizophrenia

Irving I. Gottesman and James Shields

A basic postulate of contemporary human genetics is that all of a person's characteristics are the result of interaction between his genotype and his environment. Such a statement can be taken as an exhortation to get on with the task of searching for the nature and relative importance of the factors involved and how they interact for the characteristic with which we have been concerned—schizophrenia—or it can be interpreted as an end in itself permitting peaceful coexistence between formerly warring factions. The latter option would be a false peace not in the interest of mankind; such a *laissez faire* attitude would allow the continued practice or malpractice of one's "received" ideas about the origins and treatment of schizophrenia and thus perpetuate the notoriously poor record of the helping professions in regard to sufferers from this syndrome. Ask yourself how much schizophrenia has been prevented or cured on the basis of our current understanding of the condition; the obvious answer is in no way meant to detract from the great strides made in alleviating the anguish of patients and their relatives by humanitarian treatment and advances in chemotherapy.

It should be obvious that we opted for the exhortative meaning for the "G × E" post-

ulate. From the vantage point of our twin study we could examine both genetic and environmental contributors to the schizophrenic phenotype. In our chapter on environment we pointed out that if the genes are necessary but not sufficient for the development of schizophrenia, it follows that the environment is also necessary but not sufficient. The evidence we have generated as well as that we have reviewed led us to conclude that *genetic factors specific to schizophrenia are conclusively involved in its etiology*. At no time did we imply that genetic factors were the only ones. Our evaluation of data suggested that the environmental factors were nonspecific and idiosyncratic but that the genetic contribution to the interaction resulting in schizophrenia appeared to have specificity. Even with both the genes and the environment being necessary but insufficient, the network of information above led us to the view that the genetic contribution had "privileged status" and was the "uniformly most potent" (Meehl) contributor to the etiology of schizophrenia. One of our main tasks throughout this book has been to contribute to a climate of opinion conducive to the continued, energetic application of *biological* techniques to the unsolved enigma of the etiology of schizophrenia, despite a missing *corpus delicti* so far.

We are reluctant to label schizophrenia as a disease and, even more so, as a reaction; most justice to our apprehension of the phenomenon is done by construing the disorder as an outcome of a genetically determined developmental predisposition. The word *developmental* is crucial in that it adds the dimension of time to our efforts at understanding schizophrenia; it is the ontogenetic unfolding of a particular phylogenetically given predisposition, buffeted by environmental influences with both graded and saltatory effects, that holds the attention of schizophreniologists. Some human pathologies, such as PKU and Huntington's chorea, clearly fall at one end of a continuum and are called inherited diseases because all persons with the genes develop the conditions. Other pathologies, such as cholera and plague, fall at the other end of the continuum and are called environmental diseases because virtually all persons sufficiently exposed to the vector develop the disease. Many other disorders, often common, fall in between the end points of the continuum; among these are schizophrenia, affective psychoses, diabetes, and some congenital malformations. For these latter conditions the unspecified genetic predisposition must share the spotlight with the unspecified factors in the environment which *cause* some and not others with the genotype to develop the disorder. Adding to the complexity of these middle of the continuum conditions is the probability (Shields, 1968) that the effects of environmental factors may be interaction effects only, operating on the relatively few genetically predisposed individuals to produce schizophrenia, but with no generally adverse effects on the population as a whole, unless the stressors become extreme ones.

Main Grounds for Our Emphasis on Genetic Factors

By way of review, the following are some of the many points of evidence we have presented to support our position regarding genetic factors in theories about the etiology of schizophrenia.

1. Our species is extremely diverse genetically. It is logical to expect that this genetic variability will occasionally produce a combination of genes that results in a *phenodeviant* (Lerner, 1958) at the extreme of a distribution. The work of Lewontin (1967) on blood group antigens and of Harris (1970) on enzymes suggests that about 30% of all human loci are polymorphic, i.e., two or more alleles at a given gene locus, each with frequencies greater than .01 (hence not explainable by mutation). The findings imply that 16% of the loci coding for the structure of proteins in any one person will be heterozygous; using conservative estimates for the number of such loci (50,000) each of us has about 8000 loci at which there are two different alleles, each locus resulting in a distinct protein. (Genes responsible for regulation and organization are excluded from consideration at this stage of our ignorance.) Harris calculated that the probability of two persons at random having the same type of enzymes at only eight loci was 1 in 200; the most commonly occurring types would be found in 1.8% of the population. He called the kind of diversity already demonstrated merely the tip of an iceberg.

2. Many morphological and physiological traits are known to be under some genetic control. Behavioral traits such as intelligence, social introversion, and anxiety have an appreciable genetic component, with data for some of these traits coming from animal strain difference and selection studies, as well as from work with twins and families. It would be surprising if schizophrenia were altogether exempted from analogous genetic influences.

3. No environmental causes have been found that will invariably or even with moderate probability produce schizophrenia in subjects unrelated to a schizophrenic. When cases of *folie à deux* are examined carefully, a high prevalence of schizophrenia is found among the genetic relatives of the induced (Scharfetter, 1970), thus shifting the focus from the role of inducer as a cause to one of precipitator, and a consequent refocusing on the predisposition of the induced.

4. Schizophrenia is present in all countries that have been studied extensively. In many the incidence is about the same despite great variations in ecologies such as child rearing practices. Such observations detract from assigning "culture" a major causal role in the etiology of schizophrenia.

5. Within modern urban communities there is a disproportionately higher incidence and prevalence of schizophrenia in the lowest social classes compared to the highest. On the face of it, such observations provide strong support for the role of social stressors as

causes of schizophrenia. Our considered evaluation of the data was that downward social drift of the patient was the major explanation for the excess of schizophrenia in the lower classes; however, we pointed out that some genetically predisposed individuals might have remained compensated had they been in a more sheltered class. Paradoxically, social stressors can be both predisposing and precipitating at different times. Kay and Roth (1961) in their study of late paraphrenia noted that social isolation was initially the effect of the preferences of schizoid people and secondarily a cause of their decompensation in that isolation removed various resources for adjustment in old age. Fuller and Collins (1970) provided a clear experimental model for such a phenomenon in mice susceptible to audiogenic seizures; sound as a stressor precipitated seizures in certain predisposed genotypes (DBA) on first exposure, but not in others (C57BL); on a second trial "sensitization-induced seizure susceptibility" was observed in 60% of the C57BL mice, but it was seen in even more (81%) of the hybrids carrying half their genes from the DBA's. Even when the stressor predisposed the mice to seizures, it did so as a function of the genetic predisposition.

We would like to make it clear that we would not downgrade the part played by stress—it is, after all, half of the diathesis-stress model. We, as well as others, are unable to deal adequately with the concept of stress as an explanatory construct or as an intervening variable. Many of the difficulties plaguing the concept are confronted by Levine and Scotch (1970) and their colleagues and by Selye (1956). The simplistic flow chart

$$\text{Stressor} \rightarrow \text{Stress} \rightarrow \text{Disorder}$$

is acceptable as a starting point, but denies the important role we wish to assign to the "stressee."[1] Events which are apperceived as stressors depend on the genotypic *and* experiential uniqueness (e.g., intrauterine environment, perinatal hazards, learning history, exposure to CNS toxins, etc.) of the stressee; so do the kind and degree of stress responses and so do

the various disordered outcomes of the stress responses. The problems of specificity are far from solved and we do not yet have the answers. But why might the outcomes vary from hypertension to ulcer to schizophrenia?—Perhaps the answer depends upon the specific properties of the stressee.

6. There is an increasing risk of schizophrenia to the relatives of schizophrenics as a function of the degree of genetic relatedness. The familial distribution cannot entirely be due to environmental differences between families—the MZ concordance rate is higher than the DZ—or to gross differences within families such as sex or birth order. Although there is a need for more and more detailed studies of step-sibs, sibs, and half-sibs, Rüdin (1916) found a seven-fold increase in risk for schizophrenia in the full sibs compared to the half-sibs of dementia praecox probands, despite the high proportion of shared family environment.

7. The difference in identical vs. fraternal twin concordance rates is not due to aspects of the within-family environment that are more similar for MZ than DZ twins, although there are many such aspects. Studies of MZ twins reared apart as well as adoption and fostering studies show a markedly raised incidence of schizophrenia among relatives even when they were brought up in a different home by nonrelatives.

8. Such implicitly causal constructs as schizophrenogenic mothers, doublebinding, marital skew, and communication deviance, have been found wanting (by others as well as ourselves), although we would not categorically deny them a role as possible precipitators or exacerbators of schizophrenia. The offspring of male schizophrenics are as much at risk for the disorder as are the offspring of female schizophrenics. When both parents are schizophrenic the risk to their children is about 46%; it is difficult to account for the absence of schizophrenia in the rest of the children on environmental grounds given such a schizophrenogenic environment; in what might be perceived as an even worse environment, one where one parent is a schizophrenic and the other is psychopathic, the risk of schizophrenia in the offspring is only 15%. Both sets of data are, however, compatible with genetic theories of etiology.

We close this section with yet another reminder that paradoxically it is the data showing that identical twins are as often dis-

---

[1]M. Vartanyan (personal communication) in Moscow has combined stress, neurochemical, and genetic research strategies to yield interesting preliminary data which he interprets as evidence in support of a polygenic theory for schizophrenia.

cordant as concordant for schizophrenia that provide the most impressive evidence for the important role of environmental factors in schizophrenia, whatever they may be.

Genetic Models for the Mode of Transmission

Once the existence of genetic diathesis has been established, it becomes important to provide a theory for the mode of its transmission. In the first instance theories provide a scheme for systematizing diverse pieces in a jigsaw puzzle. In the second, they encourage the formation of testable and refutable hypotheses; ideally they should compete with each other in such a fashion that one theory is made more credible and another less so when subjected to a test. Different genetic models have different implications for the kinds of studies to be conducted, for the kind of molecular pathology involved and hence the rational treatment, for possibilities of detecting premorbid cases, and for recommendations about the prevention of schizophrenia, e.g., by genetic counseling.

Models for the genetic mode of transmission in schizophrenia can be roughly classed into three categories which can in turn be divided. The broad classes are monogenic or one major locus, genetic heterogeneity, and polygenic. Monogenic theories can be divided into recessive, requiring homozygosity or a double dose of a gene at one locus (one from each parent), and dominant, requiring only a single dose of some necessary gene (from one parent). Genes themselves are neither dominant nor recessive; the terms only have meaning with respect to a particular phenotypic characteristic. John and Lewis (1966) introduced the useful distinction between exophenotype (external phenotype) and endophenotype (internal), with the latter discernible only after aid to the naked eye, e.g., a biochemical test or a microscopic examination of chromosome morphology. As endophenotypes have become more available, the distinction between recessivity and dominance has become blurred; in a sense all genes are "dominant" (cf. sickle-cell anemia vs. sickling trait) when we have a way of detecting gene action molecularly. Like most inborn errors of metabolism PKU is the result of an enzyme deficiency inherited in a recessive

fashion (two doses of a gene), but the heterozygote (one dose of the gene) can usually be identified. Enzyme deficiencies can also be inherited in a dominant fashion, e.g, porphyria. The difference depends on how far the normal homozygous state produces an excess of the minimal level needed for health. To quote Harris (1970, p. 252), "Dominant inheritance of a disease due to an enzyme deficiency is most likely to occur where the enzyme in question happens to be rate limiting in the metabolic pathway in which it takes part, because the level of activity of such enzymes in the normal organism will in general be closer to the minimum required to maintain normal function."

Dominant gene theories of schizophrenia which provide for the modifying effects on the phenotype of genes at other loci or other alleles at the same locus (cf, the G6PD polymorphism) are in practice difficult to distinguish from polygenic models; Slater's particular model (Slater, 1958; Slater & Cowie, 1971) is discussed below. A simple monogenic theory for all schizophrenic psychoses where the gene is sufficient cause for the psychosis has no advocates.

Genetic heterogeneity means different things to many people. It can mean that schizophrenia, like low-grade mental deficiency, is comprised of many rare varieties of different recessive or dominant conditions with the mutation rate at each locus maintaining the genes in the population. One form of genetic heterogeneity we can agree with is that the model is like that of mental deficiency throughout its range; a very small percentage of schizophrenic cases are due to different dominant and recessive loci, a further group is due to symptomatic phenocopies (e.g., epilepsy, use of amphetamines, or psychic trauma), but the vast majority are segregants in a normal distribution of a liability toward schizophrenia.

Polygenic models can be divided into continuous phenotypic variation and quasi-continuous variation or threshold effect. Examples of the former are height and IQ scores where extremes of a distribution may be labeled as pathological (dwarf or retardate) at some arbitrary point in the distribution; individuals just to the other side of the point are not distinctively different. The most widely known polygenic trait models posit a large number of underlying genes all of whose effects are equal; with traits so determined we would expect the phenotypic correlation between relatives to be the same as the genetic correlation if the traits are completely heritable. We find for example that the parent-child and sib-sib correlations for height or fingerprint ridge count are very close to .50. A less well known polygenic model of importance to our thinking about a model for schizophrenia permits the gene effects to be unequal. Thoday (1961, 1967) has shown that although bristle number in *Drosophila* is under polygenic control, 87.5% of the genetic difference between the means of a high and a low line could be accounted for by only five of the many genetic loci involved. The implications of such a weighted gene model for schizophrenia are to encourage searching by the usual methods of segregation analysis and linkage for the few "handleable" genes which may prove to mediate a large part of the genetic variation in the liability to schizophrenia.

A polygenic model for handling discontinuous phenotypic variation, so-called threshold or quasi-continuous characters, also forms an important background to our thinking about schizophrenia. This model has made analysis of such traits as schizophrenia, cleft palate, diabetes, and seizure susceptibility feasible, provided one accepts the working hypothesis that the underlying liability is continuously and normally distributed. Falconer (1965, 1967), Edwards (1969), Morton *et al.* (1970), and Smith (1970, 1971) have illustrated the methods involved and we (Gottesman & Shields, 1967) were the first to study psychopathology with such methods. Data on the occurrence of cleft lip with or without cleft palate, CL(P), in the relatives of probands can be used to illustrate the threshold model (Carter, 1969a; Woolf, 1971). Schizophrenia is not present at birth like cleft lip so the analogy is wanting in this respect, but such elegant data for a disorder with a variable age of onset and with the capacity for remission are not available yet.

The population incidence (q_g) of CL(P) can be taken as .001 (Woolf, 1971). The risk in sibs is .04, a low absolute value but a 40-fold increase over the population risk; in second-degree relatives it is .0065 and in third-degree (first cousins), .0036. The sharp falling off of incidence as one moves to more remote relatives is one of the tests for polygenic theory; a dominant gene theory calls for the frequency of affected relatives to decrease by one-half in

each step. An important parallel between CL(P) and schizophrenia is that the risk to parents is about one-half that in sibs although both are classes of first-degree relatives. In both disorders the reduced values probably represent the effects of social selection for who become parents; different values of q_g will be required to evaluate the significance to genetic theorizing of lower rates in parents when such selection is probable. Figure 10.1 shows a diagram for the hypothetical distribution of a genetic liability to CL(P) or other threshold character, for the general population as well as first- and third-degree relatives.

The X axis is for normal deviate values of the posited polygenically determined predisposition or liability to the threshold trait. At a point on the X axis (not drawn to scale) corresponding to a value of .001 (q_g) of the general population we can erect a vertical line (T) to represent the threshold value of liability beyond which all persons are affected; such a line would cut off 4.0% of the sibs (q_r) and only .36% of first cousins. The distances x/2 and x/8 in Figure 1 are the increased means of the liability distributions for first- and third-degree relatives and are predictable from our general knowledge about genetic correlation between relatives, once A and G, the mean liability of affected persons and of the general population, have been determined. A sharp threshold between the liability of affected and unaffected persons is artificial; the threshold

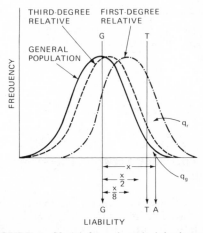

FIGURE 1. Model for polygenic inheritance of threshold characters: Three distributions of the underlying liability in the general population, in first-degree relatives, and in third-degree relatives (see text for symbol definitions).

model implies an increasing likelihood of being affected (i.e., a cumulative normal risk function) as the polygenic predisposition increases (Edwards, 1969; Smith, 1970, 1971).

Support for the threshold model arises from a demonstration of a relationship between the severity of the defect in the proband and the risk to his relatives; this is based on the assumption that the more genes involved, the more severe the condition, and the more genes involved, the more the relatives will have when the amount is halved, quartered, etc. For CL(P) unilateral and bilateral affectation form two levels of severity; in the sibs of unilateral cases the risk is 3.83%, in those of bilaterals, 6.71%; and the generalization holds for other degrees of relatives. Further support for the theory comes from the demonstration that the risk to probands' relatives, say sibs, increases with the number of other relatives affected, i.e., families with two patients are more "high risk" families than those with only one. In the case of CL(P), if no other relative is affected, the recurrence risk to a proband's sib is 2.24%; if an aunt or uncle is affected, the risk rises to 9.91%; finally, if a parent is affected, the risk to the sib rises to 15.55%. The malformation is too rare for there to have been extensive twin studies. From the available evidence Carter (1965, 1969a) estimates the risk to the identical twin of a proband to be about 40%.

From the above data, estimates of the heritability of the underlying liability to CL(P) can be made. Heritability (h^2) is defined as the proportion of the total variability of the trait in the population that is due to genetic differences, assuming the absence of dominance and interaction between genes (cf. Falconer, 1965). The risks to MZ twins, sibs, and first cousins yield h^2 estimates (Smith, 1970) of 88%, 92%, and 100%, respectively, which are reasonably consistent values.

Compatibility Between Theory and Data

We shall deal with monogenic theories first. Recessive inheritance for schizophrenia is difficult to support, since sibs are not more often affected than children. Most monogenic theories invoke a dominant gene. Slater's final version of the general theory that he first proposed in 1958 fits the pooled family data best when the population lifetime risk for developing schizophrenia is taken as .85% and the gene frequency as .03. 90% of schizophrenics will then be heterozygotes, so the trait is basically a dominant one. Only 13% of heterozygotes manifest the psychosis; however, manifestation is complete in the 10% of schizophrenics who have inherited the gene in double dose (Slater & Cowie, 1971). Elston and Campbell (1970) proposed a similar theory, derived from the application of rigorous mathematical methods to the data of Kallmann. According to this theory, the manifestation rate in heterozygotes is only 6% or 7%, even lower than the 13% "penetrance" on Slater's theory. Clearly such theories are still viable and have the merit of simplicity. They suggest that the search for a simply inherited biological error underlying all cases may not be in vain. The problem of how the abnormal gene can maintain itself in the population in view of the low fertility of schizophrenics prompts a search for compensating selective advantage, such as an increased resistance to virus infections early in life (e.g., Carter & Watts, 1971). However, no mendelizing defect has so far been identified in schizophrenia—unless it is, the theory will remain implausible for many. Anderson (1972) has pointed out that "it is difficult to estimate the degree of penetrance unless the variations in phenotype can be identified unequivocally and unless there is independent information establishing the mode of inheritance." If the mode of inheritance is independently established as the result of a dominant gene, there is no objection in principle to invoking very low penetrances; Sewall Wright himself (1963, p. 178) cited a penetrance of 2% for a gene associated with a morphological character in hybrid guinea pigs.

To avoid invoking greatly reduced penetrance Meehl (1962, 1973) and Heston (1970) have concerned themselves with a phenotype broader than schizophrenia—the schizotype and schizoid disease, respectively. Heston considers most studies to have shown about 50% of the first-degree relatives of schizophrenics to have some kind of mental abnormality. The difficulty is that there is no reliable way of defining schizoid disease without reference to relatedness to a schizophrenic. If the concept is defined broadly enough to encompass abnormalities in some 50% of schizophrenics' parents, sibs, and children, and then generalized, the population base rate will be exaggerated and include many false positives. Nevertheless there is certainly merit in carrying out family investigations based on borderline schizophrenics, schizoid personalities and the like in order to test a Mendelian hypothesis.

Heterogeneity theories are less well defined, making it more difficult to say whether they are compatible with the data or not.

One class of heterogeneity theory claims that in principle schizophrenia can be divided etiologically, though not necessarily clinically, into two groups: (1) a high-risk genetic group comprising a large number of individually rare genetic disorders, each with a very high manifestation rate and inherited as a recessive (e.g., as in severe mental retardation, Dewey, Barrai, Morton, & Mi, 1965), or as a dominant trait (Erlenmeyer-Kimling, personal communication); and (2) a residual group of sporadic cases with a low risk of recurrence consisting on the one hand of fresh mutations and on the other of a group of cases of environmental or complex etiology. Deafness, blindness, low-grade retardation, and the muscular dystrophies are conditions that belong to this first class. The theory avoids the *ad hoc* assumption of low penetrance, though in practice there are few schizophrenic families in which the risk to sibs is as high as 25%. If there were many recessive loci for schizophrenia (as there are for deafness), dual mating parents would be unlikely to be of the same type, hence less than 100% of the children would be affected, as is the case; but the observed rate in children (13.9%) when only one parent is affected still remains unaccountable. The consequences of dominant gene heterogeneity are essentially the same as those of monogenic dominance as regards the risk of recurrence in the family; but the theory can account for the continuing prevalence of schizophrenia in the population without invoking either unrealistically high mutation rates (Erlenmeyer-Kimling & Paradowski, 1966) or speculative selective advantage for the heterozygote.

A second class of genetic heterogeneity comprises theories positing that clinically different types of schizophrenia have distinct etiologies. The most fully developed theory of this kind is probably Mitsuda's (1967); see also Rosenthal (1970) and Slater and Cowie (1971). A genetic distinction between typical and atypical schizophrenias is also proposed by Inouye (1963), another Japanese psychiatrist; by the Kleist-Leonhard school (e.g., von Trostorff, 1968); by many Scandinavian psychiatrists who differentiate between "true" and reactive or schizophreniform psychoses (e.g., Welner & Strömgren, 1958); and by those who hold that process and reactive schizophrenia (cf. Garmezy, 1968) are etiologically distinct and not zones on the same continuum. These theories differ in how far they claim dominance or recessive inheritance for the clinical groups, in how far the different groups are genetically determined (if at all), and in the specificity of disorders found in relatives.

Although the hypothesis of "the schizophrenias" rather than "schizophrenia" is a popular and potentially useful one, the genetic heterogeneity hypothesis has not so far met with as much success as in the affective psychoses. The hypothesis that bipolar manic-depressive psychosis is genetically distinct from unipolar depression has received support from the work of Angst (1966), Perris (1966), Winokur et al. (1969), and others. In schizophrenia some of the clinical distinctions are of uncertain reliability, some of the genetic work claiming heterogeneity is open to criticism, and findings, if any attempt is made to replicate them, are not confirmed at different centers (e.g., van Epen, 1969).

There is increasing evidence (Davison & Bagley, 1969) that some schizophrenic syndromes—the symptomatic schizophrenias—develop on the basis of an organic pathology, including Huntington's chorea, Wilson's disease, temporal lobe epilepsy (Slater et al., 1963), and amphetamine intoxication (Connell, 1958). Slater believes the pathogenesis of such cases may give important clues to pathogenesis of schizophrenia in general.

Multiple heterogeneity implies that the bulk of cases of schizophrenia can be accounted for by pooling a number of different rare or relatively rare causes, each of which is virtually sufficient to account for an instance of the disorder. To the extent that one of the causes, a major gene, is predominant, the theory merges with the monogenic. To the extent that the different causal factors are common and insufficient, etiology will depend on the combination of several elements.

Here heterogeneity overlaps with polygenic and other multifactorial theories.

Tests of Polygenic Theory

In this section we shall muster the various lines of evidence which can be brought to bear on the relative merit of polygenic theory in accounting for the body of data on schizophrenia. One indirect approach we favored in the past was to evaluate the compatibility and consistency of independent estimates of the heritability (h^2) of the liability to schizophrenia, after assuming a graded liability for a threshold trait (Gottesman & Shields, 1967). We now present a summary in Fig. 10.2 of an updated version of this approach which uses the improvements to Falconer's method for estimating the heritability of threshold disorders devised by Smith (1970, 1971, and personal communication), our consensus diagnosis pairwise concordance rates for MZ (50%) and DZ (9%) twins, and pooled risks for sibs (10.2%), offspring of dual mating schizophrenics (46%), and for second-degree relatives (3.3%) (Zebrin-Rüdin, 1967; Slater & Cowie, 1971). Six different values of q_p (the equivalent to q_g in Falconer's notation), the population risk, ranging from .85% to 3.0% were used so as to show the effects on estimations of heritability values. Probandwise twin rates might have been more technically correct here but they would not change the overall impression; the pooled probandwise rates for MZ twins in the recent European studies approaches 50% (p. 306). The VA Hospital twin data from Chapter 2 (p. 35) lend themselves very well to an application of the technique since independent estimates of the MZ and DZ prevalence are available; the h^2 estimates for the probandwise concordance rates of 24.1% and 8.0% are 68% and 72%, respectively. For Figure 2 we have taken the rates in relatives at the level including probable schizophrenia; again the overall impression would have been little affected had we used only "strictly" diagnosed rates. Earlier questions we and others raised about the suitability of the Falconer method for MZ twin data have been resolved by Smith's refinements; and since the child regression on midparent is the same as that for one MZ twin on his co-twin (1.0), we can calculate the h^2 from risks to dual mating schizophrenics' offspring.

It is the consistency of the estimates rather than their absolute values that is our main concern. Figure 2 shows the results of this procedure; the results are most consistent at values of population risk of about 1%, yielding heritability estimates close to 85%.[2] It can be seen that the MZ and dual mating data are least sensitive to changes in q_p, while the second-degree data are very much affected by changes in q_p exceeding 1%.

When pooled data on the risk to parents is subjected to the procedure, we must take account of the lower value of q_p in a sample selected for mental health (cf. Mednick et al., 1971); by halving a risk of 1% to .5% and

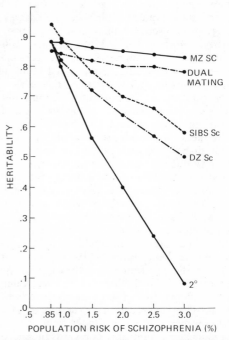

FIGURE 2. Heritabilities (Smith) of the liability to schizophrenia as a function of varying population risks, estimated from risks in different classes of probands' relatives.

[2]Nancy Mendell (personal communication) and Mendell and Elston (1971) kindly calculated the heritabilities for our data using tetrachoric functions as compared with Smith's solution by numerical integration of the normal curve; both approaches yielded very comparable results and neither implies high concordance rates in MZ twins until the heritability is virtually 100%. It should be noted that standard errors of heritability estimates are quite high since they depend on the number of affected relatives of probands.

entering Smith's nomograph with a risk q_R for parents of 5.5%, we obtain an estimate of heritability of 72%, not too much different from the values of unselected relatives at $q_p = 1\%$. The consistency of h^2 estimates across relatives sharing different amounts of environmental communality provides one line of evidence in favor of polygenic theory.

As with the example of CL(P), we can show a sharp drop in the incidence of the condition as we move to more remote relatives rather than the reduction by one-half at each step predicted by simple dominant gene theory.

MZ co-twins 50% ⟶ DZ co-twins 9% ⟶

Second-degree 3.3%   Sibs   10%
(pooled)   Children 14%

The data on cousin risks for CL(P) gave good support for its polygenic inheritance. However, the incidence of schizophrenia in the general population is too high to allow the risks in third-degree relatives to be meaningful evidence for a choice between theories; the median risk to cousins in the literature is 2.6%, based on limited data.

According to a polygenic hypothesis, affected antecedent relatives would occur less often on only *one* side of the family than under a monogenic hypothesis. Slater (1966) developed this idea to discriminate between the merits of monogenic and polygenic theories and concluded from an empirical test on family data that compatibility was somewhat better with dominant gene theory (Slater & Tsuang, 1968).

We reviewed some of the evidence which showed a higher schizophrenia risk to the children of hebephrenic and catatonic (i.e., severe) cases than to the children of paranoid and simple cases.

We showed that in most twin studies concordance was higher when the proband's illness was severe than when it was mild. The argument relating severity to risk can be extended (Kay, 1963; Shields, 1968) to disorders such as paranoia, late paraphrenia, recovered schizophrenia, and schizoaffective psychosis; in these the risk for schizophrenia in sibs was between 3% and 9%, that is, between the rate for sibs of classical schizophrenics and the population base rate. These kinds of data are analogous to the increased risk of CL(P) to relatives of bilateral over unilateral cases, and provide further support for polygenic theory. However, for a diathesis-stress disorder as opposed to a congenital malformation, considerations of the relationship between severity and risk of affectation may be confounded by environmental contributions to severity, for example in diabetes mellitus (Falconer, 1967).

Risk as a function of the number of relatives already affected with schizophrenia provides a further test of polygenic theory. We showed the increase in risk (a) to probands' sibs depending on whether a parent was schizophrenic or not and (b) to children depending on whether one or both parents were affected. Simple monogenic theory would predict no increase in the case of sibs and a rise from 50% to 75% for children. However, current modifications of monogenic theory predict a considerable rise under both (a) and (b). Slater and Cowie (1971) calculated the extent of these increases for Slater's theory. We compared the increased risks with those predicted by polygenic theory (Smith, 1971) taking q_p at 1% and h^2 at 80% as the tabled values closest to our interpretation of Figure 2. The risks are given in Table 1. For sibs, both theories are equally successful at predicting the empirical risks. In the cases of children, when one parent is affected the observed risks are too high for both theoretical predictions; if Kallmann's data were omitted or if the median empirical risk (9.7%) were used as a criterion, the fit with both theoretical predictions would be much improved.

Kallmann (1938) found a higher rate of schizophrenia (25%, 16/64) in children of schizophrenics when an uncle or aunt was also

TABLE 1   **Schizophrenia Risk as Function of Parent Status**

Risk (%)	(a) *To probands' sibs*		(b) *To probands' children*	
Number of parents affected	0	1	1	2
Observed, Table 2.4	9.7	17.2	13.9	46.3
Predicted, polygenic	6.5	18.5	8.3	40.9
Predicted, monogenic	9.4	13.5	8.8	37.1

affected than the 16.4% risk in the offspring of schizophrenics generally. Much more extensive data on risk to children or sibs, as a function of number or relatives affected, are available from Ødegaard's (1972) Norwegian study. Subdividing 1795 sibs of his probands, he found 8% were psychotic when there was no psychotic relative in the parental generation (parent, uncle, or aunt), 15% when there was one psychotic relative, and 21% when there were two or more.

Psychotic relatives in Ødegaard's study included all functional psychotics and not just schizophrenics. The presence of other abnormalities in the families of schizophrenics is taken as more consistent with polygenic than monogenic inheritance. If transmission were "simple" monogenic, we would usually expect to find (a) an excess of schizophrenia and no excess of any other abnormality and (b) an unambiguous bimodal distribution of affected and unaffected in the relatives of probands. When polygenic theories were adopted for the field of psychopathology (Slater & Slater, 1944, for psychoneurosis; and Ødegaard, 1950, 1963, for psychosis), it was on the assumption that they would account for the continuity observed from pathology to normality in both probands and relatives along more than one dimension. Such observations encouraged others to invoke a concept of schizophrenic spectrum to include some or all of the various subthreshold conditions found in the relatives of schizophrenics. Some recent proponents of a polygenic theory for schizophrenia have not explicitly rejected the equating of this view with the retrograde belief in a neuropathic taint or a unitary psychosis *(Einheitspysychose);* however, we concur with Ødegaard's (1972) rejection of the latter and with his conclusion "that there is a strong tendency for the psychotic relatives of schizophrenics to develop schizophrenia rather than other types of functional psychosis, and within the schizophrenic group, there is a tendency toward similarity in clinical picture . . . [p. 268]."

We agree with Anderson (1972) that it is not too helpful to rely on evolutionary theory in deciding among genetic models; we simply do not know enough about how any human behavior evolved (cf. Gottesman & Heston, 1972). However, data on the fertility or Darwinian fitness of schizophrenics is interesting and important in its own right. The question of how a disadvantageous genetic condition can be maintained in the population over time despite the greatly reduced fitness of both male and female schizophrenics (e.g., Slater, Hare, & Price, 1971) can perhaps be answered more readily by polygenic than monogenic theory. The former would obviate the need to find a selective advantage in gene carriers hypothesized by the balanced polymorphism theory of Huxley *et al.* (1964). Response to natural selection against a polygenic trait associated with lowered marriage and fertility rates would be very slow. Genes in the system would only be eliminated from the gene pool when they were present in the rare individual at the tail end of the distribution, while those below the threshold would not be subject to negative selection. Schizophrenics could be thought of as part of the genetic load, the price paid for conserving genetic diversity. In passing, we may note that high heritabilities suggest that the traits concerned may not have been objects of directional selection pressures and so may be irrelevant to the evolution of our species.

The evidence we have adduced in favor of polygenic threshold inheritance shows that it is an equal contender with current monogenic theories. On general grounds polygenic inheritance appears more likely to us; the commonest disorder for which single-gene inheritance has been established, cystic fibrosis of the pancreas, is about 20 times rarer than schizophrenia. However, there is considerable overlap between the two principal models, and the tests proposed for differentiating between them are far from efficient. As Slater and Cowie (1971) state, "Two genetical models are available, either of which provides an adequate framework for the observations, so that the worker is entitled to choose the model which suits his purposes best." To these we would add heterogeneity theories. Our own preference for a polygenic framework leads us to look for specific and important contributing factors on both the diathesis and the stressor sides of the model. Refutation of a polygenic theory would come about by the discovery of an endophenotype which segregated in a monogenic way in all schizophrenics.

BIBLIOGRAPHY

Anderson, V. E. Genetic hypotheses in schizophrenia. In A. R. Kaplan (Ed.), *Genetic factors in "schizophrenia."* Springfield, Illinois: Thomas, 1972. Pp. 490-494.

Angst, J. Zur Ätiologie und Nosologie endogener depressiver Psychosen. *Monographien aus dem Gesamtgebiete der Neurologie und Psychiatrie*, 1966, No. 112. Berlin and New York: Springer-Verlag.

Carter, M., & Watts, C. A. H. Possible biological advantages among schizophrenics' relatives. *British Journal of Psychiatry*, 1971, 118, 453–460

Connell, P. H. *Amphetamine psychosis*. Maudsley Monograph No. 5. London: Chapman & Hall, 1958.

Davison, K., & Bagley, C. R. Schizophrenia-like psychoses associated with organic disorders of the central nervous system: A review of the literature. In R. N. Herrington (Ed.), *Current problems in neuropsychiatry*. British Journal of Psychiatry Special Publication No. 4. Ashford, Kent: Headley, 1969. Pp. 113–184.

Dewey, W. J., Barrai, I., Morton, N. E., & Mi, M. P. Recessive genes in severe mental defect. *American Journal of Human Genetics*, 1965, 17, 237–256.

Falconer, D. S. The inheritance of liability to diseases with variable age of onset, with particular reference to diabetes mellitus. *Annals of Human Genetics*, 1967, 31, 1–20.

Fuller, J. L., & Collins, R. L. Genetics of audiogenic seizures in mice: A parable for psychiatrists. *Seminars in Psychiatry*, 1970, 2, 75–88.

Gottesman, I. I., & Heston, L. L. Human behavioral adaptations—speculations on their genesis. In L. Ehrman and G. Omenn (Eds.), *Genetic endowment and environment in the determination of behavior*. New York: Academic Press, 1972.

Harris, H. *The principles of human biochemical genetics*. Amsterdam: North-Holland Publ., 1970.

Heston, L. L. The genetics of schizophrenic and schizoid disease. *Science*, 1970, 167, 249–256.

Huxley, J., Mayr, E., Osmond, H., & Hoffer, A. Schizophrenia as a genetic morphism. *Nature (London)*, 1964, 204, 220–221.

Inouye, E. Similarity and dissimilarity of schizophrenia in twins. *Proceedings Third International Congress of Psychiatry*, 1961, 1, 524–530 (Montreal: Univ. of Toronto Press, 1963).

John, B., & Lewis, K. R. Chromosome variability and geographic distribution in insects. *Science*, 1966, 152, 711–721.

Kallmann, F. J. *The genetics of schizophrenia*. New York: Augustin, 1938.

Kay, D. W. K. Late paraphrenia and its bearing on the aetiology of schizophrenia. *Acta Psychiatrica Scandinavica*, 1963, 39, 159–169.

Kay, D. W., & Roth, M. Environmental and hereditary factors in the schizophrenias of old age ('late paraphrenia') and their bearing on the

general problem of causation in schizophrenia. *Journal of Mental Science*, 1961, 107, 649–686.

Lerner, I. M. *The genetic basis of selection*. New York: Wiley, 1958.

Levine, S. & Scotch, N. A. (Eds.) *Social stress*. Chicago, Illinois: Aldine, 1970.

Lewontin, R. C. An estimate of average heterozygosity in man. *American Journal of Human Genetics*, 1967, 19, 681–685.

Mednick, S. A., Mura, E., Schulsinger, F., & Mednick, B. Prenatal conditions and infant development in children with schizophrenic parents. In I. I. Gottesman and L. Erlenmeyer-Kimling (Eds.), *Differential reproduction in individuals with mental and physical disorders*. *Social Biology*, 1971, 18, S103–S113.

Meehl, P. E. Schizotaxia, schizotypy, schizophrenia. *American Psychologist*, 1962, 17, 827–838.

Meehl, P. E. MAXCOV—HITMAX: A taxonomic search method for loose genetic syndromes. In P. E. Meehl, *Psychodiagnosis: Selected papers*. Minneapolis: Univ. of Minnesota Press, 1973.

Mendell, N. R., & Elston, R. C. Analyses of quasicontinuous traits. *Excerpta Medica International Congress Series*, 1971, No. 233, 120.

Mitsuda, H. *Clinical genetics in psychiatry*. Tokyo: Igaku Shoin, 1967.

Morton, N. E., Yee, S., Elston, R. C., & Lew, R. Discontinuity and quasi-continuity: Alternative hypotheses of multifactorial inheritance. *Clinical Genetics*, 1970, 1, 81–94.

Ødegaard, Ø. La génétique dans la psychiatrie. *Proceedings First World Congress of Psychiatry*, Paris, 1950. Paris: Hermann, 1952. *Comptes rendus*, VI. Pp. 84–90.

Ødegaard, Ø. The psychiatric disease entities in the light of a genetic investigation. *Acta Psychiatrica Scandinavica*, 1963, Supplement 169, 94–104.

Ødegaard, Ø. The multifactorial theory of inheritance in predisposition to schizophrenia. In A. R. Kaplan (Ed.), *Genetic factors in "schizophrenia."* Springfield, Illinois: Thomas, 1972. Pp. 256–275.

Perris, C. A study of bipolar (manic-depressive) and unipolar recurrent depressive psychoses. *Acta Psychiatrica Scandinavica*, 1966, Suppl. 194.

Rosenthal, D. *Genetic theory and abnormal behavior*. New York: McGraw-Hill, 1970.

Rudin, E. *Zur Vererbung und Neuentstehung der Dementia Praecox*. Berlin and New York: Springer-Verlag, 1916.

Scharfetter, C. On the hereditary aspects of symbiontic psychoses—a contribution towards the understanding of the schizophrenia-like psychoses. *Psychiatria Clinica (Basel)* 1970, 3, 145–152.

Selye, H. *The stress of life*. New York: McGraw-

Hill, 1956.

Shields, J. Summary of the genetic evidence. In D. Rosenthal and S. S. Kety (Eds.), *The transmission of schizophrenia*. Oxford: Pergamon, 1968. Pp. 95–126.

Slater, E. The monogenic theory of schizophrenia. *Acta Genetica et Statistica Medica (Basel)*, 1958, 8, 50–56.

Slater, E. Expectation of abnormality on paternal and maternal sides: A computational model. *Journal of Medical Genetics*, 1966, 3, 159–161.

Slater, E., Beard, A. W., & Glithero, E. The schizophrenia-like psychoses of epilepsy. *British Journal of Psychiatry*, 1963, 109, 95–150.

Slater, E., & Cowie, V. A. *The genetics of mental disorders*. London and New York: Oxford Univ. Press, 1971.

Slater, E., Hare, E. H., & Price, J. S. Marriage and fertility of psychiatric patients compared with national data. In I. I. Gottesman and L. Erlenmeyer-Kimling (Eds.), *Differential reproduction in individuals with mental and physical disorders*. Social Biology, 1971, 18, S60–S73.

Slater, E., & Slater, P. A heuristic theory of neurosis. *Journal of Neurology and Psychiatry*, 1944, 7, 49–55.

Slater, E., & Tsuang, M-t. Abnormality on paternal and maternal sides: Observations in schizophrenia and manic-depression. *Journal of Medical Genetics*, 1968, 5, 197–199.

Smith, C. Heritability of liability and concordance in monozygous twins. *Annals of Human Genetics*, 1970, 34, 85–91.

Smith, C. Recurrence risks for multifactorial inheritance. *American Journal of Human Genetics*, 1971, 23, 578–588.

Thoday, J. M. Location of polygenes. *Nature (London)*, 1961, 191, 368–370.

Thoday, J. M. New insights into continuous variation. In J. F. Crow & J. V. Neel (Eds.), *Proceedings of the Third International Congress of Human Genetics*. Baltimore, Maryland: Johns Hopkins Press, 1967. Pp. 339–350.

Trostorff, S. von Über hereditäre Belastung bei den zykloiden Psychosen, den unsystematischen und systematischen Schizophrenien. *Psychiatrie, Neurologie und Medizinische Psychologie*, 1968, 20, 98–106.

Welner, J., & Strömgren, E. Clinical and genetic studies on benign schizophreniform psychoses based on a follow-up. *Acta Psychiatrica Scandinavica*, 1958, 33, 377–399.

Winokur, G., Clayton, P. J., & Reich, T. *Manic depressive illness*. St. Louis, Missouri: Mosby, 1969.

Woolf, C. M. Congenital cleft lip: A genetic study of 496 propositi. *Journal of Medical Genetics*, 1971, 8, 65–83.

Wright, S. Genetic interaction. In W. J. Burdette (Ed.), *Methodology in mammalian genetics*. San Francisco, California: Holden-Day, 1963. Pp. 159–192.

Zerbin-Rudin, E. Endogene Psychosen. In P. E. Becker (Ed.), *Humangenetik, ein kurzes Handbuch*. Vol. V/2. Stuttgart: Thieme, 1967. Pp. 446–577.

Pathological Patterns

How can the various forms of psychopathology best be classified? To the biophysical theorist, the answer lies in terms of those features of biological make-up that dispose individuals to pathology.

Emil Kraepelin, designer of the major nosological system of diagnosis, still in vogue today despite vigorous and justified criticisms, contended that all psychotic states stemmed from neurological or metabolic diseases. He briefly outlines the rationale of his position in the paper presented here and then turns to what he may be best remembered for, his ability to describe with clarity the overt clinical characteristics of his patients.

To Ernst Kretschmer, behaviors that are correlated consistently with measurable temperament characteristics offer a beginning toward a stable and scientific psychiatric classification.

William Sheldon, a disciple of Kretschmer, formulates an "operational" classification of psychiatric disorders based on his exhaustive studies of body build and temperament. In contrast to Kretschmer, Sheldon's theoretical speculations were founded on years of quantitative research.

5 Dementia Praecox and Manic-Depressive Disease

Emil Kraepelin

The subject of the following course of lectures will be the Science of Psychiatry, which, as its name implies, is that of the treatment of mental disease. It is true that, in the strictest terms, we cannot speak of the mind as becoming diseased, whether we regard it as a separate entity or as the sum total of our subjective experience. And, indeed, from the medical point of view, it is disturbances in the *physical foundations* of mental life which should occupy most of our attention. But the incidents of such diseases are generally seen in the sphere of psychical events, a department with which the art of medicine has dealt very little as yet. Here we are not so much concerned with physical changes in size, shape, firmness, and chemical composition, as with disturbances of comprehension, memory and judgment, illusions, hallucinations, depression, and morbid changes in the activity of the will. With the help of the ideas you have derived from general pathology, you will usually be able to find your way in a new department of medicine without any serious difficulty. But here you will be utterly perplexed at first by the essentially peculiar phenomena of disease with which you will meet, until you have gradually learned to a certain extent to master the special symptomatology of mental disturbances. Of course, you will sometimes have met with isolated conditions of mental disease in everyday life, or in other hospitals—intoxication, fever delirium, and delirium tremens, or even imbecility and idiocy—but they may have impressed you more as strange and incomprehensible curiosities than as adding to your stock of medical ideas.

Insanity works a change in the mental personality, that sum of characteristics which,

Excerpted from lectures given at Heidelberg University, 1902.

to our minds, represents a man's real being in a far higher degree than his physical peculiarities. Hence, our patient's whole relation to the outside world is affected in the most comprehensive way. The knowledge of all these disturbances is a fruitful field for the investigation of mental life, not only revealing many of its universal laws, but also giving a deep insight into the history of the development of the human mind, both in the individual and in the race. It also provides us with the proper scale for comprehending the numerous intellectual, moral, religious, and artistic currents and phenomena of our social life.

But it is not these variously branching scientific relations to so many of the most important questions of human existence which make a knowledge of psychical disturbances indispensable to the physician; it is rather their extraordinary *practical importance*. Insanity, even in its mildest forms, involves the greatest suffering that physicians have to meet. Only a comparatively small percentage of mental cases are permanently and completely cured in the strictest sense of the word. And the number of the insane, which will hardly be exaggerated if we estimate it as amounting at the present moment to 200,000 in Germany alone, is apparently increasing with the most unfortunate rapidity. This increase may depend, to a great extent, on our fuller knowledge of insanity, on the more highly-developed care of the insane, and on the increasing difficulty of treating them at home, and so may be only apparent. But, considering that from one-quarter to one-third of the cases admitted to our asylums are due to the abuse of alcohol or to syphilitic infection, and that these causes of which the extension is certainly not diminishing, we cannot but suppose that the number of the insane is increasing, not only in itself, but also in its proportion to the population. The growing degeneration of our race in the future may therefore still be left an open question, but certainly it might be very greatly promoted by both these causes.

All the insane are dangerous, in some degree, to their neighbours, and even more so to themselves. Mental derangement is the cause of at least a third of the total number of suicides, while sexual crimes and arson, and, to a less extent, dangerous assaults, thefts, and impostures are often committed by those whose minds are diseased. Numberless families are ruined by their afflicted members, either by the senseless squandering of their means, or because long illness and inability to work have gradually sapped the power of caring for a household. Only a certain number of those who do not recover succumb at once. The greater part live on for dozens of years, imbecile and helpless, imposing a heavy and yearly increasing burden on their families and communities, of which the effects strike deeply into our national life.

For all these reasons, it is one of the physician's most important duties to make himself, as far as possible, acquainted with the nature and phenomena of insanity. Even though the limits of his power against this mighty adversary are very narrow, opportunity enough is afforded to every practical physician to contribute his share to the prevention and alleviation of the endless misery annually engendered by mental disease. Alcoholism and syphilis undoubtedly offer the most profitable points of attack, together with the abuse of morphia and cocaine, which so clearly owes its fatal significance to the action of medical men. Family physicians, again, can often help to prevent the marriage of the insane, or of those who are seriously threatened with insanity, and to secure a proper education and choice of occupation for children predisposed to disease. But it will be their special province to recognize dangerous symptoms in time, and, by their prompt action, to prevent suicides and accidents, and obviate the short-sighted procrastination which only too often keeps patients from coming under the care of an expert alienist until the time for practically useful treatment has long been past. Even in those numerous cases which never become insane in the narrower sense, the physician who has been trained in alienism will have such an understanding of the recognition and treatment of psychical disturbances as will amply repay him for the trouble of his years of study. Even in my own experience it has happened very often that older physicians have regretted their defective knowledge of alienism, and complained that it was only in practical life that they learned how great a part is played, in the daily round of ordinary medical practice, by the correct diagnosis of more or less morbid mental incidents. I need hardly mention that, for various reasons, such a diagnosis is in constant demand by public authorities, courts of law, and trade societies.

Of course, an intimate knowledge of Psychiatry, as of every other separate branch of medicine, can only be acquired by long and thorough occupation with the subject. Yet, even in a short time, it is possible to cast at least a general and superficial glance over the commonest forms of mental disturbance. Personal investigation and continuous observation of the greatest possible number of different cases are indispensable to this, and it is only too true that, even after one or two terms of zealous clinical study, there will still be many cases which the beginner is unable to interpret correctly by means of the knowledge with which he has been furnished or which he has acquired for himself. But one important advantage to be gained comparatively quickly is a recognition of the great *difficulties* of the subject and the correction of that simple-minded ignorance, still so widely spread, which assumes that even a non-expert may give an opinion on mental cases without any more ado.

Dementia Praecox

The presentation of clinical details in the large domain of dementia praecox meets with considerable difficulties, because a delimitation of the different clinical pictures can only be accomplished artificially. There is certainly a whole series of phases which frequently return, but between them there are such numerous transitions that in spite of all efforts it appears impossible at present to delimit them sharply and to assign each case without objection to a definite form. We shall be obliged therefore, as in paralysis, to content ourselves at first for the sake of a more lucid presentation with describing the course of certain more frequent forms of the malady without attributing special clinical value to this grouping.

As such forms I have hitherto separated from each other a *hebephrenic*, a *catatonic*, and a *paranoid* group of cases. This classification has been frequently accepted with many modifications, specially concerned with the clinical position of the paranoid diseases, as also by Bleuler in his monograph on schizophrenia; he adds, however, to it the insidious 'dementia simplex' as a special form. Räcke has made other attempts at classification; he separates out 'depressive', 'confused excited', 'stuporous', 'subacute paranoid' forms and a 'catatonia in attacks'. Wieg-Wickenthal differentiates 'dementia simplex', 'hebephrenia' with pseudomanic behavior, 'depressive paranoid forms,' and catatonia.

The undoubted inadequacy of my former classification has led me once more to undertake the attempt to make a more natural grouping, as I have in hand a larger number of possibly more reliable cases. For this purpose there were at my disposal about 500 cases in Heidelberg which had been investigated by myself, in which according to their clinical features, as well as according to the length of the time that had passed, the ultimate issue of the morbid process could be accepted with considerable probability. 'Recovered' cases were not taken into account because of the uncertainty of their significance which still exists, but only such cases as had led to profound dementia or to distinctly marked and permanent phenomena of decreased function. On grounds which will be discussed later, it is, as I believe, not to be assumed that by this choice definite clinical types have quite fallen out of the scope of our consideration; at most a certain displacement in the frequency of the individual forms would be conceivable.

The result of this attempt at a classification agrees in many points with the statements of the above-mentioned investigators. First I also think that I should delimit simple insidious dementia as a special clinical form. Next in the series comes hebephrenia in the narrower sense of silly dementia which was first described by Hecker. A third group is composed of the simple depressive or stuporous forms, a fourth of states of depression with delusions. In a fifth form I have brought together the majority of the clinical cases which go along with conditions of greater excitement; one could speak of an agitated dementia praecox. To it is nearly related the sixth form, which includes essentially the catatonia of Kahlbaum, in which peculiar states of excitement are connected with stupor. A more divergent picture is seen in the seventh and eighth groups, in which the cases are placed which run a paranoid course, according to whether they end in the usual terminal states of dementia praecox or in paranoid, relatively hallucinatory, weak-mindedness. We shall then subject to special consideration the small number of observations which present the remarkable phenomenon of confusion of speech along with perfect sense and fairly reasonable activity.

Dementia Simplex

Simple insidious dementia as it was described by Diem under the name dementia simplex consists in an *impoverishment and devastation of the whole psychic life which is accomplished quite imperceptibly*. The disease begins usually in the years of sexual development, but often the first slight beginnings can be traced back into childhood. On the other hand Pick has also described a 'primary progressive dementia of adults', but it is certainly very doubtful whether it may be grouped with dementia praecox. In our patients a deterioration of mental activity becomes very gradually noticeable. The former good, perhaps distinguished scholar, fails always more conspicuously in tasks which till then he could carry out quite easily, and he is more and more outstripped by his companions. He appears absentminded, thoughtless, makes incomprehensible mistakes, cannot any longer follow the teaching rightly, does not reach the standard of the class. While pure exercises of memory are perhaps still satisfactory, a certain poverty of thought, weakness of judgement, and incoherence in the train of ideas appear always more distinctly. Many patients try by redoubled efforts to compensate for the results of their mental falling off, which is at first attributed by parents and teachers to laziness and want of good will. They sit the whole day over their work, learn by heart with all their might, sit up late at night, without being able to make their work any better. Others become idle and indifferent, stare for hours at their books without reading, give themselves no trouble with their tasks, and are not incited either by kindness or severity.

Hand in hand with this decline of mental

activity there is a change of temperament, which often forms the first conspicuous sign of the developing malady. The patients become depressed, timid, lachrymose, or impertinent, irritable, malicious; sometimes a certain obstinate stubbornness is developed. The circle of their interests becomes narrower; their relations to their companions become cold; they show neither attachment nor sympathy. Not infrequently a growing estrangement towards parents and brothers and sisters becomes noticeable. The patients remain indifferent to whatever happens in the family circle, shut themselves up, limit the contact with their relatives to the least possible. Bleuler brings forward here as a frequent explanation the 'œdipus complex', the concealed sexual inclination to one of the parents and the jealous emotions which arise from it. I consider that the generalization of that kind of case, which is certainly very rare, as belonging to the system of Freud, is wholly without foundation. It seems much more natural to me to explain the antagonism to relatives by the gloomy feeling of inferiority and the defiant resistance to it, but above all by the common experience that for a long time it has been the habit of the relatives to trace the morbid phenomena back to a moral offence, and to meet them with painful reprimands and measures. Similar antagonism is also seen quite commonly to develop in the relations with degenerate, wayward children.

Ambition and pleasure in the usual games and occasional occupations become extinct; wishes and plans for the future are silent; inclination and ability for useful occupation disappear. The patient has neither endurance nor understanding, works confusedly, begins everything the wrong way about, tries as far as possible to withdraw himself from claims on him. He remains lying in bed for days, sits about anywhere, trifles away his time in occupations of no value, devours perhaps without choice and without understanding chance and unsuitable literature, lives one day at a time without a plan. A few patients have indeed at times a certain feeling of the change, which takes place in them, often in hypochondriacal colouring; but the majority sink into dullness without being in any way sensible of it. Sometimes a certain restlessness is shown which causes the patient to take extended walks, to run away without any plan, to undertake aimless journeys. Alcohol is for him a special danger, he gives way to its temptations with-

out resistance, and then very rapidly comes down in the world, and comes into conflict with public order and criminal law. That happens the more easily as many patients are very sensitive to intoxicating drinks.

Manic-Depressive Disease

Manic-depressive insanity, as it is to be described in this section, includes on the one hand the whole domain of so-called *periodic and circular insanity*, on the other hand *simple mania*, the greater part of the morbid states termed *melancholia* and also a not inconsiderable number of cases of *amentia* (confusional or delirious insanity). Lastly, we include here certain slight and slightest colourings of *mood*, some of them periodic, some of them continuously morbid, which on the one hand are to be regarded as the rudiment of more severe disorders, on the other hand pass over without sharp boundary into the domain of *personal predisposition*. In the course of the years I have become more and more convinced that all the above-mentioned states only represent manifestations of a *single morbid process*. It is certainly possible that later a series of subordinate forms may be described, or even individual small groups again entirely separated off. But if this happens, then according to my view those symptoms will most certainly not be authoritative, which hitherto have usually been placed in the foreground.

What has brought me to this position is first the experience that notwithstanding manifold external differences certain *common fundamental features* yet recur in all the morbid states mentioned. Along with changing symptoms, which may appear temporarily or may be completely absent, we meet in all forms of manic-depressive insanity a quite definite, narrow group of disorders, though certainly of very varied character and composition. Without any one of them being absolutely characteristic of the malady, still in association they impress a uniform stamp on all the multiform clinical states. If one is conversant with them, one will in the great majority of cases be able to conclude in regard to any one of them that it belongs to the large group of forms of manic-depressive insanity by the peculiarity of the condition, and thus to gain a series of fixed points for the special clinical and prognostic significance of the case. Even a small part of the course of the disease usually enables us to arrive at this decision, just as in paralysis or dementia praecox the general psychic change often enough makes possible the diagnosis of the fundamental malady in its most different phases.

Of perhaps still greater significance than the classification of states by definite fundamental disorders is the experience that all the morbid forms brought together here as a clinical entity, *not only pass over the one into the other without recognizable boundaries, but that they may even replace each other in one and the same case.* On the one side, as will be later discussed in more detail, it is fundamentally and practically quite impossible to keep apart in any consistent way simple, periodic, and circular cases; everywhere there are gradual transitions. But on the other side we see in the same patient not only mania and melancholia, but also states of the most profound confusion and perplexity, also well developed delusions, and lastly, the slightest fluctuations of mood alternating with each other. Moreover, permanent, one-sided colourings of mood very commonly form the background on which fully developed circumscribed attacks of manic-depressive insanity develop.

A further common bond which embraces all the morbid types brought together here and makes the keeping of them apart practically almost meaningless, is their *uniform prognosis.* There are indeed slight and severe attacks which may be of long or short duration, but they alternate irregularly in the same case. This difference is therefore of no use for the delimitation of different diseases. A grouping according to the frequency of the attacks might much rather be considered, which naturally would be extremely welcome to the physician. It appears, however, that here also we have not to do with fundamental differences, since in spite of certain general rules it has not been possible to separate out definite types from this point of view. On the contrary the universal experience is striking, that the attacks of manic-depressive insanity within the delimitation attempted here never lead to profound dementia, not even when they continue throughout life almost without interruption. Usually all morbid manifestations completely disappear; but where that is exceptionally not the case, only a rather slight, peculiar psychic weakness develops, which is just as common to the types here taken together as it is different from dementias in diseases of other kinds.

As a last support for the view here represented of the unity of manic-depressive insanity the circumstance may be adduced, that the various forms which it comprehends may also apparently mutually replace one another in *heredity.* In members of the same family we frequently enough find side by side pronounced periodic or circular cases, occasionally isolated states of ill temper or confusion, lastly very slight, regular fluctuations of mood or permanent conspicuous coloration of disposition. From whatever point of view accordingly the manic-depressive morbid forms may be regarded, from that of aetiology or of clinical phenomena, the course or the issue— it is evident everywhere that here points of agreement exist, which make it possible to regard our domain as a unity and to delimit it from all the other morbid types hitherto discussed. Further experience must show whether and in what directions in this extensive domain smaller sub-groups can be separated from one another.

In the first place the difference of the states which usually make up the disease, presents itself as the most favourable ground of classification. As a rule the disease runs its course in isolated attacks more or less sharply defined from each other or from health, which are either like or unlike, or even very frequently are perfect antitheses. Accordingly we distinguish first of all manic states with the essential morbid symptoms of flight of ideas, exalted mood, and pressure of activity, and *melancholia* or *depressive states* with sad or anxious moodiness and also sluggishness of thought and action. These two opposed phases of the clinical state have given the disease its name. But besides them we observe also clinical *'mixed forms'*, in which the phenomena of mania and melancholia are combined with each other, so that states arise, which indeed are composed of the same morbid symptoms as these, but cannot without coercion be classified either with one or with the other.

6 The Schizoid Temperament

Ernst Kretschmer

Cycloid men are simple and uncomplicated beings, whose feelings rise directly, naturally, and undisguised to the surface, so that everyone can soon get a correct judgment of them. Schizoid men have a surface and a depth. Cuttingly brutal, dull and sulky, bitingly sarcastic, or timidly retiring, like a mollusc without a shell—that is the surface. Or else the surface is just nothing; we see a man who stands in our way like a question mark, we feel that we are in contact with something flavourless, boring, and yet with a certain problematic quality about it. What is there in the deep under all these masks? Perhaps there is a nothing, a dark, hollow-eyed nothing—affective anæmia. Behind an ever-silent facade, which twitches uncertainly with every expiring whim—nothing but broken pieces, black rubbish heaps, yawning emotional emptiness, or the cold breath of an arctic soullessness. But from the facade we cannot see what lurks behind. Many schizoid folk are like Roman houses and villas, which have closed their shutters before the rays of the burning sun; perhaps in the subdued interior light there are festivities.

One cannot study the schizophrenic inner life in all its fullness from peasants. Kings and poets are good enough for that. There are schizoid men with whom we can live for ten years and yet not be able to say for certain that we know them. A shy girl, pious and lamblike serves for months in the town: she is gentle and tractable with everyone. One morning the three children of the house lie murdered. The house is in flames. She has not lost her senses, she understands everything. She smiles uncertainly when she realizes her act. A young man dreams away the lovely days of his youth. He is so clumsy and loutish that one could shake him. If he is set upon a horse he falls off at once. He smiles in an embarrassed way, rather ironically. He says nothing. One day there appears a volume of poetry that he has written, full of an exquisite feeling for nature, with every blow that some fat lout has given him as he passed by moulded into an inner

Abridged from *Physique and Character*, trans. W. J. H. Sprott (London: Kegan Paul, 1925), pp. 150–174.

tragedy, and the polished rhythms flowing on full of quiet.

That is what schizoid men are like. Bleuler calls it 'Autism'—the living inside oneself. One cannot know what they feel; sometimes they don't know themselves, or only dimly—perhaps three simultaneous things, indistinct and yet with a strong emotional value, inextricably commingled one with the other in a vaguely-grasped mystical relation; or the most intimate and the most general ideas, forced together into a bizarre scheme with numbers and figures. But what their feeling is, whether it be a banality, a whim, an indecency, or a pearl of fairy lore, that is for no one—that is for them alone.

In the schizophrene group, we are less able than in the circular to separate the healthy from the diseased, the characterological from the psychotic. Circular psychoses flow in waves, which come and go in a fluid manner, compensating one another. What appears before and what after the psychoses we can regard as having the same value. Schizophrenic psychoses come in jerks. Something has got out of order in the inner structure. The whole structure may collapse inside, or perhaps only a few slanting cracks may appear. But in the majority of cases there remains something that never gets patched up. Where the attack has not been severe, we refer to a 'post-psychotic personality', and in severe cases we speak of a schizophrenic idiocy—between the two no hard-and-fast line can be drawn. But we often are not aware whether the psychosis has disappeared or not. People who for years have performed the duties connected with their calling as merely eccentric and unfriendly personalities, may one day quite by chance disclose to us that the greater part of the time they carry the most fantastic illusions about with them—here, too, no boundaries can be drawn. And besides, what, after all, is personal eccentricity, and what is to be judged the derangement of a madman? Finally, everyone alters particularly clearly at the time of puberty. Schizophrenia usually manifests itself at this period. Supposing we take people who have undergone some striking alteration at this time of life, shall we regard them as post-psychotic personalities or as undeveloped schizoids? These questions are pertinent when we are dealing with close relatives of schizophrenes. In the pubertial years the schizoid peculiarities rise to their height; but with lighter cases at this period, we often do not know (1) whether we see before us the development of a schizophrenic psychosis, or (2) whether we are in the middle of a psychosis, or (3) whether we have already the psychological results of an attack which has worn off, or finally, (4) whether it is all merely the stormy and bizarre pubertial development of a schizoid personality—for the normal effects of puberty, the shyness, the awkwardness, the sentimentality, the pathetic strainings, and the affectation, closely resemble certain traits of the schizoid temperament.

The Career of the Schizoid

Cycloid men keep, through all their manic-depressive vicissitudes, the fundamental symptoms of their temperament as a rule from the cradle to the grave. The biological influence which produces the schizophrene and schizoid personality, on the other hand, is something that is planted inside, that makes its appearance at a certain period of life, and with a certain sequence of phenomena, and then proceeds further. The most common sequence in severe cases is as follows: from earliest childhood there is a recognizable schizoid personality, at puberty a schizophrenic psychosis develops out of it, and this leaves behind it a specific deterioration or a post-psychotic personality, which does not differ in essentials from the pre-psychotic personality, though possibly it may, even apart from gross defects, in the more striking manifestation of other schizoid symptom-groups.

This typical process may, however, vary as to the times at which it makes its appearance. We sometimes find schizoids who look just as if they had already been through a schizophrenic psychosis before they were born; from infancy they are as weak in intelligence, and as obstinate, odd, hostile, and untractable as the majority of schizoids become later when they have a severe psychosis behind them.[1]

The congenitally antisocial, weak-minded individual of the schizoid genre may, in later life, on account of some katatonic jolt, betray his obvious membership in the schizophrenic group. All these severely disintegrated, defective conditions, whether they are inborn or acquired, whether they are tinged with the colour of criminal hostility to society, or sulky eccentricity, or dull-wittedness, or heboid foolishness, invariably bear the typical stamp of schizophrenic psychology, but from a characterological point of view they are so unfertile that in spite of their frequent occurrence we need only make a short mention of them; and besides, they are completely set forth in text-books of psychiatry.

While in the instances we have just mentioned the schizophrenic influence makes its appearance rather prematurely, the opposite case of its retardation is not infrequent. In my material there is a small but noteworthy number of schizophrenes, in whom no trace of a pre-psychotic personality was noticeable during the period of childhood, and who were described as being fresh, happy, sociable, and cheerful in early life. Here the pubertial psychosis breaks out suddenly, and without warning, or the pre-psychotic schizoid appears as it were, belatedly, in lingering, chronic pubertial alterations of the personality, which may simply settle down in the course of life, may persist in the characterological framework, or may turn straight away into a schizophrenic psychosis. Even from their childhood onwards, schizoids, as is well known, experience these pubertial modifications of the personality without psychoses, often after a brief and glorious flowering of all their psychic endowments. For the psychology of creativeness, this bubbling out and sudden unexpected drying up of productivity is very important, particularly in the case of poets (I would call to mind the poet Uhland, who, though healthy, was physically as well as psychically a typical schizothyme).[2]

Finally, there are a few rare instances in which the schizoid partial components of the hereditary endowment are completely retarded, e.g., until the period of involution, and can still become manifest in the character; that is to say, where you have individuals who, in early life, were bright, gay, and

---

[1] Kraepelin has advanced a similar theoretical view. It is confirmed by the physical examination, which discloses, in these schizoids who are born weak-minded, bodily stigmata of an advanced degree.

[2] The expressions 'Schizothyme' and 'Cyclothyme' refer to constitution concepts of a general character, including both healthy and diseased.

sociable, and then, after their 40th year, traits of mistrust, hypochondria, sensitive reserve, and sullen hostility towards mankind creep into the picture. We have already touched upon this process of late alternation of dominance when we were dealing with bodily constitutional stigmata.

The Psychaesthetic Proportions

The superficial schizoid peculiarities of character as they appear in our material are as follows, arranged according to their statistical frequencies:

1. Unsociable, quiet, reserved, serious (humourless), eccentric.
2. Timid, shy, with fine feelings, sensitive, nervous, excitable, fond of nature and books.
3. Pliable, kindly, honest, indifferent, dull-witted, silent.

What our statistics reflect in the first place are the pre-psychotic personalities of people who have become psychologically diseased later. We can certainly evolve the fundamental characteristics of the schizoid temperament out of them, but we shall have to fill them in with traits from schizophrenic psychoses, post-psychotic personalities, and the characters of schizoids who are not themselves psychopaths, though related to people who are, without its being possible or necessary to separate out these elements, which are inextricably mixed up with one another.

We have divided the most common schizoid peculiarities again into three groups. The characteristics in group 1 are absolutely the most common in that they run like a scarlet thread through the whole schizoid characterology, as well through group 2 as group 3. Apart from the humourless seriousness, which expresses the weak manifestation of the diathetic (cycloid) temperamental scale, they make up in its essence what Bleuler has described as 'Autism'. Groups 2 and 3 stand in a certain opposition to one another, they form a pair of contrasts similar to that which we find among cycloids in the cheerful-mobile group and the depressive-melancholic group. Group 2 contains, in all the possible shadings, the phenomena of psychic over-sensitivity, from the mimosa-like, timid fineness of feeling to a continual state of passionate excitation. Group 3 on the contrary contains indica-

tions of a certain psychic insensitivity, dullness, and lack of spontaneity. It tends, that is to say, to the pole which Kraepelin has called in the severest psychotic cases 'affective imbecility'.

If we want to give a short account of the basis of the schizoid temperament, we must say: the schizoid temperament lies between the extremes of excitability and dullness, in the same way that the cycloid temperament lies between the extremes of cheerfulness and sadness. Besides this, we shall have to lay particular stress on the symptoms of psychic overexcitability, because this has been far too little appreciated as an essential ingredient of the total schizoid psychology, while those symptoms which are to be laid to the score of insensitivity have already had their importance recognized for a long time.

He alone, however, has the key to the schizoid temperament who has clearly recognized that the majority of schizoids are not either over-sensitive or cold, but that they are over-sensitive and cold at the same time, and that in quite different relative proportions. Out of our schizoid material we can form a continuous series, beginning with what I call the 'Hölderlin type'—those extremely sensitive, abnormally tender, constantly wounded, mimosa-like natures, who are 'all nerves'— and winding up with those cold, numbed, almost lifeless ruins left by the ravages of a severe attack of dementia praecox, who hover like shades in a corner of the asylum, dull-witted as cows. And at the same time, even with the most gentle representative of that mimosa group of characteristics, we feel a light, intangible breath of aristocratic frigidity and distance, an autistic narrowing down of affective responses to a strictly limited circle of men and things, and occasionally we hear a harsh, loveless remark passed on men who lie outside this circle, and towards whose behaviour the affective resonance is damped. "There is a pane of glass between me and mankind", said such a schizoid recently—a remark of extraordinary significance. We can sense these thin, hard, cold, sharp, splintering panes of glass, when we deal with the later katatonic period of Hölderlin, who was a more than usually lovable representative of the 'mimosa' group, and even more clearly when we come to the later schizophrenic Strindberg, who said of himself, "I am hard as ice, and yet so full of feeling that I am almost sentimental". This 'mimosa' type can best be studied in schizoid men of genius, but one finds it all over the place, and also among the usual asylum material, particularly in intelligent and educated persons, in their prepsychotic states, or in the initial stages of their psychosis.

The schizoid temperaments, then, as we have said, may be ranged in a continuous ladder from this mimosa-like extreme to the insensitive and cold extreme, as the "hard as ice" (dull as leather) quality becomes ever more prominent, and "the sensitivity to the extent of sentimentality" ever less in evidence. But even in that half of our material which is primarily cold and poor in affective response, as soon as we come into close personal contact with such schizoids, we find, very frequently, behind the unresponsive, numbed exterior, in the innermost sanctuary, a tender personality-nucleus with the most vulnerable nervous sensitivity, which has withdrawn into itself, and lies there contorted. "You have no idea how miserable all that makes me", said a hebephrenic, dried-up schoolboy recently to his parents, a boy from whose external appearance no one could see anything but insuperable hard indolence, psychic paralysis, and complete lack of temperament. Bleuler was again the first to show how those mummified old asylum inmates, whom one had been accustomed to regard as the type of affective imbecility, may still have the remains of 'complexes', isolated, oversensitive portions of their psychic lives, which have remained intact, and stimulation of which may have sudden and startling results. And we are constantly coming across cases, where such an individual, who lies there apparently completely insensitive, and turned katatonically into stone, is set free by a jerk, and lets forth from his inner soul almost monumental affective outbursts; so that, in many sorts of schizophrenic states, we are unable to say straight off how much is a matter of this complete numbing and cramping of affective response, and how much is real affective imbecility.

The mixture in which, in any given schizoid, the hyperæsthetic and the anæsthetic elements are combined with one another, we call his 'psychæsthetic proportion'. And we must remember that we saw quite similar mixtures in the cycloid temperaments with regard to their diathetic or mood-proportions, in that it was only in the rarest cases that we found absolutely cheerful and absolutely miserable men, but much more prevalently combinations and alternations between cheerfulness and sadness: even the sunny, cheerful person often has a clearly depressive background, and traces of humour are to be found far down the line of the melancholic temperaments.

The mood-proportions of cycloids fluctuate in waves. The psychæsthetic proportions of schizoids get jerked out of their equilibrium. That is to say, the relation between the hyperæsthetic and the anæsthetic temperaments varies spasmodically as life goes on, in the case of many schizoids, without returning again to the position from which it started. The psychæsthesia of the healthy average man of mixed medium temperament reaches its height in the typical, sentimentally-coloured exuberance and sensitivity of the pubertal period, and then, from the age of 25, it slowly cools off until it reaches a certain quiet solidity of outlook, and often a state of sober, flat, dry immobility. The student song reflects this cooled Philistine feeling of the average man looking back at the days of his adolescence.

The displacement of the psychaesthetic proportions of the schizoids frequently proceeds on parallel lines to this normal development, and forms, as it were, an exaggerated and deepened image of it. The schizophrene, Hölderlin, displays this displacement paradigmatically, if we follow the pattern of his life from the excitable tenderness of his early years as a poet to the twilit dullwittedness of his decade-long katatonic sickliness. The transition from the hyperaesthetic to the anaesthetic pole is often experienced with terrible vividness by fully-developed personalities as a general inner cooling,[3] and

[3]What, in cases of acute schizophrenia, we call "alteration of the objective consciousness" and "alteration of the consciousness of personality", rests probably to a certain extent on the psychaesthetic displacement, since alterations in the strength of the sensational qualities and the usual feeling tone towards individual objects (hyperaesthesia, or anaesthesia) produce completely novel and unheard-of impressons (here strange noises, shrill and meaningful, there a mysterious feeling of something cold and queer, and there, again, inexplicable recognitions). The delusions of influence and persecution have probably part of their roots in these sudden mysterious modifications of the psychaesthetic illumination. In the same way, perhaps, the alterations of the internal and external sensations, of which many schizophrenes complain in the early stages, may be

Hölderlin describes it in the following verses:

> "Where art thou? But little lived I, and yet
>   breathes cold
> The evening of my life. And quiet like the
>   shadows
> I still am here; and already without song,
> Slumbers my cowering heart within my breast."

In this manner a whole group of gifted schizoids develop, even without becoming psychically diseased, men who, having been tender, shy, and nervous in their childhood, experience, in the early stages of puberty, a short hot-house-like flowering of all their capacities and affective capabilities on the basis of an enormously heightened sensitivity of their temperament, in the direction of melancholy sentimentality, or pubertial pathos with an even more exaggerated tension. After a few years, they calm down, still scarcely tolerable as average citizens, but gradually becoming ever duller and cooler, more and more individualistic, silent, and dry. The pubertial wave lifts them higher and plunges them deeper than is the case with the normal man.

Or else it may happen that the psychaesthetic displacement goes on underground over longer periods, and without choosing a particular point of time. In all these various possibilities, however, the alteration of proportions in schizoids is usually from the hyperaesthetic to the anaesthetic extreme, from excitement to emotional paralysis, in such a way that (schematically speaking), after the first stage of all-round hypersensitivity, those values which are foreign to the personality lose their affective resonance, while those values which have to do with the personality itself, becoming more and more important for it, retain their accentuation, and only when those contents which have to do with the personality itself lose their affective value, does the third stage, that of affective idiocy, set in. The allo-psychic resonance becomes obliterated before the autopsychic. The halfdead schizophrene, will, if he is educated, become an actor or a musician during this transitional stage. The exhibition of oneself is still an excitement: perhaps he will even become a futurist painter, an expressionist poet, an inventor, or a builder of abstract, schematic philosophical systems. This disproportion

biological symptoms running parallel to the psychaesthetic displacements.

caused by the dying off of the allo-psychic resonance, while the hypersensitivity of the autopsychic remains, produces extraordinary degrees of self-overvaluation, often proceeding according to fixed laws. One need go no further to perceive that a fundamentally false picture of the opposed importance of the 'I' and the 'external world' emerges out of such a psychæsthetic proportion. We can thus imagine that many schizoids, during the course of their lives, pass through a gradual temperamental cooling from without inwards, so that, side by side with an ever-increasing numbing of the outer sheath, there remains a tender hypersensitive inner nucleus which is always withdrawing into itself. This pictorial mode of expression best corresponds with the remarkable fact that those schizophrenes who are the most sensitive, and have the finest feelings, seem to have all over them on the outside a thin icy sheath, when they are with chance acquaintances; and on the other hand, lively reactions of a hypersensitive nature may occur, even where there is pronounced schizophrenic petrification, if by chance we touch on the innermost complexes of the personality. "He is a drop of fiery wine in a bowl of ice", was Hebbel's admirable remark about the healthy schizothymic Uhland.

We must supplement what we have said with the remark that the stage of absolute hypersensitivity, as also the stage of absolute affective coldness, are, indeed, in the strictest sense of the words only theoretical fictions, which hardly ever occur, to their fullest extent, in real life. What we meet with in practice is almost always certain changing relations in the psychæsthetic proportions of hypersensitivity and coldness. Only a few schizoids pass, in the course of their lives, through the typical process from extreme hyperæsthesia to the preponderatingly anæsthetic pole; some remain hyperæsthetic, some are already prevailingly torpid when they come into the world. And, finally, there are a few cases, which after a schizophrenic psychosis, are even more hyperæsthetic than before: such an one was Strindberg.

Social Reactions

Autism, regarded as a symptom of the schizoid temperament, follows in its essence the psychæsthetic scale of the individual schizoid. There are instances where autism is predominantly a symptom of hypersensitivity. Such overexcitable schizoids feel all the harsh, strong colours and tones of everyday life, which to the average man and to the cycloid are welcome and indispensably stimulating elements of existence, as shrill, ugly, and unlovable, even to the extent of being psychically painful. Their autism is a painful cramping of the self into itself. They seek as far as possible to avoid and deaden all stimulation from the outside; they close the shutters of their houses, in order to lead a dream-life, fantastic, 'poor in deeds and rich in thought' (Hölderlin) in the soft muffled gloom of the interior. They seek loneliness, as Strindberg so beautifully said of himself, in order to "spin themselves into the silk of their own souls". They have regular preferences for certain forms of milieu which do not hurt or harm: the cold aristocratic world of salons, office work that goes on mechanically, according to fixed rules and regulations, the beautiful loneliness of nature, antiquity, distant times, and the halls of learning. When a schizothyme turns from a blasé, overcivilized, society man into a hermit, like Tolstoi, the revolution inside, regarded from the point of view of the soul of the schizothyme himself, is not so great. The one milieu offers him the same as the other, the one thing that he desires above all else from the outer world: the protection of his hyperæsthesia.

The autism of the predominantly anæsthetic, on the other hand, is unfeelingness, lack of affective response to the world about him, which has no interest for his emotional life, and for whose own rightful interests he has no feeling. He draws himself back into himself because he has no reason to do anything else, because all that is about him can offer him nothing.

The autism of the majority of schizoids and schizophrenes, however, is based on mixtures, in the most varied proportions, of the two temperamental aspects; it is indolence with a streak of anxiety and animosity; it is often cold, and yet in the same breath it prays to be left in peace. Crampedness and lameness in one picture.

The nature of the social attitudes of the schizoid man, just as that of the healthy schizothymes whom we shall be describing later, springs from the above-mentioned psychæsthetic relations. Schizoid men are either unsociable or eclectically sociable within a small closed circle, or else superficially sociable, without deeper psychic rapport with their environment. The unsociability of schizoids has the most varied gradations; it is seldom mere unfeeling dullness, it usually has a clear admixture of distaste, of active turning away, of a more or less defensive or offensive character. This disinclination for human society varies from the gentlest display of anxiety, timidity, and shyness, through ironical coldness, and sulky, distorted dullness, to cutting, brutal, active hostility towards mankind. And the most remarkable thing is that the affective attitude of an individual schizoid to his fellow-men changes colour in a strange rainbow-like fashion: now timidity, irony, sulkiness, now brutality. A particularly good characterological example of this type is the schizothyme, Robespierre. Even with those who are suffering from schizophrenic insanity, the affective attitude towards the outer world has very often this quality of 'insuring' (Adler), of peeping distrustfully sideways out of half-sunken eyelids, and of tentatively projecting feelers and quickly withdrawing them. With a nervous-fingered uncertainty, especially when face to face with a newly-arrived stranger, they run over all the half-tones of the psychæsthetic scale that lies within their registers. This feeling of insecurity is often transferred to the onlooker; many a schizoid behaves so oddly, vaguely, opaquely, and strangely, or so whimsically, intriguingly, and even maliciously. But for the outside observer, there always remains, behind the 'insuring' oscillations of the schizoid affective attitude, a remnant to which he never comes nearer, which he cannot see through, which never comes to the surface.

In short, the schizoid does not get on in a crowd. The pane of glass is always there. In the hyperaesthetic type, there often develops a sharp antithesis: 'I' and 'The external world'. There is a constant excited selfanalysis and comparison: 'How do I impress people? Who is doing me an injury? In what respect have I to forgive myself something? How shall I get through?' This is particularly true of gifted, artistic natures, who have late in life fallen victims of schizophrenia, or who come from families where there is a suspicion of schizophrenic disease; Hölderlin, Strindberg, Ludwig II of Bavaria, Feuerbach, Tasso, Michelangelo, manifest this trait very significantly. They are men who have a continual psychic conflict, whose life is composed of a chain of tragedies, a single thorny path of sorrow. They have, as it were, a genius for the tragic. The pure cyclothyme is not capable of driving a situation to the point where it becomes tragic: he has already adapted himself long ago, and the environment has adapted itself to him, because he comes to meet it with understanding, and in a spirit of conciliation. A healthy individual of this type, out of the pyknic-cyclothymic group was, for example, Hans Thoma, who was as misjudged as Feuerbach, but whose life flowed on like an untroubled, contemplative brook.[4] Rugged, cold egoism, pharisaical self-satisfaction, and overwhelming, hypersensitive self-feeling, are common in all their variations in schizophrene families. But they are not the only forms of autism. Another is the striving after the theoretical amelioration of mankind, after schematic, doctrinaire rules of life, after the betterment of the world, or the model education of their own children, often involving a stoic renunciation of all needs on the part of the individuals themselves. Altruistic self-sacrifice in the grandest possible style, especially for general impersonal ideals (socialism, teetotalism), is a specific characteristic of many schizoids. In this way, in gifted schizophrenic families, we sometimes find superb characters, who leave even the most noble schizothyme far behind them in impersonal rectitude and objectivity, in unflinching fidelity to convictions, in nobility and purity of disposition, and in stubborn tenacity in the fight for their ideals, while on an average they themselves are surpassed by the cyclothymes in natural warm kind-heartedness towards individual men, and patient understanding of their peculiarities.

Psychaesthetic Variants

So far we have been looking on the hyperaesthesia and anaesthesia of schizoids as if they were single states. But they have very significant variants, about which we do not know whether they are merely quantitatively different, or whether there is a biological qualitative difference between them. At the anesthetic end we find three important temperamental variants, which, indeed, are often present simultaneously, and which show many transitional variations: dullness (with or without affective lameness), coldness, and "total indifference" (Bleuler); while at the hyper-aesthetic end the most important variations to distinguish are: sensitivity, sentimentality, and a passionate violence which springs from the presence of complexes.

Here, again, we must bring the pre-psychotics more clearly out of the general schizoid mass. We find statistically that the types corresponding to those odd eccentrics, cold-blooded, ill-tempered individuals, dry pedants, or scatter-brained wasters, who are so common among the adult relatives of schizophrenes, and among post-psychotics, do not occur nearly so often in the childhood and early pubertial stages of people who eventually become diseased. We certainly find characteristics like rudeness, stubbornness, ill-temperedness, laziness, etc., also mentioned in connection with our pre-psychotic material, in which case one can never be certain whether the relatives have really described the original personality, or its first gradual modification in the early pubertial stages. In frequency, however, they lag far behind the characteristics mentioned at the beginning of the chapter.

The commonest type in our pre-psychotic material is that in which one finds affective lameness; quiet, timid, tractable, shy people with the predicate 'good-natured'. Striking examples of 'precocious children' such as Kraepelin has given prominence to, are very common among them. The term 'affective lameness' has a close connection with popular speech, which describes those people as 'lame (contorted)' in whose behaviour it is clearly manifest that the most outstanding symptom is a psychomotor one. The expression 'affective lameness', then, does not coincide with the term 'affective dullness' which clearly lays the accent on the sensorial side. "One could have wished that he were livelier." "He is a bit tepid." "He is absolutely lacking in life and temperament." Such are the commonest descriptions of young men suffering from affective lameness. This lack of liveliness, of immediately-reacting vivacity of psychomotor expression, is found also in the most gifted members of the group with their hypersensitive inner capacities for reaction.

[4]There is no better introduction to the differences of the cyclothymic and schizothymic attitudes towards life than the comparative reading of the autobiographical sketches in Hans Thoma, *Im Herbst des Lebens*, and Anselm Feuerbach, *Ein Vermächtnis*.

The quiet cycloid is 'comfortable', the quiet type of schizoid, which we are describing here, is 'lame'. This 'comfortable' quality is the characterological expression of the lightest degree of that psychomotor type which we meet with again in the restraint of the depressive. It describes that melancholic something which takes its time for speech and activity, but where we have a warm, immediate emotional participation in every word and deed. 'The lame' have psychomotor slowness and economy in common with the 'comfortable'. But 'lameness' implies, beyond that, the loss of immediate connection between the emotional stimulus and the motor response. It is for this reason that with the 'comfortable' person we always have the feeling that we are in emotional rapport, even when he says nothing, while the 'lame' appears to us strange, unsympathetic, as we express it in German, 'nicht mitfühlend', because we often cannot read in his face, or in his movements, the expression of what he is feeling, or, above all, the adequate reaction to what we are doing and saying to him. The essential quality of the 'lame' is that he can stand there with a puzzled face and hanging arms, like a note of interrogation, in a situation that would electrify even one of the 'comfortables'.

But when the psychic expression does come to the surface in the 'lame', it is not always precisely adapted to the stimulus, or else it lags behind, until a time when it is no longer suitable. The expression of the 'lame' is very changeable and uncertain, so that one usually takes them for proud, when they are only timid, or for ironical, when they have been most deeply wounded.

In addition to this, there are often irregularities in the actual motor reactions themselves. People whom one would describe as 'lame' are quite often surprisingly reckless in their behaviour, or clumsy in their movements. They do not know what to do with their limbs. Many are also remarkably unpractical, and helpless in the ordinary matters of life, and cut an unfortunate figure when they are doing gymnastic exercises. Pronounced motor inhibitions, due to general timidity or the working of some special complex, play their part here as well. In short, even if one is looking at psychomotility from a narrower standpoint, there is again the lack of immediate working together of the processes concerned in stimulation and reaction. That is

lacking which the cycloids possess in such an outstanding degree—smoothness, naturalness, and unconstraint in affective expression and in movement.

In all this nothing has been said about the psychosensorial side of the process. The 'lameness' may be correlated with a real dullness of emotional response to the stimulus before it, or, on the other hand, processes involving the finest sensibilities, and the most extreme intrapsychic tension may be going on behind it. The simply laity, indeed, do not distinguish between these. They look on the 'lame' man as stupid, or at all events dullwitted, as an unfeeling, sleepy, boring chap, who has no snap about him, and whom one has got to wake up. He is unsympathetic to them. At school, and certainly in the barracks, the young man who is 'lame', is the queer bird, at which they all start pecking. In so far as he really has fine feelings inside and is gifted, there lies the real tragedy of such men. For many of them are far more sensitive than the average man.

On the negative side, our type of sensitive affectively lame has a characteristic in common with the whole group of schizoids. They are, on an average, devoid of humour, and often serious, without exhibiting either sorrowfulness or cheerfulness. The diathetic scale, which is the most important scale among the cycloids, finds on the whole only a weak expression in their temperament. Schizoids are very often depressed: but this depression is something quite other than the sorrowfulness of the cycloid. It has something distrustful, something ill-humoured and nervous, about it, with a clear quality of internal excitation and stress, for which reason one finds among schizoids those constitutionally depressed persons who are always on the move, while the inhibited depressive stays at home. Side by side with nervous, strained depression, we also find, among schizoids, the emotional attitude of unshakably satisfied, autistic peace of mind, while their strong positive feelings have less the quality of free gaiety, than of ecstasy, and exaggerated enthusiasm.

We must regard the type of the sensitive affectively lame, in its whole range, from the timid, impassive schizoid imbecile up to the highly differentiated Hölderlin natures, as perhaps the most important schizoid type of temperament, at any rate as one of the most frequent pre-psychotic foundations and starting points. Even among old asylum material, it still may be found in a disintegrated post-psychotic form. Similarly it occurs among the healthy members of schizophrene families.

We have already considered affective dullness as a component in the 'lame' temperament. The expression 'dullness' denotes passive lack of feeling. We find emotional dullness, as we have said, very frequently in the schizophrenic group. The light characterological form in which we often find it among the healthy members of schizophrenic families strikes one as an unshakable peace of mind, as a phlegmatic state, which may be distinguished from the cycloid 'comfortableness' by the lack of warm, emotional responsiveness towards mankind. We find the severer degrees of schizophrenic insensitivity, generally with a touch of morose brutality, or shy anxiety, congenital in schizoid imbeciles, but it is seen particularly, to a marked degree, in post-psychotics, and also after the equally significant modifications of the personality which occur at puberty. This inner blunting may betray itself in those who otherwise function perfectly well; indeed, it may be found in highly gifted individuals, manifesting itself, particularly, in surprising carelessness, and even in neglect of clothes and home. Or else it betrays itself by means of sudden and inexplicable tactlessness, and want of taste, which here and there breaks unexpectedly through the otherwise unaltered facade of good education, appearing particularly grotesque in the previously sensitive aristocratic type of schizoid. Throughout the course of his life, the poet Lenz was an excellent example of such a half-wrecked personality. One can study this disruption of the personality particularly well if one turns to the literary style of the schizophrenically diseased poets, e.g., Hölderlin. The whole personality level does not sink evenly, but an, if anything, increasing hymnic solemnity and stylistic carefulness will be broken up somewhere, in the middle of a verse, by some outrageous banality. The psychic apparatus of such men, in their style, and in their mode of life, functions like a bad sewing-machine, which keeps on making a number of fine stitches and then giving a jump. Sensitivity and absolute dullness may live here incredibly closely together: the filthiest shirt beside polished finger-nails; chaotic untidiness in a room where the most valuable and pure works of art are produced. Such instances are found not only as transitional stages towards complete schizophrenic idiocy; they may also remain intact the whole life long, as baroque types of personality. Sense and senselessness, moral suffering and banal sectarian oddity, one original thought along with two crazy ones, all in a regular mixture.

7 A Constitutional Typology

William H. Sheldon

A. Structural Concepts

Constitution

The organizational or underlying pattern. Literally, the way a thing *stands together*. The whole aggregate of the relatively fixed and deep-seated structural and behavioral characteristics that collectively differentiate a personality. Perhaps the most satisfactory way to start an examination of the constitutional pat-

Abridged from *Varieties of Delinquent Youth*, pages 14–62, 1949, by William H. Sheldon, E. M. Hartl, and Eugene McDermott. By permission of Professor Sheldon, copyright holder.

tern of a human being is photographically, although this is only a beginning and offers but an anchorage or frame of reference for constitutional description. Behind the objective and overt aspects of morphology lie individual differences first in those aspects of morphology which are not outwardly revealed, such as the structure, dysplasias, and t component of internal organs, of the nervous system, of the endocrine glands, and so on; and further, individual differences in physiology and chemistry. All of these differences contribute to and make up what is referred to as personality. The term *constitution* implies only a certain relatedness and orderliness or patterning with respect to the underlying aspects of personality. In so far as the student of constitution addresses his energies to the study of external morphology he is but trying to anchor (to something taxonomically describable) an approach to personality as a whole, in its physiological and immunological and psychological as well as morphological aspects.

The Somatotype

A quantification of the primary components determining the morphological structure of an individual. In practice the somatotype is a series of three numerals, each expressing the approximate strength of one of the primary components in a physique. The first numeral always refers to *endomorphy*, the second to *mesomorphy*, the third to *ectomorphy*. When a 7-point scale is used the somatotype $7-1-1$ is the most extreme endomorph, the $1-7-1$ is the most extreme mesomorph, and the $1-1-7$ is the most extreme ectomorph. The somatotype $4-4-4$ falls at the midpoint of the scale with respect to all three primary components.

Endomorphy, or the first component: Relative predominance in the bodily economy of structure associated with digestion and assimilation. Relatively great development of the digestive *viscera*. In embryonic life the endoderm, or inner embryonic layer, grows into what becomes the functional element in a long tube, stretched or coiled from mouth to anus with a number of appendages. This is the digestive tube. Together with its appendages it is sometimes called the vegetative system. Its organs make up the bulk of the viscera. Endomorphy means relative predominance of the vegetative system, with a consequent tendency to put on fat easily. Endomorphs have low specific gravity. They float easily in the water. When well nourished they tend toward softness and roundness throughout the body, but it should be remembered that in learning to gauge one of the components it is necessary to learn to gauge the other two at the same time.

Mesomorphy, or the second component: Relative predominance of the mesodermally derived tissues, which are chiefly bone, muscle, and connective tissue. These are the somatic structures, or the motor organ-systems. Mesomorphs tend toward massive strength and muscular development. When their endomorphy is low, so that they remain lean, they retain a hard rectangularity of outline. If endomorphy is not low, mesomorphs tend to "fill out" heavily and to grow fat in middle life. However, because of the heavy underlying skeletal and muscular structure, they remain solid. When fat they are "hard-round," in contrast with the "soft-roundness" of endomorphy, and they continue in the general mold and in the proportions of athletic shapeliness. Endomorphs get roly-poly, globular, and pendulous. Mesomorphs just swell up in their generally athletic mold. Mesomorphs are of higher specific gravity than endomorphs. They are less buoyant in water but because of superior muscular power are nevertheless often good swimmers. The mesomorphic heart and blood vessels are large, and the skin seems relatively thick because of heavy reinforcement with underlying connective tissue.

Ectomorphy, or the third component: Relative predominance of the skin and its appendages, which include the nervous system. All of these tissues are derived from the ectodermal embryonic layer. In the ectomorph there is relatively little bodily mass and relatively great surface area—therefore greater sensory exposure to the outside world. Endomorphs and mesomorphs appear to be biological conservatives, the former investing faith in superior assimilative power or digestive ability, the latter in superior resistive substance and striking power. Ectomorphs seem to have departed from *both* of these essential biological insurances and to have embarked on an exteroceptive adventure. They have given up mass for surface, in a sense suppressing the primacy of both the digestive organ-system and the motor organ-system in favor of the sensory organ-system. The Italian Schoool of Clinical Anthropology (DiGiovanni, Viola, Pende) calls them hyperevolutes, suggesting that in departing from the secure advantages of the coarser and heavier bodies of the endomorphs and mesomorphs (in favor of extending the sensorium externally), they tend to move out toward the end of an evolutionary limb whence it may be difficult to return. Morphologically, ectomorphy means flatness and fragility throughout the body, with a comparatively high height/weight index.

Mesomorphic endomorphs; endomorphic

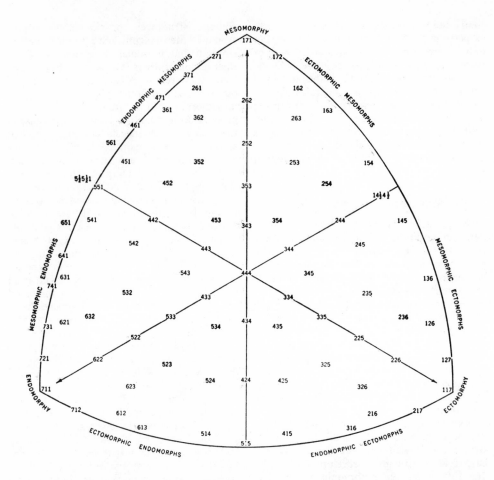

FIGURE 1. Schematic Two-Dimensional Projection of the Theoretical Spatial Relationships among the Known Somatotypes

mesomorphs; ectomorphic mesomorphs; mesomorphic ectomorphs; endomorphic ectomorphs; ectomorphic endomorphs: These terms refer to physiques in which all three of the primary morphological components are of different strength. Figure 1 is a schematic two-dimensional presentation of the somatotypes in which these six various "families" are spatially delineated. An endomorphic mesomorph is an individual in whom mesomorphy predominates, with endomorphy second in order to strength, and ectomorphy third. Example: the somatotype 3−5−2.

B. Behavioral Concepts

Temperament

According to Webster: (1) A mixing in due proportion; (2) The internal constitution with respect to balance or mixture of qualities or components; (3) The peculiar physical and mental character of an individual; (4) Frame of mind or type of mental reactions characteristic of an individual.

The original meaning of the Greek verb is to mix. As I use the term, temperament is simply some quantification of the mixture of components that a person presents. In this literal sense temperament at the morphological level is the somatotype. At a slightly more dynamic or behavioral level it is the pattern of the mixture of the three primary components *viscerotonia, somatotonia,* and *cerebrontonia.* At more complex and more culturally conditioned levels, temperament may be defined more elaborately and may embrace any schema for quantification of the manifest components of a personality that a psychologist can devise. In the academic exercise published in the second volume of this series it was shown that temperament can be measured at a level sufficiently basic to correlate about +.80 with the primary morphological components. It of course does not necessarily follow that the measurement of temperament at such a comparatively basic level is the most useful thing a psychologist can do with his time, especially if he should choose to stop at that level.

Temperament is the pattern at *all* levels. But as I use the term it is a little more specific than that. It is *the pattern quantitatively expressed, in terms of some schema of components which offers a frame of reference for an operational psychology.* The most difficult and most important task of the psychologist is that of making his choice of primary variables, or of getting down to primary components; that is to say, components which offer a basis for general quantitative comparison, and cannot be further factored.

Viscerotonia The first component of temperament, measured at the least-conditioned level of dynamic expression. Endomorphy is the same component measured at a purely structural or morphological level. Endomorphy is expressed by the morphological consequences of a predominance of the first component. Viscerotonia constitutes the primary or most general behavioral expression of the same predominance; that is to say, predominance of the digestive-assimilative function—the gut function. Twenty defining traits which when quantitatively scaled can be used to measure the first component at this level are those in the first column of Table 1.

In briefest summary viscerotonia is manifested by relaxation, conviviality, and gluttony for food, for company, and for affection or social support. When this component is predominant the primary motive in life seems to be assimilation and conservation of energy.

Somatotonia The second component of temperament, measured at the least-conditioned level of dynamic expression. Mesomorphy is the same component measured at the morphological level. Somatotonia expresses the function of movement and predation—the somatic function. Twenty defining traits which can be used to measure this component at the "lowest dynamic level" are those in the second column of Table 1.

In briefest summary somatotonia is manifested by bodily assertiveness and by desire for muscular activity. When this component is predominant the primary motive of life seems to be the vigorous utilization or expenditure of energy. Somatotonics love action and power. Their motivational organization seems dominated by the soma.

Cerebrotonia The third component of temperament, measured at the least-conditioned level of dynamic expression. Ectomorphy is the same component at the morphological level. Cerebrotonia appears to express the function of exteroception, which necessitates or involves cerebrally mediated inhibition of both of the other two primary functions. It also involves or leads to conscious attentionality and thereby to substitution of symbolic ideation for immediate overt response to stimulation. Attendant upon this latter phenomenon are the "cerebral tragedies" of hesitation, disorientation, and confusion. These appear to be by-products of overstimulation, which is doubtless one consequence of an overbalanced investment in exteroception. Twenty defining traits which can be used to measure cerebrotonia are those in the third column of Table 1.

In briefest summary cerebrotonia is manifested by (1) inhibition of both viscerotonic and somatotonic expression, (2) hyperattentionality or overconsciousness. When this component is predominant one of the principal desires of life seems to be avoidance of overstimulation—hence love of concealment and avoidance of attracting attention. While cerebrotonia seems to result from an evolutionary development in the direction of purchasing increased exteroception at the cost of *both* vegetative mass and motor strength, the

TABLE 1 The Scale for Temperament

Name	Date	Photo No.	Scored by

I Viscerotonia	II Somatotonia	III Cerebrotonia
( ) 1. Relaxation in Posture and Movement	( ) 1. Assertiveness of Posture and Movement	( ) 1. Restraint in Posture and Movement, Tightness
( ) 2. Love of Physical Comfort	( ) 2. Love of Physical Adventure	— 2. Physiological Over-response
( ) 3. Slow Reaction	( ) 3. The Energetic Characteristic	( ) 3. Overly Fast Reactions
— 4. Love of Eating	( ) 4. Need and Enjoyment of Exercise	( ) 4. Love of Privacy
— 5. Socialization of Eating	— 5. Love of Dominating, Lust for Power	( ) 5. Mental Overintensity, Hyperattentionality, Apprehensiveness
— 6. Pleasure in Digestion	( ) 6. Love of Risk and Chance	( ) 6. Secretiveness of Feeling, Emotional Restraint
( ) 7. Love of Polite Ceremony	( ) 7. Bold Directness of Manner	( ) 7. Self-conscious Motility of the Eyes and Face
( ) 8. Sociophilia	( ) 8. Physical Courage for Combat	( ) 8. Sociophobia
— 9. Indiscriminate Amiability	( ) 9. Competitive Aggressiveness	( ) 9. Inhibited Social Address
—10. Greed for Affection and Approval	—10. Psychological Callousness	—10. Resistance to Habit, and Poor Routinizing
—11. Orientation to People	—11. Claustrophobia	—11. Agoraphobia
( )12. Evenness of Emotional Flow	—12. Ruthlessness, Freedom from Squeamishness	—12. Unpredictability of Attitude
( )13. Tolerance	( )13. The Unrestrained Voice	( )13. Vocal Restraint, and General Restraint of Noise
( )14. Complacency	—14. Spartan Indifference to Pain	—14. Hypersensitivity to Pain
—15. Deep Sleep	—15. General Noisiness	—15. Poor Sleep Habits, Chronic Fatigue
( )16. The Untempered Characteristic	( )16. Overmaturity of Appearance	( )16. Youthful Intentness of Manner and Appearance
( )17. Smooth, Easy Communication of Feeling, Extraversion of Viscerotonia	—17. Horizontal Mental Cleavage, Extraversion of Somatotonia	—17. Vertical Mental Cleavage, Introversion
—18. Relaxation and Sociophilia under Alcohol	—18. Assertiveness and Aggression under Alcohol	—18. Resistance to Alcohol, and to other Depressant Drugs
—19. Need of People when Troubled	—19. Need of Action when Troubled	—19. Need of Solitude when Troubled
—20. Orientation toward Childhood and Family Relationships	—20. Orientation toward Goals and Activities of Youth	—20. Orientation toward the Later Periods of Life

Note: The thirty traits with parentheses constitute collectively the short form of the scale

manifest traits of cerebrotonia (in a crowded society) are associated largely with escaping the painful consequences of the increased exteroception thus attained. Yet cerebrotonia is probably in itself far from painful. There is a certain elemental ecstasy in the heightened attentionality just as there is a somatotonic ecstasy in vigorous muscular action and a viscerotonic ecstasy in first-rate digestive action.

The Suffix -otic

As in *viscerotic, somatorotic, cerebrotic;* also *viscerosis, somatorosis, cerebrosis*. This suffix signifies an abnormal or pathological over-manifestation of the primary component named. The extra syllable—or—is put in *somatorotic* for euphony and to maintain the syllabic parallel with *somatotonic*. Since the term *neurotic* is prepsychological in the sense that it came into use during an era before primary components had been defined, and when it was the custom to blame psychopathology vaguely on "nerves" or "glands," this term is not definitive. To call a person "neurotic" is about as meaningful as calling him "glandotic." If an individual is neurotic he is either viscerotic, somatorotic, cerebrotic, or a combination of any two or all three.

The Suffix -penic

As in *visceropenic, somatopenic, cerebropenic;* also *visceropenia, somatopenia, cerebropenia*. The suffix signifies *lack of,* or an abnormally low degree of the component named. Cf. *leukopenia,* lack of white corpuscles.

C. Babel in Psychiatry

For anyone who has had firsthand contact with problems of delinquency the point will require no urging that the criminologist and the psychiatrist are fishing in the same pond. Both are dealing with temperamental pathology in its various manifestations, and in the last analysis a psychiatry or a criminology can be only about as good, or as true and useful, as the conception of temperament which it uses for its frame of reference.

One of the major hypotheses in Constitutional Psychology is that structure and function, or somatotype and temperament, are best viewed as a continuum. We are therefore not in this study primarily concerned with correlation between somatotype and temperament, for by hypothesis such a correlation is no source of new light but only a measure of the accuracy with which quantification has been accomplished at different levels of objectivity in the measurement of the same thing. In the second volume of the series, *Varieties of*

Temperament, a crucial exercise on this correlational topic was presented. As the primary components of temperament were operationally defined and scaled in that study, the correlation between them and the primary components of the somatotype turned out to be of the order +.80. Here we are not concerned with a repetition of such an exercise but are after more elusive game than statistical correlation between structure and function. That correlation is taken for granted. The problem now is to describe temperamental pathology, and if possible thereby to reflect a little light on the vast turmoil of verbality that psychiatric thinking and writing have created.

One of the things the human clan needs urgently is an operational psychiatry. It might turn out to be a keystone for the often prayed-for science of humanics. But to get an operational psychiatry it will first be necessary to establish the habit of systematically describing psychiatric behavior. Read cases 86 through 89 and I think it will be apparent enough, even if you have been exposed to some kind of psychiatric instruction, that what you have studied is confusion. Neither the Kraepelinian typology, which is still in almost universal use, nor the currently popular psychoanalytic slang★ really brings order to the vagaries of human temperament any more than the crude morphological typologies of the Christian era, which could be called a biological age of shame, brought order to the study of human structure.

★The term *psychoanalytic slang* is used not in disparagement of Freud or of his work, for I hold both in high regard. It is used as about the most descriptive way of referring to the garbled and careless use of Freudian concepts which during the past two decades has become popular in American psychiatry and social work. On reading the biographies it will be apparent that smatterings of Freudian "language" have seeped through to half or more of the youths of the series. These boys, and many of the social workers who have coached or have ridden herd on them, "talk Freud" with about as much insight and understanding as the average city urchin has of Christianity when he "talks Jesus." In this country psychoanalytic jargon has become a superficial and a vulgar fad—a form of slang. Priests of the Freudian church are partly responsible, for they have commercialized and prostituted Freud's teaching as possibly no religious preachment was ever prostituted before.

Observation of our series of 200 boys was not begun as a psychiatric exercise. The descriptions and notations on manifest temperament were routine to constitutional study. But they soon brought us squarely against the problem of psychiatric classification. Four-fifths of the youngsters had been "seen" by one or another kind of psychiatrist, and many were under constant psychiatric observation while at the Inn. As psychiatric diagnoses and recommendations piled up, the necessity for integrating two kinds of language—our operational structure-function language and the eclectic typologizing of the psychiatric fraternity—became increasingly urgent.

It was not uncommon to find that as many as a dozen different psychiatric diagnoses and interpretations had been made on a youngster, and *sometimes the dozen would embrace the entire repertory of the Kraepelinian typology.* That is to say, the youth would at various times have been given diagnoses not only mutually contradictory and pointing in opposite directions therapeutically, but he would be taken entirely around the clock and would have *all* the possible diagnoses.

It grew clearer every day that a vocabulary problem of the most serious nature existed in the psychiatric field, that in fact the vocabulary the psychiatrists were trying to use was nonoperational. It didn't work. We held a series of seminars on the question, and invited several of our consulting psychiatrists to come and help thrash it out. One in particular, Dr. Bryant Moulton, spent many hours with us over this difficult and fascinating question.

For many years, in my attempts to correlate constitutional characteristics with psychiatric findings, I had been baffled by the lack of any quantifiable (operational) variables by which the psychiatric findings could be expressed. Patients were diagnosed as suffering from manic-depressive psychosis, *or* paranoid schizophrenia *or* hebephrenic schizophrenia, and so on. It was always a matter of either-or. Psychiatry had developed as a branch of clinical practice, where a patient either "had something" or didn't have it. If he had it, it was either measles *or* scarlet fever *or* perhaps a heat rash in Latin. In clinical medicine the either-or approach possesses a certain cogency, for there *are* disease entities which you can have or not have. But in psychology there is little use for such an approach. The constitutional psychologist tries to describe the behavior of a personality;

that is to say, of an organic structure in action. His first job (I believe) is to describe the structure, in terms of the most primary or universal components of structure that he can measure. That done, the job is to describe the behavior in terms of similarly basic behavioral components. Then the constitutional psychologist proceeds, or should proceed, to a consideration of the details of behavior in the light of the details of structure. In any event he deals mainly with components of structure and behavior, not with either-or phenomena.

We were confronted with the fact that psychiatry offered no handles that a psychologist could take hold of. It postulated no hierarchy of variables that were amenable to quantification or, therefore, to correlation. In short, psychiatry, with its either-or criteria, did not appear to present a psychologically true-to-life discipline. It seemed clear that if a psychologist were to hope to make progress in the interpretation and correlation of psychiatric phenomena, he must first translate these into a system of variables with which he could operate. Moreover this was something we had to do before the general subject of delinquency could be expected to make sense. It was clear enough that delinquent and psychopathic behavior overlapped like the shingles of a house, that to get at one was impossible without at the same time getting at the other.

In short, we found it necessary to formulate a new approach to psychiatric classification before we could integrate constitutional morphology and temperament with the vast wealth of specific information that was being accumulated through psychiatric study and referral.

D. From Disease Entities to Components

Where, then, in terms of operational concepts or in terms of structure-function language could a beginning be made toward psychiatric classification? This was a problem on which much of the potential usefulness of a study of delinquency seemed to hinge.

It was evident that in psychiatric circles there had long been a tendency to rely on some variation of a three-pole typology for a diagnostic frame of reference. At the "psychotic" level, for example, it was common to hear that, in general, three kinds of psychotic personality (together with mixtures) were to be encountered: cases showing *affective exaggeration;* those showing *paranoid projection;* and those showing *hebephrenic regression.* Also at the "psychoneurotic" level a similar tripolar typology was usually assumed to exist, and was embraced within the concepts *hysterical, psychasthenic,* and *neurasthenic* psychoneurosis.

In the closing decade of the last century Kraepelin, by including both mania and melancholia under the general heading of *manic-depressive psychosis,* and by setting this new entity off against *dementia praecox,* had postulated a fundamental dichotomy in the field of the functional psychoses. But Bleuler's conception of *schizophrenia* as a group or pattern of psychotic *reactions* soon largely supplanted the disease-entity conception of dementia praecox and led to renewed activity in the direction of classifying or "naming kinds" of schizophrenia.

Among most present-day practicing psychiatrists quite a sharp distinction is made between schizophrenic patterns in which a hostile or harsh reaction *against* seems to be the predominant temperamental "set" of the patient, and patterns characterized by reaction *away from* (i.e., by apathy, withdrawal from social contact, refusal or failure to participate or to take an interest). The reaction against is often buttressed by more or less extensive and systematized delusions in support of the central fixed idea—delusions usually of persecution and of the subject's own importance. The subject distorts his world of actual experience to fit his primary attitude. Hence the term *paranoid.* The paranoid patient, even when psychotic (which is only to say, *seriously* deranged), is "in there fighting" against something. He has not given up, has not jettisoned his cargo. There is still a somatotonic drive and it is aimed against something.

The reaction away from is of an entirely different nature, and the essential difference lies in the fact that the somatotonic drive is absent. It is as if the subject had lost, or had never had somatotonia. The drive to do things, to achieve, to dominate and triumph over others, to exercise and perfect the muscles, to compete and to fight—in short, somatotonia—is conspicuously absent. If any of this component ever was present it has been jettisoned, thrown overboard. The jettisoning

may have been necessary to save the subject from further disastrous consequences of his ill-sustained and poorly executed efforts at normal or culturally expected somatotonic aggression. This is probably as plausible a "mechanism" as any to explain the pathological somatopenia; but the essential fact is the somatopenia, whatever its origin.

One conspicuous corollary of the jettisoned pattern of personality is what psychiatrists call regressive behavior. The subject seems to regress or fall back to what is in some respects an infantile level of behavior. He may lose all ability to take care of himself, even sphincter control. There is marked lack of energy and of motivation. He may fail to respond at all to social stimulation and to conversational contact. He may have to be fed, bathed, and dressed, and in general cared for as an infant. He is then said to have regressed to a *hebephrenic* (infant mind) state.

Objections can be well taken to the use of the term hebephrenic in this sense. It is only in some respects that the subject has become like an infant; that is to say, in his helplessness. Infants, on the other hand, are normally of vigorous motivation, are alertly somatotonic and within the limits of their repertory of muscular skills are inclined to be aggressively somatotonic and to "go after" what they want. Infants—normally vigorous ones—have not jettisoned anything. It is merely that their executive department has not yet caught up with their desires. To use the idea of infant-mind or infant-like as a description of the most extreme and helpless form of mental pathology, even if it is said in Greek, is not very good semantics. These patients have not "regressed"; you can't really go back in this life. They have reacted away from the problems and competitions of life. They have jettisoned their second component and they show a pathological somatopenia. A better term than hebephrenic might be *oneirophrenic* (dream mind). However, we need not further labor the terminological aspect of the problem at this point in the development of the theme.

The distinction between mental aberration in which the *against* reaction is predominant and that in which the *away from* reaction predominates is as sharp a distinction as is to be found in psychiatry. The psychiatrically conventional single-word symbols for the two reaction patterns are, respectively, *paranoid* and *hebephrenic.*

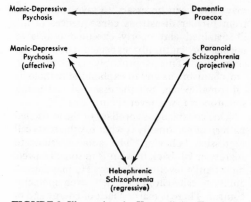

FIGURE 2. Illustrating the Kraepelinian Typology

Thus one end point of the original Kraepelinian psychotic dichotomy has as it were grown apart into two end points. Figure 2 A has grown into Figure 2 B, and a tripolar orientation has replaced a bipolar one. One of the poles, that called hebephrenic, seems to make a degree of operational sense in terms of pathological somatopenia, a concept with biological meaning. What about the other two poles? Can any sense be made of these from a biological point of view?

The reaction patterns that psychiatrists conventionally label *manic-depressive* psychosis all have one essential characteristic in common. The subject always has a low threshold of reaction. There is also a low threshold of emotional expression. He is feebly inhibited. In the "manic" state, which may be chronic or intermittent, he expresses elation and euphoria on slight provocation or without any apparent provocation. In the "depressed" state, which also may be chronic or intermittent, he similarly expresses emotional sorrow, dejection, or self-deprecation without externally apparent justification. The emotion itself may range from extreme elation to extreme dejection; indeed, it may be any emotion. It is the uninhibitedly free expression of the emotion that is constant. Similarly with respect to action of all kinds, here too it is the lack of inhibition, the lack of the cerebrotonic function, that is constant.

During the phase called manic expansiveness, that is to say, when the subject is active, the constant feature is lack of normal constraint in both emotional and somatic expression. He is maladaptively hyperactive; he is responsive, like the proverbial dog in a forest of telephone poles. There may be euphorial emotionalism, motor overactivity, flight of ideas, press of speech, poor attentional focus, hypersuggestibility, uninhibited eroticism, bizarre exhibitionism; and with it all a forceful keyed-up vigor of physical expression far beyond that for which the situation seems to call. All this is simply a description of somatotonia gone wild; pathological somatotonia, or somatorosis.

But in the phase called depression, or depressive melancholy, the dominant feature is not somatorosis but viscerosis—pathologically uncontrolled expression of viscerotonia, or lack of inhibition of affectivity. The subject is physically and mentally slowed up; overrelaxed, overly dependent, overly expressive of his now melancholy feelings. He has become untempered. In the viscerotic phase he is as uninhibitedly viscerotic as he is uninhibitedly somatorotic in the somatorotic phase.

The term manic-depressive psychosis does not then describe a disease entity, but a pattern of reaction in which the constant feature is pathological absence of inhibition. That is to say, the subject is cerebropenic. The result of the cerebropenia depends of course on the underlying temperamental endowment of the individual; that is what will determine his manner of expression. If he is mesomorphic and vigorous, strong and healthy, capable of sustained, violent exertion and of standing up well under it—if he is all this *and* cerebropenic—he will probably maintain a manic or hypomanic level of activity for long periods without recourse to rest. There are some who remain hypomanic all through life. These are athletes of a kind. One of them may exhaust a whole generation of contemporaries and two or three generations of wives or husbands, not to mention minor relatives; but they generally go out pleasantly enough in the end with a cerebral or cardiac "accident."

Such is the "pure manic," who is a comparative rarity. Similarly rare are cases of pure depression, or of "permanent aggressive melancholy." Far more common are the mixtures, and there are almost as many varieties of these as there are individuals. Typically there is some alternation between the somatorotic and the viscerotic cerebropenia, and there are cases where the individual seems to be caught in a regular rhythm or cycle of the two phases, as if he had to suspend the manic activity every so often to rest and recharge his battery. But I think that clear-cut examples of such a rhythmic cycle are less common than the term *cycloid psychosis,* which is often used instead of manic-depressive psychosis, would imply. What we find is not a disease entity but a more or less maladaptive reaction pattern characterized constantly by two things: (1) overly vigorous response, either visceral-emotional or somatic, or both; (2) feeble inhibition or lack of cerebrotonia.

We may then perhaps say that another of the poles in the tripolar schema of Figure 2 B seems to make some degree of operational sense. There may possibly be psychiatric meaning in the biological phenomenon of pathological cerebropenia. What about the third pole, which in the figure is labelled *paranoid?*

The reaction patterns that psychiatrists call paranoid, or paranoid projection—the reactions against—have as a constant characteristic a singular *lack of compassion.* The subject is without the bowels of mercy. According to his temperament and his strength he may look upon his world and his contemporaries as his persecutors or as legitimate objects of his own destructive fury. In either case his bond with his kind is one of hate, scorn, resentment, defiance; and all of this he "projects" against his environment. If he is weak the reaction pattern is more covert that overt. It then takes the form of involved delusional ideation centered particularly around the main idea of persecution. If he is strong—physically strong—overt aggression and an arrogant manner combine with opinionated superciliousness to produce quite a remarkably unpleasant personality. The strong paranoids are ugly customers, especially in a pulpit or a state legislature.

There are as many different kinds of the maladaptive paranoid-projection reaction as there are of the maladaptive affective or of the jettisoning reactions. Common to all paranoia is the lack of participant compassion. The affective psychotic on the other hand is one vast bowel of compassion. He tends to enfold his world in a cosmic Dionysian embrace, and he is so participant in *everything* that the focus of his energy is lost in ubiquity. He is at one with it all. The paranoid is unable to be at one with any of it. He cannot relax and accept; cannot accept comfort; cannot deliberately enjoy food, company, or the glories of digestion; he finds no joy in the social amenities, no "fulfillment" in knowing people and in knowing about them; he cannot express emotion

smoothly; has neither tolerance nor complacency; cannot achieve mutual dependency with other people and so cannot invest hope outside himself, except abstractly. Alcohol has no good effect—it makes him not more viscerotonic but more paranoid. These are all traits of visceropenia. But this personality cannot jettison. Cut off from the main channels of viscerotonic expression (the reaction toward), yet constrained to carry on, there is only one direction that the reaction can take. The reaction is against. It may be against at a very high and idealistic level, as in the case of Prometheus against Zeus, and this may in the long run be a "good" reaction—good for both man and Zeus. It may somehow even be good for Prometheus, and may contribute to the working out of his destiny, but Prometheus remains blood brother to Paranoius.

Biologically, the paranoid reaction seems to stem from lack of, or from interference with, the normal expression of viscerotonia. The reaction against is a visceropenic reaction. This appears to be the constant in the formula, and if the appearance is not a misleading one, it would seem possible that all three of the poles in the tripolar schema of Figure 2 B may make biological sense. Figure 2 B might then be drawn a little differently to take the form of Figure 3. Up to the present point all this is of course speculative. We are following some of the steps in the formulation of what may be called a speculative hypothesis. Hypothetically the three conventional poles for classification of the functional psychoses fall respectively *opposite* the three established poles for morphological and temperamental classification. The Dionysian affective psychoses, in this hypothetical construct, are manifestations of something gone wrong either in the constitutional endowment or in the temperamental manifestations of the third component. Similarly for the paranoid-projective psychoses with respect to the first component; and for the hebephrenic-jettisoning psychoses with respect to the second component.

In the study of morphology and temperament we had made no progress beyond the types of Hippocrates until we emerged from the idea of typologies, or of dichotomies and trichotomies, and substituted for all that the conception of components capable of multidimensional distribution and therefore leading to a morphological and a temperamental taxonomy which the familiar biological dis-

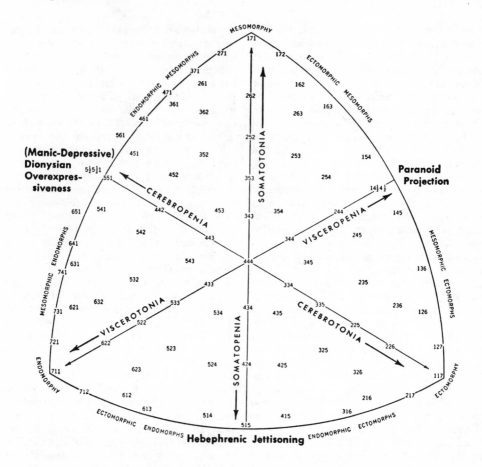

FIGURE 3. A Tripolar Psychiatric Orientation

tribution curves would fit—multidimensionally. The first two volumes of the Constitution series describe the steps leading to those two respective taxonomies. The question that now intruded itself was this: Could we take the same step in psychiatry, at last emerging from the Laocoön-like struggle to describe the mentally aberrant in terms of biologically unreal disease entities or types of reaction? Could we emerge from this and substitute for it a taxonomy psychologically operational and biologically true to life? In short, could mental aberrancy be described and diagnosed in terms of demonstrable, quantifiable components falling within a continuum with other biological phenomena? If it could, there would be a bridge between psychiatry and psychology, and the road might open to a biological humanics.

E. A Hypothetical Psychiatric Index

During the decade following 1935 I undertook exploratory constitutional studies on two groups of psychiatric patients at Worcester State Hospital, on a small group of 50 in the Army, and on 3,800 psychotic patients in the New York State mental hospitals. This latter group included all of the available male cases in the state who were under 30 and were at the time labeled dementia praecox (schizophrenia); also all available males under 45 who were labeled manic-depressive psychosis. Study of the psychiatric and diagnostic histories of these patients together with study of the physical constitution yielded a remarkable demonstration of the need for an operational frame of reference in diagnosis.

It is a common thing, not only in the New

York mental hospitals but in every other mental hospital with which I am familiar, to find that the diagnosis of a psychotic case has been changed half a dozen or more times—usually about as many times as there have been changes of diagnosing officer. Yet even in this madness there is method. One observation first struck me forcibly at Worcester and later was borne out in the New York State study and in the Army. *It is the patients who fall in a particular range of somatotypes whose diagnoses get changed the most.* These are of two groups: (1) the midrange somatotypes; and (2) those falling near the morphological poles. *There is a clearly discernible tendency toward greater diagnostic agreement when the somatotype falls near any one of the three hypothetical psychiatric poles.*

A morphological 5−5−1, 4−5−1, or 5−4−1 who is psychotic has an excellent chance to be labeled manic or manic-depressive and to keep the label. A 1−4−5 or 1−5−4 is almost equally likely to continue through his diagnostic history as a paranoid; and a 4−1−5 or 5−1−4, or even a 4−2−5 or 5−2−4 seems to be almost certain to get and to keep the tag hebephrenic schizophrenia (or schizophrenia simplex).

That this tendency toward diagnostic agreement should disappear among the midrange somatotypes, such as the 4−4−3's and 3−4−4's, or even among the 3−5−3's and 4−5−3's might well be expected. But it also disappears, and just about as conspicuously, at the morphological poles. 7−2−1's and 6−2−1's, for example, are just about as likely to get labeled hebephrenic as manic-depressive and in this somatotype area there is a remarkable tendency for hesitation and alternation between these two diagnoses.

Similarly the extreme mesomorphs 2−7−1's, 1−7−1's, 1−6−2's, and so on perplex the psychiatrists. These mesomorphs get labeled both manic and paranoid, rarely hebephrenic (although not infrequently "catatonic," which seems to be a wastebasket category). One 2−7−1 in the first series I studied at Worcester had been diagnosed as a manic-depressive psychotic five times and paranoid schizophrenic six times—ten changes of diagnosis alternating between two diagnoses. He seemed to be balanced right in the middle, between those two diagnostic typologies and I think that in fact he was so balanced. His biological position was almost perfectly centered between the two psychiatric poles.

The extreme ectomorphs, 1−1−7's, 1−2−7's, and even the far commoner 2−2−6's appear to defy diagnosis by the conventional Kraepelinian typology in about the same way. Many a dreary hour of psychiatric case conference drains off into the weighty business of deciding whether such a patient is *a* hebephrenic or *a* paranoid schizophrene; and then next month in deciding it back the other way again. The criteria on which such diagnostic decisions rest are more often derived from verbalistic hairsplitting than from inquiry into the biological nature of the patient.

For patients at all three morphological poles psychiatric diagnosis seems to run into conflict and tends to hesitate between *two* alternatives. In dealing with the midrange somatotypes the typological psychiatrist is confronted with a still more difficult diagnostic problem. The midrange people, with all three of the primary biological components more or less equally represented, tend naturally enough under varying circumstances to manifest more or less of all three of the primary psychiatric components. At times a psychotic with the somatotype 4−5−3 is very likely to behave like a manic-depressive, at times he will be singularly paranoid, at times he may be "hebephrenic as hell." Often he may be simply stuporous. His most common diagnosis is catatonic schizophrenia.

Now *catatonic* is one diagnostic term in common psychiatric use which has been defined in almost every way psychiatrically imaginable. Henderson and Gillespie[*] defined catatonia as "an alternating state characterized by a stage of depression, a stage of excitement, and a stage of stupor." Many psychiatrists, particularly those of European training, follow Kraepelin in applying the term catatonic dementia praecox (schizophrenia) to virtually all cases of functional psychosis that show a mixture or alternation of *all three* primary psychiatric components.

In the original Kraepelinian typology there was first the primary dichotomy of manic-depressive psychosis and dementia praecox; second, a division of dementia praecox into the three types, paranoid, hebephrenic, and catatonic. The catatonic type, which Kraepelin considered the most common, has always

---

[*]*A Textbook of Psychiatry* (6th ed., New York, 1946), p. 316.

been diagnosed in practice mainly by the fact of shifts between manic-like excitement, stuporous depressions, and both paranoid-like and hebephrenic-like reaction patterns—all or any of these mixed in various proportions, according to the temperament of the patient. Some of the patients with this mixed picture spend much of their time in a cataleptic state, or state of sustained immobility. Many psychiatrists have adopted that characteristic as the critical or definitive one for the diagnosis of catatonic. Others, finding that catalepsy is by no means a constant feature, have considered it incidental. Still others, especially those not trained under the Kraepelinian tradition, have looked on "catatonic" as a mere wastebasket adjective more or less synonymous with "mixed" and so have not used the term diagnostically at all. In the mental hospitals of some states today as many as 70 per cent of the schizophrenic patients are labeled catatonic; in those of some other states the term catatonic rarely appears. The consequence of all this has been rather general confusion over the term catatonic and an increasing tendency to avoid use of it, except as a synonym for mixed.

Kraepelin later added a fourth "type" of dementia praecox—the *simplex* or simple type. The identifying characteristic is absence of any definite trend; simply a general falling away of interest and a general falling back or lack of effective adaptivity. Kraepelin described this as consisting of an "impoverishment . . . of the whole psychic life, which is accomplished quite imperceptibly." No particular manic tendency, excitement or depression, or paranoid reaction. There is general apathy or emotional dulling, and a sinking away from life. The individual is born and remains a weak nonentity. A more descriptive term than schizophrenia simplex might be, simply, mental asthenia. In short, schizophrenia simplex is a term commonly applied to a psychotic personality that seems to stay in the middle with respect to all three of the primary psychiatric components, and so never shows a pronounced tendency toward any of them. The catatonic also in the long run falls in the middle, but this is because, in the course of time, he reveals all the primary psychiatric components in some strength, and all this divergent psychiatric "strength" cancels itself out.

We have now considered all the main conventional categories in the Kraepelinian diagnostic schema, which remains in almost universal psychiatric use wherever the European languages predominate. We can see that Kraepelin covered the ground remarkably well, that he included in his typology just about all of the possible main directions of variation of pattern. His is a first-rate typology. First, there is a "type of reaction pattern" extending out into each of the primary dimensions of possible extension. These are the manic-depressive, the paranoid, and the hebephrenic reaction patterns. Second, there is a name for those personalities which, upon showing tendencies along all of these dimensions, nevertheless average out somewhere near the origin or center point. These are the catatonics. Finally, there is a name for those personalities that go nowhere at all, but *simply* stay at nothingness. These are the simplexes.

But typologies do not offer an operational frame of reference for social science. Even the best of typologies can offer no more than a preliminary scaffolding which may mark out the main lines along which an operational science is to develop. The question we now have to consider is that of whether or not the whole field of psychiatric description—and therefore perhaps of psychological description in general—is ready for translation from the current typological to an operational frame of reference.

The picture as we have reviewed it can be diagrammatically summarized as in Figure 4. Here all the Kraepelin psychotic types are written into a hypothetical three-dimensional structure. But along with these typological designations there is also the suggestion of a quantitative frame of reference. At what may be called the apex or pole of the region of manic-depressive psychosis is the symbol $\psi 7-1-1$.* A personality plotted at this point on the diagram would be visualized as overwhelmingly Dionysian (a 7 in that component), and as altogether lacking in any signs of either of the other two primary psychiatric components. Similarly the symbol $\psi 1-7-1$ marks the pole for the territory of paranoid psychosis, and $\psi 1-1-7$ marks the hebephrenic pole.

---

*The Greek ψ here stands for psychiatric, and this symbol placed in front of the three familiar numerals commonly used to define the somatotype indicates that we are now considering a *psychiatric*, not a morphological index.

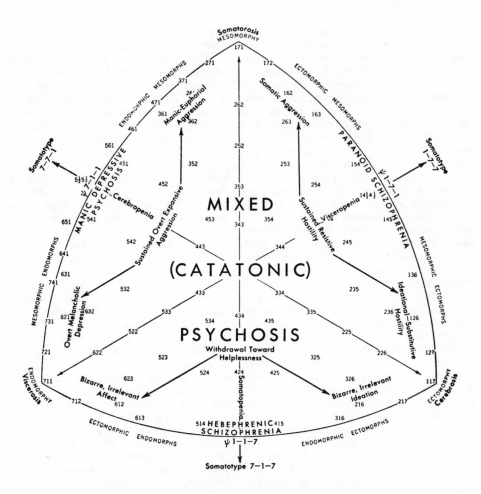

FIGURE 4. Diagram for the Psychotic Reaction Patterns

One other point of great psychiatric interest will perhaps have already occurred to anyone who in his thinking has begun to substitute the idea of a psychiatric index for the Kraepelinian typology. Psychotic personalities falling in the northwest sector of the distribution (see Figure 1) are frequently referred to as "cycloid," or manic-depressive. At times they show manic euphorial aggression, at other times overt melancholic depression. Some individuals appear to present a rhythmic alternation between the two moods. For the northwest psychiatric territory the term cycloid has long been in common use and is almost interchangeable with manic-depressive.

The psychiatric index is expressed in the same way as the morphological index, or somatotype, but the poles for the psychiatric components fall opposite those used for the morphological components. This means that the three coordinates of the psychiatric system are rotated with respect to the coordinates of the morphological system. The rotation is about the center axis determined by the points 4–4–4, 3–3–3, 2–2–2, etc. Also in this center axis are the points 7–7–7 and 1–1–1.

What has actually happened in the change over from the somatotype designations to the psychiatric designations is simply a clockwise rotation of the poles through one-sixth of a complete turn, or through 60 degrees. The *psychiatric* 7–1–1 is just 60 degrees ahead of the somatotype 7–1–1, and the same is true of other corresponding numerals except those in the center axis, which remain fixed.

But anyone who will take the trouble to observe a group of psychiatric patients, while keeping in mind the structural frame of reference of Figure 1, will soon become aware of the same cycloid phenomenon in the northeast and south that is seen in the northwest. Among paranoid schizophrenes who present about the same strength in mesomorphy as in ectomorphy there is very much the same alternation between somatic aggression and ideational substitutive hostility as there is between euphorial and melancholic expression among the patients who are well balanced in mesomorphy and endomorphy. And the same cycloid phenomenon is seen at the south, among the hebephrenic patients who show about the same strength in endomorphy and ectomorphy. These patients often alternate between bizarre, irrelevant affect and bizarre, irrelevant ideation.

When psychiatric behavior is described against an operational frame of reference the alternational or cycloid phenomenon is seen to be general—not specific to the manic-depressive pattern. Moreover the alternation is not limited to a swinging back and forth across what I have called the psychiatric poles; that is to say, across the poles of cerebropenia, visceropenia, and somatopenia. The cycloid alternation is just about as conspicuous across the poles of the primary components as across the psychiatric poles. That is to say, the swing is also seen across the poles of viscerosis, somatorosis, and cerebrosis. Endomorphs frequently show a cycloid alternation between overt melancholic depression and bizarre, irrelevant affect. Mesomorphs are likely to swing between manic-euphorial aggression and somatic aggression, and ectomorphs be-tween, ideational-substitutive hostility and bizarre, irrelevant ideation.

Among psychiatric patients of mid-range somatotype the alternations of mood and of behavior tend to become complex and some of these patients show, at different times, the definitive criteria for *all* of the Kraepelinian typological diagnoses. These are the people who get labeled catatonic. We cannot say whether or not there is usually some logical sequence, some "rhyme and reason," in their variations. There may be and somebody may find a good doctoral dissertation in the problem of working out relationships between overt constitutional factors and catatonic patterns.

In fairness to the psychiatric practitioners who have fallen into the conventional habit of applying the term cycloid only to the north-west sector, it should be pointed out that the alternation phenomenon is in fact more dramatic in that quarter than elsewhere. This is because all expressiveness reaches its maximal volume at the pole of the first psychiatric component. That is the area of pathological cerebropenia, where inhibition of expressiveness is at its physiological minimum and all reaction is therefore maximal. It was doubtless to be expected that the phenomenon of swinging back and forth between two partially incompatible kinds of reaction would first be noticed in the sector where behavior is most overtly accentuated. To point out that the cycloid pattern is seen elsewhere as well as in the northwest does not detract from the usefulness of the concept or from the brilliance of Kretschmer's classic description of the cycloid—meaning manic-depressive—temperament.

Therapeutic Approaches

It should not be surprising that biophysical theorists prefer biophysical methods for treating psychopathology. According to them, the primary source of the difficulty exists in the biophysical make-up of the patient. It follows logically, then, that efforts should be made to remedy the defect directly. The fact that few of these "defects" have been specified or even localized has not deterred the development of biophysical therapies.

The chapter of Donald Klein illustrates how pharmacological treatment can be accurately prescribed despite the lack of definitive knowledge concerning both psychiatric pathogenesis and site of drug action. The empirically derived descriptive behavioral typology he provides offers a fruitful guide to intervention decisions.

H. M. Van Praag reports on our increasing knowledge of the biophysical substrates that underlie drug action and demonstrates the growing clinical utility of understanding complex biochemical and neurophysiological processes.

8 Diagnosis and Pattern of Reaction to Drug Treatment: Clinically Derived Formulations

Donald F. Klein

I. Problem: The Indications for Drug Treatment and the Assessment of Drug Effect

The recent development of relatively effective psychopharmacological agents such as the phenothiazines and imipraminelike compounds confronted the psychiatric profession with the inadequacy of its diagnostic system for the provision of rational indications and contraindications for drug therapy. Within each standard diagnostic group there are wide variations in drug-induced behavioral reactions. Furthermore, there is a marked overlap in response patterns between diagnostic groups, although moderate statistical regularities occur. Because of these limitations, clinical treatment with psychotropic agents has been governed by rule of thumb modified by trial and error. To arrive at generally valid conclusions predictive of drug effect from such clinical empiricism is made difficult by spontaneous remissions, uncontrolled fluctuations of life circumstance, and the often meager abilities of psychiatric patients to describe their level of cognitive, affective, and social functioning objectively.

The observations and conclusions of this paper are based on experience starting in 1959, with phenothiazines and imipramine, at Hillside Hospital. Initially, we wished to gain a broad image of the patient's behavior and drug effects, avoiding simple lists of traits and symptoms. The use of psychotropic drugs

Reprinted from M. M. Katz, J. Cole, and W. Barton (Eds.), *The Role and Methodology of Classification in Psychiatry and Psychopathology*, 1968. A U.S. Public Health Service Publication.

throughout the hospital was restricted, in that they were only prescribed by a research psychiatrist, at the request of the patient's psychiatrist. Prior to starting medication, the patient's case record was reviewed and each patient was interviewed by a research psychiatrist. During drug therapy, the patient's response was assessed through weekly interviews with the patient as well as ward personnel, and through biweekly conferences with the resident and his supervising staff psychiatrist. On each such occasion, the patient's mental status, progress in psychotherapy, and utilization of hospital facilities were discussed.

When it became evident that the standard diagnostic nomenclature was of limited use in categorizing behavioral reactions to drugs, and that psychodynamic formulation lacked predictive clarity, we decided to derive a descriptive behavioral typology of drug effects. In the typological assessment, the detailed records were reviewed by three research psychiatrists, and a consensus statement was made concerning the patient's behavioral reaction during the medication period. The patients were divided into groups on the basis of changes in symptoms, affect, patterns of communication, and participation in psychotherapy and social activity. In each categorization, the behavioral reaction during drug therapy was the determining feature. No attention was paid to the patient's pretreatment behavioral pattern, except as it was relevant to the perceived changes. Inspection of these groups showed, however, that in addition to the similar behavioral changes with drug therapy, their members had similar developmental and behavioral pretreatment characteristics.

These initial studies of the phenothiazines and imipramine were conducted on approximately 200 patients. The clinical patterns of drug response reported have continued to be substantiated by further experience *(1, 2)*.

Following the clinical phase an experimental program was initiated in 1961 to study the effects of chlorpromazine and imipramine. All psychotropic drug therapy at Hillside Hospital was initiated by referral by the patient's supervising staff psychiatrist to the research team. Pretreatment examinations consisted of research psychiatrist interviews, behavioral ratings by the patient's psychiatrist and ward personnel, self-ratings of symptoms and attitudes, psychological tests, EEG, medical examination, and physiological tests, including blood pressure response to mecholyl and radioactive iodine uptake *(3–9)*.

Subjects were randomly assigned to placebo or one of two fixed dosage increment drug schedules for 4 weeks: imipramine, 75, 150, 225, and 300 mg.; chlorpromazine, 300, 600, 900, and 1,200 mg. Each dose of chlorpromazine was combined with proportionate amounts of procyclidine, 3.75, 7.5, 11.25, and 15 mg., to prevent akinesia and other extrapyramidal disorders. Each medication was dissolved in a highly flavored liquid placebo vehicle and each patient received 40 ml. per day from individually labeled bottles. Maximum dosage was maintained for 2 weeks and retesting was conducted during the sixth week of medication.

One hundred seventy-three patients started medication and 150 completed the study program. During the 7 weeks of the experimental program, the longitudinal clinical observations of the pilot phase were maintained. In addition, following the experimental period all patients were followed throughout their hospital stay so that their clinical response to other interventions could be assessed. To gain information concerning the long-term outcome, both for diagnostic clarification and estimates of treatment efficacy, all patients entered into this program were followed up by detailed interviews of themselves and informed relatives 2 and 3 years after hospital discharge *(10)*.

It should be emphasized that all referrals for psychotropic medication were accepted regardless of diagnosis or symptomatology, since it was hoped to be able to utilize the drug effects as tools for discriminating sub-

groups of patients thus requiring a large heterogeneous group. Such division of the drug groups led to small patient response subgroupings. Therefore, in an effort to expand our data the experiment was replicated, starting in 1963. This second experiment is now being terminated after an additional 150 patients completed the study.

For this presentation, the primary emphasis is on the detailed clinical psychiatric categorization of the patients in terms of drug response with its diagnostic and psychopharmacological implications. Also, certain changes in the usual study methods are described as necessary for the prediction of drug effect.

II. Clinical Groupings and Theoretical Inferences

A. Ordering Effect of Drugs on Psychiatric Data

Certain aspects of drug treatment deserve emphasis as being peculiarly useful in the attempt to understand psychiatric patients. Each patient presents a welter of unique familial relationships, developmental idiosyncracies, social aberrations, affective states, cognitive abilities, symptoms, defects, and maladaptations. The information overload upon the diagnostician is so acute that he is often led to premature closure and scotomization of the data. Furthermore, since the clinician is usually confronted with a cross-sectional picture it is very difficult to know which manifest pathological features are primary, in the sense of being tightly linked directly to the fundamental disturbances, and which are secondary in the sense of being inconstant accompaniments or sequential reverberations.

As Ledley and Lusted point out, the fundamental formula of medical diagnosis is "if medical knowledge *E* is known, then if the patient presents symptoms *G*, he had diseases *f*." Conversely, "if diseases *f* are cured then the patient's symptoms will disappear" *(11)*. Unfortunately for the neatness of this formulation, it does not distinguish reversible symptoms from irreversible effects. The persistence of painful, ineffective, and maladaptive affects, thoughts, beliefs, and behaviors in psychiatric patients, long past the period when the apparently initiating causes have ceased to operate, is one of the core problems in pathogenetic theory. If this persistence is due to a variety of causes, rather than some unitary repetition compulsion, it is possible that the identification of drug effects which terminate some persisting difficulties, ameliorate others, and are ineffective in still others may aid us in approaching this aspect of pathogenesis systematically. "Curative" drug therapy would allow us to determine which of the manifold aspects of the patient are symptoms of the illness, and which aspects are illness irrelevant.

B. Psychiatric States with Complete or Almost Complete Remission

Attention to this question of complete symptomatic remission was attracted by the frequent remarkable psychopharmacological successes in certain groups; i.e., retarded depressions, manic states, and angry hyperactive paranoid states.

1. Mood elevations in retarded depressions. These patients are depressed, inactive, self-depreciatory, hopeless, and uninterested in the environment. They relate in an apathetic, uncommunicative, and passive fashion and complain of the sudden onset of anorexia, insomnia, unhappiness, loss of interest in their activities, inability to cope with their responsibilities, to concentrate or make decisions. With imipramine treatment there is a distinct increase in environmental interaction and goal directed activity followed by a lessening of complaints and a general cheerfulness of mood. Complaints of tension and apprehension related to difficulties in discharge planning and returning to the community remain, however, with anxious procrastinating attempts to evolve a foolproof plan.

2. Reduction of anger and psychomotor acceleration in manic and angry, hyperactive, paranoid patients. One group of patients caused considerable diagnostic disagreement. Usually they were labeled manic-depressive, manic- or schizo-affective, or schizophrenic, paranoid type.

These patients approach the staff in an angry, supercilious, and manipulative manner. They are demanding of their doctors and are frequently suspicious and evasive when pressed concerning their feelings and personal relationships. There are frequent complaints of unjust confinement through the blundering errors of friends, relatives, and hospital staff. They express their anger elatedly, without marked fearfulness or depression, often revealing persecutory delusions, ideas of influence, sexual abuse, and auditory hallucinations. Flight of ideas, loss of goal orientation, and illogical associations are demonstrated. On the ward they demand attention, are meddlesome and verbally aggressive. They are generally too hyperactive and negativistic to engage in hospital activities.

The response to medication of this group is a reduction of anger, psychomotor deceleration, and increased social participation. These patients require large doses of chlorpromazine (about 2,000 mgs. per day) for effective control. This dosage is easily tolerated when given in combination with anti-parkinson medication.

Patients now approach the interviewer in an ingratiating manner, expressing the understanding that they had reacted in an emotionally disturbed way in the past. The greater their previous delusional formation, the greater their denial of illness. There is a decrease in expressions of angry frustration and an associated increase in tolerance for frustration. Psychomotor acceleration disappears and mood is more evenly maintained, with infrequent mild depressive dips. In psychotherapeutic sessions they are capable of more meaningful discussions of their interpersonal relationships and feelings.

They interact more freely with both patients and staff in a helpful but often controlling manner. They express boredom with hospital routine and contrast it unfavorably with the full and active life they would be leading at home. The staff evaluated these patients as greatly improved, and occasionally used such descriptions as "cured" or "remitted." Prognosis was also rated "hopeful."

Under drug treatment each of these groups frequently shows a complete or almost complete restitution to the premorbid status. The fact that the natural history of each of these conditions is also marked by periods of apparently complete spontaneous remission is a striking parallel that can hardly be an accident. The outstanding commonalities of these illnesses is their relatively late onset in adult patients with good premorbid social and psychological development, and the marked derangement of psychomotor activation and mood.

The fact that both drug treatment and the natural course of these diseases are marked by complete remissions lead me to postulate that the core of these illnesses lies in their common denominator, a reversible pathological mood and activation state, and that both the processes of natural repair and drug treatment operate by normalizing this central pathological state.

Cognitive defects that occur in these states seem to be either related to the state of psychomotor acceleration or mood congruent convictions. That is, both the manic and the angry, hyperactive paranoid show distractability, flight of ideas, impulsiveness, and loss of goal organization. The retarded depressive, on the other hand, has paucity of ideas, tenacious ruminations, and inability to convert ideas into action spontaneously. Delusions are mood congruent; e.g., the belief in unworthiness and physical illness in the depressives, the conviction of grandiose abilities in the manic, or the certainty of the hostility of psychiatric staff and relatives in the angry paranoids.

Both the mood disturbance and the psychomotor rate disorder appear to ameliorate simultaneously. The convictions, which initially may be attempts to conceptualize and rationalize the subjectively overwhelming, radically altered mood state, have a degree of functional autonomy persisting past the termination of the originally causative mood and cognitive disturbances. Therefore, the depressive may be left with lowered self-esteem, the manic may retain a conviction of uniqueness, special ability and creativeness, and the paranoid may remain somewhat suspicious and wary of an environment seen as potentially hostile.

C. Psychiatric States with Functionally Autonomous Residual Pathology

1. Reduction of episodic anxiety in phobic-anxious states. This schema of patients with primary reversible affective-activation disturbance and secondary affective reactions, and conceptual convictions which have relative functional autonomy received further support from the study of phobic-anxious states *(12).*

These patients also had episodic illness, in that their lives were punctuated by discrete series of overwhelming attacks of panic. Typically, subjects note the sudden onset of inexplicable "panic" attacks, accompanied by rapid breathing, palpitations, weakness, a feeling of impending death, and occasionally depersonalization. Their activities become progressively constricted, until they are no longer able to travel alone for fear of being suddenly rendered helpless while isolated from help. Depressive complaints are frequent and associated with feelings of futility. Although fear of open spaces is not the hallmark of this condition but rather expectant fear of lack of support when overwhelmed, their condition is often referred to as agoraphobia. They engage in prolonged outpatient psychotherapy, usually devoted to the exploration of unconscious sexual and aggressive impulses, with the interpretation of the phobically barred areas as situations of forbidden symbolic temptation. Hospitalization occurs after the family can no longer tolerate the restrictions placed upon it.

Under imipramine treatment the "panic" attacks cease, although both phenothiazines and sedatives had been previously ineffective. However, the patients are reluctant to change their phobic behavior pattern, having shown the same reluctance following spontaneous terminations of panic attacks. Because of the persistence of this secondary apprehensiveness, the patient may complain and behave in an unchanged fashion after imipramine treatment has terminated the panic attacks. These patients require supportive and directive treatment focussed on changing the conceptual residue of the original disturbance (i.e., "I might be overwhelmed by panic, at any moment"), for manifest behavioral change to occur. However, such supportive and directive treatment is entirely ineffective in the face of continued panic attacks.

Imipramine has been an important aid in the definition of this nosological group since these patients also present a wide array of associated obsessional, hypochondriacal, affective, dependent, passive-aggressive, addictive, histrionic, and manipulative features. Depending on the salient symptomatology, or the selective perception of the diagnostician, they may be referred to as obsessionals, hysterics, atypical depressives, passive-aggressive character disorders, pseudo-neurotic schizophrenics, acute schizophrenics, alcoholics, barbiturate addicts, anxiety states, conversion reactions, etc. This diagnostic chaos is the natural result of the psychiatrist's inability to arrive at a hierarchy of importance for this multiform symptomatology on any cross-sectional basis. Attempting to arrive at a consensus between dissenting diagnosticians usually results in a fence-straddling label; e.g., severe mixed psychoneurosis or pseudoneurotic schizophrenia or borderline state, etc.

Imipramine treatment highlights the panic attack as the proximal cause that both initiates the adaptive dependent-phobic behavioral sequence and maintains it by an irregular reinforcement schedule. Thus, it gives a marked positive weighting to such a symptom in the attempt to predict drug effect and to form homogeneous diagnostic subgroups. This is further emphasized by the fact that phenothiazines, which are often considered antianxiety agents, are positively deleterious in their effects on this syndrome although they are most helpful in "panic" episodes marked by delusions, hallucinations, or referential thought disorder. This group furnishes a good example of the utility of patterned predictors in the development of drug-relevant diagnostic categories.

2. Reduction of recurrent agitated depression in obsessive-compulsive states. This schema of primary drug responsive activation-affective disturbances and residual affective or cognitive symptoms which are functionally autonomous led to attempts to see if other disorders approximated this sequence.

Certain patients who are often diagnosed as "Agitated Depressions in Obsessive-Compulsive Personalities" may be hospitalized because of the extent of their inability to function and the manifest risk of suicide. Their self-presentations are dominated by descriptions of battles against ego-alien obsessions and compulsions. Their emotional states vary from a chronic discouragement through fearful ingratiation in the hope of help, to ludicrous outbursts of coercive agitation coupled with threats of suicide and demands for immediate succor. Their communication is well organized and no thought disorder is evident outside of the obsessional preoccupations. Psychotherapy is barren, repetitive, ruminative, intellectualized, and symptom-centered. On the ward, the patients are ritualistic and solitary but tractable, except during their demonstrations of despair and hopelessness. Insomnia is common.

Several alternative formulations concerning this cross-sectional symptom state are possible. First, the agitated depression may be a secondary psychological despair reaction to the primary life-crippling obsessions and compulsions. Another formulation might be that the obsessions and compulsions are secondary, magical, self-punitive, expiatory attempts to alleviate the primary depressions. Still another formulation might be that the obsessions, compulsions, and agitated depression are all secondary reactions to, or attempts to control, a primary underlying disturbance, e.g., breakthrough of unconscious hostility.

Phenothiazine treatment in such cases induces the following sequence of changes. The agitation and insomnia are sharply reduced within a few days so that ward personnel and family are immediately relieved by the change. The depressive complaints and lack of social participation changes more slowly, but with a stimulating environment the patients participate more actively within a few weeks and finally state they are no longer depressed. The obsessions and compulsions hardly change at all in frequency although the patients more easily disregard these symptoms *(2)*.

Again study of the natural history of the illness shows a striking parallelism with its clinical course in response to drugs. These patients were obedient, fearful, dependent children who developed lifelong obsessional traits. Later, episodic agitated depressions resulted in acute failures in psychosocial functioning followed by rather lengthy convalescences, with prolonged exacerbations of obsessive-compulsive symptoms even after the patient returned to social functioning. Drug treatment restores them to their typical obsessional mode of functioning prior to the present episode of depressive decompensation, in a fashion similar to spontaneous remission.

Both on historical and drug effect grounds, we cannot maintain that obsessions and compulsions cause depression, or that depression is necessary for obsessions and compulsions, or that both are conjointly caused by a third present factor, since the depressive state fluctuates independently of the chronic obsessive-compulsive state. Perhaps both obsessive-compulsive fixed symptomatology and recurrent agitated depressions are common enough so that they may occasionally randomly co-exist in one person. Still other data would be necessary to resolve this issue; i.e., a community survey giving the incidence of these disorders separately and jointly so as to determine if their conjoint presence is simply due to random co-existence. However, I believe most psychiatrists would hypothesize a high incidence of agitated depression in obsessional states. Both obsessive-compulsive symptomatology and recurrent agitated depressions may reflect a common early psychological and constitutional difficulty involving separation anxiety, proneness to depression, marked dependency, and severe ritualistic conscience formation. This difficulty has eventuated in both a functionally autonomous, early developed, chronic, drug-unresponsive, obsessive-compulsive symptom pattern in association with a persisting drug-responsive vulnerability to depressive disorder.

3. Affective stability reactions in emotionally unstable character disorders. Another group of patients who approximate an affective-activation disturbance with a functionally autonomous residue are often diagnosed as "Emotionally Unstable Character Disorders," although underlying or incipient schizophrenia is usually considered. The affective-activation disorder of these predominantly adolescent patients consists of alternating short periods of tense, empty dysphoria accompanied by inactivity and withdrawal, suddenly shifting to periods of impulsiveness, giddiness, low frustration tolerance, intolerance of rules, and short-sighted hedonism. This marked lability is often not immediately noted as core pathology because of the complicated self-presentations which range from a fragile, immature, dependent image, eliciting protectiveness from the observer, to a hard "wise guy" presentation appearing as independence and lack of need for support. The patients are perplexed about their goals in life, stating that they do not know who they are, what they are, or what they want to be. They are confused over issues of dependency, intimacy, and self-assertion, reacting in a disorganized, flighty, and despairing fashion. There is a pervasive feeling of being excluded from normal life and from peer groups, with a conviction of being irreparably bad. They are rational, relevant, and coherent except for periods of either giddiness or agitated fearfulness during which their speech and behavior become scattered and disorganized. Participation in hospital activities fluctuates consid-

erably, but when involved, these patients are often creative, skilled, and original.

With phenothiazine treatment there is a decrease in affective lability and impulsiveness. A bland, placid, friendly, and ingratiating manner replaces feelings of confusion, perplexity, anxiety, and depression. Feelings of role diffusion and inability to find a path in life decrease without finding specific solutions. Flight of ideas is no longer apparent, and during psychotherapy their introspective ruminations are changed to a concern for day-to-day events and for peer relationships, without interest in long-range planning. The patients rejoin their peers in a friendly fashion and are active and popular. In place of the rapidly alternating phases of activity and withdrawal there is a more uniform degree of friendly interaction, but occasional short-sighted impulsive actions may still occur.

Thus, with phenothiazine medication their lability decreases, their frustration tolerance increases, and their social behavior becomes more acceptable. However, the capacity to think of long-range goals and step-by-step achievements remains absent. They experience little distress in their present lives and are unable to view the future meaningfully. The stage is thus set for a bland denial of difficulty coupled with an indifference to productive work and planning, and occasional impulsive hedonism *(2)*.

In these cases the secondary residue consists of a mixture of sociopathic attitudes and planning defects that seem to be partly the consequence of their previous inability to rely upon themselves as a stable base, combined with the previous experience of a kaleidoscopic world. Also during phenothiazine treatment, they are particularly prone to complain of a sense of boredom, deadness, and inability to really enjoy themselves, reminiscent of the opiate addict's complaint of feeling badly when "on the natural." Their complaints of pervasive anhedonia seem not to be borne out by social observation since they frequently may be observed evidently enjoying themselves and are highly motivated to organize parties, outings, etc., that may provide them with "kicks." One may hypothesize that this complaint, which occurred prior to drug treatment, may be due to contrast with their previous episodes of gleeful elation. In a sense they are addicted to these "high" periods, miss them, and are willing to suffer the discomforts and disruptions of mood lability to regain these affective states. Therefore, another functionally autonomous residue consists of the memory of pathologically pleasant states with the contrast derogation of normal mood.

Phenothiazine treatment highlights the disruptive effect of the short-term mood swings as central to this group's psychosocial decompensation. These patients are often capable of supervised work and recreation, while receiving medication, in spite of the persistence of their social attitudes. Again there is a parallelism of drug effect and natural history. Although insufficient longitudinal data has been gathered to be definitive, these patients may have a relatively good prognosis, their lability and impulsive antisociality "burning out" with increasing age, leaving a socially acceptable citizen with somewhat deviant manipulative and irresponsible attitudes.

A patient group which resembles the "high" phase of the "Emotionally Unstable Character Disorders," are chronically ebullient, overactive, impulsive, rash, with marked lack of foresight, and intolerance of routine and rules. The qualitatively abnormal attitudes and social maneuvers are figurally salient over the background activation-affective state so that they may be diagnosed as "Passive-Aggressive Character Disorders, Aggressive Type." This diagnosis fails to recognize the chronic activation dysregulation, whereas the European term "Hyperthymic Psychopath" seems more appropriate. After phenothiazine treatment these patients are indistinguishable from the drug-treated Emotionally Unstable Character Disorders.

4. Reduction of schizophrenic disorganization. The relationship of the manic-depressive states to the schizophrenias has been a perplexing question since the original distinction was made by Kraepelin on the basis of course: Schizophrenics deteriorating and manic-depressives remitting periodically. However, the existence of remitting patients with unquestionable episodes of thought disorder caused the development of many diagnostic labels, including that of schizo-affective psychosis, which pointed to the lack of a simple correlation between disordered thinking and deteriorative course.

It is generally acknowledged that prognosis in schizophrenia, meaning remission with the relative absence of persisting deleterious residual defects, is best in patients with familial history of psychotic depression, acute adult onset, precipitating cause, affective turmoil, depressive preoccupations, confusion, good premorbid personality, and socially adequate adjustment. In other words, the prognosis is better the closer the onset, heredity, and symptomatology approximates manic-depressive illness, and to a lesser degree, toxic states. Again, prognostic criteria for phenothiazine treatment of schizophrenia are similar to those for prognosis in the natural course of the disease in that those patients with acute onset, affective turmoil, good premorbid personaltiy, and manic-depressive features respond best, with least residual defect.

The fact that both acute manic and acute schizophrenic episodes are produced by imipramine in psychotics and patients with CNS damage but not in normals, neurotics, or character disorders *(13)*, may indicate, on the grounds of parsimony, that these naturally occurring acute psychotic states share a common pathophysiological link that is sensitive to the effects of imipramine. It is often very difficult to distinguish acute manic from acute schizophrenic states and the diagnosis is frequently made on the basis of the amount of residual cognitive and affective disorder remaining after the acute flareup. The common ameliorative effects of phenothiazines in these conditions may also indicate action at a common pathological site.

One might attempt to integrate these pharmacological and nosological considerations concerning schizophrenia and manic-depressive disease by the following considerations:

(a) The common pathophysiological link in the acute psychotic state consists of a disorder in the interconnected normal neurohumoral mechanisms regulating arousal, activity, pleasure response, fear, and anger. The existence of such "activation" mechanisms has received convergent support from many sources, reviewed in Duffy's extensive monograph *(14)*. The activation mechanisms seem to have evolved in relation to states of heightened environmental interaction and organismal activity as exemplified in waking, flight, fight, and pleasurable activity. Obviously, all of these states are crucial for survival.

Duffy points out that behavioral description seems to require regularly the use of two descriptive categories: (1) "direction" (relating to selective environmental evaluation leading to approach or withdrawal) and (2) "activation" (relating to intensity of response tending towards overt expression). "Activation" should not be directly equated with overt activity because of the possibility of inhibitory intervention. "Emotion" may be considered as a compound phenomenon of "activation" and "direction," although the issue of arousal patterns specific to fear and anger remains debatable. The fact that two independent descriptive categories are necessary leads to the inference of two partially independent systems of behavioral regulation, each having specific pathological deviations.

(b) It is postulated that only the range of emotionally labile, manic, and depressive disorders will be produced if only activating mechanisms are pathologically involved. Activation dysregulation may occur in two ways. Through the postulated pathological disturbance in activation regulation or through states of extreme environmental stress producing excessively intense and prolonged activation.

(c) In some schizophrenic conditions it is postulated that there are other forms and degrees of central nervous system pathology involving cognition and selective evaluation of the environment, ranging from the severe to the subclinical, exclusive of pathology in the activating systems.

Pollack (15) has pointed out that there is a significant relationship between psychiatric patients' I.Q. and age of hospitalization. The lower the age of hospitalization (which in turn is positively correlated with the age of appearance of manifest illness), the lower the I.Q. Discharge ratings are correlated both with age and I.Q., the poorest occurring in young patients with low I.Q. This is compatible with a range of severity in CNS "directive" defects in schizophrenics, the most severe defects causing the most obvious and therefore early detected behavioral disturbances. These CNS defects induce a range of chronic disorder in the directive, integrative, cognitive functions and become more disruptive during periods of activation dysregulation.

It is postulated that in other schizophrenics, pathology in the activation system induces an endogenous toxin that causes interference with the directing system and that in these patients there is no initial defect in the directing system. Relevant to this is the finding that the plasma factor in schizophrenia is probably not present at all times and that its level is closely related to the physical activity of the subject.

(d) The schema would predict a two-stage process in the pathophysiology of some acute schizophrenias characterized by sequential pathology in both activating and directing systems. An inital stage of mood disturbance and insomnia, is superseded by angry hyperactivity, psychomotor acceleration, and flight of ideas shared by acute mania, or loss of environmental interest shared by acute depression, followed by gross psychotic perceptual and cognitive disruption, including delusions and hallucinations. This sequence has been observed by Klein and Fink (6), Pollack et al. (5) using imipramine, and Brune and Himwich (16) who used MAO inhibitors in the treatment of schizophrenics. These groups reported a biphasic psychotogenesis: a period of mood elevation approaching inappropriate euphoria and increased environmental interest, followed by angry hyperactivity and cognitive disorganization.

(e) The prognosis may be best in schizophrenic patients whose onset and symptomatology approximate manic-depressive disease, simply because they required the greatest activation dysregulation to produce cognitive disorganization. The implication is that manic-like schizophrenics have the least CNS cognitive defect and that following the period of affective turmoil they are closest to normal CNS functioning, and therefore best able to manage their lives in a fashion approximating the norm. The prognosis may be worst in schizophrenics with early, insidious onset and flattened, inappropriate affect, because the onset of cognitive disorder in the absence of activation disorder indicates a more profound CNS defect that is less likely to become compensated.

(f) The process-reactive continuum hypothesis of the schizophrenias resembles this model: process schizophrenics may be equated to patients with major CNS cognitive defects and reactive schizophrenics to those with minor CNS cognitive defects activated by a pathological arousal mechanism or an intact directing system deranged by an activation-linked toxin. It should be noted that this interpretation is at variance with the usual one that equates process-reactive with organic-psychogenic. It is generally recognized that for some remitting schizophrenias each psychotic episode is followed by a decrement in the patient's affective and cognitive level, leading to chronic defect after repeated episodes. In these cases the residual symptomatology may be a mixture of irreversible CNS defect and a functionally autonomous mixture of self-protective maneuvers such as social self-isolation, passive-dependent relationships, unwillingness to engage in problem solving activity, etc.

Again the natural course of illness and the results of drug treatment seem isomorphic, since those schizophrenic patients who most closely resemble manic-depressives respond best to phenothiazines, with minimum residual symptomatology. Therefore, one might predict that the new phenothiazine treatment of schizophrenia should result in no increase in the percentage of patients who are symptom free at followup since this would be fixed by the natural incidence of manic-depressive-like schizophrenics. However, there should be a shift in prevalence from those patients who are grossly psychotic to those who may be maintained in the community with discernible residual defect. Kelly and Sargant have reported such findings (17).

D. Drug-Refractory States

Just as patients with complete remission highlight the common denominators of drug action, drug-refractory patients highlight drug irrelevant motivational, affective, and cognitive states.

1. *Patients without manifest activation-affective dysregulation.* It follows from the theory that psychotropic agents work reparatively on activation-affective dysregulation that conditions not characterized by this defect should be refractory to these drugs. On the whole this is accurate. Dyssocial, antisocial, passive-aggressive, and narcissistic character disorders, perversions, obsessive-compulsive states, mental deficiency, conversion and hypochondriacal reactions, chronic "burned out," and pseudoneurotic schizophrenics are all refractory to phenothiazines and imipramine-like drugs. Whenever drugs have proved useful in these conditions it is in the treatment of an intercurrent affective derangement, without alteration of the patients' chronic difficulty. Again drug treatment mimics natural course; i.e., unremitting chronic symptoms with transient affective flare-ups.

2. *Patients with apparent activation-affective dysregulation.* (a) Patients whose specific de-fects elude drug treatment. It must be admitted that patients who conform exactly to the descriptions given above of affective-activation disorder may not respond to psychotropic agents. Under the usual clinical circumstances it is difficult to try one antidepressant or phenothiazine after another, methodically, in search of a suitable agent, especially since ECT is regularly effective in these drug-refractory states. However, certain depressives who are refractory to imipramine respond to desmethylimipramine or an MAO inhibitor. It seems likely that these therapeutic specificities are due to different specific defects in the basic pathophysiology that are not reflected in the manifest symptomatology. Careful comparative studies of diagnostically and phenomenally similar patients who respond differentially to drugs may help isolate such basic pathophysiological differences.

(b) The histrionic. One patient group who causes great difficulty for any theory of psychotropic drug action, as well as grave problems in clinical management, is comprised of characteristically labile, episodically agitated, erratic, unpredictable, manipulative, tense, and histrionic patients. They are usually rational, relevant, and coherent, although there are occasional paranoid and hallucinatory verbalizations. They may express themselves as being panicky and frightened to the point of suicide and several minutes later be affably laughing with other patients. Their therapists readily become emotionally involved and are frequently frustrated and perplexed by the inability to predict or modify the patient's behavior. The patients express great investment in their doctors and psychotherapy, endowing them with miraculous potentialities. They maintain a high degree of interaction with other patients, being at times sociable, friendly, and supportive, and at other times disturbing, hostile, argumentative, and demanding, and yet again pleading for help and direction.

There is no sustained response to medication, although a transient initial improvement is common. Intolerance of distressing side effects is expressed dramatically. Because of their lability, there is much uncertainty as to the effectiveness of medication, so that they tend to receive long treatment courses before the medication is found to be ineffective by the staff. However, if the patient responds in a somatizing fashion medication is terminated promptly.

Why this emotionally labile and agitated group should prove so refractory to phenothiazine medication remains a real problem. One clinical feature of predictive value and theoretical import is the marked relationship of their symptoms to environmental impact. Unlike depressed patients who may increase the vigor of their complaints in the presence of psychiatric staff in an attempt to coerce a maximum curative effort from them, but who remain inactive or unproductively agitated when not under staff observation, this group of refractory patients may appear in good spirits, when apparently unobserved by staff, engage in social games and gossip pleasantly with other patients, even shortly after an explosive affective display. The key issue may be histrionic role playing and symptom imitation, in other words, that these patients' symptoms may not be the direct external manifestations of intolerable affective states, but rather may be environmentally oriented, learned, manipulative devices. Agitation and depressive complaints in this group are not the same as similarly labeled phenomena in other patients.

Psychiatrists often comment on the disappearance of the classical hysteric; i.e., hysterical fits, paralyses, and anesthesias are conspicuously absent on our psychiatric wards. In Charcot's time the practice was to hospitalize hysterical patients with epileptic and neurological patients. It seems likely that hysterical symptomatology was modified by iatrogenic exposure. Nowadays hysterics (manipulative, histrionic, imitative, labile patients) are hospitalized with schizophrenics and it may be that we are thus producing what might be termed "pseudoschizophrenic neurotics" or "hysteroschizophrenics" in the same fashion as hystero-epilepsy was produced 80 years ago. These patients may supply a considerable proportion of the surprising aberrant somatizing and negative responses to phenothiazines on the part of apparently schizophrenic patients.

(c) The chronically anxious. Another group of patients who are comparatively refractory to phenothiazines or imipramine are those with chronic anticipatory anxiety. A pharmaco-diagnostic note is the moderate usefulness in these patients of drugs of the sedative class; i.e., alcohol, barbiturates, meprobamate, glutethimide, ethchlorvinyl, chlordiazepoxide group. The usefulness of these agents is limited by pharmacological tolerance since increasingly larger doses are required to maintain equanimity, and these patients often self-administer these compounds to the point of addiction. This is in sharp contrast to the effects of the phenothiazines and imipramine where progressively less medication is necessary to maintain remission following initial effective treatment. Also in sharp contrast is the general uselessness of these sedative agents in conditions of marked activation-affective dysregulation.

Some theories of phenothiazine effect place heavy emphasis on the central role of antianxiety actions. That is, various symptoms such as hallucinations, delusions, and agitation are seen as secondary responses to anxiety, and the ameliorative effects of the drug are ascribed to reduction of anxiety. This type of theory has been supported by the reports of supposed specific effects of phenothiazines on conditioned avoidance reactions. The clinical refractoriness of chronically anxious patients to psychotropic agents casts doubt on this.

This reinforces the necessity for discriminating among anticipatory anxiety, panic anxiety, anxiety accompanying affective dysregulation, and anxiety in acute schizophrenic psychosis.

III. Implications for Psychopharmacological and Diagnostic Research

A. *Diagnosis-Irrelevant Target Symptoms as Predictors of Drug Effect*

The poor fit between standard diagnosis and prediction of drug effect led to several attempts at solutions outside the framework of diagnosis. Describing certain invariant symptom-drug relationships, e.g., reduction of agitation, or reduction of anxiety, or mood elevation, was attempted. However, the clinical experience detailed above showed that psychopathological phenomena, often referred to as target symptoms, that were labeled identically in different patients might respond differently to the same medication. Irregularities in the drug response of phenomenally similar symptoms cast considerable doubt on the legitimacy of classifying behaviors together on the basis of gross behavioral or introspective report similarities.

Another approach is to see each symptom as a prominent aspect of an integrated disease that cannot be abstracted from the symptom complex without leading to false equivalences with similar aspects of entirely different configurations. However, this viewpoint requires that diagnostic formulation be systematic patterned multivariate descriptions. Patterned clinical diagnosis is not the same as the products of many of the currently employed multivariate techniques such as person correlations, linear additive multiple regression analysis, or canonical correlations.

For instance, when the trait of "panic" is associated with auditory hallucinations, it should be weighted positively for beneficial chlorpromazine effect. However, in the presence of agoraphobia it should be weighted negatively (1, 2, 12). The implication is that "$panic_1$" is simply not the same as "$panic_2$" and identical coding of these two phenomenally similar behaviors does violence to the possibility of determining their relationships correctly. Formulating such complexities requires interaction terms that are not part of the usual additive multivariate approach. Furthermore, these interaction terms are very difficult if not impossible to establish on a statistical inductive basis. They may require stipulation derived from clinical experience. In turn this would require a new level of creative interaction between clinicians and statisticians.

Once patterned clinical diagnoses were developed it would still be necessary to show that the application of these patterns led to predictions of drug effects on specific aspects of the pattern that would be significantly better than predictions that utilized data in univariate fashion or in the form of linear additive multiple regression equations. In any case, the issue of diagnosis has not been avoided by the attempts to relate symptom reduction directly to drug effects, but rather has been reemphasized as an investigative area.

B. Inferred Underlying Universal Variables as Sites of Drug Action

The need to diagnose so as to predict drug effect might be avoided if drug effects are mediated by certain diagnosis-irrelevant underlying variables that are either increased or decreased in their functional capacities by drugs; e.g., depressing the cortex, releasing the subcortex, depressing or stimulating the hypothalamus or reticular activating system, etc. This postulation form is not restricted to

neurophysiological hypotheses. One might postulate changes in excitatory or inhibitory processes in Pavlovian or Hullian styles, or decrease or increase in repression or psychic energy in psychoanalytic terminology.

An analogy is with an overly loud radio. The specific fault may lie in many places but simply decreasing the aerial length would provide sufficiently decreased input to compensate for many of them. The actual defects would not be specifically remedied or diagnosed. Aerial shortening may be considered analogous to symptomatic compensatory treatment. One clinical example might be aspirin, whose analgesic effect seems independent of the specific source of painful afferent input. If psychotropic drug effects follow a nonspecific compensation model, their relevance to the elucidation of specific defects is dubious.

This approach presents the same difficulties as the target-symptom approach, with the added problem of getting agreement as to the existence, or granted this, the state of the inferential underlying variable. Also, this model of unidirectional functional effect is hard to reconcile with the normalizing effects of psychotropic agents that frequently ameliorate both extremes of paired polar systems, such as mania and depression, stupor and agitation, fearful withdrawal and assaultiveness.

C. Inferred Pathological Disturbances as Sites of Drug Action

Still another alternative view is that psychotropic drugs specifically affect pathological disturbances in a normalizing reparative manner rather than a compensatory one. In a previous paper I have presented evidence that the pertinent psychiatrically relevant actions of psychotropic drugs are manifest only in pathological cases and present a cybernetic theory of the nature of the relevant pathology and treatment effect (13). Briefly, the phenothiazines and imipramine-like agents are seen as acting by repair of an impaired control mechanism, a pathologically insensitive level detector in an activation-affect controlling servomechanism. This hypothesis has the merit of accounting for the normalizing effect of these drugs, in apparently opposite pathological states, by one pharmacological action. In this view, drug effect and diagnosis are closely tied to each other, in that ameliorative effect implies a specific defect, although the specific cybernetic defect hypothesized may well be incorrect.

These views of drug effect, i.e., compensatory and reparative, are not mutually exclusive. It is possible that specific physiological drug effects are compensatory for certain pathological conditions, reparative for others, and irrelevant or toxic for still others. There is some heuristic value in this emphasis on the possibility of reparative drug action since it fosters the use of clinical drug effects as the basis for a drug-relevant psychiatric typology. That is, patients would be grouped on the basis of pattern of drug-induced changes in symptoms, affect, patterns of communication, participation in psychotherapy, and social activity. The responses to medication would be used as dissecting tools to distinguish various subpopulations and to permit the determination of specific developmental, physiological, and psychosocial commonalities within each subpopulation. Hopefully these commonalities may shed light on the question of the etiology and pathogenesis of psychiatric disorder, as well as serve the practical purpose of providing rational indications and contraindications for drug therapy.

D. Longitudinal Analysis

One aspect of diagnosis which is often insufficiently attended to is the importance of the extended time sequence of pathological manifestations. Diagnosis in general medicine is never restricted to cross-sectional evaluation but depends heavily on history. Most computer attempts at diagnosis have utilized either cross-sectional examinational material (18) or have used historical data (e.g., age of onset) as entries in a multiple-regression analysis that cannot use information derived from longitudinal ordering. Although change scores may be used as items, extended sequences cannot be put into this form. This issue has probably not been handled adequately because of the unmanageably large number of equiprobable sequences generated by a combinatorial approach.

Also sequential order may be more important than the exact timing of phases. With a form that samples the patient's history at fixed levels, the described order of the phases will vary depending on the synchrony of the sampling period with disease periodicity. One might have a patient who was functioning relatively normally until he had a three-month period of emotional lability, followed by a one month period of elation, followed by a three month period of depression, perplexity, and withdrawal, culminating in a referential and delusional psychotic state. If one were to use a fixed time-sampling period (e.g., a patient description every 6 months) quite different orders (e.g., normal depressed psychotic, normal manic psychotic, normal labile depressed psychotic, etc.) might be generated depending on the date taken as the zero point. Such fixed time-sampling approaches are less appropriate the more one is attempting to capture a rapid flux, requiring such short intervals as to approach a narrative, and of least interest when one is attempting to describe a slow-moving, nonperiodic condition.

One approach to this problem would be to formalize the descriptive psychiatric knowledge of disease courses in the form of modal sequential descriptions. The course of each patient could be rated for the overall degree it approximates known longitudinal patterns with allowance made for missed phases, and attention paid to qualitatively unique aspects and sequences. Discrepancies would be noted and cases that did not approximate known patterns would be investigated for new patterns. This diagnostic program would emphasize an interplay between the substantiation or contradiction of past beliefs and new inductive attempts rather than a *de novo* inductive attempt.

The relevance of this discussion of the methodology of handling ordered sequential data to the study of the relationship of drug effects to diagnosis is that the problem of analyzing history is formally identical to the problem of analyzing the time course of drug effect. Present psychopharmacological studies are typically before and after, two-point studies, with the examiners often completely out of contact with the patient during the intervening treatment period. The only sequence handled is from before to after, as the intervening changes remain unobserved and unanalysed. As long as the field was preoccupied with the overriding question of proving therapeutic efficacy, the use of before and after controlled studies was rational and efficient. As we are now shifting to the more refined question of which drug for which patient, we must correspondingly refine and intensify our methods, possibly using modal sequential drug-change patterns. This effort will require the intensive longitudinal study of the individual patient by the trained psychiatric clinician as he remains our only presently available tool able to recognize multivariate patterned sequences, either by comparison with specified modal sequences or inductively from atypical courses. The current organization of research into studies with large numbers of patients with brief cross-sectional examinations does not encourage such work. Even the most intensive, ambitious, scientific, and well-organized programs, such as the VA and NIMH collaborative studies, do not deal directly with the question of sequential historical and drug-effect analysis, although they point in this direction.

Furthermore, it follows from the theory presented, that for many patient groups, especially those with periodic activation-affective dysregulation, the impact of drugs is to accelerate the natural course of recovery from the illness. Therefore, in the short space of several months one is given the unusual opportunity of getting an overview of a naturally much longer process, thus allowing the sharp delineation of longitudinal patterns that would otherwise be obscured by life's vicissitudes and the usual difficulties of prolonged longitudinal observation. Critical test of this hypothesis of an isomorphism between the course of both natural recovery and drug treatment would require analyses similar to those outlined above.

These analyses would require the integrated services of a research team of skilled psychiatric clinicians, psychologists, social workers, and statisticians. Furthermore, such studies could only be carried out in an inpatient setting that would welcome and support research programs, rather than consider them interferences with the clinical process. It would appear that such intensive studies will require the development of clinical research centers devoted to the specific problem of diagnosis.

IV. Summary

The practical necessity for defining the indications for psychotropic drug treatment has reemphasized that our psychiatric diagnostic system is unsatisfactory.

A series of illustrations of typical clinical responses to drugs are presented, derived from clinical and experimental experience at Hillside Hospital. These illustrations lead to the following inferences:

1. Certain psychiatric illnesses (manic-depressive and hyperactive paranoid) are primarily caused by deranged affective-activation mechanisms and have minimal secondary, functionally autonomous, symptomatic reverberations. These illnesses have naturally occurring complete remissions and also respond best to psychotropic drugs.

2. Other psychiatric illnesses (periodic phobic-anxious states, agitated depressions in obsessional states, emotionally unstable character disorders, and the schizophrenias) are characterized both by affective-activation disorders and a secondary residue that persists after the termination of the affective derangement. Psychotropic drugs again mimic the natural course of the illness since these illnesses are characterized by naturally occurring remissions with persistent secondary symptoms.

3. Other psychiatric illnesses that are not characterized by a primary activation-affective disorder are refractory to psychotropic agents. However, histrionic-hysterical patients and chronic anticipatory anxiety states require special differentiation since their affective difficulties appear to have a different origin.

4. Psychotropic drugs may work by normalizing deranged affective-activation mechanisms. To the degree that a psychiatric illness is due to such deranged activation mechanisms, the drug effects will mimic the processes of natural remission.

5. The prediction of drug effects from target symptoms from effects on diagnosis-irrelevant control mechanisms and from specific effects on pathological states is discussed.

6. The need for study of patterned multivariate diagnosis utilizing longitudinal historical and drug effect data is emphasized. This will require much more intensive studies than were necessary for the determination of the therapeutic efficacy of psychotropic drugs. Such studies require the development of clinical research centers devoted to the specific issue of diagnosis.

REFERENCES

1. Klein, D. F., and Fink, M.: "Psychiatric Reaction Patterns to Imipramine." Amer. J. Psychiat. *119*, 432–438, 1962.
2. Klein, D. F., and Fink, M.: "Behavioral Reaction Patterns to Phenothiazines." Arch. Gen. Psych. *7*, 449–459, 1962.

3. Klein, D. F., and Fink, M.: "Multiple Item Factors as Change Measures in Psychopharmacology." Psychopharmacologia, *4*, 43–52,1963.

4. Belmont, I., Pollack, M., Willner, A., Klein, D. F., and Fink, M.: "The Effects of Imipramine and Chlorpromazine on Perceptual Analytic Ability, Perceptual Responsivity and Memory as Revealed in Rorschach Responses." J. Nerv. & Ment. Dis. *137*, 42–50, 1963.

5. Pollack, M., Klein, D. F., Willner, A., Blumberg, A. G., and Fink, M.: "Imipramine-Induced Behavioral Disorganization in Schizophrenic Patients: Physiologic and Psychologic Correlates." Rec. Adv. Biol. Psychiat. 7, 53–61, 1965.

6. Fink, M., Klein, D. F., and Kramer, J. C.: "Clinical Efficacy of Chlorpromazine-Procyclidine Combination, Imipramine and Placebo in Depressive Disorders." Psychopharmacologia, 7, 27–36, 1965.

7. Fink, M., Pollack, M., Klein, D. F., Blumberg, A. G., Belmont, I., Karp, E., Kramer, J. C., and Willner, A.: "Comparative Studies of Chlorpromazine and Imipramine. I: Drug Discriminating Patterns." Neuropsychopharmacology, *3*, 370–372, 1964.

8. Pollack, M., Karp, E., Belmont, I., Willner, A., Klein, D. F., and Fink, M.: "Comparative Studies of Chlorpromazine and Imipramine..II: Psychological Performance of Profiles." Neuropsychopharmacology, *3*, 374–376, 1964.

9. Blumberg, A. G., Klein, D. F., and Pollack, M.: "Effects of Chlorpromazine and Imipramine on Systolic Blood Pressure in Psychiat-

ric Patients: Relationships to Age, Diagnosis and Initial Blood Pressure." J. Psychiat. Res. *2*, 51–60, 1964.

10. Levenstein, S., Klein, D. F., and Pollack, M.: "Follow-up Study of Formerly Hospitalized Voluntary Psychiatric Patients: The First Two Years." (As submitted to Amer. J. Psychiat.)

11. Ledley, R. S., and Lusted, L. B.: "Reasoning Foundations of Medical Diagnosis." Science, *130*, 9–21, 1959.

12. Klein, D. F.: "Delineation of Two-Drug Responsive Anxiety Syndromes." Psychopharmacologia, *5*, 397–408, 1964.

13. Klein, D. F.: "Behavioral Effects of Imipramine and Phenothiazines, Implications for a Psychiatric Pathogenetic Theory and Theory of Drug Action." Rec. Adv. Biol. Psychiat. *1*, 273–287, 1965.

14. Duffy, E.: Activation and Behavior. John Wiley & Sons, Inc. New York, 1962.

15. Pollack, M.: "Comparison of Childhood, Adolescent and Adult Schizophrenia." Arch. Gen. Psychiat. *2*, 652–660, 1960.

16. Brune, G. G., and Himwich, H. E.: "Biogenic Amines and Behavior in Schizophrenic Patients." Rec. Adv. Biol. Psychiat. *5*, 144–160, 1963.

17. Kelly, D. H. W., and Sargant, W.: "Present Treatment of Schizophrenia. A Controlled Follow-up Study." Brit. Med. J. *1*, 147–150, 1965.

18. Warner, H. R., Toronto, A. F., Veasey, L. G., and Stephenson, R.: "A Mathematical Approach to Medical Diagnosis." J. Amer. Med. Assoc. *177*, 177–183, 1961.

9 New Developments in Human Psychopharmacology

H. M. Van Praag

The origins of psychotropic drugs are hardly aristocratic. They are products of coincidence, not of purposeful research; and this applies to all the prototypes: the neuroleptics (chlorpromazine: Largactil); the tricyclic antidepressants (imipramine: Tofranil); the monoamine oxidase (MAO) inhibitors (iproniazid: Marsilid); the ataractics (chlordiazepoxide: Librium); the lithium salts

Reprinted from *Comprehensive Psychiatry*, *115*, 387–401, 1974. By permission of Grune and Stratton, Inc. and the author.

(lithium carbonate); and the hallucinogens (LSD). This could easily have led to a status quo: application of fortuitous finds, but no research in an effort to exceed the limits of accident. This situation, however, has not transpired. The psychotropic drugs have set in motion an avalanche of research, which has moved in different directions.

Psychotropic drugs are effective on two levels: the metabolic level and the level of behavior. This has raised the question of an interrelationship between the two actions. Current brain and behavior research would be unthinkable without psychotropic drugs. Conversely, brain and behavior research have stimulated the development of compounds with more or less specific effects on the metabolic level and thereby, it is hoped, on the behavior level as well. In this manner biological psychiatry and psychopharmacology are capable of reciprocal stimulation.

Psychopathology, too, owes much to psychopharmacology. By the end of the 1940s the field of psychiatric-syndrome identification and differentiation seemed to have been fully explored. Then the psychotropic drugs arrived, and patients with apparently related syndromes were found sometimes to respond, but at other times to be unresponsive, to a certain type of drug. This observation led to an unprecedented revival of psychopathological research, but this time with the aid of advanced statistical techniques. And this brings us to the third field in which psychotropic drugs have served as the pacemaker: psychometry. When a drug is given, one wants to know (that is, to measure) what it does and what it does not do. For this purpose a range of instruments has been evolved of the type: questionnaire, self-rating scale, and standardized interview—not ideal measuring instruments, it is true, but suitable to ensure a degree of desubjectification of psychopathological research and suitable also to enhance its transferability and reproducibility. Psychometric research as it is now being done in the field of psychiatry is no longer a somewhat esoteric pastime for clinical psychologists, but an applied psychiatric auxiliary science. And we have mainly the psychotropic drugs to thank for this.

What has the practitioner derived from all this research? Not very much so far—no breakthrough, no spectacular new therapeutic possibilities—but certainly a number of promises, i.e., developments that, I expect, can enrich psychopharmacology in the near future or can lead to a more rational use of existing psychotropic drugs. It is these developments that I intend to discuss in the following sections.

Impulses from Biological Psychiatry

Antidepressants

Antidepressants increase the available amount of monoamines (MA) at the central MA-ergic receptors. MAO inhibitors achieve this through inhibition of the MA degration within the neuron, and tricyclic compounds produce this effect by blocking uptake or re-uptake of MA into the neuron after impulse transmission. It is assumed that the activity of the MA-ergic systems is consequently enhanced. The two types of antidepressants are chemically unrelated; yet their net influence on the central MA is the same, and both are therapeutically effective in (vital = endogenous) depressions. This is why an interrelationship between these actions has been postulated (1).

Another reason to relate central MA metabolism to mood regulation lies in the fact that the MA metabolism can be disturbed in depressions (2). This applies to serotonin (5-hydroxytryptamine: 5-HT) as well as to catecholamines (CA)—dopamine (DA) and noradrenaline (NA)—the three principal MA found in the brain. This conclusion is based on data collected from diverse sources: postmortem examination of the brains of suicide victims, studies of the basal concentration of MA metabolites in the CSF, and studies of the rate of accumulation of these metabolites after inhibiting their transport from the CNS to the blood stream with the aid of probenecid. This probenecid-induced accumulation is accepted as a measure of the turnover of the corresponding amine in the CNS.

Indication of a central MA deficiency has not been found in all types of depressions, but mainly in vital depressions, and not in all vital depressions, but only in a proportion of cases. This has prompted us to postulate that the group of vital depressions, although fairly homogeneous in terms of psychopathological symptoms, is biochemically heterogeneous and encompasses patients with and patients without a disturbed MA metabolism (2).

Should MA deficiency and depression indeed be related, then there is every reason for efforts to abolish this deficiency. With a view to these efforts, there is a need for drugs that selectively support one of the central MA. Current antidepressants lack this selectivity: they enhance the activity of the three MA. However, attempts are now being made to ensure a more selective effect on the central MA metabolism (1). For example, chloroamphetamines have been tested in depressions by virtue of their suspected ability to enhance the release of 5-HT from the synaptic vesicles to the synapse. With the aid of MA precursors, attempts have been made to enhance the synthesis of one particular amine. The selectivity thus achieved, however, is as yet by no means satisfactory. Chloro-amphetamines proved not to leave the CA metabolism entirely unaffected after all; and the effect of MA precursors is not "focal" either: the 5-HT precursor 5-hydroxytryptophan, for example, does increase the cerebral 5-HT concentration, but at the same time lowers that of DA; L-dopa vigorously enhances DA synthesis, but at the same time causes a corresponding decrease in 5-HT concentration.

The need for drugs with circumscribed influences on the central MA thus continues. In my view, the objective can be most closely approximated by selective inhibition of reuptake or by selective receptor stimulation. We are waiting for suitable drugs to achieve this.

Neuroleptics

Neuroleptics are a heterogeneous group of compounds in terms of chemical structure. Little is known about individual differences in effect, but experience has taught us that the same patient sometimes shows a much more favorable response to one neuroleptic than to another, and that the efficacy of a given neuroleptic can vary widely in different patients of the same diagnostic category. So far, hardly any search has been made for biological variables that might explain these obscure differences. These factors might conceivably come under three different headings.

To begin with, individual differences in intestinal absorption and degradation rate might play a role. Research into these pharmacokinetic factors stagnates, however, because determination of many neuroleptics in body fluids still poses grave technical difficulties.

A second possibility is a difference in mechanism of action between individual neuroleptics. So far as the central MA metabolism is concerned, this is a very real possibility. Neuroleptics increase the intracerebral turnover of DA and NA—an effect that is assumed to be secondary to DA receptor and NA receptor block, respectively. In man and in animals, the degree to which the DA-ergic and the NA-ergic systems are influenced varies from drug to drug. It is not inconceivable that the biochemical action profile of neuroleptics determines their therapeutic efficacy (3).

The third possibility immediately follows from the second. Should a relationship prove to exist between the occurrence of certain psychotic symptoms and disorders in the central CA metabolism, then the therapeutic efficacy of a neuroleptic could depend on the question whether its biochemical action profile and biochemical lesion are "in tune." It is possible, for example, that hyperdopaminergically determined symptoms can be more effectively controlled with the aid of a selective DA receptor antagonist than with an agent that chiefly blocks NA-ergic transmission. This question has not yet been studied. If the above suggested relationship should prove to be close to reality, then this would provide a vigorous impulse for the development of neuroleptics with selective effects on the CA metabolism and for the application of biochemical criteria in determining indications for neuroleptics.

Drugs Used against Addictions

It has been made plausible that the euphorizing and stimulant action of some habit-forming drugs are related to CA-ergic activity in the brain. Specifically, this applies to alcohol and to amphetamines.

Carlsson and Lindqvist (4) have recently demonstrated that ethanol enhances CA synthesis, probably through activation of tyrosine hydroxylase, the enzyme that transforms tyrosine into dopa. They measured the in vivo activity of this enzyme by inhibiting dopa decarboxylase (with the aid of 3-hydroxybenzylhydrazine), followed by determination of the rate of dopa accumulation. Administration of ethanol was found to cause a dose-dependent increase in dopa accumulation. No effect on the 5-HT metabolism was observed.

On the behavior level, ethanol induces increased motor activity in rodents. This stimulant effect remains absent after premedication with α-methyl-p-tyrosine (α-MT)—an inhibitor of tyrosine hydroxylase and therefore of DA and NA synthesis. This suggests that CA play a role in the stimulant action of ethanol (5).

These data prompted Ahlenius et al. (6) to study the interaction of α-MT and ethanol in human subjects. Ten normal male social drinkers were premedicated with α-MT and were then given 50 ml aquavit every 10 min for the next 40 min (thus receiving a total of 200 ml). A so-called double-blind/crossover design was used. This means that the test subject was given either a placebo or α-MT (neither he nor the observer knowing which) and that the experiment was repeated in such a manner as to ensure that the placebo group received α-MT the second time, and the α-MT group the placebo. In this design, therefore, each test subject served as his own control.

The drinking situation had few laboratory connotations and approximated a party situation. The test subjects knew one another, were seated at a round table, and had free access to garnishes. Behavior rating was done by three sober observers well acquainted with all the test subjects. It was established that α-MT reduced the stimulant and euphorizing effect of ethanol in all test subjects.

Comparable experience has been gained with amphetamines (7a). These compounds increased motor activity in all test animals studied. They enhanced CA-ergic activity in the brain, partly by promoting release of CA into the synapse and partly by blocking their re-uptake into the neuron. Both the biochemical and the behavior effect are antagonized by α-MT, so that, in this case too, an interrelationship was suspected. It seems plausible that this applies to man also, because α-MT vigorously suppresses the stimulant and euphorizing effects of amphetamines in those addicted to these agents. However, habituation to this effect occurs quickly, so that the practical importance of α-MT in this respect seems rather limited.

Be that as it may, this type of research may nevertheless herald a more purposeful contribution of drug therapy to the treatment and control of addictions.

Pharmacological Prophylaxis

Psychopharmacology has supplied psychiatry with a few methods of prophylaxis. First of all, of course, the preventive use of lithium salts. In recurrent vital depressions (so-called unipolar depressions) and in manic-depressive fluctuations (so-called bipolar depressions), long-term use of lithium salts reduces the frequency and depth of the manic and depressive phases. In view of the high incidence of these conditions and their high mortality (suicide), lithium prophylaxis can be counted among the principal medical assets of the past decade (8).

It is possible that lithium salts are not unique in this respect. Prien et al. (9) have recently demonstrated that reduction of the relapse rate can also be achieved with the aid of tricyclic antidepressants. They treated 116 patients with unipolar and bipolar depressions over a two-year period randomly with imipramine (Tofranil), lithium, or placebo. In terms of prophylactic effect, lithium and imipramine were both superior to the placebo, but their efficacies in unipolar and bipolar depressions differed. In unipolar depressions the two compounds were equivalent, but in bipolar depressions lithium was superior. Before imipramine (or perhaps other tricyclic antidepressants as well) can be accepted as a prophylactic in unipolar depressions, Prien's findings must of course be corroborated, and more information must be collected on the long-term (side) effects of this agent.

Imipramine prophylaxis would as such be an asset. To begin with, lithium is not always tolerated; tremors (for those who need manual skill in their profession) and weight gain (a primary esthetic disadvantage particularly for younger people) may necessitate discontinuation of treatment. Moreover, a tricyclic antidepressant is probably more readily processed to provide a long-acting drug than is lithium, and in chronic treatment this is a major advantage.

Long-acting neuroleptics have proven their value in the field of psychotic disorders (10). The prognosis of chronic recurrent psychoses improves when neuroleptic medication is continued for a long time. This long-term design is often frustrated because many patients, once discharged, are careless with their maintenance medication. Long-acting neuroleptics, which are given only once every 2 to 4 weeks and generally by the parenteral route, permit a long-term therapy design. In this type of neuroleptic medication, relapses and recurrences are substantially less numerous than without medication or during treatment with conventional compounds (11).

Current prophylactic drugs have as much been chance hits as the therapeutics in this field. It is conceivable that more purposeful research can be set in motion in this field also. As it is, biological psychiatric research is almost entirely confined to disease phases; hardly any research is done during periods in which the patient is free from symptoms.

Consequently it is unknown whether such metabolic or physiological disorders as are found are syndrome-dependent or syndrome-independent, that is, whether they disappear at the same time as the psychopathological disturbances or persist after clinical recovery. In the latter case they probably have no direct causative, but possibly a predisposing, significance.

Certain scattered data indicate that (continued) research after (clinical) recovery can indeed be worthwhile. According to Coppen et al. (12), the plasma concentration of free tryptophan (mother substance of 5-HT) is decreased in depressive patients. After psychological recovery this concentration rises, but it does not in all cases return to normal. The same applies to the concentration of the principal 5-HT metabolite 5-hydroxyindole-acetic acid (5-HIAA) in the CSF (13) and to accumulation of 5-HIAA in the CSF after probenecid administration (14). Decreases in these values are observed during depressive phases, and clinical recovery does not necessarily lead to their complete normalization. If it is justifiable to regard such persistent metabolic disorders as factors predisposing to depression, then their control affords a possibility of truly purposeful pharmacological prophylaxis.

Hypnotics

Sleep disorders are diagnosed chiefly on the basis of subjective data supplied by the patient. The patient indicates that he does not get enough sleep, that he does not awaken refreshed, or that he is more tired in the morning than when he went to bed. Quite surprisingly, the relation between the amount of sleep and the degree to which one feels refreshed is by no means a linear one. The amount of sleep measured (electroencephalographically or by direct visual observation) can be quite satisfactory, while the test subject nevertheless indicates that he has slept poorly and does not feel refreshed at all. A short night's sleep does not exclude a feeling of being well rested.

Hypnotics are widely prescribed, but with a rather uncertain hand. This is to be expected in view of the inadequacies of sleep diagnosis; after all, we do not know which parameters of sleep determine the subjective feelings of having slept well or poorly. We do not know which sleep parameters are disturbed in the actual case, nor how these are influenced by the hypnotic prescribed. Practically speaking, the speed with which it produces its effect is the only factor taken into account in selecting a hypnotic.

Perhaps this unsatisfactory situation can be altered with the aid of the sleep EEG. This procedure makes it possible closely to follow the sleep pattern throughout the night and to obtain data on several sleep characteristics, e.g., sleep latency, duration of sleep, number and duration of REM and non-REM phases, etc. With the aid of the sleep EEG the sleep pattern in disturbed sleep can be compared with the normal sleep pattern. This could provide a basis for sleep diagnosis. Moreover, this procedure could be used to characterize the effects of various hypnotics on various sleep parameters, and to investigate the relation between their physiological action and therapeutic effect. This would make selection of a hypnotic much more rational (15).

And there is something else: in the past few years, a biochemistry of sleep has evolved (16). MA-ergic mechanisms probably play a role in induction of sleep and in the origin of the various electroencephalographically defined sleep phases. This affords the possibility, in principle, to exert a more or less circumscribed influence on certain sleep parameters with the aid of drugs and to study the effect on sleep. For example, the notion that 5-HT is possibly involved in the production of slow-wave sleep led to research into the hypnotic effect of tryptophan and 5-hydroxytryptophan—not without encouraging results. With this I do not mean to say more, for the time being, than that sleep biochemistry points out possible approaches in the development of new and possibly more selective hypnotic agents. In research into such agents, the sleep EEG has become indispensable because it is only by this procedure that their selective actions, if any, can be demonstrated.

Sleep research is expensive, time-consuming, and difficult, particularly in methodological terms. On the other hand, sleep disorders are endemic in our society, and hypnotics are among the most widely used and abused drugs. Government and industry therefore have every reason to ensure that sleep research is vigorously stimulated in a limited number of well-equipped centers.

Impulses from Neuroendocrinology

Neuroendocrinology, a Potential Partner of Psychopharmacology

There are close relationships between psychopharmacology and transmitter chemistry. The effect of psychotropic drugs on the metabolism of various central neurotransmitters has been intensively studied. Psychotropic drugs in their turn have contributed to our knowledge of the metabolism and function of these neurotransmitters. Conversely, transmitter chemistry has supplied impulse for the development of new types of psychotropic drugs. For example: when a correlation between the therapeutic effect of antidepressants and their ability to enhance central MA activity became plausible, this stimulated the search for compounds that selectively increase DA-ergic, NA-ergic, or serotonergic activity, e.g., by receptor stimulation or inhibition of the re-uptake of the MA involved into the neuron.

It is true that primarily one group of neurotransmitters have been studied in relation to the actions of psychotropic drugs, namely that of the MA. This has not been based on any particular principle—not, for example, on the contention that MA-ergic systems play a more or less exclusive role in regulating behavior. The underlying reason is a technical and methodological one. It is relatively easy to measure MA and their metabolites. Moreover, MA metabolism is of a linear character; there is a mother substance and there are end products. Compare this with a substance such as acetylcholine, which is also a central transmitter. Its determination is difficult, and often still dependent on cumbersome biological methods. Moreover, choline is a degradation product as well as a precursor of acetylcholine, and this is why the choline concentration gives no unqualified information on acetylcholine consumption.

Relations between psychopharmacology and neuroendocrinology, however, have been scanty. The influence of psychotropic drugs on neuroendocrine systems is a theme of low "research density." Likewise, little attention has been paid to the possible action of neurohormones on behavior. The contribution of neuroendocrinology to applied psychopharmacology is therefore minimal, but there are some hopeful developments.

Thyrotropin-releasing Hormone: TRH

Prange and his co-workers have in the past few years been studying the effects of thyroid hormones on depressive symptoms. Their line of research has been prompted by the observation that the toxicity of imipramine (Tofranil) is increased in hyperthyroid patients. Their starting point was the hypothesis that thyroid hormone also enhances the therapeutic action of imipramine.

They demonstrated that triiodothyronine (liothyronine; T_3) does potentiate the effect of imipramine and may per se have a slight antidepressant effect (17). As expected, a similar effect was obtained with thyroid-stimulating hormone (thyrotropin; TSH) (18). TSH is an anterior pituitary hormone that stimulates the thyroid to increased hormone production. Finally, they tested another regulatory mechanism localized above the thyroid; thyrotropin-releasing hormone (TRH), a tripeptide produced in the hypothalamus that stimulates the pituitary to produce TSH (19). They reported that a single intravenous injection of 500 to 600 μg of this substance had a brief therapeutic effect, lasting a few hours. In normal test subjects an activating and euphorizing effect was likewise observed (20).

Prange's work was of interest for several reasons. First, the antidepressant effect ensued within a few hours, in contrast to what we are accustomed to seeing with conventional antidepressants: an effect, if any, is not observed until after 10 to 14 days, and no effect occurs after a single dose either in depressive patients or in normal test subjects.

The second interesting feature was that the effect of TRH on mood was possibly not produced via the pituitary/thyroid axis. This can be deduced from the following data: Mice premedicated with a MAO inhibitor show increased motor activity following L-dopa administration. This dopa effect is potentiated by tricyclic antidepressants. This design is used for testing and screening new potential antidepressants. In this test, TRH behaves like an antidepressant, and it retains this property in the hypophysectomized animal. If the motor activity in mice is analogous to antidepressant action in man, then this implies that the last-mentioned effect is produced apart from pituitary and thyroid and is probably based on a direct influence on the brain (21).

The third important observation was that after injection of TRH the pituitary gland in patients examined released but little TSH. This phenomenon is known from hyperthyroidism, in which case the pituitary is less susceptible to the TRH influence due to the large amount of circulating thyroid hormone. The depressive patients examined, however, showed no signs of hyperthyroidism. Then why did the pituitary release only little TSH after TRH injection? A plausible if speculative explanation is that in these patients the production of physiological TRH in the hypothalamus is diminished, and that the pituitary has consequently become "lazy," unaccustomed to responding adequately to TRH.

Prange's observations have been sustained (22, 23), and, without claiming that TRH is a practical asset (its antidepressant effect is not sufficiently pronounced for that), the significance of this hormone must not be underestimated—theoretically not because TRH has at one stroke made the neuroendocrine system a focus of psychopharmacological interest, and practically not because it is the first substance that seems capable of exerting a quick and selective influence on mood regulation.

Antiandrogens

Hypersexuality is a common source of delinquency, particularly if the sexual impulses have a strong aggressive charge. Its treatment is difficult, and methods of several different types are generally tried: psychotherapy, behavior therapy, hormonal therapy (female sex hormones), and sometimes even psychosurgery. The therapeutic efficacy of these approaches can at best be described as variable, and new methods will certainly be welcome.

A new form of hormonal therapy has recently been introduced: that with antiandrogens (24). These are synthetic compounds that inhibit the effect of natural and synthetic androgens on peripheral and central (the so-called mating centers in the hypothalamus) effector cells. Substances inhibiting the synthesis of androgens, e.g., the estrogens, are not brought under this heading. Antiandrogens have been studied for some 40 years, and in recent years one representative of this category has been used in male hypersexuality, namely the competitive androgen antagonist cyproterone acetate (Androcur).

Little controlled research has thus far been done; with this restriction in mind, the results so far can be described as encouraging (25). The compound has a physiological effect: reduced capability of erection and ejaculation. It also has a psychological effect: reduced strength of drive and vigor of sexual fantasies. The two effects are not always parallel, and this entails a risk. When potency diminishes more markedly than desire, a serious degree of frustration can result. The effects of cyproterone acetate are reversible, and symptoms of feminization (which mar the use of estrogens) are not observed.

Indications for antiandrogen therapy need not be discussed here. We are concerned only with the principle: more or less selective antagonism to a hormonal action. This appears to afford a rational possibility for selective control of behavior.

ACTH Analogues

Memory disorders are a bane for the victim and for the therapist. The former realizes that his security is undermined; the latter is powerless. The memory concept encompasses a number of processes that can be grossly divided into two groups: processes involved in storage information and processes that make it possible to retrieve stored information for use (recall). In principle, a memory disorder can be based on a defect in storage as well as on a defect in recall. Memory disorders in the context of dementia are permanent and progressive. Those following a cranial injury or ECT are generally transient.

It should in principle be possible to abolish a recall disorder with the aid of drugs. But a storage disorder equates to irreversible loss of memory and cannot be abolished, only prevented (26), at least in theory. In actual practice we have neither therapeutic nor prophylactic agents in these cases. Vasodilators have been recommended, but their efficacy is dubious. To begin with, these compounds can probably do no more than ensure brief transient dilatation of the cerebral vascular bed. Second, the degree in which such vasodilation does indeed help cognitive functions remains a moot point.

The fact that I broach this subject nevertheless is due to findings that the status quo seems to be becoming less inevitable. A not unimportant proportion of these findings come from de Wied and his co-workers (27), who a few years ago described an ACTH fragment that in animals facilitates the learning of avoidance behavior and counteracts extinction ("forgetting") of this behavior. ACTH consists of 39 amino acids; the peptide in question consists of the amino acid 4-10 of this series. ACTH has long been known to promote learning ability as well as retention of what has been learned (7), but it was uncertain whether impurities in the ACTH compound or one of the adrenocortical hormones produced this effect. ACTH 4-10 solved these questions, insofar as the purity of this synthetic compound is unquestionable, and insofar as it exerts no significant influence on the adrenal gland. Its effect on memory must therefore be a result of a direct action on the brain.

There are as yet no data on the effect of such ACTH-derived peptides on human memory disorders, and surely one need not expect drugs against (imminent) dementia to be shortly introduced. But it is important, nevertheless, to have an open mind regarding these experiments, for they demonstrate two things: (1) it is possible in principle to influence memory disorders with the aid of drugs, and (2) there are hormonal derivatives with an exclusively central, not a peripheral, action. Both conclusions open a hopeful perspective for psychopharmacology.

Impulses from Pharmacokinetics

The dosage of psychotropic drugs entails a significant factor of automatism, both as to frequency of dose and as to the amount given per dose. Doses are as a rule given three times daily. Perhaps, however, the half-value time of the agent is such that one or two doses per day would be sufficient.

The amount per dose generally varies within fairly narrow limits. Nine out of 10 patients daily receive 3 × 50 mg of an agent such as imipramine (Tofranil). The 24-hr dosage rarely exceeds 225 mg or is less than 75 mg. Medication is discontinued as ineffective when the patient shows no positive response after 4 to 6 weeks. However, this procedure ignores the possibility that the agent *can* be effective but is not because in the doses given it does not reach the effector cells in sufficient

concentration, e.g., due to poor intestinal absorption, rapid renal excretion, or rapid metabolization. The values of such factors differ, not only per drug but also per individual. This is why a much more individualized approach to dosage is required.

In human individuals, concentrations at the (cerebral) effector cells cannot be measured; but renal clearance and CSF and plasma concentrations are in principle measurable. Recently, and still on a modest scale, studies have been started of the relationship between plasma concentrations (mainly of tricyclic antidepressants) and effect (28). No data on CSF concentrations are available. In one respect these studies are remarkably unequivocal: the same dosage can produce widely different steady-state concentrations in different individuals. They can differ by a factor of 10-40. This applies to amitriptyline (Tryptizol) nortriptyline (Sensaval), desipramine (Pertofran), and maprotiline (Ludiomil). The marked disparity in plasma values is probably due to genetically determined differences in metabolic rate. In any case, one of the consequences is that the dosage warrants no prediction about the blood level attained.

Of course the cardinal question is whether plasma levels are representative of the concentration at the relevant receptors in the brain. A relationship between plasma level and therapeutic effect would be a strong positive argument. The books on this question are far from closed, because some investigators did, but others did not, establish such a relationship (29). For two reasons it is difficult to evaluate these data. First, even given an adequate plasma level, not all types of depression are equally susceptible to tricyclic antidepressants. In my view it would therefore be advisable for the time being to limit research of this type to vital depressions—the group most readily responsive to antidepressants. The second problem is that only the total concentration of the antidepressant in the plasma has so far been determined; but only the fraction not bound to plasma proteins is pharmacologically active, and this fraction has proved not to be a constant value, as it was previously believed to be (29). This factor will have to be taken into account in future research.

There is no doubt whatever about the existence of a lower limit—a concentration below which the therapeutic effect of an antidepressant is always insufficient—and it should be pointed out once again that even at an apparently adequate dosage the concentration can remain below this limit.

Corresponding results have recently been reported with reference of diazepam (Valium). This drug also has a critical plasma concentration below which the chance of an anxiolytic effect is virtually nil, and the dosage at which this limit is attained differs individually (30, 31).

Another method to compare dose and effect was chosen for phenelzine (Nardil), representative of the second main group of antidepressants, the MAO inhibitors. This method was based on determination of the MAO activity in the blood platelets. It was thus found that the chance of a therapeutic effect of this drug is substantially greater when MAO activity is inhibited at least 80% than at a smaller percentage of inhibition. In this instance, too, the dose required to attain a given degree of MAO inhibition is not a constant factor (32).

The pharmacokinetics of psychotropic drugs is still in its infancy and is handicapped by the fact that methods of determination are generally still expensive and complicated (lithium being a favorable exception). With a further elaboration of these methods, I expect progress on three fronts: individualization and therefore optimalization of dosage; limitation of polypharmacy (pharmacokinetic research can supply information on the question whether the plasma concentration of a given drug is affected by combination with a second and, if so, in which direction); and diminution of side effects, for there are indications that the risk of side effects from tricyclic anti-depressants and lithium salts increases as a given plasma concentration is exceeded (8, 28). Should these expectations be fulfilled, then determination of the plasma concentration of psychotropic drugs will have to be introduced in actual practice—if not as a routine procedure then certainly in the case of unexpected therapy resistance or inconvenient side effects.

Tomorrow's Psychotropic Drugs and the Teaching of Biological Psychiatry

The trends I have outlined may turn out to be a mirage. If they are not (and I presume they are not), then some fundamental changes will occur in psychiatric pharmacotherapy. Psy-chotropic drugs are still being prescribed on the basis of the cookbook principle: 3 × 50 mg imipramine (Tofranil) for depression; 3 × 100 mg chlorpromazine (Largactil) for psychotic disorders, etc. To prescribe for a patient, only a little knowledge about the action of a drug and the symptoms in the case is required. What one needs for this type of therapy is an iron memory or a good vade mecum; training in biological psychiatry is hardly necessary.

With tomorrow's psychotropic drugs, this approach will be possible to a steadily diminishing degree. More and more, the choice of drug will come to be determined by weighing two series of data: one on the mechanism of action of the drug prescribed, and the other on the current psychopathological, biochemical, and physiological (e.g., electroencephalographic) condition of the patient under treatment. No longer will a random antidepressant or neuroleptic be prescribed; instead, one will select the drug most likely to control the existing biological deviations. With only psychopharmacological knowledge of the cookbook type, moreover, one will be less and less able to follow and evaluate new developments in this field.

In short, if the trends outlined above continue, the all-around psychiatrist will have to have a knowledge of biological behavior determinants. The foundations for such knowledge must be laid during training, and not merely by lip service. Biological psychiatry is very much a research discipline. Teaching and research will have to be closely linked, and this takes money. Some full-time staff jobs, some research facilities, a laboratory, and a budget will have to be made available. Of course it is possible to teach biological psychiatry from a scientific vacuum, but for all who are involved it will be merely swimming dry. It will not be easy to find a competent teacher in this situation. Moreover, begetting offspring is not a solo performance.

If well planned, a biological psychiatric unit need not be large to be productive, but even standing room in this theatre costs more than merely words.

Summary

The prototypes of today's psychotropic drugs were all chance discoveries. Today, however, efforts are being made to ensure a more purposeful further evolution of psychopharmacology. Impulses to this effect come from biological psychiatric research, neuroendocrinology, and pharmacokinetics. This is elucidated on the basis of examples.

So far, psychotropic drugs have been prescribed according to the cookbook principle. This requires a very good memory (or vade mecum), but hardly any insight. However, the changes now in the process of occurring increasingly necessitate knowledge of biological determinants of (disturbed) behavior, both in order to practice pharmacotherapy on a professional level and in order to be able to follow and evaluate new trends. This is to be taken into account in the education and training of psychiatrists.

REFERENCES

1. Praag, H. M. van: New developments in the field of antidepressants. *Comm. Contemp. Psychiatry*, 1:63−78, 1971.
2. Praag, H. M. van: Towards a biochemical typology of depression? *Pharmakopsychiat.* (in press).
3. Praag, H. M. van: Neuroleptics as a guideline to biological research in psychotic disorders. *Compr. Psychiatry* (submitted for publication).
4. Carlsson, A., and Lindqvist, M.: Effects of ethanol on the hydroxylation of tyrosine and tryptophan in rat brain in vivo. *J. Pharmacol.*, 25:437−440, 1973.
5. Carlsson, A., Engel, J., and Svensson, T.: Inhibition of ethanol-induced excitation in mice and rats by α-methyl-p-tyrosine. *Psychopharmacologia*, 26:307−312, 1972.
6. Ahlenius, S., Carlsson, A., Engel, J., et al.: Antagonism by alpha methyltyrosine of the ethanol-induced stimulation and euphoria in man. *Clin. Pharmacol. Ther.*, 14:586−591, 1973.
7. Mirsky, I. A., Miller, R., and Stein, M.: Relation of adrenocortical activity and adaptive behavior. *Psychosom. Med.*, 15:574−584, 1953.
7a. Jönsson, L. E., Anggard, E., and Gunne, L. M.: Blockade of intravenous amphetamine euphoria in man. *Clin. Pharmacol. Ther.*, 12:889−896, 1971.
8. Praag, H. M. van: The use of lithium salts in psychiatry. Indications and practical guidelines. *Dis. Nerv. Syst.* (in press).
9. Prien, R. F., Caffey, E. M., and Klett, C. J.: Prophylactic efficacy of lithium carbonate in manic-depressive illness. *Arch. Gen. Psychiatry*, 28:337−341, 1973.
10. Praag, H. M. van, Schut, T., Dols, L. C. W., et al.: A controlled trial of penfluridol in acute psychosis. *Br. Med. J.*, 4:710−713, 1971.
11. Hirsch, S. R., Gaind, R., Rohde, P. D., et al.: Outpatient maintenance of chronic schizophrenic patients with long-acting fluphenazine: Double-blind placebo-trial. *Br. Med. J.*, 192:633−637, 1973.
12. Coppen, A., Eccleston, E. G., and Peet, M.: Total and free tryptophan concentration in the plasma of depressive patients. *Lancet*, II:60−63, 1973.
13. Ashcroft, C. W., Blackburn, I. M., Eccleston, D., et al.: Changes on recovery in the concentrations of biogenic amine metabolites in the cerebrospinal fluid of patients with affective illness. *Psychol. Med.*, 3:319−326, 1973.
14. Praag, H. M. van, and Korf, J.: A pilot study of some kinetic aspects of the metabolism of 5-hydroxytryptamine in depressive patients. *Biol. Psychiatry*, 3:105−112, 1971.
15. Hartmann, E.: The effect of drugs on sleep. In H. M. van Praag and H. Meinardi (Eds.), *Brain and Sleep*. Amsterdam: Erven Bohn (in press).
16. Jouvet, M.: Regulation of the sleep waking cycle by monoamines. In H. M. van Praag and H. Meinardi (Eds.), *Brain and Sleep*. Amsterdam: Erven Bohn (in press).
17. Prange, A. J., Jr., Wilson, I. C., Rabon, A. M., et al.: Enhancement of imipramine antidepressant activity by thyroid hormone. *Am. J. Psychiatry*, 126:457−469, 1969.
18. Prange, A. J., Jr., Wilson, I. C., Knox, A., et al.: Enhancement of imipramine by thyroid stimulating hormone: Clinical and theoretical implications. *Am. J. Psychiatry*, 127:191−199, 1970.
19. Prange, A. J., Jr., Lara, P. P., Wilson, I. C., et al.: Effects of thyrotropin-releasing hormone in depression. *Lancet*, II:999−1022, 1972.
20. Wilson, I. C., Prange, A. J., Jr., Lara, P. P., et al.: TRH (lopremone): Psychobiological responses of normal women. I. Subjective Experiences. *Arch. Gen. Psychiatry*, 29:15−20, 1973.
21. Plotnikoff, N. P., Prange, A. J., Jr., Breese, G. R., et al.: Thyrotropin releasing hormone: Enhancement of dopa activity by a hypothalamic hormone. *Science*, 178:417−419, 1972.
22. Burg, W. van den, Praag, H. M. van, Bos, E. R. H., et al.: TRH as a possible quick-acting but short-lasting antidepressant. *Psychol. Med.* (in press).
23. Kastin, A. J., Schalch, D. S., Ehrensing, R.

H., et al.: Improvement in mental depression with decreased thyrotropin response after administration of thyrotropin-releasing hormone. *Lancet*, II:740–742, 1972.

24. Neumann, F., and Steinbeck, H.: Antiandrogene. Tierexperimentelle Grundlagen und klinische Anwendungsmöglichkeiten. *Internist*, 12:198–200, 1971.

25. Cooper, A. J., Ismail, A. A. A., Phanjo, A. L., et al.: Antiandrogen (cyproterone acetate) therapy in deviant hypersexuality. *Brit. J. Psychiatry*, 120:59–63, 1972.

26. Ritger, H. G. M.: *Amnesie in de rat*. Proefschrift, Utrecht, 1973.

27. Wied, D. de: Effects of peptide hormones on behavior. In W. F. Ganong and L. Martini (Eds.), *Frontiers in Neuroendocrinology*. New York: Oxford University Press, 1969, pp. 97–140.

28. Praag, H. M. van: Prophylaxe van recidiverende vitale depressies en manisch-depressieve schommelingen. *Ned Tijdschr. Geneesk.*, 117:492–493, 1973.

29. Glassman, A. H., Hurwic, M. J., and Perel, J. M.: Plasma binding of imipramine and clinical outcome. *Amer. J. Psychiatry*, 130:1367–1369, 1973.

30. Dasberg, H., Kleijn, E. van der, Guelen, P. J. R., et al.: Plasmaconcentrations of diazepam and of its metabolite in desmethyl-diazepam in relation to the anxiolytic effect in clinical anxiety. *Clin. Pharmacol. Ther.*, 15:473, 1974.

31. Dasberg, H., and Praag, H. M. van: The therapeutic effect of short-term oral diazepam treatment on acute clinical anxiety in a crisis centre. *Acta Psychiatr. Scand.* (in press).

32. Angst, J., and Woggon, B.: Pharmacological treatment of affective disorders. In *Advances in Drug Therapy of Mental Illness*. WHO/Medical Tribune Genève (in press).

Critical Evaluation

The belief that tangible biophysical defects or deficiencies are the cause of mental disorders has not gone unchallenged. Evidence in support of this notion has not been demonstrated convincingly and has spurred adherents of other viewpoints to question the wisdom of pursuing the search for these defects. Thomas Szasz's article, for example, contends that the concept of mental disease itself is merely a myth, a false verbal analogy founded on the erroneous application of a medical model to psychopathology.

10 The Myth of Mental Illness

Thomas S. Szasz

My aim in this essay is to raise the question "Is there such a thing as mental illness?" and to argue that there is not. Since the notion of mental illness is extremely widely used nowadays, inquiry into the ways in which this term is employed would seem to be especially indicated. Mental illness, of course, is not literally a "thing"—or physical object—and

From *Amer. Psychol. 15*:113–118, 1960. Copyright 1960 by the American Psychological Association. Reprinted by permission of the author and the publisher.

hence it can "exist" only in the same sort of way in which other theoretical concepts exist. Yet, familiar theories are in the habit of posing, sooner or later—at least to those who come to believe in them—as "objective truths" (or "facts"). During certain historical periods, explanatory conceptions such as deities, witches, and microorganisms appeared not only as theories but as self-evident *causes* of a vast number of events. I submit that today mental illness is widely regarded in a somewhat similar fashion, that is, as the cause of innumerable diverse happenings. As an antidote to the complacent use of the notion of mental illness—whether as a self-evident phenomenon, theory, or cause—let us ask this question: What is meant when it is asserted that someone is mentally ill?

In what follows I shall describe briefly the main uses to which the concept of mental illness has been put. I shall argue that this notion has outlived whatever usefulness it might have had and that it now functions merely as a convenient myth.

Mental Illness as a Sign of Brain Damage

The notion of mental illness derives its main support from such phenomena as syphilis of the brain or delirious conditions—intoxications, for instance—in which persons are known to manifest various peculiarities or disorders of thinking and behavior. Correctly speaking, however, these are diseases of the brain, not of the mind. According to one school of thought, *all* so-called mental illness is of this type. The assumption is made that some neurological defect, perhaps a very subtle one, will ultimately be found for all the disorders of thinking and behavior. Many contemporary psychiatrists, physicians, and other scientists hold this view. This position implies that people *cannot* have troubles—expressed in what are *now called* "mental illnesses"—because of differences in personal needs, opinions, social aspirations, values, and so on. *All problems in living* are attributed to physicochemical processes which in due time will be discovered by medical research.

"Mental illnesses" are thus regarded as basically no different than all the other diseases (that is, of the body). The only difference, in this view, between mental and bodily diseases is that the former, affecting the brain, manifest themselves by means of mental symptoms; whereas the latter, affecting other organ systems (for example, the skin, liver, etc.), manifest themselves by means of symptoms referable to those parts of the body. This view rests on and expresses what are, in my opinion, two fundamental errors.

In the first place, what central nervous system symptoms would correspond to a skin eruption or a fracture? It would *not* be some emotion or complex bit of behavior. Rather, it would be blindness or a paralysis of some part of the body. The crux of the matter is that a disease of the brain, analogous to the disease of the skin or bone, is a neurological defect, and not a problem in living. For example, a *defect* in a person's visual field may be satisfactorily explained by correlating it with certain definite lesions in the nervous system. On the other hand, a person's *belief*—whether this be a belief in Christianity, in Communism, or in the idea that his internal organs are "rotting" and that his body is, in fact, already "dead"—cannot be explained by a defect or disease of the nervous system. Explanations of this sort of occurrence—assuming that one is interested in the belief itself and does not regard it simply as a "symptom" or expression of something else that is *more interesting*—must be sought along different lines.

The second error in regarding complex psychosocial behavior, consisting of communications about ourselves and the world about us, as mere symptoms of neurological functioning is *epistemological*. In other words, it is an error pertaining not to any mistakes in observation or reasoning, as such, but rather to the way in which we organize and express our knowledge. In the present case, the error lies in making a symmetrical dualism between mental and physical (or bodily) symptoms, a dualism which is merely a habit of speech and to which no known observations can be found to correspond. Let us see if this is so. In medical practice, when we speak of physical disturbances, we mean either signs (for example, a fever) or symptoms (for example, pain). We speak of mental symptoms, on the other hand, when we refer to a patient's *communications about himself, others, and the world about him.* He might state that he is Napoleon or that he is being persecuted by the Communists. These would be considered mental symptoms *only* if the observer believed that the patient was *not* Napoleon or that he was *not* being persecuted by the Communists. This makes it apparent that the statement that "*X* is a mental symptom" involves rendering a judgment. The judgment entails, moreover, a covert comparison or matching of the patient's ideas, concepts, or beliefs with those of the observer and the society in which they live. The notion of mental symptom is therefore inextricably tied to the *social* (including *ethical*) *context* in which it is made in much the same way as the notion of bodily symptom is tied to an *anatomical* and *genetic context* (Szasz, 1957a, 1957b).

To sum up what has been said thus far: I have tried to show that for those who regard mental symptoms as signs of brain disease, the concept of mental illness is unnecessary and misleading. For what they mean is that people so labeled suffer from diseases of the brain; and, if that is what they mean, it would seem better for the sake of clarity to say that and not something else.

Mental Illness as a Name for Problems in Living

The term "mental illness" is widely used to describe something which is very different than a disease of the brain. Many people today take it for granted that living is an arduous process. Its hardship for modern man, moreover, derives not so much from a struggle for biological survival as from the stresses and strains inherent in the social intercourse of complex human personalities. In this context, the notion of mental illness is used to identify or describe some feature of an individual's so-called personality. Mental illness—as a deformity of the personality, so to speak—is then regarded as the *cause* of the human disharmony. It is implicit in this view that social intercourse between people is regarded as something *inherently harmonious*, its disturbance being due solely to the presence of "mental illness" in many people. This is obviously fallacious reasoning, for it makes the abstraction "mental illness" into a *cause*, even though this abstraction was created in the first place to serve only as a shorthand expression for certain types of human behavior. It now becomes necessary to ask: "What kinds of behavior are regarded as indicative of mental illness, and by whom?"

The concept of illness, whether bodily or mental, implies *deviation from some clearly defined norm*. In the case of physical illness, the norm is the structural and functional integrity of the human body. Thus, although the desirability of physical health, as such, is an ethical value, what health *is* can be stated in anatomical and physiological terms. What is the norm deviation from which is regarded as mental illness? This question cannot be easily answered. But whatever this norm might be, we can be certain of only one thing: namely, that it is a norm that must be stated in terms of *psychosocial, ethical,* and *legal* concepts. For example, notions such as "excessive repression" or "acting out an unconscious impulse" illustrate the use of psychological concepts for judging (so-called) mental health and illness. The idea that chronic hostility, vengefulness,

or divorce are indicative of mental illness would be illustrations of the use of ethical norms (that is, the desirability of love, kindness, and a stable marriage relationship). Finally, the widespread psychiatric opinion that only a mentally ill person would commit homicide illustrates the use of a legal concept as a norm of mental health. The norm from which deviation is measured whenever one speaks of a mental illness is a *psychosocial and ethical one*. Yet, the remedy is sought in terms of *medical* measures which—it is hoped and assumed—are free from wide differences of ethical value. The definition of the disorder and the terms in which its remedy are sought are therefore at serious odds with one another. The practical significance of this covert conflict between the alleged nature of the defect and the remedy can hardly be exaggerated.

Having identified the norms used to measure deviations in cases of mental illness, we will now turn to the question: "Who defines the norms and hence the deviation?" Two basic answers may be offered: (*a*) It may be the person himself (that is, the patient) who decides that he deviates from a norm. For example, an artist may believe that he suffers from a work inhibition; and he may implement this conclusion by seeking help *for* himself from a psychotherapist. (*b*) It may be someone other than the patient who decides that the latter is deviant (for example, relatives, physicians, legal authorities, society generally, etc.). In such a case a psychiatrist may be hired by others to do something *to* the patient in order to correct the deviation.

These considerations underscore the importance of asking the question "Whose agent is the psychiatrist?" and of giving a candid answer to it (Szasz, 1956, 1958). The psychiatrist (psychologist or nonmedical psychotherapist), it now develops, may be the agent of the patient, of the relatives, of the school, of the military services, of a business organization, of a court of law, and so forth. In speaking of the psychiatrist as the agent of these persons or organizations, it is not implied that his values concerning norms, or his ideas and aims concerning the proper nature of remedial action, need to coincide exactly with those of his employer. For example, a patient in individual psychotherapy may believe that his salvation lies in a new marriage; his psychotherapist need not share this hypothesis. As the patient's agent, however, he must abstain from bringing social or legal force to bear on the patient which would prevent him from putting his beliefs into action. If his *contract* is with the patient, the psychiatrist (psychotherapist) may disagree with him or stop his treatment; but he cannot engage others to obstruct the patient's aspirations. Similarly, if a psychiatrist is engaged by a court to determine the sanity of a criminal, he need not fully share the legal authorities' values and intentions in regard to the criminal and the means available for dealing with him. But the psychiatrist is expressly barred from stating, for example, that it is not the criminal who is "insane" but the men who wrote the law on the basis of which the very actions that are being judged are regarded as "criminal." Such an opinion could be voiced, of course, but not in a courtroom, and not by a psychiatrist who makes it his practice to assist the court in performing its daily work.

To recapitulate: In actual contemporary social usage, the finding of a mental illness is made by establishing a deviance in behavior from certain psychosocial, ethical, or legal norms. The judgment may be made, as in medicine, by the patient, the physician (psychiatrist), or others. Remedial action, finally, tends to be sought in a therapeutic—or covertly medical—framework, thus creating a situation in which *psychosocial, ethical,* and/or *legal deviations* are claimed to be correctible by (so-called) *medical action.* Since medical action is designed to correct only medical deviations, it seems logically absurd to expect that it will help solve problems whose very existence had been defined and established on nonmedical grounds. I think that these considerations may be fruitfully applied to the present use of tranquilizers and, more generally, to what might be expected of drugs of whatever type in regard to the amelioration or solution of problems in human living.

The Role of Ethics in Psychiatry

Anything that people *do*—in contrast to things that *happen* to them (Peters, 1958)—takes place in a context of value. In this broad sense, no human activity is devoid of ethical implications. When the values underlying certain activities are widely shared, those who participate in their pursuit may lose sight of them altogether. The discipline of medicine, both as a pure science (for example, research) and as a technology (for example, therapy),

contains many ethical considerations and judgments. Unfortunately, these are often denied, minimized, or merely kept out of focus; for the ideal of the medical profession as well as of the people whom it serves seems to be having a system of medicine (allegedly) free of ethical value. This sentimental notion is expressed by such things as the doctor's willingness to treat and help patients irrespective of their religious or political beliefs, whether they are rich or poor, etc. While there may be some grounds for this belief—albeit it is a view that is not impressively true even in these regards—the fact remains that ethical considerations encompass a vast range of human affairs. By making the practice of medicine neutral in regard to some specific issues of value need not, and cannot, mean that it can be kept free from all such values. The practice of medicine is intimately tied to ethics; and the first thing that we must do, it seems to me, is to try to make this clear and explicit. I shall let this matter rest here, for it does not concern us specifically in this essay. Lest there be any vagueness, however, about how or where ethics and medicine meet, let me remind the reader of such issues as birth control, abortion, suicide, and euthanasia as only a few of the major areas of current ethicomedical controversy.

Psychiatry, I submit, is very much more intimately tied to problems of ethics than is medicine. I use the word "psychiatrist" here to refer to that contemporary discipline which is concerned with *problems in living* (and not with diseases of the brain, which are problems for neurology). Problems in human relations can be analyzed, interpreted, and given meaning only within given social and ethical contexts. Accordingly, it *does* make a difference—arguments to the contrary notwithstanding—what the psychiatrist's socioethical orientations happen to be; for these will influence his ideas on what is wrong with the patient, what deserves comment or interpretation, in what possible directions change might be desirable, and so forth. Even in medicine proper, these factors play a role, as for instance, in the divergent orientations which physicians, depending on their religious affiliations, have toward such things as birth control and therapeutic abortion. Can anyone really believe that a psychotherapist's ideas concerning religious belief, slavery, or other similar issues play no role in his practical work? If they do make a difference, what are we to infer from it? Does it not seem reasonable that we ought to have different psychiatric therapies—each expressly recognized for the ethical positions which they embody — for, say, Catholics and Jews, religious persons and agnostics, democrats and communists, white supremacists and Negroes, and so on? Indeed, if we look at how psychiatry is actually practiced today (especially in the United States), we find that people do seek psychiatric help in accordance with their social status and ethical beliefs (Hollingshead & Redlich, 1958). This should really not surprise us more than being told that practicing Catholics rarely frequent birth control clinics.

The foregoing position which holds that contemporary psychotherapists deal with problems in living, rather than with mental illness and their cures, stands in opposition to a currently prevalent claim, according to which mental illness is just as "real" and "objective" as bodily illness. This is a confusing claim since it is never known exactly what is meant by such words as "real" and "objective." I suspect, however, that what is intended by the proponents of this view is to create the idea in the popular mind that mental illness is some sort of disease entity, like an infection or a malignancy. If this were true, one could *catch* or *get* a "mental illness," one might *have* or *harbor* it, one might *transmit* it to others, and finally one could get *rid* of it. In my opinion, there is not a shred of evidence to support this idea. To the contrary, all the evidence is the other way and supports the view that what people now call mental illnesses are for the most part *communications* expressing unacceptable ideas, often framed, moreover, in an unusual idiom. The scope of this essay allows me to do no more than mention this alternatively theoretical approach to this problem (Szasz, 1957c).

This is not the place to consider in detail the similarities and differences between bodily and mental illnesses. It shall suffice for us here to emphasize only one important difference between them: namely, that whereas bodily disease refers to public, physicochemical occurrences, the notion of mental illness is used to codify relatively more private, sociopsychological happenings of which the observer (diagnostician) forms a part. In other words, the psychiatrist does not stand *apart* from what he observes, but is, in Harry Stack Sullivan's apt words, a "participant ob-

server." This means that he is *committed* to some picture of what he considers reality— and to what he thinks society considers reality—and he observes and judges the patient's behavior in the light of these considerations. This touches on our earlier observation that the notion of mental symptom itself implies a comparison between observer and observed, psychiatrist and patient. This is so obvious that I may be charged with belaboring trivialities. Let me therefore say once more that my aim in presenting this argument was expressly to criticize and counter a prevailing contemporary tendency to deny the moral aspects of psychiatry (and psychotherapy) and to substitute for them allegedly value-free medical considerations. Psychotherapy, for example, is being widely practiced as though it entailed nothing other than restoring the patient from a state of mental sickness to one of mental health. While it is generally accepted that mental illness has something to do with man's social (or inter-personal) relations, it is paradoxically maintained that problems of values (that is, of ethics) do not arise in this process.* Yet, in one sense, much of psychotherapy may revolve around nothing other than the elucidation and weighing of goals and values—many of which may be mutually contradictory—and the means whereby they might best be harmonized, realized, or relinquished.

The diversity of human values and the methods by means of which they may be realized is so vast, and many of them remain so unacknowledged, that they cannot fail but lead to conflicts in human relations. Indeed, to say that human relations at all levels — from mother to child, through husband and wife, to nation and nation — are fraught with stress, strain, and disharmony is, once again, making the obvious explicit. Yet, what may be obvious may be also poorly understood. This I think is the case here. For it seems to

---

*Freud went so far as to say that: "I consider ethics to be taken for granted. Actually I have never done a mean thing" (Jones, 1957, p. 247). This surely is a strange thing to say for someone who has studied man as a social being as closely as did Freud. I mention it here to show how the notion of "illness" (in the case of psychoanalysis, "psychopathology," or "mental illness") was used by Freud—and by most of his followers—as a means for classifying certain forms of human behavior as falling within the scope of medicine, and hence (by *fiat*) outside that of ethics!

me that—at least in our scientifc theories of behavior—we have failed to *accept* the simple fact that human relations are inherently fraught with difficulties and that to make them even relatively harmonious requires much patience and hard work. I submit that the idea of mental illness is now being put to work to obscure certain difficulties which at present may be inherent—not that they need be unmodifiable—in the social intercourse of persons. If this is true, the concept functions as a disguise; for instead of calling attention to conflicting human needs, aspirations, and values, the notion of mental illness provides an amoral and impersonal "thing" (an "illness") as an explanation for *problems in living* (Szasz, 1959). We may recall in this connection that not so long ago it was devils and witches who were held responsible for men's problems in social living. The belief in mental illness, as something other than man's trouble in getting along with his fellow man, is the proper heir to the belief in demonology and witchcraft. Mental illness exists or is "real" in exactly the same sense in which witches existed or were "real."

Choice, Responsibility, and Psychiatry

While I have argued that mental illnesses do not exist, I obviously did not imply that the social and psychological occurrences to which this label is currently being attached also do not exist. Like the personal and social troubles which people had in the Middle Ages, they are real enough. It is the labels we give them that concerns us and, having labelled them, what we do about them. While I cannot go into the ramified implications of this problem here, it is worth noting that a demonologic conception of problems in living gave rise to therapy along theological lines. Today, a belief in mental illness implies— nay, requires—therapy along medical or psychotherapeutic lines.

What is implied in the line of thought set forth here is something quite different. I do not intend to offer a new conception of "psychiatric illness" nor a new form of "therapy." My aim is more modest and yet also more ambitious. It is to suggest that the phenomena now called mental illnesses be looked at afresh and more simply, that they be removed from the category of illnesses, and that they be regarded as the expressions of man's struggle with the problem of *how* he

should live. The last mentioned problem is obviously a vast one, its enormity reflecting not only man's inability to cope with his environment, but even more his increasing self-reflectiveness.

By problems in living, then, I refer to that truly explosive chain reaction which began with man's fall from divine grace by partaking of the fruit of the tree of knowledge. Man's awareness of himself and of the world about him seems to be a steadily expanding one, bringing in its wake an ever larger *burden of understanding* (an expression borrowed from Susanne Langer, 1953). *This burden, then, is to be expected and must not be misinterpreted.* Our only *rational* means for lightening it is *more understanding*, and appropriate *action* based on such understanding. The main alternative lies in acting as though the burden were not what in fact we perceive it to be and taking refuge in an outmoded theological view of man. In the latter view, man does not fashion his life and much of his world about him, but merely lives out his fate in a world created by superior beings. This may logically lead to pleading nonresponsibility in the face of seemingly unfathomable problems and difficulties. Yet, if man fails to take increasing responsibility for his actions, individually as well as collectively, it seems unlikely that some higher power or being would assume this task and carry this burden for him. Moreover, this seems hardly the proper time in human history for obscuring the issue of man's responsibility for his actions by hiding it behind the skirt of an all-explaining conception of mental illness.

Conclusions

I have tried to show that the notion of mental illness has outlived whatever usefulness it might have had and that it now functions merely as a convenient myth. As such, it is a true heir to religious myths in general, and to the belief in witchcraft in particular; the role of all these belief-systems was to act as *social tranquilizers*, thus encouraging the hope that mastery of certain specific problems may be achieved by means of substitutive (symbolic-magical) operations. The notion of mental illness thus serves mainly to obscure the everyday fact that life for most people is a continuous struggle, not for biological survival, but for a "place in the sun," "peace of mind," or some other human value. For man aware of himself and the world about him, once the needs for preserving the body (and perhaps the race) are more or less satisfied, the problem arises as to what he should do with himself. Sustained adherence to the myth of mental illness allows people to avoid facing this problem, believing that mental health, conceived as the absence of mental illness, automatically insures the making of right and safe choices in one's conduct of life. But the facts are all the other way. It is the making of good choices in life that others regard, retrospectively, as good mental health!

The myth of mental illness encourages us, moreover, to believe in its logical corollary: that social intercourse would be harmonious, satisfying, and the secure basis of a "good life" were it not for the disrupting influences of mental illness or "psychopathology." The potentiality for universal human happiness, in this form at least, seems to me but another example of the I-wish-it-were-true type of fantasy. I do believe that human happiness or well-being on a hitherto unimaginably large scale, and not just for a select few, is possible. This goal could be achieved, however, only at the cost of many men, and not just a few being willing and able to tackle their personal, social, and ethical conflicts. This means having the courage and integrity to forego waging battles on false fronts, finding solutions for substitute problems—for instance, fighting the battle of stomach acid and chronic fatigue instead of facing up to a marital conflict.

Our adversaries are not demons, witches, fate, or mental illness. We have no enemy whom we can fight, exorcise, or dispel by "cure." What we do have are *problems in living*—whether these are biologic, economic, political, or sociopsychological. In this essay I was concerned only with problems belonging in the last mentioned category, and within this group mainly with those pertaining to moral values. The field to which modern psychiatry addresses itself is vast, and I made no effort to encompass it all. My argument was limited to the proposition that mental illness is a myth, whose function it is to disguise and thus render more palatable the bitter pill of moral conflicts in human relations.

REFERENCES

Hollingshead, A. B., and Redlich, F. C. *Social class and mental illness.* New York: Wiley, 1958.

Jones, E. *The life and work of Sigmund Freud.* Vol. III. New York: Basic Books, 1957.

Langer, S. K. *Philosophy in a new key.* New York: Mentor Books, 1953.

Peters, R. S. *The concept of motivation.* London: Routledge & Kegan Paul, 1958.

Szasz, T. S. Malingering: "Diagnosis" or social condemnation? *AMA Arch. Neurol. Psychiat.,* 1956, 76, 432–443.

Szasz, T. S. *Pain and pleasure: A study of bodily feelings.* New York: Basic Books, 1957. (a)

Szasz, T. S. The problem of psychiatric nosology: A contribution to a situational analysis of psychiatric operations. *Amer. J. Psychiat.,* 1957, 114, 405–413. (b)

Szasz, T. S. On the theory of psychoanalytic treatment. *Int. J. Psycho-Anal.,* 1957, 38, 166–182. (c)

Szasz, T. S. Psychiatry, ethics and the criminal law. *Columbia Law Rev.,* 1958, 58, 183–198.

Szasz, T. S. Moral conflict and psychiatry. *Yale Rev.,* 1959, in press.

Integrative Directions

There are those who contend that the major traditions of psychology and psychiatry have, for too long now, been doctrinaire in their assumptions. These critics claim that theories which focus their attention on only one level of data cannot help but generate formulations that are limited by their narrow preconceptions; moreover, their findings must, inevitably, be incompatible with the simple fact that psychological processes are multidetermined and multidimensional in expression.

Adolf Meyer, originator of the "psychobiologic" school at the turn of this century, spoke out vigorously for the principle of man's intrinsic biological and psychological unity. Writing at a time when this principle was persistently obscured and overlooked, Meyer's remained a voice in the wilderness.

Paul Meehl, in his incisive and brilliantly speculative article, illustrates the fruits of this integrative thesis. Here he formulates a model that explicates the processes by which an ostensive neurological defect can develop into a manifest clinical syndrome when activated by particular social learning regimens.

11 The Role of the Mental Factors in Psychiatry

Adolf Meyer

Nearly forty years ago John P. Gray made a plea for the view that mind cannot become diseased itself, and that there cannot be any *mental* diseases, but only diseases of the brain. To prove this, he eradicated as a superstition the idea that mental or moral causes could figure in the etiology of mental disorders. He published a table of the causes in the cases admitted during the years 1843–1870 and in these he gave the following ratio in percentages (selection from the complete table):

	1843	1851	1860	1865	1866	1867	1868
Moral causes	46.38	30.05	13.95	5.41	3.09		
Physical causes	33.70	62.57	70.33	73.35	67.78	80.05	77.49
Unascertained causes	19.93	7.37	15.73	21.24	29.12	19.95	22.51

He achieved his practical aim to harmonize the theory and the wise aspiration to obtain the supremacy of physicians in the care of the insane. But he went from one extreme—the tendency to systematic ignoring of the somatic factors in the lay public—to another extreme, the disregard of the mental factors.

Pathology also had to pass through extremes. From witchcraft and humoral pathology, it had become a study of *lesions* and their consequences. Lesions of the brain figured as the only possible explanations of disorders of its functions. So numerous were the anatomical and histological discoveries that they absorbed all the attention; and what was not known yet was nevertheless put down in terms of some kind of "lesion" and the *knowledge of the lesion* was the pathology.

In the meantime a revolution has taken place. The theory of immunity brought pathology to experimental terms. The great fact had to be accepted that an organism which had had smallpox was protected for a

From the *American Journal of Insanity*, LXV (1908), 39–52.

period. The capacity of *resistance* to degrees of virulence of anthrax became an issue greater than that of a mere knowledge of the tissue changes. The mere histologist has given way to the experimentalist; or rather, a *combination* of all the available facts, causal, functional and structural, in terms of experiments, has become the central thought of pathology.

The finest histological demonstration of the posterior column lesions of tabes—by many thought to be "the pathology of the disease"—would not tell us that if you wish to avoid tabes you must avoid syphilis. The knowledge of lesions is but *one* of the resources of the formula of real pathology, and this formula is: (1) What is the condition under study (the disturbance expressed functionally or anatomically, but at least sufficiently to distinguish it from other similar conditions)? (2) What are the conditions under which it arises? and (3) To what extent are the conditions and the developments modifiable?

We know now that the lesion itself, if we know it, is only one of the *symptoms* (although to be sure one of the type which "keep" and can be bottled up and demonstrated longer than the functional symptoms), and that the whole condition must be expressed in a lucid equation of an experiment of nature before it gives us the satisfaction of knowing the "pathology."

Hence the mere *assumption* of a hypothetical lesion is no solution and not even necessarily the most stimulating hypothesis. Thus we come to hear again of "psychogenetic developments" of cases of dementia praecox and of depressions, hysterical tantrums, etc. What can this mean?

Take the case of a woman of somewhat restricted capacity who was forced by circumstances to move on two occasions, and each time on no other occasion worked herself into a depression; she did not see how she could do the work and, instead of doing the best she could, she dropped into a state of evil anticipation, lamentation, perplexity—a typical depression of several months' duration. Her sister too had a depression of a rather different character, but also on provocation. We do well to point to the constitutional peculiarity—a lack of immunity. Since there *are* cases in which we cannot find any precipitating factors, we are apt to spread ourselves on a statement of heredity and possibly degeneracy of make-up, of possible lesions, etc., and to overemphasize these issues. What we actually know is that this patient is apt to react with a peculiar depressive reaction where others get along with fair balance. The etiology thus involves (1) constitutional make-up, and (2) a precipitating factor; and in our eagerness we cut out the latter and only speak of the heredity or constitutional make-up. It is my contention that we must use *both* facts and that of the two, for *prevention* and for the special characterization of the make-up, the precipitating factor is of the greater importance, because *it* alone gives us an idea of the actual defect and a suggestion as to how to strengthen the person that he may become resistive. It is a problem of index of resistance with regard to *certain difficulties of mental adjustment*.

Take another case: a girl taken advantage of by a neighbor's boy at six. She did not dare tell any one for shame; and without knowing what it all meant, she imagined things about it, that she had become different from others. It is difficult to know how much children can elaborate such feelings and how much they can become entangled and twisted by amplifying dreams and talk of others and what not, if once started on a track without the normal corrections. At eleven, the patient had a slight accident and limped for six months. A plain ovarialgia with typical hysterical convulsions and paraplegia followed her nursing her sister through an illness at eighteen; recovery in one year. Then at twenty-one, after nursing and losing her grandmother, she experienced a new collapse, again with recovery. At twenty-five, there came a hysterical psychosis which was mismanaged and drifted into stupor, then excitement and then a classical catatonic dementia. For every step there are adequate causes; usually causes which would not have upset you or me, but which upset the patient. Now what makes the difference between her and you and me? A different make-up, yes; but what kind? Can we expect a full answer in some general term? Do we not, to explain it usefully and practically, have to express it in the very facts of the history? Every step is like an experiment telling us the story, and giving us the concrete facts to be minded; while to speak merely of "hysteria" or later of "dementia praecox" gives us no good clue as to what to prevent, and what sore spots to protect and what weak sides to strengthen, but only a general characterization of the possible mischief and the probable *absence* of a palpable lesion, and the fact that the disorder consists of a faulty hanging together of the mental reactions or adjustments, shown by and promoted by previous maladjustments.

Some of you are probably familiar with my explanation of many of the conditions now lumped together as dementia praecox. I started from the realization that in some diseases we are continually promising ourselves lesions, and over that we neglect facts which are even now at hand and ready to be sized up and the very things we must learn to handle. Some persons are immune and readily balanced, others get wrecked. The main question is, What makes the difference? Some talk of degeneracy, others of autointoxications and still others of glia overgrowth—but these statements are often enough mere conjectures or refer to merely incidental facts and do not give us much to go by.

Take a case of catatonic stupor. There are evidently many factors involved. All I want to know is whether I can best clinch the facts actually known about the patient by using what is accessible (usually a characteristic string of habit developments and experiences and maladjustments), or by *inventing* some poisons or what not.

It has been my experience to find in many a case of dementia praecox far more forerunners of actual mischief than the average psychiatrist gets at by his examination when he avoids these facts or does not know how to use them. And it has become my conviction that the developments in some mental diseases are rather the results of peculiar mental tangles than the result of any coarsely appreciable and demonstrable brain lesion or poisoning—the natural further development of inefficient reaction types; and that I would rather look at the bird in the hand, and act on the available facts, while I can still live in hope that some day I might find an organ or poison which is more involved than another, and which might be given a prop.

I should consider it preposterously absurd to try to explain an alcoholic delirium merely on fears and psychogenetic factors, leaving out of sight the stomach condition and lack of food and sleep; and I consider it as equally absurd to disregard the experience with the moving and all it implied, the twist of the hysterical woman along the line of a supposed internal injury, and its being used in the development of a catatonia, or the weight of habitual indecision and lack of completion in psychasthenia, the habit conflicts and deterioration of sane instincts in dementia praecox, etc. Where these facts *exist*, we should use *them* rather than wholly hypothetical poisons. Where we *do* find somatic disorders we use them; where we should have to invent them first in order to get anything to work with, we had better use the facts at hand for what they are worth to reconstruct the disorder in terms of an experiment of nature.

Why the dissatisfaction with explanations of a psychogenetic nature?

(1) Because the facts are difficult to get at, and difficult to control critically, and often used for stupid inferences, for instance, a notion that a psychogenetic origin, i.e. a development out of natural mental activities which need not harm you and me, could not explain occasional lasting and frequently progressive disorders (in the face of the fact that nothing is more difficult to change than a political or religious or other deeply rooted conviction or tendency and nothing more difficult to stem than an unbalanced tendency to mysticism, lying, etc.).

(2) Because there prevail misleading dogmatic ideas about mind.

It is unfortunate that science still adheres to an effete and impossible contrast between mental and physical. More and more we realize that what figures to our mind as *matter* is much better expressed in terms of combinations of electrons, if not simply of energies, which throw off many of the forbidding and restrictive features of those masses which form the starting point of our concept of inert matter, which is practically sufficient for most demands of ordinary physics, but a hindrance to a better conception of the more complex happenings of biochemistry. Mind, on the other hand, is a *sufficiently organized living being in action;* and not a peculiar form of mind-stuff. A sufficiently organized brain is the main central link, but mental activity is really best understood in its full meaning as the adaption and adjustment of the individual as a whole, in contrast to the simple activity of single organs such as those of circulation, respiration, digestion, elimination, or simple reflex activity.

We know, of course, that in these reactions which we know as mental, the brain forms the central link at work, although we know but little of the detail working. Sensorimotor adjustments form an essential part and as soon as we pass from the simple representative reactions such as sensations and thoughts, to the affective reactions, emotions and actions, we get a distinct participation of the work of glands, of circulation, of respiration and muscular adjustments, so that organs serving *as such* more limited "infrapsychic" purposes enter as intrinsic parts into emotions, appetites, instincts and actions, so as to form the concrete *conduct and behavior,* which is the main thing deranged in our patients.

Thus we do not contrast mental activity with physical activity, which can be shown to be an artificial contrast with untenable and not truly scientific foundation, but mental activity and non-mental activity; activity of the person as a whole as mental activity, contrasted with the activity of the individual organs when working without mental links (as the heart does when removed from the body, or the various organs in the mere vegetative regulations and functions).

We do not know all the details of the modes of collaboration, but the main lines. We study their differences of various reaction types and of modifiability in various individuals and determine their chances of adjustment, and their ability to work themselves through the conflicts, tangles and temptations of usual and unusual demands. The extent to which the individual is capable of elaborating an efficient reaction determines the person's level. Our comparative measure of the various disabilities (of a patient getting through the difficulty of moving, the difficulty of getting square with an infantile trauma and its imaginary elaborations, the difficulty and twist resulting from habitual indecision and substitution of ruminations and panics and all that) is the normal complete reaction or adjustment to and of the situation. Why the tantrum? How can it be forestalled? Such would be the questions and problems uppermost in my mind.

The common reasoning is that if the patient gets through one tangle or one delusion, the disease still remains and other delusions will form. This I think is very often not correct, unless we bow dogmatically to an unwarrantedly broad notion of "disease." Mere disposition is not the disease. In practice that assumption is certainly very often *proved* to be false if we handle the conditions correctly. Very often the supposed disease back of it all is a myth and merely a self-protective term for an insufficient knowledge of the conditions of reaction and inadequacy of our present remedial skill.

Unfortunately our habits of diction lead us to call mental only the most specialized central reaction, the "thought," or at least the more essentially subjective part of the reaction. Yet as practical persons you do not take the word of an unknown person, but the act, as the real event. If you do that in psychopathology, and not before that, you also deal with conclusive factors. The act, not merely the possible step to it, counts; the *reaction* of the person as a whole, not merely one "thought," or part-step. We can under no circumstances afford to ignore the mental facts in the development of a large group of mental disorders. They *can* be the only expression of the facts to be heeded and to be worked with. But the mental facts we speak of are not mere thought but actual attitudes, affects, volitions and activities and possibly disorders of discrimination (which are oftener due to infrapsychic disturbances, as is shown by the psychosensory deliria).

Every mental adjustment must be in keeping with the laws of anabolism and catabolism; it has its somatic components. It is, therefore, intelligible that it *may* be easier

to precipitate harm than to correct it, and that some disorders or conflicts may permanently damage the processes of anabolism.

I should like to illustrate further the influence of such an event as an upsetting shame and its setting in a depression, or an anxiety—but I have used too much of your time already. I only want to say one more word and that with regard to the *test* of the whole proposition: the existence or non-existence of psychotherapeutic helps.

If mental factors meant nothing, psychotherapy would be a snare and a delusion. Is it so? What is psychotherapy? Lately I heard two papers on this question—one an excellent sketch of the history and not without an occasional emphasis on the queer and on the yellow streak in what is commonly known as psychotherapy and suggestion. The other was a simple discussion of the treatment of constipation by establishing an unshakable habit. It was psychologically interesting to watch the distinguished audience. The first paper expressed what in the main has been the general practice and the foundations of some of the more recent developments, with many sidelights but no urgent appeal to any special reform in the attitude of the physician. It elicited full appreciation as a fair and conservative general statement.

The report of the cures of even the most obstinate constipation with the simple method of Dubois and good sense and establishment of a habit met with smiles. Why? Because many men believe they *have* tried that method and have failed; and they do not realize that usually it is because they did not insist on the chief principle of psychotherapy, viz., that it is not talk or "thought" alone, but *the doing of things*, that is wanted. A physician will ask a patient whether he took his pill; but when he gives a sometimes somewhat elaborate regime of how to do things—i.e., the best psychotherapy by help and education—he often does not take correspondingly elaborate pains to control the carrying out of the plan to the dot—and he fails.

Psychotherapy is regulation of action, and only complete when action is reached. This is why we all use it in the form of occupation or rest, where it is an efficient and controllable form of regulation. This is why we teach patients actually to take different attitudes to things. Habit training is the backbone of psychotherapy; suggestion merely a step to the end, and of use only to the one who knows that the end can and *must* be *attained*. Action with flesh and bone is the only safe criterion of efficient mental activity; and actions and attitude and their adaptation is the issue in psychotherapy.

To sum up: There are conditions in which disorders of function (possibly with definite lesions) of special organs are the essential explanation of a mental disorder—a perversion of metabolism by poison, a digestive upset, a syphilitic reaction or an antisyphilitic reaction of the nervous system, an arteriosclerosis, and, in *these*, the *mental* facts are the *incidental* facts of the experimental chain.

But there *are* cases in which the apparent disorder of individual organs is merely an incident in a development which we could not understand correctly except by comparing it with the normal and efficient reaction of the individual as a whole, and for that we must use terms of psychology—not of mysterious events, but *actions* and *reactions* of which we know that they *do* things, a truly dynamic psychology. There we find the irrepressible instincts and habits at work, and finally the characteristic mental reaction type constituting the obviously pathological aberrations, and while it may be too late in many cases to stem the stream of destructive action—action beyond correction and in conflict with the laws of balance and anabolism and catabolism—seeing the facts in the right way will help us set aright what *can* be set aright, prevent what *can* be prevented and do what *can* be done to secure gymnastics and orthopaedics of mind—i.e., of the conduct and efficiency of the person as a whole.

Modern pathology sees in most "diseases" nature's way of righting inadequate balance. They are crude ways of *repair*, not the enemy itself; reactions to be guided, not to be suppressed; and to understand the whole process you can no longer get along by dreaming of lesions when your facts are too meagre; but you see the facts as they are, the reaction of the patient;—and *he* is a psychopathologist who can help nature strike the balance with the least expense to the patient. Much psychopathology and psychotherapy will depend on the bracing of weak organs; but its work is not concluded before the patient is shown the level of his mental metabolism, the level of efficient anabolism and catabolism in terms of conduct and behavior and efficient meeting of the difficulties worth meeting, and avoidance of what otherwise would be a foolish attempt.

This is a progress beyond John P. Gray, and I feel that had he seen the recent developments, man of action as he was, he would himself have subscribed to the rule that the real aim of psychiatry is to attain balance of the metabolism of conduct, obtained, according to the accessibility of the facts, from the adjustment of the individual organs, or from adjustment of the activities and attitudes which we can only size up in terms of a psychology of "activity of the individual as a whole." And, last but not least, we see that there is a deep reason for our interest in the adjustment of the *tasks* of adaptation, a straightening out of the situation outside of the patient, the family and other problems of adjustment which may be too much for the patient. These have always been the practical ways; and by dropping some unnecessary shells and traditions, we can see a psychopathology develop without absurd contrasts between mental and physical, and rather a division into adjustments of the person as a whole and adjustments of individual organs.

12 Schizotaxia, Schizotypy, Schizophrenia

Paul E. Meehl

In the course of the last decade, while spending several thousand hours in the practice of intensive psychotherapy, I have treated—

From the *Amer. Psychol.* 17:827–838, 1962. Copyright 1962 by the American Psychological Association. Reprinted by permission of the author and the publisher.

sometimes unknowingly except in retrospect—a considerable number of schizoid and schizophrenic patients. Like all clinicians, I have formed some theoretical opinions as a result of these experiences. While I have not until recently begun any systematic research efforts on this baffling disorder, I felt that to share with you some of my thoughts, based though they are upon clinical impressions in the context of selected research by others, might be an acceptable use of this occasion.

Let me begin by putting a question which I find is almost never answered correctly by our clinical students on PhD orals, and the answer which they seem to dislike when it is offered. Suppose that you were required to write down a procedure for selecting an individual from the population who would be diagnosed as schizophrenic by a psychiatric staff; you have to wager $1,000 on being right; you may not include in your selection procedure any behavioral fact, such as a symptom or trait, manifested by the individual. What would you write down? So far as I have been able to ascertain, there is only one thing you could write down that would give you a better than even chance of winning such a bet—namely, "Find an individual X who has a schizophrenic identical twin." Admittedly, there were many other facts which would raise your odds somewhat above the low base of schizophrenia. You might, for example, identify X by first finding mothers who have certain unhealthy child-rearing attitudes; you might enter a subpopulation defined jointly by such demographic variables as age, size of community, religion, ethnic background, or social class. But these would leave you with a pretty unfair wager, as would the rule, "Find an X who has a fraternal twin, of the same sex, diagnosed as schizophrenic" (Fuller & Thompson, 1960, pp. 272–283; Stern, 1960, pp. 581–584).

Now the twin studies leave a good deal to be desired methodologically (Rosenthal, 1962); but there seems to be a kind of "double standard of methodological morals" in our profession, in that we place a good deal of faith in our knowledge of schizophrenic dynamics, and we make theoretical inferences about social learning factors from the establishment of group trends which may be statistically significant and replicable although of small or moderate size; but when we come to the genetic studies, our standards of rigor suddenly increase. I would argue that the concordance rates in the twin studies need not be accepted uncritically as highly precise parameter estimates in order for us to say that their magnitudes represent the most important piece of etiological information we possess about schizophrenia.

It is worthwhile, I think, to pause here over a question in the sociology of knowledge,

namely, why do psychologists exhibit an aversive response to the twin data? I have no wish to argue *ad hominem* here—I raise this question in constructive and irenic spirit, because I think that a substantive confusion often lies at the bottom of this resistance, and one which can be easily dispelled. Everybody readily assents to such vague dicta as "heredity and environment interact," "there need be no conflict between organic and functional concepts," "we always deal with the total organism," etc. But it almost seems that clinicians do not fully believe these principles in any concrete sense, because they show signs of thinking that *if* a genetic basis were found for schizophrenia, the psychodynamics of the disorder (especially in relation to intrafamilial social learnings) would be somehow negated or, at least, greatly demoted in importance. To what extent, if at all, is this true?

Here we run into some widespread misconceptions as to what is meant by *specific etiology* in nonpsychiatric medicine. By postulating a "specific etiology" one does *not* imply any of the following:

1. The etiological factor always, or even usually, produces clinical illness.
2. If illness occurs, the particular form and content of symptoms is derivable by reference to the specific etiology alone.
3. The course of the illness can be materially influenced by procedures directed against the specific etiology.
4. All persons who share the specific etiology will have closely similar histories, symptoms, and course.
5. The largest single contributor to symptom variance is the specific etiology.

In medicine, not one of these is part of the concept of specific etiology, yet they are repeatedly invoked as arguments against a genetic interpretation of schizophrenia. I am not trying to impose the causal model of medicine by analogy; I merely wish to emphasize that *if* one postulates a genetic mutation as the specific etiology of schizophrenia, he is not thereby committed to any of the above as implications. Consequently such familiar objections as, "Schizophrenics differ widely from one another" or "Many schizophrenics can be helped by purely psychological methods" should not disturb one who opts for a genetic hypothesis. In medicine, the concept of specific etiology means the *sine qua non*—the causal condition which is necessary, but not sufficient, for the disorder to occur. A genetic theory of schizophrenia would, in this sense, be stronger than that of "one contributor to variance"; but weaker than that of "largest contributor to variance." In analysis of variance terms, it means an interaction effect such that no other variables can exert a main effect when the specific etiology is lacking.

Now it goes without saying that "clinical schizophrenia" as such cannot be inherited, because it has behavioral and phenomenal contents which are learned. As Bleuler says, in order to have a delusion involving Jesuits one must first have learned about Jesuits. It seems inappropriate to apply the geneticist's concept of "penetrance" to the crude statistics of formal diagnosis—if a specific genetic etiology exists, its phenotypic expression in *psychological* categories would be a quantitative aberration in some parameter of a behavioral acquisition function. What could possibly be a genetically determined functional parameter capable of generating such diverse behavioral outcomes, including the preservation of normal function in certain domains?

The theoretical puzzle is exaggerated when we fail to conceptualize at different levels of molarity. For instance, there is a tendency among organically minded theorists to analogize between catatonic phenomena and various neurological or chemically induced states in animals. But Bleuler's masterly *Theory of Schizophrenic Negativism* (1912) shows how the whole range of catatonic behavior, including diametrically opposite modes of relating to the interpersonal environment, can be satisfactorily explained as instrumental acts; thus even a convinced organicist, postulating a biochemical defect as specific etiology, should recognize that the causal linkage between this etiology and catatonia is indirect, requiring for the latter's derivation a lengthy chain of statements which are not even formulable except in molar psychological language.

What kind of behavioral fact about the patient leads us to diagnose schizophrenia? There are a number of traits and symptoms which get a high weight, and the weights differ among clinicians. But thought disorder continues to hold its own in spite of today's greater clinical interest in motivational (especially interpersonal) variables. If you are inclined to doubt this for yourself, consider the following indicators: Patient experiences intense ambivalence, readily reports conscious hatred of family figures, is pananxious, subjects therapist to a long series of testing operations, is withdrawn, and says, "Naturally, I am growing my father's hair."

While all of these are schizophrenic indicators, the last one is the diagnostic bell ringer. In this respect we are still Bleulerians, although we know a lot more about the schizophrenic's psychodynamics than Bleuler did. The significance of thought disorder, associative dyscontrol (or, as I prefer to call it so as to include the very mildest forms it may take, "cognitive slippage"), in schizophrenia has been somewhat deemphasized in recent years. Partly this is due to the greater interest in interpersonal dynamics, but partly also to the realization that much of our earlier psychometric assessment of the thought disorder was mainly reflecting the schizophrenic's tendency to underperform because uninterested, preoccupied, resentful, or frightened. I suggest that this realization has been overgeneralized and led us to swing too far the other way, as if we had shown that there really *is* no cognitive slippage factor present. One rather common assumption seems to be that if one can demonstrate the potentiating effect of a motivational state upon cognitive slippage, light has thereby been shed upon the etiology of schizophrenia. Why are we entitled to think this? Clinically, we see a degree of cognitive slippage not found to a comparable degree among nonschizophrenic persons. Some patients (e.g., pseudoneurotics) are highly anxious and exhibit minimal slippage; others (e.g., burnt-out cases) are minimally anxious with marked slippage. The demonstration that we can intensify a particular patient's cognitive dysfunction by manipulating his affects is not really very illuminating. After all, even ordinary neurological diseases can often be tremendously influenced symptomatically via emotional stimuli; but if a psychologist demonstrates that the spasticity or tremor of a multiple sclerotic is affected by rage or fear, we would not thereby have learned anything about the etiology of multiple sclerosis.

Consequent upon our general assimilation of the insights given us by psychoanalysis, there is today a widespread and largely unquestioned assumption that when we can trace out the motivational forces linked to the content of aberrant behavior, then we understand why the person has fallen ill. There is no compelling reason to assume this, when the evidence is mainly our dynamic understanding of the patient, however valid that may be. The phrase "why the person has fallen ill" may, of course, be legitimately taken to include these things; an account of how and when he falls ill will certainly include them. But they may be quite inadequate to answer the question, "Why does X fall ill and not Y, granted that we can understand both of them?" I like the analogy of a color psychosis, which might be developed by certain individuals in a society entirely oriented around the making of fine color discriminations. Social, sexual, economic signals are color mediated; to misuse a color word is strictly taboo; compulsive mothers are horribly ashamed of a child who is retarded in color development, and so forth. Some color-blind individuals (not all, perhaps not most) develop a color psychosis in this culture; as adults, they are found on the couches of color therapists, where a great deal of *valid* understanding is achieved about color dynamics. Some of them make a social recovery. Nonetheless, if we ask, "What was basically the matter with these patients?" meaning, "What is the specific etiology of the color psychosis?" the answer is that mutated gene on the X chromosome. This is why my own therapeutic experience with schizophrenic patients has not yet convinced me· of the schizophrenogenic mother as a specific etiology, even though the picture I get of my patients' mothers is pretty much in accord with the familiar one. There is no question here of accepting the patient's account; my point is that *given* the account, and taking it quite at face value, does not tell me why the patient is a patient and not just a fellow who had a bad mother.

Another theoretical lead is the one given greatest current emphasis, namely, *interpersonal aversiveness.* The schizophrene suffers a degree of social fear, distrust, expectation of rejection, and conviction of his own unlovability which cannot be matched in its depth, pervasity, and resistance to corrective experience by any other diagnostic group.

Then there is a quasi-pathognomonic sign, emphasized by Rado (1956; Rado & Daniels, 1956) but largely ignored in psychologists' diagnostic usage, namely, *anhedonia*—a marked, widespread, and refractory defect in pleasure capacity which, once you learn how to examine for it, is one of the most consistent

and dramatic behavioral signs of the disease.

Finally, I include *ambivalence* from Bleuler's cardinal four (1950). His other two, "autism" and "dereism," I consider derivative from the combination of slippage, anhedonia, and aversiveness. Crudely put, if a person cannot think straight, gets little pleasure, and is afraid of everyone, he will of course learn to be autistic and dereistic.

If these clinical characterizations are correct, and we combine them with the hypothesis of a genetic specific etiology, do they give us any lead on theoretical possibilities?

Granting its initial vagueness as a construct, requiring to be filled in by neurophysiological research, I believe we should take seriously the old European notion of an "integrative neural defect" as the only direct phenotypic consequence produced by the genic mutation. This is an aberration in some parameter of single cell function, which may or may not be manifested in the functioning of more molar CNS systems, depending upon the organization of the mutual feedback controls and upon the stochastic parameters of the reinforcement regime. This neural integrative effect, which I shall christen *schizotaxia*, is all that can properly be spoken of as inherited. The imposition of a social learning history upon schizotaxic individuals results in a personality organization which I shall call, following Rado, the *schizotype*. The four core behavior traits are obviously not innate; but I postulate that they are universally learned by schizotaxic individuals, given any of the actually existing social reinforcement regimes, from the best to the worst. If the interpersonal regime is favorable, and the schizotaxic person also has the good fortune to inherit a low anxiety readiness, physical vigor, general resistance to stress, and the like, he will remain a well-compensated "normal" schizotype, never manifesting symptoms of mental disease. He will be like the gout-prone male whose genes determine him to have an elevated blood uric acid titer, but who never develops clinical gout.

Only a subset of schizotypic personalities decompensate into clinical schizophrenia. It seems likely that the most important causal influence pushing the schizotype toward schizophrenic decompensation is the schizophrenogenic mother.

I hope it is clear that this view does not conflict with what has been established about the mother-child interaction. If this interaction were totally free of material ambivalence and aversive inputs to the schizotaxic child, even compensated schizotypy might be avoided; at most, we might expect to find only the faintest signs of cognitive slippage and other minimal neurological aberrations, possibly including body image and other proprioceptive deviations, but not the interpersonal aversiveness which is central to the clinical picture.

Nevertheless, while assuming the etiological importance of mother in determining the course of aversive social learnings, it is worthwhile to speculate about the modification our genetic equations might take on this hypothesis. Many schizophrenogenic mothers are themselves schizotypes in varying degrees of compensation. Their etiological contribution then consists jointly in their passing on the gene, *and* in the fact that being schizotypic, they provide the kind of ambivalent regime which potentiates the schizotypy of the child and raises the odds of his decompensating. Hence the incidence of the several parental genotypes among parent pairs of diagnosed proband cases is not calculable from the usual genetic formulas. For example, given a schizophrenic proband, the odds that mother is homozygous (or, if the gene were dominant, that it is mother who carries it) are different from those for father; since we have begun by selecting a decompensated case, and formal diagnosis as the phenotype involves a potentiating factor for mother which is psychodynamically greater than that for a schizotypic father. Another important influence would be the likelihood that the lower fertility of schizophrenics is also present, but to an unknown degree, among compensated schizotypes. Clinical experience suggests that in the semicompensated range, this lowering of fertility is greater among males, since many schizotypic women relate to men in an exploited or exploitive sexual way, whereas the male schizotype usually displays a marked deficit in heterosexual aggressiveness. Such a sex difference in fertility among decompensated cases has been reported by Meyers and Goldfarb (1962).

Since the extent of aversive learnings is a critical factor in decompensation, the inherited anxiety readiness is presumably greater among diagnosed cases. Since the more fertile mothers are likely to be compensated, hence themselves to be relatively low anxiety if

schizotaxic, a frequent parent pattern should be a compensated schizotypic mother married to a neurotic father, the latter being the source of the proband's high-anxiety genes (plus providing a poor paternal model for identification in male patients, and a weak defender of the child against mother's schizotypic hostility).

These considerations make ordinary family concordance studies, based upon formal diagnosis, impossible to interpret. The most important research need here is development of high-validity indicators for compensated schizotypy. I see some evidence for these conceptions in the report of Lidz and coworkers, who in studying intensively the parents of 15 schizophrenic patients were surprised to find that "minimally, 9 of the 15 patients had at least one parent who could be called schizophrenic, or ambulatory schizophrenic, or clearly paranoid in behavior and attitudes" (Lidz, Cornelison, Terry, and Fleck, 1958, p. 308). As I read the brief personality sketches presented, I would judge that all but two of the probands had a clearly schizotypic parent. These authors, while favoring a "learned irrationality" interpretation of their data, also recognize the alternative genetic interpretation. Such facts do not permit a decision, obviously; my main point is the striking difference between the high incidence of parental schizotypes, mostly quite decompensated (some to the point of diagnosable psychosis), and the zero incidence which a conventional study would have yielded for this group.

Another line of evidence, based upon a very small sample but exciting because of its uniformity, is McConaghy's report (1959) that among nondiagnosed parent pairs of 10 schizophrenics, subclinical thought disorder was psychometrically detectable in at least one parent of every pair. Rosenthal (1962) reports that he can add five tallies to this parent-pair count, and suggests that such results might indicate that the specific heredity is dominant, and completely penetrant, rather than recessive. The attempt to replicate these findings, and other psychometric efforts to tap subclinical cognitive slippage in the "normal" relatives of schizophrenics, should receive top priority in our research efforts.

Summarizing, I hypothesize that the statistical relation between schizotaxia, schizotypy, and schizophrenia is class inclusion: All schizotaxics become, *on all actually existing social learning regimes*, schizotypic in personality organization; but most of these remain compensated. A minority, disadvantaged by other (largely polygenically determined) constitutional weaknesses, and put on a bad regime by schizophrenogenic mothers (most of whom are themselves schizotypes) are thereby potentiated into clinical schizophrenia. What makes schizotaxia etiologically specific is its role as a *necessary* condition. I postulate that a nonschizotaxic individual, whatever his other genetic makeup and whatever his learning history, would at most develop a character disorder or a psychoneurosis; but he would become a schizotype and therefore could never manifest its decompensated form, schizophrenia.

What sort of quantitative aberration in the structural or functional parameters of the nervous system can we conceive to be directly determined by a mutated gene, and to so alter initial dispositions that affected individuals will, in the course of their childhood learning history, develop the four schizotypal source traits: cognitive slippage, anhedonia, ambivalence, and interpersonal aversiveness? To me, the most baffling thing about the disorder is the phenotypic heterogeneity of this tetrad. If one sets himself to the task of doing a theoretical Vigotsky job on this list of psychological dispositions, he may manage part of it by invoking a sufficiently vague kind of descriptive unity between ambivalence and interpersonal aversiveness; and perhaps even anhedonia could be somehow subsumed. But the cognitive slippage presents a real roadblock. Since I consider cognitive slippage to be a core element in schizophrenia, any characterization of schizophrenic or schizotypic behavior which purports to abstract its essence but does not include the cognitive slippage must be deemed unsatisfactory. I believe that an adequate theoretical account will necessitate moving downward in the pyramid of the sciences to invoke explanatory constructs not found in social, psychodynamic, or even learning theory language, but instead at the neurophysiological level.

Perhaps we don't know enough about "how the brain works" to theorize profitably at that level; and I daresay that the more a psychologist knows about the latest research on brain function, the more reluctant he would be to engage in etiological speculation. Let me entreat my physiologically expert listeners to be charitable toward this clinician's premature speculations about how the schizotaxic brain might work. I feel partially justified in such speculating because there are some well-attested general truths about mammalian learned behavior which could almost have been set down from the armchair, in the way engineers draw block diagrams indicating what kinds of parts or subsystems a physical system *must* have, and what their interconnections *must* be, in order to function "appropriately." Brain research of the last decade provides a direct neurophysiological substrate for such cardinal behavior requirements as avoidance, escape, reward, drive differentiation, general and specific arousal or activation, and the like (see Delafresnaye, 1961; Ramey & O'Doherty, 1960). The discovery in the limbic system of specific positive reinforcement centers by Olds and Milner in 1954, and of aversive centers in the same year by Delgado, Roberts, and Miller (1954), seems to me to have an importance that can scarcely be exaggerated; and while the ensuing lines of research on the laws of intracranial stimulation as a mode of behavior control present some puzzles and paradoxes, what *has* been shown up to now may already suffice to provide a theoretical framework. As a general kind of brain model let us take a broadly Hebbian conception in combination with the findings on intracranial stimulation.

To avoid repetition I shall list some basic assumptions first but introduce others in context and only implicitly when the implication is obvious. I shall assume that:

When a presynaptic cell participates in firing a postsynaptic cell, the former gains an increment in firing control over the latter. Coactivation of anatomically connected cell assemblies or assembly systems therefore increases their stochastic control linkage, and the frequency of discharge by neurons of a system may be taken as an intensity variable influencing the growth rate of intersystem control linkage as well as the momentary activity level induced in the other systems. (I shall dichotomize acquired cortical systems into "perceptual-cognitive," including central representations of goal objects; and "instrumental," including overarching monitor systems which select and guide specific effector patterns.)

Most learning in mature organisms involves altering control linkages between systems which themselves have been consolidated by previous learnings, sometimes requiring thousands of activations and not necessarily related to the reinforcement operation to the extent that perceptual-to-instrumental linkage growth functions are.

Control linkage increments from coactivation depend heavily, if not entirely, upon a period of reverberatory activity facilitating consolidation.

Feedback from positive limbic centers is facilitative to concurrent perceptual-cognitive or instrumental sequences, whereas negative center feedback exerts an inhibitory influence. (These statements refer to initial features of the direct wiring diagram, not to all long-term results of learning.) Aversive input also has excitatory effects via the arousal system, which maintain activity permitting escape learning to occur because the organism is alerted and keeps doing things. But I postulate that this overall influence is working along with an opposite effect, quite clear from both molar and intracranial experiments, that a major biological function of aversive-center activation is to produce "stoppage" of whatever the organism is currently doing.

Perceptual-cognitive systems and limbic motivational control centers develop two-way mutual controls (e.g., discriminative stimuli acquire the reinforcing property; "thoughts" become pleasantly toned; drive-relevant perceptual components are "souped-up.")

What kind of heritable parametric aberration could underlie the schizotaxic's readiness to aquire the schizotypic tetrad? It would seem, first of all, that the defect is much more likely to reside in the neurone's synaptic control function than in its storage function. It is hard to conceive of a general defect in storage which would on the one hand permit so many perceptual-cognitive functions, such as tapped by intelligence tests, school learning, or the high order cognitive powers displayed by some schizotypes, and yet have the diffuse motivational and emotional effects found in these same individuals. I am not saying that a storage deficit is clearly excludable, but it hardly seems the best place to look. So we direct our attention to parameters of control.

One possibility is to take the anhedonia as fundamental. What is *phenomenologically* a radical pleasure deficiency may be roughly identified *behaviorally* with a quantitative deficit in the positive reinforcement growth constant, and each of these—the "inner" and "outer" aspects of the organism's appetitive

control system—reflect a quantitative deficit in the limbic "positive" centers. The anhedonia would then be a direct consequence of the genetic defect in wiring. Ambivalence and interpersonal aversiveness would be quantitative deviations in the balance of appetitive-aversive controls. Most perceptual-cognitive and instrumental learnings occur under mixed positive and negative schedules, so the normal consequence is a collection of habits and expectancies varying widely in the intensity of their positive and negative components, but mostly "mixed" in character. Crudely put, everybody has *some* ambivalence about almost everything, and everybody has *some* capacity for "social fear." Now if the brain centers which mediate phenomenal pleasure and behavioral reward are numerically sparse or functionally feeble, the aversive centers meanwhile functioning normally, the longterm result would be a general shift toward the aversive end, appearing clinically as ambivalence and exaggerated interpersonal fear. If, as Brady believes, there is a wired-in reciprocal inhibiting relation between positive and negative centers, the longterm aversive drift would be further potentiated (i.e., what we see at the molar level as a sort of "softening" or "soothing" effect of feeding or petting upon anxiety elicitors would be reduced).

Cognitive slippage is not as easy to fit in, but if we assume that normal ego function is acquired by a combination of social reinforcements and the self-reinforcements which become available to the child via identification; then we might say roughly that "everybody has to learn *how* to think straight." Rationality is socially acquired: the secondary process and the reality principle are slowly and imperfectly learned, by even the most clear headed. Insofar as slippage is manifested in the social sphere, such an explanation has some plausibility. An overall aversive drift would account for the paradoxical schizotypic combination of interpersonal distortions and acute perceptiveness of others' unconscious, since the latter is really a hypersensitivity to aversive signals rather than an overall superiority in realistically discriminating social cues. On the output side, we might view the cognitive slippage of mildly schizoid speech as originating from poorly consolidated second-order "monitor" assembly systems which function in an editing role, their momentary regnancy constituting the "set to communicate." At this level, selection among competing verbal operants involves slight differences in appropriateness for which a washed-out social reinforcement history provides an insufficiently refined monitor system. However, if one is impressed with the presence of a pervasive and primary slippage, showing up in a diversity of tests (cf. Payne, 1961) and also on occasions when the patient is desperately trying to communicate, an explanation on the basis of deficient positive center activity is not too convincing.

This hypothesis has some other troubles which I shall merely indicate. Schizoid anhedonia is mainly interpersonal, i.e., schizotypes seem to derive adequate pleasure from esthetic and cognitive rewards. Secondly, some successful psychotherapeutic results include what appears to be a genuine normality of hedonic capacity. Thirdly, regressive electroshock sometimes has the same effect, and the animal evidence suggests that shock works by knocking out the aversive control system rather than by souping up appetitive centers. Finally, if the anhedonia is really general in extent, it is hard to conceive of any simple genetic basis for weakening the different positive centers, whose reactivity has been shown by Olds and others to be chemically drive specific.

A second neurological hypothesis takes the slippage factor as primary. Suppose that the immediate consequence of whatever biochemical aberration the gene directly controls were a specific alteration in the neurone's membrane stability, such that the distribution of optional transmission probabilities is more widely dispersed over the synaptic signal space than in normals. That is, presynaptic input signals whose spatio-temporal configuration locates them peripherally in the neurone's signal space yield transmission probabilities which are relatively closer to those at the maximum point, thereby producing a kind of dedifferentention or flattening of the cell's selectivity. Under suitable parametric assumptions, this synaptic slippage would lead to a corresponding dedifferentiation of competing interassembly controls, because the elements in the less frequently or intensely coactivated control assembly would be accumulating control increments more rapidly than normal. Consider a perceptual-cognitive system whose regnancy is preponderantly associated with positive-center coactivation but sometimes with aver-

sive. The cumulation of control increments will draw these apart; but if synaptic slippage exists, their difference, at least during intermediate stages of control development, will be attenuated. The intensity of aversive-center activation by a given level of perceptual-cognitive system activity will be exaggerated relative to that induced in the positive centers. For a preponderantly aversive control this will be reversed. But now the different algebraic sign of the feedbacks introduces an important asymmetry. Exaggerated negative feedback will tend to lower activity level in the predominantly appetitive case, retarding the growth of the control linkage; whereas exaggerated positive feedback in the predominantly aversive case will tend to heighten activity levels, accelerating the linkage growth. The long-term tendency will be that movement in the negative direction which I call *aversive drift*. In addition to the asymmetry generated to the difference in feedback signs, certain other features in the mixed-regime setup contribute to aversive drift. One factor is the characteristic difference between positive and negative reinforcers in their role as strengtheners. It seems a fairly safe generalization to say that positive centers function only weakly as strengtheners when "on" continuously, and mainly when they are turned on as terminators of a cognitive or instrumental sequence; by contrast, negative centers work mainly as "off" signals, tending to inhibit elements while steadily "on." We may suppose that the former strengthen mainly by facilitating postactivity reverberation (and hence consolidation) in successful systems, the latter mainly by holding down such reverberation in unsuccessful ones. Now a slippage-heightened aversive steady state during predominantly appetitive control sequences reduces their activity level, leaves fewer recently active elements available for a subsequent Olds-plus "on" signal to consolidate. Whereas a slippage-heightened Olds-plus steady state during predominantly aversive control sequences (a) increases their negative control *during* the "on" period and (b) leaves relatively more of their elements recently active and hence further consolidated by the negative "off" signal when it occurs. Another factor is exaggerated competition by aversively controlled sequences, whereby the appetitive chains do not continue to the stage of receiving socially mediated positive reinforcement, because avoidant chains (e.g.,

phobic behavior, withdrawal, intellectualization) are getting in the way. It is worth
mentioning that the schizophrenogenic
mother's regime is presumably "mixed" not
only in the sense of the frequent and unpredictable aversive inputs she provides in response to the child's need signals, but also in
her greater tendency to present such aversive
inputs *concurrently* with drive reducers—
thereby facilitating the "scrambling" of
appetitive-and-aversive controls so typical of
schizophrenia.

The schizotype's dependency guilt and aversive overreaction to offers of help are here
seen as residues of the early knitting together
of his cortical representations of appetitive
goals with punishment-expectancy assembly
systems. Roughly speaking, he has learned
that to want anything interpersonally provided is to be endangered.

The cognitive slippage is here conceived as
a direct molar consequence of synaptic slippage, potentiated by the disruptive effects of
aversive control and inadequate development
of interpersonal communication sets. Cognitive and instrumental linkages based on sufficiently massive and consistent regimes, such
as reaching for a seen pencil, will coverge to
asymptotes hardly distinguishable from the
normal. But systems involving closely competing strengths and automatized selection
among alternatives, especialy when the main
basis of acquisition and control is social reward, will exhibit evidences of malfunction.

My third speculative model revives a notion with a long history, namely, that the
primary schizotaxic defect is a quantitative
deficiency of inhibition. (In the light of
Milner's revision of Hebb, in which the inhibitory action of Golgi Type II cells is crucial
even for the formation of functionally differentiated cell assemblies, a defective inhibitory parameter could be an alternative
basis for a kind of slippage similar in its
consequences to the one we have just finished
discussing.) There are two things about this
somewhat moth-eaten "defective inhibition"
idea which I find appealing. First, it is the
most direct and uncomplicated neurologizing
of the schizoid cognitive slippage. Schizoid
cognitive slippage is neither an incapacity to
link, nor is it an unhealthy overcapacity to
link; rather it seems to be a defective *control*
over associations which are also accessible to
the healthy (as in dreams, wit, psychoanalytic
free association, and certain types of creative

work) but are normally "edited out" or "automatically suppressed" by those super-
ordinate monitoring assembly systems we
lump together under the term "set." Secondly, in working with pseudoneurotic cases
one sees a phenomenon to which insufficient
theoretical attention has been paid: Namely,
these patients cannot turn off painful
thoughts. They suffer constantly and intensely from painful thoughts about themselves, about possible adverse outcomes,
about the past, about the attitudes and intentions of others. The "weak ego" of schizophrenia means a number of things, one of
which is failure of defense; the schizophrenic
has too ready access to his own id, and is too
perceptive of the unconscious of others. It is
tempting to read "failure of defense" as
"quantitatively deficient inhibitory feedback." As mentioned earlier, aversive signals
(whether exteroceptive or internally originated) must exert both an exciting effect via
the arousal system and a quick-stoppage effect
upon cortical sequences which fail to terminate the ongoing aversive signal, leading the
organism to shift to another. Suppose the gene
resulted in an insufficient production (or too
rapid inactivation) of the specific inhibitory
transmitter substance, rendering all inhibitory
neurones quantitatively weaker than normal.
When aversively linked cognitive sequences
activate negative limbic centers, these in turn
soup up the arousal system normally but
provide a subnormal inhibitory feedback,
thereby permitting their elicitor to persist for
a longer time and at higher intensity than
normal. This further activates the negative
control center, and so on, until an equilibrium
level is reached which is above normal in
intensity all around, and which meanwhile
permits an excessive linkage growth in the
aversive chain. (In this respect the semicompensated case would differ from the late-stage
deteriorated schizophrenic, whose aversive
drift has gradually proliferated so widely that
almost any cognitive or instrumental chain
elicits an overlearned defensive "stoppage,"
whereby even the inner life undergoes a profound and diffuse impoverishment.)

The mammalian brain is so wired that
aversive signals tend to produce stoppage of
regnant cognitive or instrumental sequences
without the aversive signal having been specifically connected to their controlling cues or
motivational systems. E.g., lever pressing
under thirst or hunger can be inhibited by

shock-associated buzzer, even though the latter has not been previously connected with hunger, paired with the discriminative stimulus, nor presented as punishment for the operant. A deficient capacity to inhibit concurrent activity of fringe elements (aversively connected to ambiguous social inputs from ambivalent mother) would accelerate the growth of linkages between them and appetitive systems not hitherto punished. Sequential effects are here especially important, and combine with the schizophrenogenic mother's tendency not to provide differential cues of high consistency as predictors of whether aversive or appetitive consequences will follow upon the child's indications of demand.

Consider two cortical systems having shared "fringe" subsystems (e.g., part percepts of mother's face). When exteroceptive inputs are the elicitors, negative feedback from aversive centers cannot usually produce stoppage; in the absence of such overdetermining external controls, the relative activity levels are determined by the balance of facilitative and inhibitory feedbacks. "Fringe" assemblies which have already acquired more aversive control, if they begin to be activated by regnant perceptual-cognitive sequences, will increase inhibitory feedback; and being "fringe" they can thereby be held down. The schizotaxic, whose aversive-feedback stoppage of fringe-element activity is weakened, accumulates excessive intertrial Hebbian increments toward the aversive side, the predominantly aversive fringe elements being more active and becoming more knit into the system than normally. On subsequent exteroceptively controlled trials, whenever the overdetermining stimulus input activates predominantly aversive perceptual-cognitive assemblies, their driving of the negative centers will be heightened. The resulting negative feedback may now be strong enough that, when imposed upon "fringe" assemblies weakly activated and toward the appetitive side, it can produce stoppage. On such occasions the more appetitive fringe elements will be retarded in their linkage growth, receiving fewer Hebbian increments. And those which do get over threshold will become further linked during such trials to the concurrent negative center activity. The result is twofold: a retarded growth of appetitive perceptual-cognitive linkages; and a progressive drawing of fringe elements into the aversive ambit.

"Ambiguous regimes," where the pairing of S+ and S− inputs occurs very unpredictably, will have a larger number of fringe elements. Also, if the external schedule is dependent upon regnant appetitive drive states as manifested in the child's intrumental social acts, so that these are often met with mixed S+ (drive-relevant) and S− (anxiety-eliciting) inputs, the appetitive and aversive assemblies will tend to become linked, and to activate positive and negative centers concurrently. The anhedonia and ambivalence would be consequences of this plus-minus "scrambling," especially if the positive and negative limbic centers are mutually inhibitory but here deficiently so. We would then expect schizotypic anhedonia to be basically interpersonal, and only derivatively present, if at all, in other contexts. This would in part explain the schizotype's preservation of relatively normal function in a large body of instrumental domains. For example, the acqusition of basic motor and cognitive skills would be relatively less geared to a mixed input, since "successful" mastery is both mechanically rewarded (e.g., how to open a door) and also interpersonally rewarded as "school success," etc. The hypercathexis of intellect, often found even among nonbright schizotypes, might arise from the fact that these performances are rewarded rather "impersonally" and make minimal demands on the reinforcing of others. Also, the same cognitive and mechanical instrumental acts can often be employed both to turn on positive center feedback and to turn off negative, an equivalence much less true of purely social signals linked to interpersonal needs.

Having briefly sketched three neurological possibilities for the postulated schizotaxic aberration, let me emphasize that while each has sufficient merit to be worth pursuing, they are mainly meant to be illustrative of the vague concept "integrative neural defect." I shall myself not be surprised if all three are refuted, whereas I shall be astounded if future research shows no fundamental aberration in nerve-cell function in the schizotype. Postulating schizotaxia as an open concept seems at first to pose a search problem of needle-in-haystack proportions, but I suggest that the plausible alternatives are really somewhat limited. After all, what does a neuron do to another neuron? It excites, or it inhibits! The schizotypic preservation of relatively normal function in selected domains directs our search toward some minimal deviation in a synaptic control parameter, as opposed to, say, a gross defect in cell distribution or structure, or the kind of biochemical anomaly that yields mental deficiency. Anything which would give rise to defective storage, grossly impaired transmission, or sizable limitations on functional complexity can be pretty well excluded on present evidence. What we are looking for is a quantitative aberration in synaptic control—a deviation in amount or patterning of excitatory or inhibitory action—capable of yielding cumulative departures from normal control linkages under mixed appetitive-aversive regimes; but slight enough to permit convergence to quasinormal asymptotes under more consistent schedules (or when massive repetition with motive-incentive factors unimportant is the chief basis for consolidation). The defect must generate aversive drift on mixed social reinforcement regimes, and must yield a primary cognitive slippage which, however, may be extremely small in magnitude except as potentiated by the cumulative effects of aversive drift. Taken together these molar constraints limit our degrees of freedom considerably when it comes to filling in the neurophysiology of schizotaxia.

Leaving aside the specific nature of schizotaxia, we must now raise the familiar question whether such a basic neurological defect, however subtle and nonstructural it might be, should not have been demonstrated hitherto? In reply to this objection I shall content myself with pointing out that there are several lines of evidence which, while not strongly arguing *for* a neurological theory, are rebuttals of an argument presupposing clear and consistent *negative* findings. For example: Ignoring several early European reports with inadequate controls, the literature contains a half-dozen quantitative studies showing marked vestibular system dysfunction in schizophrenics (Angyal & Blackman, 1940, 1941; Angyal & Sherman, 1942; Colbert & Koegler, 1959; Freeman & Rodnick, 1942; Leach, 1960; Payne & Hewlett, 1960; Pollock & Krieger, 1958). Hoskins (1946) concluded that a neurological defect in the vestibular system was one of the few clear-cut biological findings in the Worcester studios. It is of prime importance to replicate these findings among compensated and pseudoneurotic cases, where the diffuse withdrawal and deactivation factor would not provide the explanation it does in the chronic, burnt-out case (cf.

Collins, Crampton, & Posner, 1961). Another line of evidence is in the work of King (1954) on psychomotor deficit, noteworthy for its careful use of task simplicity, asymptote performance, concern for patient cooperation, and inclusion of an outpatient pseudoneurotic sample. King himself regards his data as indicative of a rather basic behavior defect, although he does not hold it to be schizophrenia-specific. Then we have such research as that of Barbara Fish (1961) indicating the occurrence of varying signs of perceptual-motor maldevelopment among infants and children who subsequently manifest clinical schizophrenia. The earlier work of Schilder and Bender along these lines is of course well known, and there has always been a strong minority report in clinical psychiatry that many schizophrenics provide subtle and fluctuating neurological signs of the "soft" variety, if one keeps alert to notice or elicit them. I have myself been struck by the frequent occurrence, even among pseudoneurotic patients, of transitory neurologic-like complaints (e.g., diplopia, localized weakness, one-sided tremor, temperature dyscontrol, dizziness, disorientation) which seem to lack dynamic meaning or secondary gain and whose main effect upon the patient is to produce bafflement and anxiety. I have seen preliminary findings by J. McVicker Hunt and his students in which a rather dramatic quantitative deficiency in spatial cognizing is detectable in schizophrenics of above-normal verbal intelligence. Research by Cleveland (1960; Cleveland, Fisher, Reitman, & Rothaus, 1962) and by Arnhoff and Damianopoulos (1964) on the clinically well-known body-image anomalies in schizophrenia suggests that this domain yields quantitative departures from the norm of such magnitude that with further instrumental and statistical refinement it might be used as a quasipathognomonic sign of the disease. It is interesting to note a certain thread of unity running through this evidence, which perhaps lends support to Rado's hypothesis that a kinesthetic integrative defect is even more characteristic of schizotypy than is the radical anhedonia.

All these kinds of data are capable of a psychodynamic interpretation. "Soft" neurological signs are admittedly ambiguous, especially when found in the severely decompensated case. The only point I wish to make here is that *since* they exist and are at present unclear in etiology, an otherwise plausible neurological view cannot be refuted on the ground that there is a *lack* of any sign of neurological dysfunction in schizophrenia; there is no such lack.

Time forces me to leave detailed research strategy for another place, but the main directions are obvious and may be stated briefly: The clinician's Mental Status ratings on anhedonia, ambivalence, and interpersonal aversiveness should be objectified and preferably replaced by psychometric measures. The research findings on cognitive slippage, psychomotor dyscontrol, vestibular malfunction, body image, and other spatial aberrations should be thoroughly replicated and extended into the pseudoneurotic and semicompensated ranges. If these efforts succeed, it will be possible to set up a multiple sign pattern, using optimal cuts on phenotypically diverse indicators, for identifying compensated schizotypes in the nonclinical population. Statistics used must be appropriate to the theoretical model of a dichotomous latent taxonomy reflecting itself in otherwise independent quantitative indicators. Finally concordance studies should then be run relating proband schizophrenia to schizotypy as identified by this multiple indicator pattern. Meanwhile we should carry on an active and varied search for more direct neurological signs of schizotaxia, concentrating our hunches on novel stimulus inputs (e.g., the stabilized retinal image situation) which may provide a better context for basic neural dysfunction to show up instead of being masked by learned compensations or imitated by psychopathology.

In closing, I should like to take this unusual propaganda opportunity to play the prophet. It is my strong personal conviction that such a research strategy will enable psychologists to make a unique contribution in the near future, using psychological techniques to establish that schizophrenia, while its content is learned, is fundamentally a neurological disease of genetic origin.

REFERENCES

Angyal, A., and Blackman, N. Vestibular reactivity in schizophrenia. *Arch. Neurol. Psychiat.*, 1940, *44*, 611–620.

Angyal, A., and Blackman, N. Paradoxical reactions in schizophrenia under the influence of alcohol, hyperpnea, and CO_2 inhalation. *Amer. J. Psychiat.*, 1941, 97, 893–903.

Angyal, A., and Sherman, N. Postural reactions to vestibular stimulation in schizophrenic and normal subjects. *Amer. J. Psychiat.*, 1942, *98*, 857–862.

Arnhoff, F., and Diamianopoulos, E. Self-body recognition and schizophrenia: An exploratory study. *J. Gen. Psychol.*, 1964, *70*, 353–361.

Bleuler, E. *Theory of schizophrenic negativism.* New York: Nervous and Mental Disease Publishing, 1912.

Bleuler, E. *Dementia praecox.* New York: International Universities Press, 1950.

Cleveland, S. E. Judgment of body size in a schizophrenic and a control group. *Psychol. Rep.*, 1960, 7, 304.

Cleveland, S. E., Fisher, S., Reitman, E. E., and Rothaus, P. Perception of body size in schizophrenia. *Arch. gen. Psychiat.*, 1962, *7*, 277–285.

Colbert, G., and Koegler, R. Vestibular dysfunction in childhood schizophrenia. *AMA Arch. gen. Psychiat.*, 1959, *1*, 600–617.

Collins, W. E., Crampton, G. H., and Posner, J.B. The effect of mental set upon vestibular nystagmus and the EEG. *USA Med. Res. Lab. Rep.*, 1961, No. 439.

Delafresnaye, J. F. (Ed.) *Brain mechanisms and learning.* Springfield, Ill.: Charles C Thomas, 1961.

Delgado, J. M. R., Roberts, W. W., and Miller, N. E. Learning motivated by electrical stimulation of the brain. *Amer. J. Physiol.*, 1954, *179*, 587–593.

Fish, Barbara. The study of motor development in infancy and its relationship to psychological functioning. *Amer. J. Psychiat.*, 1961, *117*, 1113–1118.

Freeman, H., and Rodnick, E. H. Effect of rotation on postural steadiness in normal and schizophrenic subjects. *Arch. Neurol. Psychiat.*, 1942, *48*, 47–53.

Fuller, J. L., and Thompson, W. R. *Behavior genetics.* New York: Wiley, 1960, pp. 272–283.

Hoskins, R. G. *The biology of schizophrenia.* New York: Norton, 1946.

King, H. E. *Psychomotor aspects of mental disease.* Cambridge: Harvard Univer. Press, 1954.

Leach, W. W. Nystagmus: An integrative neural deficit in schizophrenia. *J. abnorm. soc. psychol.*, 1960, *60*, 305–309.

Lidz, T., Cornelison, A., Terry, D., and Fleck, S. Intrafamilial environment of the schizophrenic patient: VI. The transmission of irrationality. *AMA Arch. Neurol. Psychiat.*, 1958, *79*, 305–316.

McConaghy, N. The use of an object sorting test in elucidating the hereditary factor in schizophrenia. *J. Neurol. Neurosurg. Psychiat.*, 1959, *22*, 243–246.

Meyers, D., and Goldfarb, W. Psychiatric appraisals of parents and siblings of schizophrenic children. *Amer. J. Psychiat.*, 1962, *118*, 902–908.

Olds, J., and Milner, P. Positive reinforcement produced by electrical stimulation of septal area and other regions of rat brain. *J. comp. physiol. Psychol.*, 1954, *47*, 419–427.

Payne, R. W. Cognitive abnormalities. In H. J. Eysenck (Ed.), *Handbook of abnormal psychology*. New York: Basic Books, 1961, pp. 248–250.

Payne, R. S., and Hewlett, J. H. G. Thought disorder in psychotic patients. In H. J. Eysenck (Ed.), *Experiments in personality*. Vol. 2. London: Routledge, Kegan, Paul, 1960, pp. 3–106.

Pollack, M., and Krieger, H. P. Oculomotor and postural patterns in schizophrenic children. *AMA Arch. Neurol. Psychiat.*, 1958, *79*, 720–726.

Rado, S., and Daniels, G. *Changing concepts of psychoanalytic medicine*. New York: Grune & Stratton, 1956.

Ramey, E. R., and O'Doherty, D. S. (Ed.) *Electrical studies on the unanesthetized brain*. New York: Hoeber, 1960.

Rosenthal, D. Problems of sampling and diagnosis in the major twin studies of schizophrenia. *J. psychiat. Res.*, 1962, *1*, 16–34.

Stern, K. *Principles of human genetics*. San Francisco: Freeman, 1960, pp. 581–584.

PART II

∽

Intrapsychic Theories

Introduction

The emphasis given to early childhood experience by intrapsychic theorists represents their contention that disorders of adulthood are a direct product of the continued and insidious operation of past events. To them, knowledge of the past provides information indispensable to understanding adult difficulties. To the question "What is the basis of adult disorders?" they would answer: the anxieties of childhood and the progressive sequence of defensive maneuvers which were devised to protect against a recurrence of these feelings.

Intrapsychic theorists contend that these two determinants of adult behavior, childhood anxieties and defensive maneuvers, are unconscious, that is, cannot be brought to awareness except under unusual conditions. It is the search for these unconscious processes which is the distinguishing feature of the intrapsychic approach. The obscure and elusive phenomena of the unconscious are the data which they uncover and use for their concepts. These data consist, first, of repressed childhood anxieties that persist within the individual and attach themselves insidiously to ongoing experiences, and, second, of unconscious adaptive processes which protect the individual against the resurgence of these anxieties. The *intrapsychic* label we have attached to these theorists reflects, therefore, their common focus on these two elements of the unconscious.

Orientation

Our presentation of the intrapsychic approach begins with a contribution by Sigmund Freud for two reasons. First, in recognition of the fact that his monumental works are the foundation upon which all other intrapsychic theories are based and, second, to demonstrate the bridge he attempted to build between the biophysical and the intrapsychic orientations. Freud anchored many of his concepts to the biological make-up of man, a view that was rejected or overlooked by several of his followers. In the selection reprinted, drawn from one of his major publications, Freud attempted to summarize the central features of his theoretical work. Here he chose to stress two central ideas: the role and development of the biological instincts and the workings of unconscious processes.

13 The Metapsychology of Instincts, Repression and the Unconscious

Sigmund Freud

I. Instincts

The view is often defended that sciences should be built up on clear and sharply defined basal concepts. In actual fact no science, not even the most exact, begins with such definitions. The true beginning of scientific activity consists rather in describing phenomena and then in proceeding to group, classify and correlate them. Even at the stage of description it is not possible to avoid applying certain abstract ideas to the material in hand, ideas derived from various sources and certainly not the fruit of the new experience only. Still more indispensable are such ideas—which will later become the basal concepts of the science—as the material is further elaborated. They must at first necessarily possess some measure of uncertainty; there can be no question of any clear delimitation of their content. So long as they remain in this condition, we come to an understanding about their meaning by repeated references to the material of observation, from which we seem to have deduced our abstract ideas, but which is in point of fact subject to them. Thus, strictly speaking, they are in the nature of

From *Collected Papers*, Volume IV, Hogarth Press, 1925/1915.

conventions; although everything depends on their being chosen in no arbitrary manner, but determined by the important relations they have to the empirical material—relations that we seem to divine before we can clearly recognize and demonstrate them. It is only after more searching investigation of the field in question that we are able to formulate with increased clarity the scientific concepts underlying it, and progressively so to modify these concepts that they become widely applicable and at the same time consistent logically. Then, indeed, it may be time to immure them in definitions. The progress of science, however, demands a certain elasticity even in these definitions. The science of physics furnishes an excellent illustration of the way in which even those 'basal concepts' that are firmly established in the form of definitions are constantly being altered in their content.

A conventional but still rather obscure basal concept of this kind, which is nevertheless indispensable to us in psychology, is that of an *instinct*. Let us try to ascertain what is comprised in this conception by approaching it from different angles.

First, from the side of physiology. This has given us the concept of *stimuli* and the scheme of the reflex arc, according to which a stimulus applied *from the outer world* to living tissue (nervous substance) is discharged by action *towards the outer world*. The action answers the purpose of withdrawing the substance affected from the operation of the stimulus, removing it out of range of the stimulus.

Now what is the relation between 'instinct' and 'stimulus'? There is nothing to prevent our including the concept of 'instinct' under that of 'stimulus' and saying that an instinct is a stimulus to the mind. But we are immediately set on our guard against treating instinct and mental stimulus as one and the same thing. Obviously, besides those of instinctual origin, there are other stimuli to the mind which behave far more like physiological stimuli. For example, a strong light striking upon the eye is not a stimulus of instinctual origin; it is one, however, when the mucous membrane of the esophagus becomes parched or when a gnawing makes itself felt in the stomach.[1]

We have now obtained material necessary for discriminating between stimuli of instinctual origin and the other (physiological) stimuli which operate on our minds. First, a stimulus of instinctual origin does not arise in the outside world but from within the organism itself. For this reason it has a different mental effect and different actions are necessary in order to remove it. Further, all that is essential in an external stimulus is contained in the assumption that it acts as a single impact, so that it can be discharged by a single appropriate action—a typical instance being that of motor flight from the source of stimulation. Of course these impacts may be repeated and their force may be cumulative, but that makes no difference to our notion of the process and to the conditions necessary in order that the stimulus may be dispelled. An instinct, on the other hand, never acts as a momentary impact but always as a constant force. As it makes its attack not from without but from within the organism, it follows that no flight can avail against it. A better term for a stimulus of instinctual origin is a 'need'; that which does away with this need is 'satisfaction'. This can be attained only by a suitable (adequate) alteration of the inner source of stimulation.

We thus find our first conception of the

essential nature of an instinct by considering its main characteristics, its origin in sources of stimulation within the organism and its appearance as a constant force, and thence we deduce one of its further distinguishing features, namely, that no actions of flight avail against it. Now, in making these remarks, we cannot fail to be struck by a fact which compels us to a further admission. We do not merely accept as basal concepts certain conventions which we apply to the material we have acquired empirically, but we also make use of various complicated postulates to guide us in dealing with psychological phenomena. We have already cited the most important of these postulates; it remains for us expressly to lay stress upon it. It is of a biological nature, and makes use of the concept of 'purpose'(one might say, of adaptation of the means to the end) and runs as follows: the nervous system is an apparatus having the function of abolishing stimuli which reach it, or of reducing excitation to the lowest possible level: an apparatus which would even, if this were feasible, maintain itself in an altogether unstimulated condition. Let us for the present not take exception to the indefiniteness of this idea and let us grant that the task of the nervous system is—broadly speaking—*to master stimuli*. We see then how greatly the simple physiological reflex scheme is complicated by the introduction of instincts. External stimuli impose upon the organism the single task of withdrawing itself from their action: this is accomplished by muscular movements, one of which reaches the goal aimed at and, being the most appropriate to the end in view, is thenceforward transmitted as an hereditary disposition. Those instinctual stimuli which emanate from within the organism cannot be dealt with by this mechanism. Consequently, they make far higher demands upon the nervous system and compel it to complicated and interdependent activities, which effect such changes in the outer world as enable it to offer satisfaction to the internal source of stimulation; above all, instinctual stimuli oblige the nervous system to renounce its ideal intention of warding off stimuli, for they maintain an incessant and unavoidable afflux of stimulation. So we may probably conclude that instincts and not external stimuli are the true motive forces in the progress that has raised the nervous system, with all its incomparable efficiency, to its present high level of development. Of course there is nothing to

---

[1]Assuming, of course, that these internal processes constitute the organic basis of the needs described as thirst and hunger.

prevent our assuming that the instincts themselves are, at least in part, the precipitates of different forms of external stimulation, which in the course of phylogenesis have effected modifications in the organism.

If now we apply ourselves to considering mental life from a biological point of view, an 'instinct' appears to us as a borderland concept between the mental and the physical, being both the mental representative of the stimuli emanating from within the organism and penetrating to the mind, and at the same time a measure of the demand made upon the energy of the latter in consequence of its connection with the body.

We are now in a position to discuss certain terms used in reference to the concept of an instinct, for example, its impetus, its aim, its object and its source.

By the *impetus* of an instinct we understand its motor element, the amount of force or the measure of the demand upon energy which it represents. The characteristic of impulsion is common to all instincts, is in fact the very essence of them. Every instinct is a form of activity; if we speak loosely of passive instincts, we can only mean those whose aim is passive.

The *aim* of an instinct is in every instance satisfaction, which can only be obtained by abolishing the condition of stimulation in the source of the instinct. But although this remains invariably the final goal of every instinct, there may yet be different ways leading to the same goal, so that an instinct may be found to have various nearer or intermediate aims, capable of combination or interchange. Experience permits us also to speak of instincts which are *inhibited in respect of their aim,* in cases where a certain advance has been permitted in the direction of satisfaction and then an inhibition or deflection has occurred. We may suppose that even in such cases a partial satisfaction is achieved.

The *object* of an instinct is that in or through which it can achieve its aim. It is the most variable thing about an instinct and is not originally connected with it, but becomes attached to it only in consequence of being peculiarly fitted to provide satisfaction. The object is not necessarily an extraneous one: it may be part of the subject's own body. It may be changed any number of times in the course of the vicissitudes the instinct undergoes during life; a highly important part is played by this capacity for displacement in the instinct. It may happen that the same object may serve for the satisfaction of several instincts simultaneously, a phenomenon which Adler calls a 'confluence' of instincts. A particularly close attachment of the instinct to its object is distinguished by the term *fixation:* this frequently occurs in very early stages of the instinct's development and so puts an end to its mobility, through the vigorous resistance it sets up against detachment.

By the *source* of an instinct is meant that somatic process in an organ or part of the body from which there results a stimulus represented in mental life by an instinct. We do not know whether this process is regularly of a chemical nature or whether it may also correspond with the release of other, *e.g.* mechanical, forces. The study of the sources of instinct is outside the scope of psychology; although its source in the body is what gives the instinct its distinct and essential character, yet in mental life we know it merely by its aims. A more exact knowledge of the sources of instincts is not strictly necessary for purposes of psychological investigation; often the source may be with certainty inferred from the aims.

Now what instincts and how many should be postulated? There is obviously a great opportunity here for arbitrary choice. No objection can be made to anyone's employing the concept of an instinct of play or of destruction, or that of a social instinct, when the subject demands it and the limitations of psychological analysis allow of it. Nevertheless, we should not neglect to ask whether such instinctual motives, which are in one direction so highly specialized, do not admit of further analysis in respect of their sources, so that only those primal instincts which are not to be resolved further could really lay claim to the name.

I have proposed that two groups of such primal instincts should be distinguished: the *self-preservative* or *ego*-instincts and the *sexual* instincts. But this proposition has not the weight of a necessary postulate, such as, for instance, our assumption about the biological 'purpose' in the mental apparatus *(v. supra);* it is merely an auxiliary construction, to be retained only so long as it proves useful, and it will make little difference to the results of our work of description and classification if we replace it by another. The occasion for it arose in the course of the evolution of psychoanalysis, which was first employed upon the psychoneuroses, actually upon the group designated transference neuroses (hysteria and obsessional neurosis); through them it became plain that at the root of all such affections there lies a conflict between the claims of sexuality and those of the ego. It is always possible that an exhaustive study of the other neurotic affections (especially of the narcissistic psychoneuroses, the schizophrenias) may oblige us to alter this formula and therewith to make a different classification of the primal instincts. But for the present we do not know what this new formula may be, nor have we met with any argument which seems likely to be prejudicial to the contrast between sexual and ego-instincts.

An attempt to formulate the general characteristics of the sexual instincts would run as follows: they are numerous, emanate from manifold organic sources, act in the first instance independently of one another and only at a late stage achieve a more or less complete synthesis. The aim which each strives to attain is 'organ-pleasure'; only when the synthesis is complete do they enter the service of the function of reproduction, becoming thereby generally recognizable as sexual instincts. At their first appearance they support themselves upon the instincts of self-preservation, from which they only gradually detach themselves; in their choice of object also they follow paths indicated by the ego-instincts. Some of them remain throughout life associated with these latter and furnish them with libidinal components, which with normal functioning easily escape notice and are clearly recognizable only when disease is present. They have this distinctive characteristic—that they have in a high degree the capacity to act vicariously for one another and that they can readily change their objects. In consequence of the last-mentioned properties they are capable of activities widely removed from their original modes of attaining their aims (sublimation).

Our inquiry into the various vicissitudes which instincts undergo in the process of development and in the course of life must be confined to the sexual instincts, for these are the more familiar to us. Observation shows us that an instinct may undergo the following vicissitudes:

Reversal into its opposite,
Turning round upon the subject,
Repression,
Sublimation.

Since I do not intend to treat of sublimation here and since repression requires a spe-

cial chapter to itself, it only remains for us to describe and discuss the two first points. Bearing in mind that there are tendencies which are opposed to the instincts pursuing a straight-forward course, we may regard these vicissitudes as modes of defence against the instincts.

The *reversal* of an instinct *into its opposite* may on closer scrutiny by resolved into two different processes: a change from active to passive, and a reversal of the content. The two processes, being essentially distinct, must be treated separately.

Examples of the first process are met with in the two pairs of opposites: sadism-masochism and scoptophilia-exhibitionism. The reversal here concerns only the aims of the instincts. The passive aim (to be tortured, or looked at) has been substituted for the active aim (to torture, to look at). Reversal of content is found in the single instance of the change of love into hate.

The *turning around* of an instinct *upon the subject* is suggested to us by the reflection that masochism is actually sadism turned around upon the subject's own ego, and that exhibitionism includes the love of gazing at the subject's own body. Further, analytic observation leaves us in no doubt that the masochist also enjoys the *act* of torturing when this is being applied to himself, and the exhibitionist the exposing of someone in being exposed himself. So the essence of the process is the change of the object, while the aim remains unchanged.

The fact that, at that later period of development, the instinct in its primary form may be observed side by side with its (passive) opposite deserves to be distinguished by the highly appropriate name introduced by Bleuler: *ambivalance*.

These considerations regarding the developmental history of an instinct and the permanent character of the intermediate stages in it should make instinct-development more comprehensible to us. Experience shows that the degree of demonstrable ambivalance varies greatly in individuals, groups and races. Marked ambivalence of an instinct in a human being at the present day may be regarded as an archaic inheritance, for we have reason to suppose that the part played in the life of the instincts by the active impulses in their original form was greater in primitive times than it is on an average to-day.

The transformation of the 'content' of an instinct into its opposite is observed in a single instance only—the changing of *love into hate*. It is particularly common to find both these directed simultaneously towards the same object, and this phenomenon of their co-existence furnishes the most important example of ambivalence of feeling.

The case of love and hate acquires a special interest from the circumstance that it resists classification in our scheme of the instincts. It is impossible to doubt the existence of a most intimate relation between these two contrary feelings and sexual life, but one is naturally unwilling to conceive of love as being a kind of special component-instinct of sexuality in the same way as are the others just discussed. One would prefer to regard loving rather as the expression of the whole sexual current of feeling, but this idea does not clear up our difficulties and we are at a loss how to conceive of an essential opposite to this striving.

Loving admits of not merely one, but of three antitheses. First there is the antithesis of loving—hating; secondly, there is loving—being loved; and, in addition to these, loving and hating together are the opposite of the condition of neutrality or indifference. The second of these two antitheses, loving—being loved, corresponds exactly to the transformation from active to passive and may be traced to a primal situation in the same way as the scoptophilic instinct. This situation is that of *loving oneself*, which for us is the characteristic of narcissism. Then, according to whether the self as object or subject is exchanged for an extraneous one, there results the active aim of loving or the passive one of being loved, the latter remaining nearly related to narcissism.

Perhaps we shall come to a better understanding of the manifold opposites of loving if we reflect that our mental life as a whole is governed by *three polarities*, namely, the following antitheses:

Subject (ego)—Object (external world),
Pleasure—Pain,
Active—Passive.

The antithesis of ego—non-ego (outer), *i.e.* subject—object, is, as we have already said, thrust upon the individual being at an early stage, by the experience that it can abolish external stimuli by means of muscular action but is defenceless against those stimuli that originate in instinct. This antithesis remains sovereign above all in our intellectual activity and provides research with a fundamental situation which no amount of effort can alter.

The polarity of pleasure—pain depends upon a feeling-series, the significance of which in determining our actions (will) is paramount and has already been emphasized. The antithesis of active and passive must not be confounded with that of ego-subject—external object. The relation of the ego to the outer world is passive in so far as it receives stimuli from it, active when it reacts to these. Its instincts compel it to a quite special degree of activity towards the outside world, so that, if we wished to emphasize the essence of the matter, we might say that the ego-subject is passive in respect of external stimuli, active in virtue of its own instincts. The antithesis of active—passive coalesces later with that of masculine—feminine, which, until this has taken place, has no psychological significance. The fusion of activity with masculinity and passivity with femininity confronts us, indeed, as a biological fact, but it is by no means so invariably complete and exclusive as we are inclined to assume.

II. Repression

One of the vicissitudes an instinctual impulse may undergo is to meet with resistances the aim of which is to make the impulse inoperative. Under certain conditions, which we shall presently investigate more closely, the impulse then passes into the state of *repression*. If it were a question of the operation of an external stimulus, obviously flight would be the appropriate remedy; with an instinct, flight is of no avail, for the ego cannot escape from itself. Later on, rejection based on judgement (*condemnation*) will be found to be a good weapon against the impulse. Repression is a preliminary phase of condemnation, something between flight and condemnation; it is a concept which could not have been formulated before the time of psycho-analytic research.

It is not easy in theory to deduce the possibility of such a thing as repression. Why should an instinctual impulse suffer such a fate? For this to happen, obviously a necessary condition must be that attainment of its aim by the instinct should produce 'pain' instead of pleasure. But we cannot well imagine such a contingency. There are no such instincts; satisfaction of an instinct is always pleasurable. We should have to assume certain peculiar circumstances, some sort of process which changes the pleasure of satisfaction into 'pain'.

In order the better to define repression we may discuss some other situations in which instincts are concerned. It may happen that an external stimulus becomes internal, for example, by eating into and destroying a bodily organ, so that a new source of constant excitation and increase of tension is formed. The stimulus thereby acquires a far-reaching similarity to an instinct. We know that a case of this sort is experienced by us as *physical pain*. The aim of this pseudo-instinct, however, is simply the cessation of the change in the organ and of the pain accompanying it. There is no other direct pleasure to be attained by cessation of the pain. Further, pain is imperative; the only things which can subdue it are the effect of some toxic agent in removing it and the influence of some mental distraction.

The case of physical pain is too obscure to help us much in our purpose. Let us suppose that an instinctual stimulus such as hunger remains unsatisfied. It then becomes imperative and can be allayed by nothing but the appropriate action for satisfying it; it keeps up a constant tension of need. Anything like a repression seems in this case to be utterly out of the question.

So repression is certainly not an essential result of the tension produced by lack of satisfaction of an impulse being raised to an unbearable degree. The weapons of defence of which the organism avails itself to guard against that situation must be discussed in another connection.

Let us instead confine ourselves to the clinical experience we meet with in the practice of psycho-analysis. We then see that the satisfaction of an instinct under repression is quite possible; further, that in every instance such a satisfaction is pleasurable in itself, but is irreconcilable with other claims and purposes; it therefore causes pleasure in one part of the mind and 'pain' in another. We see then that it is a condition of repression that the element of avoiding 'pain' shall have acquired more strength than the pleasure of gratification. Psycho-analytic experience of the transference neuroses, moreover, forces us to the conclusion that repression is not a defence-mechanism present from the very beginning, and that it cannot occur until a sharp distinction has been established between what is conscious and what is unconscious; that *the essence of repression lies simply in the function of rejecting and keeping something out of consciousness*. This conception of repression would be supplemented by assuming that, before the mental organization reaches this phase, the other vicissitudes which may befall instincts, *e.g.* reversal into the opposite or turning round upon the subject, deal with the task of mastering the instinctual impulses.

It seems to us now that in view of the very great extent to which repression and the unconscious are correlated, we must defer probing more deeply into the nature of repression until we have learnt more about the structure of the various institutions in the mind—and about what differentiates consciousness from the unconscious. Till we have done this, all we can do is to put together in purely descriptive fashion some characteristics of repression noted in clinical practice, even though we run the risk of having to repeat unchanged much that has been said elsewhere.

Psycho-analysis is able to show us something else which is important for understanding the effects of repression in the psychoneuroses. It shows us, for instance, that the instinct-presentation develops in a more unchecked and luxuriant fashion if it is withdrawn by repression from conscious influence. It ramifies like a fungus, so to speak, in the dark and takes on extreme forms of expression, which when translated and revealed to the neurotic are bound not merely to seem alien to him, but to terrify him by the way in which they reflect an extraordinary and dangerous strength of instinct. This illusory strength of instinct is the result of an uninhibited development of it in phantasy and of the damming-up consequent on lack of real satisfaction. The fact that this last result is bound up with repression points the direction in which we have to look for the true significance of the latter.

In reverting to the contrary aspect, however, let us state definitely that it is not even correct to suppose that repression withholds from consciousness all the derivatives of what was primally repressed. If these derivatives are sufficiently far removed from the repressed instinct-presentation, whether owing to the process of distortion or by reason of the number of intermediate associations, they have free access to consciousness. It is as though the resistance of consciousness against them was in inverse proportion to their remoteness from what was originally repressed. During the practice of the psycho-analytic method, we continually require the patient to produce such derivatives of what has been repressed as, in consequence either of their remoteness or of distortion, can pass the censorship of consciousness. Indeed, the associations which we require him to give, while refraining from any consciously directed train of thought or any criticism, and from which we reconstruct a conscious interpretation of the repressed instinct-presentation, are precisely derivatives of this kind. We then observe that the patient can go on spinning a whole chain of such associations, till he is brought up in the midst of them against some thought-formation, the relation of which to what is repressed acts so intensely that he is compelled to repeat this attempt at repression. Neurotic symptoms, too, must have fulfilled the condition referred to, for they are derivatives of the repressed, which has finally by means of these formations wrested from consciousness the right of way previously denied it.

We can lay down no general rule concerning the degree of distortion and remoteness necessary before the resistance of consciousness is abrogated. In this matter a delicate balancing takes place, the play of which is hidden from us; its mode of operation, however, leads us to infer that it is a question of a definite degree of intensity in the cathexis of the unconscious—beyond which it would break through for satisfaction. Repression acts, therefore, in a *highly specific* manner in each instance; every single derivative of the repressed may have its peculiar fate—a little more or a little less distortion alters the whole issue. In this connection it becomes comprehensible that those objects to which men give their preference, that is, their ideals, originate in the same perceptions and experiences as those objects of which they have most abhorrence, and that the two originally differed from one another only by slight modifications. Indeed, as we found in the origin of the fetish, it is possible for the original instinct-presentation to be split into two, one part undergoing repression, while the remainder, just on account of its intimate association with the other, undergoes idealization.

The same result as ensues from an increase or a decrease in the degree of distortion may also be achieved at the other end of the apparatus, so to speak, by a modification in the conditions producing pleasure and 'pain.'

Special devices have been evolved, with the object of bringing about such changes in the play of mental forces that what usually gives rise to 'pain' may on this occasion result in pleasure, and whenever such a device comes into operation the repression of an instinct-presentation that is ordinarily repudiated is abrogated. The only one of these devices which has till now been studied in any detail is that of joking. Generally the lifting of the repression is only transitory; the repression is immediately reestablished.

Observations of this sort, however, suffice to draw our attention to some further characteristics of repression. Not only is it, as we have just explained, *variable* and *specific*, but it is also exceedingly *mobile*. The process of repression is not to be regarded as something which takes place once for all, the results of which are permanent, as when some living thing has been killed and from that time onward is dead; on the contrary, repression demands a constant expenditure of energy, and if this were discontinued the success of the repression would be jeopardized, so that a fresh act of repression would be necessary. We may imagine that what is repressed exercises a continuous straining in the direction of consciousness, so that the balance has to be kept by means of a steady counter-pressure. A constant expenditure of energy, therefore, is entailed in maintaining a repression, and economically its abrogation denotes a saving. The mobility of the repression, incidentally, finds expression also in the mental characteristics of the condition of sleep which alone renders dream-formation possible. With a return to waking life the repressive cathexes which have been called in are once more put forth.

Finally, we must not forget that after all we have said very little about an instinctual impulse when we state it to be repressed. Without prejudice to the repression such an impulse may find itself in widely different conditions; it may be inactive, *i.e.* cathected with only a low degree of mental energy, or its degree of cathexis (and consequently its capacity for activity) may vary. True, its activity will not result in a direct abrogation of the repression, but it will certainly set in motion all the processes which terminate in a breaking through into consciousness by circuitous routes. With unrepressed derivatives of the unconscious the fate of a particular idea is often decided by the degree of its activity or cathexis. It is an everyday occurrence that such a derivative can remain unrepressed so long as it represents only a small amount of energy, although its content is of such a nature as to give rise to a conflict with conscious control. But the quantitative factor is manifestly decisive for this conflict; as soon as an idea which is fundamentally offensive exceeds a certain degree of strength, the conflict takes on actuality, and it is precisely activation of the idea that leads to its repression. So that, where repression is concerned, an increase in energic cathexis operates in the same way as an approach to the unconscious, while a decrease in that energy operates like distance from the unconscious or like distortion. We understand that the repressing tendencies can find a substitute for repression in a weakening or lessening of whatever is distasteful to them.

We now wish to gain some insight into the mechanism of the process of repression, and especially we want to know whether it has a single mechanism only, or more than one, and whether perhaps each of the psycho-neuroses may be distinguished by a characteristic repression-mechanism peculiar to itself. At the outset of this inquiry, however, we encounter complications. The mechanism of a repression becomes accessible to us only when we deduce it from its final results. If we confine our observations to the results of its effect on the ideational part of the instinct-presentation, we discover that as a rule repression creates a *substitute-formation*. What then is the mechanism of such a substitute-formation, or must we distinguish several mechanisms here also? Further, we know that repression leaves *symptoms* in its train. May we then regard substitute-formation and symptom-formation as coincident processes, and, if this is on the whole possible, does the mechanism of substitute-formation coincide with that of repression? So far as we know at present, it seems probable that the two are widely divergent, that it is not the repression itself which produces substitute-formations and symptoms, but that these latter constitute indications of a *return of the repressed* and owe their existence to quite other processes. It would also seem advisable to examine the mechanisms of substitute and symptom-formation before those of repression.

Obviously there is no ground here for speculation to explore: on the contrary, the solution of the problem must be found by careful analysis of the results of repression observable in the individual neuroses. I must,

however, suggest that we should postpone this task, too, until we have formed reliable conceptions of the relation of consciousness to the unconscious.

III. The Unconscious

Psycho-analysis has taught us that the essence of the process of repression lies, not in abrogating or annihilating the ideational presentation of an instinct, but in withholding it from becoming conscious. We then say of the idea that it is in a state of 'unconsciousness', of being not apprehended by the conscious mind, and we can produce convincing proofs to show that unconsciously it can also produce effects, even of a kind that finally penetrate to consciousness. Everything that is repressed must remain unconscious, but at the very outset let us state that the repressed does not comprise the whole unconscious. The unconscious has the greater compass: the repressed is a part of the unconscious.

How are we to arrive at a knowledge of the unconscious? It is of course only as something conscious that we know anything of it, after it has undergone transformation or translation into something conscious. The possibility of such translation is a matter of everyday experience in psycho-analytic work. In order to achieve this, it is necessary that the person analysed should overcome certain resistances, the very same as those which at some earlier time placed the material in question under repression by rejecting it from consciousness.

In many quarters our justification is disputed for assuming the existence of an unconscious system in the mind and for employing such an assumption for purposes of scientific work. To this we can reply that our assumption of the existence of the unconscious is *necessary* and *legitimate*, and that we possess manifold *proofs* of the existence of the unconscious. It is necessary because the data of consciousness are exceedingly defective; both in healthy and in sick persons mental acts are often in process which can be explained only by presupposing other acts, of which consciousness yields no evidence. These include not only the parapraxes[2] and dreams of healthy persons, and everything designated a mental symptom or an obsession in the sick; our most intimate daily experience introduces

---

[2]*E.g.*, slips of the tongue, mislaying of objects, etc.

us to sudden ideas of the source of which we are ignorant, and to results of mentation arrived at we know not how. All these conscious acts remain disconnected and unintelligible if we are determined to hold fast to the claim that very single mental act performed within us must be consciously experienced; on the other hand, they fall into a demonstrable connection if we interpolate the unconscious acts that we infer. A gain in meaning and connection, however, is a perfectly justifiable motive, one which may well carry us beyond the limitations of direct experience. When, after this, it appears that the assumption of the unconscious helps us to construct a highly successful practical method, by which we are enabled to exert a useful influence upon the course of conscious processes, this success will have won us an incontrovertible proof of the existence of that which we assumed. We become obliged then to take up the position that it is both untenable and presumptuous to claim that whatever goes on in the mind must be known to consciousness.

We can go further and in support of an unconscious mental state allege that only a small content is embraced by consciousness at any given moment, so that the greater part of what we call conscious knowledge must in any case exist for very considerable periods of time in a condition of latency, that is to say, of unconsciousness, of not being apprehended by the mind. When all our latent memories are taken into consideration it becomes totally incomprehensible how the existence of the unconscious can be gainsaid. We then encounter the objection that these latent recollections can no longer be described as mental processes, but that they correspond to residues of somatic processes from which something mental can once more proceed. The obvious answer to this should be that a latent memory is, on the contrary, indubitably a residuum of a mental process. But it is more important to make clear to our minds that this objection is based on the identification—not, it is true, explicitly stated but regarded as axiomatic—of conscious and mental. This identification is either a *petitio principii* and begs the question whether all that is mental is also necessarily conscious, or else it is a matter of convention, of nomenclature. In this latter case it is of course no more open to refutation than any other convention. The only question that remains is whether it proves so useful that we must needs adopt it. To this we may reply that the conventional identification of the

mental with the conscious is thoroughly unpractical. It breaks up all mental continuity, plunges us into the insoluble difficulties of psychophysical parallelism, is open to the reproach that without any manifest grounds it overestimates the part played by consciousness, and finally it forces us prematurely to retire from the territory of psychological research without being able to offer us any compensation elsewhere.

At any rate it is clear that the question—whether the latent states of mental life, whose existence is undeniable, are to be conceived of as unconscious mental states or as physical ones—threatens to resolve itself into a war of words. We shall therefore be better advised to give prominence to what we know with certainty of the nature of these debatable states. Now, as far as their physical characteristics are concerned, they are totally inaccessible to us; no physiological conception nor chemical process can give us any notion of their nature. On the other hand, we know for certain that they have abundant points of contact with conscious mental processes; on being submitted to a certain method of operation they may be transformed into or replaced by conscious processes, and all the categories which we employ to describe conscious mental acts, such as ideas, purposes, resolutions and so forth, can be applied to them. Indeed, of many of these latent states we have to assert that the only point in which they differ from states which are conscious is just in the lack of consciousness of them. So we shall not hesitate to treat them as objects of psychological research, and that in the most intimate connection with conscious mental acts.

The stubborn denial of a mental quality to latent mental processes may be accounted for by the circumstance that most of the phenomena in question have not been objects of study outside psycho-analysis. Anyone who is ignorant of the facts of pathology, who regards the blunders of normal persons as accidental, and who is content with the old saw that dreams are froth[3] need only ignore a few more problems of the psychology of consciousness in order to dispense with the assumption of an unconscious mental activity. As it happens, hypnotic experiments, and especially post-hypnotic suggestion, had demonstrated tangibly even before the time of psycho-analysis the existence and mode of operation of the unconscious in the mind.

---

[3] ['Träume sind Schäume.']

The assumption of an unconscious is, moreover, in a further respect a perfectly *legitimate* one, inasmuch as in postulating it we do not depart a single step from our customary and accepted mode of thinking. By the medium of consciousness each one of us becomes aware only of his own states of mind; that another man possesses consciousness is a conclusion drawn by analogy from the utterances and actions we perceive him to make, and it is drawn in order that this behaviour of his may become intelligible to us. (It would probably be psychologically more correct to put it thus: that without any special reflection we impute to everyone else our own constitution and therefore also our consciousness, and that this identification is a necessary condition of understanding in us.) This conclusion—or identification—was formerly extended by the ego to other human beings, to animals, plants, inanimate matter and to the world at large, and proved useful as long as the correspondence with the individual ego was overwhelmingly great; but it became more untrustworthy in proportion as the gulf between the ego and the non-ego widened. To-day, our judgment is already in doubt on the question of consciousness in animals; we refuse to admit it in plants and we relegate to mysticism the assumption of its existence in inanimate matter. But even where the original tendency to identification has withstood criticism—that is, when the non-ego is our fellowman—the assumption of a consciousness in him rests upon an inference and cannot share the direct certainty we have of our own consciousness.

Now psycho-analysis demands nothing more than that we should apply this method of inference to ourselves also—a proceeding to which, it is true, we are not constitutionally disposed. If we do this, we must say that all the acts and manifestations which I notice in myself and do not know how to link up with the rest of my mental life must be judged as if they belonged to someone else and are to be explained by the mental life ascribed to that person. Further, experience shows that we understand very well how to interpret in others (*i.e.*, how to fit into their mental context) those same acts which we refuse to acknowledge as mentally conditioned in ourselves. Some special hindrance deflects our investigations from ourselves and interferes with our obtaining true knowledge of ourselves.

Now this method of inference, applied to oneself in spite of inner opposition, does not lead to the discovery of an unconscious, but leads logically to the assumption of another, second consciousness which is united in myself with the consciousness I know. But at this point criticism may fairly make certain comments. In the first place, a consciousness of which its own possessor knows nothing is something very different from that of another person and it is questionable whether such a consciousness, lacking, as it does, its most important characteristic, is worthy of any further discussion at all. Those who have contested the assumption of an unconscious system in the mind will not be content to accept in its place an unconscious consciousness. Secondly, analysis shows that the individual latent mental processes inferred by us enjoy a high degree of independence, as though each had no connection with another, and knew nothing about any other. We must be prepared, it would appear, to assume the existence not only of a second consciousness in us, but of a third and fourth also, perhaps of an infinite series of states of consciousness, each and all unknown to us and to one another. In the third place—and this is the most weighty argument of all—we have to take into account that analytic investigation reveals some of these latent processes as having characteristics and peculiarities which seem alien to us, or even incredible, and running directly counter to the well-known attributes of consciousness. This justifies us in modifying our inference about ourselves and saying that what is proved is not a second consciousness in us, but the existence of certain mental operations lacking in the quality of consciousness. We shall also, moreover, be right in rejecting the term 'subconsciousness' as incorrect and misleading. The known cases of '*double conscience*' (splitting of consciousness) prove nothing against our view. They may most accurately be described as cases of a splitting of the mental activities into two groups, whereby a single consciousness takes up its position alternately with either the one or the other of these groups.

In psycho-analysis there is no choice for us but to declare mental processes to be in themselves unconscious, and to compare the perception of them by consciousness with the perception of the outside world through the sense-organs; we even hope to extract some fresh knowledge from the comparison.

Etiology and Development

The key to the development of pathological behavior, according to the intrapsychic theorist, can be found in faulty experiences in early life. Each child is born with a variety of drives or instincts which require nourishment and stimulation. Deprivation or conflicts associated with these needs result in feelings of anxiety and insecurity. In an effort to handle these feelings, the child adopts a variety of defensive maneuvers which ultimately lead to maladaptive behavior.

Karl Abraham, an early disciple of Freud, was the first to undertake a full explication of the relationship between psychosexual stage experiences and later character types. Building on a prior paper by Freud, Abraham develops an intriguing model of the origins of various "oral" personalities.

Erik Erikson, one of the major contemporary figures in "ego psychology," has formulated a model for ego development which parallels Freud's conception of the stages of psychosexual development. In the selection reprinted here, he outlines, with a clarity rare among intrapsychic writers, the major phases of early interpersonal experience. Disruptions in the sequence of this developmental pattern often lead to pathological developments, according to Erikson.

14 The Influence of Oral Erotism on Character-Formation

Karl Abraham

According to the usual view the formation of character is to be traced back partly to inherited disposition, and partly to the effects of environment, among which particular significance is ascribed to upbringing. Psychoanalytical investigation has for the first time drawn attention to sources of character-formation which have not hitherto been sufficiently considered. On the basis of psychoanalytical experience we have come to take the view that those elements of infantile sexuality which are excluded from participation in the sexual life of the adult individual undergo in part a transformation into certain character-traits. As is well known, Freud was the first to show that certain elements of infantile anal erotism undergo a transformation of this kind. Some part of this anal erotism enters into the final organization of mature sexual life, some becomes sublimated,

From *Selected Papers on Psychoanalysis*, Hogarth Press, 1927/1924.

and some goes to form character. These contributions to character from anal sources are to be regarded as normal. They render it possible for the individual to adapt himself to the demands of his environment as regards cleanliness, love of order, and so on. Apart from this, however, we have learnt to recognize an 'anal character' in the clinical sense, which is distinguished by an extreme accentuation of certain character-traits; but it is to be noted that the excessive addiction to cleanliness, parsimony, and similar tendencies found in such characters never succeeds completely. We invariably find the opposite extreme more or less strongly developed in them.

Now experience teaches us that not all deviations from the final character-formation of the genital stage originate in the anal sources just mentioned. We find that oral erotism is a source of character-formation as well. Here, too, we can see that the supplies from this source can fall within the normal or can greatly exceed it. If our observations are correct, then we can speak of oral, anal, and genital sources of character-formation; in doing so, however, we quite consciously neglect one aspect of the problem, since we are only taking into consideration those contributions to the formation of character which are derived from the erotogenic zones, and not those coming from the component-instincts. This neglect is, however, more apparent than real; for example, the close connection of the component of cruelty in infantile instinctual life with oral erotism will become evident in the character-formation of the individual as elsewhere, so that it is hardly necessary to draw special attention to it.

What I shall be able to say about character-traits of oral origin will perhaps be disappointing in some respects, because I cannot offer a picture comparable in completeness to that of the anal character. I shall therefore begin by pointing out certain differences between the two which should not be lost sight of, and which will moderate our expectations as regards the oral character to more suitable proportions.

In the first place, it should be remembered that of the pleasurable tendencies that are connected with intestinal processes only a small part can come to form part of normal erotism in an *unrepressed* form; whereas an incomparably greater part of the libidinal cathexis of the mouth which characterizes infancy can still be employed in later life. Thus the oral elements of infantile sexuality do not need to be changed into character-formation or sublimated to the same extent as the anal ones.

In the second place, we must bear in mind that a retrograde transformation of character, such as is connected with the outbreak of certain nervous disturbances, in the main comes to a stop at the anal stage. If it proceeds further and a pathological intensification of oral traits such as will be described later, ensues, then these latter will show an admixture of traits belonging to the anal stage; and we should in that case expect to find a combination of the two kinds of character-traits rather than a pure culture of oral ones.

If we proceed to study these mixed products of two different sources of character-formation more deeply we make a new discovery, namely, that the origin of the anal character is very closely connected with the history of oral erotism, and cannot be completely understood without reference to it.

Clinical experience has led Freud to the view that in many people the particular libidinal emphasis that attaches to the intestinal processes is a constitutional factor. There can be no doubt that this is so. We need only call to mind how in certain families positive phenomena of anal erotism as well as anal character-traits are everywhere observable in the most different members. Nevertheless, correct as this view is, the facts admit of further explanation in the light of the following psycho-analytic observations.

In infancy the individual has an intense pleasure in the act of sucking, and we have familiarized ourselves with the view that this pleasure is not to be ascribed entirely to the process of taking food, but that it is conditioned in a high degree by the significance of the mouth as an erotogenic zone.

This primitive form of obtaining pleasure is never completely abandoned by the individual but persists under all kinds of disguises during the whole of his life, and even experiences a reinforcement at certain times and in particular circumstances. Nevertheless, as it grows up both physically and mentally, the child does effect a far-reaching renunciation of its original pleasure in sucking. Now observation shows that every such renunciation of pleasure only takes place on the basis of an exchange. It is this process of renunciation and the course it takes under different conditions which merits our attention.

First of all there is the process of the irruption of teeth, which, as is well known, causes a considerable part of the pleasure in sucking to be replaced by pleasure in biting. We need only call to mind how during this stage of development the child puts every object it can into its mouth and tries with all its strength to bite it to pieces.

In the same period of development the child begins to have ambivalent relations to external objects. It is to be noted that the friendly as well as the hostile aspect of its attitude is connected with pleasure. At about the same period a further displacement of pleasurable sensation to other bodily functions and areas occurs.

What is of particular significance is that the pleasure in sucking undertakes a kind of migration. At about the time that the child is being weaned it is also being trained in habits of cleanliness. An important prerequisite for the success of this latter process lies in the gradually developing function of the anal and urethral sphincters. The action of these muscles is the same as that of the lips in sucking, and is obviously modelled on it. The original unchecked voiding of bodily excretions was accompanied by stimulation of the apertures of the body which was undoubtedly pleasurable. If the child adapts itself to the demands of training and learns to retain its excretions this new activity also gets to be accompanied by pleasure. The pleasurable sensations in the organ connected with this process form the foundation upon which the mental pleasure in retention of every kind of possession is gradually built up. More recent investigations have shown that the possession of an object originally signified to the infantile mind the having incorporated it into its own body. Whereas to begin with, pleasure was only associated with taking in something coming from without or with expelling bodily contents, now there is added the pleasure in retaining bodily contents, which leads to pleasure in all forms of property. The relation in which these three sources of physical and mental gratification stand to one another is of the greatest practical significance for the later social conduct of the individual. If the pleasure in getting or taking is brought into the most favourable relation possible with the pleasure in possession, as well as with that in giving up, then an exceedingly important step has been made in laying the foundations of the individual's social relations. For when such a relationship between the three tendencies is present, the most important preliminary condition for overcoming the ambivalence of the individual's emotional life has been established.

In what has so far been said we have only called attention to single features of the multiform developmental process. For the purpose of our investigation it is sufficient to make clear that the first and therefore perhaps the most important step the individual makes towards attaining a normal attitude in his final social and sexual relationships consists in dealing successfully with his oral erotism. But there are numerous ways in which this important process of development may suffer disturbance. In order to understand this we must bear in mind that the pleasure of the sucking period is to a great extent a pleasure in taking, in being given something. It then becomes apparent that any quantitative divergence from the usual degree of pleasure gained can give rise to disturbances.

Given certain conditions of nourishment the sucking period can be an extremely displeasurable one for the child. In some cases its earliest pleasurable craving is imperfectly gratified, and it is deprived of the enjoyment of the sucking stage.[1] In other cases the same period is abnormally rich in pleasure. It is well known how some mothers indulge the craving for pleasure in their infants by granting them every wish. The result is that it is extraordinarily difficult to wean the child, and it sometimes takes two or three years to do it. In a few cases the child persists in taking food by sucking from a bottle until it is almost grown up.

Whether in this early period of life the child has had to go without pleasure or has been indulged with an excess of it, the effect is the same. It takes leave of the sucking stage under difficulties. Since its need for pleasure has either not been sufficiently gratified or has become too insistent, it fastens with particular intensity on the possibilities of pleasure to be got from the next stage. In doing this it finds itself in constant danger of a new disappointment, to which it will react more readily than the normal child with a regression to the earlier stage. In other words: In the child who has been disappointed or over-indulged in the sucking period the pleasure in biting, which is also the most primitive form of sadism, will be especially emphasized. Thus the formation of character in such a child begins under the influence of an abnormally pronounced ambivalence of feeling. In practice such a disturbance of the development of character expresses itself in pronounced characteristics of hostility and dislike. It accounts for the presence of the abnormally over-developed envy which is so common. Eisler has already referred this character-trait to an oral source.[2] I fully agree with his view, but would like to emphasize its relation to the later oral stage. In many cases an elder child, who is already at the stage of taking food by biting and chewing, has an opportunity of observing a younger child being suckled. In such cases the characteristic of envy receives a special reinforcement. Sometimes it is incompletely over-

---

[1] Freud made it clear long ago that stomach and bowel troubles in infancy can have a harmful effect on the mental development of the child.

[2] 'Pleasure in Sleep and Disturbed Capacity for Sleep' (1921).

come by being turned into its opposite; but the original feeling is easily seen to persist in various disguises.

But if the child escapes the Scylla of this danger, it is threatened by the Charybdis of another. It attempts to resume the abandoned act of sucking in an altered form and in another locality. We have already spoken of the sucking activity of the sphincters at the excretory apertures of the body, and have recognized that an inordinate desire to possess, especially in the form of abnormal parsimony and avarice, stands in close relation to this process. Thus we see that those traits, which belong to the clinical phenomena of the anal character, are built up on the ruins of an oral erotism whose development has miscarried. In the present paper I shall only describe this one path of defective development. The preceding remarks will suffice to show how dependent is our understanding of the anal character on an adequate knowledge of the preceding stages of development.

We will pass on to consider the direct contributions rendered by oral erotism to the formation of character, and will begin with an example taken from ordinary psycho-analytical observation.

Neurotic parsimony, which may be developed to the point of avarice, is often met with in people who are inhibited from properly earning a livelihood; and the anal sources of character-formation provide no explanation of it. It is in fact connected with an inhibition of the craving for objects, and this indicates that the libido has undergone some special vicissitude. The pleasure in acquiring desired objects seems in this case to have been repressed in favour of pleasure in holding fast to existing possessions. People in whom we find this inhibition are always haunted by a fear lest they should lose the smallest part of their possessions. This anxiety prevents them from trying to earn money, and renders them in many ways helpless in practical life. We shall understand this type of character-formation if we go on to examine related symptoms.

In certain other cases the person's entire character is under oral influence, but this can only be shown after a thorough analysis has been made. According to my experience we are here concerned with persons in whom the sucking was undisturbed and highly pleasurable. They have brought with them from this happy period a deeply-rooted conviction that everything will always be well with them. They face life with an imperturbable optimism which often does in fact help them to achieve their aims. But we also meet with less favourable types of development. Some people are dominated by the belief that there will always be some kind person—a representative of the mother, of course—to care for them and to give them everything they need. This optimistic belief condemns them to inactivity. We again recognize in them individuals who have been over-indulged in the sucking period. Their whole attitude towards life shows that they expect the mother's breast to flow for them eternally, as it were. They make no kind of effort, and in some cases they even disdain to undertake a bread-winning occupation.

This optimism, whether it is allied to an energetic conduct in life or, as in the last-mentioned aberration, to a care-free indifference to the world, stands in noteworthy contrast to a feature of the anal character that has not been sufficiently appreciated up to the present. I refer to a melancholy seriousness which passes over into marked pessimism. I must point out, however, that this characteristic is to a great extent not directly of anal origin, but goes back to a disappointment of oral desires in the earliest years. In persons of this type the optimistic belief in the benevolence of fate is completely absent. On the contrary, they consistently show an apprehensive attitude towards life, and have a tendency to make the worst of everything and to find undue difficulties in the simplest undertakings.

A character thus rooted in oral erotism influences the entire behaviour of the individual, as well as his choice of profession, his predilections, and his hobbies. We may cite as an instance the type of neurotic official who is only able to exist when all the circumstances of his life have been prescribed for him once and for all. To him the necessary condition of life is that his means of sustenance should be guaranteed to him up to the day of his death. He renounces all ideals of personal success in favour of receiving an assured and regular income.

So far we have dealt with people whose entire character is explained on the supposition that their libido has been fully gratified in the oral stage of their development. In psycho-analytic work, however, we observe other individuals who are burdened throughout their whole life with the after-effects of an ungratified sucking period. In them there is no trace of such a development having taken place.

In their social behaviour these people always seem to be asking for something, either in the form of a modest request or of an aggressive demand. The manner in which they put forward their wishes has something in the nature of persistent sucking about it; they are as little to be put off by hard facts as by reasonable arguments, but continue to plead and to insist. One might almost say that they 'cling like leeches' to other people. They particularly dislike being alone, even for a short time. Impatience is a marked characteristic with them. In some cases, those in which psycho-analytic investigation reveals a regression from the oral-sadistic to the sucking stage, their behavior has an element of cruelty in it as well, which makes them something like vampires to other people.

We meet certain traits of character in the same people which can be traced back to a peculiar displacement within the oral sphere. Their longing to experience gratification by way of sucking has changed to a need to *give* by way of the mouth, so that we find in them, besides a permanent longing to obtain everything, a constant need to communicate themselves orally to other people. This results in an obstinate urge to talk, connected in most cases with a feeling of overflowing. Persons of this kind have the impression that their fund of thought is inexhaustible, and they ascribe a special power or some unusual value to what they say. Their principal relation to other people is effected by the way of oral discharge. The obstinate insistence described above naturally occurs chiefly by means of speech. But that function serves at the same time for the act of giving. I could, moreover, regularly establish the fact that these people could not control their other activities any more than they could their speech. Thus one frequently finds in them a neurotically exaggerated need to urinate, which often appears at the same time as an outburst of talking or directly after it.

In those features of character-formation which belong to the oral-sadistic stage, too, speaking takes the place of repressed impulses from another quarter. In certain neurotics the hostile purpose of their speech is especially striking. In this instance it serves the uncon-

scious aim of killing the adversary. Psychoanalysis has shown that in such cases, in place of biting and devouring the object, a milder form of aggression has appeared, though the mouth is still utilized as the organ of it. In certain neurotics speaking is used to express the entire range of instinctual trends, whether friendly or hostile, social or asocial, and irrespective of the instinctual sphere to which they originally belonged. In them the impulse to talk signifies desiring as well as attacking, killing, or annihilating, and at the same time every kind of bodily evacuation, including the act of fertilization. In their phantasies speaking is subject to the narcissistic valuation which their unconscious applies to all physical and psychical productions. Their entire behaviour shows a particularly striking contrast to reticent people with anal character-formation.

Observations of this kind most emphatically draw our attention to the varieties and differences that exist within the realm of oral character-formation, and show that the field which we are investigating is anything but limited or poor in variations. The most important differences, however, are those which depend on whether a feature of character has developed on the basis of the earlier or the later oral stage; whether, in other words, it is the expression of an unconscious tendency to suck or to bite. In the latter case we shall find in connection with such a character-trait the most marked symptoms of ambivalence—positive and negative instinctual cravings, hostile and friendly tendencies; while we may assume on the basis of our experience that the character-traits derived from the stage of sucking are not as yet subjected to ambivalence. According to my observations, this fundamental difference extends to the smallest details of a person's behaviour. At a meeting of the British Psychological Society (Medical Section) Dr. Edward Glover recently read a paper in which he gave these differences particular consideration.[3]

The very significant contrasts found in the character-formation of different individuals can be traced psycho-analytically from the fact that decisive influences on the process of formation of character have been exercised in the one case by oral impulses, and in the other case by anal ones. Equally important is the connecting of sadistic instinctual elements

[3]'The Significance of the Mouth in Psycho-Analysis' (1924).

with the manifestation of libido flowing from the various erotogenic zones. A few examples may roughly illustrate this point. In our psycho-analyses we are able to trace phenomena of very intense craving and effort back to the primary oral stage. It need hardly be said that we do not exclude other sources of impulse as factors in those phenomena. But the desires derived from that earliest stage are still free from the tendency to destroy the object—a tendency which is characteristic of the impulses of the next stage.

The covetous impulses which are derived from the second oral stage are in strong contrast to the unassuming character of the anally constituted person. But we must not forget that the weakness of the acquisitive tendency in the latter is balanced by his obstinate holding fast to things which he has already got.

Characteristic, too, are the differences in the inclination to share one's own possessions with others. Generosity is frequently found as an oral character-trait. In this the orally gratified person is identifying himself with the bounteous mother. Things are very different in the next, oral-sadistic stage, where envy, hostility, and jealousy make such behaviour impossible. Thus in many cases generous or envious behaviour is derived from one of the two oral stages of development; and in the same way the inclination to avarice corresponds to the succeeding anal-sadistic stage of character-formation.

There are noteworthy differences in the person's social conduct, too, according to the stage of his libido from which his character is derived. People who have been gratified in the earliest stage are bright and sociable; those who are fixated at the oral-sadistic stage are hostile and malicious; while moroseness, inaccessibility, and reticence go together with the anal character.

Furthermore, persons with an oral character are accessible to new ideas, in a favourable as well as an unfavourable sense, while the anal character involves a conservative behaviour opposed to all innovations—an attitude which certainly prevents the hasty abandonment of what has been proved good.

There is a similar contrast between the impatient importunity, haste, and restlessness of people with oral character-formation, and the perseverance and persistence of the anal character, which, on the other hand, tends to procrastination and hesitation.

The character-trait of ambition, which we meet with so frequently in our psycho-analyses, has been derived long ago by Freud[4] from urethral erotism. This explanation, however, does not seem to have penetrated to the deepest sources of that characteristic. According to my experience, and also that of Dr. Edward Glover, this is rather a character-trait of oral origin which is later reinforced from other sources, among which the urethral one should be particularly mentioned.

Besides this, it has to be noted that certain contributions to character-formation originating in the earliest oral stage coincide in important respects with others derived from the final genital stage. This is probably explicable from the fact that at these two stages the libido is least open to disturbance from an ambivalence of feeling.

In many people we find, beside the oral character-traits described, other psychological manifestations which we must derive from the same instinctual sources. These are impulses which have escaped any social modification. As examples a morbidly intense appetite for food and an inclination to various oral perversions are especially to be mentioned. Further, we meet many kinds of neurotic symptoms which are determined orally; and finally there are phenomena which have come into being through sublimation. These latter products deserve a separate investigation, which, however, would exceed the limits of this paper; hence I shall only briefly give a single example.

The displacement of the infantile pleasure in sucking to the intellectual sphere is of great practical significance. Curiosity and the pleasure in observing receive important reinforcements from this source, and this not only in childhood, but during the subject's whole life. In persons with a special inclination for observing Nature, and for many branches of scientific investigation, psycho-analysis shows a close connection between those impulses and repressed oral desires.

A glance into the workshop of scientific investigation enables us to recognize how impulses pertaining to the different erotogenic zones must support and supplement one another if the most favourable results possible are to be achieved. The optimum is reached when an energetic imbibing of observations is combined with enough tenacity and ability to

---

[4]'Character and Anal Erotism' (1908).

'digest' the collected facts, and a sufficiently strong impulse to give them back to the world, provided this is not done with undue haste. Psycho-analytical experience enables us to recognize various kinds of divergences from this optimum. Thus there are people with great mental capacity for absorbing, who, however, are inhibited in production. Others again produce too rapidly. It is no exaggeration to say of such people that they have scarcely taken a thing in before it comes out of their mouths again. When they are analysed it often proves that these same persons tend to vomit food as soon as they have eaten it. They are people who show an extreme neurotic impatience; a satisfactory combination of forward-moving oral impulses with retarding anal ones is lacking in the structure of their character.

In conclusion, it seems to me particularly important to allude once more to the significance of such combinations. In the normal formation of character we shall always find derivatives from all the original instinctual sources happily combined with one another.

It is important, moreover, to consider the numerous possibilities of such combinations because it prevents us from over-estimating some one particular aspect, important though it may be. If we consider the problems of character-formation from the one large unifying point of view which psycho-analysis affords us, from that of infantile sexuality, then it is obvious how everything weaves itself into a whole in the characterological sphere. The realm of infantile sexuality extends over two quite different fields. It covers the entire unconscious instinctual life of the mature human being. It is likewise the scene of the very important mental impressions of the earliest years of the child, among which we have to reckon prenatal influences. Sometimes we may feel dismayed in face of the mass of phenomena which meets us in the wide field of human mentality, from the play of children and other typical products of the early activity of phantasy, through the first development of the child's interests and talents, up to the most highly valued achievements of mature human beings and the most extreme individual differentiations. But then we must remember that Freud has given us in the practice and theory of psycho-analysis an instrument with which to investigate this wide subject and to open up the road to infantile sexuality, that inexhaustible source of life.

15 Growth and Crises

Erik H. Erikson

Basic Trust versus Basic Mistrust

For the first component of a healthy personality I nominate a sense of *basic trust,* which I think is an attitude toward oneself and the world derived from the experiences of the first year of life. By "trust" I mean what is commonly implied in reasonable trustfulness as far as others are concerned and a simple sense of trustworthiness as far as oneself is concerned. When I say "basic," I mean that neither this component nor any of those that follow are, either in childhood or in adulthood, especially conscious. In fact, all of these criteria, when developed in childhood and when integrated in adulthood, blend into the total personality. Their crises in childhood, however, and their impairment in adulthood are clearly circumscribed.

In describing this growth and its crises as a development of a series of alternative basic attitudes, we take recourse to the term *"a sense of."* Like a "sense of health" or a "sense of not being well," such "senses" pervade surface and depth, consciousness and the unconscious. They are ways of conscious *experience,* accessible to introspection (where it develops); ways of *behaving,* observable by

Reprinted from *Identity and the Life Cycle* by Erik H. Erikson, by permission of W. W. Norton & Company, Inc. Copyright © 1980 by W. W. Norton and Company, Inc. Copyright © 1959 by International Universities Press, Inc.

others; and unconscious *inner states* determinable by test and analysis. It is important to keep these three dimensions in mind, as we proceed.

In *adults* the impairment of basic trust is expressed in a *basic mistrust*. It characterizes individuals who withdraw into themselves in particular ways when at odds with themselves and with others. These ways, which often are not obvious, are more strikingly represented by individuals who regress into psychotic states in which they sometimes close up, refusing food and comfort and becoming oblivious to companionship. In so far as we hope to assist them with psychotherapy, we must try to reach them again in specific ways in order to convince them that they can trust the world and that they can trust themselves (Fromm-Reichmann, 1950).

It is from the knowledge of such radical regressions and of the deepest and most infantile layers in our not-so-sick patients that we have learned to regard basic trust as the cornerstone of a healthy personality. Let us see what justifies our placing the crisis and the ascendancy of this component at the beginning of life.

As the newborn infant is separated from his symbiosis with the mother's body, his inborn and more or less coordinated ability to take in by mouth meets the mother's more or less coordinated ability and intention to feed him and to welcome him. At this point he lives through, and loves with, his mouth, and the mother lives through, and loves with, her breasts.

For the mother this is a late and complicated accomplishment, highly dependent on her development as a woman; on her unconscious attitude toward the child; on the way she has lived through pregnancy and delivery; on her and her community's attitude toward the act of nursing—and on the response of the newborn. To him the mouth is the focus of a general first approach to life—the *incorporative* approach. In psychoanalysis this stage is usually referred to as the "oral" stage. Yet it is clear that, in addition to the overwhelming need for food, a baby is, or soon becomes receptive in many other respects. As he is willing and able to suck on appropriate objects and to swallow whatever appropriate fluids they emit, he is soon also willing and able to "take in" with his eyes whatever enters his visual field. His tactual senses, too, seem to "take in" what feels good. In this sense, then,

one could speak of an *"incorporative stage,"* one in which he is, relatively speaking, receptive to what he is being offered. Yet many babies are sensitive and vulnerable, too. In order to ensure that their first experience in this world may not only keep them alive but also help them to coordinate their sensitive breathing and their metabolic and circulatory rhythms, we must see to it that we deliver to their senses stimuli as well as food in the proper intensity and at the right time; otherwise their willingness to accept may change abruptly into diffuse defense—or into lethargy.

Now, while it is quite clear what *must* happen to keep a baby alive (the minimum supply necessary) and what *must not* happen, lest he be physically damaged or chronically upset (the maximum early frustration tolerable), there is a certain leeway in regard to what *may* happen; and different cultures make extensive use of their prerogatives to decide what they consider workable and insist upon calling necessary. Some people think that a baby, lest he scratch his own eyes out, must necessarily be swaddled completely for the better part of the day and throughout the greater part of the first year; also, that he should be rocked or fed whenever he whimpers. Others think that he should feel the freedom of his kicking limbs as early as possible, but also that he, as a matter of course, be forced to cry "please" for his meals until he literally gets blue in the face. All of this (more or less consciously) seems related to the culture's general aim and system. I have known some old American Indians who bitterly descried the way in which we often let our small babies cry because we believe that "it will make their lungs strong." No wonder (these Indians said) that the white man, after such an initial reception, seems to be in a hurry to get to the "next world." But the same Indians spoke proudly of the way their infants (breast fed into the second year) became blue in the face with fury when thumped on the head for "biting" the mother's nipples; here the Indians, in turn, believed that "it's going to make good hunters of them."

There is some intrinsic wisdom, some unconscious planning and much superstition in the seemingly arbitrary varieties of child training: what is "good for the child," what *may* happen to him, depends on what he is supposed to become and where.

At any rate, it is already in his earliest encounters that the human infant meets up with the basic modalities of his culture. The simplest and the earliest modality is *"to get,"* not in the sense of *"go and get"* but in that of receiving and accepting what is given; and this sounds easier than it is. For the groping and unstable newborn's organism learns this modality only as he learns to regulate his readiness to get with the methods of a mother who, in turn, will permit him to coordinate his means of getting as she develops and coordinates her means of giving. The mutuality of relaxation thus developed is of prime importance for the first experience of friendly otherness: from psychoanalysis one receives the impression that in thus *getting what is given,* and in learning to *get somebody to do* for him what he wishes to have done, the baby also develops the necessary groundwork to *get to be* the giver, to "identify" with her.

Where this *mutual regulation* fails, the situation falls apart into a variety of attempts to control by duress rather than by reciprocity. The baby will try to get by random activity what he cannot get by central suction; he will activate himself into exhaustion or he will find his thumb and damn the world. The mother's reaction may be to try to control matters by nervously changing hours, formulas, and procedures. One cannot be sure what this does to a baby; but it certainly is our clinical impression that in some sensitive individuals (or in individuals whose early frustration was never compensated for) such a situation can be a model for a radical disturbance in their relationship to the "world,'" to "people," and especially to loved or otherwise significant people.

There are ways of maintaining reciprocity by giving to the baby what he can get through other forms of feeding and by making up for what is missed orally through the satiation of other than oral receptors: his pleasure in being held, warmed, smiled at, talked to, rocked, and so forth. Besides such *"horizontal"* compensation (compensation during the same stage of development) there are many *"longitudinal"* compensations in life: compensations emerging from later stages of the life cycle.[1]

During the "second oral" stage the ability

and the pleasure in a more active and more directed incorporative approach ripen. The teeth develop and with them the pleasure in biting *on* hard things, in biting *through* things, and in biting *off* things. This *active-incorporative* mode characterizes a variety of other activities (as did the first incorporative mode). The eyes, first part of a passive system of accepting impressions as they come along, have now learned to focus, to isolate, to "grasp" objects from the vaguer background and to follow them. The organs of hearing similarly have learned to discern significant sounds, to localize them, and to guide an appropriate change in position (lifting and turning the head, lifting and turning the upper body). The arms have learned to reach out determinedly and the hands to grasp firmly. We are more interested here in the over-all *configuration and final integration* of developing approaches to the world than in the *first appearance of specific abilities* which are so well described in the child-development literature.[2]

With all of this a number of interpersonal patterns are established which center in the social modality of *taking* and *holding on to* things—things which are more or less freely offered and given, and things which have more or less a tendency to slip away. As the baby learns to change positions, to roll over, and very gradually to establish himself on the throne of his sedentary kingdom, he must perfect the mechanisms of grasping and appropriating, holding and chewing all that is within his reach.

The *crisis* of the oral stage (during the

---

with the support of an expanding economy and of a generous social group, learned to compensate for grievous early misfortunes of a kind which in our clinical histories would suffice to explain malfunctioning rather convincingly. The study gave me an opportunity to chart a decade of the life histories of about fifty (healthy) children, and to remain somewhat informed about the further fortunes of some of them. However, only the development of the identity concept . . . has helped me to approach an understanding of the mechanisms involved. I hope to publish my impressions.

[2]The reader trained in child development may want to pay special attention to the fact that one can think of a stage as the time when a capacity *first appears* (or appears in testable form) or as that period when it is so well *established* and integrated (has become an available apparatus for the ego, as we would say) that the next step in development can safely be imitated.

---

[1]My participation in the longitudinal research of the Institute of Child Welfare at the University of California (see Macfarlane, 1938; Erikson, 1951b) has taught me the greatest respect for the resiliency and resourcefulness of individual children who,

second part of the first year) is difficult to assess and more difficult to verify. It seems to consist of the coincidence in time of three developments: (1) a physiological one: the general tension associated with a more violent drive to incorporate, appropriate, and observe more actively (a tension to which is added the discomfort of "teething" and other changes in the oral machinery); (2) a psychological one: the infant's increasing awareness of himself as a distinct person; and (3) an environmental one: the mother's apparent turning away from the baby toward pursuits which she had given up during late pregnancy and postnatal care. These pursuits include her full return to conjugal intimacy and may soon lead to a new pregnancy.

Where breast feeding lasts into the biting stage (and, generally speaking, this has been the rule) it is now necessary to learn how to continue sucking without biting, so that the mother may not withdraw the nipple in pain or anger. Our clinical work indicates that this point in the individual's early history provides him with some sense of basic loss, leaving the general impression that once upon a time one's unity with a material matrix was destroyed. Weaning, therefore, should not mean sudden loss of the breast and loss of the mother's reassuring presence too, unless, of course, other women can be depended upon to sound and feel much like the mother. A drastic loss of accustomed mother love without proper substitution at this time can lead (under otherwise aggravating conditions) to acute infantile depression (Spitz, 1945) or to a mild but chronic state of mourning which may give a depressive undertone to the whole remainder of life. But even under more favorable circumstances, this stage seems to introduce into the psychic life a sense of division and a dim but universal nostalgia for a lost paradise.

It is against the combination of these impressions of having been deprived, of having been divided, and of having been abandoned, all of which leave a residue of basic mistrust, that basic trust must be established and maintained.[3]

What we here call "trust" coincides with what Therese Benedek has called "confi-

dence." If I prefer the word "trust," it is because there is more naiveté and more mutuality in it: an infant can be said to be trusting, but it would be assuming too much to say that he "has confidence." The general state of trust, furthermore, implies not only that one has learned to rely on the sameness and continuity of the outer providers but also that one may trust oneself and the capacity of one's own organs to cope with urges; that one is able to consider oneself trustworthy enough so that the providers will not need to be on guard or to leave.

In the psychiatric literature we find frequent references to an "oral character," which is a characterological deviation based on the unsolved conflicts of this stage. Wherever oral pessimism becomes dominant and exclusive, infantile fears, such as that of "being left empty," or simply of "being left," and also of being "starved of stimulation," can be discerned in the depressive forms of "being empty" and of "being no good." Such fears, in turn, can give orality that particular avaricious quality which in psychoanalysis is called "oral sadism," that is, a cruel need to get and to take in ways harmful to others. But there is an optimistic oral character, too, one which has learned to make giving and receiving the most important thing in life; and there is "orality" as a normal substratum in all individuals, a lasting residuum of this first period of dependency on powerful providers.

---

an *achievement scale* out of these stages that they blithely omit all the *negative* senses (basic mistrust, etc.) which are and remain the dynamic counterpart of the positive senses throughout life. (See, for example, the "maturation chart" distributed at the National Congress of Parents and Teachers in Omaha, Nebraska [1958], which omits any reference to crises, and otherwise "adapts" the stages presented here.)

What the child acquires at a given stage is a certain *ratio* between the positive and the negative which, if the balance is toward the positive, will help him to meet later crises with a better chance for unimpaired total development. The idea that at any stage a *goodness* is achieved which is impervious to new conflicts within and changes without is a projection on child development of that success ideology which so dangerously pervades our private and public daydreams and can make us inept in the face of a heightened struggle for a meaningful existence in our time.

Only in the light of man's inner division and social antagonism is a belief in his essential resourcefulness and creativity justifiable and productive.

---

[3]One of the chief misuses of the schema presented here is the connotation that the sense of trust (and all the other *positive* senses to be postulated) is an *achievement*, secured once and for all at a given stage. In fact, some writers are so intent on making

It normally expresses itself in our dependencies and nostalgias, and in our all too hopeful and all too hopeless states. The integration of the oral stage with all the following ones results, in adulthood, in a combination of faith and realism.

The pathology and irrationality of oral trends depend entirely on the degree to which they are integrated with the rest of the personality and the degree to which they fit into the general cultural pattern and use approved interpersonal techniques for their expression. Here, as elsewhere, we must therefore consider as a topic for discussion the expression of *infantile urges* in *cultural patterns* which one may (or may not) consider a pathological deviation in the total economic or moral system of a culture or a nation. One could speak, for example, of the invigorating belief in "chance," that traditional prerogative of American trust in one's own resourcefulness and in Fate's store of good intentions. This belief, at times, can be seen to degenerate—in large-scale gambling, or in "taking chances" in the form of an arbitrary and often suicidal provocation of Fate, or in the insistence that one has not only the right to an equal chance but also the privilege of being preferred over all other investors in the same general enterprise. In a similar way all the pleasant reassurances which can be derived (especially in good company) from old and new taste sensations, from inhaling and imbibing, from munching and swallowing and digesting, can turn into mass addictions neither expressive of, nor conducive to, the kind of basic trust which we have in mind.

Here we are obviously touching on phenomena the analysis of which would call for a comprehensive approach both to personality and to culture. This would be true also for an epidemiological approach to the problem of the more or less malignant elaboration of the oral character in "schizoid" characters and the mental diseases seemingly expressive of an underlying weakness in oral reassurance and basic trust. A related problem is the belief (reflected in much of contemporary obstetric and pediatric concern with the methods of child care) that the establishment of a basic sense of trust in earliest childhood makes adult individuals less dependent on mild or malignant forms of addiction, on self-delusion, and on avaricious appropriation. Of this, little is known; and the question remains whether healthy orality makes for a healthy culture or a healthy culture makes for healthy orality—or both.

At any rate, the psychiatrists, obstetricians, pediatricians, and anthropologists, to whom I feel closest, today would agree that the *firm establishment of enduring patterns for the balance of basic trust over basic mistrust* is the first task of the budding personality and therefore first of all a task for maternal care. But it must be said that the *amount of trust* derived from earliest infantile experience does not seem to depend on absolute *quantities of food or demonstrations of love* but rather on the *quality* of the maternal relationship. Mothers create a sense of trust in their children by that kind of administration which in its quality combines sensitive care of the baby's individual needs and a firm sense of personal trustworthiness within the trusted framework of their community's life style. (This forms the basis in the child for a sense of identity which will later combine a sense of being "all right," of being oneself, and of becoming what other people trust one will become.) Parents must not only have certain ways of guiding by prohibition and permission; they must also be able to represent to the child a deep, an almost somatic conviction that there is a meaning to what they are doing. In this sense a traditional system of child care can be said to be a factor making for trust, even where certain items of that tradition, taken singly, may seem irrational or unnecessarily cruel. Here much depends on whether such items are inflicted on the child by the parent in the firm traditional belief that this is the only way to do things or whether the parent misuses his administration of the baby and the child in order to work off anger, alleviate fear, or win an argument, with the child or with somebody else (mother-in-law, doctor, or priest).

In times of change—and what other times are there, in our memory?—one generation differs so much from another that items of tradition often become disturbances. Conflicts between mother's ways and one's own self-made ways, conflicts between the expert's advice and mother's ways, and conflicts between the expert's authority and one's own self-willed ways may disturb a mother's trust in herself. Furthermore, all the mass transformations in American life (immigration, migration, and Americanization; industrialization, urbanization, mechanization, and others) are apt to disturb young mothers in those tasks which are so simple yet so far-reaching. No wonder, then, that the first section of the first chapter of Benjamin Spock's (1945) book is entitled "Trust Yourself." But while it is true that the expert obstetrician and pediatrician can do much to replace the binding power of tradition by giving reassurance and guidance, he does not have the time to become the father-confessor for all the doubts and fears, angers and arguments, which can fill the minds of lonely young parents. Maybe a book like Spock's needs to be read in study groups where the true psychological spirit of the town meeting can be created; that is, where matters are considered to be agreed upon not because somebody said so, but because the free airing of opinions and emotions, of prejudices and of errors has led to a general area of relative consent and of tolerant good will.

This chapter has become unduly long. In regard to the matters discussed here, it is too bad that one must begin with the beginning. We know so little of the beginning, of the deeper strata of the human mind. But since we have already embarked on general observations, a word must be said about one cultural and traditional institution which is deeply related to the matter of trust, namely, religion.

It is not the psychologist's job to decide whether religion should or should not be confessed and practiced in particular words and rituals. Rather the psychological observer must ask whether or not in any area under observation religion and tradition are living psychological forces creating the kind of faith and conviction which permeates a parent's personality and thus reinforces the child's basic trust in the world's trustworthiness. The psychopathologist cannot avoid observing that there are millions of people who cannot really afford to be without religion, and whose pride in not having it is that much whistling in the dark. On the other hand, there are millions who seem to derive faith from other than religious dogmas, that is, from fellowship, productive work, social action, scientific pursuit, and artistic creation. And again, there are millions who profess faith, yet in practice mistrust both life and man. With all of these in mind, it seems worth while to speculate on the fact that religion through the centuries has served to restore a sense of trust at regular intervals in the form of faith while giving tangible form to a sense of evil which it

promises to ban. All religions have in common the periodical childlike surrender to a Provider or providers who dispense earthly fortune as well as spiritual health; the demonstration of one's smallness and dependence through the medium of reduced posture and humble gesture; the admission in prayer and song of misdeeds, of misthoughts, and of evil intentions; the admission of inner division and the consequent appeal for inner unification by divine guidance; the need for clearer self-delineation and self-restriction; and finally, the insight that individual trust must become a common faith, individual mistrust a commonly formulated evil, while the indiividual's need for restoration must become part of the ritual practice of many, and must become a sign of trustworthiness in the community.

Whosoever says he has religion must derive a faith from it which is transmitted to infants in the form of basic trust; whosoever claims that he does not need religion must derive such basic faith from elsewhere.

Autonomy versus Shame and Doubt

A survey of some of the items discussed in Spock's book under the headings "The One-Year-Old" and "Managing Young Children" will enable those of us who, at this time, do not have such inquisitive creatures in our homes to remember our skirmishes, our victories, and our defeats:

> Feeling his oats.
> The passion to explore.
> He gets more dependent and more independent at the same time.
> Arranging the house for a wandering baby.
> Avoiding accidents.
> Now's the time to put poisons out of reach.
> How do you make him leave certain things alone?
> Dropping and throwing things.
> Children learn to control their own aggressive feelings.
> Biting humans.
> Keeping bedtime happy.
> The small child who won't stay in bed at night.

My selection is intended to convey the inventory and range of problems described though I cannot review here either the doctor's excellent advice or his good balance in depicting the remarkable ease and matter-of-factness with which the nursery may be governed at this as at any other stage. Nevertheless, there is an indication of the sinister forces which are leashed and unleashed, especially in the guerilla warfare of unequal wills; for the child is often unequal to his own violent drives, and parent and child unequal to each other.

The over-all significance of this stage lies in the maturation of the muscle system, the consequent ability (and doubly felt inability) to coordinate a number of highly conflicting action patterns such as "holding on" and "letting go," and the enormous value with which the still highly dependent child begins to endow his autonomous will.

Psychoanalysis has enriched our vocabulary with the word "anality" to designate the particular pleasurableness and willfulness which often attach to the eliminative organs at this stage. The whole procedure of evacuating the bowels and the bladder as completely as possible is, of course, enhanced from the beginning by a premium of "feeling good" which says in effect, "well done." This premium, at the beginning of life, must make up for quite frequent discomfort and tension suffered as the bowels learn to do their daily work. Two developments gradually give these anal experiences the necessary volume: the arrival of better formed stool and the general coordination of the muscle system which permits the development of voluntary release, of dropping and throwing away. This new dimension of approach to things, however, is not restricted to the sphincters. A general ability, indeed, a violent need, develops to drop and to throw away and to alternate withholding and expelling at will.

As far as anality proper is concerned, at this point everything depends on whether the cultural environment wants to make something of it. There are cultures where the parents ignore anal behavior and leave it to older children to lead the toddler out to the bushes so that his compliance in this matter may coincide with his wish to imitate the bigger ones. Our Western civilization, and especially certain classes within it, have chosen to take the matter more seriously. It is here that the machine age has added the ideal of a mechanically trained, faultlessly functioning, and always clean, punctual, and deodorized body. In addition it has been more or less consciously assumed that early and

rigorous training is absolutely necessary for the kind of personality which will function efficiently in a mechanized world which says "time is money" and which calls for orderliness, punctuality, and thrift. Indications are that in this, we have gone too far; that we have assumed that a child is an animal which must be broken or a machine which must be set and tuned—while, in fact, human virtues can grow only by steps. At any rate our clinical work suggests that the neurotics of our time include the "over-compulsive" type, who is stingy, retentive, and meticulous in matters of affection, time, and money, as well as in matters concerning his bowels. Also, bowel and bladder training has become the most obviously disturbing item of child training in wide circles of our society.

What, then, makes the anal problem potentially important and difficult?

The anal zone lends itself more than any other to the expression of stubborn insistence on conflicting impulses because, for one thing, it is the model zone for two contradictory modes which must become alternating; namely, *retention* and *elimination*. Futhermore, the sphincters are only part of the muscle system with its general ambiguity of rigidity and relaxation, of flexion and extension. This whole stage, then, becomes a battle for *autonomy*. For as he gets ready to stand on his feet more firmly, the infant delineates his world as "I" and "you," "me" and "mine." Every mother knows how astonishingly pliable a child may be at this stage, if and when he has made the decision that he *wants* to do what he is supposed to do. It is impossible, however, to find a reliable formula for making him want to do just that. Every mother knows how lovingly a child at this stage will snuggle and how ruthlessly he will suddenly try to push the adult away. At the same time the child is apt both to hoard things and to discard them, to cling to possessions and to throw them out of the windows of houses and vehicles. All of these seemingly contradictory tendencies, then, we include under the formula of the retentive-eliminative modes.

The matter of mutual regulation between adult and child now faces its severest test. If outer control by too rigid or too early training insists on robbing the child of his attempt *gradually* to control his bowels and other functions willingly and by his free choice, he will again be faced with a double rebellion and a double defeat. Powerless in his own body (sometimes afraid of his bowels) and powerless outside, he will again be forced to seek satisfaction and control either by regression or by fake progression. In other words, he will return to an earlier, oral control, that is, by sucking his thumb and becoming whiny and demanding; or he will become hostile and willful, often using his feces (and, later, dirty words) as ammunition; or he will pretend an autonomy and an ability to do without anybody to lean on which he has by no means really gained.

This stage, therefore, becomes decisive for the ratio between love and hate, for that between cooperation and willfulness, and for that between the freedom of self-expression and its suppression. From a sense of *self-control without loss of self-esteem* comes a lasting sense of autonomy and pride; from a sense of muscular and anal impotence, of loss of self-control, and of parental overcontrol comes a lasting sense of doubt and shame.

To develop autonomy, a firmly developed and a convincingly continued stage of early trust is necessary. The infant must come to feel that basic faith in himself and in the world (which is the lasting treasure saved from the conflicts of the oral stage) will not be jeopardized by this sudden violent wish to have a choice, to appropriate demandingly, and to eliminate stubbornly. *Firmness* must protect him against the potential anarchy of his as yet untrained sense of discrimination, his inability to hold on and to let go with circumspection. Yet his environment must back him up in his wish to "stand on his own feet" lest he be overcome by that sense of having exposed himself prematurely and foolishly which we call shame, or that secondary mistrust, that "doubletake," which we call doubt.

Shame is an infantile emotion insufficiently studied. Shame supposes that one is completely exposed and conscious of being looked at—in a word, self-conscious. One is visible and not ready to be visible; that is why we dream of shame as a situation in which we are stared at in a condition of incomplete dress, in night attire, "with one's pants down." Shame is early expressed in an impulse to bury one's face, or to sink, right then and there, into the ground. This potentiality is abundantly utilized in the educational method of "shaming" used so exclusively by some primitive peoples, where it supplants the often more destructive sense of guilt to be discussed later. The destructiveness of shaming is balanced in some civilizations by devices for *"saving face."* Shaming exploits an increasing sense of being small, which paradoxically develops as the child stands up and as his awareness permits him to note the relative measures of size and power.

Too much shaming does not result in a sense of propriety but in a secret determination to try to get away with things when unseen, if, indeed, it does not result in deliberate *shamelessness*. There is an impressive American ballad in which a murderer to be hanged on the gallows before the eyes of the community, instead of feeling appropriately afraid or ashamed, begins to berate the onlookers, ending every salvo of defiance with the words, "God damn your eyes." Many a small child, when shamed beyond endurance, may be in a mood (although not in possession of either the courage or the words) to express defiance in similar terms. What I mean by this sinister reference is that there is a limit to a child's and an adult's individual endurance in the face of demands which force him to consider himself, his body, his needs, and his wishes as evil and dirty, and to believe in the infallibility of those who pass such judgment. Occasionally he may be apt to turn things around, to become secretly oblivious to the opinion of others, and to consider as evil only the fact that they exist: his chance will come when they are gone, or when he can leave them.

Many a defiant child, many a young criminal, is of such makeup, and deserves at least an investigation into the conditions which caused him to become that way.

To repeat: muscular maturation sets the stage for experimentation with two simultaneous sets of social modalities—*holding on* and *letting go.* As is the case with all of these modalities, their basic conflicts can lead in the end either to hostile or to benign expectations and attitudes. Thus, "to hold" can become a destructive and cruel retaining or restraining, and it can become a pattern of care: "to have and to hold." To "let go," too, can turn into an inimical letting loose of destructive forces, or it can become a relaxed "to let pass" and "to let be." Culturally speaking, these modalities are neither good nor bad; their value depends on whether their hostile implications are turned against enemy or fellow man—or against the self.

The last-named danger is the one best known to psychiatry. Denied the gradual and well-guided experience of the autonomy of free choice, or weakened by an initial loss of trust, the sensitive child may turn against himself all his urge to discriminate and to manipulate. He will *overmanipulate himself*, he will develop a *precocious conscience*. Instead of taking possession of things in order to test them by repetitive play, he will become obsessed by his own repetitiveness; he will want to have everything "just so," and only in a given sequence and tempo. By such infantile obsessiveness, by dawdling, for example, or by becoming a stickler for certain rituals, the child then learns to gain power over his parents and nurses in areas where he could not find large scale mutual regulation with them. Such hollow victory, then, is the infantile model for a compulsion neurosis. As for the consequences of this for adult character, they can be observed in the classical compulsive character which we have mentioned. We must add to this the character dominated by the wish to "get away with" things—yet unable to get away even with the wish. For while he learns evasion from others, his precocious conscience does not let him really get away with anything, and he goes through life habitually ashamed, apologetic, and afraid to be seen; or else, in a manner which we call "overcompensatory," he evinces a defiant kind of autonomy. Real inner autonomy, however, is not carried on the sleeve.

But it is time to return from these considerations of the abnormal to a study of the headings which transmit the practical and benevolent advice of the children's doctor. They all add up to this: be firm and tolerant with the child at this stage, and he will be firm and tolerant with himself. He will feel pride in being an autonomous person; he will grant autonomy to others; and now and again he will even let himself get away with something.

Why, then, if we know how, do we not tell parents in detail what to do to develop this intrinsic, this genuine autonomy? The answer is: because when it comes to human values, nobody knows how to fabricate or manage the fabrication of the genuine article. My own field, psychoanalysis, having studied particularly the excessive increase of guilt feelings beyond any normal rhyme or reason, and the consequent excessive estrangement of the child from his own body, attempted at least to formulate what should *not* be done to children. These formulations, however, often aroused superstitious inhibitions in those who

were inclined to make anxious rules out of vague warnings. Actually, we are learning only gradually what exactly *not* to do with *what kind* of children at *what age*.

People all over the world seem convinced that to make the right (meaning *their*) kind of human being, one must consistently introduce the senses of shame, doubt, guilt, and fear into a child's life. Only the patterns vary. Some cultures begin to restrict early in life, some late, some abruptly, others more gradually. Until enough comparative observations are available, we are apt to add further superstitions, merely because of our wish to *avoid* certain pathological conditions, without even knowing definitely all the factors which are responsible for these conditions. So we say: Don't wean too early; don't train too early. But what is too early and what is too late seem to depend not only on the pathologies we wish to avoid but also on the values we wish to create, or, to put it more honestly, on the values we wish to live by. For no matter what we do in detail, the child will feel primarily what we live by, what makes us loving, cooperative, and firm beings, and what makes us hateful, anxious, and divided in ourselves.

There are of course a few matters of necessary avoidance which become clear from our basic epigenetic point of view. It will be remembered that every new development carries with it its own specific vulnerability. For example, at around eight months the child seems to be somehow more aware, as it were, of his *separateness;* this prepares him for the impending sense of autonomy. At the same time he becomes more cognizant of his mother's features and presence and of the strangeness of others. Sudden or prolonged separation from his mother at that time apparently can cause a sensitive child to experience an aggravation of the experience of division and abandonment, arousing violent anxiety and withdrawal. Again, in the first quarter of the second year, if everything has gone well, the infant just begins to become aware of the autonomy discussed in this chapter. The introduction of bowel training at this time may cause him to resist with all his strength and determination, because he seems to feel that his budding will is being "broken." To avoid this feeling is certainly more important than to insist on his being trained just then because there is a time for the stubborn ascendancy of autonomy and there is a time for the partial sacrifice of secure autonomy, but obviously the time for a meaningful sacrifice is *after* one has acquired and reinforced a core of autonomy and has also acquired more insight.

The more exact localization in time of the most critical growth periods of the personality is becoming established only now. Often, the unavoidable cause of trouble is not one event but the coincidence in time of a number of changes which upset the child's orientation. He may have been involved in a special growth period when the family moved to a new place. Perhaps he was forced to conceive of his first words all over again when the grandmother who had taught him these words suddenly died. A trip on the part of the mother may have exhausted her because she happened to be pregnant at the time, and thus unable, on returning, to make proper amends. Given the right spirit toward life and its vicissitudes, a parent can usually handle such matters, if necessary with the help of the pediatrician or guidance expert. The expert's job, however, should be (to quote Frank Fremont-Smith) *"to set the frame of reference within which choice is permissible and desirable."* For in the last analysis (as comparative studies in child training have convinced many of us) the kind and degree of a sense of autonomy which parents are able to grant their small children depends on the dignity and the sense of personal independence which they derive from their own lives. Again, just as the sense of trust is a reflection of the parent's sturdy and realistic faith, so is the sense of autonomy a reflection of the parents' dignity as individuals.

As was the case with "oral" personality, the compulsive personality (often referred to as "anal" in the psychiatric literature) has its normal aspects and its abnormal exaggerations. If well integrated with other compensatory traits, some compulsiveness is useful in the administration of matters in which order, punctuality, and cleanliness are essential. The question is always whether we remain the masters of the rules by which we want to make things more manageable (not more complicated) or whether the rules master the ruler. But it often happens, in the individual as well as in group life, that the letter of the rules kills the spirit which created them.

We have related basic trust to the institution of religion. The basic need of the individual for a delineation of his *autonomy* in the adult order of things seems, in turn, to be taken care of by the *principle of "law and order,"* which in daily life as well as in the high courts of law apportions to each his privileges and his limitations, his obligations and his rights. The sense of autonomy which arises, or should arise, in the second stage of childhood, is fostered by a handling of the small individual which expresses a sense of rightful dignity and lawful independence on the part of the parents and which gives him the confident expectation that the kind of autonomy fostered in childhood will not be frustrated later. This, in turn, necessitates a relationship of parent to parent, of parent to employer, and of parent to government which reaffirms the parent's essential dignity within the hierarchy of social positions. It is important to dwell on this point because much of the shame and doubt, much of the indignity and uncertainty which is aroused in children is a consequence of the parents' frustrations in marriage, in work, and in citizenship. Thus, the sense of autonomy in the child (a sense richly fostered in American childhood in general) must be backed up by the preservation in economic and political life of a high sense of autonomy and of self-reliance.

Social organization assigns with the power of government certain privileges of leadership and certain obligations of conduct; while it imposes on the ruled certain obligations of compliance and certain privileges of remaining autonomous and self-determining. Where this whole matter becomes blurred, however, the matter of individual autonomy becomes an issue of mental health, as well as one of economic reorientation. Where large numbers of people have been prepared in childhood to expect from life a high degree of personal autonomy, pride, and opportunity, and then in later life find themselves ruled by superhuman organizations and machinery too intricate to understand, the result may be deep chronic disappointment not conducive to healthy personalities willing to grant each other a measure of autonomy. All great nations (and all the small ones) are increasingly challenged by the complication and mechanization of modern life, and are being enveloped in the problems of the organization of larger units, larger spheres, and larger interdependencies which by necessity redefine the role of the individual. It is important for the spirit of this country, as it is for that of the world, that an increased consciousness of equality and individuality may grow out of the necessity for divided function within the increasing complexity of organization; for otherwise a number of fears are aroused which find expression in anxiety on a large scale, often individually slight and hardly conscious, but nevertheless strangely upsetting to people who seemingly, on the surface, have what they want or what they seem to have a right to expect. Besides irrational fears of losing one's autonomy—"don't fence me in"—there are fears of being sabotaged in one's free will by inner enemies; of being restricted and constricted in one's autonomous initiative; and, paradoxically enough, at the same time of not being completely controlled enough, of not being told what to do. While many such fears are, of course, based on the realistic appraisal of dangers inherent in complex social organizations and in the struggle for power, safety, and security, they seem to contribute to psychoneurotic and psychosomatic disturbances on the one hand, and, on the other, to the easy acceptance of slogans which seem to promise alleviation of conditions by excessive and irrational conformity.

Initiative versus Guilt

Having found a firm solution of his problem of autonomy, the child of four and five is faced with the next step—and with the next crisis. Being firmly convinced that he *is* a person, the child must now find out *what kind* of a person he is going to be. And here he hitches his wagon to nothing less than a star: he wants to be like his parents, who to him appear very powerful and very beautiful, although quite unreasonably dangerous. He "identifies with them," he plays with the idea of how it would be to be them. Three strong developments help at this stage, yet also serve to bring the child closer to his crisis: (1) he learns to *move around* more freely and more violently and therefore establishes a wider and, so it seems to him, an unlimited radius of goals; (2) his sense of *language* becomes perfected to the point where he understands and can ask about many things just enough to misunderstand them thoroughly; and (3) both language and locomotion permit him to expand his *imagination* over so many things that he cannot avoid frightening himself with what he himself has dreamed and thought up. Nevertheless, out of all this he must emerge with a sense of *unbroken initiative* as a basis for a high and yet realistic sense of ambition and independence.

One may ask here—one may, indeed—what are the criteria for such an unbroken sense of initiative? The criteria for all the senses discussed here are the same: a crisis, beset with fears, or at least a general anxiousness or tension, seems to be resolved, in that the child suddenly seems to "grow together" both psychologically and physically. He seems to be "more himself," more loving and relaxed and brighter in his judgment (such as it is at this stage). Most of all, he seems to be, as it were, self-activated; he is in the free possession of a certain surplus of energy which permits him to forget failures quickly and to approach what seems desirable (even if it also seems dangerous) with undiminished and better aimed effort. In this way the child and his parents face the next crisis much better prepared.

We are now approaching the end of the third year, when walking is getting to be a thing of ease, or vigor. The books tell us that a child "can walk" much before this; but from the point of view of personality development he cannot really walk as long as he is only able to accomplish the feat more or less well, with more or fewer props, for short spans of time. He has made walking and running an item in his sphere of mastery when gravity is felt to be *within*, when he can forget that he is doing the walking and instead can find out what he can do *with it*. Only then do his legs become an unconscious part of him instead of being an external and still unreliable ambulatory appendix. Only then will he find out with advantage what he now *may* do, along with what he *can* do.

To look back: the first way-station was prone relaxation. The trust based on the experience that the basic mechanisms of breathing, digesting, sleeping, and so forth have a consistent and familiar relation to the foods and comforts offered gives zest to the developing ability to raise oneself to a sitting and then to a standing position. The second way-station (accomplished only toward the end of the second year) is that of being able to sit not only securely but, as it were, untiringly, a feat which permits the muscle system gradually to be used for finer discrimination and for more autonomous ways of selecting and discarding, of piling things up—and of throwing them away with a bang.

The third way-station finds the child able

to move independently and vigorously. He is ready to visualize himself as being as big as the perambulating grown-ups. He begins to make comparisons and is apt to develop untiring curiousity about differences in sizes in general, and sexual differences in particular. He tries to comprehend possible future roles, or at any rate to understand what roles are worth imitating. More immediately, he can now associate with those of his own age. Under the guidance of older children or special women guardians, he gradually enters into the infantile politics of nursery school, street corner, and barnyard. His learning now is eminently intrusive and vigorous: it leads away from his own limitations and into future possibilities.

The *intrusive mode*, dominating much of the behavior of this stage, characterizes a variety of configurationally "similar" activities and fantasies. These include the intrusion into other bodies by physical attack; the intrusion into other people's ears and minds by aggressive talking; the intrusion into space by vigorous locomotion; the intrusion into the unknown by consuming curiosity.

This is also the stage of infantile sexual curiosity, genital excitability, and occasional preoccupation and overconcern with sexual matters. This "genitality" is, of course, rudimentary, a mere promise of things to come; often it is not particularly noticeable as such. If not specifically provoked into precocious manifestation by especially strict and pointed prohibitions ("if you touch it, the doctor will cut it off") or special customs (such as sex play in groups), it is apt to lead to no more than a series of fascinating experiences which soon become frightening and pointless enough to be repressed. This leads to the ascendancy of that human specialty which Freud called the "latency" period, that is, the long delay separating infantile sexuality (which in animals is followed by maturity) and physical sexual maturation.

The sexual orientation of the boy is focused on the phallus and its sensations, purposes, and meanings. While erections undoubtedly occur earlier (either reflexively or in response to things and people who make the child feel intensively), a focused interest may now develop in the genitalia of both sexes, as well as an urge to perform playful sex acts, or at least acts of sexual investigation. The increased locomotor mastery and the pride in being big now and *almost* as good as father and mother receives its severest setback in the clear fact that in the genital sphere one is vastly inferior; furthermore, it receives an additional setback in the fact that not even in the distant future is one ever going to be father in sexual relationship to mother, or mother in sexual relationship to father. The very deep emotional consequences of this insight and the magic fears associated with it make up what Freud has called the oedipus complex.

Psychoanalysis verifies the simple conclusion that boys attach their first genital affection to the maternal adults who have otherwise given comfort to their bodies and that they develop their first sexual rivalry against the persons who are the sexual owners of those maternal persons. The little girl, in turn, becomes attached to her father and other important men and jealous of her mother, a development which may cause her much anxiety, for it seems to block her retreat to that self-same mother, while it makes the mother's disapproval ever so much more magically dangerous because unconsciously "deserved."

Girls often have a difficult time at this stage, because they observe sooner or later that, although their locomotor, mental, and social intrusiveness is increased equally with, and is as adequate as, that of the boys, thus permitting them to become perfect tomboys, they lack one item: the penis; and with it, important prerogatives in some cultures and classes. While the boy has this visible, erectable, and comprehensible organ to which he can attach dreams of adult bigness, the girl's clitoris only poorly sustains dreams of sexual equality. She does not even have breasts as analogously tangible tokens of her future, her maternal drives are relegated to play fantasy or baby tending. On the other hand, where mothers dominate households, the boy, in turn, can develop a sense of inadequacy because he learns at this stage that while a boy can do well in play and work, he will never boss the house, the mother, and the older sisters. His mother and sisters, in fact, might get even with him for vast doubts in themselves by making him feel that a boy (with his snails and puppy-dog tails) is really an inferior if not a repulsive creature. Both the girl and the boy are now extraordinarily appreciative of any convincing promise of the fact that someday they will be as good as father or mother—perhaps better; and they are grateful for sexual enlightenment, a little at a time, and patiently repeated at intervals. Where the necessities of economic life and the simplicity of its social plan make the male and female roles and their specific powers and rewards comprehensible, the early misgivings about sexual differences are, of course, more easily integrated in the culture's design for the differentiation of sexual roles.

This stage adds to the inventory of basic social modalities in both sexes that of "making" in the older and today slangier sense of "being on the make." There is no simpler, stronger word to match the social modalities previously enumerated. The word suggests enjoyment of competition, insistence on goal, pleasure of conquest. In the boy the emphasis remains on "making" by head-on attack; in the girl it may change to "making" by making herself attractive and endearing. The child thus develops the prerequisites for *masculine* and *feminine initiative*, that is, for the selection of social goals and perseverance in approaching them. Thus the stage is all set for entrance into life, except that life must first be school life. The child here must repress or forget many of his fondest hopes and most energetic wishes, while his exuberant imagination is tamed and he learns the necessary self-restraint and the necessary interest in impersonal things—even the three R's. This often demands a change of personality that is sometimes too drastic for the good of the child. This change is not only a result of education but also of an inner reorientation, and it is based on a biological fact (the delay of sexual maturation) and a psychological one (the repression of childhood wishes). For those sinister oedipal wishes (so simply and so trustingly expressed in the boy's assurance that he will marry mother and make her proud of him and in the girl's that she will marry father and take much better care of him), in consequence of vastly increased imagination and, as it were, the intoxication of increased locomotor powers, seem to lead to secret fantasies of terrifying proportions. The consequence is a deep sense of *guilt*—a strange sense, for it forever seems to imply that the individual has committed crimes and deeds which, after all, were not only not committed but also would have been biologically quite impossible.

While the struggle for autonomy at its worst concentrated on keeping rivals out, and was therefore more an expression of *jealous rage* most often directed against encroachments by *younger* siblings, initiative brings with it *anticipatory rivalry* with those who were there first and who may therefore occupy with their superior equipment the field toward which one's initiative is directed. Jealousy and rivalry, those often embittered and yet essentially futile attempts at demarcating a sphere of unquestioned privilege, now come to a climax in a final contest for a favored position with one of the parents; the inevitable and necessary failure leads to guilt and anxiety. The child indulges in fantasies of being a giant and a tiger, but in his dreams he runs in terror for dear life. This, then, is the stage of fear for life and limb, including the fear of losing (or on the part of the girl the conviction that she may have lost) the male genital as punishment for the fantasies attached to infantile genital excitement.

All of this may seem strange to readers who have only seen the sunnier side of childhood and have not recognized the potential powerhouse of destructive drives which can be aroused and temporarily buried at this stage, only to contribute later to the inner arsenal of a destructiveness so ready to be used when opportunity provokes it. By using the words "potential," "provoke," and "opportunity," I mean to emphasize that there is little in these inner developments which cannot be harnessed to constructive and peaceful initiative if only we learn to understand the conflicts and anxieties of childhood and the importance of childhood for mankind. But if we should choose to overlook or belittle the phenomena of childhood, or to regard them as "cute" (even as the individual forgets the best and the worst dreams of his childhood), we shall forever overlook one of the eternal sources of human anxiety and strife.

It is at this stage of initiative that the great governor of initiative, namely, *conscience*, becomes firmly established. Only as a dependent does man develop conscience, that dependence on himself which makes him, in turn, dependable; and only when thoroughly dependable with regard to a number of fundamental values can he become independent and teach and develop tradition.

The child now feels not only ashamed when found out but also afraid of being found out. He now hears, as it were, God's voice without seeing God. Moreover, he begins automatically to feel guilty even for mere thoughts and for deeds which nobody has watched. This is the cornerstone of morality in the individual sense. But from the point of view of mental health, we must point out that if this great achievement is overburdened by all too eager adults, it can be bad for the spirit and for morality itself. For the conscience of the child *can* be primitive, cruel, and uncompromising, as may be observed in instances where children learn to constrict themselves to the point of over-all inhibition; where they develop an obedience more literal than the one the parent wishes to exact; or where they develop deep regressions and lasting resentments because the parents themselves do not seem to live up to the new conscience which they have fostered in the child. One of the deepest conflicts in life is the hate for a parent who served as the model and the executor of the conscience but who (in some form) was found trying to "get away with" the very transgressions which the child can no longer tolerate in himself. These transgressions often are the natural outcome of the existing inequality between parent and child. Often, however, they represent a thoughtless exploitation of such inequality; with the result that the child comes to feel that the whole matter is not one of universal goodness but of arbitrary power. The suspiciousness and evasiveness which is thus mixed in with the all-or-nothing quality of the superego, that organ of tradition, makes moralistic man a great potential danger to himself and to his fellow men. It is as if morality, to him, became synonymous with vindictiveness and with the suppression of others.

It is necessary to point to the source of such moralism (not to be mistaken for morality) in the child of this age because infantile moralism is a stage to be lived through and worked through. The consequences of the guilt aroused at this stage (guilt expressed in a deep-seated conviction that the child as such, or drive as such, is essentially bad) often do not show until much later, when conflicts over initiative may find expression in a self-restriction which keeps an individual from living up to his inner capacities or to the powers of his imagination and feeling (if not in relative sexual impotence or frigidity). All of this, of course, may in turn be "overcompensated" in a great show of tireless initiative, in a quality of "go-at-itiveness" at all cost. Many adults feel that their worth as people consists entirely in *what they are doing*, or rather in *what they are going to do next*, and not in what they are, as individuals. The strain consequently developed in their bodies, which are always "on the go," with the engine racing,

even at moments of rest, is a powerful contribution to the much-discussed psychosomatic diseases of our time.

Pathology, however, is only the sign that valuable human resources are being neglected, that they have been neglected first of all in childhood. The problem is again one of mutual regulation. Where the child, now so ready to overrestrict himself, can gradually develop a sense of responsibility, where he can gain some simple feeling for the institutions, functions, and roles which will permit him to anticipate his responsible participation as an adult, he will soon find pleasurable accomplishment in wielding miniature tools and weapons, in manipulating meaningful toys, and in taking care of himself—and of younger children.

For such is the wisdom of the ground plan that at no time is the individual more ready to learn quickly and avidly, to become big in the sense of sharing obligation, discipline, and performance rather than power, in the sense of *making things, instead of "making" people,* than during this period of his development. He is also eager and able to *make things together,* to combine with other children for the purpose of constructing and planning, instead of trying to boss and coerce them; and he is able and willing to profit fully by the association with teachers and ideal prototypes.

Parents often do not realize why some children suddenly seem to think less of them and seem to attach themselves to teachers, to the parents of other children, or to people representing occupations which the child can grasp: firemen and policemen, gardeners and plumbers. The point is that children do not wish to be reminded of the principal inequality with the parent of the same sex. They remain identified with this same parent; but for the present they look for opportunities where superficial identification seems to promise a field of initiative without too much conflict or guilt.

Often, however, (and this seems more typical of the American home than of any other in the world), the child can be guided by the parent himself into a second, a more realistic identification based on the spirit of equality experienced in doing things together. In connection with comprehensible technical tasks, a companionship may develop between father and son, an experience of essential *equality in worth,* in spite of the *inequality in time schedules.* Such companionship is a lasting treasure not only for parent and child but for mankind, which so sorely needs an alleviation of all those hidden hatreds which stem from the exploitation of weakness because of mere size or schedule.

Only a combination of early prevention and alleviation of hatred and guilt in the growing being, and the consequent handling of hatred in the free collaboration of people who feel *equal in worth although different in kind or function or age*, permits a peaceful cultivation of initiative, a truly free sense of enterprise. And the word "enterprise" was deliberately chosen. For a comparative view of child training suggests that it is the prevalent economic ideal, or some of its modifications, which is transmitted to the child at the time when, in identification with his parent, he applies the dreams of early childhood to the as yet dim goals of an active adult life.

Industry versus Inferiority

One might say that personality at the first stage crystallizes around the conviction "I am what I am given," and that of the second, "I am what I will." The third can be characterized by "I am what I can imagine I will be." We must now approach the fourth: "I am what I learn." The child now wants to be shown how to get busy with something and how to be busy with others.

This trend, too, starts much earlier, especially in some children. They want to watch how things are done and to try doing them. If they are lucky they live near barnyards or on streets around busy people and around many other children of all ages, so that they can watch and try, observe and participate as their capacities and their initiative grow in tentative spurts. But now it is time to *go to school*. In all cultures, at this stage, children receive some systematic instruction, although it is by no means always in the kind of school which literate people must organize around teachers who have learned how to teach literacy. In preliterate people much is learned from adults who become teachers by acclamation rather than by appointment; and very much is learned from older children. What is learned in more primitive surroundings is related to the basic skills of *technology* which are developed as the child gets ready to handle the utensils, the tools, and the weapons used by

the big people: he enters the technology of his tribe very gradually but also very directly. More literate people, with more specialized careers, must prepare the child by teaching him things which first of all make him literate. He is then given the widest possible basic education for the greatest number of possible careers. The greater the specialization, the more indistinct the goal of initiative becomes; and the more complicated the social reality, the vaguer the father's and mother's role in it. Between childhood and adulthood, then, our children go to school; and school seems to be a world all by itself, with its own goals and limitations, its achievements and disappointments.

Grammar-school education has swung back and forth between the extreme of making early school life an extension of grim adulthood by emphasizing self-restraint and a strict sense of duty in doing what one is *told* to do, and the other extreme of making it an extension of the natural tendency in childhood to find out by playing, to learn what one must do by doing steps which one *likes* to do. Both methods work for some children at times but not for all children at all times. The first trend, if carried to the extreme, exploits a tendency on the part of the preschool and grammar-school child to become entirely dependent on prescribed duties. He thus learns much that is absolutely necessary and he develops an unshakable sense of duty; but he may never unlearn again an unnecessary and costly self-restraint with which he may later make his own life and other people's lives miserable, and in fact spoil his own children's natural desire to learn and to work. The second trend, when carried to an extreme, leads not only to the well-known popular objection that children do not learn anything any more but also to such feelings in children as are expressed in the by now famous remark of a metropolitan child who apprehensively asked one morning: "Teacher, *must* we do today what we *want* to do?" Nothing could better express the fact that children at this age *do* like to be mildly but firmly coerced into the adventure of finding out that one can learn to accomplish things which one would never have thought of by oneself, things which owe their attractiveness to the very fact that they are *not* the product of play and fantasy but the product of reality, practicality, and logic; things which thus provide a token sense of participation in the real world of adults. In discussions of this kind it is common to say that one must steer a middle course between play and work, between childhood and adulthood, between old-fashioned and progressive education. It is always easy (and it seems entirely satisfactory to one's critics) to say that one plans to steer a middle course, but in practice it often leads to a course charted by avoidances rather than by zestful goals. Instead of pursuing, then, a course which merely avoids the extremes of easy play or hard work, it may be worthwhile to consider what play is and what work is, and then learn to dose and alternate each in such a way that *play is play and work is work*. Let us review briefly what play may mean at various stages of childhood and adulthood.

The adult plays for purposes of recreation. He steps out of his reality into imaginary realities for which he has made up arbitrary but nonetheless binding rules. But an adult rarely gets away with being a playboy. Only he who works shall play—if, indeed, he can relax his competitiveness.

The playing child, then, poses a problem: whoever does not work shall not play. Therefore, to be tolerant of the child's play the adult must invent theories which show either that childhood play is really the child's work or that it does not count. The most popular theory, and the easiest on the observer, is that the child is nobody yet and that the nonsense of his play reflects it. According to Spencer, play uses up surplus energy in the young of a number of mammalians who do not need to feed or protect themselves because their parents do it for them. Others say that play is either preparation for the future or a method of working off past emotion, a means of finding imaginary relief for past frustrations.

It is true that the content of the individual play often proves to be the infantile way of thinking over difficult experiences and of *restoring a sense of mastery*, comparable to the way in which we repeat, in ruminations and in endless talk, in daydreams and in dreams during sleep, experiences that have been too much for us. This is the rationale for play observation, play diagnosis, and play therapy. In watching a child play, the trained observer can get an impression of what it is the child is "thinking over," and what faulty logic, what emotional dead end he may be caught in. As a diagnostic tool such observation has become indispensable.

The small world of manageable toys is a harbor which the child establishes, returning to it when he needs to overhaul his ego. But the thing-world has its own laws: it may resist rearrangement or it may simply break to pieces; it may prove to belong to somebody else and be subject to confiscation by superiors. Thus, play may seduce the child into an unguarded expression of dangerous themes and attitudes which arouse anxiety and lead to sudden *disruption of play*. This is the counterpart, in waking life, of the anxiety dream: it can keep children from trying to play just as the fear of night terror can keep them from going to sleep. If thus frightened or disappointed, the child may regress into daydreaming, thumb sucking, masturbating. On the other hand, if the first use of the thing-world is successful and guided properly, the *pleasure of mastering toy things* becomes associated with the *mastery of the conflicts* which were projected on them and with the *prestige* gained through such mastery.

Finally, at nursery-school age playfulness reaches into the world *shared with others*. At the first these others are treated as things; they are inspected, run into, or forced to "be horsie." Learning is necessary in order to discover what potential play content can be admitted only to fantasy or only to play by and with oneself; what content can be successfully represented only in the world of toys and small things; and what content can be shared with others and even forced upon them.

What is infantile play, then? We saw that it is not the equivalent of adult play, that it is not recreation. The playing adult steps sideward into another, an artificial reality; the playing child advances forward to new stages of *real mastery*. This new mastery is not restricted to the technical mastery of toys and *things;* it also includes an infantile way of mastering *experience* by meditating, experimenting, planning, and sharing.

While all children at times need to be left alone in solitary play (or later in the company of books and radio, motion pictures and video, all of which, like the fairy tales of old, at least *sometimes* seem to convey what fits the needs of the infantile mind), and while all children need their hours and days of make-believe in games, they all, sooner or later, become dissatisfied and disgruntled without a sense of being useful, without a sense of being able to make things and make them well and even perfectly: this is what I call the *sense of industry*. Without this, the best entertained child soon acts exploited. It is as if he knows and his society knows that now that he is psychologically already a rudimentary parent, he must begin to be somewhat of a worker and potential provider before becoming a biological parent. With the oncoming latency period, then, the normally advanced child forgets, or rather "sublimates" (that is, applies to more useful pursuits and approved goals) the necessity of "making" people by direct attack or the desire to become father or mother in a hurry; he now learns to win recognition by *producing things*. He develops industry, that is, he adjusts himself to the inorganic laws of the tool world. He can become an eager and absorbed unit of a productive situation. To bring a productive situation to completion is an aim which gradually supersedes the whims and wishes of his idiosyncratic drives and personal disappointments. As he once untiringly strove to walk well, and to throw things away well, he now wants to make things well. He develops the pleasure of *work completion* by steady attention and persevering diligence.

The danger at this stage is the development of a sense of *inadequacy and inferiority*. This may be caused by an insufficient solution of the preceding conflict: he may still want his mummy more than knowledge; he may still rather be the baby at home than the big child in school; he still compares himself with his father, and the comparison arouses a sense of guilt as well as a sense of anatomical inferiority. Family life (small family) may not have prepared him for school life, or school life may fail to sustain the promises of earlier stages in that nothing that he has learned to do well already seems to count one bit with the teacher. And then, again, he may be potentially able to excel in ways which are dormant and which, if not evoked now, may develop late or never.

Good teachers, healthy teachers, relaxed teachers, teachers who feel trusted and respected by the community, understand all this and can guide it. They know how to alternate play and work, games and study. They know how to recognize special efforts, how to encourage special gifts. They also know how to give a child time, and how to handle those children to whom school, for a while, is not important and rather a matter to endure than to enjoy; or the child to whom, for a while,

other children are much more important than the teacher.

Good parents, healthy parents, relaxed parents feel a need to make their children trust their teachers, and therefore to have teachers who can be trusted. It is not my job here to discuss teacher selection, teacher training, and the status and payment of teachers in their communities—all of which is of direct importance for the development and the maintenance of children of a *sense of industry* and a positive identification with those who *know* things and know how to *do* things. Again and again I have observed in the lives of especially gifted and inspired people that one teacher, somewhere, was able to kindle the flame of hidden talent.

The fact that the majority of teachers in the elementary school are women must be considered here in passing, because it often leads to a conflict with the "ordinary" boy's masculine identification, as if knowledge were feminine, action masculine. Both boys and girls are apt to agree with Bernard Shaw's statement that those who can, do, while those who cannot, teach. The selection and training of teachers, then, is vital for the avoidance of the dangers which can befall the individual at this stage. There is, first, the above-mentioned sense of inferiority, the feeling that one will never be any good—a problem which calls for the type of teacher who knows how to emphasize what a child *can* do, and who knows a psychiatric problem when she sees one. Second, there is the danger of the child's identifying too strenuously with a too virtuous teacher or becoming the teacher's pet. What we shall presently refer to as his sense of identity can remain prematurely fixed on being nothing but a good little worker or a good little helper, which may not be all he *could* be. Third, there is the danger (probably the most common one) that throughout the long years of going to school he will never acquire the enjoyment of work and the pride of doing at least one kind of thing well. This is particularly of concern in relation to that part of the nation who do not complete what schooling is at their disposal. It is always easy to say that they are born that way; that there must be less educated people as background for the superior ones; that the market needs and even fosters such people for its many simple and unskilled tasks. But from the point of the healthy personality (which, as we proceed, must now include the aspect of playing a constructive role in a healthy society), we must consider those who have had just enough schooling to appreciate what more fortunate people are learning to do but who, for one reason or another, have lacked inner or outer support of their stick-to-itiveness.

It will have been noted that, regarding the period of a developing sense of industry, I have referred to *outer hindrances* but not to any crisis (except a deferred inferiority crisis) coming from the inventory of basic human drives. This stage differs from the others in that it does not consist of a swing from a violent inner upheaval to a new mastery. The reason why Freud called it the latency stage is that violent drives are normally dormant at that time. But it is only a lull before the storm of puberty.

On the other hand, this is socially a most decisive stage: since industry involves doing things beside and with others, a first sense of *division of labor* and of *equality of opportunity* develops at this time. When a child begins to feel that it is the color of his skin, the background of his parents, or the cost of his clothes rather than his wish and his will to learn which will decide his social worth, lasting harm may ensue for the *sense of identity*, to which we must now turn.

Identity versus Identity Diffusion

With the establishment of a good relationship to the world of skills and to those who teach and share the new skills, childhood proper comes to an end. Youth begins. But in puberty and adolescence all sameness and continuities relied on earlier are questioned again because of a rapidity of body growth which equals that of early childhood and because of the entirely new addition of physical genital maturity. The growing and developing young people, faced with this physiological revolution within them, are now primarily concerned with attempts at consolidating their social roles. They are sometimes morbidly, often curiously, preoccupied with what they appear to be in the eyes of others as compared with what they feel they are and with the question of how to connect the earlier cultivated roles and skills with the ideal prototypes of the day. In their search for a new sense of continuity and sameness, some adolescents have to refight many of the crises of earlier

years, and they are never ready to install lasting idols and ideals as guardians of a final identity.

The integration now taking place in the form of the ego identity is more than the sum of the childhood identifications. It is the inner capital accrued from all those experiences of each successive stage, when successful identification led to a successful alignment of the individual's *basic drives* with his *endowment* and his *opportunities*. In psychoanalysis we ascribe such successful alignments to "ego synthesis"; I have tried to demonstrate that the ego values accrued in childhood culminate in what I have called a *sense of ego identity*. The sense of ego identity, then, is the accrued confidence that one's ability to maintain inner sameness and continuity (one's ego in the psychological sense) is matched by the sameness and continuity of one's meaning for others. Thus, self-esteem, confirmed at the end of each major crisis, grows to be a conviction that one is learning effective steps toward a tangible future, that one is developing a defined personality within a social reality which one understands. The growing child must, at every step, derive a vitalizing sense of reality from the awareness that his individual way of mastering experience is a successful variant of the way other people around him master experience and recognize such mastery.

In this, children cannot be fooled by empty praise and condescending encouragement. They may have to accept artificial bolstering of their self-esteem in lieu of something better, but what I call their accruing ego identity gains real strength only from wholehearted and consistent recognition of real accomplishment, that is, achievement that has meaning in their culture. On the other hand, should a child feel that the environment tries to deprive him too radically of all the forms of expression which permit him to develop and to integrate the next step in his ego identity, he will resist with the astonishing strength encountered in animals who are suddenly forced to defend their lives. Indeed, in the social jungle of human existence, there is no feeling of being alive without a sense of ego identity. To understand this would be to understand the trouble of adolescents better, especially the trouble of all those who cannot just be "nice" boys and girls, but are desperately seeking for a satisfactory sense of belonging, be it in cliques and gangs here in our country or in inspiring mass movements in others.

Ego identity, then, develops out of a gradual integration of all identifications, but here, if anywhere, the whole has a different quality than the sum of its parts. Under favorable circumstances children have the nucleus of a separate identity in early life; often they must defend it against any pressure which would make them overidentify with one of their parents. This is difficult to learn from patients, because the neurotic ego has, by definition, fallen prey to overidentification and to faulty identifications with disturbed parents, a circumstance which isolated the small individual both from his budding identity and from his milieu. But we can study it profitably in the children of minority-group Americans who, having successfully graduated from a marked and well-guided stage of autonomy, enter the most decisive stage of American childhood: that of initiative and industry.

Minority groups of a lesser degree of Americanization (Negroes, Indians, Mexicans, and certain European groups) often are privileged in the enjoyment of a more sensual early childhood. Their crises come when their parents and teachers, losing trust in themselves and using sudden correctives in order to approach the vague but pervasive Anglo-Saxon ideal, create violent discontinuities; or where, indeed, the children themselves learn to disavow their sensual and over-protective mothers as temptations and a hindrance to the formation of a more American personality.

On the whole, it can be said that American schools successfully meet the challenge of training children of playschool age and of the elementary grades in a spirit of self-reliance and enterprise. Children of these ages seem remarkably free of prejudice and apprehension preoccupied as they still are with growing and learning and with the new pleasures of association outside their families. This, to forestall the sense of individual inferiority, must lead to a hope for "industrial association," for equality with all those who apply themselves wholeheartedly to the same skills and adventures in learning. Many individual successes, on the other hand, only expose the now overly encouraged children of mixed backgrounds and somewhat deviant endowments to the shock of American adolescence:

the standardization of individuality and the intolerance of "differences."

The emerging ego identity, then, bridges the early childhood stages, when the body and the parent images were given their specific meanings, and the later stages, when a variety of social roles becomes available and increasingly coercive. A lasting ego identity cannot begin to exist without the trust of the first oral stage; it cannot be completed without a promise of fulfillment which from the dominant image of adulthood reaches down into the baby's beginnings and which creates at every step an accruing sense of ego strength.

The danger of this stage is *identity diffusion;* as Biff puts it in Arthur Miller's *Death of a Salesman*, "I just can't take hold, Mom, I can't take hold of some kind of a life." Where such a dilemma is based on a strong previous doubt of one's ethnic and sexual identity, delinquent and outright psychotic incidents are not uncommon. Youth after youth, bewildered by some assumed role, a role forced on him by the inexorable standardization of American adolescence, runs away in one form or another; leaving schools and jobs, staying out all night, or withdrawing into bizarre and inaccessible moods. Once "delinquent," his greatest need and often his only salvation, is the refusal on the part of older friends, advisers, and judiciary personnel to type him further by pat diagnoses and social judgments which ignore the special dynamic conditions of adolescence. For if diagnosed and treated correctly, seemingly psychotic and criminal incidents do not in adolescence have the same fatal significance which they have at other ages. Yet many a youth, finding that the authorities expect him to be "a bum" or "a queer," or "off the beam," perversely obliges by becoming just that.

In general it is primarily the inability to settle on an occupational identity which disturbs young people. To keep themselves together they temporarily overidentify, to the point of apparent complete loss of identity, with the heroes of cliques and crowds. On the other hand, they become remarkably clannish, intolerant, and cruel in their exclusion of others who are "different," in skin color or cultural background, in tastes and gifts, and often in entirely petty aspects of dress and gesture arbitrarily selected as *the* signs of an in-grouper or out-grouper. It is important to understand (which does not mean condone or participate in) such intolerance as the necessary *defense against a sense of identity diffusion*, which is unavoidable at a time of life when the body changes its proportions radically, when genital maturity floods body and imagination with all manners of drives, when intimacy with the other sex approaches and is, on occasion, forced on the youngster, and when life lies before one with a variety of conflicting possibilities and choices. Adolescents help one another temporarily through such discomfort by forming cliques and by stereotyping themselves, their ideals, and their enemies.

It is important to understand this because it makes clear the appeal which simple and cruel totalitarian doctrines have on the minds of the youth of such countries and classes as have lost or are losing their group identities (feudal, agrarian, national, and so forth) in these times of worldwide industrialization, emancipation, and wider intercommunication. The dynamic quality of the tempestuous adolescences lived through in patriarchal and agrarian countries (countries which face the most radical changes in political structure and in economy) explains the fact that their young people find convincing and satisfactory identities in the simple totalitarian doctrines of race, class, or nation. Even though we may be forced to win wars against their leaders, we still are faced with the job of winning the peace with these grim youths by convincingly demonstrating to them (by living it) a democratic identity which can be strong and yet tolerant, judicious and still determined.

But it is increasingly important to understand this also in order to treat the intolerances of our adolescents at home with understanding and guidance rather than with verbal stereotypes or prohibitions. It is difficult to be tolerant if deep down you are not quite sure that you are a man (or a woman), that you will ever grow together again and be attractive, that you will be able to master your drives, that you really know who you are,[4] that you know what you want to be, that you know what you look like to others, and that you will know how to make the right decisions without, once for all, committing yourself to the wrong friend, sexual partner, leader, or career.

[4]On the wall of a cowboys' bar in the wide-open West hangs a saying "I ain't what I ought to be, I ain't what I'm going to be, but I ain't what I was."

Democracy in a country like America poses special problems in that it insists on *self-made identities* ready to grasp many chances and ready to adjust to changing necessities of booms and busts, of peace and war, of migration and determined sedentary life. Our democracy, furthermore, must present the adolescent with ideals which can be shared by youths of many backgrounds and which emphasize autonomy in the form of independence and initiative in the form of enterprise. These promises, in turn, are not easy to fulfill in increasingly complex and centralized systems of economic and political organization, systems which, if geared to war, must automatically neglect the "self-made" identities of millions of individuals and put them where they are most needed. This is hard on many young Americans because their whole upbringing, and therefore the development of a healthy personality, depends on a certain degree of *choice*, a certain hope for an individual *chance*, and a certain conviction in freedom of *self-determination*.

We are speaking here not only of high privileges and lofty ideas but also of psychological necessities. Psychologically speaking, a gradually accruing ego identity is the only safeguard against the *anarchy of drives* as well as the *autocracy of conscience*, that is, the cruel overconscientiousness which is the inner residue in the adult of his past inequality in regard to his parent. Any loss of a sense of identity exposes the individual to his own childhood conflicts—as could be observed, for example, in the neuroses of World War II among men and women who could not stand the general dislocation of their careers or a variety of other special pressures of war. Our adversaries, it seems, understand this. Their psychological warfare consists in the determined continuation of general conditions which permit them to indoctrinate mankind within their orbit with the simple and yet for them undoubtedly effective identities of class warfare and nationalism, while they know that the psychology, as well as the economy, of free enterprise and of self-determination is stretched to the breaking point under the conditions of long-drawn-out cold and lukewarm war. It is clear, therefore, that we must bend every effort to present our young men and women with the tangible and trustworthy promise of opportunities for a rededication to the life for which the country's history, as well as their own childhood, has prepared them. Among the tasks of national defense, this one must not be forgotten.

I have referred to the relationship of the problem of trust to matters of adult faith; to that of the problem of autonomy to matters of adult independence in work and citizenship. I have pointed to the connection between a sense of initiative and the kind of enterprise sanctioned in the economic system, and between the sense of industry and a culture's technology. In searching for the social values which guide identity, one confronts the problem of aristocracy, in its widest possible sense which connotes the conviction that the best people rule and that that rule develops the best in people. In order not to become cynically or apathetically lost, young people in search of an identity must somewhere be able to convince themselves that those who succeed thereby shoulder the obligation of being the best, that is, of personifying the nation's ideals. In this country, as in any other, we have those successful types who become the cynical representatives of the "inside track," the "bosses" of impersonal machinery. In a culture once pervaded with the value of the self-made man, a special danger ensues from the idea of a synthetic personality: as if you are what you can appear to be, or as if you are what you can buy. This can be counteracted only by a system of education that transmits values and goals which determinedly aspire beyond mere "functioning" and "making the grade."

Pathological Patterns

Intrapsychic theorists recognize that pathological behavior represents, in large measure, an adaptive strategy developed by individuals in response to feelings of anxiety and threat. The bizarre and maladaptive behavior they display is not viewed as functionless or random, but as an intricate, albeit self-defeating, maneuver to relieve oneself of anguish, humiliation, and insecurity. In childhood, a youngster will cope with anxiety by a variety of spontaneous strategies; he may be submissive, hostile, ambitious, avoidant, exploitive, or independent, shifting from one to another at different times. Eventually, a dominant pattern of adaptive behavior emerges, a pattern termed the individual's character structure or style by psychoanalysts.

Carl Jung, an early disciple of Freud who broke from the main stream of psychoanalysis, retained Freud's focus on the role of unconscious processes. He posited the existence of a collective unconscious to represent a hypothetical pattern of inborn dispositions bequeathed by the ancestral past of mankind. Failure to find adequate expression for these dispositions was viewed by Jung to be the crux of psychopathology. In the paper presented here, Jung summarizes the major variants of his personality typology.

The second article is an excerpt from the writings of Wilhelm Reich. Drawing upon earlier work by Freud and Abraham, Reich provides a fully developed characterology based on the vicissitudes of psychosexual development. The astuteness of Reich's observations is most impressive.

Erich Fromm's excerpt further illustrates the richness of the intrapsychic approach to personality and its maladaptive variants. Notable in Fromm's formulations is his grasp of the role of social forces in shaping the characterological pattern.

16 Psychological Types

Carl G. Jung

The Extraverted Type

In our descriptions of this and the following type it will be necessary, in the interest of lucid and comprehensive presentation, to discriminate between the conscious and unconscious psychology. Let us first lend our minds to a description of the *phenomena of consciousness.*

The General Attitude of Consciousness

Everyone is, admittedly, orientated by the data with which the outer world provides him; yet we see that this may be the case in a way that is only relatively decisive. Because it is cold out of doors, one man is persuaded to wear his overcoat, another from a desire to become hardened finds this unnecessary; one man admires the new tenor because all the world admires him, another withholds his approbation not because he dislikes him but because in his view the subject of general admiration is not thereby proved to be admirable; one submits to a given state of affairs because his experience argues nothing else to be possible, another is convinced that, although it has repeated itself a thousand times in the same way, the thousand and first will be different. The former is orientated by the objective data; the latter reserves a view which is, as it were, interposed between himself and the objective fact. Now, when the orientation to the object and to the objective facts is so predominant that the most frequent and essential decisions and actions are determined, not by subjective values but by objective relations, one speaks of an extraverted attitude. When this is habitual, one speaks of an extraverted type. If a man so thinks, feels, and acts, in a word so *lives*, as to correspond *directly* with objective conditions and their claims, whether in a good sense or ill, he is extraverted. His life makes it perfectly clear that it is the objective rather than the subjective value which plays the greater role as the determining factor of his consciousness. He

Abridged from *Psychological Types*, Kegan Paul, 1923/1921.

naturally has subjective values, but their determining power has less importance than the external objective conditions. Never, therefore, does he expect to find any absolute factors in his own inner life, since the only ones he knows are outside himself. Epimetheus-like, his inner life succumbs to the external necessity, not of course without a struggle; which, however, always ends in favor of the objective determinant. His entire consciousness looks outwards to the world, because the important and decisive determination always comes to him from without. But it comes to him from without only because that is where he expects it. All the distinguishing characteristics of his psychology, in so far as they do not arise from the priority of one definite psychological function or from individual peculiarities, have their origin in this basic attitude. *Interest* and *attention* follow objective happenings and, primarily, those of the immediate environment. Not only persons but things seize and rivet his interest. His *actions*, therefore, are also governed by the influence of persons and things. They are directly related to objective data and determinations, and are, as it were, exhaustively explainable on these grounds. Extraverted action is recognizably related to objective conditions. In so far as it is not purely reactive to environmental stimuli, its character is constantly applicable to the actual circumstances, and it finds adequate and appropriate play within the limits of the objective situation. It has no serious tendency to transcend these bounds. The same holds good for interest: objective occurrences have a well-nigh inexhaustible charm, so that in the normal course the extravert's interest makes no other claims.

The moral laws which govern his action coincide with the corresponding claims of society, i.e., with the generally valid moral viewpoint. If the generally valid view were different, the subjective moral guiding line would also be different, without the general psychological *habitus* being in any way changed. It might almost seem, although it is by no means the case, that this rigid determination by objective factors would involve an altogether ideal and complete adaptation to general conditions of life. An *accommodation* to objective data, such as we have described, must, of course, seem a complete adaptation to the extraverted view, since from this standpoint no other criterion exists. But from a higher point of view, it is by no means granted that the standpoint of objectively given facts is the normal one under all circumstances. Objective conditions may be either temporarily or locally abnormal. An individual who accommodated to such conditions certainly conforms to the abnormal style of his surroundings, but, in relation to the universally valid laws of life, he is, in common with his milieu, in an abnormal position. The individual may, however, thrive in such surroundings, but only to the point when he, together with his whole milieu, is destroyed for transgressing the universal laws of life. He must inevitably participate in this downfall with the same completeness as he was previously adjusted to the objectively valid situation. He is adjusted, but not adapted, since adaptation demands more than a mere frictionless participation in the momentary conditions of the immediate environment. (Once more I would point to Spitteler's Epimetheus.) Adaptation demands an observance of laws far more universal in their application than purely local and temporary conditions. Mere adjustment is the limitation of the normal extraverted type. On the one hand, the extravert owes his normality to his ability to fit into existing conditions with relative ease. He naturally pretends to nothing more than the satisfaction of existing objective possibilities, applying himself, for instance, to the calling which offers sound prospective possibilities in the actual situation in time and place. He tries to do or to make just what his milieu momentarily needs and expects from him, and abstains from every innovation that is not entirely obvious, or that in any way exceeds the expectation of those around him. But on the other hand, his normality must also depend essentially upon whether the extravert takes into account the actuality of his subjective needs and requirements; and this is just his weak point, for the tendency of his type has such a strong outward direction that even the most obvious of all subjective facts, namely the condition of his own body, may quite easily receive inadequate consideration. The body is not sufficiently objective or "external," so that the satisfaction of simple elementary requirements which are indispensable to physical well-being is no longer given its place. The body accordingly suffers, to say nothing of the soul. Although, as a rule, the extravert takes small note of this latter circumstance, his intimate domestic circle perceives it all the more keenly. His loss of equilibrium is perceived by himself only when abnormal bodily sensations make themselves felt.

These tangible facts he cannot ignore. It is natural he should regard them as concrete and "objective," since for his mentality there exists only this and nothing more—in himself. In others he at once sees "imagination" at work. A too extraverted attitude may actually become so regardless of the subject that the latter is entirely sacrificed to so-called objective claims; to the demands, for instance, of a continually extending business, because orders lie claiming one's attention or because profitable possibilities are constantly being opened up which must instantly be seized.

This is the extravert's danger: he becomes caught up in objects, wholly losing himself in their toils. The functional (nervous) or actual physical disorders which result from this state have a compensatory significance, forcing the subject to an involuntary self-restriction. Should the symptoms be functional, their peculiar formation may symbolically express the psychological situation; a singer, for instance, whose fame quickly reaches a dangerous pitch tempting him to a disproportionate outlay of energy, is suddenly robbed of his high tones by a nervous inhibition. A man of very modest beginnings rapidly reaches a social position of great influence and wide prospects, when suddenly he is overtaken by a psychogenic state, with all the symptoms of mountain sickness. Again, a man on the point of marrying an idolized woman of doubtful character, whose value he extravagantly overestimates, is seized with a spasm of the esophagus, which forces him to a regimen of two cups of milk in the day, demanding his three-hourly attention. All visits to his fiancée are thus effectually stopped, and no choice is left to him but to busy himself with his bodily nourishment. A man who through his own energy and enterprise has built up a vast business, entailing an intolerable burden of work, is afflicted by nervous attacks of thirst, as a result of which he speedily falls a victim to hysterical alcoholism.

Hysteria is, in my view, by far the most frequent neurosis with the extraverted type.

The classical example of hysteria is always characterized by an exaggerated rapport with the members of his circle, and a frankly imitatory accommodation to surrounding conditions. A constant tendency to appeal for interest and to produce impressions upon his milieu is a basic trait of the hysterical nature. A correlate to this is his proverbial suggestibility, his pliability to another person's influence. Unmistakable extraversion comes out in the communicativeness of the hysteric, which occasionally leads to the divulging of purely fantastic contents; whence arises the reproach of the hysterical lie.

To begin with, the "hysterical" character is an exaggeration of the normal attitude; it is then complicated by compensatory reactions from the side of the unconscious, which manifests its opposition to the extravagant extraversion in the form of physical disorders, whereupon an introversion of psychic energy becomes unavoidable. Through this reaction of the unconscious, another category of symptoms arises which have a more introverted character. A morbid intensification of fantasy activity belongs primarily to this category. From this general characterization of the extraverted attitude, let us now turn to a description of the modifications which the basic psychological functions undergo as a result of this attitude.

The Attitude of the Unconscious

It may perhaps seem odd that I should speak of an "attitude of the unconscious." As I have already sufficiently indicated, I regard the relation of the unconscious to the conscious as compensatory. The unconscious, according to this view, has as good a claim to an "attitude" as the conscious.

In the foregoing section I emphasized the tendency to a certain one-sidedness in the extraverted attitude, because of the controlling power of the objective factor in the course of psychic events. The extraverted type is constantly tempted to give himself away (apparently) in favor of the object, and to assimilate his subject to the object. I have referred in detail to the ultimate consequences of this exaggeration of the extraverted attitude, viz., to the injurious suppression of the subjective factor. It is only to be expected, therefore, that a psychic compensation of the conscious extraverted attitude will lay especial weight upon the subjective factor, i.e., we shall have

to prove a strong egocentric tendency in the unconscious. Practical experience actually furnishes this proof. I do not wish to enter into a casuistical survey at this point, so must refer my readers to the ensuing sections, where I shall attempt to present the characteristic attitude of the unconscious from the angle of each function type. In this section we are merely concerned with the compensation of a general extraverted attitude; I shall, therefore, confine myself to an equally general characterization of the compensating attitude of the unconscious.

The attitude of the unconscious as an effective complement to the conscious extraverted attitude has a definitely introverting character. It focuses libido upon the subjective factor, i.e., all those needs and claims which are stifled or repressed by a too extraverted conscious attitude. It may be readily gathered from what has been said in the previous section that a purely objective orientation does violence to a multitude of subjective emotions, intentions, needs, and desires, since it robs them of the energy which is their natural right. Man is not a machine that one can reconstruct, as occasion demands, upon other lines and for quite other ends, in the hope that it will then proceed to function, in a totally different way, just as normally as before. Man bears his age-long history with him; in his very structure is written the history of mankind.

The historical factor represents a vital need, to which a wise economy must respond. Somehow the past must become vocal, and participate in the present. Complete assimilation to the object, therefore, encounters the protest of the suppressed minority, elements belonging to the past and existing from the beginning. From this quite general consideration it may be understood why it is that the unconscious claims of the extraverted type have an essentially primitive, infantile, and egoistical character. When Freud says that the unconscious is "only able to wish," this observation contains a large measure of truth for the unconscious of the extraverted type. Adjustment and assimilation to objective data prevent inadequate subjective impulses from reaching consciousness. These tendencies (thoughts, wishes, affects, needs, feelings, etc.) take on a regressive character corresponding with the degree of their repression, i.e., the less they are recognized, the more infantile and archaic they become. The conscious attitude robs them of their relatively disposable energy charge, only leaving them the energy of which it cannot deprive them. This remainder, which still possesses a potency not to be underestimated, can be described only as primeval instinct. Instinct can never be rooted out from an individual by any arbitrary measures; it requires the slow, organic transformation of many generations to effect a radical change, for instinct is the energic expression of a definite organic foundation.

The Introverted Type

The General Attitude of Consciousness

The introverted is distinguished from the extraverted type by the fact that, unlike the latter, who is prevailingly oriented by the object and objective data, he is governed by the subjective factors. In the section alluded to I mentioned, *inter alia*, that the introvert interposes a subjective view between the perception of the object and his own action, which prevents the action from assuming a character that corresponds with the objective situation. Naturally, this is a special case, mentioned by way of example, and merely intended to serve as a simple illustration. But now we must go in quest of more general formulations.

Introverted consciousness doubtless views the external conditions, but it selects the subjective determinants as the decisive ones. The type is guided, therefore, by that factor of perception and cognition which represents the receiving subjective disposition to the sense stimulus. Two persons, for example, see the same object, but they never see it in such a way as to receive two identically similar images of it. Quite apart from the differences in the personal equation and mere organic acuteness, there often exists a radical difference, both in kind and degree, in the psychic assimilation of the perceived image. Whereas the extraverted type refers preeminently to that which reaches him from the object, the introvert principally relies upon that which the outer impression constellates in the subject. In an individual case of apperception the difference may, of course, be very delicate, but in the total psychological economy it is extremely noticeable, especially in the form of a *reservation of the ego*. Although it is anticipating somewhat, I consider that point

of view which inclines, with Weininger, to describe this attitude as philautic, or, with other writers, as autoerotic, egocentric, subjective, or egoistic, to be both misleading in principle and definitely depreciatory. It corresponds with the normal bias of the extraverted attitude against the nature of the introvert. We must not forget—although extraverted opinion is only too prone to do so—that all perception and cognition is not purely objective: it is also subjectively conditioned. The world exists not merely in itself, but also as it appears to me. Indeed, at bottom, we have absolutely no criterion that could help us to form a judgment of a world whose nature was unassimilable by the subject. If we were to ignore the subjective factor, it would mean a complete denial of the great doubt as to the possibility of absolute cognition. And this would mean a *rechute* into that stale and hollow positivism which disfigured the beginning of our epoch—an attitude of intellectual arrogance that is invariably accompanied by a crudeness of feeling, and an essential violation of life, as stupid as it is presumptuous. Through an overvaluation of the objective powers of cognition, we repress the importance of the subjective factor, which simply means the denial of the subject. But what is the subject? The subject is man—we are the subject. Only a sick mind could forget that cognition must have a subject, for there exists no knowledge and, therefore, for us, no world where "I know" has not been said, although with this statement one has already expressed the subjective limitation of all knowledge.

The same holds good for all the psychic functions: they have a subject which is just as indispensable as the object. It is characteristic of our present extraverted valuation that the word "subjective" occasionally rings almost like a reproach or blemish; but in every case the epithet "merely subjective" means a dangerous weapon of offense, destined for that daring head that is not unceasingly convinced of the unconditional superiority of the object. We must, therefore, be quite clear as to what meaning the term "subjective" carries in this investigation. As the subjective factor, then, I understand that psychological action or reaction which, when merged with the effect of the object, makes a new psychic fact. Now, in so far as the subjective factor, since oldest times and among all peoples, remains in a very large measure identical with itself—since elementary perceptions and cognitions are almost universally the same—it is a reality that is just as firmly established as the outer object. If this were not so, any sort of permanent and essentially changeless reality would be altogether inconceivable, and any understanding with posterity would be a matter of impossibility. Thus far, therefore, the subjective factor is something that is just as much a fact as the extent of the sea and the radius of the earth. Thus far, also, the subjective factor claims the whole value of a world-determining power which can never, under any circumstances, be excluded from our calculations. It is the other world law, and the man who is based upon it has a foundation just as secure, permanent, and valid as the man who relies upon the object. But, just as the object and objective data remain by no means always the same, inasmuch as they are both perishable and subject to chance, the subjective factor is similarly liable to variability and individual hazard. Hence its value is also merely relative. The excessive development of the introverted standpoint in consciousness, for instance, does not lead to a better or sounder application of the subjective factor, but to an artifical subjectification of consciousness, which can hardly escape the reproach "merely subjective." For, as a countertendency to this morbid subjectification, there ensues a desubjectification of consciousness in the form of an exaggerated extraverted attitude which richly deserves Weininger's description "misautic." Inasmuch as the introverted attitude is based upon a universally present, extremely real, and absolutely indispensable condition of psychological adaptation, such expressions as "philautic," "egocentric," and the like are both objectionable and out of place, since they foster the prejudice that it is invariably a question of the beloved ego. Nothing could be more absurd than such an assumption. Yet one continually meets it when examining the judgments of the extravert upon the introvert. Not, of course, that I wish to ascribe such an error to individual extraverts; it is rather the present generally accepted extraverted view which is by no means restricted to the extraverted type; for it finds just as many representatives in the ranks of the other type, albeit very much against its own interest. The reproach of being untrue to his own kind is justly leveled at the latter, whereas this, at least, can never be charged against the former.

The introverted attitude is normally governed by the psychological structure, theoretically determined by heredity, but which to the subject is an ever-present subjective factor. This must not be assumed, however, to be simply identical with the subject's ego, an assumption that is certainly implied in the above-mentioned designations of Weininger; it is rather the psychological structure of the subject that precedes any development of the ego. The really fundamental subject, the Self, is far more comprehensive than the ego, because the former also embraces the unconscious, while the latter is essentially the focal point of consciousness. Were the ego identical with the Self, it would be unthinkable that we should be able to appear in dreams in entirely different forms and with entirely different meanings. But it is a characteristic peculiarity of the introvert, which, moreover, is as much in keeping with his own inclination as with the general bias, that he tends to confuse his ego with the Self, and to exalt his ego to the position of subject of the psychological process, thus effecting that morbid subjectification of consciousness, mentioned above, which so alienates him from the object.

The psychological structure is the same. Semon has termed it "mneme," whereas I call it the *collective unconscious*. The individual Self is a portion, or excerpt, or representative, of something universally present in all living creatures, and, therefore, a correspondingly graduated kind of psychological process, which is born anew in every creature. Since earliest times, the inborn manner of *acting* has been called *instinct*, and for this manner of psychic apprehension of the object I have proposed the term *archetype*. I may assume that what is understood by instinct is familiar to everyone. It is another matter with the archetype. This term embraces the same idea as is contained in "primordial image" (an expression borrowed from Jakob Burckhardt), and as such I have described it in this book.

The archetype is a symbolical formula, which always begins to function whenever there are no conscious ideas present, or when such as are present are impossible upon intrinsic or extrinsic grounds. The contents of the collective unconsciousness are represented in consciousness in the form of pronounced tendencies, or definite ways of looking at things. They are generally regarded by the individual as being determined by the object—incorrectly, at bottom—since they have their source in the unconscious structure of the psyche, and are only released by the operation of the object. These subjective tendencies and ideas are stronger than the objective influence; because their psychic value is higher, they are superimposed upon all impressions. Thus, just as it seems incomprehensible to the introvert that the object should always be decisive, it remains just as enigmatic to the extravert how a subjective standpoint can be superior to the objective situation. He reaches the unavoidable conclusion that the introvert is either a conceited egoist or a fantastic doctrinaire. Recently he seems to have reached the conclusion that the introvert is constantly influenced by an unconscious power complex. The introvert unquestionably exposes himself to this prejudice; for it cannot be denied that his definite and highly generalized mode of expression, which apparently excludes every other view from the outset, lends a certain countenance to this extraverted opinion. Furthermore, the very decisiveness and inflexibility of the subjective judgment, which is superordinated to all objective data, is alone sufficient to create the impression of a strong egocentricity. The introvert usually lacks the right argument in presence of this prejudice; for he is just as unaware of the unconscious, though thoroughly sound, presuppositions of his subjective judgment, as he is of his subjective perceptions. In harmony with the style of the times, he looks without, instead of behind his own consciousness, for the answer. Should he become neurotic, it is the sign of a more or less complete unconscious identity of the ego with the Self, whereupon the importance of the Self is reduced to nil, while the ego becomes inflated beyond reason. The undeniable, world-determining power of the subjective factor then becomes concentrated in the ego, developing an immoderate power claim and a downright foolish egocentricity. Every psychology which reduces the nature of man to unconscious power instinct springs from this foundation. For example, Nietzsche's many faults in taste owe their existence to this subjectification of consciousness.

The Unconscious Attitude

The superior position of the subjective factor in consciousness involves an inferiority of the objective factor. The object is not given that importance which should really belong to it. Just as it plays too great a role in the extraverted attitude, it has too little to say in the introverted. To the extent that the introvert's consciousness is subjectified, thus bestowing undue importance upon the ego, the object is placed in a position which in time becomes quite untenable. The object is a factor of undeniable power, while the ego is something very restricted and transitory. It would be a very different matter if the Self opposed the object. Self and world are commensurable factors; hence a normal introverted attitude is just as valid, and has as good a right to existence, as a normal extraverted attitude. But, if the ego has usurped the claims of the subject, a compensation naturally develops under the guise of an unconscious reinforcement of the influence of the object. Such a change eventually commands attention, for often, in spite of a positively convulsive attempt to ensure the superiority of the ego, the object and objective data develop an overwhelming influence, which is all the more invincible because it seizes upon the individual unawares, thus effecting an irresistible invasion of consciousness. As a result of the ego's defective relation to the object—for a will to command is not adaptation—a compensatory relation to the object develops in the unconscious, which makes itself felt in consciousness as an unconditional and irrepressible tie to the object. The more the ego seeks to secure every possible liberty, independence, superiority, and freedom from obligations, the deeper does it fall into the slavery of objective facts. The subject's freedom of mind is chained to an ignominious financial dependence, his unconcernedness of action suffers, now and again, a distressing collapse in the face of public opinion, his moral superiority gets swamped in inferior relationships, and his desire to dominate ends in a pitiful craving to be loved. The chief concern of the unconscious in such a case is the relation to the object, and it affects this in a way that is calculated to bring both the power illusion and the superiority fantasy to utter ruin. The object assumes terrifying dimensions, in spite of conscious depreciation. Detachment from, and command of, the object are, in consequence, pursued by the ego still more violently. Finally, the ego surrounds itself by a regular system of safeguards (Adler has ably depicted these) which shall at least preserve the illusion of superiority. But, therewith, the introvert severs himself completely from the object, and either squanders his energy in defensive measures or makes fruitless attempts to impose his power upon the object and successfully assert himself. But these efforts are constantly being frustrated by the overwhelming impressions he receives from the object. It continually imposes itself upon him against his will; it provokes in him the most disagreeable and obstinate effects, persecuting him at every step. An immense inner struggle is constantly required of him, in order to "keep going." Hence *psychoasthenia* is his typical form of neurosis, a malady which is characterized on the one hand by an extreme sensitiveness, and on the other by a great liability to exhaustion and chronic fatigue.

An analysis of the personal unconscious yields an abundance of power fantasies coupled with fear of the dangerously animated objects, to which, as a matter of fact, the introvert easily falls a victim. For a peculiar cowardliness develops from his fear of the object; he shrinks from making either himself or his opinion effective, always dreading an intensified influence on the part of the object. He is terrified of impressive affects in others, and is hardly ever free from the dread of falling under hostile influence. For objects possess terrifying and powerful qualities for him—qualities which he cannot consciously discern in them, but which, through his unconscious perception, he cannot choose but believe in. Since his conscious relation to the object is relatively repressed, its exit is by way of the unconscious, where it becomes loaded with the qualities of the unconscious. These qualities are primarily infantile and archaic. His relation to the object, therefore, becomes correspondingly primitive, taking on all those peculiarities which characterize the primitive object relationship. Now it seems as though objects possessed magical powers. Strange new objects excite fear and distrust, as though concealing unknown dangers; objects long rooted and blessed by tradition are attached to his soul as by invisible threads; every change has a disturbing, if not actually dangerous, aspect, since its apparent implication is a magical animation of the object. A lonely island where only what is permitted to move moves, becomes an ideal. *Auch Einer*, the novel by F. Th. Vischer, gives a rich insight into this side of the introvert's psychology, and at the same time shows the underlying symbolism of the collective unconscious, which in this description of types I am leaving on one side, since it is a universal phenomenon with no especial connection with types.

17 Some Circumscribed Character Forms

Wilhelm Reich

The Hysterical Character

In our investigation of the various character types, we proceeded from the assumption that every character form, in terms of its basic function, represents an armoring against the stimuli of the outer world and the repressed inner drives. The external form of this armoring, however, is always historically determined. We also endeavored to cite a few conditions which determine different character types. Perhaps the most important of

these, apart from the character of the person most responsible for the child's upbringing, is the stage of development in which the instinctual apparatus meets its most crucial frustration. Definite relations must always exist between the external appearance of the character, its inner mechanism, and the specific history of its origin.

The hysterical character, as complicated as the pathological symptoms and reactions pertaining to it may often be, represents the simplest, most transparent type of character armor. If one disregards the differences existing within this type, if one condenses what is common to all of them, the most conspicuous characteristic of both male and female examples of this type is an importunate *sexual attitude*. This is combined with a specific kind of *physical agility* exhibiting a distinct sexual nuance, which explains the fact that the connection between female hysteria and sexuality was recognized very early. Disguised or undisguised coquetry in gait, look, or speech betrays, especially in women, the hysterical character type. In the case of men, besides softness and excessive politeness, a feminine facial expression and a feminine bearing also appear.

These characteristics appear with more or less distinct anxiousness that is manifested most strongly when the goal sought by the sexual behavior is close at hand. At such a time, the hysterical character will always shrink back or assume a passive, apprehensive attitude. There is a quantitative correlation between hysterical coquetry and the passivity which follows it. In the sexual experience, however, there is another variation: overt displays of excitation in the act without corresponding gratification. Under analysis, these pseudo-passionate displays turn out to be the expression of a severe anxiety, which is overcome by activity.

The facial expression and the gait of the hysterical character are never severe and heavy, as they are in the compulsive character; never arrogant and self-confident, as they are in the phallic-narcissistic character. The movements of the archetype have a kind of lilting quality (not to be confused with elastic), are supple and sexually provocative. That the hysterical character is easily excited can be inferred from the appearance as a whole. The appearance of the compulsive character, on the other hand, suggests restraint.

Whereas shyness and anxiousness paired with coquetry as well as physical agility are conspicuous in the behavioral expressions of a hysterical character, the additional specific hysterical character traits are concealed. Among these we find fickleness of reactions, i.e., a tendency to change one's attitudes unexpectedly and unintentionally; a strong suggestibility, which never appears alone but is coupled with a strong tendency to reactions of disappointment. A hysterical character, as opposed to a compulsive character, can be easily persuaded of the most improbable things. By the same token he will readily give up his beliefs when others, just as easily acquired, replace them. Hence, an attitude of compliance is usually followed by its opposite, swift deprecation and groundless disparagement. The hysterical character's openness to

suggestion accounts for his susceptibility to passive hypnosis on the one hand and his propensity for fantastic ideas on the other hand. This is related to the exceptional capacity for hypnosis on the one hand and his propensity for fantastic ideas on the other hand. This is related to the exceptional capacity for sexual attachment of a childish nature. The vivid imagination can easily lead to pseudologia; that is, fantasized experiences are reproduced and grasped as real experiences.

While it is true that many hysterical characteristics are expressed in the physical bearing, there is also a strong tendency to embody pyschic conflicts in somatic symptoms. This is easily explained in terms of the libido structure.

Specifically, the hysterical character is determined by a fixation in the genital stage of childhood development, with its incestuous attachment. From this fixation the hysterical character derives his strong genital aggression as well as his anxiety. The genital incest ideas are of course repressed, but they are in full possession of their cathexis; they have not, as in the case of the compulsive character, been replaced by pregenital strivings. Inasmuch as pregenital, oral, anal, and urethral strivings form a part of the hysterical character—as is always the case—they are embodiments of genitality or at least allied with it. In the hysterical character, the mouth and the anus always stand for the female genital organ. In other character types, e.g., melancholia, these zones fulfill their original pregenital function. The hysterical character, as Ferenczi put it, "genitalizes" everything; the other forms of neuroses substitute pregenital mechanisms for genitality or, as opposed to hysteria, allow genitalia to function as breast, mouth, or anus. Elsewhere I called this the flooding of the genital with pregenital libido. As a result of the genital anxiety which operates both as a genital fixation and as an inhibition of the genital function, the hysterical character always suffers from a severe sexual disturbance. At the same time he is plagued by an acute stasis of unabsorbed genital libido. Hence, his sexual agility has to be as vehement as his tendency to anxiety reactions. In contrast to the compulsive character, the hysterical character is overladen with *unabsorbed* sexual tension.

This leads us to the nature of his armoring. It is far less compact and stable than the armoring of the compulsive character. In the hysterical character, the armoring constitutes, in the simplest possible way, an anxious ego defense against the genital incest strivings. While it is certainly strange, it cannot be denied that, in archetypes of the hysterical character, genital sexuality places itself at the service of its own defense. The more anxiety-ridden the attitude as a whole is, the more urgent the sexual manifestations appear. Generally, the meaning of this function is as follows: the hysterical character has exceptionally strong and ungratified genital impulses that are inhibited by genital anxiety. Thus, he always feels himself at the mercy of dangers which correspond to his infantile fears. The original genital striving is used, as it were, to explore the source, magnitude, and proximity of the danger. For instance, if a hysterical woman displays strong sensuality, it would be wrong to assume that she is expressing genuine sexual willingness. Quite the contrary: on the first attempt to take advantage of this apparent willingness, one would find that, in cases of extreme hysteria, the overt expression would be immediately transformed into its opposite, that the sexual manifestations would be replaced by anxiety or defense in some other form, including precipitate flight. Thus, the sexual displays in the hysterical character are an attempt to find out whether dangers are present and where they might be coming from. This is also clearly demonstrated in the transference reaction in the analysis. The hysterical character never recognizes the meaning of his sexual behavior; he violently refuses to take cognizance of it and is shocked by "such insinuations." In short, one soon sees that what stands out here as sexual striving is basically sexuality in the service of defense. Not until this defense has been unmasked and the childhood genital anxiety analytically taken apart does the genital object striving emerge in its original function. As this occurs, the patient also loses his exaggerated sexual agility. That other secondary impulses are expressed in this sexual behavior, e.g., primitive narcissism or the desire to dominate and impress, is of little importance.

Insofar as mechanisms other than genital mechanisms or their substitute formations are found in the hysterical character, they do not belong specifically to this type. For example, we often encounter depressive mechanisms. In these cases, the genital incestuous fixation is replaced by regressions to oral mechanisms or by new formations in the course of the process. The hysterical character's strong inclination to regress, especially to oral stages, can be accounted for by the sexual stasis in this zone as well as by the fact that the mouth, in its role as a genital organ, attracts a great deal of libido to itself in the "displacement from below upwards." In this process, melancholia-like reactions, which belong to the original oral fixation, are also activated. Thus, the hysterical character presents himself in a pure form when he play-acts, and is nervous and vivacious. When he is depressive, introverted, autistic, however, he betrays mechanisms other than those which specifically belong to him. Yet one can speak of hysterical depression as opposed to melancholic depression. The difference lies in the degree to which genital libido and object relationship are combined with oral attitudes. At the one extreme, we have unadulterated melancholia; at the other, where genitality predominates, we have unadulterated hysteria.

One final characteristic must be stressed: the hysterical character exhibits little interest in sublimations and intellectual accomplishments, and reaction formations are much fewer than in other forms of neurotic characters. This, too, ties in with the fact that, in the hysterical character, the libido does not advance toward sexual gratification, which could reduce the hypersexuality, nor is sexual energy adequately bound. Rather, this energy is partially discharged in somatic innervations or partially transformed into fear or anxiety. From these libido mechanisms of the hysterical character, some people like to deduce the alleged antithesis between sexuality and social accomplishments. But they overlook the fact that the extreme disturbance of the ability to sublimate is the direct result of the sexual inhibition with unattached genital libido and that social accomplishments and interests are possible only after the capacity for gratification has been realized.

In terms of the prophylaxis of neurosis and sexual economy, it becomes meaningful to ask why the hysterical character cannot somehow transform his genital stasis, in the same way that other character types transform their pregenital strivings. The hysterical character uses his genital libido neither for reaction formations nor for sublimations. Indeed, not even the character armoring is solidly developed. If these facts are considered together with other characteristics of the genital libido, we arrive at the conclusion that fully developed genital excitations are ill suited for purposes other than direct gratification. Their inhibition severely hinders the sublimation of other libidinal strivings because it imbues them with too much energy. Although the specific quality of genitality might be the reason for this process, the more likely explanation is the quantity of the libido used in the excitation of the genital zone. The genital apparatus, as opposed to all the other partial drives, is physiologically the most strongly equipped because it has the capacity for *orgastic* discharge; and in terms of libido economy, it is the most vital. Thus, we can assume that its impulses have a far greater similarity with hunger, as far as inflexibility and tenacity are concerned, than they have with impulses from other erogenous zones. This may well be a powerful blow to certain ethical concepts—but that cannot be helped. Indeed, the resistance to these findings can also be explained: their recognition would have revolutionary consequences.

The Compulsive Character

If the character's most general function is to ward off stimuli and to secure psychic balance, this should not be difficult to prove in the compulsive character. For this type is one of the most thoroughly studied psychic formations. There are fluid transitions from the known compulsive symptoms to the character's mode of behavior. Even if the neurotic compulsive sense of order is not present, a *pedantic sense of order* is typical of the compulsive character. In both big and small things, he lives his life according to a preconceived, irrevocable pattern. A change in the prescribed order causes at the very least an unpleasant sensation. In cases which can already be regarded as neurotic, a change arouses anxiety. If this trait constitutes an improvement of one's capacity for work because it is combined with thoroughness, it entails an extreme limitation of the capacity for work because it does not allow any spontaneity in one's reaction. Advantageous to an official, this trait will prove to be detrimental to productive work, to the play of new ideas. Hence, compulsive characters are seldom

found among great statesmen. They are more likely to be encountered among scientists, whose work is not incompatible with such a trait even though it wholly precludes speculation and will stand in the way of fundamentally new discoveries. This is related to another character trait, the ever-present penchant for *circumstantial, ruminative thinking.* There is a marked inability to focus attention on what is rationally important about an object and to disregard its superficial aspects. Attention is evenly distributed; questions of secondary importance are accorded the same thoroughness as those at the center of professional interests. The more pathological and rigid this trait is, the more attention is concentrated on things of secondary importance and the rationally more important matters are sidetracked. This is the result of a well-understood process, the displacement of unconscious cathexes, the replacement of unconscious ideas which have become important, by irrelevant, secondary matters. This is part of the larger process of progressive repression directed against repressed ideas. Usually, these ideas, childish musings on forbidden things, are not allowed to penetrate to the real issue. This thinking and musing also move along prescribed paths, in accordance with definite, historically determined schemata, and considerably obstruct the flexibility of one's thinking. In some cases, an above-average capacity for abstract, logical thinking compensates for this rigidity. The critical capacities—within the framework of logic—are better developed than the creative capacities.

Frugality, often pushed to the point of *parsimony*, is a character trait in all compulsive characters and is intimately related to the others we have named. Pedantry, circumstantiality, tendency to compulsive rumination, and frugality are all derived from a single instinctual source: anal eroticism. For the most part, they represent the direct derivatives of reaction formations against the childhood tendencies prevalent during the period of toilet training. Insofar as these reaction formations have not been wholly successful, traits having a nature completely opposite to the ones already discussed exist and constitute an inherent part of the compulsive character. In more concrete terms, they constitute breakthroughs of the original tendencies. Then we have manifestations of extreme sloppiness, inability to husband money, thorough thinking only within circumscribed limits. If one adds the strong passion for *collecting* things, then the ensemble of the anal-erotic derivatives in the character is complete. Whereas we can easily grasp the qualitative connection between these traits and the interest in the functions of evacuation, the connection between compulsive rumination and anal eroticism is not obvious. While we always find ruminations about where babies come from, the transformation of the interest in defecation to a definite kind of thinking, whose existence is unquestioned, appears to be subject to unknown laws. The investigations of Abraham, Jones, Ophuijsen, and others built upon Freud's first work on this subject offer the most complete orientation in this area.

We will briefly name a few other character traits which derive not from the anal but from the sadistic impulses pertaining specifically to this stage. Compulsive characters always exhibit a marked proclivity for reactions of *pity* and *guilt feelings*. This of course is not a refutation of the fact that their other traits are not exactly pleasant for their fellow man. In their exaggerated sense of order, pedantry, etc., their hostility and aggression often extort a direct gratification. In keeping with the compulsive character's fixation on the anal-sadistic stage of libido development, we find in these traits all the reaction formations against the original contrary tendencies. We must emphasize, however, that we are justified in speaking of a compulsive character only when the full ensemble of these traits is present—not when someone is merely pedantic and does not exhibit any of the other traits of the compulsive character. Thus, it would be incorrect to speak of a compulsive neurosis when a hysterical character is orderly or ruminative.

Whereas the character traits that we have named so far are manifestations of direct transformations of certain partial drives, there are other typical traits which demonstrate a more complicated structure and are the results of a series of interacting forces. Among these we have *indecision, doubt, and distrust*. In external appearance, the compulsive character exhibits strong *reserve* and *self-possession;* he is just as ill disposed toward affects as he is acutely inaccessible to them. He is usually even-tempered, lukewarm in his displays of both love and hate. In some cases, this can develop into a complete *affect-block*. These latter traits are already a matter of form rather than content and thus lead us to our actual theme, the dynamics and economy of the character.

The reserve and methodicalness in life and thought that go together with indecisiveness indeed have a definite relation to it and constitute the point of departure for our analysis of the form of the character. They cannot, as in the case of character traits imbued with a specific content, be derived directly from individual drives. Rather, these traits give the person his distinctive quality. In analysis, they constitute the central element of the character resistance as well as the tendency to avoid the termination of a situation, including the analytic treatment. We learn from clinical experience that the traits of doubt, distrust, etc., operate as a resistance in the analysis and cannot be eliminated until the pronounced affect-block has been broken through. Hence, this deserves our special attention. We shall limit our discussion to those phenomena which are expressed as form, especially in view of the fact that the other traits are well known. This investigation is new territory.

To begin with, we have to refresh our memory regarding what is known about the libido development of the compulsive character. Historically, we have a central fixation on the anal-sadistic stage, i.e., in the second or third year of life. Toilet training, because of the mother's own particular character traits, is carried out too soon. This leads to powerful reaction formations, e.g., extreme self-control, even at an early age. With the rigid toilet training, a powerful anal obstinacy develops and mobilizes the sadistic impulses to strengthen itself. In the typical compulsion neurosis, the development continues to the phallic phase, i.e., genitality is activated. However, partially because of the person's previously developed inhibitions and partially because of the parents' antisexual attitude, it is soon relinquished. Insofar as genitality is developed, it is dependent upon the prior development of the anality and sadism in the form of phallic-sadistic aggression. Needless to say, a male child will sacrifice his genital impulses to the castration anxiety—i.e., will repress them—that much more readily, the more aggressive his acquired sexual constitution and the more extensive the character inhibitions and guilt feelings from earlier periods which impinge upon the new phase. Hence, in the compulsion neurosis the repression of the genitality is typically followed by a withdrawal to the immediately preceding stage of feces interest and the aggression of this stage. From now on, i.e., during the so-called latency period[1]—which is especially pronounced in the compulsive character—the anal and sadistic reaction formations usually grow more intense and mold the character into a definite form.

When such a child reaches puberty, when he is exposed to the most powerful stresses of physical maturation, he will, if the armoring of his character is strong, have to repeat briefly the old process, without attaining the fulfillment of the demands of sexual maturity. Usually, in the beginning, there are violent fits of sadism against women (beating and rape fantasies, etc.) which are accompanied by feelings of affective weakness and inferiority. These feelings cause the youth to make narcissistic compensations in the form of strongly emphasized ethical and aesthetic strivings. The fixations on the anal and sadistic position are strengthened or regressively reactivated following a brief, usually unsuccessful advance toward genital activity; this causes further elaborations of the corresponding reaction formations. As a result of these in-depth processes, the pubertal and post-pubertal period of the compulsive character proceeds in a typical way, and we are therefore able to draw definite a posteriori conclusions about this period. There is, first of all, a progressive stunting of the emotional capacity, a stunting which sometimes impresses the average person as a mark of especially good social "adjustment." This may also appear to be the case to the person himself, as, indeed, in a certain sense it is. Simultaneously with the affect-block, however, there is a feeling of inner desolation and an intense desire "to begin a new life," which is usually attempted with the most absurd means. One such patient constructed a complicated system for the purpose of dealing with his small and large tasks. He had to master them so he could begin a new life on a certain day; he even went so far as to calculate the exact second at which his new life would begin to take shape. Since he was never able to fulfill the prescribed conditions, he always had to begin anew.

As a prototype of disturbances in the compulsive character manifested as a "form" of the character rather than as a "content" of a character trait, we would do well to investigate his affect-block. Although it impresses us as a helpless attitude on the part of the ego, this is not at all the case. On the contrary, in almost no other character formation does analysis show such intense and avid defense work. What is warded off, and how is it done? The compulsive character's typical means of repression is to separate the affects from the ideas, thus very often allowing the latter to emerge into consciousness without interference. One such patient dreamed and thought about incest with his mother and even about violent rapes, yet he remained unaffected. Genital and sadistic excitation was totally absent. If such patients are analyzed without at the same time concentrating on the affect-block, additional unconscious material is obtained—occasionally even a weak excitation—but never the affects which would correspond to the ideas. What has become of these? When symptoms exist, the affects are partially absorbed in them; when there are no symptoms, they are mainly absorbed in the affect-block itself. The proof of this assertion is immediately evident when one succeeds in breaking through the block by means of consistent isolation and interpretation. When this has been accomplished, the sought-after affects reappear spontaneously, at first usually in the form of anxiety.

It is noteworthy that at first only aggressive impulses are set free; the genital impulses appear much later. Thus, we can say that bound aggressive energy makes up the outer layer of the character armor. By what is it bound? The aggression is bound with the help of anal-erotic energies. The affect-block represents one enormous *spasm of the ego*, which makes use of somatic spastic conditions. All the muscles of the body, but especially those of the pelvic floor and pelvis, the muscles of the shoulders, and those of the face (cf. the "hard," almost mask-like physiognomy of compulsive characters), are in a state of chronic hypertonia.[2] This ties in with the physical awkwardness so often encountered in the compulsive character. Hence, the ego, to put it graphically, has taken anal holding-back tendencies from the repressed layers and put them to use in its own interest as a means of warding off sadistic impulses. Whereas

---

[1]The latency period, as we learn from the sexual development of children of primitive peoples, is not a biological but a sociological phenomenon, created by sexual suppression.

[2]Cf. Fenichel's excellent presentation in "Über organlibinöse Begleiterscheinungen der Triebabwehr" *Internationalen Zeitschrift für Psychoanalyse*, 1928.

anality and aggression are parallel forces in the unconscious, anality, i.e., holding back, operates against aggression (and vice versa) in the function of defense. Thus, unless we break down the affect-block, we shall not get at the anal energies either. We are reminded of our affect-blocked patient who, for months on end, passed his hand over the fly of his pants three times before each session while reciting the Götz quotation three times. It was as if he wanted to say: "I would so much like to kill you, but I have to control myself—so you know what you can do . . ."

The passive-feminine character also wards off aggression with the help of anal tendencies, but in a way different from the compulsive character. In the former, anality operates in the original direction as an object-libido striving; in the latter, it is manifested in the form of anal holding back, i.e., already as a reaction formation. In the purely developed compulsive character, therefore, passive homosexuality (which of course belongs to the category of the hysterical character) is not so close to the surface and relatively unrepressed as it is in the passive-feminine character.

How is it possible that anal holding back in the character can have such far-reaching ramifications, causing those who suffer from it to become living machines? This is not solely because of the anal reaction formation. The sadism which is bound in the affect-block is not only its object but also the means it employs to ward off anality. Thus, interests in anal functions are also warded off with the help of aggressive energy. Every affective, lively expression arouses in the unconscious the old excitations that had never been resolved. The result is a constant anxiety that a misfortune could take place, that something might preclude the reestablishment of self-possession. We observe that this is the point of departure for the unraveling of the whole childhood conflict between urge to evacuate and the need to hold back, out of fear of punishment. And we learn from clinical experience that, if the analysis of the affect-block is carried out correctly, the breakthrough into the central conflict is a success and the corresponding cathexes are restored to the old positions. This is equivalent to the dissolving of the armor.

By way of the affect-block, we also arrive at the affective anchoring of the first identifications and the superego: the demand to exercise control, originally imposed by the outer world upon a rebelling ego, is complied with. But this compliance does not stop there;

it becomes a chronic, inflexible mode of reaction. And this can be accomplished only with the help of the repressed energies of the id.

Further probing into the dynamics of the affect-block shows that two kinds of sadistic impulses are consumed in it. Through systematic resistance analysis, they can be extracted in fairly pure, separate forms. Usually, anal sadism, whose goal is beating, stomping, crushing, etc., is liberated first. After it has been worked through and the anal fixations have been loosened, *phallic*-sadistic impulses move more and more into the foreground (sticking, piercing, etc.). That is, the regression is eliminated; the road to the cathexis of the phallic position is paved. At this point usually, *affective* castration anxiety finally becomes manifest and the analysis of the genital repressions begins. In compulsive characters, the old childhood phobia often reappears in this stage.

Hence, we find two layers of repressions in the compulsive character: the outer layer consists of sadistic and anal impulses, while the deeper layer is made up of phallic impulses. This corresponds to the inversion which takes place in the regression process: those impulses which receive a new cathexis lie closest to the surface; whereas object-libidinal genital strivings are deeply repressed, "covered over" by layers of pregenital positions. These structural relations reveal that it would be a serious technical error, through interpretations, to make the patient affectively aware of the weak manifestations of genital-object strivings *before* the superimpositions have been worked through. Everything would be received coldly, warded off with doubt and distrust.

We have in this connection to pause a moment to consider ambivalence and doubt. They constitute the severest obstructions to analysis if we do not succeed, from the outset, in disentangling the various strivings that comprise ambivalent emotions. Ambivalence reflects a conflict between two simultaneously present potentials, one to love and the other to hate the same person; at a deeper layer it is an inhibition of the libidinal as well as aggressive strivings by the existing fear of punishment. If all manifestations are indiscriminately and simultaneously analyzed, the ambivalence will hardly be mastered. And this could easily lead one to assume that man is biologically, i.e., immutably, ambivalent. If, on the other hand, we proceed in keeping with the structural and dynamic relations, hate will soon move into the foreground and can be resolved with relative ease through analysis, thus paving the way to the extrication of the libidinal strivings. The best procedure to effect this *separation of the ambivalent strivings* is to analyze thoroughly the contemporary distrust, right at the outset of the analysis.

In this discussion we have had to restrict ourselves to the essential traits of the compulsive character, leaving many secondary features untouched. It is enough if we have succeeded in explaining the basic makeup of the character.

18 Non-Productive Character Orientations

Erich Fromm

Freud tried to account for this dynamic nature of character traits by combining his characterology with his libido theory. In accordance with the type of materialistic thinking prevalent in the natural sciences of the late nineteenth century, which assumed the energy in natural and psychical phenomena to be a substantial not a relational entity, Freud believed that the sexual drive was the source of energy of the character. By a number of complicated and brilliant assumptions he explained different character traits as "sublimations" of, or "reaction formations" against, the various forms of the sexual drive. He interpreted the *dynamic nature* of character traits as an expression of their *libidinous source.*

The progress of psychoanalytic theory led, in line with the progress of the natural and social sciences, to a new concept which was based, not on the idea of a primarily isolated individual, but on the *relationship* of man to others, to nature, and to himself. It was assumed that this very relationship governs and regulates the energy manifest in the passionate strivings of man. H. S. Sullivan, one of the pioneers of this new view, has accordingly defined psychoanalysis as a "study of interpersonal relations."

The theory presented in the following pages follows Freud's characterology in essential points: in the assumption that character traits underlie behavior and must be inferred from it; that they constitute forces which, though powerful, the person may be entirely unconscious of. It follows Freud also in the assumption that the fundamental entity in

From *Man For Himself* by Erich Fromm. Copyright 1947, © 1975 by Erich Fromm. Reprinted by permission of Holt, Rinehart and Winston, Inc.

character is not the single character trait but the total character organization from which a number of single character traits follow. These character traits are to be understood as a syndrome which results from a particular organization or, as I shall call it, orientation of character. I shall deal only with a very limited number of character traits which follow immediately from the underlying orientation. A number of other character traits could be dealt with similarly, and it could be shown that they are also direct outcomes of basic orientations or mixtures of such primary traits of character with those of temperament. However, a great number of others conventionally listed as character traits would be found to be not character traits in our sense but pure temperament or mere behavior traits.

The main difference in the theory of character proposed here from that of Freud is that the fundamental basis of character is not seen in various types of libido organization but in specific kinds of a person's relatedness to the world. In the process of living, man relates himself to the world (1) by acquiring and assimilating things, and (2) by relating himself to people (and himself). The former I shall call the process of assimilation; the latter, that of socialization. Both forms of relatedness are "open" and not, as with the animal, instinctively determined. Man can acquire things by receiving or taking them from an outside source or by producing them through his own effort. But he must acquire and assimilate them in some fashion in order to satisfy his needs. Also, man cannot live alone and unrelated to others. He has to associate with others for defense, for work, for sexual satisfaction, for play, for the upbringing of the young, for the transmission of knowledge and material possessions. But beyond that, it is necessary for him to be related to others, one with them, part of a group. Complete isolation is unbearable and incompatible with sanity. Again man can relate himself to others in various ways: he can love or hate, he can compete or cooperate; he can build a social system based on equality or authority, liberty or oppression; but he must be related in some fashion and the particular form of relatedness is expressive of his character.

These orientations, by which the individual relates himself to the world, constitute the core of his character; character can be defined as the *(relatively permanent) form in which human energy is canalized in the process of assimilation and socialization.* This canalization of psychic energy has a very significant biological function. Since man's actions are not determined by innate instinctual patterns, life would be precarious, indeed, if he had to make a deliberate decision each time he acted, each time he took a step. On the contrary, many actions must be performed far more quickly than conscious deliberation allows. Furthermore, if all behavior followed from deliberate decision, many more inconsistencies in action would occur than are compatible with proper functioning. According to behavioristic thinking, man learns to react in a semiautomatic fashion by developing habits of action and thought which can be understood in terms of conditioned reflexes. While this view is correct to a certain extent, it ignores the fact that the most deeply rooted habits and opinions which are characteristic of a person and resistant to change grow from his character structure: they are expressive of the particular form in which energy has been canalized in the character structure. The character system can be considered the human substitute for the instinctive apparatus of the animal. Once energy is canalized in a certain way, action takes place "true to character." A particular character may be undesirable ethically, but at least it permits a person to act fairly consistently and to be relieved of the burden of having to make a new and deliberate decision every time. He can arrange his life in a way which is geared to his character and thus create a certain degree of compatibility between the inner and the outer situation. Moreover, character has also a selective function with regard to a person's ideas and values. Since to most people ideas seem to be independent of their emotions and wishes and

the result of logical deduction, they feel that their attitude toward the world is confirmed by their ideas and judgments when actually these are as much a result of their character as their actions are. This confirmation in turn tends to stabilize their character structure since it makes the latter appear right and sensible.

Not only has character the function of permitting the individual to act consistently and "reasonably"; it is also the basis for his adjustment to society. The character of the child is molded by the character of its parents in response to whom it develops. The parents and their methods of child training in turn are determined by the social structure of their culture. The average family is the "psychic agency" of society, and by adjusting himself to his family the child acquires the character which later makes him adjusted to the tasks he has to perform in social life. He acquires that character which makes him want to do what he has to do and the core of which he shares with most members of the same social class or culture. The fact that most members of a social class or culture share significant elements of character and that one can speak of a "social character" representing the core of a character structure common to most people of a given culture shows the degree to which character is formed by social and cultural patterns. But from the social character we must differentiate the individual character in which one person differs from another within the same culture. These differences are partly due to the differences of the personalities of the parents and to the differences, psychic and material, of the specific social environment in which the child grows up. But they are also due to the constitutional differences of each individual, particularly those of temperament. Genetically, the formation of individual character is determined by the impact of its life experiences, the individual ones and those which follow from the culture, on temperament and physical constitution. Environment is never the same for two people, for the difference in constitution makes them experience the same environment in a more or less different way. Mere habits of action and thought which develop as the result of an individual's conforming with the cultural pattern and which are not rooted in the character of a person are easily changed under the influence of new social patterns. If, on the other hand, a person's behavior is rooted in his character, it is charged with energy and changeable only if a fundamental change in a person's character takes place.

In the following analysis *nonproductive orientations* are differentiated from the *productive orientation*. It must be noted that these concepts are "ideal-types," not descriptions of the character of a given individual. Furthermore, while, for didactic purposes, they are treated here separately, the character of any given person is usually a blend of all or some of these orientations in which one, however, is dominant. Finally, I want to state here that in the description of the nonproductive orientations only their negative aspects are presented.

The Receptive Orientation

In the receptive orientation a person feels "the source of all good" to be outside, and he believes that the only way to get what he wants—be it something material, be it affection, love, knowledge, pleasure—is to receive it from that outside source. In this orientation the problem of love is almost exclusively that of "being loved" and not that of loving. Such people tend to be indiscriminate in the choice of their love objects, because being loved by anybody is such an overwhelming experience for them that they "fall for" anybody who gives them love or what looks like love. They are exceedingly sensitive to any withdrawal or rebuff they experience on the part of the loved person. Their orientation is the same in the sphere of thinking: if intelligent, they make the best listeners, since their orientation is one of receiving, not of producing, ideas; left to themselves, they feel paralyzed. It is characteristic of these people that their first thought is to find somebody else to give them needed information rather than to make even the smallest effort of their own. If religious, these persons have a concept of God in which they expect everything from God and nothing from their own activity. If not religious, their relationship to persons or institutions is very much the same; they are always in search of a "magic helper." They show a particular kind of loyalty, at the bottom of which is the gratitude for the hand that feeds them and the fear of ever losing it. Since they need many hands to feel secure, they have to be loyal to numerous people. It is difficult for them to say "no," and they are easily caught between conflicting loyalties and promises. Since they cannot say "no," they love to say "yes" to everything and everybody, and the resulting paralysis of their critical abilities makes them increasingly dependent on others.

They are dependent not only on authorities for knowledge and help but on people in general for any kind of support. They feel lost when alone because they feel that they cannot do anything without help. This helplessness is especially important with regard to those acts which by their very nature can only be done alone—making decisions and taking responsibility. In personal relationships, for instance, they ask advice from the very person with regard to whom they have to make a decision.

This receptive type has great fondness for food and drink. These persons tend to overcome anxiety and depression by eating or drinking. The mouth is an especially prominent feature, often the most expressive one; the lips tend to be open, as if in a state of continuous expectation of being fed. In their dreams, being fed is a frequent symbol of being loved; being starved, an expression of frustration or disappointment.

By and large, the outlook of people of this receptive orientation is optimistic and friendly; they have a certain confidence in life and its gifts, but they become anxious and distraught when their "source of supply" is threatened. They often have a genuine warmth and a wish to help others, but doing things for others also assumes the function of securing their favor.

The Exploitative Orientation

The exploitative orientation, like the receptive, has as its basic premise the feeling that the source of all good is outside, that whatever one wants to get must be sought there, and that one cannot produce anything oneself. The difference between the two, however, is that the exploitative type does not expect to receive things from others as gifts, but to take them away from others by force or cunning. This orientation extends to all spheres of activity.

In the realm of love and affection these people tend to grab and steal. They feel attracted only to people whom they can take away from somebody else. Attractiveness to them is conditioned by a person's attachment to somebody else; they tend not to fall in love with an unattached person.

We find the same attitude with regard to thinking and intellectual pursuits. Such people will tend not to produce ideas but to steal them. This may be done directly in the form of plagiarism or more subtly by repeating in different phraseology the ideas voiced by others and insisting they are new and their own. It is a striking fact that frequently people with great intelligence proceed in this way, although if they relied on their own gifts they might well be able to have ideas of their own. The lack of original ideas or independent production in otherwise gifted people often has its explanation in this character orientation, rather than in any innate lack of originality. The same statement holds true with regard to their orientation to material things. Things which they can take away from others always seem better to them than anything they can produce themselves. They use and exploit anybody and anything from whom or from which they can squeeze something. Their motto is: "Stolen fruits are sweetest." Because they want to use and exploit people, they "love" those who, explicitly or implicitly, are promising objects of exploitation, and get "fed up" with persons whom they have squeezed out. An extreme example is the kleptomaniac who enjoys things only if he can steal them, although he has the money to buy them.

This orientation seems to be symbolized by the biting mouth which is often a prominent feature in such people. It is not a play upon words to point out that they often make "biting" remarks about others. Their attitude is colored by a mixture of hostility and manipulation. Everyone is an object of exploitation and is judged according to his usefulness. Instead of the confidence and optimism which characterizes the receptive type, one finds here suspicion and cynicism, envy and jealousy. Since they are satisfied only with things they can take away from others, they tend to overrate what others have and underrate what is theirs.

The Hoarding Orientation

While the receptive and exploitative types are similar inasmuch as both expect to get things from the outside world, the hoarding orientation is essentially different. This orientation makes people have little faith in anything new they might get from the outside world; their security is based upon hoarding and saving, while spending is felt to be a threat. They have surrounded themselves, as it were, by a protective wall, and their main aim is to bring as much as possible into this fortified position and to let as little as possible out of it. Their miserliness refers to money and material things as well as to feelings and thoughts. Love is essentially a possession; they do not give love but try to get it by possessing the "beloved." The hoarding person often shows a particular kind of faithfulness toward people and even toward memories. Their sentimentality makes the past appear as golden; they hold on to it and indulge in the memories of bygone feelings and experiences. They know everything but are sterile and incapable of productive thinking.

One can recognize these people too by facial expressions and gestures. Theirs is the tight-lipped mouth; their gestures are characteristic of their withdrawn attitude. While those of the receptive type are inviting and round, as it were, and the gestures of the exploitative type are aggressive and pointed, those of the hoarding type are angular, as if they wanted to emphasize the frontiers between themselves and the outside world. Another characteristic element in this attitude is pedantic orderliness. The hoarder will be orderly with things, thoughts, or feelings, but again, as with memory, his orderliness is sterile and rigid. He cannot endure things out of place and will automatically rearrange them. To him the outside world threatens to break into his fortified position; orderliness signifies mastering the world outside by putting it, and keeping it, in its proper place in order to avoid the danger intrusion. His compulsive cleanliness is another expression of his need to undo contact with the outside world. Things beyond his own frontiers are felt to be dangerous and "unclean"; he annuls the menacing contact by compulsive washing, similar to a religious washing ritual prescribed after contact with unclean things or people. Things have to be put not only in their proper place but also into their proper time; obsessive punctuality is characteristic of the hoarding type; it is another form of mastering the outside world. If the outside world is experienced as a threat to one's fortified position, obstinacy is a logical reaction. A constant "no" is the almost automatic defense against intrusion; sitting tight, the answer to the danger of being pushed. These people tend to feel that they possess only a fixed quantity of strength, energy, or mental capacity, and that this stock is diminished or exhausted by use and can never be replenished. They cannot understand the self-replenishing function of all living substance and that activity and the use of one's powers increase strength while stagnation paralyzes; to them, death and destruction have more reality than life and growth. The act of creation is a miracle of which they hear but in which they do not believe. Their highest values are order and security; their motto: "There is nothing new under the sun." In their relationship to others intimacy is a threat; either remoteness or possession of a person means security. The hoarder tends to be suspicious and to have a particular sense of justice which in effect says: "Mine is mine and yours is yours."

The Marketing Orientation

The marketing orientation developed as a dominant one only in the modern era. In order to understand its nature one must consider the economic function of the market in modern society as being not only analogous to this character orientation but as the basis and the main condition for its development in modern man.

Barter is one of the oldest economic mechanisms. The traditional local market, however, is essentially different from the market as it has developed in modern capitalism. Bartering on a local market offered an opportunity to meet for the purpose of exchanging commodities. Producers and customers became acquainted; they were relatively small groups; the demand was more or less known, so that the producer could produce for this specific demand.

The modern market is no longer a meeting place but a mechanism characterized by abstract and impersonal demand. One produces for this market, not for a known circle of customers; its verdict is based on laws of supply and demand; and it determines whether the commodity can be sold and at what price. No matter what the *use value* of a pair of shoes may be, for instance, if the supply is greater than the demand, some shoes will be sentenced to economic death; they might as well not have been produced at all. The market day is the "day of judgment" as far as the exchange *value* of commodities is concerned.

The reader may object that this description of the market is oversimplified. The producer does try to judge the demand in advance, and under monopoly conditions even obtains a certain degree of control over it. Nevertheless, the regulatory function of the market has been, and still is, predominant enough to have a profound influence on the character formation of the urban middle class and, through the latter's social and cultural influence, on the whole population. The market concept of value, the emphasis on exchange value rather than on use value, has led to a similar concept of value with regard to people and particularly to oneself. The character orientation which is rooted in the experience of oneself as a commodity and of one's value as exchange value I call the marketing orientation.

In our time the marketing orientation has been growing rapidly, together with the development of a new market that is a phenomenon of the last decades—the "personality market." Clerks and salesmen, business executives and doctors, lawyers and artists all appear on this market. It is true that their legal status and economic positions are different: some are independent, charging for their services; others are employed, receiving salaries. But all are dependent for their material success on a personal acceptance by those who need their services or who employ them.

The principle of evaluation is the same on both the personality and the commodity market: on the one, personalities are offered for sale; on the other, commodities. Value in both cases is their exchange value, for which use value is a necessary but not a sufficient condition. It is true, our economic system could not function if people were not skilled in the particular work they have to perform and were gifted only with a pleasant personality. Even the best bedside manner and the most beautifully equipped office on Park Avenue would not make a New York doctor successful if he did not have a minimum of medical knowledge and skill. Even the most winning personality would not prevent a secretary from losing her job unless she could type reasonably fast. However, if we ask what the respective weight of skill and personality as a condition for success is, we find that only in exceptional cases is success predominantly the result of skill and of certain other human qualities like honesty, decency, and integrity. Although the proportion between skill and human qualities on the one hand and "personality" on the other hand as prerequisites for success varies, the "personality factor" always plays a decisive role. Success depends largely on how well a person sells himself on the market, how well he gets his personality across, how nice a "package" he is; whether he is "cheerful," "sound," "aggressive," "reliable," "ambitious"; furthermore what his family background is, what clubs he belongs to, and whether he knows the right people. The type of personality required depends to some degree on the special field in which a person works. A stockbroker, a salesman, a secretary, a railroad executive, a college professor, or a hotel manager must each offer different kinds of personality that, regardless of their differences, must fulfill one condition: to be in demand.

The fact that in order to have success it is not sufficient to have the skill and equipment for performing a given task but that one must be able to "put across" one's personality in competition with many others shapes the attitude toward oneself. If it were enough for the purpose of making a living to rely on what one knows and what one can do, one's self-esteem would be in proportion to one's capacities, that is, to one's use value; but since success depends largely on how one sells one's personality, one experiences oneself as a commodity or rather simultaneously as the seller *and* the commodity to be sold. A person is not concerned with his life and happiness, but with becoming salable. This feeling might be compared to that of a commodity, of handbags on a counter, for instance, could they feel and think. Each handbag would try to make itself as "attractive" as possible in order to attract customers and to look as expensive as possible in order to obtain a higher price than its rivals. The handbag sold for the highest price would feel elated, since that would mean it was the most "valuable" one; the one which was not sold would feel sad and convinced of its own worthlessness. This fate might befall a bag which, though excellent in appearance and usefulness, had the bad luck to be out of date because of a change in fashion.

Like the handbag, one has to be in fashion on the personality market, and in order to be in fashion one has to know what kind of personality is most in demand. This knowledge is transmitted in a general way throughout the whole process of education, from kindergarten to college, and implemented by the family. The knowledge acquired at this early stage is not sufficient, however; it emphasizes only certain general qualities like adaptability, ambition, and sensitivity to the changing expectations of other people. The more specific picture of the models for success one gets elsewhere. The pictorial magazines, newspapers, and newsreels show the pictures and life stories of the successful in many variations. Pictorial advertising has a similar function. The successful executive who is pictured in a tailor's advertisement is the image of how one should look and be, if one is to draw down the "big money" on the contemporary personality market.

The most important means of transmitting the desired personality pattern to the average man is the motion picture. The young girl tries to emulate the facial expression, coiffure, gestures of a high-priced star as the most promising way to success. The young man tries to look and be like the model he sees on the screen. While the average citizen has little contact with the life of the most successful people, his relationship with the motion-picture stars is different. It is true that he has no real contact with them either, but he can see them on the screen again and again, can write them and receive their autographed pictures. In contrast to the time when the actor was socially despised but was nevertheless the transmitter of the works of great poets to his audience, our motion-picture stars have no great works or ideas to transmit, but their function is to serve as the link an average person has with the world of the "great." Even if he can not hope to become as successful as they are, he can try to emulate them; they are his saints and because of their success they embody the norms for living.

Since modern man experiences himself both as the seller and as the commodity to be sold on the market, his self-esteem depends on conditions beyond his control. If he is "successful," he is valuable; if he is not, he is worthless. The degree of insecurity which results from this orientation can hardly be overestimated. If one feels that one's own value is not constituted primarily by the human qualities one possesses, but by one's success on a competitive market with ever-changing conditions, one's self-esteem is bound to be shaky and in constant need of confirmation by others. Hence one is driven to strive relentlessly for success, and any setback is a severe threat to one's self-esteem;

helplessness, insecurity, and inferiority feelings are the result. If the vicissitudes of the market are the judges of one's value, the sense of dignity and pride is destroyed.

But the problem is not only that of self-evaluation and self-esteem but of one's experience of oneself as an independent entity, of one's *identity with oneself.* The mature and productive individual derives his feeling of identity from the experience of himself as the agent who is one with his powers; this feeling of self can be briefly expressed as meaning "*I am what I do.*" In the marketing orientation

man encounters his own powers as commodities alienated from him. He is not one with them but they are masked from him because what matters is not his self-realization in the process of using them but his success in the process of selling them. Both his powers and what they create become estranged, something different from himself, something for others to judge and to use; thus his feeling of identity becomes as shaky as his self-esteem; it is constituted by the sum total of roles one can play: "*I am as you desire me.*"

Therapeutic Approaches

Pathological behavior, according to the intrapsychic theorists, reflects the operation of unconscious anxieties and defensive maneuvers that have persisted from early childhood. The task of therapy, then, is to bring these residues of the past into consciousness where they can be reevaluated and reworked in a constructive fashion. The excerpts chosen for this section are drawn from two of the more prominent contemporary psychoanalytic theorists, Otto Kernberg and Heinz Kohut. Together, they have stimulated a renewed vitality in analytic circles.

Kernberg's contribution is of particular value in that he not only discusses issues relevant to treatment, but does so with reference to what is perhaps the most "popular" diagnostic syndrome of the day, the borderline condition.

Another major new syndrome, the narcissistic personality, is the object of Kohut's essay on intrapsychic treatment approaches. Somewhat esoteric and stylistically turbid, Kohut's work is a prime illustration of contemporary analytic thought.

19 Borderline Personality Organization: Diagnosis and Treatment

Otto Kernberg

In this chapter, I use the term ego weakness to refer to structural alterations of the ego derived from early ego disturbances, and will

From *Borderline Conditions and Psychological Narcissism* (New York: Jason Aronson, 1975), pp. 161–177. Reprinted by permission of the publisher.

examine briefly, 1) the clinical manifestations of ego weakness which is typical for borderline personality organization, 2) some hypotheses regarding the origin of ego weakness, 3) complications arising from efforts to analyze patients with ego weakness and some technical implications for the treatment of these patients and, 4) some conditions improving or worsening analyzability in these cases. I will introduce at several points new material to the respective analyses developed in earlier chapters, emphasizing the diagnostic and therapeutic features of borderline personality organization. Finally, I will summarize some clinical and theoretical implications of transference psychosis and clarify further the differential diagnosis with schizophrenia.

The Clinical Manifestations of Borderline Personality Organization

Clinically, when we speak of patients with borderline personality organization, we refer to patients who present serious difficulties in their interpersonal relationships and some alteration of their experience of reality but with essential preservation of reality testing. Such patients also present contradictory character traits, chaotic coexistence of defenses against and direct expression of primitive "id contents" in consciousness, a kind of pseudo-insight into their personality without real concern for nor awareness of the conflictual nature of this material, and a lack of clear identity and lack of understanding in depth of other people. These patients present primitive defensive operations rather than repression and related defenses, and above all, mutual dissociation of contradictory ego states reflecting what might be called a "nonmetabolized" persistence of early, pathological internalized object relationships. They also show "non-specific" manifestations of ego weakness. The term "nonspecific" refers to lack of impulse control, lack of anxiety tolerance, lack of sublimatory capacity, and presence of primary process thinking, and indicates that these manifestations of ego weakness represent a general inadequacy of normal ego functions. In contrast, the primitive defensive constellation of these patients and their contradictory, pathological character traits are "specific" manifestations of ego weakness. In short, they represent highly individualized, active compromise formations of impulse and defense.

Hypotheses Regarding the Origin of Ego Weakness

Two essential tasks that the early ego has to accomplish in rapid succession are (1) the differentiation of self-images from object-images, and (2) integrating libidinally determined and aggressively determined self- and object-images.

The first task is accomplished in part under the influence of the development of the apparatuses of primary autonomy: perception and memory traces help to sort out the origin of stimuli and gradually differentiate self-from object-images. This first task fails to a major extent in the psychoses, in which a pathological fusion between self- and object-images determines a failure in the differentiation of ego boundaries and, therefore, in the differentiation of self from nonself. In contrast, in the case of borderline personality organization, differentiation of self- from object-images has occurred to a sufficient degree to permit the establishment of integrated ego boundaries and a concomitant differentiation between self and others.

The second task, however, of integrating self- and object-images built up under the influence of libidinal drive derivatives and their related affects with their corresponding self- and object-images built up under the influence of aggressive drive derivatives and related affects, fails to a great extent in borderline patients, mainly because of the pathological predominance of pregenital aggression. The resulting lack of synthesis of contradictory self- and object-images interferes with the integration of the self-concept and with the establishment of object-constancy or "total" object relationships. I will now examine these hypotheses in more detail.

Good enough mothering implies that mother evokes, stimulates, and complements ego functions which are not yet available to the infant. For example, mother's intuitive handling of the baby permits the early detection of sources of pain, fear, and frustration, in addition to providing an optimum of gratifying, pleasurable experiences while satisfying the baby's basic needs. Intrapsychically, this means that a core experience of satisfaction and pleasure is set up in the baby, powerfully reinforced by the pleasurable affects thus released and gradually also by the proprioceptive and exteroceptive perceptions linked with such experiences. Out of this core will come the basic, fused self-mother image which in turn determines basic trust. Basic trust involves recognition, and, later, anticipation of a pleasurable mother-child relationship. The basic ego disturbance is the failure to build up a sufficiently strong fused "all good" self-object image or "good internal object."

The libidinally determined good self-object image permits some attenuation or neutralization of the anxiety producing and disorganizing effects of excessive frustration, with which "bad," fused self-object images are set up. The normal relationship with mother reinforces, as well as depends upon, the buildup of this good internal fused self-object image.

Severe frustrations and the consequent predominance of aggressively-determined, "all bad" fused self-object images may interfere with the next stage of development, namely, the gradual sorting out of self from object components in the realm of the good self-object image. As Jacobson points out, defensive refusion of primitive, all good self- and object-images as a protection against excessive frustration and rage is the prototype of what constitutes, if prolonged beyond the early infantile stages of development, a psychotic identification.

If and when self-images have been differentiated from object-images in the area of libidinally determined ego nuclei and, later, in the area of aggressively determined ego nuclei, a crucial step has been taken which differentiates future psychotic from nonpsychotic ego structures. The next step is the gradual integration of contradictory (that is, libidinally determined and aggressively determined) self-images, with the crystallization of a central self surrounded, we might say, by object-images which in turn become integrated (in the sense that good and bad object representations related to the same external objects are integrated). This is also the point where tolerance of ambivalence begins to develop. When such integration is achieved, an integrated self-image or self-concept relates to integrated object-images and there is also a continuous reshaping and reconfirmation of both self-concept and object-images by means of mechanisms of projection and introjection linked with actual interpersonal relationships with mother and other human beings surrounding the child.

The integrated self-concept and the related integrated representation of objects constitutes ego identity in its broadest sense. A stable ego identity, in turn, becomes a crucial determinant of stability, integration, and flexibility of the ego, and also influences the full development of higher level superego func-

tions (abstraction, depersonification, and individualization of the superego).

Failure to integrate the libidinally determined and the aggressively determined self- and object-images is the major cause for nonpsychotic ego disturbances which, in turn, determine limits in analyzability. Such lack of integration derives from a pathological predominance of aggressively determined self- and object-images and a related lack of establishment of a sufficiently strong ego core around the originally fused good self-object image. However, in contrast to conditions in which self-images have not been differentiated from object-images (the psychoses), there has been at least sufficient differentiation between self- and object-images for the establishment of firm ego boundaries in cases of ego distortion which are generally designated as borderline conditions. The problem at this point is that the intensity of aggressively determined self- and object-images, and of defensively idealized all good self- and object-images makes integration impossible. Bringing together extremely opposite loving and hateful images of the self and of significant others would trigger unbearable anxiety and guilt because of the implicit danger to the good internal and external object relations; therefore, there is an active defensive separation of such contradictory self- and object-images; in other words, primitive dissociation or splitting becomes a major defensive operation.

Lack of integration of self- and object-representations is at first a normal characteristic of early development; but, later, such lack of integration is used actively to separate contradictory ego states. Splitting refers to the active, defensive separation of contradictory ego states. Primitive defensive operations linked to splitting (denial, primitive idealization, omnipotence, projection, and projective identification) powerfully reinforce splitting, and protect the ego from unbearable conflicts between love and hatred by sacrificing its growing integration. Clinically, the child who is going to become a borderline patient lives from moment to moment, actively cutting off the emotional links between what would otherwise become chaotic, contradictory, highly frustrating and frightening emotional experiences with significant others in his immediate environment.

There are several significant structural consequences of these primitive defensive operations set up to protect the ego against unbearable conflict and the related pathology of internalized object relationships. First, an integrated self-concept cannot develop, and chronic overdependence on external objects occurs in an effort to achieve some continuity in action, thought, and feeling in relating to them. Lack of integration of the self-concept determines the syndrome of identity-diffusion. Second, contradictory character traits develop, representing the contradictory self- and object-images, further creating chaos in the interpersonal relationship of the future borderline patient. Third, superego integration suffers because the guiding function of an integrated ego identity is missing; contradictions between exaggerated, all good ideal object-images and extremely sadistic, all bad superego forerunners interfere with superego integration. Therefore, the superego functions which would further facilitate ego integration also are missing and this reinforces the pathological consequences of excessive reprojection of superego nuclei in the form of paranoid trends. Fourth, a lack of integrated object-representations interferes with deepening of empathy with others as individuals in their own right; lack of integration of the self-concept further interferes with full emotional understanding of other human beings; the end result is defective object-constancy or incapacity to establish total object relationships. Fifth, nonspecific aspects of ego strength (anxiety tolerance, impulse control, sublimatory potential) suffer because of the weakness of ego and superego integration. Ego strength depends on the neutralization of instinctual energy; such neutralization takes place essentially in the integration of libidinally and aggressively derived self- and object-images.

Complications in Analyzing Patients with Borderline Personality Organization, and Technical Implications for Their Treatment

In patients with ego weakness, primitive, early conflicts are not repressed; conscious mutual dissociation among contradictory primitive contents replaces repression and the normal "resistance versus content" organization of defenses and impulses. Consciousness of primitive material does not reflect insight but the predominance of splitting mechanisms—a different set of defensive constellations from those centering around repression seen in neurotic patients.

Also, deficit in nonspecific manifestations of ego strength interferes with the necessary tolerance of increased conflict awareness during treatment, and provokes excessive acting-out tendencies.

In addition, lack of differentiation of the self-concept and the lack of differentiation and individualization of objects interfere with the differentiation of present from past object relationships. Transference and reality are confused; also, the analyst is not differentiated from the transference object because of the prevalence of primitive projection. Furthermore, the lack of capacity for seeing the analyst as an integrated object in his own right, and the pathologically increased, alternating projection of self- and object-images (so that reciprocal roles are easily interchanged in the transference) weakens ego boundaries in the transference and promotes transference psychosis.

Finally, the therapeutic relationship easily replaces ordinary life, because its gratifying and sheltered nature further intensifies the temptation to gratify primitive pathological needs in the transference and acting out.

This summary reflects the typical structure of borderline personality organization and the typical treatment difficulties these patients present. Although some authors believe that a standard psychoanalysis can and should be carried out under these conditions, others, including myself, question this. However, the treatment I suggest as ideally suited for these patients is a psychoanalytically derived procedure which strongly emphasizes the interpretation of resistances and of the transference and the adherence to an essentially neutral position of the analyst.

I have suggested the following technical requirements for the psychoanalytic psychotherapy of borderline patients: (1) systematic elaboration of the negative transference in the "here and now" only, without attempting to achieve full genetic reconstructions; (2) interpretation of the defensive constellations of these patients as they enter the negative transference; (3) limit-setting in order to block acting out of the transference, with as much structuring of the patient's life outside the hours as necessary to protect the neutrality of the analyst; (4) noninterpretation of the less primitively determined, modulated aspects of the positive transference to foster the gradual development of the therapeutic alliance.

Some Conditions under Which Analyzability Improves or Worsens

Improvement or worsening of the prognosis for psychoanalysis within the context of serious ego distortions of borderline personality organization depends on structural developments which complicate borderline personality organization and which, in turn, largely depend upon further vicissitudes of internalized object relationships.

If the borderline patient has achieved some higher level of superego integration, abstraction, and depersonification, the superego may still be sufficiently strong to carry out functions fostering ego integration at large, thus compensating for the lack of integration of the self-concept (identity diffusion). Some infantile personalities have developed surprisingly good internalized value systems; the capacity to identify with ethical, professional, and/or artistic values beyond satisfaction of their own needs; and a personal integrity in dealing with these values, professions, or arts. Although a high intelligence and particular talents may be helpful elements, most important for such a development to occur seems to be the availability of object relations at the height of the development of advanced superego structures (around ages 4 to 6 and/or throughout adolescence) which were not completely controlled by their primitive conflicts and which permitted more harmonious integration of some realistic superego demands and prohibitions. Honesty and integrity in the ordinary sense of these words are also valuable prognostic factors which may permit some infantile personalities and other borderline personality structures to undergo a nonmodified psychoanalytic procedure.

A prognostically negative development complicating borderline personality organization is a pathological fusion of "all good" self-images with early ideal self-images and early ideal object-images. Such a pathological fusion of all the "good" aspects of internalized object relationships crystallizes into an an idealized, highly unrealistic self-concept which, if fostered by some realistic circumstances (such as an unusual talent, physi-

cal beauty, or intelligence), may be reinforced by reality and, paradoxically, foster better reality adaptation to "specialness." This development characterizes the narcissistic personality. Social functioning may improve greatly under these circumstances, but at the cost of the loss of the normal differentiation between self on the one hand, and ego ideal on the other (at the cost, therefore, of a most important superego structure). Serious superego defects are typical of narcissistic personalities and compromise their analyzability.

It hardly needs to be stressed that the idealized self-concept requires even stronger activation of primitive defensive operations to deny and project the devaluated, bad aspects of the self; therefore, these defenses perpetuate a lack of realistic integration of the self-concept. However, the very improvement in surface functioning may obscure the severity of the underlying psychopathology, and narcissistic personalities may undergo years of psychoanalysis without change. Elsewhere, I refer to the fact that these patients should, however, be treated with psychoanalysis, and I also stress the special technical requirements of their analysis.

A particularly ominous development worsening the prognosis for both psychoanalysis and psychoanalytic psychotherapy is the development, within the character structure of borderline patients, of identification with primitive superego forerunners of a highly sadistic kind. Under these circumstances, primitive destructiveness and self-destructiveness are built into the ego structure, are sanctioned by the superego, and permit direct expression of aggressive impulses under conditions which can seriously threaten the physical as well as the psychic life of these patients. Self-destruction, originally expressing primitive, pregenital aggression, may become an ego ideal and gratify the patient's sense of omnipotence in that he no longer needs to fear frustration and suffering (suffering is now an enjoyment in itself). Such aggression is expressed not only by random destructiveness, but by selective destructiveness toward those on whom the patient depends for his gratification (and his improvement). Therefore, he particularly envies those on whom he depends because these objects have an internal sense of love and they even want to provide goodness for others, including the patient. These patients represent prognostically the most ominous type of identification with the aggressor.

Further Considerations about Treatment

Transference Interpretation, Regression, and Reconstruction

I would now like to stress the following aspects of the treatment of these patients: first, one has to keep in mind that ego weakness does not reflect absence of a solid defensive organization of the ego, but represents the very active presence of a rigid constellation of primitive defenses; these defenses by their effects contribute to producing and maintaining such ego weakness. Second, rather than attempting to reinforce higher level defenses or to support the patient's adaptation directly, it is helpful to consistently interpret these primitive defensive operations, especially as they enter the transference, because the interpretation of these defenses permits ego growth to resume and higher level defensive operations to take over. Third, interpretations have to be formulated so that the patient's distortions of the analyst's intervention can be simultaneously and systematically examined, and the patient's distortion of present reality and especially of his perceptions in the hour can be systematically clarified. This clarification does not mean suggestion, advice giving, or revelation regarding personal matters of the analyst to the patient, but a clear explanation of how the analyst sees the "here and now" interaction with the patient in contrast to how the analyst assumes the patient is interpreting this "here and now" interaction. Clarification of perceptions and of the patient's relationship to the interpretation is, therefore, an important component of an essentially interpretive approach which attempts to systematically analyze the primitive defensive constellation as it enters the transference.

Often, in advanced stages of treatment of borderline patients, it turns out that while the traumatic circumstances patients reported earlier were unreal, there were other, very real, chronically traumatizing parent-child interactions which they had never been consciously aware of before. It turns out that the most

damaging influences were those which the patient had taken as a matter of course, and the absence of these influences are often experienced by the patient as an astonishing opening of new perspectives on life. The following case illustrates the relationship between distortion of present reality and distortion of the past in the transference of a borderline patient, and the need to clarify the patient's perceptions in the hours.

A patient reminisced about having intimate physical contact with both parents which in her mind amounted to a family shared orgy. Gradually she became aware of the fantastic nature of these memories but later she recalled experiences she had not reported because they seemed such a matter of course. The patient reacted angrily whenever the analyst stated he did not understand some verbal or nonverbal communication of hers. She did not believe him; she thought he really could read her mind and that he only pretended he could not because he wanted to make her angry. After she consistently explored her assumption that the analyst could read her mind, she remembered that her mother had told her that she could indeed read the patient's mind. The patient's rejection of interpretations that seemed false to her was experienced by her as rebelliousness against mother. The implicit omnipotence of mother, her sadistic intrusion, the patient's passive acceptance of such a style of communication during childhood and adolescence, and her secondary omnipotent utilization of this pattern, turned out to reflect the real, highly traumatic aspects of her childhood. After working through in the transference the fantastic experiences with the parents—and the defenses against them—the patient was able to perceive the more realistic aspects of the therapeutic relationship. She became aware of the real, pathological interactions with her parents, which previously had seemed natural to her.

The implications of this observation that I wish to stress are that the disturbance in reality testing of this patient was related to a double layer of transference phenomena: a) the highly distorted transference (at times of an almost psychotic nature) reflecting fantastic internal object-relationships related to early ego disturbances, and b) the more "realistic" transference related to real experiences—the highly inappropriate parent-child interactions.

Interpretation of primitive defensive operations as they are activated in the therapeutic relationship may bring about immediate, impressive improvement in the patient's psychological functioning to such an extent that such a method in itself may be used in the diagnostic process when trying to differentiate borderline from psychotic patients. Systematic probing of primitive defensive operations, such as interpretation of splitting mechanisms in the hour, will tend to improve immediately the functioning of the borderline patient, but will bring about further regression into manifest psychotic symptomatology in the psychotic patient. The following cases illustrate such improvement or regression in the diagnostic process:

In the hospital, I examined a college student, a single girl in her early twenties, with awkward and almost bizarre behavior, childlike theatrical gestures, emotional outbursts, suicidal ideation, and breakdown in her social relations and scholastic achievements. Her initial diagnosis was hysterical personality. She was very concerned about social and political matters, cried over the fact that she needed to be in the hospital, but simultaneously acted completely indifferent while talking about her suicidal fantasies, acted as if she were drowsy or drugged, gave clear indication of boredom with the interviews, and complained about her inability to make up her mind about herself. I pointed out to her the displacement of her concern over herself to the social and political situation, the expression of depreciation of the interviewer, the effective avoidance of taking responsibility for herself by dissociating her concern for herself from the chaotic, easy-go-lucky behavior geared to force others to take over for her.

In technical terms, I interpreted primitive defensive operations (splitting, denial, omnipotence, and devaluation) as they were apparent in the "here and now" interaction with me. In the course of the interviews, the patient changed from an almost psychotic appearance to that of a rather thoughtful, perceptive although highly anxious neurotic patient. The final diagnosis was: infantile personality, with borderline features.

In contrast to this case, I examined another college student in her early twenties, also single, whose initial diagnosis was that of an obsessive-compulsive neurosis, probably functioning on a borderline level. The entire interaction was filled with highly theoretical,

philosophical considerations, and efforts to examine more personal, emotional material only intensified the abstract nature of the comments that followed. I attempted to interpret to the patient the avoidance function of her theorizing, and explored some of the emotional experiences which she expressed in theoretical, philosophical terms. I also wondered with her whether the direct, personal impact of those experiences was too much for her, her theorizing providing her with some safety by distance. For example, when exploring the unhappy nature of a relationship with a boyfriend, she discussed the theological theories about guilt; and I wondered whether it was hard for her to explore guilt feelings she might have had in connection with that relationship. As I confronted the patient with her defensive maneuvers, she became more disturbed, openly distrustful, and even more abstract. Toward the end of the interviews, there was direct evidence of formal thought disorder and the diagnosis of schizophrenic reaction was eventually confirmed.

The implications of these observations that I wish to stress are (1) interpretation of the predominant defensive operations in borderline patients may strengthen ego functioning, while the same approach to psychotic patients may bring about further regression; (2) the intimate relationship between reality testing, the effectiveness of defensive operations, and the immediate interpersonal interaction.

The fact that interpretation of these defensive operations may increase regression in psychotic patients does not imply that interpretive approaches should not be attempted with them; but such approaches do require particular modifications of the analytic technique which contraindicate both psychoanalysis as such, and the modified approach recommended for borderline patients. The psychotic patient, with his blurring of limits between self and object-images and the subsequent loss of ego boundaries, also utilizes splitting and other related primitive defensive operations; but he uses them to keep a surface adaptation in the face of threatening primitive dangers of complete engulfment or ego-dissolution. His problem is not only to separate hatred and love completely from each other but to avoid any intensification of awareness of affects, because the very intensity of any emotional relationship in itself may trigger off the refusion of self- and object-images. Therefore, interpretation of the psychotic patient's primitive defensive operations may bring about further loss of reality testing and psychotic regression.

Primitive defensive operations, and especially pathological forms of splitting and projection which bring about total dispersal of emotional awareness, protect the tenuous social adaptation of the psychotic patient: the underlying lack of self–object differentiation is thus obscured. Intensive psychotherapy with psychotic patients highlights this self–object fusion and requires a therapeutic approach which is different from that required with borderline conditions.

The intensive, psychoanalytic psychotherapy of psychotic, particularly schizophrenic, patients requires a tolerance, on the therapist's part, of the powerful countertransference reactions triggered off by the patient's fusion experiences in the transference. The therapist has to make maximal use of his countertransference experiences to understand the patient's experience, to convey to the patient his understanding in verbal communications, and to map out gradually in these communications the implicit differences existing between the patient's experiences and the therapist's reality, and between the patient's past and the present in the transference. In contrast, the therapist working with borderline patients, needs to interpret the primitive projective mechanisms, particularly projective identification, which contribute powerfully to the alternating projection of self- and object-images, and therefore, to blurring the boundary between what is "inside" and "outside" in the patient's experience of his interactions with the therapist. Acting out of the transference and excessive gratification of primitive emotional needs in the transference of borderline conditions need to be controlled while preserving an essentially neutral attitude of the therapist.

The following, concluding comments refer specifically to borderline patients. Working through of the primitive level of internalized object relationships activated in the transference gradually permits a shift in the transference into a predominance of the higher level, more realistic type of internalized object relations related to real childhood experiences. In order to achieve improvement in distorted ego functions, the patient must come to terms at some point with very real, serious limitations of what life has given him in his early years. Here the issue of coming to terms with physical and psychological defects converge. It is probably as difficult for borderline patients eventually to come to terms with the fact of failure in their early life as it is for patients with inborn or early determined physical defects to acknowledge, mourn, and come to terms with their defects. Borderline patients gradually have to become aware of how their parents failed them—not in the distorted, monstrous ways which existed in their fantasies when beginning treatment, but failed them in simple human ways of giving and receiving love, and providing consolation and understanding, and intuitively lending a helping hand when the baby, or the child, was in trouble. Borderline patients also have to learn to give up the highly idealized, unrealistically protective fantasies about perfect past relationships with their parents; for them to really separate from their parents is a much more difficult and frightening prospect than for the neurotic patient. These patients also have to work through the corresponding idealizations and magical expectations in the transference, and learn to acccept the analyst realistically as a limited human being. This painful learning process is achieved by means of eventual analysis of parameters of technique, or by means of realistically examining in the treatment situation modifications of technique and why the analyst used them. Coming to terms with severe defects in one's past requires the capacity to mourn and to work through such mourning; to accept aloneness; and to realistically accept that others may have what the patient himself may never be able to fully compensate for. Hopefully, such capacity will develop throughout the treatment, but it is hard to foretell to what extent this development will take place.

Transference Psychosis

I mentioned earlier that the lack of differentiation of the self-concept and the lack of differentiation and individualization of objects interfere with the differentiation of present from past object-relationships, and contribute to the development of transference psychosis. Transference psychosis is a characteristic complication in the treatment of patients with borderline personality organization. There are similarities and differences between the transference psychosis that borderline patients develop and the psychotic transference characteristic of psychotic patients in intensive treatment.

The similarities of transference psychosis in borderline and psychotic patients are: 1) In both, there is a loss of reality testing in the transference situation, and the development of delusional thoughts involving the therapist; hallucinatory or pseudo-hallucinatory experiences may develop in the hours. 2) In both, primitive object relationships of a fantastic nature predominate in the transference; these relationships are characterized by multiple self-images and multiple object-images, that is, fantasy structures reflecting the earliest layers of internalized object relationships which represent a deeper layer of the mind than the dyadic and oedipal-triangular relationships characteristic of transference neurosis. This is in contrast to the predominance in the transference neurosis of less severely ill patients, of later, more realistic, internalized self- and object-representations in the context of an integrated ego and superego, reflecting more realistic, past interactions with the parents. 3) In borderline and psychotic patients, there develops an activation of primitive, overwhelming affective reactions in the transference, and a loss of sense of having a separate identity from the therapist.

The differences between the transference psychosis of borderline patients and the psychotic transference of psychotic, particularly schizophrenic, patients who undergo intensive psychotherapy are:

1. In borderline patients, the loss of reality testing does not strikingly affect the patient's functioning outside the treatment setting; these patients may develop delusional ideas and psychotic behavior within the treatment hours over a period of days and months without showing these manifestations outside the hours. Also, the transference psychosis of patients with borderline personality organization responds dramatically to the treatment previously outlined. In contrast, the psychotic transference of schizophrenic patients reflects their general loss of reality testing, and the psychotic thinking, behavior, and affect ex-

pression of their life outside the treatment hours. The initial detachment of the schizophrenic patient is usually reflected in psychotic behavior in the hours which is not markedly different from his psychotic behavior outside the treatment hours. It may take a long time for psychotic patients to develop a particular, intensive emotional relationship to the therapist, differentiated from all other interactions: when this finally does happen, the psychotic transference becomes particularly different from that of borderline patients, our next point.

2. Psychotic patients, particularly at more advanced states of development of their psychotic transference, have fusion experiences with the therapist by which they feel a common identity with him. In contrast to borderline patients, this identity confusion in the transference is not due to rapid oscillation of projection of self- and object-images (so that object relationships are activated with rapidly alternating, reciprocal role enactment on the part of patient and therapist), but is a consequence of refusion of self- and object-images, so that separateness between self and nonself no longer obtains: this reflects their regression to a more primitive stage of symbiotic self-object fusion. Borderline patients, even in the course of a transference psychosis, do experience a boundary of a sort between themselves and the therapist: it is as if the patient maintains a sense of being different from the therapist at all times, but concurrently he and the therapist are interchanging aspects of their personalities. In contrast, psychotic patients experience themselves as one with the therapist at all times; however, the nature of this oneness changes from a frightening, dangerous experience of raw aggression and confused engulfment (without differentiating who engulfs and who is the engulfed) to that of an exalted, mystical experience of oneness, goodness, and love. In short, the underlying mechanisms determining loss of ego boundaries, loss of reality testing, and delusion formation are different in the psychotic transferences of borderline and psychotic patients.

20 The Psychoanalytic Treatment of Narcissistic Personality Disorders

Heinz Kohut

Introductory Considerations

The classification of the transferencelike structures mobilized during the analysis of narcissistic personalities presented here is based on previous conceptualizations (Kohut, 1966) of which only the following brief summary can be given. It was suggested that the child's original narcissistic balance, the perfection of his primary narcissism, is disturbed by the unavoidable shortcomings of maternal care, but that the child attempts to save the original experience of perfection by assigning it on the one hand to a grandiose and exhibitionistic image of the self: the *grandiose self*, and, on the other hand, to an admired you: the *idealized parent imago*. The central mechanisms which these two basic narcissistic configurations employ in order to preserve a part of the original experience are, of course, antithetical. Yet they coexist from the beginning and their individual and largely independent lines of development are open to separate scrutiny. At this moment it can only be pointed out that, under optimum developmental conditions, the exhibitionism and grandiosity of the archaic grandiose self are gradually tamed, and that the whole structure ultimately becomes integrated into the adult personality and supplies the instinctual fuel for our ego-syntonic ambitions and purposes, for the enjoyment of our activities, and for important aspects of our self-esteem. And, under similarly favorable circumstances, the idealized parent imago, too, becomes integrated into the adult personality. Introjected as our idealized superego, it becomes an important component of our psychic organization by holding up to us the guiding leadership of its ideals. If the child, however, suffers severe narcissistic traumata, then the grandiose self does not merge into the relevant ego content but is retained in its unaltered form and strives for the fulfillment of its archaic aims. And if the child experiences traumatic disappointments in the admired adult, then

Reprinted from *Psychoanal. Study Child*, 23, 86–104, 1968, by permission of International Universities Press, Inc., and Elizabeth Kohut.

the idealized parent imago, too, is retained in its unaltered form, is not transformed into tension-regulating psychic structure but remains an archaic, transitional object that is required for the maintenance of narcissistic homeostasis.

Severe regressions, whether occurring spontaneously or during therapy, may lead to the activation of unstable, prepsychological fragments of the mind-body-self and its functions which belong to the stage of *autoerotism* (cf. Nagera, 1964). The pathognomonically specific, transferencelike, therapeutically salutary conditions, however, on which I am focusing, are based on the activation of psychologically elaborated, cohesive configurations which enter into stable amalgamations with the *narcissistically* perceived psychic representation of the analyst. The relative stability of this narcissistic transference-amalgamation, however, is the prerequisite for the performance of the analytic task in the pathogenic narcissistic areas of the personality.

The Narcissistic Transferences

I shall now examine the two narcissistic transferences delimited in accordaance with the previously given conceptualizations: the therapeutic activation of the idealized parent imago for which the term *idealizing transference* will be employed, and the activation of the grandiose self which will be called the *mirror transference*.

Therapeutic Activation of the Idealized Parent Imago: The Idealizing Transference

The *idealizing transference* is the therapeutic revival of the early state in which the psyche saves a part of the lost experience of global narcissistic perfection by assigning it to an archaic (transitional) object, the idealized parent imago. Since all bliss and power now reside in the idealized object, the child feels empty and powerless when he is separated from it and he attempts, therefore, to maintain a continuous union with it.

Idealization, whether it is directed at a dimly perceived archaic mother-breast or at the clearly recognized oedipal parent, belongs genetically and dynamically in a narcissistic context. The idealizing cathexes, however, although retaining their narcissistic character, become increasingly neutralized and aim-inhibited. It is especially in the most advanced stages of their early development that the idealizations (which now coexist with powerful object-instinctual cathexes) exert their strongest and most important influence on the phase-appropriate internalization processes. At the end of the oedipal period, for example, the internalization of object-cathected aspects of the parental imago accounts for the contents (i.e., the commands and prohibitions) and functions (i.e., praise, scolding, punishment) of the superego; the internalization of the narcissistic aspects, however, for the exalted position of these contents and functions. It is from the narcissistic instinctual component of their cathexes that the aura of absolute perfection of the values and standards of the superego and of the omniscience and might of the whole structure are derived. That stream of narcissism, however, which is subsumed under the term idealized parent imago remains vulnerable throughout its whole early development, i.e., from the stage of the incipient, archaic idealized object (which is still almost merged with the self) to the time of the massive reinternalization of the idealized aspect of the imago of the oedipal parent (who is already firmly established as separate from the self). The period of greatest vulnerability ends when an idealized nuclear superego has been formed, since the capacity for the idealization of his central values and standards which the child thus acquires exerts a lasting beneficial influence on the psychic economy in the narcissistic sectors of the personality.

The beginning of latency, however, may be considered as still belonging to the oedipal phase. It constitutes the last of the several periods of greatest danger in early childhood during which the psyche is especially susceptible to traumatization because after a spurt of development a new balance of psychological forces is only insecurely established. If we apply this *principle of the vulnerability of new structures* to the superego at the beginning of latency and, in particular, to the newly established idealization of its values and standards and of its rewarding and punishing functions,

it will not surprise us to learn from clinical experience that a severe disappointment in the idealized oedipal object, even at the beginning of latency, may yet undo a precariously established idealization of the superego, may recathect the imago of the idealized object, and thus lead to a renewed insistence on finding an external object of perfection.

Under optimal circumstances the child experiences gradual disappointment in the idealized object—or, expressed differently: the child's evaluation of the idealized object becomes increasingly realistic—which leads to a withdrawal of the narcissistic idealizing cathexes from the object imago and to their gradual (or more massive but phase-appropriate) internalization, i.e., to the acquisition of permanent psychological structures which continue, endopsychically, the functions which had previously been fulfilled by the idealized object. If the child's relationship to the idealized object is, however, severely disturbed, e.g., if he suffers a traumatic (intense and sudden, or not phase-appropriate) disappointment in it, then the child does not acquire the needed internal structure, but his psyche remains fixated on an archaic object imago, and the personality will later, and throughout life, be dependent on certain objects in what seems to be an intense form of object hunger. The intensity of the search for and of the dependency on these objects is due to the fact that they are striven for as a substitute for missing segments of the psychic structure. These objects are not loved for their attributes, and their actions are only dimly recognized; they are needed in order to replace the functions of a segment of the mental apparatus which had not been established in childhood.

The structural defects which are the result of early disturbances in the relationship with the idealized object cannot be discussed within the confines of this essay. The following clinical illustration will instead focus on the effect of later traumatic disappointments, up to and including early latency.

Mr. A., a tall, asthenic man in his late twenties, was a chemist in a pharmaceutical firm. Although he entered analysis with the complaint that he felt sexually stimulated by men, it soon became apparent that his homosexual preoccupations constituted only one of the several indications of an underlying broad personality defect. More important were periods of feeling depressed (with an associated drop in his work capacity); and, as a trigger to the preceding disturbance, a specific vulnerability of his self-esteem, manifested by his sensitivity to criticism, or simply to the absence of praise, from the people whom he experienced as his elders or superiors. Thus, although he was a man of considerable intelligence who performed his tasks with skill and creative ability, he was forever in search of approval: from the head of the research laboratory where he was employed, from a number of senior colleagues, and from the fathers of the girls whom he dated. He was sensitively aware of these men and of their opinion of him. So long as he felt that they approved of him, he experienced himself as whole, acceptable, and capable; and was then indeed able to do well in his work and to be creative and successful. At slight signs of disapproval of him, however, or of lack of understanding for him, he would become depressed, would tend to become first enraged and then cold, haughty, and isolated, and his creativeness deteriorated.

The cohesive transference permitted the gradual reconstruction of a certain genetically decisive pattern. Repeatedly, throughout his childhood, the patient had felt abruptly disappointed in the power of his father just when he had (re-)established him as a figure of protective strength and efficiency. As is frequent, the first memories which the patient supplied subsequent to the transference activations of the crucial pattern referred to a comparatively late period. The family had come to the United States when the patient was nine and the father, who had been prosperous in Europe, was unable to repeat his earlier successes in this country. Time and again, however, the father shared his newest plans with his son and stirred the child's fantasies and expectations; but time and again he sold out in panic when the occurrence of unforeseen events and his lack of familiarity with the American scene combined to block his purposes. Although these memories had always been conscious, the patient had not previously appreciated the intensity of the contrast between the phase of great trust in the father, who was most confidence-inspiring while he was forging his plans, and the subsequent disappointment.

Most prominent among the patient's relevant recollections of earlier occurrences of the idealization-disappointment sequence were those of two events which affected the family

fortunes decisively when the patient was six and eight years old respectively. The father who, during the patient's early childhood, had been a virile and handsome man had owned a small but flourishing industry. Judging by many indications and memories, father and son had been very close emotionally and the son had admired his father greatly. Suddenly, when the patient was six, German armies invaded the country, and the family, which was Jewish, fled. Although the father had initially reacted with helplessness and panic, he had later been able to re-establish his business, though on a much reduced scale, but, as a consequence of the German invasion of the country to which they had escaped (the patient was eight at that time), everything was again lost and the family had to flee once more.

The patient's memories implicated the beginning of latency as the period when the structural defect was incurred. There is no doubt, however, that earlier experiences, related to his pathological mother, had sensitized him and accounted for the severity of the later acquired structural defect.

Described in metapsychological terms, his defect was the insufficient idealization of the superego and, concomitantly, a recathexis of the idealized parent imago of the late preoedipal and the oedipal stages. The symptomatic result of this defect was circumscribed yet profound. Since the patient had suffered a traumatic disappointment in the narcissistically invested aspects of the father imago, his superego did not possess the requisite exalted status and was thus unable to raise the patient's self-esteem. In view of the fact, however, that the patient had not felt equally deprived of those aspects of the father imago that were invested with object-instinctual cathexes, his superego was relatively intact with regard to those of its contents and functions that were built up as the heir to the object-instinctual dimensions of the oedipal father relationship. His nuclear goals and standards were indeed those of his cultural background transmitted by his father; what he lacked was the ability to feel more than a fleeting sense of satisfaction when living up to his standards or reaching his goals. Only through the confirmatory approval of external admired figures was he able to obtain a sense of heightened self-esteem. In the transference he seemed thus insatiable in two demands that he directed toward the idealized analyst: that the analyst share the patient's values, goals, and standards (and thus imbue them with significance through their idealization); and that the analyst confirm through the expression of a warm glow of pleasure and participation that the patient had lived up to his values and standards and had successfully worked toward a goal. Without the analyst's expression of his empathic comprehension of these needs, the patient's values and goals seemed trite and uninspiring to him and his successes were meaningless and left him feeling depressed and empty.

The Genesis of the Pathogenic Fixation on the Idealized Parent Imago

As can be regularly ascertained, the essential genetic trauma is grounded in the parents' own narcissistic fixations, and the parents' narcissistic needs contribute decisively to the child's remaining enmeshed within the narcissistic web of the parents' personality until, for example, the sudden recognition of the shortcomings of the parent, or the child's sudden desperate recognition of how far out of step his own emotional development has become, confronts him with the insuperable task of achieving the wholesale internalization of a chronic narcissistic relationship. The complexity of the pathogenic interplay between parent and child, and the varieties of its forms, defy a comprehensive description. Yet in a properly conducted analysis, the crucial pattern will often emerge with great clarity.

Mr. B., for example, established a narcissistic transference in which the analyst's presence increased and solidified his self-esteem and thus, secondarily, improved his ego functioning and efficiency.[1] To any impending disruption of this beneficial deployment of narcissistic cathexes, he responded with rage, and with a decathexis of the narcissistically invested analyst, and a hypercathexis of his grandiose self, manifested by cold and imperious behavior. But, finally (after the analyst had gone away, for example), he reached a comparatively stable balance: he withdrew to lonely intellectual activities which, although pursued with less creativity than before, provided him with a sense of self-sufficiency. In his words, he "rowed out

---

[1]The episode described here concerns a patient who was treated by a colleague (a woman) in regular consultation with the author.

alone to the middle of the lake and looked at the moon." When, however, the possibility of re-establishing the relationship to the narcissistically invested object offered itself, he reacted with the same rage that he had experienced when the transference—to use his own significant analogy—had become "unplugged." At first I thought that the reaction was nonspecific, consisting of yet unexpressed rage about the analyst's leaving, and of anger at having to give up a newfound protective balance. These explanations were, however, incomplete since the patient was in fact by his reactions describing an important sequence of early events. The patient's mother had been intensely enmeshed with him, and had supervised and controlled him in a most stringent fashion. His exact feeding time, for example, and in later childhood, his eating time, was determined by a mechanical timer—reminiscent of the devices which Schreber's father employed with his children (Niederland, 1959)—and thus the child felt that he had no mind of his own and that his mother was continuing to perform his mental functions long beyond the time when such maternal activities, carried out empathically, are indeed phase-appropriate and required. Under the impact of the anxious recognition of the inappropriateness of this relationship, he would in later childhood withdraw to his room to think his own thoughts, uninfluenced by her interference. When he had just begun to achieve some reliance on this minimum of autonomous functioning, his mother had a buzzer installed. From then on, she would interrupt his attempts of internal separation from her whenever he wanted to be alone. The buzzer summoned him more compellingly (because the mechanical device was experienced as akin to an endopsychic communication) than would have her voice or knocking. No wonder, then, that he reacted with rage to the return of the analyst after he had "rowed to the center of the lake to look at the moon."

The Process of Working Through and Some Other Clinical Problems in the Idealizing Transference

Little need be said concerning the beginning of the analysis. Although there may be severe resistances, especially those motivated by apprehensions about the extinction of individuality due to the wish to merge into the idealized object, the pathognomonic regression will establish itself spontaneously if the analyst does not interfere by premature transference interpretations. The working-through phase of the analysis can, however, begin only after the pathognomonic idealizing transference has been firmly established. It is set into motion by the fact that the instinctual equilibrium which the analysand aims to maintain is sooner or later disturbed. In the undisturbed transference the patient feels powerful, good, and capable. Anything, however, that deprives him of the idealized analyst creates a disturbance of his self-esteem: he feels powerless and worthless, and if his ego is not assisted by interpretations concerning the loss of the idealized parent imago, the patient may turn to archaic precursors of the idealized parent imago or may abandon it altogether and regress further to reactively mobilized archaic stages of the grandiose self. The retreat to archaic idealizations may manifest itself in the form of vague, impersonal, trance-like religious feelings; the hypercathexis of archaic forms of the grandiose self and of the (autoerotic) body self will produce the syndrome of emotional coldness, tendency toward affectation in speech and behavior, shame propensity, and hypochondria.

Although such temporary cathectic shifts toward the archaic stages of the idealized parent imago and of the grandiose self are common occurrences in the analysis of narcissistic personalities, they may be precipitated by seemingly minute narcissistic injuries the discovery of which may put the analyst's empathy and clinical acumen to a severe test.

The essence, however, of the curative process in the idealizing transference can be epitomized in a few comparatively simple principles. A working-through process is set in motion in which the repressed narcissistic strivings with which the archaic object is invested are admitted into consciousness. Although the ego and superego resistances with which we are familiar from the analysis of the transference neuroses also do occur here, and although there are in addition specific ego resistances (motivated by anxiety concerning hypomanic overstimulation) which oppose the mobilization of the idealizing cathexes, the major part of the working-through process concerns the loss of the narcissistically experienced object. If the repeated interpretations of the meaning of separations from the analyst on the level of the idealizing narcissistic libido are given with correct empathy for the analysand's feelings—in particular for what

appears to be his lack of emotions, i.e., his coldness and retreat, e.g., in response to separations—then there will gradually emerge a host of meaningful memories which concern the dynamic prototypes of the present experience. The patient will recall lonely hours during his childhood in which he attempted to overcome a feeling of fragmentation, hypochondria, and deadness which was due to the separation from the idealized parent. And he will remember, and gratefully understand, how he tried to substitute for the idealized parent imago and its functions by creating erotized replacements and through the frantic hypercathexis of the grandiose self: how he rubbed his face against the rough floor in the basement, looked at the mother's photograph, went through her drawers and smelled her underwear; and how he turned to the performance of grandiose athletic feats in which flying fantasies were being enacted by the child, in order to reassure himself. Adult analogues in the analysis (during the weekend, for example) are intense voyeuristic preoccupations, the impulse to shoplift, and recklessly speedy drives in the car. Childhood memories and deepening understanding of the analogous transference experiences converge in giving assistance to the patient's ego, and the formerly automatic reactions become gradually more aim-inhibited.

The ego acquires increasing tolerance for the analyst's absence and for the analyst's occasional failure to achieve a correct empathic understanding. The patient learns that the idealizing libido need not be immediately withdrawn from the idealized imago and that the painful and dangerous regressive shifts of the narcissistic cathexes can be prevented. Concomitant with the increase of the ability to maintain a part of the idealizing investment despite the separation, there is also an enhancement of internalization, i.e., the analysand's psychic organization acquires the capacity to perform some of the functions previously performed by the idealized object.

Therapeutic Activation of the Grandiose Self: The Mirror Transference

Analogous to the idealized object in the idealizing transference, it is the grandiose self which is reactivated in the transferencelike condition referred to as the *mirror transference*.

The mirror transference constitutes the therapeutic revival of the developmental stage in which the child attempts to retain a part of the original, all-embracing narcissism by concentrating perfection and power upon a grandiose self and by assigning all imperfections to the outside.

The mirror transference occurs in three forms which relate to specific stages of development of the grandiose self:

1. An archaic form in which the self-experience of the analysand includes the analyst; it will be referred to as *merger through the extension of the grandiose self.*

2. A less archaic form in which the patient assumes that the analyst is like him or that the analyst's psychological makeup is similar to his; it will be called the *alter-ego transference* or *twinship.*

3. A still less archaic form in which the analyst is experienced as a separate person who, however, has significance to the patient only within the framework of the needs generated by his therapeutically reactivated grandiose self. Here the term *mirror transference* is most accurate and will again be employed. In this narrower sense the mirror transference is the reinstatement of the phase in which the gleam in the mother's eye, which mirrors the child's exhibitionistic display, and other forms of maternal participation in the child's narcissistic enjoyment confirm the child's self-esteem and, by a gradually increasing selectivity of these responses, begin to channel it into realistic directions. If the development of the grandiose self is traumatically disturbed, however, then this psychic structure may become cut off from further integrative participation in the development of the personality. Insecurely repressed in an archaic form, it is, on the one hand, removed from further external influence; yet, on the other hand, continues to disturb realistic adaptation by its recurrent intrusions into the ego. In the mirror transference, however, it may become cohesively remobilized, and a new road to its gradual modification is opened.

The central activity in the clinical process during the mirror transference concerns the raising to consciousness of the patient's infantile fantasies of exhibitionistic grandeur. In view of the strong resistances which oppose this process and the intensive efforts required in overcoming them, it may at times be disappointing for the analyst to behold the apparently trivial fantasy which the patient has ultimately brought into the light of day.

True, at times even the content of the fantasy permits an empathic understanding of the shame and hypochondria, and of the anxiety which the patient experiences: shame, because the revelation is at times still accompanied by the discharge of unneutralized exhibitionistic libido; and anxiety because the grandiosity isolates the analysand and threatens him with permanent object loss.

Patient C., for example, told the following dream during a period when he was looking forward to being publicly honored: "The question was raised of finding a successor for me. I thought: How about God?" The dream was partly the result of the attempt to soften the grandiosity through humor; yet it aroused excitement and anxiety, and led, against renewed resistances, to the recall of childhood fantasies in which he had felt that he was God.

In many instances, however, the nuclear grandiosity is only hinted at. Patient D., for example, recalled with intense shame and resistance that as a child he used to imagine that he was running the streetcars in the city. The fantasy appeared harmless enough; but the shame and resistance became more understandable when the patient explained that he was operating the streetcars via a "thought control" which enamated from his head, above the clouds.

Although the content of the grandiose fantasy cannot be further discussed here, it is important to clarify the role of the mirror transference which enables its emergence. As indicated before, the patient's major resistances are motivated by his attempt to escape from the uneasy elation alternating with fear of permanent object loss, painful self-consciousness, shame-tension, and hypochondria which is due to the dedifferentiating intrusions of grandiose fantasies and narcissistic-exhibitionistic libido into the ego. The transference, however, functions as a specific therapeutic buffer. In the mirror transference, in the narrower sense, the patient is able to mobilize his grandiose fantasies and exhibitionism on the basis of the hope that the therapist's empathic participation and emotional response will not allow the narcissistic tensions to reach excessively painful or dangerous levels. In the twinship and the merger, the analogous protection is provided by the long-term deployment of the narcissistic cathexes upon the therapist, who now is the carrier of the patient's infantile greatness and exhibitionism.

Later, especially with the aid of the very last clinical example referred to in this presentation, some of the specific, concrete clinical steps by which the mobilized infantile narcissistic demands gradually become tamed and neutralized will be demonstrated. Here, however, the general significance of the mirror transference in the context of therapy will be examined.

The rational aims of therapy could not, by themselves, persuade the vulnerable ego of the narcissistically fixated analysand to forego denial and acting out and to face and to examine the needs and claims of the archaic grandiose self. In order to actuate, and to maintain in motion, the painful process which leads to the confrontation of the grandiose fantasies with a realistic conception of the self, and to the realization that life offers only limited possibilities for the gratification of the narcissistic-exhibitionistic wishes, a mirror transference must be established. If it does not develop, the patient's grandiosity remains concentrated upon the grandiose self, the ego's defensive position remains rigid, and ego expansion cannot take place.

The mirror transference rests on the therapeutic reactivation of the grandiose self. That the analyst can be enlisted in the support of this structure is an expression of the fact that the formation of a cohesive grandiose self was indeed achieved during childhood; the listening, perceiving, and echoing-mirroring presence of the analyst now reinforces the psychological forces which maintain the cohesiveness of the self-image, archaic and (by adult standards) unrealistic though it may be. Analogous to the therapeutically invaluable, controlled, temporary swings toward the disintegration of the idealizing parent imago when the idealizing transference is disturbed, we may encounter as a consequence of a disturbance of the mirror transference the temporary fragmentation of the narcissistically cathected, cohesive (body-mind) self and a temporary concentration of the narcissistic cathexes on isolated body parts, isolated mental functions, and isolated actions, which are then experienced as dangerously disconnected from a crumbling self. As is the case in the idealizing transference, these temporary disturbances of the transference equilibrum occupy in the analysis of narcissistic personalities a central position of stategic importance which corresponds to the place of the structural conflict in the ordinary transference neuroses; and their analysis tends to elicit the deepest insights and leads to the most solid accretions of psychic structure.

The following constitutes an especially instructive illustration of such a temporary regressive fragmentation of the therapeutically activated grandiose self.

Mr. E. was a graduate student whose psychopathology and personality structure will not be discussed except to say that he sought relief from painful narcissistic tension states by a number of perverse means in which the inconstancy of his objects and sexual goals were indicative of the fact that he could trust no source of satisfaction. This brief report concerns a weekend during an early phase of the long analysis when the patient was already beginning to realize that separations from the analyst[2] upset his psychic equilibrium, but when he did not yet understand the specific nature of the support which the analysis provided. During earlier weekend separations a vaguely perceived inner threat had driven him to dangerous voyeuristic activities in public toilets during which he achieved a feeling of merger with the man at whom he gazed. This time, however, he was able, through an act of artistic sublimation, not only to spare himself the aforementioned cruder means of protection against the threatened dissolution of the self, but also to explain the nature of the reassurance he was receiving from the analyst. During this weekend, the patient painted a picture of the analyst. The key to the understanding of this artistic production lay in the fact that in it the analyst had neither eyes nor nose—the place of these sensory organs was taken by the analysand. On the basis of this evidence and of additional corroborative material, the conclusion could be reached that a decisive support to the maintenance of the patient's narcissistically cathected self-image was supplied by the analyst's perception of him. The patient felt whole when he thought that he was acceptingly looked at by an object that substituted for an insufficiently developed endopsychic function: the analyst provided a replacement for the lacking narcissistic cathexis of the self.

Some General Therapeutic Considerations Concerning the Mirror Transference

The analysand's demands for attention, admiration, and for a variety of other forms of mirroring and echoing responses to the

---

[2]This analysis was carried out by a senior student at the Chicago Institute for Psychoanalysis under regular supervision by the author.

mobilized grandiose self, which fill the mirror transference in the narrow sense of this term, do not usually constitute great cognitive problems for the analyst, although he may have to mobilize much subtle understanding to keep pace with the patient's defensive denials of his demands or with the retreat from them when the immediate empathic response to them is not forthcoming. Here it is of decisive importance that the analyst comprehend and acknowledge the phase-appropriateness of the demands of the grandiose self and that he grasp the fact that for a long time it is a mistake to emphasize to the patient that his demands are unrealistic. If the analyst demonstrates to the patient that the narcissistic needs are appropriate within the context of the total early phase that is being revived in the transference and that they have to be expressed, then the patient will gradually reveal the urges and fantasies of the grandiose self, and the slow process is thus initiated that leads to the integration of the grandiose self into the realistic structure of the ego and to an adaptively useful transformation of its energies.

The empathic comprehension of the reactivation of the earlier developmental stages (the alter-ego transference or twinship; the merger with the analyst through the extension of the grandiose self) is, however, not achieved easily. It is, for example, usually difficult for the analyst to hold fast to the realization that the meagerness of object-related imagery with regard to current and past figures as well as with regard to the analyst himself is the appropriate manifestation of an archaic narcissistic relationship. A frequent misunderstanding of the mirror transference in general and of the therapeutic activation of the most archaic stages of the grandiose self in particular thus consists in its being mistaken for the outgrowth of a widespread resistance against the establishment of an object-instinctual transference. And many analyses of narcissistic personality disorders are either short-circuited at this point (leading to a brief analysis of subsidiary sectors of the personality in which ordinary transferences do occur while the principal disturbance, which is narcissistic, remains untouched) or are forced into a mistaken and unprofitable direction against diffuse, nonspecific, and chronic ego resistances of the analysand.

If the establishment of a mirror transference is, however, not prevented, the gradual mobilization of the repressed grand-iose self will take place and a number of specific, pathognomonic, and therapeutically valuable resistances will be set in motion. The principal end of the working-through processes in the idealizing transference is the internalization of the idealized object which leads to the strengthening of the matrix of the ego and to the strengthening of the patient's ideals; the principal end of the working-through processes in the mirror transference is the transformation of the grandiose self which results in a firming of the ego's potential for action (through the increasing realism of the ambitions of the personality) and in increasingly realistic self-esteem.

An important question posed by the analysis of narcissistic personalities, especially in the area of the grandiose self, concerns the degree of therapeutic activity which needs to be employed by the analyst. In applying Aichhorn's technique with juvenile delinquents (1936), for example, the analyst offers himself actively to the patient as a replica of his grandiose self, in a relationship which resembles the twinship (or alter-ego) variant of a mirror transference (see also A. Freud's illuminating summary [1951]). A delinquent's capacity to attach himelf to the analyst in admiration indicates, however, that an idealized parent imago and the deep wish to form an idealizing transference are (preconsciously) present, but, in consequence of early disappointments, they are denied and hidden. It was Aichhorn's special understanding for the delinquent that led him to offer himself first as a mirror image of the delinquent's grandiose self. He was thus able to initiate a veiled mobilization of idealizing cathexes toward an idealized object without yet disturbing the necessary protection of the defensively created grandiose self and its activities. Once a bond is established, however, a gradual shift from the omnipotence of the grandiose self to the more deeply longed-for omnipotence of an idealized object (and the requisite therapeutic dependence on it) can be achieved.

In the analytic treatment of the ordinary cases of narcissistic personality disturbance, however, the active encouragement of idealization is not desirable. It leads to the establishment of a tenacious transference bondage, bringing about the formation of a cover of massive identification and hampering the gradual alteration of the existing narcissistic structures. But a spontaneously occurring therapeutic mobilization of the idealized parent imago or of the grandiose self is indeed to be welcomed and must not be interfered with.

There are two antithetical pitfalls concerning the form of the interpretations which focus on the narcissistic transferences: the analyst's readiness to moralize about the patient's narcissism; and his tendency toward abstractness of the relevant interpretations.

The triad of value judgments, moralizing, and therapeutic activism in which the analyst steps beyond the basic analytic attitude to become the patient's leader and teacher is most likely to occur when the psychopathology under scrutiny is not understood metapsychologically. Under these circumstances the analyst can hardly be blamed when he tends to abandon the ineffective analytic armamentarium and instead offers himself to the patient as an object to identify with in order to achieve therapeutic changes. If lack of success in areas that are not yet understood metapsychologically is tolerated, however, without the abandonment of analytic means, then the occurrence of new analytic insights is not prevented and scientific progress can be made.

Where metapsychological understanding is not entirely lacking but is incomplete, analysts tend to supplement their interpretations with suggestive pressure and the weight of the personality of the therapist becomes of greater importance. There are thus certain analysts who are said to be exceptionally gifted in the analysis of "borderline" cases and anecdotes about their therapeutic activities become widely known in analytic circles. But just as the surgeon, in the heroic era of surgery, was a charismatically gifted individual who performed great feats of courage and skill, while the modern surgeon tends to be a calm, well-trained craftsman, so also with the analyst. As our knowledge about the narcissistic disorders increases, their treatment becomes the work of analysts who do not employ any special charisma of their personalities but restrict themselves to the use of the tools that provide rational success: interpretations and reconstructions. There are, of course, moments when a forceful statement is indicated as a final move in persuading the patient that the gratifications obtained from the unmodified narcissistic fantasies are spurious. A skillful analyst of an older generation, for example, as asserted by local psychoanalytic lore, would make his point at a strategic juncture by silently handing over a crown and sceptor to his unsuspecting analysand instead of confronting him with yet another verbal interpretation. In general, however, the psychoanalytic process is most enhanced if we trust the spontaneous synthetic functions of the patient's ego to integrate the narcissistic configurations gradually, in an atmosphere of analytic-empathic acceptance, instead of driving the analysand toward an imitation of the analyst's scornful rejection of the analysand's lack of realism.

The second danger, namely, that interpretations regarding the narcissistic transference might become too abstract, can be much diminished if we avoid falling victim to the widespread confusion between object relations and object love. We must bear in mind that our interpretations about the idealizing transference and the mirror transference are statements about an intense object relationship, despite the fact that the object is invested with narcissistic cathexes, and that we are explaining to the analysand how his very narcissism leads him to a heightened sensitivity about certain specific aspects and actions of the object, the analyst, whom he experiences in a narcissistic mode.

If the analyst's interpretations are noncondemnatory; if he can clarify to the patient in concrete terms the significance and the meaning of his (often acted-out) messages, of his seemingly irrational hypersensitivity, and of the back-and-forth flow of the cathexis of the narcissistic positions; and especially, if he can demonstrate to the patient that these archaic attitudes are comprehensible, adaptive, and valuable within the context of the total state of personality development of which they form a part—then the mature segment of the ego will not turn away from the grandiosity of the archaic self or from the awesome features of the overestimated, narcissistically experienced object. Over and over again, in small, psychologically manageable portions, the ego will deal with the disappointment at having to recognize that the claims of the grandiose self are unrealistic. And, in response to this experience, it will either mournfully withdraw a part of the narcissistic investment from the archaic image of the self, or it will, with the aid of newly acquired structure, neutralize the associated narcissistic energies or channel them into aim-inhibited pursuits. And over and over again, in small, psychologically manageable portions, the ego will deal with the disappointment at having to recognize that the idealized object is unavailable or imperfect. And, in response to this experience, it will withdraw a part of the idealizing investment from the object and strengthen the corresponding internal structures. In short, if the ego learns first to accept the presence of the mobilized narcissistic structures, it will gradually integrate them into its own realm, and the analyst will witness the establishment of ego dominance and ego autonomy in the narcissistic sector of the personality.

Concluding Remarks

The foregoing examination must, in its entirety, be considered a summarizing preview of a broader study; no retrospective survey of the findings and opinions that have been presented will, therefore, be given. It must be stressed, however, that there are some important aspects of the subject matter which either could only be mentioned briefly or had to be disregarded altogether.

Thus, as mentioned initially, it was necessary to omit almost all references to the work of others, such as, for example, the significant contributions by H. Hartmann (1953), K. R. Eissler (1953), E. Jacobson (1964), and A. Reich (1960); furthermore, it was not possible to compare the approach toward our subject matter taken in the present study with that chosen by such important authors as Federn (1952) on the one hand and Mahler (1952) on the other; and, finally, still within the same context, it was not possible to discuss the work of Melanie Klein and her school which often appears to be concerned with disorders that are related to those scrutinized in this essay.

No attempt was made to define and delimit the area of psychopathology with which this study is dealing; the question of the appropriateness of the use of the term transference in the present context could not be taken up; the discussion of the role of aggression had to be bypassed; the recurrent traumatic states in which the focus of the analysis shifts tem-porarily to the near-exclusive consideration of the overburdenedness of the psyche could not be illuminated; many other difficulties, therapeutic limitations and failures were not considered; and, most regrettably it was not possible to demonstrate the specific wholesome changes that occur as the result of the transformation of the narcissistic structures and of their energies. In all: it was the aim of this contribution to give the outline of a systematic approach to the psychoanalytic treatment of narcissistic personalities; a thorough scrutiny of the subject could not be undertaken.

BIBLIOGRAPHY

Aichhorn, A. (1936), The Narcissistic Transference of the "Juvenile Imposter." In: *Delinquency and Child Guidance*, ed. O. Fleischmann, P. Kramer, & H. Ross. New York: International Universities Press, 1964, pp. 174–191.

Eissler, K. R. (1953), Notes upon the Emotionality of a Schizophrenic Patient and Its Relation to Problems of Technique. *This Annual*, 8:199–251.

Federn, P. (1952), *Ego Psychology and the Psychoses*, ed. E. Weiss. New York: Basic Books.

Freud, A. (1951), Obituary: August Aichhorn. *Int. J. Psa.*, 32:51–56.

Hartmann, H. (1953), Obituary: August Aichhorn. *Int. J. Psa.*, 32:51–56.

Hartmann, H. (1953), Contribution to the Metapsychology of Schizophrenia. *This Annual*, 8:177–198.

Jacobson, E. (1964), *The Self and the Object World*. New York: International Universities Press.

Kohut, H. (1966), Forms and Transformations of Narcissism. *J. Amer. Psa. Assn.*, 14:243–272.

Mahler, M. S. (1952), On Child Psychosis and Schizophrenia: Autistic and Symbiotic Infantile Psychoses. *This Annual*, 7:286–305.

Nagera, H. (1964), Autoerotism, Autoerotic Activities, and Ego Development. *This Annual*, 19:240–255.

Niederland, W. G. (1959), Schreber: Father and Son. *Psa. Quart.*, 28:151–169.

Reich, A. (1960), Pathologic Forms of Self-esteem Regulation. *This Annual*, 15:215–232.

Critical Evaluation

Intrapsychic theorists have created a highly complicated superstructure of concepts and propositions to amplify their notions. Although the intricacies of man's behavior are infinite, intrapsychic theorists appear to incorporate an excessive number of principles and terms to account for them. Critics are especially prone to note the rather shoddy empirical foundation upon which these concepts are based. They contend that the line of reasoning connecting dubious clinical observations to the theory progresses through a series of highly tenuous and obscure steps. In short, not only is the source of intrapsychic data suspect, but the sequence of reasoning which ties it to the conceptual system seems excessively involved and imprecise. The paper by Adolf Grünbaum, the distinguished philosopher of science, persuasively argues these points in an elucidation of the logical shortcomings of analytic concepts such as repression, parapraxes, and dreamwork.

21 Logical Foundations of Psychoanalytic Theory

Adolf Grünbaum

1. Introduction

Freud has emphasized that Breuer's "cathartic method [of therapy and clinical investigation] was the immediate precursor of psychoanalysis; and, in spite of every exten-

[1]Sigmund Freud, "A Short Account of Psychoanalysis." In *Standard Edition of the Complete Psychological Works of Sigmund Freud*, trans. J. Strachey et al. (London: Hogarth Press, 1924), vol. 19, p. 194. Hereafter any references given to Freud's writings in English will be to this *Standard Edition* under its acronym "S.E." followed by the year of first appearance, the volume number, and the page(s). Thus, the 1924 paper just cited in full would be cited within the text in abbreviated fashion as follows: S.E. 1924, 19:194.

Copyright © Adolf Grünbaum 1983; by permission of the author.

This paper is based on an invited address to the session of the Committee on Philosophy and Medicine, held at the December 1981 meeting of the American Philosophical Association in Philadelphia. I wish to thank Benjamin B. Rubinstein and Rosemarie Sand for their valuable comments on the first draft of this paper. I am also indebted to the Fritz Thyssen Stiftung for its support of work in the philosophy of psychoanalysis.

sion of experience and of every modification of theory, is still contained within it as its nucleus" (S.E. 1924, 19:194).[1] Josef Breuer used hypnosis to revive and articulate the patient's memory of a *repressed* traumatic experience which had presumably occasioned the first appearance of a particular hysterical symptom. Thereby Freud's mentor induced a purgative release of the pent-up emotional distress that had been originally bound to the trauma. And since such cathartic reliving of a repressed trauma seemed to yield relief from the particular hysterical symptom, Breuer and Freud hypothesized that repression is the *sine qua non* for the pathogenesis of the patient's psychoneurosis (S.E. 1893, 2:6-7; 1893, 3:29-30).

This *aetiologic* role of repressed ideation then became prototypic for much of Freud's own theory of unconscious motivations. Repressed *wishes* were postulated to be the motives of *all* dreaming. And sundry repressed mentation was deemed to cause the *bungling* of actions at which the subject is normally successful ("parapraxes" such as slips of the tongue or pen, instances of mishearing or misreading, cases of forgetting of words, intentions or events, and mislaying or losing of objects) (S.E. 1916, 15:25, 67). Thus, even in the case of "normal" people, Freud saw manifest dream content and various sorts of "slips" as the tell-tale symptoms of (temporary) *mini*-neuroses, engendered by repressions.

He arrived at the purported sexual repression-aetiologies of the psychoneuroses, as well as at the supposed causes of dreams and parapraxes, by lifting presumed repressions via the patient's allegedly "free" associations. At the same time, excavation of the pertinent repressed ideation was to remove the pathogens of the patient's afflictions. Hence scientifically, Freud deemed the psychoanalytic method of investigation to be both heuristic *and* probative, over and above being a method of therapy. By the same token, he declared that "the theory of repression is the cornerstone on which the whole structure of psychoanalysis rests. It is the most essential part of it" (S.E. 1914, 14:16). And he claimed that clinical evidence furnishes compelling support for this theoretical cornerstone.

Therefore we can scrutinize the logical foundations of psychoanalytic theory by examining Freud's clinical arguments for the repression-aetiology of ⌐he psychoneuroses and for the cardinal causal role of repressed ideation in committing "Freudian slips" and in dreaming. This paper is devoted to just such a scrutiny. And its upshot will be that the reasoning by which Freud sought to justify the very foundation of his theory was grievously flawed.

2. The Repression-Aetiology of the Psychoneuroses

Breuer and Freud explicitly adduced the separate *therapeutic* removal of particular neurotic symptoms, by means of undoing repressions having a thematic and associative affinity to these very symptoms, as their *evidence* for attributing a cardinal *causal* role in symptom formation to the repression of traumatic events. Let us look at the intermediate reasoning on which the founders of psychoanalysis relied to claim therapeutic support for their aetiologic identification of an original act of repression as the specific pathogen initially responsible for the formation of the neurotic symptom.

They extrapolated this account of the first origination of the symptom backward from the dynamics they had postulated for the subsequently continuing existence of the symptom. And they had been led to attribute the *maintenance* of the symptom, in turn, to a *coexisting* ongoing repression of the traumatic *memory* which "acts like a foreign body which long after its entry must continue to be regarded as an agent that is still at work." But what is their basis for this attribution? As they tell us at once: "we find the evidence for this in a highly remarkable phenomenon," which they describe in italics as follows: *"each individual hysterical symptom immediately and permanently disappeared when we had succeeded in bringing clearly to light the memory of the event by which it was provoked and in arousing its accompanying effect"* (S.E. 1893, 2:6; italics in original).

What then is the evidence they give for their aetiologic identification of the repressed experience of a particular traumatic event *E* as the pathogen — avowedly *not* as the mere precipitator!—of a given symptom *S* that first appeared at the time of *E*? Plainly and emphatically, they predicate their identification of the repression of *E* as the pathogen of *S* on the fact that the abreactive lifting of that repression issued in the durable *removal* of *S*. And, as their wording shows, they appreciate all too well that *without* this symptom removal, neither the mere painfulness of the event *E*, nor its temporal coincidence with *S*'s first appearance, nor yet the mere fact that the hysteric patient had *repressed* the trauma *E* could justify, even together, blaming the pathogenesis of *S* on the repression of *E*. Thus, the credibility of the repression aetiology is crucially dependent on the reportedly durable separate removal of various particular symptoms, a therapeutic outcome deemed supportive, because it appears to have been wrought by *separately* lifting particular repressions!

This epistemic dependence of the repression aetiology on the presumed cathartic dynamics of effecting positive therapeutic outcome is further accentuated by the pains which Breuer and Freud take promptly to argue that their symptom removals are due to the lifting of repressions rather than to suggestion: "It is plausible to suppose that . . . the patient expects to be relieved of his sufferings by this procedure, and it is this expectation . . . which is the [therapeutically] operative factor. This, however, is not so . . . the symptoms, which sprang from separate causes were separately removed" (S.E. 1893, 2:7). Thus, the separate symptom removals are made to carry the vital probative burden of discrediting the threatening rival hypothesis of placebo effect, wrought by mere suggestion.

Believing to have met this challenge, Breuer and Freud at once reiterate their epoch-making repression-aetiology. Let us now recapitulate the essential steps of the reasoning that prompted them to postulate this aetiology. First they attributed their positive therapeutic results to the lifting of repressions. Having assumed such a *therapeutic connection*, they wished to *explain* it. And then they saw that it would indeed be explained deductively by the following aetiologic hypothesis: The particular repression whose undoing removed a given symptom *S* is *causally necessary* for the initial formation *and* maintenance of *S*. Thus, the nub of their inductive argument for inferring a repression-aetiology can be formulated as follows: The *removal* of a hysterical symptom *S* by means of *lifting* a repression *R* is *cogent evidence* that the repression *R* was *causally necessary* for the formation of the symptom *S* (S.E. 1893, 2:7).

Clearly, the attribution of *therapeutic* success to the undoing of repressions—rather than to mere suggestion—was the foundation, both logically and historically, for the central dynamical significance that unconscious ideation acquired in psychoanalytic theory: Without reliance on the presumed dynamics of their *therapeutic* results, Breuer and Freud could never have propelled clinical data into repression aetiologies.

As we saw, they had argued pointedly that the therapeutic gains made by their cathartically treated patients were *not* wrought by suggestion. Instead, they attributed these remedial results to the abreactive recall of those *repressed* traumata during which the distressing symptoms had first presented themselves. Since these traumata occasioned the onset of the hysterical symptoms, I shall refer to them as "occasioning" traumata. Hence we can say that Breuer and Freud had credited the patient's improvements to the *lifting* of the particular repression by which he had sequestered the memory of the *occasioning* trauma in his unconscious. And yet, when Freud himself treated additional patients by Breuer's cathartic method, this treatment failed to achieve *lasting* therapeutic gains. Indeed, the ensuing correlation of symptom relapses and intermittent removals, on the one hand, with the vicissitudes of his personal relations to the

patient, on the other, led him to *repudiate* the *decisive* therapeutic role that Breuer and he had attributed to undoing the repression of the *occasioning* trauma!

The evidence and reasoning that had driven Freud to this repudiation by 1896 are poignantly recalled by him in his 1925 Autobiographical Study:

> . . . even the most brilliant [therapeutic] results were liable to be suddenly wiped away if my personal relation with the patient became disturbed. It was true that they would be reestablished if a reconciliation could be effected; but such an occurrence proved that the personal emotional relation between doctor and patient was after all stronger than the whole cathartic process. [S.E. 1925, 20:27]

Freud's therapeutic repudiation of abreactively retrieving the memory of the *occasioning* trauma also had a momentous corollary: He likewise renounced the major *aetiologic* significance that he and Breuer had originally attributed to the *repression* of *this* trauma (S.E. 1896, 3:194-195). Yet he adhered undauntedly to the research program of seeking the pathogens of neuroses among *some* repressed traumata *or other* (S.E. 1896, 3:195–99). And, though the disappointments of cathartic treatment outcome had undercut the very basis for giving decisive remedial credit to the lifting of repressions, he unflinchingly clung to the therapeutic view that the excavation of *some* repression or *other* would remove the pathogen of the patient's affliction. But as I shall now argue, the empirical rationale that Breuer and Freud had used for postulating a *repression*-aetiology *at all* was altogether undermined by just the findings that induced Freud himself to repudiate the attribution of therapeutic gain to the undoing of the repression of the occasioning trauma.

The aforementioned symptom *relapses*, which ensued after Freud had lifted the patient's repression of the occasioning trauma, showed him that the undoing of this repression failed to uproot the *cause* of the neurotic symptoms. Moreover, the fragile, ephemeral symptom remissions achieved by patients who received Breuer's cathartic treatment could hardly be credited to the lifting of this repression. By Freud's own 1925 account, giving such therapeutic credit had very soon run afoul of a stubborn fact: "The personal emotional relation between doctor and patient was after all [therapeutically] stronger than the whole cathartic process" (S.E. 1925, 20:27).

For even *after* the patient's repression of the occasioning trauma had indeed been undone cathartically, the alternation between his remissions and relapses still depended *decisively* on the ups and downs of how well he got along emotionally with his doctor.

Yet, as we saw earlier, the 1893 postulation of a repression aetiology of neurosis in Breuer's and Freud's foundational communication had rested *crucially* on the premise that the patient's symptom removals had actually been wrought by lifting his repression of the memory of the occasioning trauma. And thus Freud's own abandonment of just this therapeutic premise completely negated the very reason that Breuer and he had invoked for postulating the pathogenicity of repression at all. In short, I claim that *the moral of Freud's therapeutic disappointments in the use of the cathartic method after 1893 was nothing less than the collapse of the epoch-making 1893 argument for the repression-aetiology of neurosis*, which Breuer and he had propounded.

Why, I ask, did Freud adamantly retain the generic repression aetiology instead of allowing that this aetiology itself had simply become baseless? And why, in the face of this baselessness, was he content with his mere aetiologic demotion of the repressed *occasioning* trauma, while clinging to the view that the pathogen is bound to be some other earlier repressed trauma of a sexual nature, to be excavated via free associations (S.E. 1896, 3:195–199)? Whatever his reason, he seemingly did not appreciate that the aetiologic fiasco suffered by Breuer's account in the wake of the disappointingly fragile therapeutic results had made a shambles of the very cornerstone of this psychoanalytic edifice. For such an appreciation would have been tantamount to his realization that the aetiology of neurosis still posed the same fundamental challenge as it had *before* Anna O. enabled Breuer to stumble upon the alleged "talking cure." Instead, Freud avowedly committed himself to a "prolonged search for the traumatic experience from which hysterical symptoms appeared to be derived" (S.E. 1923, 18:243), just when the initially plausible traumatic aetiology had been found to be baseless after all.

I have stressed the collapse of the 1893 therapeutic argument on which Breuer and Freud rested their originally hypothesized repression-aetiology of neurosis. Yet I need to forestall a possible misunderstanding of my methodological complaint against Freud's tenacious search for evidence that might warrant the *rehabilitation* of the repression-aetiology in a *new* version. Hence let me emphasize that I do *not* fault the pursuit of this research program *per se* after the demise of the cathartic method. What I do find objectionable, however, is Freud's all too ready willingness—once he was no longer collaborating with Breuer—to claim pathogenicity for purported childhood repressions on evidence *far less cogent* than the *separate* symptom removals that Breuer and he had pointedly adduced in 1893. In short, having embarked on the program of retaining the repression-aetiology *somehow*, Freud was prepared to draw aetiologic conclusions whose credentials just did not live up to Breuer's initial 1893 standard. And even that higher original standard, I contend, was still not high enough. Indeed I maintain that the repression-aetiology of neurosis would have lacked adequate empirical credentials, even if the therapeutic gains from cathartic treatment had turned out to be both durable and splendid. Even such impressive results may not be due to all to the lifting of pathogenic repressions; instead they may be a *placebo effect* (Grünbaum 1980, pp. 325–343), resulting from the congeniality of the rationale given to the patient for his affliction. Moreover, as I have argued elsewhere in detail (Grünbaum 1982a), the retrospective validation of repression as the initial pathogen lacks the sort of controls that are needed to attest *causal relevance*. And there is doubt about the reliability of purported memories elicited under the suggestive conditions of hypnosis. Incidentally, despite the replacement of hypnosis by free association in psychoanalytic treatment, Freudian therapy has retained an important tenet of its cathartic predecessor: "Recollection without affect almost invariably produces no [therapeutic] result" (S.E. 1893, 2:6).

Elsewhere (Grünbaum 1980, §II; Grünbaum 1982, §3) I have shown in detail that Freud's own subsequent (1917) *therapeutic* defense of his sexual version of the repression-aetiology—a defense that I dubbed "The Tally Argument"—has fared no better empirically than the original reliance on cathartic treatment success as evidence for the pathogenicity of repression. Hence, whatever his own evidential or personal motivations for retaining the repression-aetiology, I claim that it should now be regarded as *generically* devoid of clinical evidential support, no less than Breuer's particular version of it, which Freud repudiated as clinically unfounded. And, by the same token, I maintain that the demise of the therapeutic justification for the repression aetiology fundamentally impugns the *investigative* utility of lifting repressions (via "free" associations) in the conduct of aetiologic inquiry. In short, the collapse of the therapeutic argument for the repression-aetiology seriously undermines the purported *clinical research* value of free associations, which are given pride of place as an epistemic avenue to the presumed pathogens.

Though the repression aetiology of psychoneurotic disorders was thus itself in grave jeopardy from lack of cogent clinical support, Freud extrapolated it by postulating that repressions engender "slips" (parapraxes) and dreams no less than they spawn full-blown neuroses. For example, he assimilated a slip of the tongue to the status of a mini-neurotic symptom by viewing the slip as a *compromise* between a repressed motive that crops out in the form of a disturbance, on the one hand, and the conscious intention to make a certain utterance, on the other. But as against this generalized explanatory reliance on repressed mentation, I shall argue for the following thesis: Even if the original *therapeutic* defense of the repression-aetiology of neuroses had actually turned out to be empirically viable, Freud's compromise-models of parapraxes and of manifest dream content would be *misextrapolations* of that aetiology, precisely because they lacked any corresponding therapeutic base at the outset. For in 1900 Freud defended the heuristic and probative use of free association in *interpreting dreams* by pointing to its primary use in *aetiologic* inquiry. And he explicitly adduced *therapeutic* results, in turn, to legitimate free association as a reliable means of identifying the pathogens aetiologically. As he put it: "We might also point out in our defense that our procedure in interpreting dreams [by means of free association] is identical with the procedure by which we resolve hysterical symptoms; and there the correctness of our method is warranted by the coincident emergence and disappearance of the symptoms" (S.E. 1900, 5:528).

3. Parapraxes as Mini-Neurotic Symptoms

One of Freud's paradigm cases of a slip of the tongue will now serve to exhibit the poverty of the empirical credentials of his compromise-model of parapraxes. The example involves the forgetting of a pronoun in a Latin quotation.

On one of his trips, Freud became reacquainted with an academically trained young man who was familiar with some of his psychoanalytic writings. The young man, an Austrian Jew whom we shall call "AJ," conveys to Freud that he resented the social and career handicaps resulting from religious discrimination. To vent this frustration, he *tries* to quote the line from Virgil's *Aeneid* in which the despairing and abandoned Dido exclaims: *Exoriare aliquis nostris ex ossibus ultor* (Would that someone arise from our bones as an avenger!). But AJ's memory is defective, and he not only inverts the word order of *nostris ex* but altogether *omits* the indefinite pronoun *"aliquis"* (someone). Aware that something was missing in the line, AJ asks for help, whereupon Freud quotes the line correctly (S.E. 1901, 6:9ff).

His interlocutor asks Freud to explain his memory lapse. Being glad to oblige, Freud then enjoins him to associate freely, whereupon AJ begins by decomposing *"aliquis"* into *"a"* and *"liquis."* After a series of intermediate associations, the young man comes up with the thought of St. Januarius, the Christian martyr who became the patron saint of Naples. And AJ brings up the purported miracle of this saint's clotted blood. Freud points out that St. Januarius and St. Augustine, whom AJ had mentioned earlier, "both have to do with the calendar." Then Freud asks: "But won't you remind me about the miracle of his blood?" After responding that this relic is kept in a vial stored in a Neapolitan church and liquifies at regular intervals, AJ pauses. Thereupon Freud says, "Well, go on. Why do you pause?" And after AJ responds "Well, something *has* come into my mind . . . but it's too intimate to pass on . . . Besides, I don't see any connection, or any necessity for saying it" (ellipses are Freud's), Freud assures him in a schoolmasterly manner: "You can leave the connection to me" (S.E. 1901, 6:10−11).

When AJ then volunteers that his intimate sudden thought was "of a lady from whom I might easily hear a piece of news that would be very awkward for both of us," Freud asked rhetorically: "That her periods have stopped?" And he explains reasonably enough that he had interpreted the young man's prior association to the miracle of St.

Januarius' blood as an allusion to a woman's period.

AJ did actually have good reason to fear that his paramour was pregnant by him. And the anxiety he had felt because of this ominous possibility had indeed emerged, however tortuously, from the process of association in which he had engaged. Moreover, AJ himself was well aware of these facts. Yet he was prompted to query the alleged *causal bearing* of his genuine worry on his *aliquis* lapse: "And you really mean to say that it was this anxious expectation that made me unable to produce an unimportant word like aliquis?" With sovereign confidence, Freud retorted: "It seems to me undeniable."

Judging by Freud's account, it is unclear whether AJ had actually *repressed* his fear of pregnancy rather than merely relegated it to his own so-called preconscious by diverting his attention to other stimuli. But let us assume that this thought had been in a repressed state, at least prior to the time t_1 when AJ committed the parapraxis of forgetting *"aliquis."* Soon after Freud restored this forgotten word to AJ's awareness, the young man used the restored word as the point of departure for associations, which he began to generate at time t_2. Then the anxiety-laden thought of a confirmed unwanted pregnancy emerged at time t_3. For brevity, I shall say that there was a "memory lapse" at time t_1, a triggering restored awareness at time t_2, and a (tortuously) ensuing "terminal emergence" of repressed anxiety-content at time t_3.

As Timpanaro (1976, p. 51) has noted, Freud did not hesitate to intervene occasionally in the flow of AJ's associations. Hence Timpanaro has charged that Freud thereby subtly steered the associations in a manner akin to the Socratic method of eliciting answers to leading questions.

But let us grant here, at least for argument's sake, that there is some kind of *uncontaminated causal linkage* between the restored awareness of *"aliquis"* at time t_2, which triggers the labyrinthine sequence of associations, on the one hand, and the emerging anxiety-thought in which this sequence terminated at time t_3, on the other. Then we must ask the following *question:* On what grounds does Freud, or anyone else, take *this* assumed causal linkage to be *evidence* at all for the further claim that the repressed thought harbored by AJ before t_1 was the *cause* of his memory-lapse at time t_1? More explicitly, why

should the ultimately ensuing elicitation of AJ's previously repressed pregnancy fear via circuitous intermediate associations starting from the restored *"aliquis,"* bespeak that this very fear—while as yet being repressed—had *caused* him to forget this word, as well as to invert *"nostris ex"*? Why indeed should the *repressed* fear be held to have caused the *forgetting* of *"aliquis"* at the outset just because meandering associations starting out from the restored memory of *"aliquis"* issued in the conscious emergence of the fear?

It would be untutored, besides being uncharitable, to suppose that Freud did not draw on some auxiliary hypotheses to fill the *prima facie* glaring inferential gap to which our question has called attention. Indeed, he *extrapolated* from his repression-aetiology of neuroses, much as he had already done quite explicitly when claiming to explain manifest dream content (S.E. 1900, 4:101 and 5:528). Thus, he postulated that the compromise-formation model of neurotic symptoms—in which *repressed* contents are deemed *causally necessary* for symptom-formation—may also be warrantedly extrapolated to cover parapraxes. And once these bungled actions had thus been conceptualized as mini-neurotic symptoms, Freud felt entitled to make a further assumption: If a repression emerges into consciousness via free associations triggered by the subject's awareness of his parapraxis, then the prior presence of *that* repression was the cause of the parapraxis. *Mutatis mutandis*, he had already taken both of these hypotheses to apply to manifest dream contents, as we shall see in some detail later on.

Yet I maintain that the reasoning by which Freud thought he had supported these important postulates is grievously flawed. Note first that it was Freud's correct statement of the quotation from Virgil, but *not* the undoing of AJ's repression of his pregnancy fear, which served to *remove* the mnemonic lacuna of aliquis in the young man's awareness. Hence it would plainly be altogether wrong-headed to credit the lifting of the repression of AJ's fear with filling the quite *different* memory gap constituting AJ's "slip." Indeed, let us suppose that Freud had *not* filled this gap for AJ by supplying the omitted *"aliquis"* to him. And assume further that AJ had taken *other* words in his defectively recalled Latin line as the point of departure for his associations. Then let us even postulate *without* evidence that the *latter* associations would have eventuated in AJ's recall of the forgotten word *"aliquis"* only *after* the conscious emergence of his repressed fear of the pregnancy. Even then, it would be quite unclear that the posited unaided filling of AJ's memory gap can be credited causally to the lifting of his repressed fear! In any case, Freud did not adduce any evidence that the permanent lifting of a repression to which he had attributed a parapraxis will be "therapeutic" in the sense of enabling the person himself to correct the parapraxis *and* to avoid its repetition or other parapraxes in the future. While the hypothesized repression-"aetiology" of parapraxes thus lacked "therapeutic" support, it was precisely such *prima facie* impressive support which Breuer and Freud had marshaled to show that the removal of neurotic symptoms is attributable to the lifting of repressions, so that repressions are presumably pathogens. In short, there is a striking disparity in regard to the adduced evidential support between the hypothesis that parapraxes are due to repressions, on the one hand, and that repressions are the pathogens of neurotic symptoms, on the other.

Yet once Freud's postulational abandon was no longer daunted by Breuer's known theoretical restraint, Freud unabashedly enunciated his repression-theory of parapraxes. He did so despite the lack of any counterpart to the evidential support from therapeutic outcome on which Breuer and he had emphatically grounded their repression-aetiology of neurotic afflictions. Instead of being given pause by this patent discrepancy, in 1900 and 1901 Freud assimilated manifest dream content, and then also parapraxes to neurotic symptoms by construing them alike as compromise-formations engendered by repressions (cf. S.E. 1900, 4:144). Hence I view his theory of parapraxes and of dreams as *misextrapolations* of the generic repression aetiology of neurotic symptoms, which had at least had *prima facie* therapeutic support.

But, as I argued in Section 2, this very aetiology, with its compromise-model of symptoms, is itself devoid of adequate clinical credentials. And we saw that, by the same token, Freud failed to sustain the investigative utility of lifting repressions (via "free" associations) in the conduct of aetiologic inquiry. *A fortiori*, he has given us no *cogent* reason to infer that lifting repressions is a means of fathoming the causes of parapraxes and of

dreaming. For the repression-"aetiology" of parapraxes just turned out to be a gratuitous extrapolation from the compromise-formation model of neurotic symptoms. And thus even *bona fide* repressions uncovered by means of free associations can be presumed to be causally *irrelevant* to parapraxes and dreams, at least until and unless *additional* grounds for such relevance are shown to exist in particular cases.

This presumption of causal irrelevance has recently been further strengthened by the detailed and well-supported *alternative* causal explanations of parapraxes that have been put forward by Timpanaro (1976) in his important book *The Freudian Slip*. The highly instructive *non*-Freudian psychological hypotheses employed by him were evolved by philologists to carry out textual criticism. And the various "aetiologic" categories of errors he employs fully allow for causation by unconscious mechanisms. But instead of having the status of Freudian *repressions*, these hypothesized mental processes qualify technically as "preconscious" in the vocabulary of psychoanalysis. And Timpanaro (1976, p. 95) expects a deepening of his non-Freudian psychological explanations of slips from the currently developing study of the physiological mechanisms underlying memory, forgetfulness, and concentration as well as of their liability to emotional influences. Additional non-Freudian psycholinguistic explanations for errors in linguistic performance are offered in Fromkin (1980).

Freud discusses some of the non-psychoanalytic approaches to an understanding of slips made by his own contemporaries. But he belittles the causal factors singled out by them as merely generic and shallow (S.E. 1901, 6:21−22 and 80−81). Indeed, he indicts them for being satisfied with accepting factors that merely *favor* the commission of a parapraxis in lieu of causally necessary or sufficient conditions (S.E. 1916, 15:45−46 and 61). Prompted by this, I say: Whatever the incompleteness or other defects of the more recent non-psychoanalytic explanations of slips offered by Timpanaro or by psycholinguists, their deficits are not remedied at all by the psychoanalytic explanations. Thus, these deficits do not redound to the credibility of Freud's thesis that all parapraxes are due to repressions. For, to take Freud's earlier example, let it be granted that AJ's chain of associations from his corrected parapraxis issued causally in the disclosure of the repressed anxiety afflicting him, *and* that this unconscious fear of pregnancy had been clamoring for overt expression. How then does this assumed motive serve to explain even probabilistically why AJ committed any parapraxis at all, let alone why he forgot *"aliquis"*? *A fortiori*, how does Freud's claim that AJ's unconscious anxiety is the *"sense"* or *intention* behind his slip (S.E. 1916, 15:40) even match, let alone excel Timpanaro's explanation (1976, chap. 3), which invoked the tendencies to effect mental economies by syntactic and stylistic banalization, coupled with the elimination of the superfluous? Yet Freud downgrades psycholinguistic explanations generically. As he remarks, after such explanations were offered, "on the whole . . . we were further than ever from understanding slips of the tongue" (S.E. 1916, 15:34). For he claims that the purported motives of parapraxes are "more interesting than . . . the circumstances in which they come about" (S.E. 1916, 15:40). And furthermore, he maintains that, unlike psychophysiological accounts, his motivational elucidations address the question of "why it is that the slip occurred in this particular way and no other" (S.E. 1916, 15:32; cf. also p. 36).

More fundamentally, suppose that Freud did use AJ's repressed anxiety to give a hypothetico-deductive explanation of his slip. Then the *causal nexus* between the repression and the slip asserted in its *explanans* would have been *epistemically unacceptable*. For, as I have argued above and also indicated elsewhere (Grünbaum 1980, pp. 377–378), Freud has offered nothing better than *post hoc ergo propter hoc* toward the evidential support needed for *that* causal nexus, even if we grant him that the sequence of AJ's associations was an entirely uncontaminated causal chain.

The *aliquis* example is representative of other cases in which Freud fallaciously trades on the genuineness of a fear (or wish) with which the subject is preoccupied, and on its elicitation by associations initiated by a given parapraxis, to gain plausibility for the causal attribution of that parapraxis to the elicited fear (or wish). Even the unique elicitation-capacity presumed for these particular associations can be spurious. For, as Timpanaro (1976, p. 143) has rightly stressed, genuine preoccupations or obsessions tend to be evoked by a great *many* stimuli, even or especially when they are devoid of any foundation.

The psychoanalytic theory of slips, which offers explanations based on repressions unearthed via free associations, ought *not* to be allowed to benefit from such credibility as is possessed by other explanations having only a limited similarity to them! One species of such different explanations features mental states of which the subject who committed the slip was clearly *conscious*. Another species features mental states that, though not at the *focus* of the subject's consciousness, were readily available to his conscious awareness: These states were "preconscious" in Freud's parlance, as opposed to being repressed (*dynamically* unconscious). Being the adroit pedagogue and even deft expository promoter that he was, Freud exemplifies both of these sorts of slips by way of *didactic prolegomena* (e.g. in S.E. 1916, 15:64–65). But neither of these two species can be credited to psychoanalytic theory, because—as Timpanaro (1976) put it concisely:

> The truly Freudian "slip" or instance of forgetting presupposes the existence of psychic material which my conscious ego has repressed because it proved *displeasing*—or, given it was desirable from a hedonistic point of view, because my moral inhibitions prevented my confession of it even to myself, let alone to others. [P. 122]

Thus, suppose that in the course of giving a lecture on human sexuality, a person misspeaks himself by saying "orgasm" instead of "organism." Then it is *not* a *bona fide* "Freudian" explanation to remark that conceptual preoccupation with the overall topic of the lecture combined with phonetic similarity to generate the slip. And, by the same token, Freudians should not trade on cases in which a slip may be plausibly held to bespeak the presence of a *conscious* thought that the subject wishes to conceal. Nor on instances of slips in which there is little evidence for the prior repression of a thought which a speaker tried unsuccessfully to hide. An example of this, which I owe to Rosemarie Sand, would be the man who turns from the exciting view of a lady's exposed bosom muttering "excuse me, I have got to get a *breast* of *flesh* air!"

Since these embarrassing losses of control appear to have psychological causes, they do call for corresponding psychological explanations. And hence they indeed militate *against* the view, which Freud decried as widely avowed, "that a mistake in speaking is a *lapsus linguae* and of no psychological significance" (S.E. 1901, 6:94). For these cases of mis-speaking do qualify as "serious mental acts; they have a sense [motive]" (S.E. 1916, 15:44). Furthermore, as Benjamin Rubinstein has pointed out illuminatingly, these sorts of "slips"—though *not* bespeaking repressions—share two significant features of the genuinely "Freudian" ones: (i) They exhibit intrusions upon the agent's control of his own behavior, and (ii) the intruding element is a wish or an affect. But despite being psychologically revealing, such cases are not supportive of the psychoanalytic theory of parapraxes, in which repression is held to play the cardinal explanatory role. For, in the concluding chapter of his *magnum opus* on slips, one of the three necessary conditions that Freud explicitly laid down for inclusion of a slip in the purview of his theory is as follows: "If we perceive the parapraxis at all, we must not be aware in ourselves of any motive for it. We must rather be tempted to explain it by 'inattentiveness,' or to put it down to 'chance' " (S.E. 1901, 6:239). Indeed, the avowed contribution of Freud's theory to our understanding of various sorts of "slips" is to explain those species "in which the parapraxis produces nothing that has any sense of its own" for either the subject who commits the slip or for others (S.E. 1916, 15:41). Thus, when Freud lists parapraxes *violating* his requirement that they be devoid of a sense of their own, these violations furnish mere didactic prolegomena: They serve the explicitly stated "limited aim of using the study of these phenomena as a help towards a preparation for psycho-analysis" (S.E. 1916, 15:55).

Freud's illustrations of such propaedeutic cases include instances of nonsensical misspoken words such that the speaker who uttered them knows at once when asked "what he had really meant to say" (S.E. 1916, 15:42; cf. also p. 47). In fact, "the disturbing purpose is known to the speaker and moreover had been noticed by him before he made the slip of the tongue" (S.E. 1916, 15:64). More generally, as Freud explains, "we shall find whole categories of cases in which the intention, the sense, of the slip is plainly visible" (S.E. 1916, 15:40). For in such instances "the parapraxis itself brings its sense to light" so as to be perspicuous to the subject no less than to others (S.E. 1916, 15:41; cf. also p. 47). Emphasizing the propaedeutic role of all such perspicuous cases, Freud declares: "My

choice of these examples has not been unintentional, for their origin and solution [motivational explanation] come neither from me nor from any of my followers" (S.E. 1916, 15:47).

One such example features a German-speaking anatomy professor who misspoke himself in a lecture as follows: "In the case of the female genitals, in spite of many *Versuchungen* [temptations]—I beg your pardon, *Versuche* [experiments] . . ." (S.E. 1901, 6:78–79; also 1916, 15:33). When the anatomist himself thus corrected his slip, he patently had no need of lifting a repression to disclose to him that *erotic interest* was a possible contributing motive for his use of a sex-oriented term instead of the phonetically similar neutral term he had expected to utter. Yet in a paper "On the Freudian Theory of Speech," the psycholinguist A. W. Ellis (1980, p. 124) overlooks the propaedeutic role of the anatomist's slip and of all the other motivationally perspicuous illustrations given by Freud. Drawing an exegetically incorrect conclusion from these transparent examples, Ellis tells us: "It is not necessary that the speaker should be unaware of the activity of the disturbing purpose [motive] within him before it reveals itself in the slip." But, qua characterization of the scope of the *psycho-analytic* theory of slips, this formulation contravenes Freud's aforecited restriction as to the purview of this theory. For he demanded that the speaker *not* be aware of any motive for his slip (S.E. 1901, 6:239, condition *c*). Hence the inferred perturbing intention had to be sequestered in the speaker's unconscious. Having overlooked Freud's restriction, Ellis violates it anew when he proceeds to give purported illustrations of "Freud's mode of explanation" (1980, p. 124). Thus, his *prime* example is the anatomist's perspicuous temptation slip rather than one "in which the parapraxis produces nothing that has any sense of its own" (S.E. 1916, 15:41).

Yet Ellis does inquire whether "depth-analytic explanations are needed in addition to the mechanical-psycholinguistic explanations proposed more recently" (1980, p. 123). His domain of inquiry consists of 51 word substitution slips, which he selected from Freud's 1901 index of speech lapses. The closest he comes to considering whether *repressed* ideation might generate slips is in his remarks on word blend errors, which result from the blending of two words (1980, §5). Ellis notes that the speaker can attest introspectively to the prearticulatory presence of thoughts that he wished to conceal. And Ellis allows that the word which the speaker intended to utter blended with a lingering phonemic trace of the disturbing thoughts, thereby betraying their presence. But, as he hastens to point out, "those thoughts could not have been truly unconscious prior to manifesting themselves in the slip" (1980, p. 129). Indeed, since he took a word blend example in which the subject's unaided introspection did disclose a prearticulatory disturbing motive, it was evident from the start that this motive did not qualify as repressed.

Unfortunately, Ellis does not tell us whether *any* of the 51 word substitution slips examined by him were of the *opaque* sort required by Freud's restriction. But unless this requirement is demonstrably met, it is at best unclear whether Freud's repression-theory of parapraxes is damaged by Ellis' findings. Yet he claims such damage in virtue of the feasibility of giving psycholinguistic explanations of a *non*-motivational kind for the 51 substitution slips he had selected. Thus, he notes that the erroneously substituted words are either phonetically similar to the target words, semantically related closely to them, or are perseverations from prior utterances in the given lexical context.

Psychoanalysts have rightly complained that as friendly an experimental psychologist as Saul Rosenzweig had simply failed to test Freud's 1915 conception of repression, when Rosenzweig claimed to have found experimental support for it in 1934 (cf. Grünbaum 1982, § I). Alas, the same type of complaint is appropriate to M. T. Motley's (1980) interpretation of his ingenious laboratory investigations. He did furnish telling experimental evidence for the *causal relevance* of cognitive-affective mental sets, and even of personality dispositions, to the production of verbal misreadings. These influences acted via prearticulatory semantic editing of the words to be read. And thus, semantic influences external to the speaker's intended utterance effected verbal slips that were "closer in meaning to those semantic influences than to the originally intended utterance" (Motley 1980, p. 145). The pertinent misreadings were phoneme-switching errors of the sort known as "spoonerisms" (Fromkin 1980, p. 11; Motley 1980, p. 134).

But, like Ellis, Motley misconstrues the probative relevance of his otherwise valuable findings to Freud's psychoanalytic theory of slips. In Motley's case, the crucial question is: Do the cognitive-affective mental sets and/or personality dispositions he manipulated as the independent variable in his experiments qualify as *repressed*, rather than as focally conscious or preconscious? I shall argue that, in all three of his experiments, the answer is plainly negative. The semantic prearticulatory editing manifested in these experiments occurs at three corresponding levels as follows: consonance with the immediate verbal context in Experiment 1, with the speaker's sociosituational context in Experiment 2, and with one of the speaker's specified personality traits in Experiment 3. And Motley (p. 136) views these three experiments sequentially as *ascendingly* **qualified to serve as** *bona fide* tests of Freud's own theory of parapraxes. By contrast, I claim that none of them reaches even the threshold of being a test of psychoanalytic theory, as distinct from a rival theory that *denies* the causal relevance of repressed ideation. For Motley's findings could *all* be explained by the sort of rival psychological theory—that countenances *only conscious* motivational influences as generators of slips. To substantiate my claim that Motley's results are probatively irrelevant in the stated sense, let me comment briefly on the pertinent salient features of his three experiments in turn.

1. He himself describes Experiment 1 as only a partial realization of Freud's initial conditions (pp. 138–39). But he nonetheless invokes it as generic support for psychoanalytic theory. And his grounds for this tribute are that, in Freud's account, the adduced motives operate in the production of slips via prearticulatory editing of a kind which is *generically* semantic rather than just phonological (p. 136). But note that the semantic interfering stimuli in this experiment were word-pairs, each of which was presented tachistoscopically for one second. And such exposure is long enough for conscious or at worst preconscious cognitive registration. Furthermore, Motley gives no evidence at all for the prearticulatory *repression* of these interfering semantic stimuli.

True enough, his Experiment 1 does attest that semantic influences from the immediate verbal context of a slip are causally relevant to the commission of the slip. But, as we just saw, in this experiment these influences are preconscious, if not outright focally conscious. Hence I deem the causal relevance demonstrated in Motley's first experiment to be probatively unavailing as distinctive support for the psychoanalytic theory of slips, in the sense of being support for those of its consequences that are *not* likewise consequences of *any* rival theories eschewing repressed motives. For brevity, I shall speak of such distinctive support as support for psychoanalytic theory *"as such."*

2. Motley regards Experiment 2 as "virtually a direct test of Freud's theory" (p. 139). Yet in this second experiment no less than in the first, the cognitive-affective situational sets he manipulated in the treatment groups can hardly be claimed to have been repressed by the subjects. In one group, the situational mental set was conscious anticipation of experiencing an electric shock on the part of subjects who had been explicitly told to be prepared for it, and who were *ostensibly* connected to electrodes (p. 139). In another group, there was no electrical set, but the male subjects were pointedly stimulated sexually by "a female confederate experimenter who was by design attractive, personable, very provocatively attired, and seductive in behavior" (p. 140). The ensuing arousal was all too present in the subjects' conscious awareness. And there was a third "neutral set" control group.

True enough, "Experiment 2 demonstrates that subjects' speech encoding systems were sensitive to semantic influence from their situational cognitive [electric or sex] set" (p. 141). And, as in Freud's theory, that influence originated *outside* the total semantic context of the intended utterance. All the same, since the influence was not repressed, the results of Experiment 2, no less than those of Experiment 1, are seen to be probatively unavailing as support for psychoanalysis as such. Hence there is no foundation for Motley's conclusion that "Experiment 2 provides strong support for Freud's view of verbal slips" (p. 141).

3. Motley sees Experiment 3 as the best of his three purported tests of Freudian theory. Male heterosexual anxiety was manipulated as the independent variable. And the experiment did succeed in exhibiting the influence of the subject's personality on his verbal slips. But, qua support for Freud, that demonstration is futile, unless the relevant personality disposition bespeaks the operation of repressed ideation. Motley gives us every reason to claim that it does not.

As he explains, the personality trait of sex anxiety "was operationalized as Mosher Sex-

Guilt Inventory scores" (p. 142). Using these scores, Motley selected three treatment groups of high, medium, and low sex anxiety. But Mosher used a sentence-completion questionnaire filled out by none other than the subjects *themselves* to develop scales for sex-guilt, hostile guilt, and morality-guilt. And if the subjects who rate high, medium, and low on the sex-guilt scale are to furnish responses probatively relevant to the repression-theory of parapraxes, these ratings would need to betoken degrees of (sexual) repression somehow, perhaps inversely or directly.

Yet I submit the true-false and forced-choice answers given by the subjects on the questionnaire fail to be a gauge of (sexual) repression. Plainly one reason for this failure is that a person who has guilt feelings that qualify psychoanalytically as repressed will not consciously know or admit it when simply asked. Indeed, he(she) will even deny it in good faith, sometimes vehemently! Motley seems to have overlooked that insofar as the Mosher scores can be held to measure "psychodynamic conflict," what they measure is *conscious* conflict, *not* psychoanalytically pertinent conflict. It is as if one had devised a questionnaire to measure the *conscious* "income tax conflict" experienced by a person who is torn between the conscious temptation to cheat on his tax return and the equally conscious fear of legal prosecution for having done so. By contrast, Freudian psychodynamic conflict is a clash between a repressed thought clamoring for conscious recognition, on the one hand, and the ego or superego which denies that thought entry into awareness, on the other. When depicting Mosher sex-guilt scores to be measures of "psychodynamic conflict," Motley (p. 144) unfortunately pays no heed to the crucially pertinent difference between the conscious and the Freudian sorts of conflict. For he gives no reason at all to suppose that the subjects who scored high, medium, and low on Mosher's sex-guilt scale had repressed the sexual impulse aroused in them by the provocative voluptuous female experimenter. Hence, by using the Mosher scale ratings as a gauge of personality disposition, Motley forfeited the probative relevance of his otherwise valuable findings to the repression-theory of slips.

He did find (p. 142) that high Mosher-guilt subjects committed more sex-error spoonerisms than medium-guilt ones, whose errors, in turn, exceeded those of the low-guilt ones. And, as he rightly maintains (p. 143), he has thereby shown that—within the given situational cognitive set of sex arousal—personality-disposition can issue in verbal slips via semantic prearticulatory editing. Thus, Motley's results emerge as quantitatively modulated instances of the same motivational genre as the speech error of the consciously aroused man who declared that he wants "to get a *breast* of *flesh* air." By the same token, Motley's findings are just as probatively unavailing for buttressing the psychoanalytic theory of parapraxes as this "breast-flesh" slip. Indeed, despite claiming support for Freudian theory from the outcome of Experiment 3, Motley issues the following concluding disclaimer, among others: "Whereas Freud would claim that *all* verbal slips are semantic manifestations of a speaker's private cognitive-affective state, the present study makes no such claim (and this writer would expect such manifestations to be rare)" (p. 145). As I have argued, the design of Motley's three experiments lend substance to the complaint that experimental psychologists tend to overlook the initial conditions required by a genuine test of Freud's theory. Yet, in addition to yielding otherwise interesting results, these imaginative designs seem to point the way to devising genuine tests.

The restricted purview that Freud enunciated for the *psychoanalytic* contribution to the motivational elucidation of parapraxes has often been overlooked especially because Freud genuinely psychoanalyzes merely some parapraxes, as in the *aliquis* case, while essentially only reporting others are largely letting them speak for themselves, as it were. In this way, the reader is tempted to conclude incorrectly that if these others are of the plausible sort which I have exemplified, then they automatically bespeak support for Freud's theory. Thus, Freud relates how a speaker in the German parliament asked for a demonstration of "unreserved" ("rückhaltslos") loyalty to the Kaiser, but betrayed the hypocrisy of his subservience by saying "spineless" ("rückratslos") instead (S.E. 1901, 6:95). Another case of self-betrayal of a *conscious* thought, which was reported to Freud by Theodor Reik, is that of a young girl who did not intend to reveal to her parents her antipathy to the young man whom they wished her to marry. But when asked by her mother how she felt about him, she described him by coining the neologism "sehr liebens*widrig*"

(very love-repelling), though she had meant to be insincere and say "sehr liebens*würdig*" (very worthy of love) (S.E. 1901, 6:91). And, as Timpanaro (1976, pp. 151–53, 144–45, 178–79) has shown illuminatingly, Freud describes other episodes in which a slip *might* be due to the cunning of a repression but assumes *tout court* that is definitely *must* be, especially if the interpretation depicts individual motivations as misanthropic. Hence Timpanaro concludes that "all the really persuasive examples" in Freud's writings are what, *faute de mieux*, he calls "gaffes" (pp. 126–27):

> 'Slips' of this kind certainly presuppose that something has been suppressed, but the speaker is fully conscious of, and currently preoccupied with, whatever it is that he wants to conceal from those to whom he is speaking. It is not something which has genuinely been 'repressed' (forgotten) and re-emerges from the depths of his unconscious.[P. 127]

And Timpanaro remarks perceptively (p. 105) that Freud's explanations increasingly forfeit cogency according as the slips to which they pertain differ from the "gaffe" type, being alleged to have a more recondite, unconscious genesis. Indeed, he points out (p. 104) that, as Freud fully appreciated, nonpsychoanalytic accounts of gaffes have long been clichés in the folklore of common sense psychology. For instance, such expressions as "he gave himself away" betoken the recognition that, lacking complete control of what we say, we sometimes fail to conceal from others what is not meant for them and we would even prefer not to know ourselves, although we *are* conscious of it. And the vexation that often accompanies the slip may well be due to the unexpected realization of just this incomplete control, rather than to the unconscious appreciation of the tainted origin of the slip, as claimed by Freud (p. 157n).

But the important conclusion is this: *If there are any slips which are actually caused by genuine repressions, Freud did not give us any good reason to think that his clinical methods can identify and certify their causes as such,* no matter how interesting the elicited "free" associations might otherwise be. And as is apparent from my arguments, this adverse upshot seems indefeasible even if one were to grant that the analyst does not influence the subject's "free" associations. Besides, such an absence of influence would be utopian (cf. Grünbaum 1982, §III, 3).

The psychoanalytic explanations of other species of parapraxes by means of repressed motivations are just as tenuously founded as in the cases we have discussed. For example, the same unfavorable verdict applies to Freud's account of *misreadings*. For, as he tells us:

If we want to discover the disturbing purpose which produced the misreading, we must leave the text that has been misread entirely aside and we may begin the analytic investigation with the two questions: what is the first association to the product of the misreading? and in what situation did the misreading occur? [S.E. 1916, 15:70]

And, as he explains further:

What we ought to read is something unwished-for, and analysis will convince us that an intense wish to reject what we have read must be held responsible for its alternation. [P. 71]

I do not deny that "an intense wish to reject what we have read" *may* be "responsible for its alteration." But I deny that Freud's reliance on the method of free association furnished a sound reason for making this causal attribution, let alone for concluding—as he did—that the wish to reject "must" be held responsible. Hence I claim that his method for identifying and certifying the purported motive ought *not* to "convince us," as he thinks. Yet I *allow*, of course, that genuinely probative methods of causal inquiry may turn out to vindicate, at least in some cases, Freud's imputations of unconscious motivations for the commission of parapraxes.

Can any of the above array of doubts as to the *repression* genesis of a slip be validly gainsaid by claiming, as Freud did, that the alleged cause of the slip is established to *be* its cause by the *introspective* confirmation of the subject who committed it? As he put it: "You shall grant me that there can be no doubt of a parapraxis having sense if the subject himself admits it" (S.E. 1916, 15:50). Thus, when an examinee attributed his own penchant to forget Gassendi's name to a guilty conscience, Freud took it for granted that this "very subtle motivation" had to be responsible, because it was one "which the subject of it has explained himself" (S.E. 1901, 6:27). And he reports parapraxes by Storfer, himself, and Andréas Salomé, claiming that self-observation was able to certify the actual repressed cause of the bungled action in each case (S.E. 1901, 6:118, 163, 168; but cf. Timpanaro (1976, p. 146) for a rival account

of Storfer's slip by reference to linguistic banalization, as well as phonic and conceptual similarity). But it is probatively unavailing that AJ can confirm having put his genuine anxiety about the Neapolitan woman's pregnancy out of his mind—if indeed he had—at least temporarily, when he discussed his resentment of religious discrimination with Freud just before quoting Virgil. For such confirmation is patently a far cry from certifying the alleged *causal nexus* between the given fear and the slip. And even if the person who "slipped" were not under the suggestive, intimidating influence of the analyst, how could the subject possibly know any better than any of the rest of us that the pertinent unconscious fear had actually caused his slip?

On the face of it, it would seem that the privileged epistemic access which introspection afforded these subjects to the existence of their anxieties hardly extends to the certification of the wholly unvalidated causal nexus. More significantly, this indictment of Freud's appeal to introspective confirmation is well supported. For substantial evidence recently marshaled by cognitive psychologists tells against a subject's privileged epistemic access to the identification of the causes of his own behavior (Grünbaum 1980, sec. III, pp. 354–67).

4. Manifest Dream Contents as Mini-Neurotic Symptoms

So far, the criticism I have offered of Freud's theory of dreams has been just a corollary, generated *mutatis mutandis* from the failure of free associations to validate the psychoanalytic theory of parapraxes. But the psychoanalytic interpretation of dreams calls for some further scrutiny in its own right, if only because Freud regarded it as "*the royal road to a knowledge of the unconscious activities of the mind*" (S.E. 1900, 5:608; italics in original).

As Freud tells us, "the idea that *some* dreams are to be regarded as wish-fulfillments" had been commonplace in *pre*-psychoanalytic psychology (S.E. 1900, 4:134). Hence, Freud propounded a distinctive and exciting thesis about dreaming only when he *universalized* this commonsensical idea: "the meaning [motive force for the formation] of *every* dream is the fulfillment of a wish." And, as he is the first to recognize, *prima facie* this completely general thesis is impugned by sundry wish-*contravening* and distressing manifest dream contents (e.g. anxiety-dreams). Besides nightmares and examination dreams, for instance, "nonsensical" dreams also challenge Freud's account.

Even in the pre-psychoanalytic dream theories mentioned by Freud, the claim that a *particular* dream is "wish-fulfilling" goes beyond maintaining that the specifics of the dream's content *depict* the realization of some antecedent hope or desire. For, in the case of such a dream, these preanalytic psychological theories maintain furthermore that once the pertinent desires had not been satisfied in waking life, they *caused* the formation of a dream content in which they achieved vicarious consumption. And perhaps the common sense credibility of this pre-analytic causal attribution of *some* dreams to wishes derives from those familiar *waking fantasies* in which unrequited love and other desires find vicarious consumption. In any event, Freud relies on this common sense credibility of the motivational role of wishes in the formation of *some* dreams. Thus, in the case of one of his specimen dreams—the Irma dream—he plainly trades on the conviction carried by just this credibility to authenticate the trustworthiness of his method of free association as a means of identifying the motivational causes of *any and all* dreams. And his reason for endeavoring to establish this trustworthiness was that free association seemed to him to yield repressed wishes as the motives of even those dreams whose manifest contents are anything but wish-fulfilling. In this way, he thought he had legitimated his *universalization* of wish-fulfillment as being the formative cause of any and all manifest dream contents.

True, in 1933, he acknowledged the existence of some exceptions to this universal claim (S.E. 1933, 22:28–30). And thus he modified his wish-fulfillment hypothesis. While retaining wish-fulfillment as the function of dreaming, he acknowledged that it does miscarry with fair frequency. Hence, he then concluded that "the dream may aptly be characterized as an *attempt* at the fulfilment of a wish" (S.E. 1925, 20:46n. This footnote was added in 1935). In short, the motive for dreaming is still held to be a wish, but the actually ensuing dream is no longer claimed to qualify universally as its fulfillment. But let us disregard this rather minor modification for now and deal with Freud's earlier unqualified generalization.

Freud relies on two avenues to ascertain the purported motivational cause (or "meaning") of a dream: (i) The free associations of the individual dreamer, which originate at the separate elements of the manifest content (usually visual images), and (ii) dream symbolism whose unconscious motivational significance is claimed to be independent of individual and even cultural differences. Freud does explain that when gleaning the "sense" of a dream, the translation of interpersonal dream symbolism complements the method of free association (S.E. 1900, 5:341–42, 359; 1916, 15:150). But he emphasizes that the interpersonally significant symbols play only an auxiliary, subordinate role in dream interpretation vis-à-vis the "decisive significance" of the dreamer's free associations (S.E. 1900, 5:360; 1916, 15:151).

Indeed, in the magisterial digest of the dream theory he gave in his "Autobiographical Study," which he revised in 1935, he even seems to deny the probative value of dream symbolism by implication. True, he there makes passing mention of the role of symbolism in the dreamwork (S.E. 1925, 20:45). But he does so after having told us that the "manifest content was simply a make-believe, a façade, which could serve as a starting point for the associations but not for the interpretation" (S.E. 1925, 20:44). Thus, when interpersonal dream symbolism is present in the manifest content, its interpretative translation can yield only *bits* for the interpretation. Hence, for the purpose of examining the credentials of his interpretation of dreams, it will suffice to confine our comments to his reliance on the method of free association as an epistemic avenue to the purported motivational cause of dreaming.

As he explains, free associations setting out from the manifest content of any dream yield a repressed wish and other assorted repressed content, commingled with miscellaneous thoughts that qualify as "preconscious" in his familiar technical sense (S.E. 1900, 5:552–553; 1916, 15:224–226; 1923, 19:114; 1925, 20:44 and 46). Being the presumed residues of the dreamer's waking life before the dream, the emerging preconscious thoughts may well *happen* to include a *non*-repressed wish. And he then identifies the repressed wish yielded by the associations as the agency to which the dream owes its initial formation.

I shall examine Freud's interpretation of his Irma dream. This scrutiny will hardly vindicate his claim that this specimen dream authenticates free association as a reliable means of fathoming the formative causes of *all* dreams (S.E. 1900, 4:chap. II). Far from supplying such vindication, I shall maintain that even when common sense psychology regards a given dream as patently wish-fulfilling, psychoanalytically conducted free association does not have the probative resources to *underwrite* this verdict!

In his preamble to his own dream about his patient Irma, Freud details the events of the previous day that avowedly provided its point of departure (S.E. 1900, 4:106). And it is clear from this account that these events left him with *conscious* feelings of frustration and aggressive desires, which clamored for expression: Annoyance with Irma because she had rejected Freud's conjecture as to the unconscious cause of her hysterical symptoms; frustration because, as the presumed consequence of her rejection of his "solution," her somatic symptoms had persisted; irritation by his junior colleague Otto, who had implied censure of his handling of Irma's therapeutic expectations, and the desire "to justify" his treatment of Irma for the benefit of his respected senior colleague Dr. M., who has since been revealed to be his mentor Breuer (Grinstein 1980, chap. 1).

The aggressive wishes which had remained unfulfilled by the end of the day in question are then patently acted out or realized in the manifest dream content that Freud goes on to report (p. 107). For early within the dream, Freud is avowedly rebuking Irma for her resistance to his "solution." And he explicitly blames *her* for the persistence of her pains. Then, at the end of the dream, Dr. M. and he are condemning Otto for negligently causing Irma to become infected by his use of a dirty syringe. Thus, after recapitulating the conscious motives specified in the preamble, and the manifest content, Freud tells us convincingly that the following motivational interpretation "leapt to the eyes" from these data: The dream *"content was the fulfillment of a wish and its motive was a wish"* (S.E. 1900, 4:119; italics in original).

Now, if a dreamer remembers on the day after the dream what *conscious* thoughts he had on the day before his dream, it is true enough that this recollection *may* occur *in the wake* of thinking of the dream, thereby qualifying as a kind of association to the dream. Yet this sort of association clearly differs from the recovery of a *repressed* thought, first achieved if the dreamer takes elements of the manifest content as points of departure *and* is careful to heed the demanding injunctions of Freud's "fundamental rule" of "free association" (S.E. 1923, 18:238). This distinction does indeed matter in the context of Freud's attempted use of the Irma dream to authenticate free association as a trustworthy avenue for identifying repressed wishes as the formative causes of manifest dream contents. For he traded on the label "association" to insinuate the falsehood that the plainly *conscious* aggressive wishes of the prior day, which he specifies in his preamble, were first excavated associatively in the manner of a repressed thought. That this suggested conclusion is mere pretense is evident from his own report. For when speaking of the events on the day and evening *before* the dream, he says: "The same evening I wrote out Irma's case history, with the idea of giving it to Dr. M. (a common friend [of Otto's and Freud's] who was at that time the leading figure in our circle) in order to justify myself [in the face of Otto's implied reproof]" (S.E. 1900, 4:106).

In sum, though the aggressive conscious wishes that Freud had on the day before his Irma dream were then patently fulfilled in its manifest content, free association played *no excavating role* in his recall of these wishes after the dream. For he had been avowedly conscious of them the evening before. Hence for this reason alone, the purportedly paradigmatic Irma dream cannot serve to authenticate free association as a trustworthy avenue for certifying that *repressed infantile* wishes are the formative *causes* of manifest dream content, as claimed by Freud's theory. Yet he relies on free association to make just this claim (S.E. 1900, 5:546, 548–549, 552–554, 567–568, and 583–584). For example, he does so to make the following assertions *in italics*: ". . . *a conscious wish can only become a dream-instigator if it succeeds in awakening an unconscious wish with the same tenor and in obtaining reinforcement from it. . . . a wish which is represented in a dream must be an infantile one*" (S.E. 1900, 5:553). And fully *thirty years* after he had had a childhood dream at about age seven whose dominant theme was anxiety, he was satisfied that his analysis of this dream warranted the following conclusion: "The anxiety can be traced back, when repression is taken into account, to an obscure and evidently sexual craving that had found appropriate expression in the visual content of the dream" (S.E. 1900, 5:584). Since he invoked free association crucially to draw these causal inferences, I maintain that *Freud has indeed failed to sustain the major thesis of his dream theory*, a theory in which he took special pride. Yet even in a quite recent paper, the analysts Frank and Trunnel (1978) describe a training procedure based on the assumption that an archaic wish is the universal motive force of dreaming.

Thus to this day, Freudians claim that repressed *infantile* wishes are the primogenitors of *all* dreams. Yet, judging by Freud's own report on his celebrated Irma Injection Dream, there is no evidence at all that he ever carried his analysis of it far enough to extend to his childhood wishes (S.E. 1900, 4:120–21). Hence, if one of his infantile wishes is to have been the instigator of his Irma dream, his own published analysis of this dream cannot possibly underwrite the principal substantive tenet of his dream theory. How then can his disciples justify hailing it as *"the"* dream specimen of psychoanalysis, instead of demoting it to a mere popularized example? Over fifty years after the publication of *The Interpretation of Dreams* in 1900, Erik Erikson made a strenuous effort to rise to this challenge in a paper entitled "The Dream Specimen of Psychoanalysis" (1954). In this way, *Irma* is supposed to retain pride of place as the prototypic dream of psychoanalysis.

But if it was thus not until fifteen years after Freud's death that an orthodox interpretation of the Irma dream was even proposed, how did Freud himself justify using this particular dream "specimen" to *introduce* his analysis of dreams? The answer is encapsulated in the word *"method"* within the title of the pertinent chapter II of his *magnum opus* on the subject: "The Method of Interpreting Dreams: An Analysis of a Specimen Dream" (S.E. 1900, 4:96). Early in this chapter (pp. 100–102), he tells us clearly in what manner his "knowledge of that procedure [method of dream interpretation] was reached" (p. 100). As he explains there, it was a matter of *simply enlarging* the epistemic role of *free association* from being only a method of *aetiologic* inquiry aimed at therapy, to serving likewise as an avenue for interpreting dreams:

> My patients were pledged to communicate to me every idea or thought that occurred to them in connection with some particular subject; amongst other things they told me their dreams and so taught me that a dream can be inserted into the psychical chain that has to be traced backwards in the memory from a pathological idea. It was then only a short step to treating the dream itself as a symptom and to applying to dreams the method of interpretation that had been worked out for symptoms. [S.E. 1900, 4:100–101]

Note how here Freud makes light of the epistemically dubious nature of this momentous extension by vastly understating its gaping pitfalls as "only a short step." Yet he apparently wanted this step to carry conviction for his readers as well.

Thus, his initial accent in the opening presentation of his dream theory was on authenticating the *method* of interpreting dreams. For even if one grants that the method of free association ("fundamental rule of psychoanalysis") can fathom and certify the pathogens of neuroses as such, it is anything but obvious that this method can reliably perform the same epistemic service in identifying the causes (motives) of our dreams. And it would beg the question to *assume outright* that any dream can be regarded as a kind of neurotic symptom. Hence Freud's strategy was to argue first that, in the case of the Irma dream, the use of free association does yield motives independently countenanced by common sense psychology as having patently engendered *this* dream. Thereafter, he is prepared to rest his *substantive* theory of dreams as *universally* wish-fulfilling on the deliverances of the method purportedly authenticated by the analysis of his Irma dream. This order of argument is recapitulated in the very last sentences of the pertinent chapter, which read:

> For the moment I am satisfied with the achievement of this one piece of fresh knowledge. If we adopt the method of interpreting dreams which I have indicated here, we shall find that dreams really have a meaning and are far from being the expression of a fragmentary activity of the brain, as the authorities have claimed. *When the work of interpretation has been completed, we perceive that a dream is the fulfilment of a wish* (italics in original). [S.E. 1900, 4:121]

Accordingly, as I already indicated early on, this dream earned its laurels of being "*the* dream specimen of psychoanalysis" on methodological rather than substantive grounds. The more so, since the wishes that had been *shown* to be fulfilled by it were hardly repressed infantile ones, but *only* adult conscious desires!

As for the substantive conclusions derived from the published analysis of this paradigmatic dream, Freud issues a disclaimer in regard to the completeness of his account of it:

> I will not pretend that I have completely uncovered the meaning of this dream or that its interpretation is without a gap. I could spend much more time over it, derive further information from it and discuss fresh problems raised by it. I myself know the points from which further trains of thought could be followed. [S.E. 1900, 4:120—21]

Given the principally methodological basis of the exemplar-status accorded to the Irma dream, it is very disappointing that psychoanalysts have not *scrutinized* its purported authentication of free association as the method of dream analysis. One's disappointment is the greater because—of all of Freud's own dreams—the Irma dream has spawned a larger literature than any other (cf. Grinstein 1980, p. 22 for some citations). Though the aforementioned paper by Erikson (1954) is just as insouciant epistemologically as the rest of this literature, it warrants comment. For its avowed burden is to give the Irma dream the *infantile* motivational underpinning required by orthodox doctrine. Thus, he sees himself as having made good on his conclusion that "the latent infantile wish that provides the energy . . . for the dream is embedded in a manifest dream structure which on every level reflects significant trends of the dreamer's total situation" (p. 55). Let us examine his reasoning.

After quoting from Freud's own lengthy summary of *Irma*, Erikson (p. 15) points out that it does not contain any *repressed* motive: "We note that the wish demonstrated here is not more than preconscious." And the conscious wishes detailed by Freud are all adult rather than infantile ones. Indeed, nowhere in his *magnum opus* on dream interpretation does he explicitly offer a repressed wish for *this* dream, let alone an infantile one. Hence Erikson (pp. 15—16) proposes to supply a missing latent dream motive satisfying both of these theoretical desiderata and featuring sexual themata.

Erikson develops the hypothesized sexual origin by pointing to colloquial, sexually allusive overtones ("double meanings") of several German words in Freud's original. In the 1938 English translation cited by Erikson, the rendition of these German words was "so literal that an important double meaning gets lost" (Erikson, p. 24). The original German words, he tells us, "allude to sexual meanings, as if the Irma Dream permitted a complete sexual interpretation alongside the professional one—an inescapable expectation in any case" (p. 26).

Our focus is on Erikson's quest for the purported "infantile meaning of the Irma Dream" (p. 27), *not* on the *pansexual* significance that he claimed for it as well. Hence I shall forgo making a methodological complaint against the alleged inescapability of the expectation that "a complete sexual interpretation" of the dream is feasible. What does matter is that *only* the sexual allusion of the German word "*Spritze*" figures in Erikson's account as a clue to the conjectured infantile meaning of *Irma*. Stressing the unique allusive role of this one word in Freud's original, Erikson explains: "The recognition of this double meaning is absolutely necessary for a pursuit of the infantile meaning of the Irma Dream" (p. 27).

What then is the presumed sexual significance of "*Spritze*" on which Erikson rests his entire case for an infantile interpretation? He articulates the sexual and infantile overtones of "*Spritze*" in turn before they can be seen to merge.

First he explains the phallic-urinary tinge of the word's colloquial allusion:

> The German word . . . "*Spritze*" . . . is, indeed, used for syringes, but has also the colloquial meaning of "squirter." . . . squirter is an instrument of many connotations; of these, the phallic-urinary one is most relevant, for the use of a dirty syringe makes Otto a "dirty squirter," or "a little squirt," not just a careless physician. [P. 26]

It is undeniable that this sexual overtone is one of Erikson's *own* associations to the word "*Spritze*." But, according to the psychoanalytic methodology of dream interpretation, the interpretively relevant associations are those of the dreamer *himself*. For if a repressed infantile wish is to emerge as the motive for a given dream, it can be *certified* as its primogenitor only by probing the dreamer's *own* associations to elements of the manifest content. And it was Freud, not Erikson, who had the *Irma* dream. Hence, even according to the inferential standards countenanced by psychoanalytic theory, the sexual allusion of *Spritze* has probative merit only if it was one of Freud's *own* associations. But that is still not enough. If a thought revealed by an association is to be adduced as a motive for the *Irma* dream, it must be shown to be one of Freud's associations to *this* particular dream. Therefore, those of Freud's associations that he himself linked to elements of *other* dreams, as far as we know, cannot be adduced as motives for *this* dream.

Yet Erikson's phallic-urethral association to *"Spritze"* is conspicuously absent from Freud's own account of the associations evoked in *him* by Otto's syringe as part of the manifest content of *Irma*. Here is what Freud himself has to say:

> *And probably the syringe had not been clean.* This was yet another accusation against Otto, but derived from a different source. I had happened the day before to meet the son of an old lady of eighty-two, to whom I had to give an injection of morphia twice a day [footnote omitted]. At the moment she was in the country and he told me that she was suffering from phlebitis. I had at once thought it must be an infiltration caused by a dirty syringe. I was proud of the fact that in two years I had not caused a single infiltration; I took constant pains to be sure that the syringe was clean. In short, I was conscientious. [S.E. 1900, 4:118; italics in original]

So far, at any rate, Erikson has come up empty-handed. But the success of his endeavor to legitimate *Irma* as a doctrinal centerpiece does not turn on finding a sexual overtone for the dream motive. Mindful of the theory's call for a repressed infantile theme, Erikson offers "the dream's [sexual] allusion to a childhood problem" (p. 27) as his clincher. But unfortunately, he relies on speculation instead of clear evidence that Freud himself ever linked Dr. Otto's *"Spritze"* associatively to the memory of the childhood episode in question.

In the Section entitled "Infantile Material as a Source of Dreams" (S.E. 1900, 4:189–219), Freud does indeed relate the episode adduced by Erikson to a dream. But one looks in vain for *Irma* in the whole series of dreams he interprets there. Nor is there even any passing mention of *Irma*, let alone of Dr. Otto's *Spritze*. When the childhood

episode invoked by Erikson is discussed near the end of the Section (p. 216), its explicit associative context (pp. 215–16) is a dream relating to the 1848 Revolution (pp. 209–11) in central Europe.

At best, Freud's own report of the associative linkages of the given episode to dreams allows Erikson to *speculate* as follows: Freud *may* perhaps *also* have associated that childhood scene with repaying Otto in kind by having him malpractice with a dirty syringe. For notice Freud's own wording:

> When I was seven or eight years old there was another domestic scene, which I can remember very clearly. One evening before going to sleep I disregarded the rules which modesty lays down and obeyed the calls of nature [in a chamber pot] in my parents' bedroom while they were present. In the course of his reprimand, my father let fall the words: 'The boy will come to nothing.' This must have been a frightful blow to my ambition, for references to this scene are still constantly recurring in my dreams and are always linked with an enumeration of my achievements and successes, as though I wanted to say: 'You see, I *have* come to something.' [S.E. 1900, 4:216]

It is, of course, quite true that there is a good deal of *thematic* affinity between this humiliating paternal rebuke for immodest urination and the Otto syringe motif in Irma. But surely this thematic affinity alone is not evidence that the memory of the childhood scene was the motivational primogenitor of having dreamt the Irma Injection Dream in particular. Thematic affinity alone fails to bespeak such primogenesis, if only because it is not a reason for giving *psychodynamic priority* to the childhood memory over the actual *adult* thought of a syringe that Freud himself gave as the explanation for the dream-syringe! Flawed though it is as a method of *certifying causes*, even free association does not give epistemic sanction to Erikson's psychodynamic attribution on the flimsy basis used by him. For even if one deems the method of free association competent to identify the agencies of dream formation for any given dream, Erikson's use of Freud's reported associations is too speculative to sustain the hypothesized motivational origin of *Irma*.

As if to acknowledge the tenuous character of his documentation, Erikson proceeds gingerly when he conjectures what infantile experience engendered the Otto syringe motif:

If his father told little Freud under the embarrassing circumstance of the mother's presence in the parental bedroom, that he would never amount to anything, i.e., that the intelligent boy did not hold what he promised—is it not suggestive to assume that the tired doctor [Sigmund Freud] of the night before the dream had gone to bed with a bitter joke in his preconscious mind: yes, maybe I did promise too much when I said I could cure hysteria; maybe my father was right after all, I do not hold what I promised [P. 42]

Here the interrogative phrase "is it not suggestive to assume" has a commendably tentative tenor. But ironically, Erikson himself undermines the probative value of the childhood memory, even if its genetic relevance is granted. For he explicitly places it in the dreamer's "preconscious mind" on the eve of the dream. Though Freud's wish to prove his father wrong meets the requirement of being a childhood vestige, it does not lend support to the *psychoanalytic* dream theory, unless it was also *repressed* when Freud was on the verge of having the Irma dream.

Yet despite having declared Freud's childhood memory to have been preconscious on the eve of the dream (p. 42), Erikson does not hesitate to transform it into a *latent* infantile wish in the concluding paragraph of his essay (p. 55). And unmindful of his initial caution in proposing *infantile* primogenesis, he goes on to affirm it categorically in the metapsychological idiom of "energy" (p. 55): "The Irma Dream," he maintains, "illustrates how the latent infantile wish that provides the energy for . . . the dream, is imbedded in a manifest dream structure." But for all of Erikson's impressive sensitivity to associative nuances, he offers nothing to justify thus giving *psychodynamic priority* to the infantile urination experience over the waking adult thought of a *dirty syringe*, which Freud reported from the day before the dream. Indeed, even as regards mere thematic affinity to the Otto syringe motif, the thoughts Freud reported having on the day before the dream seem closer than the childhood memory adduced by Erikson.

Moreover, the temporal priority of the infantile wish over the adult one hardly vouches for a corresponding *psychodynamic* primacy. Why then does Erikson, no less than other Freudians, insist (p. 34) that dreams owe their very occurrence dynamically to "an id wish and all of its infantile energy"? Let me

suggest that this strained insistence on infantile causes becomes more intelligible—albeit *not* cogent—if one bears in mind that Freud explicitly modeled his interpretation of dreams on his repression-aetiology of neuroses (S.E. 1900, 4:100−101 and 5:528). As I recounted earlier, when Breuer postulated the *adult* occasioning traumata to be the primogenetic pathogens of hysteria, this aetiologic version was discredited by therapeutic failures. Yet Freud was determined to retain a repression-aetiology in some form. Hence he was driven to demote the *adult* occasioning traumata aetiologically to mere *precipitators* of neurosis, and to claim that childhood repressions were the *essential* pathogens. But, as he told us (S.E. 1900, 4:100−101), he developed his theory of dreams by assimilating manifest dream content to neurotic symptoms at the outset. And having downgraded adult occasioning traumata aetiologically in favor of childhood pathogens, he presumably felt entitled, by analogy, to give repressed *infantile* wishes psychodynamic primacy over adult ones.

Perhaps we should assume that the conclusion of this rationale was a tacit premise of Erikson's account. For in the absence of such an assumption, Erikson's entire case for attributing the occurrence of *Irma* to the "energy" from a childhood motive dangles ever so precariously from the thin thread of a colloquial allusion of "*Spritze.*" Indeed, it appears as a product of scraping the bottom of the epistemic barrel, unless infantile motives *generically* have psychodynamic primacy over adult ones. But, as I have argued, Freud's analogical rationale is not viable. Hence it cannot serve to underwrite the psychodynamic primacy of infantile wishes.

So much then for Erikson's imaginative but abortive attempt to provide a doctrinally orthodox infantile underpinning for Freud's own interpretation of *Irma*.

It so happens that in the case of the Irma dream, there are actually grounds from common sense psychology for regarding the aggressive motives reported in Freud's preamble as having engendered the manifest dream content. But free association did not first uncover these motives. Hence their common sense causal credentials cannot serve at all as evidence that, for any and all dreams, if certain repressed wishes reentered consciousness via a tortuous causal chain of free associations initiated by the manifest content, then the latter emergence would itself reliably identify these wishes as the initial motivational causes of the dream. Yet it is presumably just this probative reliance on free association that Erikson is extolling, in the context of interpreting Irma, by speaking breezily of "the necessity to abandon well-established methods of sober investigation (invented to find out a few things exactly and safely to overlook the rest) for a method of self-revelation apt to open the floodgates of the unconscious" (p. 54).

Nor did Freud offer a cogent reason, in the case of dreams, for resting the interpretive use of free association on an extrapolation from the repression-aetiology of neuroses. For the reasoning he did offer begs the question as follows: "We might also point out in our defense that our procedure in interpreting dreams [by means of free association] is identical with the procedure by which we resolve hysterical symptoms; and there the correctness of our method is warranted by the coincident emergence and disappearance of the symptoms" (S.E. 1900, 5:528). Indeed, as I have already explained in conjunction with my criticism of Freud's repression theory of parapraxes, his argument here is a misextrapolation. For he does not even try to adduce any counterpart to the therapeutic support that Breuer and he had claimed to have for the repression-aetiology of hysteria and for the investigative utility of lifting repressions via free associations to fathom the pathogens. Therefore I conclude that Freud's reliance on free association as a means of fathoming the causes of dreams is just as grievously flawed epistemically as his use of free association to identify the causes of parapraxes.

One must deplore some of the transparent inconsistency incurred by Freud in offering the Irma dream to underwrite his epistemic trust in free association as a causally probative tool of inquiry. Thus first he tells us (S.E. 1900, 4:107) that the Irma dream is unusual in the sense that "It was immediately clear [from his preamble] what events of the previous day provided its starting point." And three chapters later, he acknowledges: "the connection with the previous day is so obvious as to require no further comment" (p. 165). Having himself pointed out this transparency, he declares all the same: "Nevertheless no one who had only read the preamble and the [manifest] content of the dream could have the slightest notion of what the dream meant"

(p. 108). One is immediately taken aback by this puzzling declaration of obscurity precisely because, as we saw, the preamble clearly reveals that the events of the preceding day had left Freud with conscious aggressive desires (wishes), which are then patently fulfilled in the manifest dream content reported by him. And even on the heels of claiming that without free association, the dream's wish motives would be utterly obscure, he belies this claim as follows: "the words which I spoke to Irma in the dream showed that I was specially anxious not to be responsible for the pains which she still had" (p. 108). But worse, he waits until after he detailed his associations to contradict flatly his declaration of initial obscurity as to the dream's motive. For he then tells us convincingly that the wish character of that motive had "leapt to the eyes" (p. 119) from the conscious motives specified in the preamble and the description of the manifest content.

How, I must ask, can the critique I gave of Freud's dream theory, for example, possibly be seen as an illicit extrapolation of standards of appraisal appropriate only to the physical sciences? I am prompted to ask this rhetorical question, because the inveterate complaint of just such methodological transgression has again been leveled in a recent paper by Jane Flax (1981), which is directed against my views on psychoanalysis.

A second specimen dream discussed by Freud is one whose manifest content clearly depicts the thwarting of the very wish consciously felt by the dreamer in the dream itself (S.E. 1900, 4:146−49). And Freud presents the analysis of this dream to illustrate his contention that the manifest content of the dream is wish-fulfilling despite its distressing content.

The dreamer, "a clever woman patient" challenged Freud to show how his wish-fulfillment theory can accommodate the thwarting of just the desire she felt within the dream itself. For she dreamt that on a Sunday afternoon, she found herself wishing to give a dinner party. Having nothing but a little smoked salmon in the house, she had to buy some food. Yet, since it was Sunday, the stores were closed. The attempt to enlist the service of some caterers failed, since the telephone was out of order, thus aborting the plan to give the dinner party.

The frustrated hostess reported to Freud that in her waking life, she had had a longstanding craving to "have a caviare sandwich every morning but had grudged the expense" (p. 147). And on the day before the dream, she had asked her husband *not* to indulge this desire of hers, although he would readily have done so. Allegedly, she had made this request "so that she could go on teasing him about it," as she was wont to do generally. Furthermore, as Freud relates:

> ... the day before she had visited a woman friend of whom she confessed she felt jealous because her (my patient's) husband was constantly singing her praises. Fortunately this friend of hers is very skinny and thin and her husband admires a plumper figure. I asked her what she had talked about to her thin friend. Naturally, she replied, of that lady's wish to grow a little stouter. Her friend had enquired, too: 'When are you going to ask us to another meal? You always feed one so well. [P.148]

And when Freud asked her how she would account for the presence of the smoked salmon in the manifest dream content, she replied that this delicacy is her female friend's favorite dish.

Initially, Freud identified the dream motive as the wish to lessen the rival's chances of becoming plumper, since that would have made her still more attractive to the dreamer's husband. And thus the inability to give a dinner party is conducive to the fulfillment of the patient's aim. But Freud appreciates that this account has not dealt with an uncomfortable detail: Since the rival had expressed the wish to gain weight,

> ... it would not have been surprising if my patient had dreamt that her friend's wish was unfulfilled; for my patient's own wish was that her friend's wish (to put on weight) should not be fulfilled. But instead of this she dreamt that one of her *own* wishes was not fulfilled.[P.149]

How then does he propose to deal with this recalcitrant datum?

An auxiliary hypothesis is brought to the rescue. Freud postulates that instead of being the patient herself, the person who figures in the dream is actually her rival, with whom she had "identified" herself to the extent of putting herself into the rival's place. And he seems to be well aware that a rescuing auxiliary can be indicted as *ad hoc*, unless it is buttressed by *independent* evidential support. Thus, he goes on to claim at once (p. 149) that just such support is supplied by the patient's

request to her husband in waking life *not* to cater to her craving for caviar. For, under the collateral hypothesis that the patient can assume her rival's identity even in waking life, her avowed conscious desire to deprive the rival of food would make sense of her renunciatory request to her husband.

In this way, Freud believes to have shown that even a dream depicting the *thwarting* of a wish felt in the dream does qualify after all as the fulfillment of another wish, which is only latent, being a residue from the day before. And, as he sees it, his auxiliary hypothesis of interpersonal identification contributed to an understanding of a datum from the patient's behavior in waking life, besides enabling his major postulate of wish-fulfillment to explain the initially refractory feature of the manifest dream content.

Glymour (unpublished) has discussed the aborted dinner party dream as an illustration of Freud's device "to confirm an interpretation by finding two or more elements of the dream which are independently associated with a key figure in the interpretation of the dream." This dream illustrates this device, because after Freud had inferred the aim to thwart the dreamer's rival as the dream-motive, he had said: "All that was now lacking was some coincidence to confirm the solution" (S.E. 1900, 4:148). And when his patient reported her rival's fondness for smoked salmon, he had seized on the role of this delicacy in the manifest dream content as the confirming coincidence.

Glymour challenges this claim of confirmation as spurious. As he points out, Freud's conclusion as to the motivational cause had asserted an order of cause and effect that is the *reverse* of the causal order exhibited by the free associations. For associations generated by two manifest dream elements (the dinner party and the salmon) had *each* prompted his patient to think of her rival. But Freud took this to be evidence that the affect bound to that rival was the motivational cause for the thematic occurrence of both a dinner party and salmon in the manifest dream content. And Glymour objects that "Evidence for the first causal model is not necessarily evidence for the second," a causal reversal which he indicts as "one of Freud's favorite fallacies." Hence Glymour rejects Freud's invocation of the "coincidence" that both a dinner party and salmon figured in the manifest dream content: "the coincidence is manufactured:

one associates, at Freud's direction, until one thinks of something which has connections with several elements in one's dream; the several elements cause the common thought, not vice-versa, and the coincidence requires no further explanation. The method of manufacture is all the explanation required." Indeed, Freud thus argues fallaciously from the confluence of associations to a causal reversal in *explicitly generalized* form (S.E. 1900, 5:528, lines 1−7).

As the reader will recall from Section 3, it was in the context of my critique of Freud's theory of parapraxes that I argued for the rejection of his inference of causal reversal, *while emphasizing its fallacious origination in his repression-aetiology of the psychoneuroses.* And, as a corollary to my historico-logical discreditation of his causal inference, I objected to his commission of the same fallacy in his theory of dreams. Glymour independently uncovered the fallacy in the context of the dream theory by pointing out illuminatingly that it lurked behind Freud's reliance on a coincidence in the manifest dream content to *confirm* his analysis of the dream. But, as I showed in Section 3, Freud's fallacious causal inference is not quite the glaringly crude blunder that it appears to be. This flagrant appearance results from seeing that inference in the context of the dream theory alone, as Glymour did.

For such an *isolated* appraisal neglects that Freud speaks of dreams as being "like all other psychopathological structures" (S.E. 1900, 4:149). Twenty-five years later, he stressed this assimilation of manifest dream content to his compromise model of neurotic symptoms: "dreams are constructed like a neurotic symptom: they are compromises between the demands of a repressed impulse and the resistance of a censoring force in the ego" (S.E. 1925, 20:45). Thus, as I explained earlier, he did believe that the legacy of Breuer's method vouches for free association as an avenue to the identification of repressed dream motives. And, as I showed furthermore, Freud was led to this conclusion by misextrapolation from a flawed repression-aetiology of the neuroses. All the same, it emerges that Freud's causal reversal inference in his dream theory is not quite as devoid of a plausible rational motivation as Glymour makes it appear to be.

The objections I have raised so far against Freud's dream theory would hold, even if the method of free association were not flawed epistemically by the analyst's overt and covert interventions. But this method is considerably impaired by the defects I have charged against it elsewhere (Grünbaum 1982, §III,3): manipulative adulteration as well as selection bias. And these liabilities vitiate it, regardless of whether the repressions it yields are deemed the pathogens of neurotic symptoms, the causes of slips, or the motives for dream constructions. Indeed, as I have also explained in another place (Grünbaum 1982, §III,5), this conclusion bespeaks the spuriousness of the consilience of clinical inductions that Freud adduced late in life (S.E. 1937, 23:257−69) to validate analytic interpretations.

Clark Glymour (unpublished) has rightly complained that the contrived manner of selecting from the products of free association has enabled Freud's method to function *ad hoc* when generating the elements belonging to the purported *latent* dream content. For, as Glymour argues cogently, Freud so selected the latent content as to preserve his wish-fulfillment hypothesis from refutation by such *prima facie* counterexamples as nightmares and diffuse anxiety dreams. Freud gave no justificatory criteria in advance for weaving *particular* associations together to make *one* sort of story. Instead, he begged the question by tailoring his selections from the patient's associative output *ad hoc* to the preservation of his wish-fulfillment hypothesis, whenever the manifest dream-content was anything but wish-fulfilling. A suitably different set of selections from the associations could have been made to yield other motives, such as fear or disgust. Thus Freud failed to sustain his account of the latent content by *warrantedly* selected evidence. But since this account was *essential* to evading refutation by anxiety dreams, Glymour concludes reasonably enough that the universal wish-fulfillment hypothesis of psychoanalytic dream theory ought to be presumed false rather than unfalsifiable.

Freud of course did not come to grips with the objections to his dream theory that I developed in the present Section 4. To recapitulate, my principal complaint was that his *universal* wish-fulfillment theory of dreaming is ill-founded. For it was an *extrapolation* from the generic repression-aetiology of neurotic symptoms. But in the absence of a counterpart to the therapeutic moorings which had supplied the *crucial* evidence for the repression-aetiology of neuroses, it was wanton for Freud to engage in this extrapolation. By the same token, he misextrapolated the investigative use of free association in aetiologic inquiry by drawing the following conclusion: The motivational cause of a dream can be reliably identified on the strength of being a repressed thought, emerging from free associations triggered by the manifest dream content.

These fundamental doubts are not allayed by the quite limited qualification to which Freud was driven in his late "Revision of the Theory of Dreams" (S.E. 1933, 22:28–30). There he unequivocally exempted only one class of dreams from the otherwise universal purview of his wish-fulfillment hypothesis: Chronic dreams that regularly feature the painful reliving of severely traumatic episodes, such as the psychic traumata suffered by soldiers in combat.

5. Conclusion

Freud told us that the theory of repression is the cornerstone of the entire psychoanalytic theory of unconscious motivations. And he claimed that his clinical evidence furnishes compelling support for this cornerstone. Thus, I was able to scrutinize the logical foundations of the psychoanalytic edifice by examining Freud's clinical arguments for the repression-aetiology of the psychoneuroses, and for the cardinal causal role of repressed ideation in committing parapraxes ("slips") and in dreaming. The upshot of this scrutiny was that the reasoning by which he thought to justify the very foundation of his theory was grievously flawed.

Plainly, this conclusion leaves quite open whether some other, genuinely probative evidence will turn out to lend significant support at least to the repression-aetiology of psychoneuroses, which is *the* major pillar of the Freudian structure.

Though I have given a critique of the basic pillars of psychoanalysis, it might be asked: Why its anachronistic focus on Freud's reasoning to the exclusion of the modifications and elaborations by those post-Freudians whose doctrines are recognizably psychoanalytic in content rather than only in name? Latter day psychoanalytic theoreticians that come to mind are the very influential Heinz Kohut, who pioneered the so-called "self-

psychology" and the so-called "object relations" theorists, who include not only the leading Otto Kernberg but also Harry Guntrip, W. R. D. Fairbairn, Donald Winnicott, and others. Thus, Heinz Kohut, for example, downgrades Freud's Oedipal, *instinctual* factors in favor of pre-Oedipal, *environmental* ones as the sources of the purported *unconscious* determinants of personality structure. More generally, insofar as these post-Freudian theories are indeed recognizably psychoanalytic, they do of course embrace some version of the repression-aetiology. And, furthermore, they rely epistemically on free association in the clinical investigation of purported pathogens and other unconscious determinants of behavior, while lifting repressions to effect therapy.

But, I submit, precisely to the extent that these outgrowths of Freud's ideas are thus recognizably psychoanalytic in content as well as in method of inquiry and therapy, my epistemic critique of Freud's original hypotheses applies with equal force to the aetiologic, developmental, and therapeutic tenets of these successors. How, I ask, for example, can Kohut possibly claim better validation for his species of unconscious determinants than Freud can for the sexual ones? Moreover, it is just ludicrous to pretend with Flax (1981, p. 564) that my focus on Freud in appraising psychoanalytic theory epistemically is akin to the anachronistic procedure of "throwing out physics because there are unresolved problems in Newton's theory." For this purported analogy suggests misleadingly that the epistemic difficulties which beset Freud's original formulations have been overcome by the much vaunted post-Freudian formulations of self-psychology and object relations theory. And it overlooks the logical incompatibility of the most influential of these versions: As Robbins (1980, p. 477) points out, Kohut's and Kernberg's views are "fundamentally antagonistic" to one another, being rooted in a schism between Melanie Klein and W. R. D. Fairbairn.

True, there are elements in some of the post-Freudian theories that give less emphasis to repression, both aetiologically and therapeutically, than the received doctrine. For example, self-psychology gives significant aetiologic weight to the absence of empathic mirroring in early childhood. Yet, as Morris Eagle has shown (private communication, and in press), these ingredients of the post-

Freudian theories are at least as flawed epistemologically as the repression model that was found seriously wanting in this essay. Hence it is futile to adduce these modifications, as the disciples of self-psychology and object relations theory are wont to do, as improvements upon Freud's original hypotheses, whose articulations were more lucid and more amenable to scrutiny.

Indeed, there is not even agreement among the post-Freudians in regard to the probative value that may be assigned to *one and the same case study material:* While Kohut claimed clinical support for his theory from his re-analysis of Mr. Z.—a patient whose prior analysis had been a traditional one—the contemporary Chicago analyst Gedo (1980) harshly discounts the scientific quality of Kohut's case study material. And he concludes (p. 382) that the "theoretical inferences" drawn by Kohut from his clinical observations "fail to carry scientific conviction." A similarly negative assessment is reached by the psychoanalytic psychologist F.J. Levine (1979), an ardent exponent of psychoanalytic methods of investigation and therapy. On the other hand, Ferguson (1981, pp. 135–36) believes that Kohut's case history of Mr. Z. is "a crystalline example of the *fact* that a progressive theory change [in L. Laudan's sense] has taken place in psychoanalysis." But, Ferguson then seems to damn it with faint praise, saying "the case of Mr. Z. provides something of a 'confirming instance' of the new theory."

No wonder that the psychodynamically-oriented psychologists Fisher and Greenberg (1977) reached the following verdict: "The diversity of the secondary elaborations of Freud's ideas is so Babel-like as to defy the derivation of sensible deductions that can be put to empirical test" (p. ix).

REFERENCES

Eagle, M. "Psychoanalysis and Modern Psychodynamic Theories." In *Personality and the Behavior Disorders*, rev. ed., ed. N.S. Endler and J. McV. Hunt. New York: Wiley (in press).

Ellis, A. W. 1980. "On the Freudian Theory of Speech Errors." In *Errors in Linguistic Performance: Slips of the Tongue, Ear, Pen, and Hand*, ed. V. A. Fromkin, pp. 123–31. New York: Academic Press.

Erikson, E. H. 1954. "The Dream Specimen of Psychoanalysis." *Journal of the American Psychoanalytic Association* II:5–56.

Ferguson, M. 1981. "Progress and Theory Change: The Two Analyses of Mr. Z." *Annual of Psychoanalysis* 9:133–60.

Flax, J. 1981. "Psychoanalysis and the Philosophy of Science: Critique or Resistance?" *Journal of Philosophy* 78:561–69.

Frank, A. and E. E. Trunnell 1978. "Conscious Dream Synthesis as a Method of Learning About Dreaming: A Pedagogic Experiment." *The Psychoanalytic Quarterly* 47:103–12.

Fromkin, V. A. (ed.) 1980. *Errors in Linguistic Performance: Slips of the Tongue, Ear, Pen, and Hand*. New York: Academic Press.

Gedo, J. E. 1980. "Reflections on Some Current Controversies in Psycho-Analysis." *Journal of the American Psychoanalytic Association* 28:363–83.

Glymour, C. Unpublished Lectures on Freud.

Grinstein, A. 1980. *Sigmund Freud's Dreams*, 2nd ed. New York: International Universities Press.

Grünbaum, A. 1980. "Epistemological Liabilities of the Clinical Appraisal of Psychoanalytic Theory." *Noûs* 14:307–85.

Grünbaum, A. 1982. "Can Psychoanalytic Theory Be Cogently Tested 'On the Couch' "? In *Explanation and Evaluation in Psychiatry and Medicine*, Pittsburgh Series in Philosophy and History of Science, ed. L. Laudan, vol. 8. Berkeley: University of California Press.

Grünbaum, A. 1982a. "Retrospective Versus Prospective Testing of Aetiological Hypotheses in Freudian Theory." In *Minnesota Studies in the Philosophy of Science*, ed. J. Earman, vol. X. Minneapolis: University of Minnesota Press.

Levine, F. J. 1979. "On the Clinical Application of Heinz Kohut's Psychology of the Self: Comments on Some Recently Published Case Studies." *Journal of the Philadelphia Association for Psychoanalysis* 6:1–19.

Motley, M. T. 1980. "Verification of 'Freudian Slips' and Semantic Prearticulatory Editing via Laboratory-Induced Spoonerisms." In *Errors in Linguistic Performance: Slips of the Tongue, Ear, Pen, and Hand*, ed. V. A. Fromkin, pp. 133–47. New York: Academic Press.

Robbins, M. 1980. "Current Controversy in Object Relations Theory as Outgrowth of a Schism Between Klein and Fairbairn." *International Journal of Psychoanalysis* 61:477–92.

Timpanaro, S. 1976. *The Freudian Slip*, trans. Kate Soper. Atlantic Highlands, NJ: Humanities Press.

Integrative Directions

Among the earliest efforts to provide a bridge between psychoanalytic formulations and those of other theoretical schools were the writings of Thomas French in the 1930s. He saw a natural synthesis between Freudian processes and the experimental conditioning studies of Pavlov, influencing thereby such notable contributors as Franz Alexander, Norman Cameron, and Jules Masserman.

The paper by Alexander reprinted in this section was among the first by a psychoanalyst who sought to align psychotherapeutic processes with concepts derived from learning theory. Although maintaining an analytic stance, he recognized that dynamic therapies could be enhanced by the explicit introduction of principles of change derived from learning concepts.

More contemporaneously, Judd Marmor, an American psychoanalyst, acknowledges several realms within which behavioral techniques can fruitfully be employed. Although open to alternative models and methods, he elucidates the view in his paper that the processes comprising behavioral therapies are much more complex and "dynamic" in character than their adherents are ready to admit.

22 The Dynamics of Psychotherapy in the Light of Learning Theory

Franz Alexander

Most of what we know about the basic dynamic principles of psychotherapy is derived from the psychoanalytic process.

One of the striking facts in this field is that the intricate procedure of psychoanalytic treatment underwent so few changes since its guiding principles were formulated by Freud between 1912 and 1915.[7-11] Meanwhile, substantial developments took place in theoretical knowledge, particularly in ego psychology. Moreover, in all other fields of medicine, treatments underwent radical changes resulting from a steadily improving understanding of human physiology and pathology. No medical practitioner could treat patients with the same methods he learned 50 years ago without being considered antiquated. In contrast, during the same period the standard psychoanalytic treatment method as it is taught today in

From *American Journal of Psychiatry*, *120:*440–448, November 1963. Copyright 1963 by the American Psychiatric Association. Reprinted by permission.

psychoanalytic institutes remained practically unchanged.

It is not easy to account for this conservatism. Is it due to the perfection of the standard procedure, which because of its excellence does not require reevaluation and improvement, or does it have some other cultural rather than scientific reasons?

Among several factors one is outstanding: to be a reformer of psychoanalytic treatment was never a popular role. The need for unity among the pioneer psychoanalysts, who were universally rejected by outsiders, is one of the deep cultural roots of this stress on conformity. The majority of those who had critical views became "dissenters" either voluntarily or by excommunication. Some of these became known as neo-Freudians. Some of the critics, however, remained in the psychoanalytic fold.

(Some analysts jocularly expressed the view that the stress on conformity was a defense against the analyst's unconscious identification with Freud, each wanting to become himself a latter-day Freud and founder of a new school. Conformity was a defense against too many prima donnas.) Another important factor is the bewildering complexity of the psychodynamic processes occurring during treatment. It appears that the insecurity which this intricate field necessarily provokes creates a defensive dogmatism which gives its followers a pseudosecurity. Almost all statements concerning technique could be legitimately only highly tentative. "Tolerance of uncertainty" is generally low in human beings. A dogmatic reassertion of some traditionally accepted views—seeking for a kind of consensus—is a common defense against uncertainty.

In spite of all this, there seems to be little doubt that the essential psychodynamic principles on which psychoanalytic treatment rests have solid observational foundations. These constitute the areas of agreement among psychoanalysts of different theoretical persuasion. Briefly, they consist in the following observations and evaluations:

1. During treatment unconscious (repressed) material becomes conscious. This increases the action radius of the conscious ego: the ego becomes cognizant of unconscious impulses and thus is able to coordinate (integrate) the latter with the rest of conscious content.

2. The mobilization of unconscious materials is achieved mainly by two basic therapeutic factors: interpretation of material emerging during free association and the patient's emotional interpersonal experiences in the therapeutic situation (transference). The therapist's relatively objective, nonevaluative, impersonal attitude is the principal factor in mobilizing unconscious material.

3. The patient shows resistance against recognizing unconscious content. Overcoming this resistance is one of the primary technical problems of the treatment.

4. It is only natural that the neurotic patient will sooner or later direct his typical neurotic attitude toward his therapist. He develops a transference which is the repetition of interpersonal attitudes, mostly the feelings of the child to his parents. This process is favored by the therapist encouraging the patient to be himself as much as he can during the interviews. The therapist's objective, nonevaluative attitude is the main factor, not only in mobilizing unconscious material during the process of free association, but also in facilitating the manifestation of transference. The original neurosis of the patient, which is based on his childhood experiences, is thus transformed in an artificial "transference neurosis" which is a less intensive repetition of the patient's "infantile neurosis." The resolution of these revived feelings and behavior patterns—the resolution of the transference neurosis—becomes the aim of the treatment.

There is little disagreement concerning these fundamentals of the treatments. Controversies, which occur sporadically, pertain primarily to the technical means by which the transference neurosis can be resolved. The optimal intensity of the transference neurosis is one of the points of contention.

This is not the place to account in detail the various therapeutic suggestions which arose in recent years. Most of these modifications consisted in particular emphases given to certain aspects of the treatment. There are those who stressed interpretation of resistance (Wilhelm Reich, Helmuth Kaiser), while others focused on the interpretation of repressed content. Fenichel stated that resistance cannot be analyzed without making the patient understand what he is resisting.[6]

It is most difficult to evaluate all these modifications because it is generally suspected that authors' accounts about their theoretical views do not precisely reflect what they are actually doing while treating patients. The reason for this discrepancy lies in the fact that the therapist is a "participant observer" who is called upon constantly to make decisions on the spot. The actual interactional process between therapist and patient is much more complex than the theoretical accounts about it. In general there were two main trends: (1) emphasis on cognitive insight as a means of breaking up the neurotic patterns and (2) emphasis upon the emotional experiences the patient undergoes during treatment. These are not mutually exclusive, yet most controversies centered around emphasis on the one or the other factor: cognitive versus experiential.

While mostly the similarity between the transference attitude and the original pathogenic childhood situation has been stressed, I emphasized the therapeutic significance of the difference between the old family conflicts and the actual doctor-patient relationship. This difference is what allows "corrective emotional experience" to occur, which I consider as the central therapeutic factor both in psychoanalysis proper and in analytically oriented psychotherapy. The new settlement of an old unresolved conflict in the transference situation becomes possible not only because the intensity of the transference conflict is less than that of the original conflict, but also because the therapist's actual response to the patient's emotional expressions is quite different from the original treatment of the child by the parents. The fact that the therapist's reaction differs from that of the parent, to whose behavior the child adjusted himself as well as he could with his own neurotic reactions, makes it necessary for the patient to abandon and correct these old emotional patterns. After all, this is precisely one of the ego's basic functions—adjustment to the existing external conditions. As soon as the old neurotic patterns are revived and brought into the realm of consciousness, the ego has the opportunity to readjust them to the changed external and internal conditions. This is the essence of the corrective influence of those series of experiences which occur during treatment.[2, 3] As will be seen, however, the emotional detachment of the therapist turned out under observational scrutiny to be less complete than this idealized model postulates.

Since the difference between the patient-therapist and the original child-parent relationship appeared to me a cardinal therapeutic agent, I made technical suggestions derived from these considerations. The therapist in order to increase the effectiveness of the corrective emotional experiences should attempt to create an interpersonal climate which is suited to highlight the discrepancy between the patient's transference attitude and the actual situation as it exists between patient and therapist. For example, if the original childhood situation which the patient repeats in the transference was between a strict punitive father and a frightened son, the therapist should behave in a calculatedly permissive manner. If the father had a doting, all-forgiving attitude toward his son, the therapist should take a more impersonal and reserved attitude. This suggestion was criticized by some authors, that these consciously and purposefully adopted attitudes are artificial and will be recognized as such by the patient. I maintained, however, that the

therapist's objective, emotionally not participating attitude is itself artificial inasmuch as it does not exist between human beings in actual life. Neither is it as complete as has been assumed. This controversy will have to wait to be decided by further experiences of practitioners.

I made still other controversial technical suggestions aimed at intensifying the emotional experiences of the patient. One of them was changing the number of interviews in appropriate phases of the treatment in order to make the patient more vividly conscious of his dependency needs by frustrating them.

Another of my suggestions pertains to the ever-puzzling question of termination of treatment. The traditional belief is that the longer an analysis lasts, the greater is the probability of recovery. Experienced analysts more and more came to doubt the validity of this generalization. If anything, this is the exception; very long treatments lasting over many years do not seem to be the most successful ones. On the other hand, many so-called transference cures after very brief contact have been observed to be lasting. A clear correlation between duration of treatment and its results has not been established. There are no reliable criteria for the proper time of termination. Improvements observed during treatment often prove to be conditioned by the fact that the patient is still being treated. The patient's own inclination to terminate or to continue the treatment is not always a reliable indication. The complexity of the whole procedure and our inability to estimate precisely the proper time of termination induced me to employ the method of experimental temporary interruptions, a method which in my experience is the most satisfactory procedure. At the same time it often reduces the total number of interviews. The technique of tentative temporary interruptions is based on trusting the natural recuperative powers of the human personality, which are largely underestimated by many psychoanalysts. There is an almost general trend toward "overtreatment." A universal regressive trend in human beings has been generally recognized by psychoanalysts. Under sufficient stress everyone tends to regress to the helpless state of infancy and seek help from others. The psychoanalytic treatment situation caters to this regressive attitude. As Freud stated, treatments often reach a point where the patient's will to be cured is outweighed by his wish to be treated.

In order to counteract this trend a continuous pressure on the patient is needed to make him ready to take over his own management as soon as possible. During temporary interruptions patients often discover that they can live without their analyst. When they return, the still not worked out emotional problems come clearly to the forefront.*

Furthermore, I called attention to Freud's distinction between two forms of regression. He first described regression to a period of ego-development in which the patient was still happy, in which he functioned well. Later he described regressions to traumatic experiences, which he explained as attempts to master subsequently an overwhelming situation of the past. During psychoanalytic treatment both kinds of regression occur. Regressions to pretraumatic or preconflictual periods—although they offer excellent research opportunity for the study of personality development—are therapeutically not valuable. Often we find that the patient regresses in his free associations to preconflictual early infantile material as a maneuver to evade the essential pathogenic conflicts. This material appears as "deep material" and both patient and therapist in mutual self-deception spend a great deal of time and effort to analyze this essentially evasive material. The recent trend to look always for very early emotional conflicts between mother and infant as the most common source of neurotic disturbances is the result of overlooking this frequent regressive evasion of later essential pathogenic conflicts. Serious disturbances of the early symbiotic mother-child relation occur only with exceptionally disturbed mothers. The most common conflicts begin when the child has already a distinct feeling of being a person (ego-awareness) and relates to his human environment, to his parents and siblings as to individual persons. The oedipus complex and sibling rivalry are accordingly the common early sources of neurotic patterns. There are many exceptions, of course, where the personality growth is disturbed in very early infancy.

Another issue which gained attention in

*This type of "fractioned analysis," which was practiced in the early days of the Outpatient Clinic of the Berlin Institute, is an empirical experimental way to find the correct time for termination.

the post-Freudian era is the therapist's neglect of the actual present life situation in favor of preoccupation with the patient's past history. This is based on the tenet that the present life circumstances are merely precipitating factors, mobilizing the patient's infantile neurosis. In general, of course, the present is always determined by the past. Freud in a rather early writing proposed the theory of complementary etiology. A person with severe ego defects acquired in the past will react to slight stress situations in his present life with severe reactions; a person with a relatively healthy past history will require more severe blows of life to regress into a neurotic state.[12] Some modern authors, like French, Rado, myself, and others feel that there is an unwarranted neglect of the actual life circumstances.[1,15] The patient comes to the therapist when he is at the end of his rope, is entangled in emotional problems which have reached a point when he feels he needs help. These authors feel that the therapist never should allow the patient to forget that he came to him to resolve his present problem. The understanding of the past should always be subordinated to the problems of the present. Therapy is not the same as genetic research. Freud's early emphasis upon the reconstruction of past history was the result of his primary interest in research. At first he felt he must know the nature of the disease he proposes to cure. The interest in past history at the expense of the present is the residue of the historical period when research in personality dynamics of necessity was a prerequisite to develop a rational treatment method.

These controversial issues will have to wait for the verdict of history. Their significance cannot yet be evaluated with finality. One may state, however, that there is a growing inclination to question the universal validity of some habitual practices handed down by tradition over several generations of psychoanalysts. There is a trend toward greater flexibility in technique, attempting to adjust the technical details to the individual nature of the patient and his problems. This principle of flexibility was explicitly stressed by Edith Weigert, Thomas French, myself, and still others.

While there is considerable controversy concerning frequency of interviews, interruptions, termination, and the mutual relation between intellectual and emotional factors in treatment, there seems to be a universal consensus about the significance of the therapist's individual personality for the results of the treatment. This interest first manifested itself in several contributions dealing with the therapist's own emotional involvement in the patient—"the countertransference phenomenon." Freud first used the expression, countertransference, in 1910. It took, however, about 30 years before the therapist's unconscious, spontaneous reactions toward the patient were explored as to their significance for the course of the treatment. The reasons for this neglect were both theoretical and practical. Originally Freud conceived the analyst's role in the treatment as a blank screen who carefully keeps his incognito and upon whom the patient can project any role, that of the image of his father (father transference), of mother (mother transference), or of any significant person in his past. In this way the patient can reexperience the important interpersonal events of his past undisturbed by the specific personality of the therapist. The phenomenon called "countertransference," however, contradicts sharply the "blank screen" theory.

It is now generally recognized that in reality the analyst does not remain a blank screen, an uninvolved intellect, but is perceived by the patient as a concrete person. There is, however, a great deal of difference among present-day authors in the evaluation of the significance of the therapist's personality in general and his countertransference reactions in particular.

Some authors consider countertransference as an undesirable impurity just as the patient's emotional involvement with his therapist (transference) originally was considered as an undesirable complication. The ideal model of the treatment was that the patient should freely associate and thus reveal himself without controlling the train of his ideas, and should consider the therapist only as an expert who is trying to help him. Later, as is well known, the patient's emotional involvement turned out to be the dynamic axis of the treatment. So far as the therapist's involvement is concerned, it is considered by most authors as an unwanted impurity. The therapist should have only one reaction to the patient, the wish to understand him and give him an opportunity for readjustment through the insight offered to him by the therapist's interpretations. The latter should function as a pure intellect without being disturbed by

any personal and subjective reactions to the patient.

The prevailing view is that the analyst's own emotional reactions should be considered as disturbing factors of the treatment.

Some authors, among them Edith Weigert, Frieda Fromm-Reichmann, Heimann, Benedek, and Salzman, however, mention certain assets of the countertransference; they point out that the analyst's understanding of his countertransference attitudes may give him a particularly valuable tool for understanding the patient's transference reactions.[5,13,14,16] As to the therapeutic significance of the countertransference, there is a great deal of disagreement. While Balint and Balint consider this impurity as negligible for the therapeutic process,[4] Benedek states in her paper on countertransference that the therapist's personality is the most important agent of the therapeutic process.[5] There is, however, general agreement that a too intensive emotional involvement on the therapist's part is a seriously disturbing factor. Glover speaks of the "analyst's toilet" which he learns in his own personal analysis, which should feee him from unwanted emotional participation in the treatment. This is, indeed, the most important objective of the training analysis; it helps him to know how to control and possibly even to change his spontaneous countertransference reactions.

I believe that the countertransference may be helpful or harmful. It is helpful when it differs from that parental attitude toward the child which contributed to the patient's emotional difficulties. The patient's neurotic attitudes developed not in a vacuum but as reactions to parental attitudes. If the therapist's reactions are different from these parental attitudes, the patient's emotional involvement with the therapist is not realistic. This challenges the patient to alter his reaction patterns. If, however, the specific countertransference of the therapist happens to be similar to the parental attitudes toward the child, the patient's neurotic reaction patterns will persist and an interminable analysis may result. There is no incentive for the patient to change his feelings. I recommended therefore that the therapist should be keenly aware of his own spontaneous—no matter how slight—feelings to the patient and should try to replace them by an interpersonal climate which is suited to correct the original neurotic patterns.

One of the most systematic revisions of the standard psychoanalytic procedure was undertaken by Sandor Rado, published in several writings, beginning in 1948.[15] His critical evaluation of psychoanalytic treatment and his suggested modifications deserve particular attention because for many years Rado has been known as one of the most thorough students of Freud's writings.

As years went on, Rado became more and more dissatisfied with the prevailing practice of psychoanalysis, and proposed his adaptational technique based on his "adaptational psychodynamics." As it is the case with many innovators, some of Rado's formulations consist in new terminology. Some of his new emphases, however, are highly significant. He is most concerned, as I am, with those features of the standard technique of psychoanalysis which foster regression without supplying a counterforce toward the patient's progression, that is to say, to his successful adaptation to the actual life situation. He raises the crucial question: Is the patient's understanding of his past development sufficient to induce a change in him? "To overcome repressions and thus be able to recall the past is one thing; to learn from it and be able to act on the new knowledge, another."[15]

Rado recommends, as a means to promote the goal of therapy, raising the patient from his earlier childlike adaptations to an appropriate adult level—"to hold the patient as much as possible at the adult level of cooperation with the physician." The patient following his regressive trend "parentifies" the therapist but the therapist should counteract this trend and not allow himself to be pushed by the patient into the parent role. Rado criticizes orthodox psychoanalytic treatment as furthering the regressive urge of the patient by emphasizing the "punitive parentifying" transference (the patient's dependence upon the parentalized image of the therapist).[15] Rado points out that losing self-confidence is the main reason for the patient to build up the therapist into a powerful parent figure. Rado's main principle, therefore, is to "bolster up the patient's self-confidence on realistic grounds." He stresses the importance of dealing with the patient's actual present life conditions in all possible detail. Interpretations must always embrace the conscious as well as unconscious motivations. In concordance with mine and French's similar emphasis[1] Rado succinctly states: "Even when the bio-graphic material on hand reaches far into the past, interpretation must always begin and end with the patient's present life performance, his present adaptive task. The significance of this rule cannot be overstated."

Rado considers his adaptational technique but a further development of the current psychoanalytic technique, not something basically contradictory to it. It should be pointed out that while criticizing the standard psychoanalytic procedure, Rado in reality criticizes current practice, but not theory. According to accepted theory, the patient's dependent—in Rado's term—"parentifying" transference should be resolved. The patient during treatment learns to understand his own motivations; this enables him to take over his own management. He assimilates the therapist's interpretations and gradually he can dispense with the therapist, from whom he has received all he needs. The therapeutic process thus recapitulates the process of emotional maturation; the child learns from the parents, incorporates their attitude, and eventually will no longer need them for guidance. Rado's point becomes relevant when one points out that the current procedure does not always achieve this goal, and I may add, it unnecessarily prolongs the procedure. The reason for this is that the exploration of the past became an aim in itself, indeed the goal of the treatment. The past should be subordinated to a total grasp of the present life situation and serve as the basis for future adaptive accomplishments.

At this point my emphasis is pertinent, that it is imperative for the therapist to correctly estimate the time when his guidance becomes not only unnecessary but detrimental, inasmuch as it unnecessarily fosters the very dependency of the patient on the therapist which the latter tries to combat. I stated that deeds are stronger than words; the treatment should be interrupted at the right time in order to give the patient the experience that he can now function on his own and thus gain that self-confidence which Rado tries to instill into the patient by "positive interpretations." No matter, however, what technical devices they emphasize, the goal of these reformers is the same: to minimize the danger implicit in the psychotherapeutic situation, namely, encouraging undue regression and evasion of the current adaptive tasks. It is quite true that regression is necessary in order to give the patient opportunity to reexperience his early maladaptive patterns and grapple with them anew to find other more appropriate levels of feeling and behavior. The key to successful psychoanalytic therapy is, however, not to allow regression in the transference to become an aim in itself. It is necessary to control it.

In view of these controversies the need for a careful study of the therapeutic process became more and more recognized. Different research centers initiated programs from grants given by the Ford Foundation to study the therapeutic process. At the Mount Sinai Hospital in Los Angeles, under my direction, we undertook a study of the therapeutic process, in which a number of psychoanalysts observe the therapeutic interaction between therapist and patient in several treatment cases. All interviews were sound-recorded and both the participant observer—that is the therapist—and the nonparticipant observers recorded their evaluation of the process immediately after each interview. Our assumption was that the therapist, being an active participant in the interactional process, is not capable of recognizing and describing his own involvements with the same objectivity as those who observe him. His attention is necessarily focused on patient's material and, being himself involved in this complex interaction, cannot fully appreciate his own part in it. This expectation was fully borne out by our study.

As was expected the processing of the voluminous data thus collected proved to be a prolonged affair, which will require several years of collaborative work. Yet even at the present stage of processing, several important conclusions emerge. The most important of these is the fact that the traditional descriptions of the therapeutic process do not adequately reflect the immensely complex interaction between therapist and patient. The patient's reactions cannot be described fully as transference reactions. The patient reacts to the therapist as to a concrete person and not only as a representative of parental figures. The therapist's reactions also far exceed what is usually called countertransference. They include, in addition to this, interventions based on conscious deliberations and also his spontaneous idiosyncratic attitudes. Moreover, his own values are conveyed to the patient even if he consistently tries to protect his incognito. The patient reacts to the therapist's overt but also to his nonverbal hidden intentions and the therapist reacts to the patient's reaction to him. It is a truly transactional process.

In studying this transactional material I came to the conviction that the therapeutic process can be best understood in the terms of learning theory. Particularly the principle of reward and punishment and also the influence of repetitive experiences can be clearly recognized. Learning is defined as a change resulting from previous experiences. In every learning process, one can distinguish two components. First the motivational factor, namely, the subjective needs which activate the learning process and second, certain performances by which a new behavioral pattern suitable to fill the motivational need is actually acquired. In most general terms unfulfilled needs no matter what their nature may be—hunger for food, hunger for love, curiosity, the urge for mastery—initiate groping trial and error efforts which cease when an adequate behavioral response is found. Adequate responses lead to need satisfaction which is the reward for the effort. Rewarding responses are repeated until they become automatic and their repetition no longer requires effort and further experimentation. This is identical with the feedback mechanisms described in cybernetics. Every change of the total situation requires learning new adequate responses. Old learned patterns which were adequate in a previous situation must be unlearned. They are impediments to acquiring new adequate patterns.

I am not particularly concerned at this point with the controversy between the more mechanistic concepts of the older behaviorist theory and the newer Gestalt theory of learning. The controversy pertains to the nature of the process by which satisfactory behavior patterns are acquired. This controversy can be reduced to two suppositions. The older Thorndike and Pavlov models operate with the principle of contiguity or connectionism. Whenever a behavioral pattern becomes associated with both a specific motivating need and need satisfaction, the organism will automatically repeat the satisfactory performance whenever the same need arises. This view considers the organism as a passive receptor of external and internal stimuli, which become associated by contiguity. The organism's own active organizing function is neglected. The finding of the satisfactory pattern, according to the classical theory, takes place through blind trial and error.

In contrast, the Gestalt theoretical model operates with the supposition that the trials by which the organism finds satisfactory behavioral responses are not blind but are aided by cognitive processes. They are intelligent trials which are guided by certain generalizations arrived at with the aid of the memory of previous experiences. They imply an active organization of previous experiences. This organizational act amounts to a cognitive grasp of the total situation. I am not concerned at this juncture with the seemingly essential difference between the connectionistic and Gestalt theories of learning. Probably both types of learning exist. The infant learns without much help from previous experiences. In this learning blind trials and errors must of necessity prevail. Common basis in all learning, whether it takes place through blind trials and errors or by intelligent trials, is the forging of a connection between three variables: a specific motivating impulse, a specific behavioral response, and a gratifying experience which is the reward.

Accepting Freud's definition of thinking as a substitute for acting, that is to say, as acting in phantasy, the reward principle can be well applied to intellectual solutions or problems. Groping trials and errors in thought—whether blind or guided by cognitive processes—lead eventually to a solution which clicks. Finding a solution which satisfies all the observations without contradictions is accompanied by a feeling of satisfaction. After a solution is found—occasionally it may be found accidentally—the problem-solving urge, as everyone knows who has tried to solve a mathematical equation or a chess puzzle, ceases and a feeling of satisfaction ensues. The tension state which prevails as long as the problem is not solved yields to a feeling of rest and fulfillment. This is the reward for the effort, whether it consists of blind or intelligent trials. The principle of reward can be applied not only to a rat learning to run a maze, but to the most complex thought processes as well. The therapeutic process can be well described in these terms of learning theory. The specific problem in therapy consists in finding an adequate interpersonal relation between therapist and patient. Initially this is distorted because the patient applies to this specific human interaction feeling-patterns and behavior-patterns which were formed in the patient's past and do not apply either to the actual therapeutic situation or to

his actual life situation. During treatment the patient unlearns the old patterns and learns new ones. This complex process of relearning follows the same principles as the more simple relearning process hitherto studied by experimental psychologists. It contains cognitive elements as well as learning from actual interpersonal experiences which occur during the therapeutic interaction. These two components are intricately interwoven. They were described in psychoanalytic literature with the undefined, rather vague term *emotional insight*. The word *emotional* refers to the interpersonal experiences; the word *insight* refers to the cognitive element. The expression does not mean more than the recognition of the presence of both components. The psychological process to which the term refers is not yet spelled out in detail. Our present observational study is focused on a better understanding of this complex psychological phenomenom—emotional insight—which appears to us as the central factor in every learning process including psychoanalytic treatment. Every intellectual grasp, even when it concerns entirely nonutilitarian preoccupations such as playful puzzle-solving efforts, is motivated by some kind of urge for mastery and is accompanied with tension resolution as its reward. In psychotherapy the reward consists in less conflictful, more harmonious interpersonal relations, which the patient achieves first by adequately relating to his therapist, then to his environment, and eventually to his own ego ideal. At first he tries to gain the therapist's approval by living up to the supreme therapeutic principle—to the basic rule of frank self-expression. At the same time he tries to gain acceptance by living up to the therapist's expectations of him, which he senses in spite of the therapist's overt nonevaluating attitude. And finally, he tries to live up to his own genuine values, to his cherished image of himself. Far-reaching discrepancy between the therapist's and the patient's values is a common source of therapeutic impasse.

This gradually evolving dynamic process can be followed and described step by step in studies made by nonparticipant observers. Current studies give encouragement and hope that we shall eventually be able to understand more adequately this intricate interpersonal process and to account for therapeutic successes and failures. As in every field of science, general assumptions gradually yield to more specific ones which are obtained by meticulous controlled observations. The history of sciences teaches us that new and more adequate technical devices of observation and reasoning are responsible for advancement. In the field of psychotherapy the long overdue observation of the therapeutic process by nonparticipant observers is turning out to be the required methodological tool. This in itself, however, is not sufficient. The evaluation of the rich and new observational material calls for new theoretical perspectives. Learning theory appears to be at present the most satisfactory framework for the evaluation of observational data and for making valid generalizations. As it continuously happens at certain phases of thought development in all fields of science, different independent approaches merge and become integrated with each other. At present, we are witnessing the beginnings of a most promising integration of psychoanalytic theory with learning theory, which may lead to unpredictable advances in the theory and practice of the psychotherapies.

REFERENCES

1. Alexander, F., and French, T. M.: *Psychoanalytic Therapy. Principles and Application.* New York: Ronald Press, 1946.
2. Alexander, F.: *Psychoanalysis and Psychotherapy.* New York: W. W. Norton, 1956.
3. Alexander, F.: *Behav. Sci., 3;* Oct. 1958.
4. Balint, A., and Balint, M.: *Int. J. Psychoanal., 20;* 1939.
5. Benedek, T.: *Bull. Menninger Clin., 17:6,* 1953.
6. Fenichel, O.: *The Psychoanalytic Theory of Neurosis.* New York: W W. Norton, 1945.
7. Freud, S.: The Dynamics of the Transference (1912). *Collected Papers, Vol. II.* London: Hogarth Press, 1924.
8. Freud, S.: Recommendations for Physicians on the Psychoanalytic Method of Treatment (1912). *Collected Papers, Vol. II.* London: Hogarth Press, 1924.
9. Freud, S.: Further Recommendations in the Technique of Psychoanalysis on Beginning the Treatment. The Question of the First Communications. The Dynamics of the Cure (1913). *Collected Papers, Vol. II.* London: Hogarth Press, 1924.
10. Freud, S.: Further Recommendations in the Technique of Psychoanalysis. Recollection, Repetition and Working Through (1914). *Collected Papers, Vol. II.* London: Hogarth Press, 1924.
11. Freud, S.: Further Recommendations in the Technique of Psychoanalysis. Observations on Transference-Love (1915). *Collected Papers, Vol. II.* London: Hogarth Press, 1924.
12. Freud, S.: *New Introductory Lectures on Psychoanalysis.* New York: W. W. Norton, 1933.
13. Fromm-Reichmann, F.: *Principles of Intensive Psychotherapy.* London: Allen & Unwin, 1957.
14. Heimann, P.: *Int. J. Psychoanal., 31:* 1950.
15. Rado, S.: *Psychoanalysis of Behavior: Collected Papers, Vol. I* (1922–1956); Vol. II (1956–1961). New York: Grune and Stratton, Vol. I, 1956, Vol. II, 1962.
16. Weigert, E.: *J. Am. Psychoanal. Ass., 2:4,* 1954.

23 Dynamic Psychotherapy and Behavior Therapy: Are They Irreconcilable?

Judd Marmor

In the course of psychiatric training and practice our professional identities become so intimately linked to what we have learned and how we practice that we are prone to extol uncritically the virtues of our own techniques and to depreciate defensively those techniques that are different. The dialogue that has gone on between most behavior therapists and

Reprinted by permission from *Archives of General Psychiatry*, 24:22–28, January 1971. Copyright 1971 by the American Medical Association.

dynamic psychotherapists has been marred by this kind of bias, and claims as well as attacks have been made on both sides that are exaggerated and untenable. Science is not served by such emotional polemics but rather by objective efforts to evaluate and extend our knowledge.

Part of the confusion that exists in discussing these two basic approaches to therapy is that they are often dealt with as though each group represents a distinct entity when, in fact, they are anything but monolithic. The various schools of thought among dynamic psychotherapists are too well known to require elaboration. They cover a wide range from classical Freudians to adherents of other major theorists to eclectics who borrow from all of them to still others who try to adapt their concepts to correspond with modern learning theories, information theory, game theory, or general systems theory.

What is less well known is that among behavior therapists also there is a broad range of differences, from adherents of Pavlov and Hull to Skinnerians to eclectics and to those who lean toward information theory and general systems theory. At one end of each spectrum the theories of behavioral and dynamic psychotherapists tend to converge, while at the other end their divergence is very great. It is because adherents of these two approaches tend to define each other stereotypically in terms of their extremes that so much misunderstanding and heat are often generated between them.

It would further serve to clarify the discussion of this problem if we distinguish between investigative methods, therapeutic techniques, and theoretical formulations. A good investigative technique is not necessarily a good therapeutic technique, nor is the reverse true. By the same token, as we have long known, the success of a psychotherapeutic method for any particular condition does not in itself constitute a validation of its theoretical framework; indeed, exactly why and how any particular psychotherapeutic method works and what it actually accomplishes within the complex organization of drives, perception, integration, affect, and behavior that we call personality is itself a major research challenge.

In the remarks that follow, therefore, I shall not concern myself with the knotty issues of the comparison of results between behavior and psychodynamic therapies or of their validation. The problem of how to measure or evaluate psychotherapeutic change is still far from clear, and a matter for much-needed research. Moreover, comparisons of results between these two approaches are unsatisfactory because different criteria of efficacy are applied, and different techniques of investigation are employed, even if complete objectivity on the part of the various protagonists could be assumed—which is doubtful!

In addition, I shall not get into the oft-argued issue of whether or not simple symptom removal inevitably leads to symptom substitution. Long before behavior therapists began to question this hoary assumption, hypnotherapists had presented evidence that symptom substitution did not always take place when a symptom was removed by hypnosis.[1] Indeed, I would agree, on purely theoretical grounds, that symptom substitution is *not* inevitable. Earlier psychoanalytic assumptions concerning symptom substitution were based on what we now know was an erroneous closed-system theory of personality dynamics. If the conflictual elements involved in neurosis formation are assumed to be part of a closed system, it follows logically that removal of the symptomatic consequences of such an inner conflict without altering the underlying dynamics should result in some other symptom manifestation. If, however, personality dynamics are more correctly perceived within the framework of an open system, then such a consequence is not inevitable. Removal of an ego-dystonic symptom may, on the contrary, produce such satisfying feedback from the environment that it may result in major constructive shifts within the personality system, thus leading to modification of the original conflictual pattern. Removal of a symptom also may lead to positive changes in the perception of the self, with resultant satisfying *internal* feedbacks, heightening of self-esteem, and a consequent restructuring of the internal psychodynamic system.

Psychodynamic theorists have been aware of this possibility for many years, dating back at least to 1946 when Alexander and French[2] published their book entitled *Psychoanalytic Therapy*. In this volume a number of cases of brief psychotherapy are described, some of them involving only one to three interviews, following which the patients were not only dramatically relieved of their presenting symptoms but were then able to go on to achieve more effective adaptive patterns of functioning than they had previously displayed. In the years that followed this important publication, dynamic psychotherapists have become increasingly involved with techniques of brief psychotherapy and of crisis intervention, with a growing body of evidence that in many instances such interventions can have long-lasting positive consequences for personality integration.

Where I part company with most behavior therapists is not in questioning their therapeutic claims—although I would offer the caution that many of them are repeating the error of the early psychoanalysts of promising more than they can deliver—but in what I consider to be their oversimplified explanations of what goes on in the therapeutic transaction between patient and therapist. The explanations to which I refer are those which assume that the essential and central core of their therapeutic process rests on Pavlovian or Skinnerian conditioning and, incidentally, is therefore more "scientific" than the traditional psychotherapies. With these formulations often goes a conception of neurosis that seems to me to be quite simplistic. Thus, according to Eysenck, "Learning theory [note that he uses the singular— actually there are many theories of learning] regards neurotic symptoms as simply learned habits; there is no *neurosis* underlying the symptom but merely the symptom itself. *Get rid of the symptom and you have eliminated the neurosis.*"[3] Such an explanation is like evaluating the contents of a package in terms of its wrapping, and represents a regrettable retrogression from the more sophisticated thinking that has begun to characterize dynamic psychiatry in recent years; an approach that recognizes that "psychopathology" does not reside solely in the individual but also has significant roots in his system of relationships with his milieu and with other persons within his milieu. Hence the growing emphasis on family therapy, on conjoint marital therapy, on group therapy, and on dealing with the disordered socioeconomic conditions which constitute the matrix of so many personality disorders. To see the locus of psychopathology only in the individual leads to an emphasis on techniques of adjusting the individual to his environment regardless of how distorted, intolerable, or irrational that environment might be. Such an emphasis brings

us uncomfortably close to the dangerous area of thought and behavior control.

However, I do not wish to overemphasize this ethical issue. The fact that a technical method may lend itself to being misused does not constitute an argument against its scientific validity. My major point is that the *theoretical* foundation of Eysenck's formulation is scientifically unsound. Even if we deliberately choose to restrict our focus only to what goes on within the individual himself, the Eysenckian point of view has profound limitations. It overlooks all of the complexities of thought, symbolism, and action which must be accounted for in any comprehensive theory of psychology and psychopathology. To assume that what goes on subjectively within the patient is irrelevant and that all that matters is how he behaves is to arbitrarily disregard all of the significant psychodynamic insights of the past 75 years. In saying this, I am not defending all of psychoanalytic theory. I have been as critical as anyone of certain aspects of classical Freudian theory and I am in full accord with those who argue that psychodynamic theory needs to be reformulated in terms that conform more closely to modern theories of learning and of neurophysiology. Current researches strongly suggest that the brain functions as an extremely intricate receiver, retriever, processor, and dispatcher of information. A stimulus-response theory of human behavior does not begin to do justice to this complex process. It is precisely what goes on in the "black box" *between* stimulus and response that is the central challenge of psychiatry, and no theory that ignores the complexities of the central processes within that "black box" can be considered an adequate one. It is to Freud's eternal credit, regardless of the limitations of some of his hypotheses, that he was the first to develop a rational investigative technique for, and a meaningful key to, the understanding of this uncharted realm that exerts so profound an influence on both our perceptions and our responses.

Evidence from learning theories themselves reveals that neurotic disorders are not necessarily the simple product of exposure to traumatic conditioning stimuli or to the operant conditioning of responses. The work of Pavlov, Liddell, Masserman, and others has clearly demonstrated that neurotic symptoms can ensue when an animal is faced with incompatible choices between simultaneous approach and avoidance reactions, or with confusing conditioned stimuli which it is unable to differentiate clearly. This corresponds to the psychodynamic concept of conflict as being at the root of the vast majority of human neurotic disorders. Once such a neurotic conflict is set up in a human being, secondary elaborations, defensive adaptations, and symbolic distortions may become extensively and indirectly intertwined with almost every aspect of the individual's perceptual, cognitive, and behavioral process.

A behavioral approach alone cannot encompass these complexities. Granting that Skinnerians include verbal speech as an aspect of behavior that may require modification, what shall we say about subjective *fantasies*, concealed *thoughts*, and hidden *feelings?* Are they totally irrelevant? What about problems involving conflicts in value systems, disturbances in self-image, diffusion of identity, feelings of anomie, or even concealed delusions and hallucinations? Are they less important than specific symptom entities of a behavioral nature? No comprehensive theory of psychopathology or of the nature of the psychotherapeutic process can properly ignore these aspects of man's subjective life.

To illustrate my point that much more goes on between therapist and patient than most behavior therapists generally recognize, I should like now to briefly focus on three contrasting behavioral therapeutic approaches: (1) Wolpe's technique of reciprocal inhibition, (2) aversive conditioning treatment of homosexuality, and (3) the Masters and Johnson technique of treating sexual impotence and frigidity. In discussing these three approaches, I wish to emphasize that it is not my intention to denigrate their usefulness as therapeutic modalities or to question their results, but solely to present some of the diverse variables that I believe are involved in their therapeutic effectiveness.

Wolpe has elaborated his technique in many publications as well as in at least one film that I have seen. Although he considers the crux of his technique to be the development of a hierarchical list of graded anxieties which are then progressively dealt with by his technique of "reciprocal inhibition," the fact is that a great deal more than this takes place in the patient-therapist transaction in the Wolpe technique. Most significantly, in the orientation period of the first session or two the patient is informed not only of the treatment method per se, but also of the fact that it has yielded successful results with comparable patients, and it is indicated implicitly, if not explicitly, that the patient can expect similar success for himself if he is cooperative. Wolpe, moreover, is warm, friendly, and supportive. At the same time he is positive and authoritative in such a way as to reinforce the patient's expectations of therapeutic success. During this introductory period a detailed history is taken and even though the major emphasis is on the symptom with all of its manifestations and conditions for appearance, a detailed genetic history of personality development is usually taken also.

Following this a hierarchical list of the patient's anxieties is established. The patient is then taught a relaxation technique which is remarkably similar to what is traditionally employed in inducing hypnosis. After complete relaxation is achieved, the patient is instructed to create in fantasy these situations of graded anxiety beginning at the lowest level of anxiety, and is not permitted to go to the next level until he signals that he is completely relaxed. This procedure is repeated over and over again in anywhere from 12 to 60 or more sessions until the patient is able to fantasy the maximally phobic situation and still achieve muscular relaxation. Throughout this procedure the patient receives the strong implication, either explicitly or implicitly, that this procedure will cause his symptoms to disappear.

Wolpe attributes the success of his technique to "systematic desensitization" and explains it on the basis of Pavlovian counterconditioning. He asserts that any "activities that might give any grounds for imputations of transference, insight, suggestion, or dedepression," are either "omitted or manipulated in such a way as to render the operation of these mechanisms exceedingly implausible."[4] This kind of claim that Wolpe repeatedly makes in his writings clearly reflects his failure to appreciate the complexity of the variables involved in the patient-therapist transaction. I cannot believe that anyone who watches Wolpe's own film demonstration of his technique would agree that there are no elements of transference, insight, or suggestion in it. Indeed, one could make as plausible a case for the overriding influence of suggestion in his technique as for the influence of desensitization. In saying this I am not being pejorative about Wolpe's technique. Suggestion, in my opinion, is an integral part of every psychotherapeutic technique, behavioral or psychodynamic. It need not be overt; indeed, it probably works most potently when it is covert. Suggestion is a complex process in which elements of transference, expectancy, faith, and hope all enter. To the degree that a patient is receptive and perceives the therapist as a powerful help-giving figure, he is more likely to accept the suggestions he is being given and to try to conform to them. This process is most obvious in hypnosis but it is equally present in all psychotherapeutic techniques, where the suggestion is usually more covert. Wolpe's technique abounds in covert as well as overt suggestion. It is questionable, moreover, whether the fantasies that Wolpe has his patients create are actual substitutes for the phobic reality situations, as he would have us believe. It may well be that what is really taking place is not so much desensitization to specific stimuli as repeated reassurance and strong systematic suggestion, within a setting of heightened expectancy and faith.

However, even the combination of *desensitization* (assuming that it is taking place) and *suggestion* do not begin to cover all the elements that are present in the Wolpe method. There is also the *direct transmission of values* as when Wolpe says to a young patient, "You must learn to stand up for yourself." According to Ullmann and Krasner,[5] Wolpe hypothesizes that if a person can assert himself, anxiety will automatically be inhibited. (Parenthetically, one might question whether this is inevitably so. One frequently sees patients who assert themselves regularly, but always with enormous concomitant anxiety.) In any event, Ullmann and Krasner say: "The therapist provides the motivation by pointing out the irrationality of the fears and encouraging the individual to insist on his legitimate human rights."[5] Obviously this is not very different from what goes on in dynamic psychotherapy and it is not rendered different by virtue of the fact, according to Ullmann and Krasner, that it is "given a physiological basis by Wolpe, who refers to it as excitatory."[5] Still another variable which cannot be ignored is Wolpe's manner, which, whether he realizes it or not, undoubtedly facilitates a "positive transference" in his patients. In his film he is not only kindly and empathic to his female patient, but occasionally reassuringly touches her. Does Wolpe really believe that a programmed computer repeating his instruc-

tions to a patient who had had no prior contact with the doctor himself would achieve the identical therapeutic results?

The second behavioral technique that I would like to briefly consider is that of the aversion treatment of homosexuals. I had occasion to explore this technique some time ago with Dr. Lee Birk, of the Massachusetts Mental Health Center, who was kind enough to demonstrate his technique and go over his results with me.

Dr. Birk's method is based on the anticipatory avoidance conditioning technique introduced by Feldman and MacCulloch.[6] The patient is seated in a chair in front of a screen with an electrode cuff attached to his leg. The method involves the use of patient-selected nude and seminude male and female pictures which are flashed onto the screen. The male pictures (and presumably the fantasies associated with them) become aversive stimuli by linkage with electric shocks which are administered to the leg whenever these pictures appear on the screen. On the other hand, the female pictures become discriminative stimuli signaling safety, relief, and protection from the shocks.

In Dr. Birk's hands, as in others, the use of this method has apparently produced a striking reversal of sexual feelings and behavior in more than one-half of the male homosexuals so treated. On the face of it, this would seem to be the result of a relatively simple negative conditioning process to aversive "male" stimuli, with concomitant positive conditioning to "female" stimuli.

Closer inspection will reveal, however, that the process is considerably more complex. I wonder whether most psychiatrists realize what is actually involved in such aversive conditioning. I know that I, for one, did not, until I asked Dr. Birk to permit me to experience the kind of shock that he administered to his patients—the least intense, incidentally, of the graded series that he employed. I can only say that if that was a "mild" shock, I never want to be subjected to a "severe" one! I do not have a particularly low threshold for pain, but it was a severe and painful jolt—much more than I had anticipated—and it made me acutely aware of *how strongly motivated toward change a male homosexual would have to be to subject himself to a series of such shocks visit after visit.*

The significance of this variable cannot be ignored. Once it is recognized, the results of aversive therapy, although still notable, become less remarkable. The fact is that if other forms of psychotherapy were limited only to such a select group of exceptionally motivated homosexuals, the results also would be better than average. Although one might assume that in dynamic psychotherapies the cost of therapy in itself should insure equally good motivation, this is not always the fact. Costs of therapy may not be sacrificial, or they may be borne or shared by others, but no one else can share the pain involved in the aversive conditioning process.

Again, then, it becomes clear that we are dealing with something that is much more complicated than a simple conditioning process. The patient's intense wish to change, and his faith and expectation that this very special technique will work for him—as the doctor himself implicitly or explicitly suggests—are important factors in the total therapeutic gestalt of this aversive technique, as they are in successful dynamic psychotherapies also.

But more than this, the transference–countertransference transaction between therapist and subject is also of paramount importance. Dr. Birk communicated two interesting experiences he had which underline this point. Two of his subjects who had had very favorable responses to the "conditioning" procedure suffered serious relapses immediately after becoming angry at him. The first patient became upset because of what he considered a breach in the privacy of his treatment. Before this, he had not only been free from homosexual contacts for the first time in many years, but also free of conscious homosexual urges. When he became angry, he immediately went and sought out a homosexual partner because he wanted to see "how really good" the treatment was. Dr. Birk was aware that his patient obviously wanted to show him up and prove that the treatment was no good. Although the patient remained improved as compared to his previous homosexual behavior, *he was never again,* despite many more conditioning treatments, completely free from conscious homosexual urges and continued to act them out although less frequently than in the past. The second patient became angry with Dr. Birk because he concluded that the therapist seemed to be more interested in the results he was obtaining than he was in the patient as a person. Immediately after expressing this irritation the patient regressed to a series of homosexual encounters.

These striking examples illustrate that a simple conditioning explanation does not fit the complex process that goes on in such techniques of therapy. Aversive conditioning that has been solidly established would not be expected to disappear on the basis of such experiences unless there is something that goes on centrally in the patient that is a very important factor in the therapeutic modifications achieved. A basic aspect of this central process is in the patient–physician interpersonal relationship and it cannot and must not be ignored even in behavior therapies. I have recently encountered a number of instances where patients who were referred to behavior therapists failed to return to them after the initial sessions because the behavior therapists involved ignored this essential factor and related to the patients as though they were dealing with experimental animals.

Let us now turn to a consideration of the Masters and Johnson[7] technique of treating disorders of sexual potency. In many ways this technique falls midway between a behavioral and a psychodynamic approach and illustrates one of the ways in which a fusion of both can be successfully employed. The Masters and Johnson technique is behavioral in the sense that it is essentially symptom-focused, and that one of its most important technical tools is desensitization of the performance anxieties of the patients.

Conceptually, however, the Masters and Johnson approach to their patients goes considerably beyond simple conditioning or desensitization processes. For one thing, Masters and Johnson recognize that the problem of impotency or frigidity does not exist merely in the symptomatic individual but in his relationship with his partner. Therefore, they insist on treating the couple as a unit, and the symptom as a problem of the unit. This constitutes a systems approach in contrast to a strictly intrapsychic or behavioral one.

Secondly, Masters and Johnson are acutely aware of the influence of psychodynamic factors on the sexual behavior of their couples. In their preliminary interviews they carefully assess and evaluate the importance of these factors, and if they consider the neurotic components or interpersonal difficulties to be too great, they may refuse to proceed with their method and will refer the couple back to their physicians for appropriate psychotherapy.

This kind of selective procedure has an effect, of course, on their percentage of successful results, as does the high degree of motivation that their patients must have to come to St. Louis (who, after all, goes to St. Louis for a two-week vacation?) and to commit themselves to the considerable expense and inconvenience that is involved.

The fact, also, that Masters and Johnson insist that the therapeutic team consist of a man and a woman reveals their sensitivity to the transference implications of their relationship to their couples. They function as a sexually permissive and empathic mother-surrogate and father-surrogate who offer not only valuable technical advice and suggestions concerning sexual behavior, but also a compassion and understanding that constitute a corrective emotional experience for their patients.

Finally, the tremendous charisma and authority of this highly publicized therapeutic team must inevitably have an enormous impact on the expectancy, faith, and hope with which their patients come to them. This cannot help but greatly accentuate the suggestive impact of the given instructions in facilitating their patients' therapeutic improvement. This improvement is then reinforced by subsequent follow-up telephone calls which, among other things, confirm to the patient the empathic interest, concern, and dedication of these parent-surrogates.

I am all too aware that these brief and summary remarks cannot begin to do justice to the three above-mentioned behavioral techniques. I hope, however, that I have succeeded in making the point that in each of these instances, complex variables are involved that go beyond any simple stimulus-response conditioning model.

The research on the nature of the psychotherapeutic process in which I participated with Franz Alexander beginning in 1958 has convinced me that all psychotherapy, regardless of the techniques used, is a learning process.[8-10] Dynamic psychotherapies and behavior therapies simply represent different teaching techniques, and their differences are based in part on differences in their goals and in part on their assumptions about the nature of psychopathology. Certain fundamental elements, however, are present in both approaches.

In any psychotherapeutic relationship, we start with an individual who presents a problem. This problem may be in the form of behavior that is regarded as deviant, or it may be in the form of subjective discomfort, or in certain distortions of perception, cognition, or affect, or in any combination of these. Usually, but not always, these problems motivate the individual or someone in his milieu to consider psychiatric treatment. This decision in itself establishes an *expectancy* in the individual which is quite different than if, say, "punishment" rather than "treatment" were prescribed for his problems. This expectancy is an essential part of *every* psychotherapeutic transaction at its outset, regardless of whether the patient presents himself for behavioral or dynamic psychotherapy. The patient, in other words, is *not* a neutral object in whom certain neurotic symptoms or habits have been mechanically established and from whom they can now be mechanically removed.

Expectancy is a complex process. It encompasses factors that Frank[11] has demonstrated as being of major significance in psychotherapy—the degree of faith, trust, and hope that the patient consciously or unconsciously brings into the transaction. It is based in large part on previously established perceptions of authority or help-giving figures, perceptions that play a significant role in the degree of receptivity or non-receptivity that the patient may show to the message he receives from the psychotherapist. Psychoanalysts have traditionally referred to these presenting expectations as aspects of "transference," but regardless of what they are called, they are always present. Transference is not, as some behavior therapists seem to think, something that is "created" by the therapist—although it is true that transference distortions may be either increased or diminished by the technique the therapist employs. The way in which the therapist relates to the patient may reinforce certain maladaptive perceptions or expectations, or it may teach the patient that his previously learned expectations in relation to help-giving or authority figures are incorrect. The latter teaching is part of what Alexander and French[2] called the "corrective emotional experience."

Even in "simple" conditioning studies, experimenters like Liddell, Masserman, and Pavlov have called attention to the significance of the relationship between the experimental animal and the experimenter. In humans the problem is more complex, however. Thus, a therapist who behaves in a kindly but authoritarian manner may confirm the patient's expectancies that authority figures are omnipotent and omniscient. This increases the patient's faith and may actually facilitate his willingness to give up his symptoms to please the powerful and good parent-therapist, but it does *not* alter his childlike self-image in relation to authority figures. Depending on the therapist's objectives, this may or may not be of importance.

What I am indicating, in other words, is that a positive transference facilitates symptom removal, but if the patient's *emotional maturation, rather than just symptom removal, is the goal of therapy*, what is necessary eventually is a "dissolution" of this positive transference—which means teaching the patient to feel and function in a less childlike manner, not only in relation to the therapist but also to other authority figures.

Closely related and interacting with the patient's motivations and expectancies is the therapist's social and professional role, by virtue of which the help-seeking patient endows him with presumptive knowledge, prestige, authority, and help-giving potential. These factors play an enormous role in strengthening the capacity of the therapist to influence the patient, and constitute another element in the complex fabric that makes up the phenomenon of positive transference.

Also, the *real persons* of both patient and therapist, their actual physical, intellectual, and emotional assets and liabilities, and their respective *value systems* enter into the therapeutic transaction. Neither the patient nor the therapist can be regarded as a stereotype upon whom any particular technique will automatically work. Their idiosyncratic variables are always an important part of their transaction.

Given the above factors, a number of things begin to happen more or less simultaneously, in varying degrees, in behavior therapies as well as in dynamic psychotherapies. I have discussed these factors in detail elsewhere and will merely summarize them here. They are: *(1) Release of tension* through catharsis and by virtue of the patient's hope, faith, and expectancy; *(2) cognitive learning*, both of the trial-and-error variety and of the gestalt variety; (3) reconditioning by virtue of *operant conditioning*, by virtue of subtle reward-punishment cues from the therapist, and by corrective emotional experiences; (4) identification with the therapist; (5) repeated *reality testing*, which is the equivalent of *practice* in the learning process. These five elements encompass the most significant factors on the basis of which change takes place in a psychotherapeutic relationship.[10]

As I have mentioned above, suggestion takes place in all of these, covertly or overtly. Furthermore, as can be seen, a conditioning process takes place in dynamic psychotherapies as well as in behavior therapies, except that in the latter this process is intentional and more structured, while in the former it has not been generally recognized. In focusing on this conditioning process, behavior therapists have made a valuable contribution to the understanding of the therapeutic process. It is the thrust of this paper, however, that in so doing they have tended to minimize or ignore other important and essential elements in the therapeutic process, particularly the subtle but critical aspects of the patient–therapist interpersonal relationship.

In the final analysis, the technique of therapy that we choose to employ must depend on what aspect of man's complex psychic functioning we address ourselves to. If we choose to focus on the patient's overt symptoms or behavior patterns, some kind of behavior therapy may well be the treatment of choice. On the other hand, if the core of his problems rests in symbolic distortions of perception, cognition, affect, or subtle disturbances in interpersonal relationships, the source and nature of which he may be totally unaware, then the more elaborate reeducational process of dynamic psychotherapy may be necessary.

Moreover, indications for one approach do not necessarily rule out the other. Marks and Gelder[12, 13] and Brady,[14] among others, have demonstrated that the use of both behavior therapy and dynamic therapy in the same patient either concurrently or in sequence often brings about better therapeutic results than the use of either approach alone. Indeed, many dynamic psychotherapists have for years been unwittingly using such a combination of approaches when they prescribe drugs for the direct control of certain symptoms while concurrently pursuing a psychotherapeutic approach.

To conclude, then, in my opinion behavior therapies and dynamic psychotherapies, far from being irreconcilable, are complementary psychotherapeutic approaches. The line of demarcation between them is by no means a sharp one. As Breger and McGaugh[15] and others have shown, behavior therapists do many things in the course of their conditioning procedures that duplicate the activities of dynamic psychotherapists including "discussions, explanation of techniques and of the unadaptiveness of anxiety and symptoms, hypnosis, relaxation, 'nondirective cathartic discussions,' and 'obtaining an understanding of the patient's personality and background.' "[15] The process in both approaches is best explicable in terms of current theories of learning which go beyond simple conditioning explanations and encompass central cognitive processes also. The fact that in some disorders one or the other approach may be more effective should not surprise us and presents no contradiction. Just as there is no single best way of teaching all pupils all subjects, there is no single psychotherapeutic technique that is optimum for all patients and all psychiatric disorders.

Within this total context, it seems to me that behavior therapists deserve much credit for having opened wide the armamentarium of therapeutic strategies. By so doing, they have forced dynamic psychotherapists into a reassessment of their therapeutic techniques and their effectiveness—a reassessment that in the long run can only be in the best interests of all psychiatrists and their patients. The psychotherapeutic challenge of the future is to so improve our theoretical and diagnostic approaches to psychopathology as to be able to most knowledgeably and flexibly apply to each patient the particular treatment technique and the particular kind of therapist that together will most effectively achieve the desired therapeutic goal.

Since completing this paper, I have come across the excellent article by Klein et al.[16] in which many of the conclusions I have set forth are confirmed by them as a result of five days of direct observation of the work of Wolpe and his group at the Eastern Pennsylvania Psychiatric Institute. The authors also point out that as a consequence of their increasing popularity, behavior therapists are now beginning to treat a broader spectrum of more "difficult" patients (complex psychoneurotic problems, character neuroses, or borderline psychotic problems) with the result that their treatment procedures are "becoming longer

and more complicated, with concomitant lowering of success rates."

REFERENCES

1. Wolberg LR: Hypnotherapy, in McCary JL (ed): *Six Approaches to Psychotherapy*. New York, Dryden Press, 1955, pp 63–126.
2. Alexander F, French TM, et al: *Psychoanalytic Therapy*. New York, Ronald Press Co, 1946.
3. Eysenck HJ (ed): *Behavior Therapy and the Neuroses*. New York, Pergamon Press, 1960.
4. Wolpe J: *Psychotherapy by Reciprocal Inhibition*. Stanford, Calif, Stanford University Press, 1958.
5. Ullmann LP, Krasner L (eds): *Case Studies in Behavior Modification*. New York, Holt, Rinehart & Winston, Inc, 1965.
6. Feldman MP, MacCulloch MI: The application of anticipatory avoidance learning to the treatment of homosexuality. *Behav Res Ther* 2:165–183, 1965.
7. Masters WH, Johnson VE: *Human Sexual Response*. Boston, Little, Brown & Co, 1965.
8. Marmor J: Psychoanalytic therapy as an educational process, in Masserman J, Salzman L (eds): *Modern Concepts of Psychoanalysis*. New York, Philosophical Library Inc, 1962, pp 189–205.
9. Marmor J: Psychoanalytic therapy and theories of learning, in Masserman J (ed): *Science and Psychoanalysis*. New York, Grune and Stratton Inc, 1964, vol 7, pp 265–279.
10. Marmor J: The nature of the psychotherapeutic process, in Usdin G (ed): *Psychoneurosis and Schizophrenia*. New York, JB Lippincott Co, 1966, pp 66–75.
11. Frank JD: *Persuasion and Healing*. Baltimore, Johns Hopkins Press, 1961.
12. Marks IM, Gelder MG: A controlled retrospective study of behavior therapy in phobic patients. *Brit J Psychiat* 111:561–573, 1965.
13. Marks IM, Gelder MG: Common ground between behavior therapy and psychodynamic methods. *Brit J Med Psychol* 39:11–23, 1966.
14. Brady JP: Psychotherapy by a combined behavioral and dynamic approach. *Compr Psychiat* 9:536–543, 1968.
15. Breger L, McGaugh JL: Critique and reformulation of learning theory approaches to psychotherapy and neurosis. *Psychol Bull* 63:338–358, 1965.
16. Klein MH, Dittman AT, Parloff MB, et al: Behavior therapy: Observations and reflections. *J Consult Clin Psychol* 3:259–266, 1969.

PART III
Phenomenological Theories

Introduction

Phenomenologists stress that each individual reacts to the world in terms of his unique perception of it. No matter how transformed or unconsciously distorted this perception may be, it is the person's way of construing events which determines his behavior. Concepts and propositions must be formulated, therefore, not in terms of objective realities or unconscious processes, but in accordance with how events actually are cognitively perceived by the individual; concepts must not disassemble these experiences into depersonalized or abstract categories.

The phenomena of cognition and consciousness are among the most controversial topics in both psychological and philosophical literature. No one doubts that awareness exists, but how can phenomenological reality as experienced by another person by categorized, measured, or even sensed? At best, observers must adopt an empathic attitude, a sensing in one's self of what another may be thinking and experiencing. But this method is justly suspect, fraught with the distortions and insensitivities of the observer. To obviate this difficulty, phenomenologists assume that the verbal statements of the individual accurately reflect his phenomenal reality. Any datum which represents the individual's cognitive portrayal of his experience is grist, therefore, for the phenomenologist's mill. They contend that an individual's verbal reports reveal the most important influences upon his behavior. Is it not simple efficiency to ask a person directly what is disturbing him and how this disturbance came to pass? Is his report more prone to error than an observer's speculations gathered from the odds and ends of a case history study? Is it less reliable than deductions which are drawn from dreams and free-associations? The fact that some cognitions and recollections are misleading is not reason to dismiss them as useless; they summarize events in terms closest to the individual's experience of them and often embody knowledge that is not otherwise available.

Orientation

Phenomenologists believe that the distinctive characteristics of each individual's conscious experience should be the primary focus of clinical science. George Kelly, originator of the "personal construct" theory, provides a detailed exposition of the essential themes of this position. In the paper published here, he argues clearly for the view that psychological science can best develop from a framework of systematic phenomenological principles and hypotheses.

24 Personal Construct Theory

George A. Kelly

Who can say what nature is? Is it what now exists about us, including all the tiny hidden things that wait so patiently to be discovered? Or is it the vista of all that is destined to occur, whether tomorrow or in some distant eon of time? Or is nature, infinitely more varied than this, the myriad trains of events that might ensue if we were to be so bold, ingenious, and irreverent as to take a hand in its management?

Personal construct theory neither offers nor demands a firm answer to any of these questions, and in this respect it is unique. Rather than depending upon bedrock assumptions about the inherent nature of the universe, or upon fragments of truth believed to have been accumulated, it is a notion about how man may launch out from a position of admitted ignorance, and how he may aspire from one day to the next to transcend his own dogmatisms. It is, then, a theory of man's personal inquiry—a psychology of the human quest. It does not say what has or will be found, but proposes rather how we might go about looking for it.

Philosophical Position

Like other theories, the psychology of personal constructs is the implementation of a philosophical assumption. In this case the assumption is that whatever nature may be, or

Excerpted from J. Mancuso, *Readings for a Cognitive Theory of Personality*, New York: Holt, Rinehart and Winston, 1970, pp. 27–47. Reprinted by permission of Mrs. Gladys T. Kelly; copyright, Gladys T. Kelly.

howsoever the quest for truth will turn out in the end, the events we face today are subject to as great a variety of constructions as our wits will enable us to contrive. This is not to say that one construction is as good as any other, nor is it to deny that at some infinite point in time human vision will behold reality out to the utmost reaches of existence. But it does remind us that all our present perceptions are open to question and reconsideration, and it does broadly suggest that even the most obvious occurrences of everyday life might appear utterly transformed if we were inventive enough to construe them differently.

This philosophical position we have called *constructive alternativism*, and its implications keep cropping up in the psychology of personal constructs. It can be contrasted with the prevalent epistemological assumption of *accumulative fragmentalism*, which is that truth is collected piece by piece. While constructive alternativism does not argue against the collection of information, neither does it measure truth by the size of the collection. Indeed it leads one to regard a large accumulation of facts as an open invitation to some far-reaching reconstruction which will reduce them to a mass of trivialities.

A person who spends a great deal of his time hoarding facts is not likely to be happy at the prospect of seeing them converted into rubbish. He is more likely to want them bound and preserved, a memorial to his personal achievement. A scientist, for example, who thinks this way, and especially a psychologist who does so, depends upon his facts to furnish the ultimate proof of his propositions. With these shining nuggets of truth in his grasp it seems unnecessary for him to take responsibility for the conclusions he claims they thrust upon him. To suggest to him at this point that further human reconstruction can completely alter the appearance of the precious fragments he has accumulated, as well as the direction of their arguments, is to threaten his scientific conclusions, his philosophical position, and even his moral security. No wonder, then, that in the eyes of such a conservatively minded person, our assumption that all facts are subject—are wholly subject—to alternative constructions looms up as culpably subjective and dangerously subversive to the scientific establishment.

The Meaning of Events

Constructive alternativism stresses the importance of events. But it looks to man to propose what the character of their import shall be. The meaning of an event—that is to say, the meaning we ascribe to it—is anchored in its antecedents and its consequents. Thus meaning displays itself to us mainly in the dimension of time. This is much more than saying that meanings are rehearsals of outcomes, a proposition implicit in behavioristic theory, or that the ends justify the means—the ethical statement of the same proposition.

Besides including anticipated outcomes, meaning includes also the means by which events are anticipated. This is to suggest that different meanings are involved when identical events are correctly anticipated by different sets of inferences. It suggests also the implication of quite different meanings when the basic assumptions are different, even when the chains of inference are otherwise more or less similar.

In all of this we look to events to confirm our predictions and to encourage our venturesome constructions. Yet the same events may confirm different constructions, and different, or even incompatible, events may appear to validate the same construction. So, for each of us, meaning assumes the shape of the arguments which lead him to his predictions, and the only outside check on his personal constructions are the events which confirm or disconfirm his expectations. This is a long way from saying that meaning is revealed by what

happens, or that meaning is something to be discovered in the natural course of events, or that events shape men and ideas. Thus in constructive alternativism events are crucial, but only man can devise a meaning for them to challenge.

When we place a construction of our own upon a situation, and then pursue its implications to the point of expecting something to happen, we issue a little invitation to nature to intervene in our personal experience. If what we expect does happen, or appears to happen, our expectation is confirmed and we are likely to think that we must have had a pretty good slant on the trend of affairs, else we would have lost our bet. But if we think the matter over carefully we may begin to have doubts. Perhaps a totally different interpretation would have led to an equally successful prediction; and it may, besides, have been more straightforward, or more consistent with our conscience. Or perhaps our vivid expectations overlaid our perception of what actually happened.

So, on second thought, even when events are reconciled with a construction, we cannot be sure that they have proved it true. There are always other constructions, and there is the lurking likelihood that some of them will turn out to be better. The best we can ever do is project our anticipations with frank uncertainty and observe the outcomes in terms of which we have a bit more confidence. But neither anticipation nor outcome is ever a matter of absolute certainty from the dark in which we mortals crouch. And, hence, even the most valuable construction we have yet contrived—even our particular notion of God Himself—is one for which we shall have to continue to take personal responsibility—at least until someone turns up with a better one. And I suspect he will! This is what we mean by *constructive alternativism*. Our view might even be called a philosophical position of *epistemological responsibility*.

Basic Postulate

A person's processes are psychologically channelized by the ways in which he anticipates events. This is what we have proposed as a fundamental postulate for the psychology of personal constructs. The assumptions of constructive alternativism are embedded in this statement, although it may not be apparent until later in our exposition of the theme just how it is that they are.

We start with a *person*. Organisms, lower animals, and societies can wait. We are talking about someone we know, or would like to know—such as you, or myself. More particularly, we are talking about that person as an event—the processes that express his personality. And, since we enter the system we are about to elaborate at the point of a process—or life—rather than at the point of a body or a material substance, we should not have to invoke any special notions, such as dynamics, drives, motivation, or force to explain why our object does not remain inert. As far as the theory is concerned, it never was inert. As we pursue the theoretical line emerging from this postulate I think it becomes clear also why we do not need such notions to account for the direction of movement—any more than we need them to explain the movement itself.

This is to be a psychological theory. Mostly this is a way of announcing in the basic postulate that we make no commitment to the terms of other disciplines, such as physiology or chemistry. Our philosophical position permits us to see those other disciplines as based on man-made constructions, rather than as disclosures of raw realities, and hence there is no need for the psychologist to accept them as final, or to limit his proposals to statements consistent with them. In addition, I think the theory sounds more or less like the other theories that are known as psychological. This gives me an inclusive, as well as an exlusive reason for calling it a psychological theory, although this is more or less a matter of taste rather than of definition. Certainly I have no intention of trying to define psychology; there are just too many things called psychological that I do not care to take responsibility for.

Some have suggested that personal construct theory not be called a psychological theory at all, but a metatheory. That is all right with me. It suggests that it is a theory about theories, and that is pretty much what I have in mind. But I hope that it is clear that it is not limited to being a metatheory of formal theories, or even of articulate ones.

There is also the question of whether or not it is a cognitive theory. Some have said that it was; others have classed it as existential. Quite an accomplishment; not many theories have been accused of being both cognitive and existential! But this, too, is all right with me. As a matter of fact, I am delighted. There are categorical systems in which I think the greater amount of ambiguity I stir up, the better. Cognition, for example, strikes me as a particularly misleading category, and, since it is one designed to distinguish itself from affect and conation, those terms, too, might well be discarded as inappropriately restrictive.

Personal construct theory has also been categorized by responsible scholars as an emotional theory, a learning theory, a psychoanalytic theory (Freudian, Adlerian, and Jungian—all three), a typically American theory, a Marxist theory, a humanistic theory, a logical positivistic theory, a Zen Buddhistic theory, a Thomistic theory, a behavioristic theory, an Apollonian theory, a pragmatistic theory, a reflexive theory, and no theory at all. It has also been classified as nonsense, which indeed, by its own admission, it will likely some day turn out to be. In each case there were some convincing arguments offered for the categorization, but I have forgotten what most of them were. I fear that no one of these categorizations will be of much help to the reader in understanding personal construct theory, but perhaps having a whole lap full of them all at once will suggest what might be done with them.

The fourth term in the postulate—channelized—was chosen as one less likely than others to imply dynamics. This is because there is no wish to suggest that we are dealing with anything not already in motion. What is to be explained is the direction of the processes, not the transformation of states into processes. We see states only as an *ad interim* device to get time to stand still long enough for us to see what is going on. In other words, we have assumed that a process can be profitably regarded as more basic than an inert substance. We have had to do this notwithstanding the commitments of the centuries to quite another kind of language system. There are some disadvantages that come with this notion of what is basic, but we are willing to accept them for the time being in order to explore the heraclitean implications more fully than psychologists have ever done before.

In specifying *ways of anticipating events* as the directive referent for human processes we cut ourselves free of the stimulus–response version of nineteenth century scientific determinism. I am aware that this is a drastic step indeed, and I suspect that others who claim to have taken similar steps have not always seriously taken stock of the difficulties to be encountered. For one thing the very syntax of the language we must employ to voice our protest is built on a world view that regards objects as agents and outcomes as the products of those agents.

In our present undertaking the psychological initiative always remains a property of the person—never the property of anything else. What is more, neither past nor future events are themselves ever regarded as basic determinants of the course of human action—not even the events of childhood. But one's way of anticipating them, whether in the short range or in the long view—this is the basic theme in the human process of living. Moreover, it is that events are anticipated, not merely that man gravitates toward more and more comfortable organic states. Confirmation and disconfirmation of one's predictions are accorded greater psychological significance than rewards, punishments, or the drive reduction that reinforcements produce.

There are, of course, some predictions we would like to see disconfirmed, as well as some we hope will indeed materialize. We should not make the mistake of translating personal construct theory back into stimulus–response theory and saying to ourselves that confirmation is the same as positive reinforcement, and that disconfirmation nullifies the meaning of an experience. Disconfirmation, even in those cases where it is disconcerting, provides grounds for reconstruction—or of repentance, in the proper sense of that term—and it may be used to improve the accuracy and significance of further anticipations. Thus we envision the nature of life in its outreach for the future, and not in its perpetuation of its prior conditions or in its incessant reverberation of past events.

Personal construct theory is elaborated by a string of eleven corollaries which may be loosely inferred from its basic postulate. Beyond these are certain notions of more limited applicability which fall in line with personal construct thinking—notions about such matters as anxiety, guilt, hostility, decision making, creativity, the strategy of psychological research, and other typical concerns of professional psychologists. These latter notions need not be considered part of the formal structure of the theory, although our theoretical efforts may not come to life in the mind of the reader

until he has seen their applicability to the daily problems he faces.

Construction Corollary

A person anticipates events by construing their replications. Since events never repeat themselves, else they would lose their identity, one can look forward to them only by devising some construction which permits him to perceive two of them in a similar manner. His construction must also permit him to be selective about which two are to be perceived similarly. Thus the same construction that serves to infer their similarity must serve also to differentiate them from others. Under a system that provides only for the identification of similarities the world dissolves into homogeneity; under one that provides only for differentiation it is shattered into hopelessly unrelated fragments.

Perhaps it is true that events, as most of us would like to believe, really do repeat aspects of previous occurrences. But unless one thinks he is precocious enough to have hit upon what those aspects will ultimately turn out to be, or holy enough to have had them revealed to him, he must modestly concede that the appearance of replication is a reflection of his own fallible construction of what is going on. Thus the recurrent themes that make life seem so full of meaning are the original symphonic compositions of a man bent on finding the present in his past, and the future in his present.

Individuality Corollary

Persons differ from each other in their constructions of events. Having assumed that construction is a personal affair, it seems unlikely that any two persons would ever happen to concoct identical systems. I would go further now than when I originally proposed this corollary and suggest that even particular constructions are never identical events. And I would extend it the other way too, and say that I doubt that two persons ever put their construction systems together in terms of the same logical relationships. For myself, I find this a most encouraging line of speculation, for it seems to open the door to more advanced systems of thinking and inference yet to be devised by man. Certainly it suggests that scientific research can rely more heavily on individual imagination than it usually dares.

Organization Corollary

Each person characteristically evolves, for his convenience in anticipating events, a construction system embracing ordinal relationships between constructs. If a person is to live actively within his construction system it must provide him with some clear avenues of inference and movement. There must be ways for him to resolve the more crucial contradictions and conflicts that inevitably arise. This is not to say that all inconsistencies must be resolved at once. Some private paradoxes can be allowed to stand indefinitely, and, in the face of them, one can remain indecisive or can vacillate between alternative expectations of what the future holds in store for him.

So it seems that each person arranges his constructions so that he can move from one to another in some orderly fashion, either by assigning priorities to those which are to take precedence when doubts or contradictions arise, or by arranging implicative relationships, as in boolean algebra, so that he may infer that one construction follows from another. Thus one's commitments may take priority over his opportunities, his political affiliations may turn him from compassion to power, and his moral imperatives may render him insensitive to the brute that tugs at his sleeve. These are the typical prices men pay to escape inner chaos.

Dichotomy Corollary

A person's construction system is composed of a finite number of dichotomous constructs. Experience has shown me that this is the point where many of my readers first encounter difficulty in agreeing with me. What I am saying is that a construct is a "black and white" affair, never a matter of shadings, or of "grays." On the face of it, this sounds bad, for it seems to imply categorical or absolutistic thinking rather than any acceptance of relativism or conditionalism. Yet I would insist that there is nothing categorical about a construct.

When we look closely the initial point of difficulty in following personal construct theory usually turns out to lie in certain unrecognized assumptions made earlier while reading the exposition, or even carried over from previous habits of thought. Let us see if we can get the matter straightened out before any irreparable damage is done.

Neither our constructs nor our construing systems come to use from nature, except, of course, from our own nature. It must be noted that this philosophical position of constructive alternativism has much more powerful epistemological implications than one might at first suppose. We cannot say that constructs are essences distilled by the mind out of available reality. They are imposed *upon* events, not abstracted *from* them. There is only one place they come from; that is from the person who is to use them. He devises them. Moreover, they do not stand for anything or represent anything, as a symbol, for example, is supposed to do.

So what are they? They are reference axes, upon which one may project events in an effort to make some sense out of what is going on. In this sense they are like cartesian coordinates, the x, y, and z axes of analytic geometry. Events correspond to the point plotted within cartesian space. We can locate the points and express relations between points by specifying x, y, and z distances. The cartesian axes *do not represent* the points projected upon them, but serve as guidelines for locating those points. That, also, is what constructs do for events, including ones that have not yet occurred. They help us locate them, understand them, and anticipate them.

But we must not take the cartesian analogy too literally. Descartes' axes were lines or scales, each containing in order an infinite number of imaginary points. Certainly his x- or y-axis embodied well enough the notion of shadings or a succession of grays. Yet a construct is not quite such an axis.

A construct is the basic contrast between two groups. When it is imposed it serves both to distinguish between its elements and to group them. Thus constructs refer to the nature of the distinction one attempts to make between events, not to the array in which his events appear to stand when he gets through applying the distinction between each of them and all the others.

Suppose one is dealing with the construct of good versus bad. Such a construct is not a representation of all things that are good, and an implicit exclusion of all that are bad. Nor is it a representation of all that are bad. It is not even a representation of all things that can be called either good or bad. The construct, of itself, is the kind of contrast one perceives and not in any way a representation of objects. As far as the construct is concerned there is no good-better-best scale, or any bad-worse-worst array.

But, while constructs do not represent or symbolize events, they do enable us to cope with events, which is a statement of quite a different order. They also enable us to put events into arrays or scales, if we wish. Suppose, for example, we apply our construct to elements, say persons, or to their acts. Consider three persons. One may make a good-bad distinction between them which will say that two of them are good in relation to the third, and the third is bad in relation to the two good ones. Then he may, in turn, apply his construct between the two good ones and say one of them is good with respect to the other formerly "good" one and the one already labeled "bad."

This, of course, makes one of the persons, or acts, good in terms of one cleavage that has been made and bad in relation to the other. But this relativism applies only to the objects; the construct of good versus bad is itself absolute. It may not be accurate, and it may not be stable from time to time, but, as a construct, it has to be absolute. Still, by its successive application to events one may create a scale with a great number of points differentiated along its length. Now a person who likes grays can have them—as many as he likes.

But let us make no mistake: A scale, in comparison to a construct, is a pretty concrete affair. Yet one can scarcely have himself a scale unless he has a construct working for him. Only if he has some basis for discrimination and association can he get on with the job of marking off a scale.

Now note something else. We have really had to fall back on our philosophical position of constructive alternativism in order to come up with this kind of an abstraction. If we had not first disabused ourselves of the idea that events are the source of our construct, we would have had a hard time coming around to the point where we could envision the underlying basis of discrimination and association we call the construct.

Choice Corollary

A person chooses for himself that alternative in a dichotomized construct through which he antici-

pates the greater possibility for the elaboration of his system. It seems to me to follow that if a person makes so much use of his constructs, and is so dependent upon them, he will make choices which promise to develop their usefulness. Developing the usefulness of a construction system involves, as far as I can see, two things: defining it and extending it. One defines his system, by extension at least, by making it clear how its construct components are applied to objects or are linked with each other. He amplifies his system by using it to reach out for new fields of application. In the one case he consolidates his position and in the other he extends it.

Note that the choice is between alternatives expressed in the construct, not, as one might expect, between objects divided by means of the construct. There is a subtle point here. Personal construct theory is a psychological theory and therefore has to do with the behavior of man, not with the intrinsic nature of objects. A construct governs what the man does, not what the object does. In a strict sense, therefore, man makes decisions which initially affect himself, and which affect other objects only subsequently—and then only if he manages to take some effective action. Making a choice, then, has to do with involving oneself, and cannot be defined in terms of the external object chosen. Besides, one does not always get the object he chooses to gain. But his anticipation does have to do with his own processes, as I tried to say in formulating the basic postulate.

So when a man makes a choice what he does is align himself in terms of his constructs. He does not necessarily succeed, poor fellow, in doing anything to the objects he seeks to approach or avoid. Trying to define human behavior in terms of the externalities sought or affected, rather than the seeking process, gets the psychologist pretty far off the track. It makes more of a physicist of him than a psychologist, and a rather poor one, at that. So what we must say is that a person, in deciding whether to believe or do something, uses his construct system to proportion his field, and then moves himself strategically and tactically within its presumed domain.

Men change things by changing themselves first, and they accomplish their objectives, if at all, only by paying the price of altering themselves—as some have found to their sorrow and others to their salvation. The choices that men make are choices of their own acts, and the alternatives are distinguished by their own constructs. The results of the choices, however, may range all the way from nothing to catastrophe, on the one hand, or to consummation, on the other.

Experience Corollary

A person's construction system varies as he successively construes the replications of events. The tendency is for personal constructs to shift when events are projected upon them. The distinctions they implement are likely to be altered in three ways: (1) The construct may be applied at a different point in the galaxy, (2) it may become a somewhat different kind of distinction, and (3) its relations to other constructs may be altered.

In the first of these shifts it is a matter of change in the location of the construct's application, and hence not exactly an intrinsic change in the construct itself. In the second case, however, it is the abstraction itself which is altered, although the change may not be radical enough for the psychologist to say a new construct has been substituted. Finally, in the third case, the angular relations with other constructs are necessarily affected by the transition, unless, by some chance, the construct system were rotated as a whole. But that is not a very likely contingency.

The first kind of shift might be observed when a person moves to an urban community. Some of the actions he once regarded as aloof and unneighborly he may come to accept as relatively friendly in the new social context. But he may also rotate the axis of his construct as he gains familiarity with city life, and, as a result, come to see "aloofness" as a neighborly respect for his privacy, something he had never had very clearly in mind before. This would be an example of the second kind of shift. The third kind of shift comes when he alters his notion of respect as a result of the experience, perhaps coming to sense it not so much a matter of subservience or adulation but more a matter of empathy and consideration. As a matter of fact, we might regard the whole transition as leading him in the direction of greater maturity.

Keeping in mind that events do not actually repeat themselves and that the replication we talk about is a replication of ascribed aspects only, it begins to be clear that the succession we call experience is based on the constructions we place on what goes on. If those constructions are never altered, all that happens during a

man's years is a sequence of parallel events having no psychological impact on his life. But if he invests himself—the most intimate event of all—in the enterprise, the outcome, to the extent that it differs from his expectation or enlarges upon it, dislodges the man's construction of himself. In recognizing the inconsistency between his anticipation and the outcome, he concedes a discrepancy between what he was and what he is. A succession of such investments and dislodgments constitutes the human experience.

A subtle point comes to light at this juncture. Confirmation may lead to reconstruing quite as much as disconfirmation—perhaps even more. A confirmation gives one an anchorage in some area of his life, leaving him free to set afoot adventuresome explorations nearby, as, for example, in the case of a child whose security at home emboldens him to be the first to explore what lies in the neighbor's yard.

The unit of experience is, therefore, a cycle embracing five phases: anticipation, investment, encounter, confirmation or disconfirmation, and constructive revision. This is followed, of course, by new anticipations, as the first phase of a subsequent experiential cycle gets underway. Certainly in personal construct theory's line of reasoning experience is not composed of encounters alone.

Stated simply, the amount of a man's experience is not measured by the number of events with which he collides, but by the investments he has made in his anticipations and the revisions of his constructions that have followed upon his facing up to consequences. A man whose only wager in life is upon reaching heaven by immunizing himself against the miseries of his neighbors, or upon following a bloody party-line straight to utopia, is prepared to gain little experience until he arrives—either there, or somewhere else clearly recognized as not the place he was looking for. Then, if he is not too distracted by finding that his architectural specifications have been blatantly disregarded, or that the wrong kind of people have started moving in, I suppose he may begin to think of some other investments he might better have been making in the meantime. Of course, a little hell along the way, if taken more to heart than most heaven-bound people seem to take it, may have given him a better idea of what to expect, before it was too late to get a bit of worthwhile experience and make something out of himself.

Etiology and Development

Phenomenologists stress that every individual is the center of his changing world of experiences; experiences must be viewed, therefore, only in terms of their relevance to the individual. As the individual matures, a portion of experience becomes differentiated into cognitive attitudes toward events and persons, as well as a sense of the self-as-object. Once established, they influence the perceptions, memories, and thoughts of the individual. If experiences are inconsistent with these images, they are ignored or disowned.

An early disciple of Freud, Alfred Adler, gradually shifted his views on several major notions following his break from the psychoanalytic movement. Best known is his stress on compensatory and social, rather than sexual, factors in shaping character and pathology. Less well known is his assertion that subjective attributions give experience the meaning they have to the individual.

More current is the contribution of Aaron Beck to a systematic cognitive–phenomenological view. In the paper reprinted here, Beck elucidates how the cognitive distortions a patient exhibits can exacerbate a depressed mood.

25 The Nature and Origin of Character

Alfred Adler

What we call a character trait is the appearance of some specific mode of expression on the part of an individual who is attempting to adjust himself to the world in which he lives. Character is a social concept. We can speak of a character trait only when we consider the relationship of an individual to his environment. It would make very little difference what kind of character Robinson Crusoe had. Character is a psychic attitude, it is the quality and nature of an individual's approach to the environment in which he moves. It is the behavior pattern according to which his striving for significance is elaborated in the terms of his social feeling.

We have already seen how the goal of superiority, of power, of the conquest of others, is the goal which directs the activity of most human beings. This goal modifies the world philosophy and the behavior pattern and directs the various psychic expressions of an individual into specific channels. Traits of character are only the external manifestations of the style of life, of the behavior pattern, of

From *Understanding Human Nature*, Greenberg Publishing Co., 1927/1924.

any individual. As such they enable us to understand his attitude towards his environment, towards his fellow men, towards the society in which he lives, and towards the challenge of existence in general. Character traits are instruments, the tricks which are used by the total personality in the acquisition of recognition and significance; their configuration in the personality amounts to a "technique" in living.

Traits of character are not inherited, as many would have it, nor are they congenitally present. They are to be considered as similar to a pattern for existence which enables every human being to live his life and express his personality in any situation without the necessity of consciously thinking about it. Character traits are not the expressions of inherited powers nor predispositions but they are acquired for the purpose of maintaining a particular habitus in life. A child, for instance, is not born lazy but is lazy because laziness seems to him the best adapted means of making life easier, while it enables him at the same time to maintain his feeling of significance. The power attitude can be expressed in a certain degree, in the pattern of laziness. An individual may draw attention to a congenital defect and thus save his face before a defeat. The end result of such introspection is always something like this: "If I did not have this defect my talents would develop brilliantly. But unfortunately I *have* the defect!" A second individual who is involved in a long-standing war with his environment because of his undisciplined striving for power, will develop whatever power expressions are adequate to his battle, such as ambition, envy, mistrust, and the like. We believe that such traits of character are indistinguishable from the personality, but are not inherited nor unchangeable. Closer observation shows us that they have been found necessary and adequate for the behavior pattern and have been acquired to this end, sometimes very early in life. They are not primary factors, but secondary ones, which have been forced into being by the secret goal of the personality. They must be judged from the standpoint of teleology.

Let us recall our previous explanations in which we have shown how the style of an individual's life, his actions, his behavior, his standpoint in the world, are all closely connected with his goal. We cannot think anything, nor set anything into motion, without having some distinct purpose in mind. In the dark background of the child's soul this goal is already present, directing his psychic development from his earliest days. It gives form and character to his life and is responsible for the fact that every individual is a particular and discreet unity, different from all other personalities, because all his movements and all the expressions of his life are directed toward a common, unique, goal. To realize this is to know that we can always recognize a human being, wherever we find him in the course of his behavior, once we know his pattern.

So far as psychic phenomena and character traits are concerned, heredity plays a relatively unimportant rôle. There are no points of contact with reality which might support a theory of inherited acquired traits. Investigate any particular phenomenon in one's psychic life, and you arrive at his first day, and it would seem, indeed, as though everything were inherited. The reason that there are character traits which are common for a whole family, or a nation, or a race, lies simply in the fact that one individual acquires them from another by imitation or by the process of identifying himself with the other's activity. There are certain realities, certain peculiarities, expres-

sions and forms in the physical and psychic life, which have an especial significance in our civilization for all adolescents. Their common characteristic is that they stimulate imitation. Thus the thirst for knowledge which is expressed sometimes as a desire to see, can lead to curiosity as a character trait in such children as have difficulties with their optic apparatus, but there is no *necessity* for the development of this character trait. If the behavior pattern of this child should demand it, this same thirst for knowledge might develop into quite another character trait. The same child might satisfy himself by investigating all things, and taking them apart, or breaking them into pieces. Or such a child might, under other circumstances, become a bookworm.

We may evaluate the mistrust of those who have difficulties in hearing in much the same way. In our civilization they are exposed to a greater danger and they sense that danger with a particularly sharpened attention. They are also exposed to ridicule, degradation, and are frequently considered as cripples. These are factors of the utmost importance in the development of a mistrustful character. Since the deaf are excluded from many pleasures, it is not surprising that they should be hostile to them. But the assumption that they were born with a mistrustful character would be unwarranted. The theory that criminal character traits are congenital, is equally fallacious. The argument that many criminals are to be found in one family may be effectively countered by drawing attention to the fact that a tradition and attitude toward the world, and a bad example, go hand in hand in these cases. Children in these families are taught from early childhood the fact that thievery is a possibility for gaining a livelihood.

The striving for recognition may be considered in much the same way. Every child is faced with so many obstacles in life that no child ever grows up without striving for some form of significance. The form which this striving will take is interchangeable, and every human being approaches the problem of his personal significance in an individual way. The assertion that children are similar to their parents in their character traits, is easily explained by the fact that the child, in his striving for significance, seizes upon the example of those individuals in his environment who are already significant and demand respect, as an ideal model. Every generation learns from its ancestors in this way, and it maintains what it has learned in the greatest difficulties and complexities to which this striving for power may lead it.

The goal of superiority is a secret goal. The existence of a social feeling prevents its frank development. It must grow in secret and hide itself behind a friendly mask! We must reaffirm however that it would not grow with such tropic luxuriance if we humans understood one another better. If we could go so far that each of us developed better eyes and could more transparently view the character of his neighbor, then we should not only be able to protect ourselves better, but simultaneously make it so difficult for another to express his striving for power, that it would not pay him to do so. Under such circumstances the veiled striving for power would disappear. It pays us therefore to look into these relationships more closely and make use of the experimental evidence which we have won.

We live under such complicated cultural circumstances that proper schooling for life is made very difficult. The most important means for the development of psychological acuity have been denied the people, and up to the present the only value of schools has been that they have spread the raw stuff of knowledge before children and allowed them to eat of it what they could or would, without especially stimulating their interest in it. And even a sufficient number of these schools was but a pious wish! The most important premise for the acquisition of an understanding of human nature has been hitherto much neglected. We too have learned our standards for measuring human beings in the old schools. Here we have learned to divide good from bad, and to distinguish them. What we have not learned is how to revise our concepts, and consequently we have carried this defect into life and are laboring under it to this day.

As grown-ups we are still making use of the prejudices and fallacies of our childhood as though they were sacred laws. We are not yet aware that we have been drawn into the confusion of our complicated culture, that we have assumed standpoints which a true recognition of things as they are, would make impossible.

Human beings live in the realm of *meanings*. We do not experience pure circumstances; we always experience circumstances in their significance for men. Even at its source our experience is qualified by our human purposes. "Wood" means "wood in its relation to mankind," and "stone" means "stone as it can be a factor in human life." If a man should try to escape meanings and devote himself only to circumstances he would be very unfortunate: he would isolate himself from others: his actions would be useless to himself or to any one; in a word, they would be meaningless. But no human being can escape meanings. We experience reality always through the meaning we give it; not in itself, but as something interpreted. It will be natural to suppose, therefore, that this meaning is always more or less unfinished, incomplete; and even that it is never altogether right. The realm of meanings is the realm of mistakes.

If we asked a man, "What is the meaning of life?", he would perhaps be unable to answer. For the most part people do not bother themselves with the question or try to formulate replies. It is true that the question is as old as human history and that in our own time young people—and older people as well—will often break out with the cry, "But what is life for? What does life mean?" We can say, however, that they ask only when they have suffered a defeat. So long as everything is plain sailing and no difficult tests are set before them the question is never put into words. It is in his actions that every man inevitably puts the question and answers it. If we close our ears to his words and observe his actions, we shall find that he has his own individual "meaning of life" and that all his postures, attitudes, movements, expressions, mannerisms, ambitions, habits, and character traits accord with this meaning. He behaves as if he could rely upon a certain interpretation of life. In all his actions there is an implicit reckoning up of the world and of himself; a verdict, "I am like this and the universe is like that"; a meaning given to himself and a meaning given to life.

There are as many meanings given to life as there are human beings, and, as we have suggested, perhaps each meaning involves more or less of a mistake. No one possesses the absolute meaning of life, and we may say that any meaning which is at all serviceable cannot be called absolutely wrong. All meanings are varieties between these two limits. Among these varieties, however, we can distinguish some which answer better and some which answer worse; some where the mistake is small and some where it is large. We can discover what it is that the better meanings share in common, what it is that the worse meanings lack. In this way we can obtain a scientific "meaning of life," a common measure of true meanings, a meaning which enables us to meet reality insofar as it concerns mankind. Here again we must remember that "true" means true for mankind, true for the purposes and aims of human beings. There is no other truth than this; and if another truth existed, it could never concern us; we could never know it; it would be meaningless.

Since the meaning given to life works out as if it were the guardian angel or pursuing demon of our careers, it is very clearly of the highest importance that we should understand how these meanings come to be formed, how they differ from one another, and how they can be corrected if they involve big mistakes. This is the province of psychology, as distinct from physiology or biology—the use for human welfare of an understanding of *meanings* and the way in which they influence human actions and human fortunes. From the first days of childhood we can see dark gropings after this "meaning of life." Even a baby is striving to make an estimate of its own powers and its share in the whole life which surrounds it. By the end of the fifth year of life a child has reached a unified and crystallized pattern of behavior, its own style of approach to problems and tasks. It has already fixed its deepest and most lasting conception of what to expect from the world and from itself. From now on, the world is seen through a stable scheme of apperception: experiences are interpreted before they are accepted, and the interpretation always accords with the original meaning given to life. Even if this meaning is very gravely mistaken, even if the approach to our problems and tasks brings us continually into misfortunes and agonies, it is never easily relinquished. Mistakes in the meaning given to life can be corrected only by reconsidering the situation in which the faulty interpretation was made, recognizing the error, and revising the scheme of apperception. In rare circumstances, perhaps, an individual may be forced by the consequences of a mistaken approach to revise the meaning he has given to life and may succeed in accomplishing the change by himself. He will never do it, however, without some social pressure, or without finding that if he proceeds with the old approach he is at the end of his tether: and for the most part the approach can best be revised with the assistance of someone trained in the understanding of these meanings, who can join in discovering the original error and help to suggest a more appropriate meaning.

Let us take a simple illustration of the different ways in which childhood situations may be interpreted. Unhappy experiences in childhood may be given quite opposite meanings. One man with unhappy experiences behind him will not dwell on them except as they show him something which can be remedied for the future. He will feel, "We must work to remove such unfortunate situations and make sure that our children are better placed." Another man will feel, "Life is unfair. Other people always have the best of it. If the world treated me like that, why should I treat the world any better?" It is in this way that some parents say of their children, "I had to suffer just as much when I was a child, and I came through it. Why shouldn't they?" A third man will feel, "Everything should be forgiven me because of my unhappy childhood." In the actions of all three men their interpretations will be evident; and they will never change their actions unless they change their interpretations. It is here that individual psychology breaks through the theory of determinism. No experience is a cause of success or failure. We do not suffer from the shock of our experiences—the so-called *trauma*—but we make out of them just what suits our purposes. We are *self-determined* by the meaning we give to our experiences; and there is probably something of a mistake always involved when we take particular experiences as the basis for our future life. Meanings are not determined by situations, but we determine ourselves by the meanings we give to situations.

26 The Development of Depression: A Cognitive Model

Aaron T. Beck

Depression and the Nature of Man

A scientist, shortly after assuming the presidency of a prestigious scientific group, gradually became morose and confided to a friend that he had an overwhelming urge to leave his career and become a hobo.

A devoted mother who had always felt strong love for her children started to neglect them and formulated a serious plan to destroy them and then herself.

An epicurean who relished eating beyond all other satisfactions developed an aversion for food and stopped eating.

A wealthy businessman publicly proclaimed his guilt over a few minor misdemeanors of some decades before, put on a beggar's clothes and begged for food.

A woman, on hearing of the sudden death of a close friend, smiled for the first time in several weeks.

These strange actions, completely inconsistent with the individual's previous behavior and values, are all expressions of the same underlying condition—depression.

By what perversity does depression mock the most hallowed notions of human nature and biology?

The instinct for self-preservation and the maternal instincts appear to vanish. Basic biological drives such as hunger and sexual drive are extinguished. Sleep, the easer of all woes, is thwarted. Social instincts such as attraction to other people, love, and affection evaporate. The "pleasure principle" and "reality principle," the goals of maximizing pleasure and minimizing pain, are turned around. Not only is the capacity for enjoyment stifled, but the victims of this odd malady appear driven to behave in ways that enhance their suffering. Capacity to respond with mirth to humorous situations or with anger to situations that would ordinarily infuriate seems lost.

At one time, this strange affliction was

From *The Psychology of Depression*, 1974, edited by R. J. Friedman and M. M. Katz, pp. 3–16, by permission of the publisher, Hemisphere Publishing Corporation.

ascribed to demons that allegedly took possession of the victim. Theories advanced since then have not yet provided a more durable solution to the problem of depression. We are still encumbered by a disorder that seems to discredit the most firmly entrenched concepts of the nature of man. Paradoxically, the anomalies of depression may provide the clues for understanding this mysterious condition.

The complete reversal in the patient's behavior in depression would seem, initially, to defy explanation. During his depression, the patient's personality is far more like that of other depressives than like his previous personality. A close examination of the personality and behavioral changes can illuminate the baffling disorder, however. Feelings of pleasure and joy are replaced by sadness and apathy; the broad range of spontaneous desires and involvement in activities are eclipsed by passivity and desires to escape; hunger and sexual drive are replaced by revulsion toward food and sex; interest and involvement in usual activities are converted into avoidance and withdrawal. Finally, the desire to live is switched off and replaced by the wish to die (see Table 1).

As an initial step in understanding a baffling condition such as depression, we can attempt to arrange the various phenomena into some kind of understandable sequence. At various times, writers have assigned primacy to the intense sadness, wishes to "hibernate," self-destructive wishes, or physiological disturbance.

Is the painful emotion the catalytic agent? Certainly distress or suffering in themselves can hardly be considered the stimulus for the other depressive symptoms. Other unpleasant states such as physical pain, nausea, dizziness, shortness of breath, or anxiety rarely, if ever, lead to typical depressive symptoms such as renunciation of major objectives in life, obliteration of affectionate feelings, or wishes to die. In fact, under the influence of pain, people seem to treasure more than ever those aspects of life that they have found meaningful. Nor does sadness appear to have specific

TABLE 1 Changes from Normal to Depressed State

Items	Changes	
	Normal state	Depressed state
Stimulus	*Response*	
Loved object	Affection	Loss of feeling, revulsion
Favorite activities	Pleasure	Boredom
New opportunities	Enthusiasm	Indifference
Humor	Amusement	Mirthlessness
Novel stimuli	Curiosity	Lack of interest
Abuse	Anger	Self-criticism, sadness
Goal or drive	*Direction*	
Gratification	Pleasure	Avoidance
Welfare	Self-care	Self-neglect
Self-preservation	Survival	Suicide
Achievement	Success	Withdrawal
Thinking	*Appraisal*	
About self	Realistic	Self-devaluating
About future	Hopeful	Hopeless
About environment	Realistic	Overwhelming
Biological and physiological activities	*Symptom*	
Appetite	Spontaneous hunger	Loss of appetitie
Sexuality	Spontaneous desire	Loss of desire
Sleep	Restful	Disturbed
Energy	Spontaneous	Fatigued

qualities that can account for the self-castigations, the distortions in thinking, or loss of drive for gratifications that typify depression.

Similar difficulties are encountered in assigning primacy to other characteristics of depression. Some writers have seized on the passivity and the withdrawal of attachments to other people as forms of an atavistic wish to hibernate. If the desire to conserve energy is its goal, why does the human organism experience increased suffering and why does it seek and occasionally attain death by suicide? Ascribing the primary role to physiological symptoms such as the disturbances in sleep, appetite, and sexuality poses even greater difficulties. It is difficult to understand the sequence by which these physiological disturbances can account for such varied phenomena such as self-criticism, negative view of the world, and loss of the anger and mirth responses. Certainly when loss of appetite or sleep occurs as the result of a debilitating physical illness it does not produce the other symptoms of depression.

The Clue: The Sense of Loss

The problem of sorting the phenomena of depression into an understandable sequence may be attacked by simply asking the patient why he feels sad or by encouraging him to express his repetitive ideas. Depressed patients often provide essential information in spontaneous statements such as "I'm sad because I'm worthless," "I have no future," "I've lost everything," "My family is gone—I have nobody," or "Life has nothing for me."

It is relatively easy to detect the dominant theme in the statements of the moderately or severely depressed patient. He regards himself as lacking some element or attribute he considers essential for his happiness: competence in attaining his goals, attractiveness to other people, closeness to family or friends, tangible possessions, good health, or status or position. Such self-appraisals reflect the way the depressed patient perceives his life situation.

Although many nondepressed people experience similar deprivations, the depressed patient differs from them in the way he construes this experience: he either misinterprets or exaggerates the loss, or he attaches overgeneralized or extravagant meanings to the loss. In a long-term study of depressed patients, we found that each of the patients presented distortion and illogical thinking centering on the theme of loss (Beck 1963). These aberrations included selective abstraction, arbitrary inferences, and magnification.

In exploring the theme of loss, we once again find that a psychological disorder revolves around a *cognitive problem;* in the case of the depressed patient, distortions regarding the patient's evaluations of his world, of himself, and of his future.

The content of the distorted evaluations is relevant to the concept of shrinkage of the domain as the stimulus for the arousal of sadness (Beck 1971). The depressive's view of his valued attributes, relationships, and achievements is saturated with the notion of loss—past, present, and future. When he considers his present status, he sees a barren world; he feels pressed to the wall by external demands that cheat him of his meager resources and thwart him from attaining what he wants.

The term "loser" captures the flavor of the depressive's appraisal of himself and his experience. He agonizes over the notion that he has experienced significant losses, such as his friends, his health, or his prized possessions. He also regards himself as a "loser" in the colloquial sense: he is a misfit, an inferior and inadequate being unable to meet his responsibilities and reach his goals. If he undertakes a project or seeks some gratification, he expects to be defeated or disappointed. He finds no respite in his dreams: he is portrayed as a misfit and thwarted in his attempts to achieve his goals.

In considering the concept of loss, we should be sensitive to the crucial importance of meanings and connotations. What represents a painful loss for one person may be trivial to another. It is important to recognize that the depressed patient dwells on "hypothetical losses" and "pseudo-losses." When he thinks about a possible loss, he treats his conjecture as though it were an established fact.

A depressed man, for example, characteristically reacted to his wife's tardiness in meeting him with the thought, "She might have died on the way." He then construed the *hypothesized loss* as an actual event and became forlorn. Pseudo-loss is the incorrect labeling of any event as a loss; for example, a change in status that may actually be a gain. A depressed patient who sold some shares of stock at a large profit experienced a prolonged sense of deprivation over eliminating the securities from his portfolio and ruminated over the notion that the sale had impoverished him.

Granted that the perception of loss produces sadness, how does this sense of loss engender other symptoms of depression such as pessimism, self-criticism, escape-avoidance-giving up, suicidal wishes, and the physiological disorder?

To illuminate this problem, it would be useful to explore the chronology of depression, the onset and full development of symptoms. This sequence is most clearly demonstrated in cases of "reactive depression;" that is, depression in which there is a clearcut precipitating factor.

Development of Depression

In the course of his development, the depression-prone person may become sensitized by certain unfavorable types of life situations such as the loss of a parent or chronic rejection by his peers. Other unfavorable conditions of a more insidious nature may similarly produce vulnerability to depression. These traumatic experiences predispose the individual to overreact to analogous conditions later in life. He has a tendency to make extreme, absolute judgments when such situations occur. A loss is viewed as irrevocable; indifference, as total rejection. Other depression-prone individuals spend their childhood setting rigid, perfectionistic goals for themselves so that their universe collapses when they confront inevitable disappointments later in life (see Beck [1972] for further discussion of predisposition to depression).

The specific stresses responsible for adult depressions impinge on the individual's specific vulnerability. Numerous clinical and research reports agree on the following types of precipitating events: the disruption of a relationship with a person to whom the patient is attached, failure to attain an important goal, loss of a job, financial reverses, unexpected physical disability, and loss of social status or reputation. When such events are construed as a subtraction from the individual's personal domain, they may trigger a depression.

To justify the label "precipitating event," the experience of loss must have substantial significance to the patient. The precipitating factor, however, is not always a discrete event; insidious stresses such as the gradual withdrawal of affection by a spouse or a chronic discrepancy between goals and achievements in valued activities at work or at home may also erode the personal domain enough to produce depression. The individual, for example, may be continually dissatisfied with his or her performance as a parent, housewife, income producer, student, or creative artist. The repetitive recognition of a gap between what a person expects and what he receives from an important interpersonal relationship, from his career, or from other activities may topple him into a depression. In brief, the sense of loss may be the inevitable result of unrealistically high goals and expectations.

The manner in which traumatic circumstances involving a loss lead to the constellation of depressive symptoms may be delineated by an illustrative case: a man whose wife has unexpectedly deserted him.

The effect on the deserted mate cannot necessarily be predicted in advance. Obviously, not every person deserted by a spouse becomes depressed. He may have other sources of satisfaction—other members of his family and friends, as well as other sources of help. In fact, our deserted husband may have led a reasonably happy life before he ever met his wife. If the problem were simply a new hiatus in his life, it would seem plausible that in the course of time he would be able to compensate, at least in part, for the loss without becoming clinically depressed. Nonetheless, we know that certain vulnerable individuals respond to such a loss with the profound psychological disturbance called depression.

The impact of the loss depends in part on the kind and intensity of the meanings attached to the key person. The deserting wife has been the hub of shared experiences, fantasies, and expectations. The deserted husband (in our example) has built a network of associations around his wife, such as "She is part of me," "She is everything to me," "I enjoy life because of her," "She is my mainstay," or "She comforts me when I am down." These positive associations range from the realistic to the extremely unrealistic or imaginary. The more absolute these positive concepts, the greater the damage.

If the damage to the domain is great enough, it sets off a chain reaction. The positive values attached to the wife are totally wiped out. The greater and more absolute these positive associations, the greater the sense of loss. The extinction of "assets" such as "the only person who can make me happy" or "the essence of my existence" magnifies the impact of the loss and generates further sadness. Consequently, our deserted husband makes extreme, negative conclusions that parallel the extreme positive associations to his wife. He interprets the consequences of the loss as "I am nothing without her," "I can never be happy again," and "I can't go on without her."

The further reverberations of the desertion lead the husband to question his validity and worth: "If I had been a better person, she wouldn't have left me." Further, he foresees other negative consequences of the breakup of the marriage: "All of our friends will go over to her side," "The children will want to live with her, not with me," and "I will go broke trying to maintain two households."

As the chain reaction progresses to a full-blown depression, the husband's self-doubts and gloomy predictions expand into negative generalizations about himself, his world, and his future. He starts to see himself as permanently impoverished both in terms of emotional satisfactions and in money. In addition, he exacerbates his suffering by over-dramatizing the event: "It is too much for a person to bear" or "This is a terrible disaster." Such ideas undermine his ability and motivation to absorb the shock.

The husband—we can now refer to him as a "patient"—divorces himself from activities and goals that formerly gave him satisfaction. He is likely to withdraw from his career goals ("because they are meaningless without my wife"). He is not motivated to work or even to take care of himself ("because it isn't worth the effort"). His distress is aggravated by the physiological concomitants of depression, such as loss of appetite and sleep disturbances. Finally, he thinks of suicide as an escape ("because life is too painful").

Since the chain reaction feeds upon itself, the depression goes into a downward spiral. The various symptoms—sadness, decreased physical activity, sleep disturbance—feed back into the psychological system. Hence, as the patient experiences sadness his pessimism leads him to conclude, "I will always be sad."

This leads to more sadness, that is further interpreted in a negative way. Similarly, he thinks, "I will never be able to eat again or to sleep again" and concludes that he is rotting or deteriorating physically. As the patient observes the various manifestations of his disorder (decreased productivity, avoidance of responsibility, withdrawal from other people), he becomes increasingly critical of himself. His self-criticisms lead to deeper sadness and we thus see a continuing vicious cycle.

The same kind of chain reaction may be triggered by other kinds of losses such as failure at school or on a job. More chronic deprivations may also provide triggers: disturbance in key interpersonal relations or failure to attain certain academic goals.

This sketch of the chain reaction may be expanded to provide more complete answers to the following problems: Why does the depressed patient have such low self-esteem? Why is he pervasively pessimistic? Why does he berate himself so viciously? Why does he give up? Why does he believe no one can help him?

Low Self-Esteem

As the traumatized person reflects about adverse events (such as a separation, rejection, defeat, not achieving his expectations), he wonders what it tells him about himself. The tendency to extract personally relevant meanings from unpleasant situations is particularly characteristic of the depression-prone individual. Moreover, a special impetus to ascribing negative meanings to a loss is produced by the tendency to find some personal explanation for important life events. Usually such determinations of causality are very simplistic and may be quite erroneous.

The depression-prone individual is likely to assign the cause of an adverse event to some shortcoming in himself. The deserted husband concludes, "I have lost her *because* I am unlovable." In reality, this conclusion is only one of a number of possible explanations, such as basic incompatibility of their personalities, the wife's own problems, or her desire for an adventure which may be related more to thrill-seeking than to a change in her feelings for her husband.

When the person attributes the cause of the loss to himself, the rift in his domain becomes a chasm: He suffers not only the loss itself but he "discovers" a deficiency in himself. He tends to view this presumed deficiency in greatly exaggerated terms. A woman reacted to desertion by her lover with the thought, "I'm getting old and ugly and I must be repulsive looking." A man who lost his job due to a general decline in the economy thought, "I'm inept and too weak to make a living."

By erroneously explaining reversals as due to a defect in himself, the person produces additional undesirable effects. His awareness of the presumed defect becomes so intense that it infiltrates every thought about himself. In the course of time, his picture of his negative attributes expands to the point that it completely occupies his concept of himself. When asked to describe himself he can think only of this "bad" trait. He has great difficulty in shifting his attention to his other abilities or achievements and he glosses over or discounts attributes that he may have highly valued in the past.

The patient's preoccupation with his presumed deficiency assumes many forms. He appraises each experience in terms of the deficiency. He interprets ambiguous or slightly negatively toned experiences as evidence of this deficiency. For instance, following an argument with her brother, a mildly depressed woman concluded, "I am incapable of being loved and of giving love," and she felt more depressed. In reality, she had a number of intimate friends and a loving husband and children. When a friend was too busy to chat with her on the phone, she thought, "She doesn't want to talk to me any more." If her husband came home late from the office, she decided that he was staying away to avoid her. When her children were ill natured at dinnertime, she thought, "I have failed them." In reality, there were more plausible explanations for these events but the patient had difficulty in even considering other explanations that did not reflect badly on her.

The tendency to make comparisons with other people further lowers the self-esteem. Every encounter with another person may be turned into some negative evaluation of himself. Thus, when talking to other people the depressed patient thinks, "I'm not a good conversationalist. I'm not as interesting as the other people." As he walks down the street, he thinks: "Those people look attractive, but I am unattractive." "I have bad posture and bad breath." He sees a mother with a child and thinks, "She's a much better parent than I am." He sees another patient working industriously in the hospital and thinks, "He's a hard worker. I'm lazy and helpless."

Self-Reproaches and Self-Criticisms

The harshness and inappropriateness of the self-reproaches in depression have either been ignored by writers or have produced very abstract speculations. Freud postulated that the bereaved patient has a pool of unconscious hostility toward the deceased "loved object." Since he cannot allow himself to experience his hostility, the patient directs the anger toward himself and accuses himself of faults that appropriately belong to the loved object. The concept of inverted rage has remained firmly entrenched in many theories of depression. Freud's convoluted pathway is so removed from information obtained from patients that it defies empirical validation.

Yet a careful examination of the patient's statements can yield a more parsimonious explanation of the self-reproaches which add insult to the injury inflicted by the loss. A clue to the genesis of the self-criticisms is found in the observation that many depressed patients are critical of a certain attribute that they had previously valued highly. These qualities have often been sources of gratification. For example, a woman who had enjoyed looking at herself in the mirror berated herself with indignities such as "I'm getting old and ugly." Another acutely depressed woman, who had always traded on her personal attractiveness and had enjoyed the resulting attention, castigated herself with the thought, "I have lost my ability to entertain people," and "I cannot even carry on a decent conversation." In both cases, the depression had been precipitated by disruption of an important interpersonal relationship.

In reviewing the history of depressed patients, we often find that the depressed patient has counted on this attribute, which he now debases, for balancing the usual stresses of life, mastering new problems, and attaining important objectives. When he believes that he will not be able to master a serious problem, to reach his goals, or to forestall a loss, he downgrades the asset. As this attribute appears to sour, he comes to the conclusion that he cannot get satisfaction out of life and that all

he can expect is pain and suffering. The depressed patient proceeds from disappointment to self-blame to pessimism.

To illustrate the mechanism of self-blame, we might consider the sequence in which the average person blames and punishes somebody else who has offended him. First, he tries to find (or manufactures) some bad trait in the offender to account for his noxious behavior—as insensitivity or selfishness. He then generalizes this character flaw to occupy his global image of the offender—"He's a selfish person. He's bad." After such moral judgment, he may consider ways to punish the offender. He not only downgrades the other individual, but given the opportunity, he will strike out at some quality so as to hurt him. Finally, because the offender has brought him pain, he may want to sever the relationship and reject the other person totally.

The self-castigating depressed patient reacts similarly to his own presumed deficiency, except that he makes himself the target for attack. He regards himself as at fault and deserving of blame. He goes beyond the biblical injunction, "If thine eye offends then pluck it out." His moral condemnation spreads from the particular trait to the totality of his self-concept and is often accompanied by feelings of revulsion for himself. The ultimate of his self-condemnation is total self-rejection—just as though he were rejecting another person.

Consider the effects of self-criticism, self-condemnation, and self-rejection. The patient reacts to these self-instigated onslaughts just as he would if they were directed at him by another person: he feels hurt, sad, humiliated.

Freud and many more-recent writers have held that the sadness is a transformation of anger turned inward. By a kind of "alchemy" the anger is supposedly converted into depressive feelings. A more plausible explanation is that the sadness is the result of the self-instigated lowering of the self-esteem. Suppose I inform a student that his performance is inferior and that he accepts the assessment as fair. Even though I communicate my evaluation without anger and may, in fact, express regret or empathy, he is likely to feel sad. The lowering of his self-esteem by my objective evaluation is sufficient to make him sad—even though I am not angry at him. Similarly, if the student makes a negative evaluation of himself, he feels sad. The depressed patient is like the self-devaluating student; he feels sad because he lowers his sense of worth by his negative evaluations. There is no reason to postulate that he is unconsciously angry at someone else and that his anger is transformed into sadness.

When a depressed patient makes a negative evaluation of himself, he generally does not feel anger at himself; he is, in his frame of reference, simply making an objective judgment. Similarly he reacts with sadness when he believes that somebody else is devaluating him, even though this external devaluation may be devoid of any anger.

Pessimism

Pessimism sweeps like a tidal wave over the thought content of depressed patients. To some degree, we all tend to "live in the future." We interpret experience not only in terms of what the event means right now, but also in terms of its possible consequences. A young man who had just received a compliment from his girl friend might look forward to receiving more compliments; he might think "She really likes me," and thus foresee a more intimate relationship with her. Similarly, if he has been disappointed or rejected, he is likely to anticipate a repetition of this type of unpleasant experience.

Depressed patients have a special penchant for expecting future adversities and experiencing them as though they were happening in the present or had already occurred. For example, a man who suffered a mild business reversal began to think of ultimate bankruptcy. As he dwelt on the theme of bankruptcy, he began to regard himself as already bankrupt. Consequently, he started to feel the same degree of sadness he would had he already suffered bankruptcy. In this respect, the depressed patient is different from the anxious patient whose "catastrophes" are always in the future and consequently do not produce a sense of loss in the present.

The predictions of depressed patients tend to be overgeneralized and extreme. Since the patients regard the future as an extension of the present, they expect a deprivation or defeat to continue permanently. If a patient feels miserable now, he assumes he will always feel miserable. The absolute, global pessimism is expressed in statements such as: "Things won't ever work out for me," "Life is meaningless. It's never going to be any

different." The depressed patient judges that, since he cannot reach a major goal now, he never will be able to achieve it. Nor can he see the possibility of substituting other rewarding goals. Moreover, if a problem appears insoluble now, he assumes that he will never be able to find a way of working it out or somehow bypassing it.

Another stream leading to pessimism arises from the negative self-concept described previously. As already mentioned, the trauma of a loss is especially damaging because it implies to the patient that he is defective in some way. Moreover, because the deficiency is regarded as an integral part of him he sees it as permanent and enduring. He often regards his "flaw" as becoming progressively worse. Since the defect is within him, nobody else can help him nor can he do anything about it.

Such kinds of pessimism are especially prominent when the individual sees himself as the essential force in reaching important life goals: if he has lost these instrumental abilities, then he is beyond redemption. A mildly depressed writer, for instance, did not receive the degree of acclaim that he expected for one of his works. His failure to live up to his expectations led him to two conclusions: first, that his writing ability was deteriorating; second, since creative ability is intrinsic, his loss could not be salvaged by anybody else. The loss was therefore irreversible.

A similar reaction was reported by a student who was unsuccessful in a competition for an academic award; his reaction was, "I lost because I'm weak and inferior. I'm never going to do well in a competitive situation." Since not winning was tantamount (for him) to complete failure, this meant that his whole life—past, present, and future—was a failure.

Similarly, a woman who developed transitory back trouble and had to be confined to bed for a few weeks became depressed. She concluded from her ailment that she would always be bedridden. She incorrectly regarded her "disease" as permanent and irremediable.

As pessimism envelops the patient's total future orientation, his thinking is dominated by ideas such as: "The game is over—I don't have a second chance." "Life has passed me by. It's too late to do anything about it." His losses are irreparable; his problems are unsolvable.

Pessimism not only engulfs the distant future, but permeates every specific wish and specific task the patient undertakes. A housewife who was listing her domestic duties automatically predicted before starting each new activity that she would be unable to do it. A depressed physician expected, before seeing each new patient, that he would be unable to make a diagnosis. The negative expectancies are so strong that even though the patient may be successful in each specific task (for example, the doctor's making the diagnosis), he expects to fail the very next time. He reacts as though he screened out or failed to integrate any successful experiences.

Snowballing of Sadness and Apathy

Although the onset of depression may be sudden, its full development spreads over a period of days or weeks. The patient experiences a gradual increase in intensity of sadness and of other symptoms until he "hits bottom." Each repetition of the idea of loss constitutes a fresh experience of loss which is added to the previous reservoir of perceived losses. With each successive "loss" further sadness is generated.

As described previously (Beck 1971), any psychopathological condition is characterized by a specific sensitivity to particular types of experiences. The depressed person tends to extract elements suggestive of loss and to gloss over other features that are not consonant with or are contradictory to this interpretation. As a result of such "selective abstraction," the patient overinterprets daily events in terms of loss and is oblivious to more-positive interpretations; he is hypersensitive to stimuli suggestive of loss and is blind to stimuli representing gain. He shows the same type of selectivity in recalling past experiences. He is facile in recalling unpleasant experiences but "draws a blank" when questioned about positive experiences.

As a result of this "tunnel vision," the patient becomes impermeable to stimuli that can arouse pleasant emotions. Although he may be able to acknowledge that certain events are favorable, his attitudes block any happy feelings: "I don't deserve to be happy." "I'm different from other people, and I can't feel happy over the things that make them happy." "How can I be happy when everything else is bad?" Similarly, comical situations do not strike him as funny because of his negative set and his tendency toward self-reference: "There is nothing funny about my life." He has difficulty in experiencing anger, since he views himself as responsible for and deserving of any rude or insulting actions of other people.

The tendency to think in absolute terms contributes to the cumulative arousal of sadness. The patient tends to dwell increasingly on extreme ideas such as "Life is meaningless." "Nobody loves me." "I'm totally inadequate." or "I have nothing left."

By downgrading qualities that are closely linked with gratification, the patient is in effect taking gratification away from himself. In calling herself unattractive, the woman is in effect saying, "I no longer can enjoy my physical appearance, or compliments I receive for it, or friendships that it helped me to form and maintain."

The loss of gratification apparently trips a mechanism leading to the opposite of happiness, namely, sadness. The prevailing wind of pessimism maintains a continual state of sadness. If the usual consequence of loss is sadness, then giving up is followed by apathy. When the depressed patient regards himself as defeated or at least thwarted in his life's major goals, he is apt to experience the emotion that goes with this—indifference or apathy.

Motivational Changes

The reversals in major goals and objectives are among the most puzzling characteristics of the seriously depressed patient. He not only desires to avoid experiences that formerly gratified him or represented the mainstream of his life, but he is drawn toward a state of inactivity. He even seeks to withdraw from life completely through suicide.

To understand the link between the changes in motivation and the patient's perception of loss, it is valuable to consider the ways in which the patient has "given up." He no longer feels attracted to the kinds of enterprises that ordinarily he would engage in spontaneously. In fact, he finds that he has to force himself into any undertaking. He goes through the motions of attending to his routine affairs because he believes he should, or because he knows it is "the right thing to do," or because others urge him to do it, but not because he wants to. He finds that he has to work against a powerful inner resistance as though he were trying to drive an automobile with the brakes on or to swim upstream.

In the most extreme cases, the patient experiences "paralysis of the will": He is (completely) devoid of any spontaneous desire to do anything except remain in a state of passive inertia. Nor can he mobilize "will power" to force himself to do what he believes he "ought to do."

From this description of the motivational changes, one might surmise that perhaps some physically depleting disease had overwhelmed the patient so that he did not have the strength or resources to make even a minimal exertion. An acute or debilitating illness such as pneumonia or advanced cancer could conceivably reduce a person to such a state of immobility.

However, the physical-depletion notion is contradicted by the patient's own observation that he feels a strong drive to *avoid* constructive or normal activities. His inertia is deceptive in that it derives not only from a desire to be passive, but also from a less obvious desire to shrink from any situation that he regards as unpleasant. He feels repelled by the thought of performing even elementary functions such as getting out of bed, dressing himself, and attending to personal needs. A retarded, depressed woman would rapidly dive under the covers of her bed whenever I entered the room. She would become exceptionally aroused and even energetic in attempting to escape from an activity that she was pressed to engage in.

In contrast to the depressed patient, the physically ill person generally would like to be active and to participate in his usual activities, and it is often necessary to enforce bed rest to keep him from taxing himself.

The depressed patient's desires to avoid activity and escape from his present environment are the consequences of his peculiar constructions—negative view of future, of his environment, and of himself (the cognitive triad).

Everyday experience, as well as a number of well-designed experiments, demonstrate that when a person believes he cannot succeed at a task, he is likely to give up or not even attempt to work at it. He adopts the attitude that "There's no use in trying" and does not feel much spontaneous drive. Moreover, the belief that the task is pointless and that even successful completion is meaningless minimizes his motivation.

An analogous situation is typical of depression. The depressed patient expects negative outcomes, so he does not experience ordinary mobilization of the drive to make an effort. Furthermore, he does not see any point in trying because he believes the goals are meaningless. There is a general tendency for people to avoid situations they expect to be painful. The depressed patient perceives most situations as onerous, boring, or painful. Hence, he desires to avoid even the usual amenities of living. These avoidance desires are powerful enough to override any tendencies toward constructive, goal-directed activity.

The background setting for the patient's powerful desire to seek a passive state is illustrated by this sequence of thoughts: "I'm too fatigued and sad to do anything. If I am active I will only feel worse. But if I lie down, I can conserve my strength and my bad feeling will go away." Unfortunately, his attempt to escape from the unpleasant feeling by being passive does not work; if anything, it enhances the dysphoria. The patient finds that far from getting respite from his unpleasant thoughts and feelings, he becomes more preoccupied with them.

REFERENCES

Beck, A. T. A systematic investigation of depression. *Comprehensive Psychiatry*, 1961, 2, 162–170.

Beck, A. T. Thinking and depression. 1. Idiosyncratic content and cognitive distortions. *Archives of General Psychiatry*, 1963, 9, 324–333.

Beck, A. T. Thinking and depression. 2. Theory and therapy. *Archives of General Psychiatry*, 1964, 10, 561–571.

Beck, A. T. Cognition, affect, and psychopathology. *Archives of General Psychiatry*, 1971, 24, 495–500.

Beck, A. T. *Depression: Causes and treatment.* Philadelphia: University of Pennsylvania Press, 1972.

Beck, A. T. & Hurvich, M. S. Psychological correlates of depression. 1. Frequency of "masochistic" dream content in a private practice sample. *Psychosomatic Medicine*, 1959, 21, 50–55.

Beck, A. T. & Ward, C. H. Dreams of depressed patients: Characteristic themes in manifest content. *Archives of General Psychiatry*, 1961, 5, 462–467.

Cropley, A. J. & Weckowicz, T. E. The dimensionality of clinical depression. *Australian Journal of Psychology*, 1966, 18, 18–25.

Loeb, A., Beck, A. T., & Diggory, J. C. Differential effects of success and failure on depressed and nondepressed patients. *Journal of Nervous and Mental Disease*, 1971, 152, 106–114.

Loeb, A., Feshbach, S., Beck, A. T., & Wolf, A. Some effects of reward upon the social perception and motivation of psychiatric patients varying in depression. *Journal of Abnormal Psychology*, 1964, 68, 609–616.

Pichot, P. & Lempérière, T. Analyse factoriella d'un questionnaire d'autoevaluation des symptomes dépressifs. *Revue de Psychologie Appliquee*, 1964, 14, 15–29.

Minkoff, K., Bergman, E., Beck, A. T., & Beck, R. Hopelessness, depression, and attempted suicide. *American Journal of Psychiatry*, 1973, 130, 455–459.

Pathological Patterns

Phenomenological theorists oriented to an existential philosophy express particular concern that contemporary man is trapped in a mechanistic mass society. Exposure to such an impersonal atmosphere results in feelings of social isolation and a sense of alienation from one's "true" self. Without a sure grasp of self, the individual lacks an identity and cannot experience what is termed "being in the world." Unable to sense his own inner world, he cannot sense the inner world of others, and without meaningful social relationships, cannot break the vicious circle to expand experience and develop a sense of identity. Eventually, he may succumb to "nothingness" and disorder.

Viktor Frankl has been a leading European exponent of the phenomenological approach to the study of psychopathology and society. Associated with the existential school, he believes that it is more fruitful to understand and treat patients in terms of the personal character of their experience than in terms of abstract theoretical concepts and diagnostic categories.

The selection by Rollo May, the primary exponent of the existential school in America, represents a direct and convincing application of phenomenological philosophy to the study of mental disorders. In it, he draws upon his own experiences to illustrate the central phenomenological concepts of anxiety and self.

The paper by R. D. Laing, a British existential psychiatrist, illuminates the nature of these personal experiences of isolation and anxiety. Beneath the sense of social loneliness lies a deep and profound alienation from one's self.

27 Meaninglessness: A Challenge to Psychologists[1]

Viktor E. Frankl

Contemporary psychiatrists are more and more confronted with patients who complain of an abysmal feeling of meaninglessness, of a sense that their lives are completely futile, of what might be called an abyss experience in contradistinction to those peak experiences

[1]Parts of this article are reproduced from Frankl, V. E. (1968). *The task of education in an age of meaninglessness*. Letter, S. S. ed., Institute of

From *Psychologia Africana*, 1970, *13*, 87–95. Reprinted by permission.

Higher Education. New York, Columbia University, Teachers College Press. Professor Frankl's English language publications include *Man's Search for Meaning, Psychotherapy and Existentialism, The Will of Meaning*, and *The Doctor and the Soul*.

that have been investigated and so beautifully described by Abraham Maslow. These patients also speak of a feeling of emptiness, of an inner void, a condition which I have described and termed "the existential vacuum."[2]

If I were asked for a short explanation of the origins of the existential vacuum, I would refer to two facts: first, that man, unlike an animal, is not told by his drives and instincts what he must do; and second, that, unlike man in former times, he is no longer told by his traditions and values what he should do. Not knowing what he must do, not knowing what he should do, he often does not even know what he basically wishes to do. The danger in this is that either he will wish to do simply what other people do, and this makes for conformism, or he will simply do what other people wish him to do, and this makes for totalitarianism.

In other words, two outstanding phenomena observable in the Western and Eastern parts of the world respectively may well be explained, to some extent at least, by these effects of the existential vacuum. Recent literature available from behind the Iron Curtain reveals that, according to Stanislav Kratochvil, a Czechoslovakian psychologist, this existential frustration is by no means restricted to the capitalist states, but may be observed in communist countries, particularly among the youth.

A similar statement was made by the late Dr. Vymetal, psychiatrist of Olomouc University. He said, at a meeting of psychiatrists held behind the Iron Curtain, that we can no longer be content with psychotherapy that is based solely on Pavlovian concepts. "I am an old Pavlovian," he stated, "but I declare: sticking to the concepts of conditioned and/or unconditioned reflexes we can no longer cope with those patients who now complain of a sense of meaninglessness."

The existential vacuum is, of course, not the only origin and cause of totalitarianism and/or conformism, but it might well be a component within the etiology, within the pathogenesis. In addition to totalitarianism and conformism, there is a third result of the existential vacuum; this is neuroticism. There is a certain new kind of neurotic illness, a new syndrome, that I have termed the noögenic neurosis.[3] It is a neurosis deriving from existential frustration, from despair over the apparent meaninglessness of life. It is a neurosis that is not to be traced back to complexes or to conflicts between the ego and the superego, etc., but to spiritual and existential problems, and last but not least to the existential vacuum—to the sense of meaninglessness that is overwhelming so many people today.

James C. Crumbaugh,[4] the research director of an American hospital, has worked out a special test that he calls the PIL (Purpose in Life) test in order to differentiate diagnostically the neuroses in the traditional or conventional sense—that is to say, psychogenic neuroses—from the new, the noögenic neuroses. He has now obtained results from nearly twelve hundred subjects and the results show that the noögenic neurosis may well be differentiated from the conventional type. It is a new syndrome and it is by no means completely identical with the human condition. Based on similar results obtained in Europe and America, it would appear that about 20 per cent of neurotic cases should properly be diagnosed as noögenic.

As a kind of first aid in such cases, it seems to me to be necessary to show young people that their despair over the apparent meaninglessness of life is nothing to be ashamed of, but rather it is something of which to be proud. It is a human achievement because it is a prerogative of man not to take for granted that there is a meaning to life, but rather to venture to question this meaning. It is his prerogative not only to quest for meaning, but even to question it and to challenge the meaning of life. It is right if young people have the courage to do this. However, they should also have patience enough to wait until, sooner or later, meaning becomes clear to them, rather than commit suicide immediately out of this existential despair. In the first place, they should recognize that the fact that they venture to question the meaning of life is, after all, the manifestation of intellectual sincerity and honesty. Therefore it is truly something of which to be proud. However, they must first objectify; they must gain perspective by viewing this overwhelming

[2]Frankl, V. E. (1962) *Man's Search for Meaning, an Introduction to Logotherapy.* Boston, Beacon Press.

[3]Frankl, V. E. (1965) *The Doctor and the Soul.* New York, Alfred A. Knopf.

[4]Crumbaugh, J. C., and L. T. Maholick (1967) An experimental study in existentialism: The psychometric approach to Frankl's concept of noögenic neurosis. *In:* Frankl, V. E. *Psychotherapy and Existentialism.* New York, Simon and Schuster.

problem from a distance. This in itself is beneficial in terms of mental hygiene. And they must realize the positive aspect, the fact that their questioning is something to be proud of.

The existential vacuum might also be understood and explained and interpreted as the frustration of what I personally regard to be the primary motivational force operant in man. As a deliberate oversimplification, I have called this the will to meaning.[5] Heuristically and for didactic purposes, it is opposed to the will to power (the concept that plays such an important rôle in the neurosis theory offered by Alfred Adler's individual psychology) and to the pleasure principle on which the whole psychoanalytic system developed by Freud is still based. Freud also recognized a reality principle counteracting, in a way, the operations and the strivings of the pleasure principle, but this does not alter this state of affairs because, according to Freud's own explicit statement, the reality principle is a servant and also seeks pleasure, delayed but secure pleasure. Nevertheless, psychoanalysis is still based on the validity of that concept called the pleasure principle.

You might conceive of the pleasure principle as a will to pleasure. There is, as I have mentioned, the will to power, and I have introduced the concept of a will to meaning by which I really mean the intrinsic self-transcendent quality of human existence. It is my contention that being human always points or is directed toward something other than itself, or to someone other than oneself. I deny that man really, basically, is striving to obtain, establish, or restore any state within himself. Such a concept is a monadologistic concept of man. It is a concept of man along the lines of a closed system. Man, on the contrary, is primarily reaching out for a meaning to fulfil out there in the world, reaching out to encounter another human being out there in the world, but he is never primarily concerned with anything within himself.

This is the basic feature of human existence, this self-transcendence as I call it, and it is only after man has once renounced his primary strivings that he comes back, he returns, and reflects upon himself. I would venture to say that whenever we observe in human beings the prevalence of a will to

power and/or a will to pleasure rather than a will to meaning, it indicates that we are dealing with substitutes. The frustrated will to meaning makes a man long for pleasure and/or power, but primary man is concerned with finding and fulfilling a meaning out there in the world, with encountering other beings. Man is never concerned primarily with himself but, by virtue of his self-transcendent quality, he endeavours to serve a cause higher than himself, or to love another person. Loving and serving a cause on the command of one's conscience are the principal manifestations of this self-transcendent quality of human existence that has been totally neglected by closed-system concepts such as the homeostasis principle. This principle is based on the presupposition that an organism, and also the human psyche, are primarily concerned with and striving to maintain or restore an inner equilibrium, a state without tension, regardless of whether these tensions are aroused by inner drives and instincts, by still unsatisfied needs, or by the clashes between ego and superego or between the interests of the societal environment and those of one's own psyche. This homeostasis principle has already been abandoned for many years, even in biology, as Ludwig von Bertalanffy in Canada could show. In neurology it was disproved and abandoned by the late Kurt Goldstein, the brain pathologist, and in psychology by the late Gordon Allport, by Charlotte Buhler and by Abraham Maslow. In education, however, it is still presupposed as a valid tenet.

This self-transcendent quality of human existence gives rise to a fact which a clinician can observe day by day, namely that the pleasure principle is actually self-defeating. In other words the "pursuit of happiness"[6] is self-defeating; it is a contradiction in itself. I daresay that precisely to the extent to which an individual sets out to pursue or to strive directly for happiness, to this same extent he cannot attain it. The more he strives to attain it, the further he misses it. How can this be understood?

Once a man has a reason to be happy, whether he has fulfilled a meaning or has lovingly encountered another human being, this makes him happy. Happiness ensues, happiness happens, and one must let happi-

[5]Frankl, V. E. (1969) *The Will to Meaning.* New York, The World Publishing Company.

[6]Fabry, J. E. (1968) *The Pursuit of Meaning: Logotherapy Applied to Life.* Boston, Beacon Press.

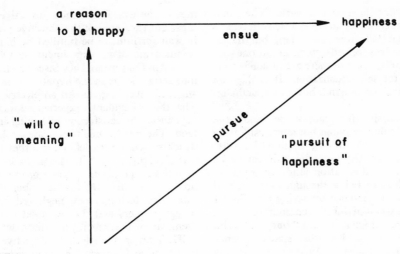

FIGURE 1.

ness happen. What happens when a man strives directly for happiness? As illustrated by Figure 1, the more he pays attention to happiness or the more he embarks on a direct quest for happiness, precisely to this extent he loses sight of the reason to be happy and, consequently, happiness fades away because for him there is no longer any reason to be happy. He has shut out the reason for happiness. He no longer cares for meaning, for other beings; he cares for happiness by way of a direct intention. This we observe in sexual neuroses. I venture to say, based on decades of practice, that more than 95 per cent of the cases of impotence or frigidity may well be traced back to the fact that the male patient is directly striving to demonstrate his potency and the female patient is directly striving to demonstrate to herself that she is capable of experiencing full orgasm. They are striving for happiness instead of letting happiness happen. They are "pursuing" happiness instead of letting happiness occur as a side effect. Pleasure is a side effect, not the goal, of human strivings; it is the side effect of fulfilling meaning, the side effect of a loving encounter with another human being. The moment one strives directly to attain pleasure, the goal is missed, because primarily man is concerned with a reason to become happy rather than with being happy. He is concerned with other human beings, with meanings; he is transcending himself rather than being a closed system that simply cares about

reinstating in his brain or psyche a certain condition called pleasure, or homeostasis, or whatever concepts have been developed in the setting of those monadologistic concepts that treat man as if he were a closed system. In other words, happiness ensues as a side effect of fulfilling a meaning, of encountering another human being, of living out this self-transcendent quality of a human being, but it fades away to the extent that it is pursued or directly sought.

The two outstanding classical schools of psychotherapy developed the will to pleasure concept and the will to power concept when *both had to deal with neurotic individuals.* Only those neurotic people who have been frustrated in their primary and original striving for the fulfillment of meaning, only those frustrated personalities are either intent on pleasure or content with power. They are intent on the effect rather than on the primary goal, or content with the means to the end because they have been frustrated in their strivings for the end itself, which is meaning.

The self-defeating quality of a direct striving for a side effect rather than a concern with the primary goal of human existence that is dictated by its self-transcendent quality, recurs in matters that are widely discussed. I am referring to the slogan of self-actualization. Self-transcendence implies that man is not capable of directly striving for self-actualization. One can actualize oneself only to the extent to which one is fulfilling a meaning out there in the world. Then self-actualization occurs, again as a side effect. It is a gift that falls into one's lap, but if one directly strives for self-actualization, one cannot obtain it, because there are no longer any grounds for self-actualization. If he has not fulfilled the task at hand, how can he actualize himself?

Self-actualization cannot be made the target of human strivings but must result from other sources, among which is self-transcendence through the fulfillment of meaning, or dedication and devotion to another human being through love. I could put it in one sentence by saying that Pindar was right when giving the admonition, "You should become what you are," but this is valid only when you add another statement once made by Karl Jaspers: "What a man is he only becomes through that cause which he has made his own."

We started with the proposition that the traditional values are on the wane, so let us ask ourselves whether it is not justifiable to contend that life is meaningless. This is not true because there is a distinction between values and meanings. Only values are affected by the wane of traditions, while meanings are spared. Values, I would say, are universal meanings. But meanings themselves are unique insofar as they refer to a unique person engaged in a unique situation. Meanings change from moment to moment, from situation to situation, and from person to person.

Meanings are unique and in this sense it might well be said that meanings are relative. They relate to a situation and to a person involved in this situation. The question is now raised whether they are also subjective, as is generally contended. Max Wertheimer, the founder of Gestalt psychology, once said explicitly that the requirement of a situation, that is to say what the situation means to the individual, is an objective quality. My great teacher, the late Rudolf Allers of Georgetown University (a philosopher rather than an experimental psychologist), was more cautious in just saying that it is a trans-subjective quality. Meanings, I would say, are objective in that they must be responsibly discovered rather than arbitrarily invented. (This, of course, is opposed to a view such as that developed by Jean-Paul Sartre.)

Incidentally, there are also subjective meanings. The person who is in the intoxicated state induced by LSD attributes meanings to the world. He finds subjective meanings, but they are not the objective meanings in wait for him, to be fulfilled by him. This reminds me of an experiment by Olds and Milner in California. They inserted electrodes into certain spots in the hypothalamus of rats and whenever they closed an electric circuit what the rats evidently experienced was sexual orgasm or the satisfaction of having ingested food. The rats learned to activate the lever by which the circuit was closed and they pressed this lever up to fifty thousand times a day, each time experiencing orgasm or the satisfaction of nutrition. After they obtained this subjective feeling, they neglected the real sexual partners and the real food offered to them. It is the same with those who take LSD. They may neglect the objective meanings waiting for them (the unique meanings they have to find) because they have restricted themselves merely to attributing meanings—profoundly subjective meanings—and they bypass their actual, their true, meanings and assignments (out there in the world) by only caring for subjective meanings.

In an age like ours, an age of the existential vacuum, man must be equipped with the capacity to discover meaning, to find for himself the individual meanings of the singular situations that together form a string called human life. He must be equipped with the means to find meaning in an age of meaninglessness. It is the particular task and assignment of education not only to content itself with transmitting traditions and values and knowledge, but also to see as one of its principal assignments the development and refining of that capacity always to find out, to smell out, the unique meanings of a given situation. This capacity is called conscience. In an age in which the Ten Commandments apparently are losing their unconditional validity for so many people, more than ever man must be equipped with the capacity to listen to the ten thousand commandments involved in the ten thousand of his life situations and mediated by his conscience. In other words, education must refine and sharpen the capacity of man to hear the voice of his conscience. Only when man has this capacity is he capable of counteracting those two effects which result from the existential vacuum—conformism and totalitarianism. Only a man with a vivid and alert conscience is capable of resisting totalitarianism and conformism.

We often see that, instead of embarking on

this business of refining man's conscience, education is rather reinforcing the existential vacuum in the young people. This occurs as a result of that reductionism along the lines of which science is so often taught on campuses. I remember when I was thirteen years of age, in junior high school, our science teacher walked up and down the rows and taught or offered us the definition of what life ultimately is. "In the final analysis," he said, "Life is nothing but a combustion, an oxidation process." Without asking permission, I sprang to my feet and threw the question into his face, "If this is true, then, Dr. Fritz, what meaning does life have?" It is a typical reductionist theory that life is nothing but an oxidation process. Actually, it is an example of oxidationism rather than reductionism.

In the United States the trend toward reductionist indoctrination is even more observable than it is elsewhere. At the University of Vienna, I found, for example, that 40 per cent of the German, Swiss, and Austrian students attending my lectures confessed that they had experienced this existential despair over the apparent meaninglessness of their own lives. In comparison, in a similar sample of American students attending my lectures, fully 81 per cent reported that they had experienced despair of this kind. I would say that the high incidence of existential despair among American students stems largely from the prevalence in the United States of the reductionist way of presenting facts and scientific data.

What is reductionism? I would define it thus: Reductionism is a pseudoscientific procedure according to which a human phenomenon (such as love or conscience) is made into a mere epiphenomenon. It is thereby deprived of its very humanness. More specifically, human phenomena are deprived of their very humanness by being dynamically reduced to, or genetically deduced from, essentially subhuman phenomena. In other words, reductionism is a subhumanism.

Let me give an example. If love is defined as the sublimation of sex, it is reduced from a human phenomenon to a subhuman phenomenon, sexual instinct. Actually, love is not and never can be the mere sublimation of sex, simply because whenever sublimation is to take place the capacity to love is presupposed. In the final analysis, a person is capable of integrating his sexuality into the whole makeup of his personality only for the sake of another person whom he loves. Stated somewhat differently, the ego is capable of integrating its id only to the extent that it is lovingly directed toward a thou. Therefore, if sublimation of sex is only possible on the basis of the capacity to love, love can never be the result of sublimation.

As to conscience, something similar must be said by way of criticism. In the same way as love has been reduced to the id (sexuality) conscience is often reduced to or even identified with the superego, but there is an essential difference. Conscience can never be identical with or reduced to the superego simply because it is not the last and certainly not the least assignment of true conscience to contradict and oppose precisely those conventions and ideals and traditions that are channelled and transmitted through the superego. Thus if the superego must sometimes be contradicted and opposed by the conscience, the conscience cannot be identical with the superego.

Time and again it is said that conscience is the result of conditioning processes. This might be correct when it is applied, for example, to a dog that has wet the floor and then slinks under the couch with its tail between its legs. The animal undoubtedly displays something that resembles conscience, but it is not true conscience. I would say it is anticipatory anxiety, the fearful expectation of punishment, and this might well be the result of certain conditioning processes. When a man "hears the voice of his conscience," however, this has nothing to do with fear of punishment. This is something different, and it is only when this difference comes to the fore that the human dimension has been entered and the human quality of this phenomenon called conscience has been envisaged at all.

There are many persons who presuppose that, if there is anything such as conscience, it must be explainable in terms of the conditioning processes observable in animals. They reduce conscience to a conditioning process by their *a priori* assumption that what is human can be explained along the lines of animal psychology and animal behaviour. In this connection I am reminded of a Viennese joke about two neighbours who were quarrelling because one said that the other's cat had eaten two pounds of butter. The other neighbour denied that the cat ever ate butter and they went to the rabbi, asking him for a Solomonic judgment.

The rabbi pondered and said, "So you contend that two pounds of butter have been eaten by this cat?"

"Yes, two pounds of butter."

"Bring me the cat."

They brought him the cat. "Bring me scales," he said.

They brought him the scales and the rabbi put the cat on the scales and, believe it or not, the weight was exactly two pounds.

"Now I have the butter," said the rabbi, "but where is the cat?"

There was the *a priori* conviction on the part of the rabbi that if there is something which weighs two pounds it must be butter. Then he was searching in vain for the cat. The same is true of the animal behaviourists; they say that if there is anything in man it must be explainable by way of animal behaviour—reflexes, conditioning processes—and they have their conditioning processes, but where then is man? The *a priorism* which contradicts any true empiricism rests with the scientists who are reductionists rather than with the man who envisages the full scope of what is going on in man, who experiences conscience not as a conditioning process, but as something he has to follow because of his humanness—unless he just does away with his own humanness, and this would be contradicting his own self.

Why are we more and more confronted with reductionistically oriented scientists? This is because we are living in an age of specialists. I would say that a specialist is a man who no longer sees the forest of truth for the trees of facts. In other words, he is concerned with the scattered facts and data furnished by a compartmentalized science and is no longer capable of arriving at a unified concept of man.[7]

The problem is whether disparate visions of man, or of a particular phenomenon in man, necessarily preclude our arriving at a unified concept of man. They do not. Consider the problem of stereoscopic vision. In stereoscopic vision two different pictures are given to the viewer. The pictures are disparate, but it is precisely this fact that opens up a new dimension—the dimension of space. In other words, the fact that the pictures obtained from scientific research are disparate need not necessarily make for confusion; all that is needed is what in physiology is called the fusion of the pictures at the retina. In other words, the fact that the pictures provided by science are disparate need not result in loss of knowledge, but may produce a gain in knowledge, provided that we arrive at a fusion of the pictures which leads us to a unified *Weltanschauung*, or concept of man.

We cannot reverse the wheel of history; society cannot do without the specialist today. The style of modern research is profoundly characterized by what is called teamwork, that is by cooperative effort by teams of specialists. As I see it, the ultimate threat and danger do not lie in the fact that scientists more and more are specializing. The loss and consequent lack of universality are not what makes for reductionism. It is rather the totality of knowledge pretended by those specialists that makes for reductionism. In other words, we do not deplore the fact that more and more scientists are specializing, but rather that more and more specialists are generalizing. Specialists are making overgeneralized statements. For example, a biologist who contends that man's human life and existence can be explained entirely on the grounds of his biology, in merely biological terms, is making biology into biologism. Likewise, a specialist may make sociology into sociologism, psychology into psychologism, and so forth. At the very moment when we make such an overgeneralized statement on man, at the same moment we have turned our science into a mere idealogy. In other words, what has been called the *terrible simplificateur* may well be complemented by a notion of the *terrible généralisateur*.

For instance "Man is nothing but a computer" is an overgeneralized statement. As a neurologist, I can vouch for the legitimacy of using the model of a computer as an analogy to explain the mode of functioning of the human central nervous system. But the error is in the phrase "nothing but" which is not true because man is infinitely more than a computer.

Formerly, nihilism was masked behind the term "nothingness." Today nihilism unmasks itself by the use of the phrase "nothing but." This is the "nothing-butness" that characterizes nihilism today and it should not be confounded with existentialism. The true

[7]Frankl, V. E. (1965) The concept of man in logotherapy. *In:* Dreyer, P.S., and S.J. Schoeman, eds. *Homo Viator: Fecsbundel Oberholzer.* Cape Town, Hollandsch Afrikaansche Uitgevers Maatschappij.

message delivered by existentialism is by no means the nothingness of man. I would say the true message of existentialism is the "nothingness" of man, the idea that a human being is not a thing, that a human being must never be reified, never totally objectified.

Let me return to reductionism. The devastating impact of an indoctrination along the lines of reductionism must not be underrated. Here I confine myself to quoting from a study by R. N. Gray and associates on 64 physicians, 11 of them psychiatrists. The study showed that during medical school, cynicism as a rule increases while humanitarianism decreases. Only after completion of medical studies is this trend reversed but unfortunately not in all subjects. Ironically, the author of the paper which reports these results, himself defines man as nothing but "an adaptive control system" and defines values as "homeostatic restraints in a stimulus-response process." According to another reductionist definition of values, they are nothing but reaction formations and defence mechanisms. My reaction to this theory was that I am not prepared to live for the sake of my reaction formations, even less to die for the sake of my defence mechanisms. Such reductionist interpretations are likely to undermine and erode the appreciation of values. As an exam-

ple, let me report the following observation. A young American couple returned from Africa where they had served as Peace Corps volunteers, completely fed up and disgusted. At the outset, they had had to participate in mandatory group sessions led by a psychologist who played a game somewhat as follows: "Why did you join the Peace Corps?" "We wanted to help people less privileged." "So you must be superior to them." "In a way." "So there must be in you, in your unconscious, a need to prove to yourself that you are superior." "Well, I never thought of it that way but you are a psychologist, you certainly know better." And so it went on. The group was indoctrinated in interpreting their idealism and altruism as hang-ups. Even worse, the volunteers "were constantly on each other's backs, playing the 'what's *your* hidden motive' game," according to the report of a Fulbright fellow who studied in Vienna at my hospital last year. Here we are dealing with an instance of what I would call hyper-interpretation. Unmasking is perfectly legitimate but it must stop as soon as one is confronted with what is genuine, genuinely human, in man. If it does not, the only thing that is unmasked is the unmasking psychologist's own "hidden motive," namely, his unconscious need to belittle the greatness of man.

28 Existential Psychology

Rollo May

Existentialism means centering upon the *existing* person; it is the emphasis on the human being as he is *emerging, becoming*. The word "existence" comes from the root *ex-sistere*, meaning literally "to stand out, emerge." Traditionally in Western culture, *existence* has been set over against *essence*, the latter being the emphasis upon immutable principles, truth, logical laws, etc., that are supposed to stand above any given existence. In endeavoring to separate reality into its discrete parts and to formulate abstract laws for these parts,

Western science has by and large been *essentialist* in character; mathematics is the ultimate, pure form of this essentialist approach. In psychology, the endeavors to see human beings in terms of forces, drives, conditioned reflexes, and so on illustrate the approach via essences.

The emphasis on essences was dominant in Western thought and science—with such notable exceptions, to name only a few, as Socrates, Augustine, and Pascal—until roughly a hundred years ago. The "peak" was reached, the most systematic and comprehensive expression of "essentialism," in Hegel's pan-rationalism, an endeavor to encompass all reality in a system of concepts that identified reality with abstract thought. It was against

Hegel that Kierkegaard, and later Nietzsche, revolted so strenuously.

But in the decades since World War I, the existential approach has emerged from the status of stepchild of Western culture to a dominant position in the center of Western art, literature, theology, and philosophy. It has gone hand in hand with the new developments in science, particularly the physics of Bohr and Heisenberg.

The extreme of the existentialist position is found in Jean Paul Sartre's statement that "existence precedes essence," the assertion that only as we affirm our existence do we have any essence at all. This is a consistent part of Sartre's great emphasis on decision: "We *are* our choices."

My own position, and that of most psychologists who appreciate the great value of this existential revolution, is not so extreme as Sartre's. "Essences" must not be ruled out—they are presupposed in logic, mathematical forms, and other aspects of truth which are not dependent upon any individual's decision or whim. But that is not to say that you can adequately describe or understand a living human being, or any living organism, on an "essentialist" basis. *There is no such thing as truth or reality for a living human being except as he participates in it, is conscious of it, has some relationship to it.* We can demonstrate at every moment of the day in our psychotherapeutic work that only the truth that comes alive, becomes more than an abstract idea, and is "felt on the pulse," only the truth that is genuinely experienced on all levels of being, including what is called subconscious and unconscious and never excluding the element of conscious decision and responsibility—only this truth has the power to change a human being.

The existentialist emphasis in psychology does not, therefore, deny the validity of the approaches based on conditioning, the formulation of drives, the study of discrete mechanisms, and so on. It only holds that you can never explain or understand any *living* human being on that basis. And the harm arises when the image of man, the presuppositions about man himself are exclusively based on such methods. There seems to be the following "law" at work: the more accurately and comprehensively you can describe a given mechanism, the more you lose the existing person. *The more absolutely and completely you formulate the forces or drives, the more you are talking about abstractions and not the existing, living human being.* For the living person (who is not hypnotized or drugged or in some other way placed in an artificial position, such as in a laboratory, in which his element of decision and his responsibility for his own existence are temporarily suspended for the purposes of the experiment) always transcends the given mechanism and always experiences the "drive" and "force" in his unique way. The distinction is whether the "person has meaning in terms of the mechanism" or the "mechanism has meaning in terms of the person." The existential emphasis is firmly on the latter. And it holds that the former can be integrated within the latter.

True, the term "existentialist" is dubious and confused these days, associated as it is with the beatnik movement at one extreme and with esoteric, untranslatable, Germanic, philosophical concepts at the other. True also, the movement collects the "lunatic fringe" groups—to which existential psychology and psychiatry are by no means immune. I often ask myself whether in some quarters the term has become so dubious as to be no longer useful. But "existence" does have the important historical meanings outlined above and probably, therefore, can and ought to be saved from its deteriorated forms.

In psychology and psychiatry, the term demarcates an *attitude*, an approach to human beings, rather than a special school or group. It is doubtful whether it makes sense to speak of "*an* existential psychologist or psychotherapist" in contradistinction to other schools; it is not a system of therapy but an attitude toward therapy, not a set of new techniques but a concern with the understanding of the structure of the human being and his experience that must underlie all techniques. This is why it makes sense, if I may say so without being misunderstood, to say that every psychotherapist is existential to the extent that he is a good therapist, i.e., that he is able to grasp the patient in his reality and is characterized by the kinds of understanding and presence that will be discussed below.

I wish, after these sallies at definition, to *be* existentialist in this essay and to speak directly from my own experience as a person and as a practicing psychoanalytic psychotherapist. Some fifteen years ago, when I was working on my book, *The Meaning of Anxiety*, I spent a year and a half in bed in a tuberculosis sanitorium. I had a great deal of time to ponder the meaning of anxiety—and plenty of first hand data in myself and my fellow patients. In the course of this time, I studied the only two books written on anxiety till our day, *The Problem of Anxiety* by Freud and *The Concept of Dread* by Kierkegaard. I valued Freud's formulations: namely, his first theory, that anxiety is the re-emergence of repressed libido, and his second, that anxiety is the ego's reaction to the threat of the loss of the loved object. Kierkegaard, on the other hand, described anxiety as the struggle of the living being against non-being—which I could immediately experience there in my struggle with death or the prospect of being a life-long invalid. He went on to point out that the real terror in anxiety is not this death as such, but the fact that each of us within himself is on both sides of the fight, that "anxiety is a desire for what one dreads," as he put it; thus, like an "alien power it lays hold of an individual, and yet one cannot tear one's self away."

What struck me powerfully then, was that Kierkegaard was writing about *exactly what my fellow patients and I were going through.* Freud was not; he was writing on a different level, giving formulations of the psychic mechanisms by which anxiety comes about. Kierkegaard was portraying what is immediately experienced by human beings in crisis. It was, specifically, the crisis of life against death, which was completely real to us patients, but he was writing about a crisis that I believe is not in its essential form different from the various crises of people who come for therapy, or the crises that all of us experience in much more minute form a dozen times a day, even though we push the ultimate prospect of death far from our minds. Freud was writing on the technical level, where his genius was supreme; perhaps more than any man up to his time, he *knew about anxiety.* Kierkegaard, a genius of a different order, was writing on the existential, ontological level; he *knew anxiety.*

This is not a value dichotomy; obviously both are necessary. Our real problem, rather, is given us by our cultural-historical situation. We in the Western world are the heirs of four centuries of technical achievement in power over nature and now over ourselves; this is our greatness and, at the same time, it is also our greatest peril. We are not in danger of repressing the technical emphasis (of which Freud's tremendous popularity in this country is proof if any were necessary). But rather we repress the opposite. If I may use terms which I shall be discussing and defining more fully later, we repress the *sense of being,* the *ontological sense.* One consequence of this repression of the sense of being is that modern man's image of himself, his experience and concept of himself as a responsible individual have likewise disintegrated.

I make no apologies in admitting that I take very seriously, as will have been evident already, the dehumanizing dangers in our tendency in modern science to make man over into the image of the machine, into the image of the techniques by which we study him. This tendency is not the fault of any "dangerous" men or "vicious" schools; it is rather a crisis brought upon us by our particular historical predicament. Karl Jaspers, both psychiatrist and existentialist philosopher, holds that we are actually in process of losing self-consciousness and that we may well be in the last age of historical man. William Whyte, in his *Organization Man,* cautions that modern man's enemies may turn out to be a "mild-looking group of therapists, who . . . would be doing what they did to help you." He refers here to the tendency to use the social sciences in support of the social ethic of our historical period; and thus the process of helping people may actually make them conform and tend toward the destruction of individuality. We cannot brush aside the cautions of such men as unintelligent or antiscientific; to try to do so would make *us* the obscurantists. There is a real possibility that we may be helping the individual adjust and be happy at the price of loss of his being.

One may agree with my sentiments here but hold that the existentialist approach, with these terms "being" and "non-being," may not be of much help. Some readers will already have concluded that their suspicion was only too right, that this so-called existential approach to psychology is hopelessly vague and horribly muddled. Carl Rogers remarks in a later chapter that many American psychologists must find these terms abhorrent because they sound so general, so philosophical, so untestable. Rogers goes on to point out, however, that he had no difficulty in putting the existential principles in therapy into empirically testable hypotheses.

But I would go further and hold that *without* some concepts of "being" and "non-being" we cannot even understand our most commonly used psychological mechanisms.

Take for example, *repression, resistance,* and *transference.* The usual discussions of these terms hang in midair, it seems to me, unconvincing and psychologically unreal, precisely because we have lacked an underlying structure on which to base them. The term "repression," for example, obviously refers to a phenomenon we observe all the time, a dynamism which Freud clearly, and in many forms, described. The mechanism is generally explained by saying that the child represses into unconsciousness certain impulses, such as sex and hostility, because the culture, in the form of parental figures, disapproves, and the child must protect his own security with those figures. But this culture which assumedly disapproves is made up of the very same people who do the repressing. Is it not an illusion, therefore, and much too simple to speak of the culture over and against the individual in such fashion and to make it our whipping boy? Furthermore, where did we get the idea that children or adults are so concerned with security and libidinal satisfactions? Are these not carryovers from our work with the *neurotic, anxious* child and the *neurotic* adult?

Certainly the neurotic, anxious child *is* compulsively concerned with security, for example; and certainly the neurotic adult, and we who study him, read our later formulations back into the unsuspecting mind of the child. But is not the normal child just as truly interested in moving out into the world, exploring, following his curiosity and sense of adventure—going out "to learn to shiver and to shake," as the nursery rhyme puts it? And if you block these needs of the child, do you not get a traumatic reaction from him just as you do when you take away his security? I, for one, believe we vastly overemphasize the human being's concern with security and survival satisfactions because they so neatly fit our cause-and-effect way of thinking. I believe Nietzsche and Kierkegaard were more accurate when they described man as *the organism who makes certain values—prestige, power, tenderness, love—more important than pleasure and even more important than survival itself.*†

†This is the point Binswanger is making in the case of *Ellen West,* translated in the volume *Existence.* By means of the discussion of the psychological illness and suicide of Ellen West, he asks whether there are times when an existence, in order to fulfill itself, must destroy its existence. In this case, Binswanger, like so many of his European psychiatric and psy-

The implication of our argument here is that we can understand such a mechanism as repression, for example, only on the deeper level of the meaning of the human being's potentialities. In this respect, "being" is to be defined as the *individual's unique pattern of potentialities.* These potentialities will be partly shared with other individuals but will in every case form a unique pattern for this particular person.

We must ask these questions, therefore, if we are to understand repression in a given person: What is this person's relation to his own potentialities? What goes on that he chooses, or is forced to choose, to block off from his awareness something that he knows, and on another level *knows that he knows?* In my own work in psychotherapy, there appears more and more evidence that anxiety in our day arises not so much out of fear of lack of libidinal satisfactions or security, but rather out of the patient's fear of his own powers and the conflicts that arise from that fear. This may well be the particular "neurotic personality of our time"—the neurotic pattern of contemporary "outer-directed," organizational man.

The "unconscious," then, is not to be thought of as a reservoir of impulses, thoughts, and wishes that are culturally unac-

chological colleagues, discusses a case for the purpose of delving into the understanding of some problem about human beings rather than for the purpose of illustrating how the case should or should not be managed therapeutically. In presenting the case, we assumed, as editors of *Existence,* that it, like the other cases, would be understood on the basis of the purposes and assumptions of its authors in writing it; this was an unrealistic assumption. The case is almost universally discussed—and from that point of view justly criticized—in this country from the point of view of what therapy should have been given Ellen West. If it had been Binswanger's purpose to discuss techniques of therapy, he would not have taken a case from the archives of four and a half decades ago in his sanatorium. He seeks, rather, to ask this most profound of all questions: Does the human being have needs and values that transcend its own survival, and are there not situations when the existence, in order to fulfill itself, needs to destroy itself? The implication of this question is in the most radical way to question simple adaptation, length of life, and survival as ultimate goals. It is similar to Nietzsche's point referred to above, and also similar to Maslow's emphasis when he brings out that the "self-actualizing personalities" that he studied resist acculturation.

ceptable. I define it rather as *those potentialities for knowing and experiencing that the individual cannot or will not actualize.* On this level, we shall find that the simple mechanism of repression, which we blithely started with, is infinitely less simple than it looks; that it involves a complex struggle of the individual's *being* against the possibility of *non-being;* that it cannot be adequately comprehended in "ego" and "not-ego" terms, or even "self" and "not-self"; and that it inescapably raises the question of the human being's freedom with respect to his own potentialities. This margin of freedom must be assumed if one is to deal with an existing person. In this margin resides the individual's responsibility for himself, which even the therapist cannot take away.

Thus, every mechanism or dynamism, every force or drive, presupposes an underlying structure that is infinitely greater than the mechanism, drive, or force itself. And note that I do not say it is the "sum total" of the mechanisms, et cetera. It is not the "sum total," though it includes all the mechanisms, drives, or forces: it is the underlying structure from which they derive their meaning. This structure is, to use one definition proposed above, the *pattern of potentiality* of the living individual man *of whom* the mechanism is one expression; the given mechanism is one of a multitude of ways in which he actualizes his potentiality. Surely, you can abstract a given mechanism like "repression" or "regression" for study and arrive at formulations of forces and drives which seem to be operative; but your study will have meaning only if you say at every point, "I am abstracting such and such a form of behavior," and if you also make clear at every point *what* you are abstracting *from,* namely the living man who *has* these experiences, the man *to whom* these things happen.

In a similar vein, I have, for a number of years, been struck, as a practicing therapist and teacher of therapists, by now often our concern with trying to understand the patient in terms of the mechanisms by which his behavior takes place blocks our understanding of what he really is experiencing. Here is a patient, Mrs. Hutchens, who comes into my office for the first time, a suburban woman in her middle thirties, who tries to keep her expression poised and sophisticated. But no one could fail to see in her eyes something of the terror of a frightened animal or a lost child. I know from what her neurological specialists have already told me, that her presenting problem is hysterical tenseness of the larynx, as a result of which she can talk only with a perpetual hoarseness. I have been given the hypothesis from her Rorschach that she has felt all her life, "If I say what I really feel, I'll be rejected; under these conditions it is better not to talk at all." During this first hour with her, I also get some hints of the genetic *why* of her problem as she tells me of her authoritarian relation with her mother and grandmother and of *how* she learned to guard firmly against telling any secrets at all.

But if, as I sit here, I am chiefly thinking of these *whys* and *hows* of the way the problem came about, I will have grasped everything *except the most important thing of all, the existing person.* Indeed, I will have grasped everything except the only real souce of data I have, namely, this experiencing human being, this person now emerging, becoming, "building world," as the existential psychologists put it, immediately in this room with me.

This is where *phenomenology*, the first stage in the existential psychotherapeutic movement, has been a helpful breakthrough for many of us. Phenomenology is the endeavor to take the phenomena as given. It is the disciplined effort to clear one's mind of the presuppositions that so often cause us to see in the patient only our own theories or the dogmas of our own systems, the effort to experience instead the phenomena in their full reality as they present themselves. It is the attitude of openness and readiness to hear—aspects of the art of listening in psychotherapy that are generally taken for granted and sound so easy but are exceedingly difficult.

Note that we say *experience* the phenomena and not *observe;* for we need to be able, as far as possible, to catch what the patient is communicating on many different levels; these include not only the words he utters but his facial expressions, his gestures, the distance from us at which he sits, various feelings which he will have and communicate subtly to the therapist and will serve as messages even though he cannot verbalize them directly, ad infinitum. And there is always a great deal of subliminal communication on levels below what either the patient or therapist may be conscious of at the moment. This points toward a controversial area in therapy which is most difficult in the training and practice of therapists, but which is unavoidable because it is so important, namely, subliminal, empathic, "telepathic" communication. We shall not go into it here; I wish only to say this experiencing of the communications of the patient on many different levels at once is one aspect of what the existential psychiatrists like Binswanger call *presence*.

Phenomenology requires an "attitude of disciplined naïveté," in Robert MacLeod's phrase. And commenting on this phrase, Albert Wellek adds his own, "an ability to *experience critically*." It is not possible, in my judgment, to listen to any words or even to give one's attention to anything without some assumed concepts, some constructs in one's own mind by which he hears, by which he orients himself in his world at that moment. But the important terms "disciplined" in MacLeod's phrase and "critically" in Wellek's refer, I take it, to the difficult attainment of objectivity—that while one must have constructs as he listens, one's aim in therapy is to make one's own constructs sufficiently flexible so that he can listen in terms of the patient's constructs and hear in the patient's language.

Phenomenology has many complex ramifications, particularly as developed by Edmund Husserl, who decisively influenced not only the philosophers Heidegger and Sartre but also the psychiatrists Minkowski, Straus, and Binswanger, the psychologists Buytendijk, Merleau-Ponty, and many others. We shall not go into these ramifications here.

Sometimes the phenomenological emphasis in psychotherapy is used as a disparagement of the learning of technique or as a reason for not studying the problems of diagnosis and clinical dynamics. I think this is an error. What is important, rather, is to apprehend the fact that the technical and diagnostic concerns are on a different level from the understanding that takes place in the immediate encounter in therapy. The mistake is in confusing them or letting one absorb the other. The student and practicing psychologist must steer his course between the Scylla of letting knowledge of techniques be a substitute for direct understanding and communication with the patient and the Charybdis of assuming that he acts in a rarified atmosphere of clinical purity without any constructs at all.

Certainly it is true that students learning therapy often become preoccupied with techniques; this is the strongest anxiety-allaying mechanism available to them in the turmoil-fraught encounters in psychotherapy. Indeed, one of the strongest motivations for dogmatism and rigid formulations among psychotherapeutic and analytic schools of all sorts lies right here—the technical dogma protects the psychologist and psychiatrist from their own anxiety. But to that extent, the techniques also protect the psychologist or psychiatrist from understanding the patient; they block him off from the full presence in the encounter which is essential to understanding what is going on. One student in a case seminar on existential psychotherapy put it succinctly when he remarked that the chief thing he had learned was that "understanding does not follow knowledge of dynamics."

There is, however, a danger of "wild eclecticism" in these phenomenological and existential approaches to therapy when they are used without the rigorous clinical study and thought which precedes any expertness. Knowledge of techniques and the rigorous study of dynamics in the training of the psychotherapist should be presupposed. Our situation is analogous to the artist: long and expert training is necessary, but if, at the moment of painting, the artist is preoccupied with technique or technical questions—a preoccupation every artist knows arises exactly at those points at which some anxiety overtakes him—he can be sure nothing creative will go on. Diagnosis is a legitimate and necessary function, particularly at the beginning of therapy; but it is a function different from the therapy itself and requires a different attitude and orientation to the patient. There is something to be said for the attitude that once one gets into therapy with a patient and has decided on the general direction, one forgets for the time being the diagnostic question. By the same token, questions of technique will arise in the therapist's mind from time to time as the therapy proceeds, and one of the characteristics of existential psychotherapy is that the technique changes. These changes will not be hit and miss, however, but will depend on the needs of the patient at given times.

If this discussion sounds unconcluded and gives the appearance of straddling the issue of "technique" on one side and "understanding" on the other, the appearance is indeed correct. The whole topic of the "technical-objective" versus the "understanding-subjective" has been on a false dichotomized basis in our psychological and psychiatric discussions. It needs to be restated on the basis of the concept of the existence of the patient as *being-in-the-world*, and the therapist as existing in and participating in this world. I shall not essay such a restatement here, but I wish only to state my conviction that such a reformulation is possible and gives promise of taking us out of our present dichotomy on this topic. And in the meantime, I wish as a practical expedient to take my stand against the nascent antirational tendencies in the existential approach. Though I believe that therapists are born and not made, it inheres in one's integrity to be cognizant of the fact that there also is a great deal we can learn!

Another question that has perennially perplexed many of us in psychology has already been implied above, and we now turn to it explicitly. What are the presuppositions which underlie our science and our practice? I do not say "scientific method" here; already a good deal of attention has been paid, and rightly, to the problem of methodology. But every method is based on certain presuppositions—assumptions about the nature of man, the nature of his experience, and so forth. These presuppositions are partially conditioned by our culture and by the particular point in history at which we stand. As far as I can see, this crucial area is almost always covered over in psychology: we tend to assume uncritically and implicitly that our particular method is true for all time. The statement that science has built-in self-corrective measures—which is partially true—cannot be taken as a reason for overlooking the fact that our particular science is culturally and historically conditioned and is thereby limited even in its self-corrective measures.

At this point, the existential insistence is that, because every psychology, every way of understanding man, is based upon certain presuppositions, the psychologist must continually analyze and clarify his own presuppositions. One's presuppositions always limit and constrict what one sees in a problem, experiment, or therapeutic situation; from this aspect of our human "finiteness" there is no escape. The naturalist perceives in man what fits his naturalistic spectacles; the positivist sees the aspects of experience that fit the logical forms of his propositions; and it is well known that different therapists of different schools will see in the same dream of a single patient the dynamics that fit the theory

of their particular school The old parable of the blind men and the elephant is writ large on the activities of men in the enlightened twentieth century as well as those of earlier, more "benighted" ages. Bertrand Russell puts the problem well with respect to physical science: "Physics is mathematical not because we know so much about the physical world but because we know so little; it is only its mathematical properties that we can discover."

No one, physicist, psychologist, or anyone else, can leap out of his historically conditioned skin. But the one way we can keep the presuppositions underlying our particular method from undue biasing effect is to know consciously what they are and so not to absolutize or dogmatize them. Thus we have at least a chance of refraining from forcing our subjects or patients upon our "procrustean couches" and lopping off, or refusing to see, what does not fit.

In Ludwig Binswanger's little book relating his conversations and correspondence with Freud, *Sigmund Freud: Reminiscences of a Friendship*, there are some interesting interchanges illustrating this point. The friendship between Freud, the psychoanalyst, and Binswanger, a leading existential psychiatrist of Switzerland, was lifelong and tender, and it marks the only instance of Freud's continuing friendship with someone who differed radically with him.

Shortly before Freud's eightieth birthday, Binswanger wrote an essay describing how Freud's theory had radically deepened clinical psychiatry, but he added that Freud's own existence as a person pointed beyond the deterministic presuppositions of his theory. "Now [with Freud's psychoanalytic contribution] man is no longer merely an animated organism, but a 'living being' who has origins in the finite life process of this earth, and who dies its life and lives its death; illness is no longer an externally or internally caused disturbance of the 'normal' course of a life on the way to its death." But Binswanger went on to point out that as a result of his interest in existential analysis, he believed that in Freud's theory man is not yet man in the full sense of the word:

> . . . for to be a man does not mean merely to be a creature begotten by living-dying life, cast into it and beaten about, and put in high spirits or low spirits by it; it means to be a being that

looks its own and mankind's fate in the face, a being that is "steadfast," i.e., one taking its own stance, or one standing on its own feet. . . . The fact that our lives are determined by the forces of life, is only one side of the truth; the other is that we determine these forces as our fate. Only the two sides together can take in the full problem of sanity and insanity. Those who, like Freud, have forged their fates with the hammer—the work of art he has created in the medium of language is sufficient evidence of this—can dispute this fact least of all.

Then, on the occasion of Freud's eightieth birthday, the Viennese Medical Society invited Binswanger, along with Thomas Mann, to deliver papers at the anniversary celebration. Freud himself did not attend, not being in good health and also, as he wrote Binswanger, not being fond of anniversary celebrations. ("They seem to be on the American model.") Binswanger spent two days with Freud in Vienna at the time of this birthday and remarked that in these conversations he was again impressed by how far Freud's own largeness and depth of humanity as a man surpassed his scientific theories.

In his paper at the celebration, Binswanger gave credit to Freud for having enlarged and deepened our insight into human nature more, perhaps, than anyone since Aristotle. But he went on to point out that these insights wore "a theoretic-scientific garb that as a whole appeared to me too 'one-sided' and narrow." He held that Freud's great contribution was in the area of *homo natura*, man in relation to nature (*Umwelt*)—drives, instincts, and similar aspects of experience. And as a consequence, Binswanger believed that in Freud's theory there was only a shadowy, epiphenomenal understanding of man in relation to his fellowmen (*Mitwelt*) and that the area of man in relation to himself (*Eigenwelt*) was omitted entirely.

Binswanger sent a copy of the paper to Freud and a week later received a letter from him containing the following sentences:

As I read it I was delighted with your beautiful language, your erudition, the vastness of your horizon, your tactfulness in contradicting me. As is well known, one can put up with vast quantities of praise. . . . *Naturally, for all that you have failed to convince me.** I have always

confined myself to the ground floor and basement of the edifice. You maintain that by changing one's point of view, one can also see the upper story, in which dwell such distinguished guests as religion, art, etc. . . . I have already found a place for religion, but putting it under the category of "the neurosis of mankind." But probably we are speaking at cross purposes, and our differences will be ironed out only after centuries. In cordial friendship, and with greetings to your charming wife, your Freud.

Binswanger then adds in his book—and this is the central reason we quote the interchange—"As can be seen from the last sentence, Freud looked upon our differences as something to be surrounded by empirical investigation, not as something bearing upon the transcendental** conceptions that underly all empirical research."

In my judgment, Binswanger's point is irrefutable. One can gather empirical data, let us say on religion and art, from now till doomsday, and one will never get any closer to understanding these activities if, to start with, his presuppositions shut out what the religious person is dedicated to and what the artist is trying to do. Deterministic presuppositions make it possible to understand everything about art except the creative act and the art itself; mechanistic naturalistic presuppositions may uncover many facts about religion, but, as in Freud's terms, religion will always turn out to be more or less a neurosis, and what the genuinely religious person is concerned with will never get into the picture at all.

The point we wish to make in this discussion is the necessity of analyzing the presuppositions one assumes and of making allowance for the sectors of reality—which may be large indeed—that one's particular approach necessarily leaves out. In my judgment, we in psychology have often truncated our understanding and distorted our perception by failure consciously to clarify these presuppositions.

I vividly recall how, back in my graduate days of psychology some twenty years ago, Freud's theories tended to be dismissed as

---

*Binswanger's italics.

**By "transcendental," Binswanger of course does not refer to anything ethereal or magical; he means the underlying presuppositions which "point beyond" the given fact, the presuppositions which determine the goals of one's activity.

"unscientific" because they did not fit the methods then in vogue in graduate schools of psychology. I maintained at the time that this missed the point: Freud had uncovered realms of human experience of tremendous importance, and if they did not fit our methods, so much the worse for our methods; the problem was to devise new ones. In actual fact, the methods did catch up—perhaps, one should add, with a vengeance, until, as Rogers has stated, Freudianism is now the dogma of American clinical psychology. Remembering my own graduate-school days, I am therefore inclined to smile when someone says that the concepts of existential psychology are "unscientific" because they do not fit the particular methods *now* in vogue.

It is certainly clear that the Freudian mechanisms invite the separation into discrete cause-and-effect formulations which fit the deterministic methodology dominant in American psychology. But what also needs to be seen is that this making of Freudianism into the dogma of psychology has been accomplished at the price of omitting essential and vitally important aspects of Freud's thought. There is at present a three-cornered liaison, in tendency and to some extent in actuality, between Freudianism, behaviorism in psychology, and positivism in philosophy. An example of the first side of the liaison is the great similarity between Hull's drive-reduction theory of learning and Freud's concept of pleasure, the goal of behavior, as consisting of the reduction of stimuli. An example of the second is the statement of the philosopher Herman Feigl in his address at a recent annual convention of the American Psychological Association, that Freud's specific mechanisms could be formulated and used scientifically, but such concepts as the "death instinct" could not be.

But the trouble there is that such concepts as the "death instinct" in Freud were precisely what saved him from the full mechanistic implications of his system; these concepts always point beyond the deterministic limitations of his theory. They are, in the best sense of the word, a mythology. Freud was never content to let go of this mythological dimension to his thinking despite his great effort at the same time to formulate psychology in terms of his nineteenth-century biological presuppositions. In my judgment, his mythology is fundamental to the greatness of his contribution and essential to his central discoveries, such as "the unconscious." It was likewise essential to his radical contribution to the new image of man, namely, man as pushed by demonic, tragic, and destructive forces. I have tried elsewhere to show that Freud's tragic concept of the Oedipus complex is much closer to the truth than our tendency to interpret the Oedipus complex in terms of discrete sexual and hostile relationships in the family. The formulation of the "death instinct" as a biological instinct makes no sense, of course, and in this sense is rightly rejected by American behaviorism and positivism. But as a psychological and spiritual statement of the tragic nature of man, the idea has very great importance indeed and transcends any purely biological or mechanistic interpretation.

Methodology always suffers from a cultural lag. Our problem is to open our vision to more of human experience, to develop and free our methods so that they will as far as possible do justice to the richness and breadth of man's experience.

29 Ontological Insecurity

R. D. Laing

A man may have a sense of his presence in the world as a real, alive, whole, and, in a temporal sense, continuous person. As such, he can live out into the world and meet others: a world and others experienced as equally real, alive, whole, and continuous.

From *The Divided Self,* chapter 3, copyright 1960, by permission of the author, Pantheon Books and Tavistock Publications, Limited.

Such a basically *ontologically*[1] secure person will encounter all the hazards of life, social, ethical, spiritual, biological, from a centrally firm sense of his own and other

[1]Despite the philosophical use of "ontology" (by Heidegger, Sartre, Tillich, especially), I have used the term in its present empirical sense because it appears to be the best adverbial or adjectival derivative of "being."

people's reality and identity. It is often difficult for a person with such a sense of his integral selfhood and personal identity, of the permanency of things, of the reliability of natural processes, of the substantiality of natural processes, of the substantiality of others, to transpose himself into the world of an individual whose experiences may be utterly lacking in any unquestionable self-validating certainties.

This study is concerned with the issues involved where there is the partial or almost complete absence of the assurances derived from an existential position of what I shall call *primary ontological security:* with anxieties and dangers that I shall suggest arise *only* in terms of *primary ontological insecurity;* and with the consequent attempts to deal with such anxieties and dangers.

The literary critic, Lionel Trilling (1955), points up the contrast that I wish to make between a *basic existential position of ontological security* and one of *ontological insecurity* very clearly in comparing the worlds of Shakespeare and Keats on the one hand, and of Kafka on the other:

> . . . for Keats the awareness of evil exists side by side with a very strong sense of personal identity and is for that reason the less immediately apparent. To some contemporary readers, it will seem for the same reason the less intense. In the same way it may seem to a contemporary reader that, if we compare Shakespeare and Kafka, leaving aside the degree of genius each has, and considering both only as expositors of man's suffering and cosmic alienation, it is Kafka who makes the more intense and complete exposition. And, indeed, the judgment may be correct, exactly because for Kafka the sense of evil is not contradicted by the sense of personal identity. Shakespeare's world, quite as much as Kafka's, is that prison cell which Pascal says the world is, from which daily the inmates are led forth to die; Shakespeare no less than Kafka forces upon us the cruel irrationality of the conditions of human life, the tale told by an idiot, the puerile gods who torture us not for punishment but for sport; and no less than Kafka, Shakespeare is revolted by the fetor of the prison of this world, nothing is more characteristic of him than his imagery of disgust. But in Shakespeare's cell the company is so much better than in Kafka's, the captains and kings and lovers and clowns of Shakespeare are alive and complete before they die. In Kafka, long

before the sentence is executed, even long before the malign legal process is even instituted, something terrible has been done to the accused. We all know what that is—he has been stripped of all that is becoming to a man except his abstract humanity, which, like his skeleton, never is quite becoming to a man. He is without parents, home, wife, child, commitment, or appetite; he has no connection with power, beauty, love, wit, courage, loyalty, or fame, and the pride that may be taken in these. So that we may say that Kafka's knowledge of evil exists without the extradictory knowledge of the self in its health and validity, that Shakespeare's knowledge of evil exists with that contradiction in its fullest possible force (pp. 38–39).

We find, as Trilling points out, that Shakespeare does depict characters who evidently experience themselves as real and alive and complete however riddled by doubts or torn by conflicts they may be. With Kafka this is not so. Indeed, the effort to communicate what being alive is like in the absence of such assurances seems to characterize the work of a number of writers and artists of our time. Life, without feeling alive.

With Samuel Beckett, for instance, one enters a world in which there is no contradictory sense of the self in its "health and validity" to mitigate the despair, terror, and boredom of existence. In such a way, the two tramps who wait for Godot are condemned to live:

> ESTRAGON: We always find something, eh, Didi, to give us the impression that we exist?
> VLADIMIR (impatiently): Yes, yes, we're magicians. But let us persevere in what we have resolved, before we forget.

In painting, Francis Bacon, among others, seems to be dealing with similar issues. Generally, it is evident that what we shall discuss here clinically is but a small sample of something in which human nature is deeply implicated and to which we can contribute only a very partial understanding.

To begin at the beginning:

Biological birth is a definitive act whereby the infant organism is precipitated into the world. There it is, a new baby, a new biological entity, already with its own ways, real and alive, from *our* point of view. But what of the baby's point of view? Under usual circumstances, the physical birth of a new living organism into the world inaugurates rapidly ongoing processes whereby within an amazingly short time the infant *feels* real and alive and has a *sense* of being an entity, with continuity in time and a location in space. In short, physical birth and biological aliveness are followed by the baby becoming existentially born as real and alive. Usually this development is taken for granted and affords the certainty upon which all other certainties depend. This is to say, not only do adults see children to be real biologically visible entities but they experience themselves as whole persons who are real and alive, and conjunctively experience other human beings as real and alive. These are self-validating data of experience.

The individual, then, may experience his own being as real, alive, whole; as differentiated from the rest of the world in ordinary circumstances so clearly that his identity and autonomy are never in question; as a continuum in time; as having an inner consistency, substantiality, genuineness, and worth; as spatially co-extensive with the body; and, usually, as having begun in or around birth and liable to extinction with death. He thus has a firm core of ontological security.

This however, may not be the case. The individual in the ordinary circumstances of living may feel more unreal than real; in a literal sense, more dead than alive; precariously differentiated from the rest of the world, so that his identity and autonomy are always in question. He may lack the experience of his own temporal continuity. He may not possess an over-riding sense of personal consistency or cohesiveness. He may feel more insubstantial than substantial, and unable to assume that the stuff he is made of is genuine, good, valuable. And he may feel his self as partially divorced from his body.

It is, of course, inevitable that an individual whose experience of himself is of this order can no more live in a "secure" world than he can be secure "in himself." The whole "physiognomy" of his world will be correspondingly different from that of the individual whose sense of self is securely established in its health and validity. Relatedness to other persons will be seen to have a radically different significance and function. To anticipate, we can say that in the individual whose own being is secure in this primary experiential sense, relatedness with others is potentially gratifying; whereas the ontologically preserving rather than gratifying insecure person is preoccupied with himself: the ordinary circumstances of living threaten his *low threshold* of security.[2]

If a position of primary ontological security has been reached, the ordinary circumstances of life do not afford a perpetual threat to one's own existence. If such a basis for living has not been reached, the ordinary circumstances of everyday life constitute a continual and deadly threat.

Only if this is realized is it possible to understand how certain psychoses can develop.

If the individual cannot take the realness, aliveness, autonomy, and identity of himself and others for granted, then he has to become absorbed in contriving ways of trying to be real, of keeping himself or others alive, of preserving his identity, in efforts, as he will often put it, to prevent himself losing his self. What are to most people everyday happenings, which are hardly noticed because they have no special significance, may become deeply significant insofar as they either contribute to the sustenance of the individual's being or threaten him with non-being. Such an individual, for whom the elements of the world are coming to have, or have come to have, a different hierarchy of significance from that of the ordinary person, is beginning, as we say, to "live in a world of his own," or has already come to do so. It is not true to say, however, without careful qualification that he is losing "contact with" reality, and withdrawing into himself. External events no longer affect him in the same way as they do others: it is not that they affect him less; on the contrary, frequently they affect him more. It is frequently not the case that he is becoming "indifferent" and "withdrawn." It may, however, be that the world of his experience comes to be one he can no longer share with other people.

But before these developments are explored, it will be valuable to characterize under three headings three forms of anxiety encountered by the ontologically insecure person: engulfment, implosion, petrification.

[2]This formulation is very similar to those of H. S. Sullivan, Hill, F. Fromm-Reichmann, and Arieti in particular. Federn, although expressing himself very differently, seems to have advanced a closely allied view.

Engulfment

An argument occurred between two patients in the course of a session in an analytic group. Suddenly, one of the protagonists broke off the argument to say, "I can't go on. You are arguing in order to have the pleasure of triumphing over me. At best you win an argument. At worst you lose an argument. *I am arguing in order to preserve my existence.*"

This patient was a young man who I would say was sane, but, as he stated, his activity in the argument, as in the rest of his life, was not designed to gain gratification but to "preserve his existence." Now, one might say that if he did, in fact, really imagine the loss of an argument would jeopardize his existence, then he was "grossly out of touch with reality" and was virtually psychotic. But that is simply to beg the question without making any contribution towards understanding the patient. It is, however, important to know that if you were to subject this patient to a type of psychiatric interrogation recommended in many psychiatric textbooks, within ten minutes his behaviour and speech would be revealing "signs" of psychosis. It is quite easy to evoke such "signs" from such a person whose threshold of basic security is so low that practically any relationship with another person, however tenuous or however apparently "harmless," threatens to overwhelm him.

A firm sense of one's own autonomous identity is required in order that one may be related as one human being to another. Otherwise, any and every relationship threatens the individual with loss of identity. One form this takes can be called engulfment. In this the individual dreads relatedness as such, with anyone or anything or, indeed, even with himself, because his uncertainty about the stability of his autonomy lays him open to the dread lest in any relationship he will lose his autonomy and identity. Engulfment is not simply envisaged as something that is liable to happen willy-nilly despite the individual's most active efforts to avoid it. The individual experiences himself as a man who is only saving himself from drowning by the most constant, strenuous, desperate activity. Engulfment is felt as a risk in being understood (thus grasped, comprehended), in being loved, or even simply in being seen. To be hated may be feared for other reasons, but to be hated as such is often less disturbing than to be destroyed, as it is felt, through being engulfed by love.

The main manoeuvre used to preserve identity under pressure from the dread of engulfment is isolation. Thus, instead of the polarities of separateness and relatedness based on individual autonomy, there is the antithesis between complete loss of being by absorption into the other person (engulfment), and complete aloneness (isolation). There is no safe third possibility of a dialectical relationship between two persons, both sure of their own ground and, on this very basis, able to "lose themselves" in each other. Such merging of being can occur in an "authentic" way only when the individuals are sure of themselves. If a man hates himself, he may wish to lose himself in the other: then being engulfed by the other is an escape from himself. In the present case it is an ever-present possibility to be dreaded. It will be shown later, however, that what at one "moment" is most dreaded and strenuously avoided can change to what is most sought.

This anxiety accounts for one form of a so-called "negative therapeutic reaction" to apparently correct interpretation in psychotherapy. To be understood correctly is to be engulfed, to be enclosed, swallowed up, drowned, eaten up, smothered, stifled in or by another person's supposed all-embracing comprehension. It is lonely and painful to be always misunderstood, but there is at least from this point of view a measure of safety in isolation.

The other's love is, therefore, feared more than his hatred, or rather all love is sensed as a version of hatred. By being loved one is placed under an unsolicited obligation. In therapy with such a person, the last thing there is any point in is to pretend to more "love" or "concern" than one has. The more the therapist's own necessarily very complex motives for trying to "help" a person of this kind genuinely converge on a concern for him which is prepared to "let him be" and is not *in fact* engulfing or merely indifference, the more hope there will be in the horizon.

There are many images used to describe related ways in which identity is threatened which may be mentioned here, as closely related to the dread of engulfment, e.g., being buried, being drowned, being caught and dragged down into quicksand. The image of fire recurs repeatedly. Fire may be the uncertain flickering of the individual's own inner aliveness. It may be a destructive alien power which will devastate him. Some psychotics say in the acute phase that they are on fire, that their bodies are being burned up. A patient describes himself as cold and dry. Yet he dreads any warmth or wet. He will be engulfed by the fire or the water, and either way be destroyed.

Implosion

This is the strongest word I can find for the extreme form of what Winnicott terms the *impingement* of reality. Impingement does not convey, however, the full terror of the experience of the world as liable at any moment to crash in and obliterate all identity, as a gas will rush in and obliterate a vacuum. The individual feels that, like the vacuum, he is empty. But this emptiness is him. Although in other ways he longs for the emptiness to be filled, he dreads the possibility of this happening because he has come to feel that all he can be is the awful nothingness of just this very vacuum. Any "contact" with reality is then in itself experienced as a dreadful threat because reality, as experienced from this position, is necessarily *implosive* and thus, as was relatedness in engulfment, *in itself* a threat to what identity the individual is able to suppose himself to have.

Reality, as such, threatening engulfment or implosion, is the persecutor.

In fact, we are all only two or three degrees Fahrenheit from experiences of this order. Even a slight fever, and the whole world can begin to take on a persecutory, impinging aspect.

Petrification and Depersonalization

In using the term "petrification," one can exploit a number of the meanings embedded in this word:

1. A particular form of terror, whereby one is petrified, i.e., turned to stone.
2. The dread of this happening: the dread, that is, of the possibility of turning, or being turned, from a live person into a dead thing, into a stone, into a robot, an automation, without personal autonomy of action, an *it* without subjectivity.
3. The "magical" act whereby one may attempt to turn someone else into stone, by "petrifying" him; and, by extension, the act whereby one negates the other person's autonomy, ignores his feelings, regards him as a thing, kills the life in him. In this sense one may perhaps better say that one depersonalizes him, or reifies him. One treats him not as a person, as a free agent, but as an *it*.

Depersonalization is a technique that is universally used as a means of dealing with the other when he becomes too tiresome or disturbing. One no longer allows oneself to be responsive to his feelings and may be prepared to regard him and treat him as though he had no feelings. The people in focus here both tend to feel themselves as more or less depersonalized and tend to depersonalize others; they are constantly afraid of being depersonalized by others. The act of turning him into a thing is, *for him,* actually petrifying. In the face of being treated as an *it*, his own subjectivity drains away from him like blood from the face. Basically he requires constant confirmation from others of his own existence as a person.

A partial depersonalization of others is extensively practised in everyday life and is regarded as normal if not highly desirable. Most relationships are based on some partial depersonalizing tendency insofar as one treats the other not in terms of any awareness of who or what he might be in himself but as virtually an android robot playing a role or part in a large machine in which one too may be acting yet another part.

It is usual to cherish if not the reality, at least the illusion that there is a limited sphere of living free from this dehumanization. Yet it may be in just this sphere that the greater risk is felt, and the ontologically insecure person experiences this risk in highly potentiated form.

The risk consists in this: if one experiences the other as a free agent, one is open to the possibility of experiencing oneself as an *object* of his experience and thereby of feeling one's own subjectivity drained away. One is threatened with the possibility of becoming no more than a thing in the world of the other, without any life for oneself, without any being for oneself. In terms of such anxiety, the very act of experiencing the other as a person is felt as virtually suicidal. Sartre discusses this experience brilliantly in Part 3 of *Being and Nothingness*.

The issue is in principle straightforward. One may find oneself enlivened and the sense of one's own being enhanced by the other, or one may experience the other as deadening and impoverishing. A person may have come to anticipate that any possible relationship with another will have the latter consequences. Any other is then a threat to his "self" (his capacity to act autonomously) not by reason of anything he or she may do or not do specifically, but by reason of his or her very existence.

Some of the above points are illustrated in the life of James, a chemist, aged twenty-eight.

The complaint he made all along was that he could not become a "person." He had "no self." "I am only a response to other people, I have no identity of my own." He felt he was becoming more and more "a mythical person." He felt he had no weight, no substance of his own. "I am only a cork floating on the ocean."

This man was very concerned about not having become a person: he reproached his mother for this failure. "I was merely her emblem. She never recognized my identity." In contrast to his own belittlement of and uncertainty about himself, he was always on the brink of being over-awed and crushed by the formidable reality that other people contained. In contrast to his own light weight, uncertainty, and insubstantiality, *they* were solid, decisive, emphatic, and substantial. He felt that in every way that mattered others were more "large scale" than he was.

At the same time, in practice he was not easily overawed. He used two chief manoeuvres to preserve security. One was an outward compliance with the other. The second was an inner intellectual Medusa's head he turned on the other. Both manoeuvres taken together safeguarded his own subjectivity which he had never to betray openly and which thus could never find direct and immediate expression for itself. Being secret, it was safe. Both techniques together were designed to avoid the dangers of being engulfed or depersonalized.

With his outer behaviour he forestalled the danger to which he was perpetually subject, namely that of becoming someone else's *thing*, by pretending to be no more than a cork. (After all, what safer thing to be in an ocean?) At the same time, however, he turned the other person into a thing in his own eyes, thus magically nullifying any danger to himself by secretly totally disarming the enemy. By destroying, in his own eyes, the other person as a person, he robbed the other of his power to crush him. By depleting him of his personal aliveness, that is, by seeing him as a piece of machinery rather than as a human being, he undercut the risk to himself of this aliveness either swamping him, imploding into his own emptiness, or turning him into a mere appendage.

This man was married to a very lively and vivacious woman, highly spirited, with a forceful personality and a mind of her own. He maintained a paradoxical relationship with her in which, in one sense, he was entirely alone and isolated and, in another sense, he was almost a parasite. He dreamt, for instance, that he was a clam stuck to his wife's body.

Just because he could dream thus, he had the more need to keep her at bay by contriving to see her as no more than a machine. He described her laughter, her anger, her sadness, with "clinical" precision, even going so far as to refer to her as "it," a practice that was rather chilling in its effect. "It then started to laugh." She was an "it" because everything she did was a predictable, determined response. He would, for instance, tell her (it) an ordinary funny joke and when she (it) laughed this indicated her (its) entirely "conditioned," robot-like nature, which he saw indeed in much the same terms as certain psychiatric theories would use to account for all human actions.

I was at first agreeably surprised by his apparent ability to reject and disagree with what I said as well as to agree with me. This seemed to indicate that he had more of a mind of his own than he perhaps realized and that he was not too frightened to display some measure of autonomy. However, it became evident that his apparent capacity to act as an autonomous person with me was due to his secret manoeuvre of regarding me not as a live human being, a person in my own right with my own selfhood, but as a sort of robot interpreting device to which he fed input and which after a quick commutation came out with a verbal message to him. With this secret outlook on me as a thing he could appear to be a "person." What he could not sustain was a person-to-person relationship, experienced as such.

Dreams in which one or other of the above forms of dread is expressed are common in such persons. These dreams are not variations on the fears of being eaten which occur in ontologically secure persons. To be eaten does not necessarily mean to lose one's identity. Jonah was very much himself even within the belly of the whale. Few nightmares go so far as to call up anxieties about actual loss of identity, usually because most people, even in their dreams, still meet whatever dangers are to be encountered as persons who may perhaps be attacked or mutilated but whose basic existential care is not itself in jeopardy. In the classical nightmare the dreamer wakes up in terror. But this terror is not the dread of losing the "self." Thus a patient dreams of a fat pig which sits on his chest and threatens to suffocate him. He wakes in terror. At worst, in this nightmare, he is threatened with suffocation, but not with the dissolution of his very being.

The defensive method of turning the threatening mother- or breast-figure into a *thing* occurs in patients' dreams. One patient dreamt recurrently of a small black triangle which originated in a corner of his room and grew larger and larger until it seemed about to engulf him—whereupon he always awoke in great terror. This was a psychotic young man who stayed with my family for several months, and whom I was thus able to get to know rather well. There was only one situation as far as I could judge in which he could let himself "go" without anxiety at not recovering himself again, and that was in listening to jazz.

The fact that even in a dream the breast-figure has to be so depersonalized is a measure of its potential danger to the self, presumably on the basis of its frightening original personalizations and the failure of *a normal process of depersonalization.*

Medard Boss (1957) gives examples of several dreams heralding psychosis. In one, the dreamer is engulfed by fire:

A woman of hardly thirty years dreamt, at a time when she still felt completely healthy, that she was afire in the stables. Around her, the fire, an ever larger crust of lava was forming. Half from the outside and half from inside her own body she could see how the fire was slowly becoming choked by this crust. Suddenly she

was entirely outside this fire and, as if possessed, she beat the fire with a club to break the crust and to let some air in. But the dreamer soon got tired and slowly she (the fire) became extinguished. Four days after this dream she began to suffer from acute schizophrenia. In the details of the dream the dreamer had exactly predicted the special course of her psychosis. She became rigid at first and, in effect, encysted. Six weeks afterwards she defended herself once more with all her might against the choking of her life's fire, until finally she became completely extinguished both spiritually and mentally. Now, for some years, she has been like a burnt-out crater.

In another example, petrification of others occurs, anticipating the dreamer's own petrification:

. . . a girl of twenty-five years dreamt that she had cooked dinner for her family of five. She had just served it and she now called her parents and her brothers and sisters to dinner. Nobody replied. Only her voice returned as if it were an echo from a deep cave. She found the sudden emptiness of the house uncanny. She rushed upstairs to look for her family. In the first bedroom, she could see her two sisters sitting on two beds. In spite of her impatient calls they remained in an unnaturally rigid position and did not even answer her. She went up to her sisters and wanted to shake them. Suddenly she noticed that they were stone statues. She escaped in horror and rushed into her mother's room. Her mother too had turned into stone and was sitting inertly in her armchair staring into the air with glazed eyes. The dreamer escaped into the room of her father. He stood in the middle of it. In her despair she rushed up to him and, desiring his protection, she threw her arms round his neck. But he too was made of stone and, to her utter horror, he turned into sand when she embraced him. She awoke in absolute terror, and was so stunned by the dream experience that she could not move for some minutes. This same horrible dream was dreamt by the patient on four successive occasions within a few days. At that time she was apparently the picture of mental and physical health. Her parents used to call her the sunshine of the whole family. Ten days after the fourth repetition of the dream, the patient was taken ill with an acute form of schizophrenia displaying severe catatonic symptoms. She fell into a state which was remarkably similar to the physical petrification of her family that she had dreamt about. She was now overpowered in waking life by behaviour patterns that in her dreams she had merely observed in other persons.

It seems to be a general law that at some point those very dangers most dreaded can themselves be encompassed to forestall their actual occurrence. Thus, to forgo one's autonomy becomes the means of secretly safeguarding it; to play possum, to feign death, becomes a means of preserving one's aliveness (see Oberndorf, 1950). To turn oneself into a stone becomes a way of not being turned into a stone by someone else. "Be thou hard," exhorts Nietzsche. In a sense that Nietzsche did not, I believe, himself intend, to be stony hard and thus far dead forestalls the danger of being turned into a dead thing by another person. Thoroughly to understand oneself (engulf oneself) is a defense against the risk involved in being sucked into the whirlpool of another person's way of comprehending oneself. To consume oneself by one's own love prevents the possibility of being consumed by another.

It seems also that the preferred method of attack on the other is based on the same principle as the attack felt to be implicit in the other's relationship to oneself. Thus, the man who is frightened of his own subjectivity being swamped, impinged upon, or congealed by the other is frequently to be found attempting to swamp, to impinge upon, or to kill the other person's subjectivity. The process involves a vicious circle. The more one attempts to preserve one's autonomy and identity by nullifying the specific human individuality of the other, the more it is felt to be necessary to continue to do so, because with each denial of the other person's ontological status, one's own ontological security is decreased, the threat to the self from the other is potentiated and hence has to be even more desperately negated.

In this lesion in the sense of personal autonomy there is both a failure to sustain the sense of oneself as a person with the other, and a failure to sustain it alone. There is a failure to sustain a sense of one's own being without the presence of other people. It is a failure *to be* by oneself, a failure to exist alone. As James put it, "Other people supply me with my existence." This appears to be in direct contradiction to the aforementioned dread that other people will deprive him of his existence. But contradictory or absurd as it

may be, these two attitudes existed in him side by side, and are indeed entirely characteristic of this type of person.

The capacity to experience oneself as autonomous means that one has really come to realize that one is a separate person from everyone else. No matter how deeply I am committed in joy or suffering to someone else, he is not me, and I am not him. However lonely or sad one may be, one can exist alone. The fact that the other person in his own actuality is not me, is set against the equally real fact that my attachment to him is a part of me. If he dies or goes away, he has gone, but my attachment to him persists. But in the last resort I cannot die another person's death. For that matter, as Sartre comments on this thought of Heidegger's, he cannot love for me or make my decisions, and I likewise cannot do this for him. In short, he cannot be me, and I cannot be him.

If the individual does not feel himself to be autonomous this means that he can experience neither his separateness from, nor his relatedness to, the other in the usual way. A lack of sense of autonomy implies that one feels one's being to be bound up in the other, or that the other is bound up in oneself, in a sense that transgresses the actual possibilities within the structure of human relatedness. It means that a feeling that one is in a position of ontological dependency on the other (i.e., dependent on the other for one's very being), is substituted for a sense of relatedness and attachment to him based on genuine mutuality. Utter detachment and isolation are regarded as the only alternatives to a clam- or vampire-like attachment in which the other person's lifeblood is necessary for one's own survival, and yet is a threat to one's survival. Therefore, the polarity is between complete isolation or complete merging of identity rather than between separateness and relatedness. The individual oscillates perpetually between the two extremes, each equally unfeasible. He comes to live rather like those mechanical toys which have a positive tropism that impels them towards a stimulus until they reach a specific point, whereupon a built-in negative tropism directs them away until the positive tropism takes over again, this oscillation being repeated *ad infinitum*.

Other people were necessary for his existence, said James. Another patient, in the same basic dilemma, behaved in the following way: he maintained himself in isolated detachment from the world for months, living alone in a single room, existing frugally on a few savings, day-dreaming. But in doing this, he began to feel he was dying inside; he was becoming more and more empty, and observed "a progressive impoverishment of my life mode." A great deal of his pride and self-esteem was implicated in thus existing on his own, but as his state of depersonalization progressed he would emerge into social life for a brief foray in order to get a "dose" of other people, but "not an overdose." He was like an alcoholic who goes on sudden drinking orgies between dry spells, except that in his case his addiction, of which he was as frightened and ashamed as any repentant alcoholic or drug-addict, was to other people. Within a short while, he would come to feel that he was in danger of being caught up or trapped in the circle he had entered and he would withdraw again into his own isolation in a confusion of frightened hopelessness, suspicion, and shame.

Some of the points discussed above are illustrated in the following two cases:

CASE 1. Anxiety at Feeling Alone

Mrs. R.'s presenting difficulty was a dread of being in the street (agoraphobia). On closer inspection, it became clear that her anxiety arose when she began to feel on her own in the street or elsewhere. She could *be* on her own, as long as she did not feel that she was really alone.

Briefly, her story was as follows: she was an only and a lonely child. There was no open neglect or hostility in her family. She felt, however, that her parents were always too engrossed in each other for either of them ever to take notice of her. She grew up wanting to fill this hole in her life but never succeeded in becoming self-sufficient, or absorbed in her own world. Her longing was always to be important and significant *to someone* else. There always had to be someone else. Preferably she wanted to be loved and admired, but, if not, then to be hated was much to be preferred to being unnoticed. She wanted to be *significant* to someone else in whatever capacity, in contrast to her abiding memory of herself as a child that she did not really matter to her parents, that they neither loved nor hated, admired nor were ashamed of her very much.

In consequence, she tried looking at herself in her mirror but never managed to convince herself that she was *somebody*. She never got over being frightened if there was no one there.

She grew into a very attractive girl and was married at seventeen to the first man who really noticed this. Characteristically, it seemed to her, her parents had not noticed that any turmoil had been going on in their daughter until she announced that she was engaged. She was triumphant and self-confident under the warmth of her husband's attentions. But he was an army officer and shortly posted abroad. She was not able to go with him. At this separation she experienced severe panic.

We should note that her reaction to her husband's absence was not depression or sadness in which she pined or yearned for him. It was panic (as I would suggest) because of the dissolution of something in her, which owed its existence to the presence of her husband and his continued attentions. She was a flower that withered in the absence of one day's rain. However, help came to her through a sudden illness of her mother. She received an urgent plea for help from her father, asking her to come to nurse her mother. For the next year, during her mother's illness, she had never been, as she put it, so much herself. She was the pivot of the household. There was not a trace of panic until after her mother's death when the prospect of leaving the place where she had at last come to mean so much, to join her husband, was very much in her mind. Her experience of the last year had made her feel for the first time that she was now her parents' child. Against this, being her husband's wife was now somehow superfluous.

Again, one notes the absence of grief at her mother's death. At this time she began to reckon up the chances of her being alone in the world. Her mother had died; then there would be her father; possibly her husband: "beyond that—nothing." This did not depress her, it frightened her.

She then joined her husband and led a gay life for a few years. She craved for all the attention he could give her but this became less and less. She was restless and unsatisfied. Their marriage broke up and she returned to live in a flat in London with her father. While continuing to stay with her father she became the mistress and model of a sculptor. In this way she had lived for several years before I saw her when she was twenty-eight.

This is the way she talked of the street: "In

the street people come and go about their business. You seldom meet anyone who recognizes you; even if they do, it is just a nod and they pass on or at most you have a few minutes' chat. Nobody knows who you are. Everyone's engrossed in themselves. No one cares about you." She gave examples of people fainting and everyone's casualness about it. "No one gives a damn." It was in this setting and with these considerations in mind that she felt anxiety.

This anxiety was at being in the street alone or rather at feeling on her own. If she went out with or met someone who really knew her, she felt no anxiety.

In her father's flat she was often alone but there it was different. There she never felt *really* on her own. She made his breakfast. Tidying up the beds, washing up, was protracted as long as possible. The middle of the day was a drag. But she didn't mind too much. "Everything was familiar." There was her father's chair and his pipe rack. There was a picture of her mother on the wall looking down at her. It was as though all these familiar objects somehow illumined the house with the presence of the people who possessed and used them or had done so as a part of their lives. Thus, although she was by herself at home, she was always able to have someone with her in a magical way. But this magic was dispelled in the noise and anonymity of the busy street.

An intensive application of what is often supposed to be the classical psychoanalytic theory of hysteria to this patient might attempt to show this woman as unconsciously libidinally bound to her father; with, consequently, unconscious guilt and unconscious need and/or fear of punishment. Her failure to develop lasting libidinal relationships away from her father would seem to support the first view, along with her decision to live with him, to take her mother's place, as it were, and the fact that she spent most of her day, as a woman of twenty-eight, actually thinking about him. Her devotion to her mother in her last illness would be partly the consequences of unconscious guilt at her unconscious ambivalence to her mother; and her anxiety at her mother's death would be anxiety at her unconscious wish for her mother's death coming true. And so on.[3]

[3]For extremely valuable psychoanalytic contributions to apparently "hysterical" symptom-formation, see Segal (1954).

However, the central or pivotal issue in this patient's life is not to be discovered in her "unconscious"; it is lying quite open for her to see, as well as for us (although this is not to say that there are not many things about herself that this patient does not realize).

The pivotal point around which all her life is centered is her *lack of ontological autonomy*. If she is not in the actual presence of another person who knows her, or if she cannot succeed in evoking this person's presence in his absence, her sense of her own identity drains away from her. Her panic is at the fading away of her being. She is like Tinker Bell. In order to exist she needs someone else to believe in her existence. How necessary that her lover should be a sculptor and that she should be his model! How inevitable, given this basic premise of her existence, that when her existence was not recognized she should be suffused with anxiety. For her, *esse* is *percipi*; to be seen, that is, not as an anonymous passer-by or casual acquaintance. It was just that form of seeing which *petrified* her. If she was seen *as* an anonymity, *as* no one who especially mattered or as a *thing*, then she *was* no one in particular She was as she was seen to be. If there was no one to see her, at the moment, she had to try to conjure up someone (father, mother, husband, lover, at different times in her life) to whom she felt she mattered, for whom she was a *person*, and to imagine herself in his or her presence. If this person on whom her being depended went away or died, it was not a matter for grief, it was a matter for panic.

One cannot transpose her central problem into "the unconscious." If one discovers that she has an unconscious phantasy of being a prostitute, this does not explain her anxiety about street-walking, or her preoccupation with women who fall in the street and are not helped to get on their feet again. The conscious phantasy is, on the contrary, to be explained by and understood in terms of the central issue implicating her self-being, her being-for-herself. Her fear of being alone is not a "defense" against incestuous phantasies or masturbation. She had incestuous phantasies. *These phantasies were a defense against the dread of being alone*, as was her whole "fixation" on being a daughter. They were a means of overcoming her anxiety at being by herself. The unconscious phantasies of this patient would have an entirely different meaning if her basic existential position were such that she had a starting-point in herself that she could leave behind, as it were, in pursuit of gratification. As it was, *her sexual life and phantasies were efforts, not primarily to gain gratification, but to seek first ontological security.* In love-making an illusion of this security was achieved, and on the basis of this illusion gratification was possible.

It would be a profound mistake to call this woman narcissistic in any proper application of the term. She was unable to fall in love with her own reflection. It would be a mistake to translate her problem into phases of psychosexual development, oral, anal, genital. She grasped at sexuality as at a straw as soon as she was "of age." She was not frigid. Orgasm could be physically gratifying if she was temporarily secure in the prior ontological sense. In intercourse with someone who loved her (and she was capable of believing in being loved by another), she achieved perhaps her best moments. But they were short-lived. She could not be alone or let her lover be alone with her.

Her need to be taken notice of might facilitate the application of a further cliché to her, that she was an exhibitionist. Once more, such a term is only valid if it is understood existentially. Thus, and this will be discussed in greater detail subsequently, she "showed herself off" while never "giving herself away." That is, she exhibited herself while always holding herself in (inhibited). She was, therefore, always alone and lonely although superficially her difficulty was not in being together with other people; her difficulty was *least in evidence* when she was most together with another person. But it is clear that her realization of the autonomous existence of other people was really quite as tenuous as her belief in her own autonomy. If they were not there, they ceased to exist for her. Orgasm was a means of possessing herself, by holding in her arms the man who possessed her. But she could not be herself, by herself, and so could not really be herself at all.

CASE 2

A most curious phenomenon of the personality, one which has been observed for centuries, but which has not yet received its full explanation, is that in which the individual seems to be the vehicle of a personality that is not his own. Someone else's personality seems to "possess" him and to be finding expression through his words and action, whereas the

individual's own personality is temporarily "lost" or "gone." This happens with all degrees of malignancy. There seem to be all degrees of the same basic process from the simple, benign observation that so-and-so "takes after his father," or "That's her mother's temper coming out in her," to the extreme distress of the person who finds himself under a compulsion to take on the characteristics of a personality he may hate and/or feel to be entirely alien to his own.

This phenomenon is one of the most important in occasioning disruption in the sense of one's own identity when it occurs unwanted and compulsively. The dread of this occurring is one factor in the fear of engulfment and implosion. The individual may be afraid to like anyone, for he finds that he is under a compulsion to become like anyone he likes.

The way in which the individual's self and personality are profoundly modified even to the point of threatened loss of his or her own identity and sense of reality by engulfment by such an alien subidentity, is illustrated in the following case:

Mrs. D., a woman of forty, presented the initial complaint of vague but intense fear. She said she was frightened of everything, "even of the sky." She complained of an abiding sense of dissatisfaction, of unaccountable excesses of anger towards her husband, in particular of a "lack of a sense of responsibility." Her fear was "as though somebody was trying to rise up inside and was trying to get out of me." She was very afraid that she was like her mother, whom she hated. What she called "unreliability" was a feeling of bafflement and bewilderment which she related to the fact that nothing she did had ever seemed to please her parents. If she did one thing and was told it was wrong, she would do another thing and would find that they still said that was wrong. She was unable to discover, as she put it, "what they wanted me to be." She reproached her parents for this above all, that they hadn't given her any way of knowing who or what she really was or had to become. She could be neither bad nor good with any "reliability" because her parents were, or she felt they were, completely unpredictable and unreliable in their expressions of love or hatred, approval or disapproval. In retrospect, she concluded that they hated her; but at the time, she said, she was too baffled by them and too anxious to discover what she was expected to be to have been able to hate them, let alone love them. She now said that she was looking for "comfort." She was looking for a line from me that would give her an indication of the path she was to follow. She found my nondirective attitude particularly hard to tolerate since it seemed to her to be so clearly a repetition of her father's attitude: "Ask no questions and you'll be told no lies." For a spell, she became subject to compulsive thinking, in which she was under a necessity to ask such questions as, "What is this for?" or "Why is this?" and to provide herself with the answers. She interpreted this to herself as her effort to get comfort from her own thoughts since she could derive comfort from no one. She began to be intensely depressed and to make numerous complaints about her feelings, saying how childish they were. She spoke a great deal about how sorry she was for herself.

Now it seemed to me "she" was not really sorry for her own true self. She sounded to me much more like a querulous mother complaining about a difficult child. Her mother, indeed, seemed to be "coming out of her" all the time, complaining about "her" childishness. Not only was this so as regards the complaints which "she" was making about herself, but in other respects as well. For instance, like her mother, she kept screaming at her husband and child; like her mother,[4] she hated everyone; and like her mother she was forever crying. In fact, life was a misery to her by the fact that she could never be herself but was always being her mother. She knew, however, that when she felt lonely, lost, frightened, and bewildered she was more her true self. She knew also that she gave her complicity to becoming angry, hating, screaming, crying, or querulous, for if she worked herself up into being like that (i.e., being her mother), she did not feel frightened any more (at the expense, it was true, of being no longer herself). However, the backwash of this manoeuvre was that she was oppressed,

[4]That is, like her notion of what her mother was. I never met her mother and have no idea whether her phantasies of her mother bore any resemblance to her mother as a real person.

when the storm had passed, by a sense of futility (at not having been herself) and a hatred of the person she had been (her mother) and of herself for her self-duplicity. To some extent this patient, once she had become aware of this false way of overcoming the anxiety she was exposed to when she was herself, had to decide whether avoiding experiencing such anxiety, by avoiding being herself, was a cure worse than her disease. The frustration she experienced with me, which called out intense hatred of me, was not fully to be explained by the frustration of libidinal or aggressive drives in the transference, but rather it was what one could term the existential frustration that arose out of the fact that I, by withholding from her the "comfort" she sought to derive from me, in that *I did not tell her what she was to be*, was imposing upon her the necessity to make her own decision about the person she was to become. Her feeling that she had been denied her birthright because her parents had not discharged their responsibility towards her by giving her a definition of herself that could act as her starting-point in life was intensified by my refusal to offer this "comfort." But only by withholding it was it possible to provide a setting in which she could take this responsibility into herself.

In this sense, therefore, the task in psychotherapy was to make, using Jasper's expression, an appeal to the freedom of the patient. A good deal of the skill in psychotherapy lies in the ability to do this effectively.

REFERENCES

Boss, M., *Analysis of Dreams*, London, Rider & Co., 1957.

Oberndorf, C. P., "The Role of Anxiety in Depersonalization," *International Journal of Psychoanalysis*, 1950, Vol. 31.

Segal, H., "Schizoid Mechanisms Underlying Phobia Formation," *International Journal of Psychoanalysis*, 1954, Vol. 35.

Trilling, Lionel, *The Opposing Self*, London, 1955, Secker & Warburg.

Therapeutic Approaches

The goal of therapy, according to phenomenological theorists, should not be to understand the causes or to remove the symptoms of pathological behavior, but rather to free patients to develop a constructive and confident image of their self-worth. They should be led to appreciate their "true identity" and encouraged to venture forth to test their personal tastes and values.

The Swiss psychiatrists Ludwig Binswanger and Medard Boss have modified Freudian psychoanalytic therapy in line with this philosophy. In this recent essay, Binswanger summarized his position on *Daseinsanalysis* and compares it with traditional intrapsychic therapy. The development of Boss' ideas are remarkably similar to those of Binswanger. In the present paper, he argues for a new basis of psychotherapy, one founded on the therapist's appreciation of the patient's total personality. Only by assuming a phenomenological attitude can the therapist, according to Boss, grasp the full nature of the patient's dilemmas and anxieties.

Carl Rogers is the major exponent in the United States of self theory and nondirective therapy. In this brief essay he provides a thoughtful summary of his views concerning the essential qualities of the therapeutic enterprise, arguing passionately that the direct, experiential and sharing qualities of the relationship may lie at the heart of what makes it effective.

30 Existential Analysis and Daseinsanalysis

Ludwig Binswanger and Medard Boss

Part I

Zürich is the birthplace of existential analysis (*Daseinsanalyse*) as a psychiatric-phenomenologic research method. I emphasize the term *research method*, for if the psychoanalytic theory of Freud or the teaching of Jung arose out of a dissatisfaction with preceding psychotherapy, thus owing their origin and development predominantly to psychotherapeutic impulses and aims, the existential research orientation in psychiatry arose from dissatisfaction with the prevailing efforts to gain scientific understanding in psychiatry; so that existential analysis owes its origin and development to an attempt to gain a new scientific understanding of the concerns of

From *Progress in Psychotherapy* edited by F. Fromm-Reichmann and J.L. Moreno, 1956, 1957, Grune and Stratton, Inc., Vol. I and Vol. II, by permission of the publisher.

psychiatry, psychopathology and psychotherapy, on the basis of the analysis of existence (*Daseinsanalytik*) as it was developed in the remarkable work of Martin Heidegger: "Being and time" (*Sein und Zeit*), in the year 1927. Psychology and psychotherapy, as sciences, are admittedly concerned with "man," but not at all primarily with mentally *ill* man, but with *man as such*. The new understanding of man, which we owe to Heidegger's analysis of existence, has its basis in the new conception that man is no longer understood in terms of some theory—be it a mechanistic, a biologic or a psychological one—but in terms of a purely phenomenologic elucidation of the total structure or total articulation of existence as BEING-IN-THE-WORLD (*In-der-Welt-sein*). What this expression, fundamental for existential analysis, means, I unfortunately cannot develop here; be it only emphasized that it encompasses alike the individual's own world and the simultaneous and coextensive relationships with and to other people and things. Nor can I go into the difference between an ontologic-phenomenologic analysis of existence, an empiric-phenomenologic existential analysis, and an empiric discursive description, classification and explanation.

Once, in his interpretation of dreams, Freud said that psychiatrists had "forsaken the stability of the psychic structure too early." Existential analysis could say the same thing, albeit with an altogether different meaning. Freud, as is well known, had in mind the stability of the articulation of the life-history with the psychic structure, in contrast to the psychiatrists of his day who, at the very first opportunity, considered the psychic structure to be disrupted, and who resorted instead to physiologic processes in the cerebral cortex. Existential analysis, on the other hand, does not have in mind the solidity of the structure of the inner life-history, but rather the solidity of the transcendental structure preceding or underlying, a priori, all psychic structures as the very condition of this possibility. I regret that I cannot explain in fuller detail these philosophic expressions, already employed by Kant but here used in a much wider sense; those among you conversant with philosophy will readily understand me. I want to emphasize only that philosophy is not here in any way being introduced into psychiatry or psychotherapy, but rather that the philosophic bases of these sciences are being laid bare. Obviously, this in turn has an effect upon one's understanding of what constitutes their scientific object or field. This effect reveals itself in the fact that we have learned to understand and to describe the various psychoses and neuroses as specific *deviations* of the a priori, or the transcendental, structure of man's humanity, of the *condition humaine*, as the French say.

Be it noted in passing that the existential-analytic research method in psychiatry had to investigate the structure of existence as being-in-the-world, as Heidegger had outlined and delineated it still further and along various new paths. Such, for instance, are its studies of various existential "dimensions," i.e., height, depth and width, thingness and resistance *(Materialität)*, lighting and coloring of the world, fullness or emptiness of existence, etc. The investigation of psychotic or neurotic world-projects and existential structures such as, for example, those which we

designate as manic, depressive, schizophrenic, or compulsive, have so occupied all of us who are engaged upon this work that only suggestions are at hand with regard to the significance of existential-analytic research for psychotherapy. I should like now very cursorily to indicate a few of the main trends of this relationship.

(1) A psychotherapy on existential-analytic bases investigates the life-history of the patient to be treated, just as any other psychotherapeutic method, albeit in its own fashion. It does not explain this life-history and its pathologic idiosyncrasies according to the teachings of any school of psychotherapy, or by means of its preferred categories. Instead, it *understands* this life-history as modifications of the total structure of the patient's being-in-the-world, as I have shown in my studies "On Flight of Ideas" (*Über Ideenflucht*), in my studies of schizophrenia, and most recently in the case of "Suzanne Urban."

(2) A psychotherapy on existential-analytic bases thus proceeds *not* merely by showing the patient where, when and to what extent he has failed to realize the fullness of his humanity, but it tries to make him *experience* this as radically as possible—how, like Ibsen's masterbuilder, Solness, he has lost his way and footing in "airy heights" or "ethereal worlds of fantasy." In this case the psychotherapist could be compared to someone who is informed, e.g., a mountain guide, familiar with the particular terrain, who attempts the trip back to the valley with the unpracticed tourist who no longer dares either to proceed or to return. And inversely, the existential-analytically-oriented therapist seeks to enable the depressed patient to get out of his cavernous subterranean world, and to gain footing "upon the ground" once more, by revealing it to him as being the only mode of existence in which the fullness of human possibilities can be realized. And further, the existential-analytically-oriented therapist will lead the twisted schizophrenic out of the autistic world of distortion and askewness in which he lives and acts, into the shared worlds, the *koinos kosmos* of Heraclitus; or he will strive to help a patient who, in her own words, lives "in two speeds" to "synchronize" these (again using her own expression). Yet, another time the therapist will see (as happened in one of Roland Kuhn's cases of

anorexia mentalis) that the goal may be reached much more rapidly if one explores not the temporal but the spatial structures of a particular patient's world. It came as a surprise to us to find how easily some otherwise not particularly intelligent or educated patients proved accessible to an existential-analytic kind of exploration, and how thoroughly they felt understood by it in their singularity. This is, after all, an altogether indispensable prerequisite for any kind of psychotherapeutic success.

(3) Regardless of whether the existential analyst is predominantly psychoanalytic or predominantly Jungian in orientation, he will always stand on the same plane with his patients—the plane of common existence. He will therefore not degrade the patient to an object toward which he is subject, but he will see in him an existential partner. He will therefore not consider the bond between the two partners to be as that of two electric batteries—a "psychic contact"—but as an *encounter* on what Martin Buber calls the "sharp edge of existence," an existence which *essentially* "is in the world," not merely as a self but also as a being-together with one another—relatedness and love. Also what has, since *Freud*, been called transference is, in the existential-analytic sense, a kind of encounter. For encounter is a being-with-others in *genuine presence*, that is to say, in the present which is altogether continuous with the *past* and bears within it the possibilities of a *future*.

(4) Perhaps you will also be interested in hearing what is the position of existential analysis toward the *dream*, and this again particularly with regard to psychotherapy. Here again it is removed from any theoretic "explanation" of the dream, especially from the purely sexual exegesis of dream contents in psychoanalysis; rather, it understands the dream, as I emphasized a long time ago, as a specific way of being-in-the-world, in other words, as a specific world and a specific way of existing. This amounts to saying that in the dream we see the whole man, the *entirety* of his problems, in a different existential modality than in waking, but against the background and with the structure of the a priori articulation of existence, and therefore the dream is also of paramount therapeutic importance for the existential analyst. For precisely by means of the structure of dreams he is enabled first of all to show the patient the structure of his

being-in-the-world in an over-all manner, and secondly, he can, on the basis of this, free him for the *totality* of existential possibilities of being, in other words, for open resoluteness *(Entschlossenheit)*; he can, to use Heidegger's expression, "retrieve" *(zurückholen)* existence from a dream existence to a genuine capacity for being itself. For the time being, I will refer you to Roland Kuhn's paper, "On the Existential Structure of a Neurosis" in Gebsattel's *Jahrbuch fur Psychologie und Psychotherapie.* I only ask of you not to imagine existential structure as something static, but as something undergoing constant change. Similarly, what we call neurosis represents a changed existential *process*, as compared with the healthy. Thus, existential analysis understands the task of psychotherapy to be the opening up of new structural possibilities to such altered existential processes.

As you see, existential analysis, instead of speaking in theoretic concepts, such as "pleasure principle" and "reality principle," investigates and treats the mentally-ill person with regard to the structures, structural articulations and structural alterations of his existence. Hence, it has not, by any means, consciousness as its sole object, as has been erroneously stated, but rather the whole man, prior to any distinction between conscious and unconscious, or even between body and soul; for the existential structures and their alterations permeate man's entire being. Obviously, the existential analyst, insofar as he is a therapist, will not, at least in the beginning of his treatment, be able to dispense with the distinction between conscious and unconscious, deriving from the psychology of consciousness and bound up with its merits and its drawbacks.

(5) Taking stock of the relationship between existential analysis and psychotherapy, it can be said that existential analysis cannot, over long stretches, dispense with the traditional psychotherapeutic methods; that, however, it can, as such, be therapeutically effective only insofar as it succeeds in opening up to the sick fellow man an understanding of the structure of human existence, and allows him to find his way back from his neurotic or psychotic, lost, erring, perforated or twisted mode of existence and world into the freedom of being able to utilize his own capacities for existence. This presupposes that the existential analyst, insofar as he is a psychotherapist,

not only is in possession of existential-analytic and psychotherapeutic competence, but that he must dare to risk committing his own existence in the struggle for the freedom of his partner's.

Part II

Modern Psychotherapy in Need of a Basis

All problems, answers and resulting actions are invariably guided by the prescientific notions about the general nature and goal of man which each investigator carries within himself. No matter whether he is explicitly aware of his "philosophical" assumptions or whether he rejects all "philosophy" and attempts to be a "pure empiricist," the fact remains that such more or less hidden philosophical presuppositions, which are at the root of all science, are of fundamental importance. Up to now modern psychologists believed that their therapeutic approaches had found a sound basis in terms of their various psychodynamic theories about the human psyche. Freud thought of the human being as a telescope-like psychic apparatus; Reich, Alexander and Horney on the other hand attempt to explain all instinctual reactions in terms of a Total I or a Total Personality; for Jung the "psyche" is a self-regulating libidinal system controlled by the archetypes of the "Collective Unconscious"; Sullivan conceives of man as the product of interactions between him and his fellowmen; Fromm and others speak of man as a Self molded by society. Yet all these modern anthropologic theories can't possibly warrant an adequate understanding of the psychotherapeutic processes. For none of them answers what ought to be the first and foremost questions: what would have to be the nature of such a "Psyche," such a psychic apparatus, such a human I or Self or total personality in order that something like a mere perception of an object and of a human being, or even something like object relations and interpersonal and social relations, be at all possible? How should a telescope-like psychic apparatus or a self-regulating libidinal system be able to perceive or understand the meaning of anything, or to love or to hate somebody? Even less can such anonymous psychic structures or forces develop a transference or a

resistance in the course of psychotherapy. Yet all these phenomena are central factors for a true healing.

Martin Heidegger's "Daseinsanalysis" Revealing Man's Basic Nature

The eminent importance of the "Daseinsanalysis" in the sense of Martin Heidegger's fundamental ontology for psychology and psychotherapy lies in the fact that it helps overcome just these shortcomings of the basic anthropologic concepts of our psychological thinking, shortcomings which until now actually kept us groping in the dark. The "Daseinsanalysis" is able to do so because its concept of man's basic nature is nothing more or less than an explicit articulation of that understanding of man which has always guided our therapeutic actions, independent of all secondary theories, although secretly only and without our awareness. Therefore, the daseinsanalytic understanding of man helps us comprehend directly and fundamentally why therapists *can* demand of their patients what they have in fact been asking all along, and why they even *must* demand it if they want to cure at all. In all their endeavors psychotherapists rely on the peculiar ability of man to exist in a variety of instinctual, feeling, thinking and acting relationships to the things and in social and interpersonal patterns of behavior towards the fellowmen of his world. The therapist tacitly counts on this human ability when he asks of his patient—and tries to help him achieve it by this or that psychotherapeutic method—that he knowingly and responsibly seize and adopt all his potentialities of relationships so that they no longer remain frozen in unconscious neurotic mental or physical symptoms because of early childhood inhibitions and repressions.

In order to gain real insight into these preconditions and this goal of all practical psychotherapeutic approaches, the daseinsanalytic thinking had to guard against approaching man dogmatically with preconceived notions about his reality, no matter how self-evident they might seem. It also had to avoid forcing man blindly, by means of such preconceived ideas, into categories whereby he would be nothing but a "Psyche," a "Person" or "Consciousness." On the contrary, the daseinsanalysis had to learn again to see man unbiased, in the manner in which he directly reveals himself, and, in so doing, it made a very simple but all the more significant discovery about the fundamental nature of man. It found that man exists only *in* his relations and *as* his relations to the objects and fellowmen of his world. In order to exist in such manner, however, man must intrinsically possess a fundamental understanding of the fact that something *is* and can *be* at all. Man's special manner of being-in-the-world can therefore only be compared to the shining of a light, in the brightness of which the presence of all that is can occur, in which all things can appear and reveal themselves in their own, proper nature. Man is fundamentally an essentially spiritual brightness and as such he genuinely exists in the world. As this world-revealing brightness he is claimed by the ultimate be-ness. If a primordial understanding of be-ness were not the very essence of man, where would he suddenly find the ability to acquire any special knowledge and insight? In fact, each single comprehension of the meaning of all the different encountering objects and all actual dealing with them is possible only because man is intrinsically "brightness" in the sense of being a primordial understanding of be-ness. This holds true in an all-embracing way; it is the prerequisite for the possibility to be concretely touched and affected by something as well as for all emotional experience and all conscious or unconscious instinctual behavior toward something: without it there can be no handling and grasping of mechanical tools, nor can there be conceptual grasping of scientific matters. This also refutes the widely heard objection that the daseinsanalysis is relevant only for the psychology of the conscious mind. The intrinsic ability of the human "dasein" to be open to the world in this way does not just discover things which can be located somewhere in space and time. It also opens up ways for the direct and immediate understanding of beings, who, as human beings, not only are altogether different from the things, but who, according to their manner of being as "dasein," are in the world in the same way as I am. These other human beings are likewise there and together with me. Humanity, as a whole, therefore, is best comparable to the full brightness of the day which also consists of the shining-together of all individual sun rays. Because of this being-together-in-the-world the world is al-

ways that which I share with others, the world of "dasein" is world-of-togetherness ("Mitwelt").[1]

Just as the objects cannot reveal themselves without such brightness of man, man cannot exist as that which he is without the presence of all he encounters. For if he did not find his proper place in the encounter with the objects, plants, animals and fellowmen, in his ability to be with them, in his relationship to them, how else could men be in this world as such brightening understanding of be-ness? Even physical light cannot appear as light unless it encounters an object and can make it shine.

The Daseinsanalytically Oriented Psychotherapist

This then, is the anthropological essense of Martin Heidegger's Existential Analysis (Daseinsanalysis). Meanwhile, the term "existential analysis" has come to include a variety of philosophical, scientific, psychopathologic and psychotherapeutic schools of thought. Although they differ in their methods and goals, they are all derivatives of Heidegger's Daseinsanalysis. At least they received from it their initial impetus even if, as in the case of J.-P. Sartre's philosophy, they have turned the real substance of the "Daseinsanalysis" into its complete opposite, namely, an extreme, subjectivistic Cartesianism.

The psychotherapist who lets himself be thoroughly pervaded by Heidegger's ontologic insight will not be able to derive new words or phrases from the daseinsanalysis for his psychopathologic descriptions. But he will win by it a tacit, but all the more reliable and all-embracing attitude toward his patient and the therapeutic process. If the therapist really understands that man is intrinsically a world-unfolding and world-opening being in the sense that in him, as the bright sphere of be-ness, comparable to a glade in a forest, all things, plants, animals and fellowmen can show and reveal themselves directly and immediately in all their significance and correlations, then he will have an unceasing reverence for the proper value of each phenomenon he encounters. At the same time he will have become aware that this way of being is the prerequisite that our destiny could claim man

[1] M. Heidegger: *Sein und Zeit.* Halle, 1927. p. 118.

as a being who should care for the things and his fellowmen in the manner that all that is and may be can best unfold and develop. To exist in this sense is man's intrinsic task in life. How else could it be that his conscience tells him so relentlessly whenever he falls short of fulfilling it? This call from the conscience and this guilt feeling will not abate until man has taken over and responsibly accepted all those possibilities which constitute him, and has borne and carried them out in taking care of the things and fellowmen of his world. Thus, he has completed his full dasein and hence can consummate his individual, intrinsic temporality in a good death. The daseinsanalytic understanding of man makes the analyst gain so deep a respect for all phenomena he encounters that it bids him to abide even more fully and more firmly by the chief rule of psychoanalysis than Freud himself could, handicapped as he still was by theoretical prejudices. The therapist will now, according to Freud's technical prescriptions, really be able to accept as equally genuine all the new possibilities for communication which grow "on the playground of transference," without mutilating them through his own intellectual and theoretical prejudices and his personal affective censure. The daseinsanalytically oriented psychoanalyst will have a clear conscience if he remains impartial to all unproved scientific theories and abstractions and therefore refrains from attributing sole and only reality to one kind of behavior—the instinctual reactions, for instance—and does not consider them more "real" than all other potentialities. Thus, the danger of a so-called unresolved transference can often be avoided. This therapeutic difficulty usually develops only because the analyst has attempted to interpret and thereby reduce a new possibility of communication which unfolded for the first time in the therapeutic situation to a mere repetition of a relationship which existed earlier in life, considering this one primary and causal. Therefore, this new possibility can never properly unfold and mature and thus must inevitably remain in its embryonic state, i.e., the "transference fixation." How different, though, if one respects for instance the divine, which also reveals itself during psychoanalysis, in its divineness, just as one is ready to concede to the earthly its earthliness, and does not degrade the divine to a mere product of sublimation of an infantile-libidinal fixation, nor to a mere subjectivistic "psychic reality" produced by some supposed archetypal structure in the psyche of a human subject.

Of equally decisive influence on the attitude of the analyst is a thorough daseinsanalytic understanding of the fact that man is intrinsically and essentially always together with others. Heidegger's fundamental ontology helps us understand this in terms of a primary participation of all men in being the same open sphere of the be-ness. This insight teaches us that there is a being-together which is of such intrinsic and essential nature that no man can in fact perceive another even in the distance, without being already—through the mere art of perceiving—involved in the other's particular world-relatedness in some specific way. Thus, from the very first encounter between the therapist and patient the therapist is already together with his patient in the patient's way of existing, just as the patient already partakes in the therapist's manner of living, no matter whether, either on the part of the therapist or the patient, their being-together manifests itself for some time only in aloof observation, indifference or even intense resistance.

Already the knowledge of just this one essential trait of man provides an enormous impetus and a firm basis even for psychotherapeutic endeavors which formerly were a venture requiring an almost blind courage. For, only in the primordial being-together as it was brought to light by Heidegger's "Daseinsanalysis" we are able now to recognize the very foundation of all psychotherapeutic possibilities. Owing to this basic structure of man's existence, the most seriously ill schizophrenic patient, for instance, partakes in some way or other as human being in the wholesome mode of living of his psychotherapist; hence, such a patient's fundamental possibility of being cured by the adequate being-together of a psychotherapeutic situation through which he may recollect his true self again.[2]

Apart from the confidence which we derive from the daseinsanalytic insights for our practical dealings with such difficult patients, the daseinsanalytic way of thinking affords us also some important "theoretical" gain. For

[2]M. Boss: *Psychoanalyse und Daseinsanalytik*. Bern, Hans Huber, 1957.

example, it helps us understand such central phenomena as "psychic projection" and "transference." Until now modern psychology could conceive of them only in terms of a tossing-out and carrying-over of psychic contents from within a "psyche" into something in the external world. Those concepts, however, are entirely unexplainable and can only be maintained on the basis of abstract intellectual constructions. The daseinsanalytic thinking allows us to understand these phenomena simply and with full justice to reality out of the primary, intrinsic being-together of all men in the same world.[3]

REFERENCES

Boss, M.: The Dream and Its Interpretation. London, Rider, 1957.
Heidegger, M.: Sein und Zeit. Tübingen, Niemeyer, 1927.

[3]M. Boss: *The Dream and Its Interpretation.* London, 1957.

31 Persons or Science? A Philosophical Question

Carl R. Rogers

This is a highly personal document, written primarily for myself, to clarify an issue which has become increasingly puzzling. It will be of interest to others only to the extent that the issue exists for them. I shall therefore describe first something of the way in which the paper grew.

As I have acquired experience as a therapist, carrying on the exciting, rewarding experience of psychotherapy, and as I have worked as a scientific investigator to ferret out some of the truth about therapy, I have become increasingly conscious of the gap between these two roles. The better therapist I have become (as I believe I have), the more I have been vaguely aware of my complete subjectivity when I am at my best in this function. And as I have become a better investigator, more "hardheaded" and more scientific (as I believe I have) I have felt an increasing discomfort at the distance between the rigorous objectivity of myself as scientist and the almost mystical subjectivity of myself as therapist. This paper is the result.

What I did first was to let myself go as therapist, and describe, as well as I could do in a brief space, what is the essential nature of psychotherapy as I have lived it with many clients. I would stress the fact that this is a

From *The American Psychologist,* 1955, *10,* 267–278. Copyright © 1955 by the American Psychological Association. Reprinted by permission.

very fluid and personal formulation, and that if it were written by another person, or if it were written by me two years ago, or two years hence, it would be different in some respects. Then I let myself go as scientist—as tough-minded fact-finder in this psychological realm—and endeavored to picture the meaning which science can give to therapy. Following this I carried on the debate which existed in me, raising the questions which each point of view legitimately asks the other.

When I had carried my efforts this far I found that I had only sharpened the conflict. The two points of view seemed more than ever irreconcilable. I discussed the material with a seminar of faculty and students, and found their comments very helpful. During the following year I continued to mull over the problem until I began to feel an integration of the two views arising in me. More than a year after the first sections were written I tried to express this tentative and perhaps temporary integration in words.

Thus the reader who cares to follow my struggles in this matter will find that it has quite unconsciously assumed a dramatic form—all of the dramatis personae being contained within myself; First Protagonist, Second Protagonist, The Conflict, and finally, The Resolution. Without more ado let me introduce the first protagonist, myself as therapist, portraying as well as I can, what the *experience* of therapy seems to be.

The Essence of Therapy in Terms of Its Experience

I launch myself into the therapeutic relationship having a hypothesis, or a faith, that my liking, my confidence, and my understanding of the other person's inner world, will lead to a significant process of becoming. I enter the relationship not as a scientist, not as a physician who can accurately diagnose and cure, but as a person, entering into a personal relationship. Insofar as I see him only as an object, the client will tend to become only an object.

I risk myself, because if, as the relationship deepens, what develops is a failure, a regression, a repudiation of me and the relationship by the client, then I sense that I will lose myself, or a part of myself. At times this risk is very real, and is very keenly experienced.

I let myself go into the immediacy of the relationship where it is my total organism which takes over and is sensitive to the relationship, not simply my consciousness. I am not consciously responding in a planful or analytic way, but simply in an unreflective way to the other individual, my reaction being based (but not consciously) on my total organismic sensitivity to this other person. I live the relationship on this basis.

The essence of some of the deepest parts of therapy seems to be a unity of experiencing. The client is freely able to experience his feeling in its complete intensity, as a "pure culture," without intellectual inhibitions or cautions, without having it bounded by knowledge of contradictory feelings; and I am able with equal freedom to experience my understanding of this feeling, without any conscious thought about it, without any apprehension or concern as to where this will lead, without any type of diagnostic or analytic thinking, without any cognitive or emotional barriers to a complete "letting go" in understanding. When there is this complete unity, singleness, fullness of experiencing in the relationship, then it acquires the "out-of-this-world" quality which many therapists have remarked upon, a sort of trance-like feeling in the relationship from which both the client and I emerge at the end of the hour, as if from a deep well or tunnel. In these moments there is, to borrow Buber's phrase, a real "I-Thou" relationship, a timeless living in the experience which is *between* the client and me. It is at the opposite pole from seeing the client, or myself, as an object. It is the height of personal subjectivity.

I am often aware of the fact that I do not *know*, cognitively, where this immediate relationship is leading. It is as though both I and the client, often fearfully, let ourselves slip into the stream of becoming, a stream or process which carries us along. It is the fact that the therapist has let himself float in this stream of experience or life previously, and found it rewarding, that makes him each time less fearful of taking the plunge. It is my confidence that makes it easier for the client to embark also, a little bit at a time. It often seems as though this stream of experience leads to some goal. Probably the truer statement, however, is that its rewarding character lies within the process itself, and that its major reward is that it enables both the client and me, later, independently, to let ourselves go in the process of becoming.

As to the client, as therapy proceeds he finds that he is daring to become himself, in spite of all the dread consequences which he is sure will befall him if he permits himself to become himself. What does this becoming one's self mean? It appears to mean less fear of the organismic, nonreflective reactions which one has, a gradual growth of trust in and even affection for the complex, varied, rich assortment of feelings and tendencies which exist in one at the organic or organismic level. Consciousness, instead of being the watchman over a dangerous and unpredictable lot of impulses, of which few can be permitted to see the light of day, becomes the comfortable inhabitant of a richly varied society of impulses and feelings and thoughts, which prove to be very satisfactorily self-governing when not fearfully or authoritatively guarded.

Involved in this process of becoming himself is a profound experience of personal choice. He realizes that he can choose to continue to hide behind a facade, or that he can take the risks involved in being himself; that he is a free agent who has it within his power to destroy another, or himself, and also the power to enhance himself and others. Faced with this naked reality of decision, he chooses to move in the direction of being himself.

But being himself doesn't "solve problems." It simply opens up a new way of living in which there is more depth and more height in the experience of his feelings, more breadth and more range. He feels more unique and hence more alone, but he is so much more real that his relationships with others lose their artificial quality, become deeper, more satisfying, and draw more of the realness of the other person into the relationship.

Another way of looking at this process, this relationship, is that it is a learning by the client (and by the therapist, to a lesser extent). But it is a strange type of learning. Almost never is the learning notable by its complexity, and at its deepest the learnings never seem to fit well into verbal symbols. Often the learnings take such simple forms as "I *am* different from others"; "I do feel hatred for him"; "I *am* fearful of feeling dependent"; "I do feel sorry for myself"; "I am self-centered"; "I do have tender and loving feelings"; "I could be what I want to be"; etc. But in spite of their seeming simplicity these learnings are vastly significant in some way which is very difficult to define. We can think of it in various ways. They are self-appropriated learnings, for one thing, based somehow in experience, not in symbols. They are analogous to the learning of the child who knows that "two and two make four" and who one day playing with two objects and two objects, suddenly realizes in *experience* a totally new learning, that "two and two *do* make four."

Another manner of understanding these learnings is that they are a belated attempt to match symbols with meanings in the world of feelings, an undertaking long since achieved in the cognitive realm. Intellectually, we match carefully the symbol we select with the meaning which an experience has for us. Thus I say something happened "gradually," having quickly (and largely unconsciously) reviewed such terms as "slowly," "imperceptibly," "step-by-step," etc., and rejected them as not carrying the precise shade of meaning of the experience. But in the realm of feelings, we have never learned to attach symbols to experience with any accuracy of meaning. This something which I feel welling up in myself, in the safety of an acceptant relationship—what is it? Is it sadness, is it anger, is it regret, is it sorrow for myself, is it anger at lost opportunities—I stumble around trying out a wide range of symbols, until one "fits," "feels right," seems really to match the organismic experience. In doing this type of

thing the client discovers that he has to learn the language of feeling and emotion as if he were an infant learning to speak; often, even worse, he finds he must unlearn a false language before learning the true one.

Let us try still one more way of defining this type of learning, this time by describing what it is not. It is a type of learning which cannot be taught. The essence of it is the aspect of self-discovery. With "knowledge" as we are accustomed to think of it, one person can teach it to another, providing each has adequate motivation and ability. But in the significant learning which takes place in therapy, one person *cannot* teach another. The teaching would destroy the learning. Thus I might teach a client that it is safe for him to be himself, that freely to realize his feelings is not dangerous, etc. The more he learned this, the less he would have learned it in the significant, experiential, self-appropriating way. Kierkegaard regards this latter type of learning as true subjectivity, and makes the valid point that there can be no direct communication of it, or even about it. The most that one person can do to further it in another is to create certain conditions which make this type of learning *possible*. It cannot be compelled.

A final way of trying to describe this learning is that the client gradually learns to symbolize a total and unified state, in which the state of the organism, in experience, feeling, and cognition may all be described in one unified way. To make the matter even more vague and unsatisfactory, it seems quite unnecessary that this symbolization should be expressed. It usually does occur, because the client wishes to communicate at least a portion of himself to the therapist, but it is probably not essential. The only necessary aspect is the inward realization of the total, unified, immediate, "at-the-instant," state of the organism which is me. For example, to realize fully that at this moment the oneness in me is simply that "I am deeply frightened at the possibility of becoming something different" is of the essence of therapy. The client who realizes this will be quite certain to recognize and realize this state of his being when it recurs in somewhat similar form. He will also, in all probability, recognize and realize more fully some of the other existential feelings which occur in him. Thus he will be moving toward a state in which he is more truly himself. He will *be*, in more unified fashion, what he organismically *is*, and this seems to be the essence of therapy.

The Essence of Therapy in Terms of Science

I shall now let the second protagonist, myself as scientist, take over and give his view of this same field.

In approaching the complex phenomena of therapy with the logic and methods of science, the aim is to work toward an u derstanding of the phenomena. In science this means an objective knowledge of events and of functional relationships between events. Science may also give the possibility of increased prediction of and control over these events, but this is not a necessary outcome of scientific endeavor. If the scientific aim were fully achieved in this realm, we would presumably know that, in therapy, certain elements were associated with certain types of outcomes. Knowing this it is likely that we would be able to predict that a particular instance of a therapeutic relationship would have a certain outcome (within certain probability limits) because it involved certain elements. We could then very likely control outcomes of therapy by our manipulation of the elements contained in the therapeutic relationship.

It should be clear that no matter how profound our scientific investigation, we could never by means of it discover any absolute truth, but could only describe relationships which had an increasingly high probability of occurrence. Nor could we discover any underlying reality in regard to persons, interpersonal relationships, or the universe. We could only describe relationships between observable events. If science in this field followed the course of science in other fields, the working models of reality which would emerge (in the course of theory building) would be increasingly removed from the reality perceived by the senses. The scientific description of therapy and therapeutic relationships would become increasingly *unlike* these phenomena as they are experienced.

It is evident at the outset that since therapy is a complex phenomenon, measurement will be difficult. Nevertheless "anything that exists can be measured," and since therapy is judged to be a significant relationship, with implications extending far beyond itself, the difficulties may prove to be worth surmounting in order to discover laws of personality and interpersonal relationships.

Since, in client-centered therapy, there already exists a crude theory (though not a theory in the strictly scientific sense), we have a starting point for the selection of hypotheses. For purposes of this discussion, let us take some of the crude hypotheses which can be drawn from this theory, and see what a scientific approach will do with them. We will, for the time being, omit the translation of the total theory into a formal logic which would be acceptable, and consider only a few of the hypotheses.

Let us first state three of these in their crude form.

1. Acceptance of the client by the therapist leads to an increased acceptance of self by the client.

2. The more the therapist perceives the client as a person rather than as an object, the more the client will come to perceive himself as a person rather than an object.

3. In the course of therapy an experiential and effective type of learning about self takes place in the client.

How would we go about translating each of these[1] into operational terms and how would we test the hypotheses? What would be the general outcomes of such testing?

This paper is not the place for a detailed answer to these questions, but research already carried on supplies the answers in a general way. In the case of the first hypothesis, certain devices for measuring acceptance would be selected or devised. These might be attitude tests, objective or projective, Q technique or the like. Presumably the same instruments, with slightly different instructions or mind set, could be used to measure the therapist's acceptance of the client, and the client's acceptance of self. Operationally then, the degree of therapist acceptance would be equated to a certain score on this instrument. Whether

---

[1] I believe it is now commonly accepted that the most subjective feelings, apprehensions, tensions, satisfactions, or reactions, may be dealt with scientifically, providing only that they may be given clear-cut operational definition. William Stephenson, among others, presents this point of view forcefully (in his "Postulates of Behaviorism," 1953), and, through his Q technique, has contributed importantly to the objectification of such subjective materials for scientific study.

client self-acceptance changed during therapy would be indicated by pre- and post-measurements. The relationship of any change to therapy would be determined by comparison of changes in therapy to changes during a control period or in a control group. We would finally be able to say whether a relationship existed between therapist acceptance and client self-acceptance, as operationally defined, and the correlation between the two.

The second and third hypotheses involve real difficulty in measurement, but there is no reason to suppose that they could not be objectively studied, as our sophistication in psychological measurement increases. Some type of attitude test or Q sort might be the instrument for the second hypothesis, measuring the attitude of therapist toward client, and of client toward self. In this case the continuum would be from objective regard of an external object to a personal and subjective experiencing. The intrumentation for hypothesis there might be physiological, since it seems likely that experiential learning has physiologically measurable concomitants. Another possibility would be to infer experiential learning from its effectiveness, and thus measure the effectiveness of learning in different areas. At the present stage of our methodology hypothesis three might be beyond us, but certainly within the foreseeable future, it too could be given operational definition and tested.

The findings from these studies would be of this order. Let us become suppositious, in order to illustrate more concretely. Suppose we find that therapist acceptance leads to client self-acceptance, and that the correlation is in the neighborhood of .70 between the two variables. In hypothesis two we might find the hypothesis unsupported, but find that the more the therapist regarded the client as a person, the more the client's self-acceptance increased. Thus we would have learned that person-centeredness is an element of acceptance, but that it has little to do with the client becoming more of a person to himself. Let us also suppose hypothesis three upheld with experiential learning of certain describable sorts taking place much more in therapy than in the control subjects.

Glossing over all the qualifications and ramifications which would be present in the findings, and omitting reference to the unex-pected leads into personality dynamics which would crop up (since these are hard to imagine in advance), the preceding paragraph gives us some notion of what science can offer in this field. It can give us a more exact description of the events of therapy and the changes which take place. It can begin to formulate some tentative laws of the dynamics of human relationships. It can offer public and replicable statements, that if certain operationally definable conditions exist in the therapist or in the relationship, then certain client behaviors may be expected with a known degree of probability. It can presumably do this for the field of therapy and personality change as it is in the process of doing for such fields as perception and learning. Eventually theoretical formulations should draw together these different areas, enunciating the laws which appear to govern alteration in human behavior, whether in the situations we classify as perception, those we classify as learning, or the more global and molar changes which occur in therapy, involving both perception and learning.

Some Issues

Here are two different methods of perceiving the essential aspects of psychotherapy, two different approaches to forging ahead into new territory in this field. As presented here, and as they frequently exist, there seems almost no common meeting ground between the two descriptions. Each represents a vigorous way of seeing therapy. Each seems to be an avenue to the significant truths of therapy. When each of these is held by a different individual or group, it constitutes a basis of sharp disagreement. When each of these approaches seems true to one individual, like myself, then he feels himself conflicted by these two views. Though they may superficially be reconciled, or regarded as complementary to each other, they seem to me to be basically antagonistic in many ways. I should like to raise certain issues which these two viewpoints pose for me.

The Scientist's Questions

First let me pose some of the questions which the scientific viewpoint asks of the experiential (using scientific and experiential simply as loose labels to indicate the two views). The hardheaded scientist listens to the experiential account, and raises several searching questions.

1. First of all he wants to know, "How can you know that this account, or any account given at a previous or later time, is true? How do you know that it has any relationship to reality? If we are to rely on this inner and subjective experience as being the truth about human relationships or about ways of altering personality, then Yogi, Christian Science, dianetics, and the delusions of a psychotic individual who believes himself to be Jesus Christ, are all true, just as true as this account. Each of them represents the truth as perceived inwardly by some individual or group of individuals. If we are to avoid this morass of multiple and contradictory truths, we must fall back on the only method we know for achieving an ever-closer approximation to reality, the scientific method."

2. "In the second place, this experiential approach shuts one off from improving his therapeutic skill, or discovering the less than satisfactory elements in the relationship. Unless one regards the present description as a perfect one, which is unlikely, or the present level of experience in the therapeutic relationship as being the most effective possible, which is equally unlikely, then there are unknown flaws, imperfections, blind spots, in the account as given. How are these to be discovered and corrected? The experiential approach can offer nothing but a trial-and-error process for achieving this, a process which is slow and which offers no real guarantee of achieving this goal. Even the criticisms or suggestions of others are of little help, since they do not arise from within the experience and hence do not have the vital authority of the relationship itself. But the scientific method, and the procedures of a modern logical positivism, have much to offer here. Any experience which can be described at all can be described in operational terms. Hypotheses can be formulated and put to test, and the sheep of truth can thus be separated from the goats of error. This seems the only sure road to improvement, self-correction, growth in knowledge."

3. The scientist has another comment to make. "Implicit in your description of the therapeutic experience seems to be the notion that there are elements in it which *cannot* be predicted—that there is some type of spontaneity or (excuse the term) free will operative here. You speak as though some of the client's behavior—and perhaps some of the therapist's—is not caused, is not a link in a sequence of cause and effect. Without desiring to become metaphysical, may I raise the question as to whether this is defeatism? Since surely we can discover what causes *much* of behavior—you yourself speak of creating the conditions where certain behavioral results follow—then why give up at any point? Why not at least *aim* toward uncovering the causes of *all* behavior? This does not mean that the individual must regard himself as an automaton, but in our search for the facts we shall not be hampered by a belief that some doors are closed to us."

4. Finally, the scientist cannot understand why the therapist, the experientialist, should challenge the one tool and method which is responsible for almost all the advances which we value. "In the curing of disease, in the prevention of infant mortality, in the growing of larger crops, in the preservation of food, in the manufacture of all the things that make life comfortable, from books to nylon, in the understanding of the universe, what is the foundation stone? It is the method of science, applied to each of these, and to many other problems. It is true that it has improved methods of warfare, too, serving man's destructive as well as his constructive purposes, but even here the potentiality for social usefulness is very great. So why should we doubt this same approach in the social science field? To be sure advances here have been slow, and no law as fundamental as the law of gravity has as yet been demonstrated, but are we to give up this approach out of impatience? What possible alternative offers equal hope? If we are agreed that the social problems of the world are very pressing indeed, if psychotherapy offers a window onto the most crucial and significant dynamics of change in human behavior, then surely the course of action is to apply to psychotherapy the most rigorous canons of scientific method, on as broad a scale as possible, in order that we may most rapidly approach a tentative knowledge of the laws of individual behavior and of attitudinal change."

The Questions of the Experientialist

While the scientist's questions may seem to some to settle the matter, his comments are far from being entirely satisfying to the therapist who has lived the experience of therapy. Such an individual has several points to make in regard to the scientific view.

1. "In the first place," this "experientialist" points out, "science always has to do with the other, the object. Various logicians of science, including Stevens, show that it is a basic element of science that it always has to do with the observable object, the observable other. This is true, even if the scientist is experimenting on himself, for to that degree he treats himself as the observable other. It never has anything to do with the experiencing me. Now does not this quality of science mean that it must forever be irrelevant to an experience such as therapy, which is intensely personal, highly subjective in its inwardness, and dependent entirely on the relationship of two individuals each of whom is an experiencing me? Science can of course study the events which occur, but always in a way which is irrelevant to what is occurring. An analogy would be to say that science can conduct an autopsy of the dead events of therapy, but by its very nature it can never enter into the living physiology of therapy. It is for this reason that therapists recognize—usually intuitively—that any advance in therapy, any fresh knowledge of it, any significant new hypotheses in regard to it must come from the experience of the therapists and clients, and can never come from science. Again, to use an analogy, certain heavenly bodies were discovered solely from examination of the scientific measurements of the courses of the stars. Then the astronomers searched for these hypothesized bodies and found them. It seems decidedly unlikely that there will ever be a similar outcome in therapy, since science has nothing to say about the internal personal experience which 'I' have in therapy. It can only speak of the events which occur in 'him.' "

2. "Because science has as its field the 'other,' the 'object,' it means that everything it touches is transformed into an object. This has never presented a problem in the physical sciences. In the biological sciences it has caused certain difficulties. A number of medical men feel some concern as to whether the increasing tendency to view the human organism as an object, in spite of its scientific efficacy, may not be unfortunate for the patient. They would prefer to see him again regarded as a person. It is in the social sci-

ences, however, that this becomes a genuinely serious issue. It means that the people studied by the social scientist are always objects. In therapy, both client and therapist become objects for dissection, but not persons with whom one enters a living relationship. At first glance, this may not seem important. We may say that only in his role as scientist does the individual regard others as objects. He can also step out of this role and become a person. But if we look a little further we will see that this is a superficial answer. If we project ourselves into the future, and suppose that we had the answers to most of the questions which psychology investigates today, what then? Then we would find ourselves increasingly impelled to treat all others, and even ourselves, as objects. The knowledge of all human relationships would be so great that we would know it rather than live the relationships unreflectively. We see some foretaste of this in the attitude of sophisticated parents who know that affection 'is good for the child.' This knowledge frequently stands in the way of their being themselves, freely, unreflectively, affectionate or not. Thus the development of science in a field like therapy is either irrelevant to the experience, or may actually make it more difficult to live the relationship as a personal, experiential event."

3. The experientialist has a further concern. "When science transforms people into objects, as mentioned above, it has another effect. The end result of science is to lead toward manipulation. This is less true in fields like astronomy, but in the physical and social sciences, the knowledge of the events and their relationships leads to manipulation of some of the elements of the equation. This is unquestionably true in psychology, and would be true in therapy. If we know all about how learning takes place, we use that knowledge to manipulate persons as objects. This statement places no value judgment on manipulation. It may be done in highly ethical fashion. We may even manipulate ourselves as objects, using such knowledge. Thus, knowing that learning takes place more rapidly with repeated review rather than long periods of concentration of one lesson, I may use this knowledge to manipulate my learning of Spanish. But knowledge is power. As I learn the laws of learning I use them to manipulate others through advertisements, through propaganda, through prediction of their responses, and the control of those responses. It is not

too strong a statement to say that the growth of knowledge in the social sciences contains within itself a powerful tendency toward social control, toward control of the many by the few. An equally strong tendency is toward the weakening or destruction of the existential person. When all are regarded as objects, the subjective individual, the inner self, the person in the process of becoming, the unreflective consciousness of being, the whole inward side of living life, is weakened, devalued, or destroyed. Perhaps this is best exemplified by two books. Skinner's *Walden Two* is a psychologist's picture of paradise. To Skinner it must have seemed desirable, unless he wrote it as a tremendous satire. At any rate it is a paradise of manipulation, in which the extent to which one can be a person is greatly reduced, unless one can be a member of the ruling council. Huxley's *Brave New World* is frankly satire, but portrays vividly the loss of personhood which he sees as associated with increasing psychological and biological knowledge. Thus, to put it bluntly, it seems that a developing social science (as now conceived and pursued) leads to social dictatorship and individual loss of personhood. The dangers perceived by Kierkegaard a century ago in this respect seem much more real now, with the increase in knowledge, than they could have then."

4. "Finally," says the experientialist, "doesn't all this point to the fact that ethics is a more basic consideration than science? I am not blind to the value of science as a tool, and am aware that it can be a very valuable tool. But unless it is the tool of ethical *persons*, with all that the term persons implies, may it not become a Juggernaut? We have been a long time recognizing this issue, because in physical science it took centuries for the ethical issue to become crucial, but it has at last become so. In the social sciences the ethical issues arise much more quickly, because persons are involved. But in psychotherapy the issue arises most quickly and most deeply. Here is the maximizing of all that is subjective, inward, personal; here a relationship is lived, not examined, and a person, not an object, emerges; a person who feels, chooses, believes, acts, not as an automaton, but as a person. And here too is the ultimate in science—the objective exploration of the most subjective aspects of life; the reduction to hypotheses, and eventually to theorems, of all that has been regarded as most personal, most

completely inward, most thoroughly a private world. And because these two views come so sharply into focus here, we must make a choice—an ethical personal choice of values. We may do it by default, by not raising the question. We may be able to make a choice which will somehow conserve both values—but choose we must. And I am asking that we think long and hard before we give up the values that pertain to being a person, to experiencing, to living a relationship, to becoming, that pertain to one's self as a process, to one's self in the existential moment, to the inward subjective self that lives."

The Dilemma

There you have the contrary views as they occur sometimes explicitly, more often implicitly, in current psychological thinking. There you have the debate as it exists in me. Where do we go? What direction do we take? Has the problem been correctly described or is it fallacious? What are the errors of perception? Or if it is essentially as described, must we choose one or the other? And if so, which one? Or is there some broader, more inclusive formulation which can happily encompass both of these views without damage to either?

A Changed View of Science

In the year that has elapsed since the foregoing material was written, I have from time to time discussed the issues with students, colleagues, and friends. To some of them I am particularly indebted for ideas which have taken root in me.[2] Gradually I have come to believe that the most basic error in the original formulation was in the description of science. I should like, in this section, to attempt to correct that error, and in the following section to reconcile the revised points of view.

[2]I would like to mention my special debt to discussions with, and published and unpublished papers by, Robert M. Lipgar, Ross L. Mooney, David A. Rodgers, and Eugene Streich. My own thinking has fed so deeply on theirs, and become so intertwined with theirs, that I would be at a loss to acknowledge specific obligations. I only know that in what follows there is much which springs from them, through me. I have also profited from correspondence regarding the paper with Anne Roe and Walter Smet.

The major shortcoming was, I believe, in viewing science as something "out there," something spelled with a capital S, a "body of knowledge," existing somewhere in space and time. In common with many psychologists I thought of science as a systematized and organized collection of tentatively verified fact, and saw the methodology of science as the socially approved means of accumulating this body of knowledge, and continuing its verification. It has seemed somewhat like a reservoir into which all and sundry may dip their buckets to obtain water—with a guarantee of 99% purity. When viewed in this external and impersonal fashion, it seems not unreasonable to see Science not only as discovering knowledge in lofty fashion, but as involving depersonalization, a tendency to manipulate, a denial of the basic freedom of choice which I have met experientially in therapy. I should like now to view the scientific approach from a different, and I hope, a more accurate perspective.

Science in Persons

Science exists only in people. Each scientific project has its creative inception, its process, and its tentative conclusion, in a person or persons. Knowledge—even scientific knowledge—is that which is subjectively acceptable. Scientific knowledge can be communicated only to those who are subjectively ready to receive its communication. The utilization of science also occurs only through people who are in pursuit of values which have meaning for them. These statements summarize very briefly something of the change in emphasis which I would like to make in my description of science. Let me follow through the various phases of science from this point of view.

The Creative Phases

Science has its inception in a particular person who is pursuing aims, values, purposes, which have personal and subjective meaning for him. As a part of this pursuit, he, in some area, "wants to find out." Consequently, if he is to be a good scientist, he immerses himself in the relevant experience, whether that be the physics laboratory, the world of plant or animal life, the hospital, the psychological laboratory or clinic, or whatever. This immersion is complete and subjec-

tive, similar to the immersion of the therapist in therapy, described previously. He senses the field in which he is interested. He lives it. He does more than "think" about it—he lets his organism take over and react to it, both on a knowing and on an unknowing level. He comes to sense more than he could possibly verbalize about his field, and reacts organismically in terms of relationships which are not present in his awareness.

Out of this complete subjective immersion comes a creative forming, a sense of direction, a vague formulation of relationships hitherto unrecognized. Whittled down, sharpened, formulated in clearer terms, this creative forming becomes a hypothesis—a statement of a tentative, personal, subjective faith. The scientist is saying, drawing upon all his known and unknown experience, that "I have a hunch that such and such a relationship exists, and the existence of this phenomenon has relevance to my personal values."

What I am describing is the initial phase of science, probably its most important phase, but one which American scientists, particularly psychologists, have been prone to minimize or ignore. It is not so much that it has been denied as that it has been quickly brushed off. Kenneth Spence has said that this aspect of science is "simply taken for granted."[3] Like many experiences taken for granted, it also tends to be forgotten. It is indeed in the matrix of immediate personal, subjective experience that all science, and each individual scientific research, has its origin.

Checking with Reality

The scientist has then creatively achieved his hypothesis, his tentative faith. But does it check with reality? Experience has shown each one of us that it is very easy to deceive

[3]It may be pertinent to quote the sentences from which this phrase is taken. ". . . the data of all sciences have the same origin—namely, the immediate experience of an observing person, the scientist himself. That is to say, immediate experience, the initial matrix out of which all sciences develop, is no longer considered a matter of concern for the scientist. He simply takes it for granted and then proceeds to the task of describing the events occurring in it and discovering and formulating the nature of the relationships holding among them." Kenneth W. Spence, in *Psychological Theory*, M. H. Marx (Ed.), Macmillan, 1951, p. 173.

himself, to believe something which later experience shows is not so. How can I tell whether this tentative belief has some real relationship to observed facts? I can use, not one line of evidence only, but several. I can surround my observation of the facts with various precautions to make sure I am not deceiving myself. I can consult with others who have also been concerned with avoiding self-deception, and learn useful ways of catching myself in unwarranted beliefs, based on misinterpretation of observations. I can, in short, begin to use all the elaborate methodology which science has accumulated. I discover that stating my hypothesis in operational terms will avoid many blind alleys and false conclusions. I learn that control groups can help me to avoid drawing false inferences. I learn that correlations, and *t* tests and critical ratios and a whole array of statistical procedures can likewise aid me in drawing only reasonable inferences.

Thus scientific methodology is seen for what it truly is—a way of preventing me from deceiving myself in regard to my creatively formed subjective hunches which have developed out of the relationship between me and my material. It is in this context, and perhaps only in this context, that the vast structure of operationism, logical positivism, research design, tests of significance, etc., have their place. They exist, not for themselves, but as servants in the attempt to check the subjective feeling or hunch or hypothesis of a person with the objective fact.

And even throughout the use of such rigorous and impersonal methods, the important choices are all made subjectively by the scientist. To which of a number of hypotheses shall I devote time? What kind of control group is most suitable for avoiding self-deception in this particular research? How far shall I carry the statistical analysis? How much credence may I place in the findings? Each of these is necessarily a subjective personal judgment, emphasizing that the splendid structure of science rests basically upon its subjective use by persons. It is the best instrument we have yet been able to devise to check upon our organismic sensing of the universe.

The Findings

If, as scientist, I like the way I have gone about my investigation, if I have been open to all the evidence, if I have selected and used intelligently all the precautions against self-deception which I have been able to assimilate from others or to devise myself, then I will give my tentative belief to the findings which have emerged. I will regard them as a springboard for further investigation and further seeking.

It seems to me that in the best of science, the primary purpose is to provide a more satisfactory and dependable hypothesis, belief, faith, for the investigator himself. To the extent that the scientist is endeavoring to prove something to someone else—an error into which I have fallen into more than once—then I believe he is using science to bolster a personal insecurity, and is keeping it from its truly creative role in the service of the person.

In regard to the findings of science, the subjective foundation is well shown in the fact that at times the scientist may refuse to believe his own findings. "The experiment showed thus and so but I believe it is wrong," is a theme which every scientist has experienced at some time or other. Some very fruitful scientific discoveries have grown out of the persistent *disbelief*, by a scientist, in his own findings and those of others. In the last analysis he may place more trust in his total organismic reactions than in the methods of science. There is no doubt that this can result in serious error as well as in scientific discoveries, but it indicates again the leading place of the subjective in the use of science.

Communication of Scientific Findings

Wading along a coral reef in the Caribbean this morning, I saw a blue fish—I think. If you, quite independently, saw it too, then I feel more confidence in my own observation. This is what is known as intersubjective verification, and it plays an important part in our understanding of science. If I take you (whether in conversation or in print or behaviorally) through the steps I have taken in an investigation, and it seems to you too that I have not deceived myself, and that I have indeed come across a new relationship which is relevant to my values, and that I am justified in having a tentative faith in this relationship, then we have the beginnings of Science with a capital S. It is at this point that we are likely to think we have created a body of scientific knowledge. Actually there is no such body of knowledge. There are only tentative beliefs, existing subjectively, in a number of different persons. If these beliefs are not tentative, then what exists is dogma, not science. If on the other hand, no one but the investigator believes the finding, then this finding is either a personal and deviant matter, an instance of psychopathology, or else it is an unusual truth discovered by a genius, which as yet no one is subjectively ready to believe. This leads me to comment on the group which can put tentative faith in any given scientific finding.

Communication to Whom?

It is clear that scientific findings can be communicated only to those who have agreed to the same ground rules of investigation. The Australian bushman will be quite unimpressed with the findings of science regarding bacterial infection. He knows that illness truly is caused by evil spirits. It is only when he too agrees to scientific method as a good means of preventing self-deception, that he will be likely to accept its findings.

But even among those who have adopted the ground rules of science, tentative belief in the findings of a scientific research can only occur where there is a subjective readiness to believe. One could find many examples. Most psychologists are quite ready to believe evidence showing that the lecture system produces significant increments of learning, and quite unready to believe that the turn of an unseen card may be called through an ability labeled extrasensory perception. Yet the scientific evidence for the latter is considerably more impeccable than for the former. Likewise when the so-called "Iowa studies" first came out, indicating that intelligence might be considerably altered by environmental conditions, there was great disbelief among psychologists, and many attacks on the imperfect scientific methods used. The scientific evidence for this finding is not much better today than it was when the Iowa studies first appeared, but the subjective readiness of psychologists to believe such a finding has altered greatly. A historian of science has noted that empiricists, had they existed at the time, would have been the first to disbelieve the findings of Copernicus.

It appears then that whether I believe the scientific findings of others, or those of my own studies, depends in part on my readiness to put a tentative belief in such findings.[4] One reason we are not particularly aware of this subjective fact is that in the physical sciences particularly, we have gradually agreed that in a very large area of experience we are ready to believe any finding which can be shown to rest upon the rules of the scientific game, properly played.

The Use of Science

But not only is the origin, process, and conclusion of science something which exists only in the subjective experience of persons—so also is its utilization. "Science" will never depersonalize, or manipulate, or control individuals. It is only persons who can and will do that. This is surely a most obvious and trite observation, yet a deep realization of it has had much meaning for me. It means that the use which will be made of scientific findings in the field of personality is and will be a matter of subjective personal choice—the same type of choice as a person makes in therapy. To the extent that he has defensively closed off areas of his experience from awareness, the person is more likely to make choices which are socially destructive. To the extent that he is open to all phases of his experience we may be sure that this person will be more likely to use the findings and methods of science (or any other tool or capacity) in a manner which is personally and socially con-

---

[4]One example from my own experience may suffice. In 1941 a research study done under my supervision showed that the future adjustment of delinquent adolescents was best predicted by a measure of their realistic self-understanding and self-acceptance. The instrument was a crude one, but it was a better predictor than measures of family environment, hereditary capacities, social milieu, and the like. At that time I was simply not ready to believe such a finding, because my own belief, like that of most psychologists, was that such factors as the emotional climate in the family and the influence of the peer group were the real determinants of future delinquency and nondelinquency. Only gradually, as my experience with psychotherapy continued and deepened, was it possible for me to give my tentative belief to the findings of this study and of a later one (1944) which confirmed it. (For a report on these two studies see "The role of self understanding in the prediction of behavior" by C. R. Rogers, B. L. Kell, and H. McNeil, *Journal of Consulting Psychology*, 1948, *12*, 174–186.)

structive.[5] There is, in actuality then, no threatening entity of "Science" which can in any way affect our destiny. There are only people. While many of them are indeed threatening and dangerous in their defensiveness, and modern scientific knowledge multiplies the social threat and danger, this is not the whole picture. There are two other significant facets. (1) There are many other persons who are relatively open to their experience and hence likely to be socially constructive. (2) Both the subjective experience of psychotherapy and the scientific findings regarding it indicate that individuals are motivated to change, and may be helped to change, in the direction of greater openness to experience, and hence in the direction of behavior which is enhancing of self and society, rather than destructive.

To put it briefly, Science can never threaten us. Only persons can do that. And while individuals can be vastly destructive with the tools placed in their hands by scientific knowledge, this is only one side of the picture. We already have subjective and objective knowledge of the basic principles by which individuals may achieve the more constructive social behavior which is natural to their organismic process of becoming.

A New Integration

What this line of thought has achieved for me is a fresh integration in which the conflict between the "experientialist" and the "scientific" tends to disappear. This particular integration may not be acceptable to others, but it does have meaning to me. Its major tenets have been largely implicit in the preceding section, but I will try to state them here in a way which takes cognizance of the arguments between the opposing points of view.

Science, as well as therapy, as well as all other aspects of living, is rooted in and based upon the immediate, subjective experience of a person. It springs from the inner, total, organismic experiencing which is only partially and imperfectly communicable. It is one phase of subjective living.

[5] I have spelled out much more fully the rationale for this view in two recent papers: "The Concept of the Fully Functioning Person" (unpublished manuscript), and "Toward a Theory of Creativity" *ETC*, 1954, *11*, 249–260.

It is because I find value and reward in human relationships that I enter into a relationship known as therapeutic, where feelings and cognition merge into one unitary experience which is lived rather than examined, in which awareness is nonreflective, and where I am participant rather than observer. But because I am curious about the exquisite orderliness which appears to exist in the universe and in this relationship I can abstract myself from the experience and look upon it as an observer, making myself and/or others the objects of that observation. As observer I use all of the hunches which grow out of the living experience. To avoid deceiving myself as observer, to gain a more accurate picture of the order which exists, I make use of all the canons of science. Science is not an impersonal something, but simply a person living subjectively another phase of himself. A deeper understanding of therapy (or of any other problem) may come from living it, or from observing it in accordance with the rules of science, or from the communication within the self between the two types of experience. As to the subjective experience of choice, it is not only primary in therapy, but it is also primary in the use of scientific method by a person. I have even come to see that freedom of choice is not necessarily antithetical to the determinism which is a part of our framework for thinking scientifically. Since I have recently tried to spell out this relationship elsewhere,[6] I will not take the space to do so here.

What I will do with the knowledge gained through scientific method—whether I will use it to understand, enhance, enrich, or use it to control, manipulate, and destroy—is a matter of subjective choice dependent upon the values which have personal meaning for me. If, out of fright and defensiveness, I block out from my awareness large areas of experience—if I can see only those facts which support my present beliefs, and am blind to all others—if I can see only the objective aspects of life, and cannot perceive the subjective—if in any way I cut off my perception from the full range of its actual sensitivity—then I am likely to be socially destructive, whether I use as tool the knowledge and instruments of science, or the power and emotional strength of a subjective rela-

[6] In my paper on "The Concept of the Fully Functioning Person."

tionship. And on the other hand if I am open to my experience, and can permit all of the sensings of my intricate organism to be available to my awareness, then I am likely to use myself, my subjective experience, *and* my scientific knowledge, in ways which are realistically constructive.

This, then, is the degree of integration I have currently been able to achieve between two approaches first experienced as conflicting. It does not completely resolve all the issues posed in the earlier section, but it seems to point toward a resolution. It rewrites the problem or reperceives the issue, by putting the subjective, existential person, with the values which he holds, at the foundation and the root of the therapeutic relationship and of the scientific relationship. For science too, at its inception, is an "I-Thou" relationship with the world of perceived objects, just as therapy at its deepest is an "I-Thou" relationship with

a person or persons. And only as a subjective person can I enter either of these relationships.

REFERENCES

Rogers, C. R. The concept of the fully functioning person. Unpublished manuscript, n.d.

Rogers, C. R. Toward a theory of creativity. *ETC: A Review of General Semantics*, 1954, *11*, 249–260.

Rogers, C. R., Kell, B., & McNeil, H. The role of self-understanding in the prediction of behavior. *Journal of Consulting Psychology*, 1948, *12*, 174–186.

Spence, K. W. Types of constructs in psychology. In M. H. Marx (Ed.), *Psychological Theory*. New York: Macmillan, 1951.

Stephenson, W. Postulates of behaviorism. *Philosophy of Science*, 1953, *20*, 110–120.

Critical Evaluation

The phenomenologist's portrayal of the dilemmas of man is striking, but we must distinguish between skillful literary depiction and effective theorizing. No matter how compelling and vivid a theory may be, the crucial test does not lie in elegant persuasion, but in explicit hypothesis. Although phenomenologists are among the most acute observers of the human condition, their formulation of these observations into a theory is sporadic and casual. Perhaps these formulations should not be thought of as theory, but as a set of loosely connected observations and notions. So discursive a body of work, little concerned with problems of integration, structure, and continuity, lacking in tautness of systematic argument, cannot be viewed as a scientific theory at all. At best, it represents a consistent point of view; at worst, it is an ill-constructed social commentary.

Other critics object not to the loose structure of phenomenological theory but to what these theories propose. Particular exception is taken to their idealistic conception of man's inherent nature. The notion that man would be a constructive, rational, and socially conscious being, were he free of malevolent distortions of society, seems not only sentimental but invalid. There is something grossly naïve in exhorting man to live life to the fullest and then expecting socially beneficial consequences to follow. What evidence is there that one's inherent self-interest would not clash with the self-interests of others? There is something as banal as the proverbialism of a fortune cookie in the suggestion "be thyself." Conceiving man's emotional disorders as a failure to "be thyself" seems equally naïve and banal.

The critique by M. Brewster Smith presented here is not entirely unfriendly to the phenomenological position. Rather it argues against a number of naïve assumptions common among phenomenologists which would preclude the development of an adequate science of personality and psychopathology.

32 The Phenomenological Approach in Personality Theory: Some Critical Remarks

M. Brewster Smith

The "phenomenological approach" has recently come to be something of a rallying cry to a number of psychologists who share the "tender-minded" bias that psychology must, after all, come to terms with human experience, and who go so far as to believe that careful attention to this experience will leave the science of psychology not merely more satisfying to like-minded people, but also better science. Sharing this point of view and agreeing heartily with the program recommended by MacLeod (1947) in his article on "The Phenomenological Approach in Social Psychology," the present writer has been dismayed by some recent publications which, it seems to him, misconstrue the appropriate role of a phenomenological approach in a way that invites the critical to reject a humanized psychology lock, stock, and barrel. Since the writer would regard such an outcome as highly unfortunate, he feels that a clarification of the issues is badly needed, and herewith makes an attempt in this direction.

The position with which he would take particular issue is that of Snygg and Combs (1949; Combs, 1949) whose point of view has also been espoused by Rogers (1947). These authors contrast the objective or external frame of reference in psychology with the phenomenological, or internal frame of reference, and, declaring their stand firmly with phenomenology, proceed to muster on their side the names of Lewin, Lecky, Allport, Murphy, and Angyal, among others, even including the seemingly less tractable father-figure of Freud. In essence, their contention is that the locus of psychological causation lies entirely within the phenomenal field of conscious experience, and that it therefore be-

From *J. Abnormal & Social Psychol.* 45: 516–522, 1950, by permission of the American Psychological Association and the author.

hooves the psychological theorist—and therapist—to formulate his problems and concepts accordingly. Snygg and Combs give much attention to the individual's perceptual-cognitive field, particularly to the *self*, as its most salient feature. Written from this standpoint, psychology comes close to a rapprochement with common sense.

While applauding their emphasis on perception and the self, the present writer proposes that they are confusing phenomenology with what may be termed the subjective frame of reference. Sharply maintained, this distinction further helps to clarify certain persistent ambiguities in the theory of ego and self.

Phenomenology and Common Sense

One of the genuine merits of the phenomenological approach is that it brings psychology somewhat closer to the world of common sense. There is always the danger that psychology, in its concern for rigor and neatness, may divorce itself too completely from this source of problems and partial insights. Focussing scientific attention on the phenomenal world as it is presented to us, the world from which common sense also takes its start, the phenomenological approach can bring into the ken of the psychologist data and problems too often left to common sense by default. Like common sense, and unlike some current varieties of psychological theory, it does deal with experience, and thus presents itself as an attractive alternative to those who find a behavioristic psychology uncongenial.

But phenomenology is not common sense, nor can it rightly be called upon to justify a common-sense psychology. In MacLeod's phrase, the phenomenological approach "involves the adoption of what might be called an attitude of disciplined naïvete" (1947, p. 194). In many respects, its result may run exactly counter to common-sense conclusions. Common sense, with its preconceived categories and stock explanations, neither disciplined nor naïve, is full of pseudo-scientific theory, while phenomenology limits its concern to the unprejudiced *description* of the world of phenomena. To take the phenomenal world presented in conscious experience as completely explanatory of behavior is closer to common sense than to phenomenology or adequate science.

Yet this is essentially what Snygg and Combs have done in their attempt to rewrite psychology in a "phenomenological frame of reference." "*All behavior, without exception,*" they say, "*is completely determined by and pertinent to the phenomenal field of the behaving organism*" (1949, p. 15, italics theirs). And they go on to explain that

> by the phenomenal field we mean the entire universe, including himself, as it is experienced by the individual at the instant of action. . . . Unlike the "objective" physical field, the phenomenal field is not an abstraction or an artificial construction. It is simply the universe of naïve experience in which each individual lives, the everyday situation of self and surroundings which each person takes to be reality (1949, p. 15).

While they bow unnecessarily to current prejudice in avoiding the word *consciousness*, their meaning is clear, and their index spells it out: "Consciousness, *see* Phenomenal field."

It is one variant of common sense that consciousness completely explains behavior, but at this juncture, it is hard to see how such a view can be regarded as an acceptable scientific postulate. Quite apart from the metaphysical controversy about the status of consciousness as "real" or respectable, we have behind us Würzburg and we have behind us Freud, to mention but two major sources of evidence that a psychology of experience or consciousness has distinct explanatory limits. Where is the determining tendency represented in the phenomenal field? What of the inacceptable strivings that warp our behavior, what of our defensive techniques of adjustment that so often prove most effective precisely when we are least aware of them? It is no satisfactory solution to speak, as Snygg and Combs do, of a "unified field of figure-ground phenomena of which the individual is more or less conscious . . . [in which] the vague and fuzzy aspects of behavior correspond to and are parts of the vague and incompletely differentiated aspects of the field" (1949, p. 17). The clinical literature abounds with instances of unconsciously determined behavior which, far from being "vague and fuzzy," is on the contrary highly differentiated.

One suspects that such a psychology of consciousness has an element of common-sense appeal not unlike the attraction of allied forms of psychotherapy. It does make sense to the layman: it accords with what he is ready and able to recognize in himself. And it has distinct value within limits that it refuses to recognize. Because it over-states its claims, however, it may tend to promote the state of affairs away from which we have been striving—every man his own psychologist.

But McLeod has already made the relevant point succinctly: "The phenomenological method, in social psychology as in the psychology of perception [and we would add, psychology generally] can never be more than an approach to a scientific inquiry" (1947, p. 207). It provides certain kinds of data, not *all* the data. It furnishes the basis for certain valuable theoretical constructs; it does not give birth to them in full concreteness. It sets some problems and provides some clues; the psychologist, theorist or clinician, must *infer* the answers.

Subjective Constructs and the Observer's Frame of Reference

Here we reach the crux of the matter. If a psychology of consciousness is necessarily incomplete yet we do not abandon our hope for a psychology that comes to terms with human experience, what is the solution? A discussion of two lesser questions may indicate the nature of the answer. In the first place, does the decision to frame our psychological concepts and theories in terms appropriate to the "private world" of the behaving person commit us to the exclusive use of phenomenal concepts? Secondly, what is the appropriate role of the phenomenological approach in the service of this kind of theory-building?

Lewin, whose psychological life space Snygg and Combs equate to their phenomenal field (1949, p. 15), was entirely clear in maintaining a sharp distinction between the two concepts. He said:

It is likewise doubtful whether one can use consciousness as the sole criterion of what belongs to the psychological life space at a given moment in regard to social facts and relationships. The mother, the father, and brothers and sisters are not to be included as real facts in the psychological situation of the child only when they are immediately present. For example, the little child playing in the garden behaves differently when he knows his mother is at home than when he knows she is out. One cannot assume that this fact is continually in the child's consciousness. Also a prohibition or a goal can play an essential role in the psychological situation without being clearly present in consciousness. . . . Here, as in many other cases it is clear that one must distinguish between "appearance" and the "underlying reality" in a dynamic sense. In other words, the phenomenal properties are to be distinguished from the conditional-genetic characteristics of objects and events, that is, from the properties which determine their casual relationships. . . . As far as the conceptual derivation is concerned for existence: "*What is real is what has effects*" (1936, p. 19).

Lewin's life space, then, is *not* merely the phenomenal field. And he adds to our previous considerations cogent reasons for thinking that a psychology of the phenomenal field cannot be adequately explanatory. His life space is not immediately given in the concreteness of experience; it is an abstract, hypothetical construct, inferred by the psychologist-observer to account for the individual's behavior.

It is, however, a construct of a type that differs from constructs of behavioristic psychology. It is formulated in terms of what is behaviorally real to the acting individual, not primarily in terms of what is physically observable to the scientist. Hence it is legitimate to speak of theories like Lewin's as anchored in a *subjective* (not phenomenological) *frame of reference*. Lewin's concepts and many of Freud's are in this sense *subjective constructs*, not because they are built of the stuff of conscious experience, but because they attempt to deal with what is effectively real to the individual, even when it is real to the scientific observer only in this secondary, indirect way.

The subjective frame of reference in theory construction is to be contrasted with the *objective frame of reference*, wherein concepts are chosen so as to be rooted as closely as possible in effective realities shared by any qualified observer. This is the distinction that Snygg and Combs seek, which makes them see both Freud and Lewin as precursors. There is no absolute difference between the two frames of reference; it is rather a question of which criteria are weighted most strongly in the selection of constructs.

Both the subjective and objective frames of reference pertain to the choice of constructs and the theoretical context in which they are embedded. They in no sense conflict with what has been called the *observer's frame of reference*, which indeed, lies at the foundation of all science. The problem of establishing a bridge between the point of view of the observer and *either* subjective or objective inferential constructs is the familiar one of operational definition. It cannot, in the last analysis, be avoided unless one chooses the alternative of claiming *direct* access to the point of view of the observed. This is the position of intuitionism, which asserts that the observer's and subject's points of view can be merged. But is this science? Not in the sense of a systematic search for understanding that can withstand the equally systematic doubt of the man from Missouri.

Subjective constructs framed in terms of the "private world" of the behaving individual remain constructs, and as such must ultimately be rooted in data accessible to the observer's frame of reference. There is no reason at all why their source should be restricted to the data of communicated conscious experience, in answer to our first question. But the phenomenological approach, or, more generally, any means of access to the experience of the subject, is of course crucial to the formulation of subjective constructs and the investigation of their relationships. Perhaps the point has been labored, but it is an essential one: the phenomenological approach, the clinical interview, the projective protocol, the behavioral observation—none of these yield direct knowledge of psychological constructs, subjective or objective, while all of them can provide the basis for inferring explanatory constructs and their relationships. If the canons of inference can be made sufficiently explicit, they provide the operational definitions that secure the constructs in the scientific home base of the observer's frame of reference.

Methods that get the subject to reveal his private world as he sees it need to be supplemented by others which permit the observer to infer effective factors that are distorted or disguised in the subject's awareness. But the broadly phenomenological methods remain a signally important source of data. Certain important subjective constructs such as the *self*, moreover, are anchored fairly directly in the data of phenomenological report.

Ego, Self, and Phenomenology

Although there is still considerable confusion in usage, a degree of consensus seems to be emerging to employ the term *self* for the phenomenal content of the experience of personal identity. A salient feature of the phenomenal field that has figured largely in personality theory, the self in this sense has the conceptual properties of a phenomenal object. Murphy (1947) and Chein (1944) use it with this meaning. Snygg and Combs agree, writing with somewhat franker circularity:

> Of particular importance in the motivation of behavior will be those parts of the phenomenal field perceived by him to be part or characteristic of himself. To refer to this important aspect of the total field we have used the term *phenomenal self* (1949, p. 111).

Within the phenomenal self, they distinguish as a stable core the *self-concept:* "Those parts of the phenomenal field which the individual has differentiated as definite and fairly stable characteristics of himself" (1949, p. 112).

Sharing with Murphy a strong emphasis on responses to the self as fundamental to motivational theory, Snygg and Combs go so far as to state that the basic human need is "the preservation and enhancement of the phenomenal self" (1949, p. 58). Changes in the perception of the self play a major role in the theory of the therapeutic process that they share with Rogers (1947).

Let us look more closely, however, at how these writers actually use the term. Passages like the following can readily be found:

> . . . when the self is free from any threat of attack or likelihood of attack, then it is possible for the self to consider these hitherto rejected perceptions, to make new differentiations, and to reintegrate the self in such a way as to include them (Rogers, 1947, p. 365).

A self threatened by its perceptions may deny the perception by simply refusing to enter the situation where such a perception is forced upon him (Snygg and Combs, 1947, p. 148).

Can a phenomenal self consider perceptions and reintegrate itself; can a threatened phenomenal self deny perceptions; or is this rather double-talk resulting from the attempt to make one good concept do the work of two? If, as this writer suspects, the latter is the case, what is the nature of the hidden second concept, which evidently is not merely a percept or phenomenal entity? To give it a name he would suggest the conventional term *ego*, realizing that usage in this respect is even more ambiguous than with the term *self*. The important point is that the concept, implicit in the writings of Rogers and of Snygg and Combs, is a subjective construct but does not refer to a phenomenal entity, whereas the self, on the other hand, is a coordinate subjective construct that does. The relation between the two will bear closer examination.

It is not necessary, at this juncture, to propose a definitive theory of the ego, nor to enter into an involved discussion of alternative views about its nature. What is relevant is that starting from an attempt to write a psychology in phenomenal terms, our authors in spite of themselves give implicit recognition to organizing, selective processes in the personality which are somehow guided by the nature and status of the self (among other things) and somehow, in turn, have an influence in its nature and status. So conceived, the relation of ego and self is highly interdependent[1] but by no means an indentity. The distinction is that between a dynamic configuration of ongoing processes, inferred from many facts of biography and behavior, and a phenomenal entity resulting from these processes and affecting them in turn, inferred primarily (but not exclusively) from phenomenological report.

Approaching the problem on a slightly different tack, we may find it rewarding to consider three of the eight conceptions of the ego listed by Allport (1943, p. 459) in the light of the distinction just made: the ego "as one segregated behavioral system among others," "as knower," and "as object of knowledge." The fundamental conception advanced here is not unlike the first of these senses, if one reads

---

[1] The writer doubts that it is advisable to construct the ego as narrowly around the self as do Chein (1944) and Murphy (1947).

into it a dynamic quality not expressed in Allport's formulation. As an on-going system of organizing and selective processes mediating the individual's intercourse with reality, it includes a variety of processes without being coterminous with the total personality.[2] Among these processes or functions is that of the ego as "knower," which the writer would take in a less metaphysical sense than Allport's to embrace the cognitive-perceptual functions of personality. These have been described with reason in psychoanalytic theory (Freud, 1933, pp. 105–106) as an integral aspect of the ego system. Among the phenomena that the ego "knows" is the *self*, Allport's "ego as object of knowledge." Like any cognitive-perceptual object, the self only imperfectly mirrors the physical, psychological, and social facts that underlie the perception. And also like similar phenomenal objects it serves as a guide to appropriate behavior. But the relation of self to ego-processes is no more and no less obscure than the relation of cognitive structures to behavior generally.

"Ego-Involvements" and "Ego Defense"

We have sought to reinstate the ego as a subjective but non-phenomenal construct mainly through an examination of the pitfalls encountered by the attempt to avoid such a concept. If the ego–self distinction as outlined above is worth making, however, it should make a difference in the formulation of other knotty problems. Does it? Two such problems—the nature of "ego-involvements" and of the "mechanisms of defense"—will be examined briefly as test cases.

As it emerges in the work of Sherif and Cantril (1947), the concept of ego-involvement lacks clarity and focus. Widely divergent sorts of psychological facts turn out to be embraced by the term, which, like so many in popular psychological currency, rather identifies a disparate group of problems than clarifies them. More often than not,

[2]How to distinguish within the personality between *ego* and *non-ego* is, of course, an important problem, though it will not be attempted here. The distinction, however, is not the same as the phenomenal one between the *self* and *notself* (often described, confusingly, as *ego-alien*).

ego-involvement means the involvement of a person's pride and self-esteem in a task; he feels put to the test and ready to be ashamed of a poor performance. In other instances, the term is invoked to cover immersion in a cause, or falling in love—cases in which the person, to be sure, cares as deeply about outcomes as in the first type, but may be engrossed to the point of losing self-awareness.

Now the present self–ego distinction makes excellent sense when applied here. Since the distinctive character of the first sort of examples lies in the fact that the individual's conception of his self and its worth is at stake, these can aptly be described as *self-involvement*. The second type of case can often still be called ego-involvement without inconsistency. The situation in the latter instances touches on the person's central system of on-going psychological processes so closely that he may lose himself in it. Similar engrossment can, to be sure, result from the involvement of equally imperative non-ego processes: who is to say, without intimate acquaintance with the principals, whether being in love should be called ego-involvement or "id-involvement"! However that may be, note that self-involvement and ego-involvement thus conceived may vary independently. A person may care about a task both because of its intrinsic meaning for him and with after-thought for its bearing on his prestige and self-esteem. Or either or neither may be the case. The behavioral conditions and consequences of ego- and self-involvement should furthermore be quite distinct.

The situation is somewhat different in regard to the theoretical status of the mechanisms of defense. Here the classical formulation by Anna Freud (1946) regards the defense mechanisms as employed by the ego (the term is used essentially in our sense) to protect itself, primarily from disruption by strong unassimilated urges, but also from threats from the external world. As a more or less precariously balanced system mediating between inner strivings and outer reality, the ego, in this view, has recourse to these sometimes drastic techniques in order to preserve its balance, and maintain the course of behavior at a lower level of adjustment if need be rather than run the risk of its catastrophic disruption. Murphy (1947), and later Snygg and Combs (1949), on the other hand, say in effect that it is rather the self that is defended. Under conditions of threat, enhancement and preservation of the self may be achieved by the classical defense mechanisms. Is it necessary to choose between these divergent formulations, or can the conflict be resolved?

The present writer would maintain that the mechanisms of defense can ultimately all be conceived as defenses of the ego, since they serve to bolster up the ego's adjustive compromise. As contributors to this compromise, they can also best be regarded as a part of the activity included in the ego system. But in a more immediate sense, any particular one of an individual's defenses may or may *not* be a *self*-defense mechanism. Since the maintenance of a favorable self-image is important to sound ego functioning, though not its only requisite, the end of ego defense can often be served most efficiently by self-defense mechanisms. Certain mechanisms, like identification, may, indeed, always take effect through the defense of the self. There are, however, instances of ego-defense mechanisms which involve the self only indirectly if at all. In regression, for example, one can hardly suppose that the self is enhanced in any way. What is more likely is that by retreating to an earlier, more deeply established, or simpler level of ego organization, the person seeks, perhaps ineptly, to cope with disturbing experiences that, by reason of circumstance, constitution, or previous learning, he has not the strength to meet maturely. In most cases, the relative significance of the self in the defensive process probably cannot be assessed in any simple way, since changes in the self for better or worse may be the *consequence* of the fortunes of the ego and its defenses, as well as the focus of defensive techniques.

A formulation of this sort, which seems to agree with present clinical experience, again suggests the usefulness of a distinction between phenomenal and non-phenomenal (shall we say *functional?*) subjective constructs, with both employed in proper coordination. A purely phenomenological psychology, on the other hand, cannot adequately describe *all* the defensive processes, since neither all the effective threats to the ego nor all the defenses against them are registered accurately in conscious awareness. Indeed, it is largely the consequence of "silent" defensive processes that phenomenological reports must be viewed with so much circumspection in personality research.

Conclusions

Starting from a discussion of Snygg and Combs' proposal of a phenomenological frame of reference for psychology (1949) the writer has sought to establish the following major points:

1. While common sense may favor an explanatory psychology framed entirely in terms of conscious experience, such a psychological system does violence to currently available knowledge.

2. Phenomenology, as distinct from common sense, is descriptive, not explanatory. It is an approach or method ancillary to the formulation of problems and derivation of constructs, and does not give birth to these constructs full blown.

3. The subjective and objective frames of reference, which denote relatively different alternative contexts within which constructs may be selected, are both entirely compatible with the observer's frame of reference. Subjective constructs to be scientifically admissible must ultimately be anchored in the data of observation.

4. The phenomenological approach provides one method of deriving subjective constructs. But not all subjective constructs need represent phenomenal entities. They may, thus, denote functional entities that are either absent from the phenomenal field or inaccurately presented in it.

5. The coordinate use of phenomenal and non-phenomenal subjective constructs, maintained in clear distinction from one another, serves to clarify the theory of the ego and the self. It is proposed that an adequate theory of personality must distinguish, among other constructs.

  a. the *ego*, a *non-phenomenal* subjective construct representisng a configuration of ongoing processes, among which is the cognitive-perceptual function. Through exercise of this function, the ego "knows," among other things,

  b. the *self*, a *phenomenal* subjective construct.

6. When carried into current problems concerning the nature of "ego-involvement"

and of the "mechanisms of defense," the above distinction seems productive.

REFERENCES

Allport, G. W. The ego in contemporary psychology. *Psychol. Rev.*, 1943, *50*, 451–478.

Chein, I. The awareness of self and the structure of the ego. *Psychol. Rev.*, 1944. *51*, 304–314.

Combs, A. W. A phenomenological approach to adjustment. *J. abnorm. soc. Psychol.*, 1949, *44*, 29–35.

Freud, A. *The ego and the mechanisms of defense.* New York: International University Press, 1946.

Freud, S. *New introductory lectures on psychoanalysis.* New York: Norton, 1933.

Lewin, K. *Principles of topological psychology.* New York: McGraw-Hill, 1936.

MacLeod, R. B. The phenomenological approach to social psychology. *Psychol. Rev.*, 1947, *54*, 193–210.

Murphy, G. *Personality: A biosocial approach to origins and structure.* New York: Harper, 1947.

Rogers, C. R. Some observations on the organization of personality. *Amer. Psychologist*, 1947, *2*, 358–368.

Sherif, M., and Cantril, H. *The psychology of ego-involvements.* New York: Wiley, 1947.

Snygg, D., and Combs, A. W. *Individual behavior: A new frame of reference for psychology.* New York: Harper, 1949.

Integrative Directions

The two theorists represented in this section are men of strong and independent inclinations. Both were trained originally as intrapsychic therapists, having made significant early contributions from that perspective. Neither had the temperament or intellect to remain constrained within the procrustean confines of orthodox psychoanalysis, breaking out in not dissimilar, yet highly original ways.

"Fritz" Perls turned increasingly existential in his approach, developing along with a coterie of younger disciples a model that sought to fuse intrapsychic depths with a phenomenological focus on the here-and-now, a theory and technique he labeled Gestalt therapy.

Crossing a wide band of schools and treatment philosophies, Albert Ellis has synthesized the recently emergent phenomenological-cognitive and behavioral-learning approaches into what he previously termed rational-emotive therapy. Ellis argues persuasively that man must judge his behaviors, not in terms of what others wish or expect, but in terms of what he believes and senses is right for him.

33   From Orthodox Psychoanalysis to the Gestalt Approach

Frederick S. Perls

Introduction

Ego, Hunger, and Aggression represents the transition from orthodox psychoanalysis to the Gestalt approach. It contains many ideas which even now—after twenty years—have not found their way into modern psychiatry.

The concepts of here-and-now reality, the organism-as-a-whole, and the dominance of the most urgent need are being accepted. However, the significance of aggression as a biological force, the relation of aggression to assimilation, the symbolic nature of the Ego, the phobic attitude in neurosis, the organism-environment unity are far from being understood.

In the last decade the awareness theory has been widely accepted, and is practiced under the names of sensitivity training and T-groups. The significance of spontaneous non-verbal expression (such as movements of the hands and eyes, posture, voice, etc.) has been recognized. In the therapeutic setting, the emphasis begins to shift from the phobic (so-called objective) couch situation to the encounter of a human therapist with, not a case, but another human being.

These are good beginnings, but there is still much to do. The probability that individual and long-range therapy might both be obsolete has not yet dawned upon the vast majority of therapists and patients. True enough, groups and workshops find increasing acceptance, but more for their economic feasibility than for their efficacy. Yet the individual session should be the exception rather than the rule. Perhaps this sounds as heretical as a proposal I made some time ago: Dealing with behavior out of the here-and-now is a waste of time.

Great strides have been made since Freud's monumental discoveries. To note a few important ones: Sullivan's emphasis on the self-esteem; Berne's concept of game playing; Roger's of feed-back; and, especially, Reich's bringing down to earth the psychology of resistances. The development from symptom

From *Ego, Hunger, and Aggression*, 1969, by permission of the publisher, Random House.

to character to existential therapy to the arrival of humanistic psychology is most promising. But. . . the majority swallowed Freud's theories hook, line and sinker, without realizing that this blind acceptance formed the root of a narrow-mindedness paralysing many of the potentialities of his ingenious discoveries. A sectarianism resulted, characterized by an almost religious credulity, by a passionate search for further proofs and by a patronizing refusal of any facts apt to disturb these sacrosanct ways of thinking. Additional theories complicated the original system, and, as always with sects, each one became intolerant of any other which deviated from the accepted principles. If anybody did not believe in the "absolute truth," a theory was handy which put the responsibility on the complexes and resistances of the sceptic.

There is another point in classical psychoanalysis which cannot stand the scrutiny of dialectical thinking—Freud's "archaeological" complex, his one-sided interest in the past. No objectivity, no real insight into the working of the dynamics of life is possible, without taking into account the counter-pole, that is the future, and, above all, the present as zero-point of past and future. We find the condensation of Freud's historic outlook in the concept of transference.[1]

The other day, whilst waiting for a tram, I pondered over the word transference, and I realized that there would have been no tram, if it had not been transferred from the factory or other tramway lines to the rails in front of me. But the running of a tramway line is not explained by this transference alone. It is a coincidence of several factors, e.g. functioning of electric current and the presence of a staff. These factors, however, are only "means whereby," while the decisive factor is the need for conveyance. Without the passengers' requirements the tram service would be quickly abolished. It would not even have been created.

It is unfortunate that one has to mention such platitudes to demonstrate how selected

[1] According to Freud, a neurosis rests on three pillars; sex instinct, repression and transference.

and comparatively unimportant a part the transference plays in the whole complex. And yet, whatever happens in psychoanalysis is not interpreted as a spontaneous reaction of the patient in answer to the analytical situation, but is supposed to be dictated by the repressed past. Freud even goes so far as to maintain that a neurosis is cured once the childhood amnesia is undone, once the patient has gained a continuous knowledge of his past. If a young man, who has never found anybody to understand his difficulties, develops a feeling of gratitude towards the analyst I doubt whether there exists a person in his past from whom he transfers his thankfulness to the analyst.

On the other hand it is silently acknowledged that the futuristic, the teleological thinking plays its part in psychoanalysis. We analyse a patient *in order* to cure him. The patient says many things *for the purpose* of covering up essential things. The analyst *aims at* stimulating and completing developments which have been arrested.

Besides transference, spontaneous reactions and futuristic thinking, there are the projections which play a very great part in the analytical situation. The patient visualizes disagreeable parts of his own unconscious personality in the analyst, who can often search till he is blue in the face for the original from whom the patient has transferred his image.

A mistake similar to the over-estimation of causes and transference occurs in the concept of "regression." Regression in the psychoanalytical sense is a historical regression, a sliding back to infancy. Is there not a possibility of interpreting it differently? Regression might mean nothing more than a falling back to the true Self, a breakdown of pretences and of all those character features which have not become part and parcel of the personality and which have not been assimilated into the neurotic's "whole."

In order to understand the decisive difference between *actual* and *historical* regression and *actual* and *historical* analysis we have to direct our attention first of all to the time factor.

Time

Einstein is of the opinion that the time sense is a matter of experience. The small child has not yet developed it. The awakening of a suckling occurs when the hunger tension has become so high as to interrupt sleep. This is not due to any sense of time: on the contrary, the hunger helps to create such a sense. Although we do not know of any organic equivalents of the time sense, its existence has to be assumed, if not by anything else than by the accuracy with which some people can tell the correct time.

The longer the delay of wish gratification, the greater the impatience, when the concentration remains on the object of gratification. The impatient person wants the immediate, *timeless* joining of his vision with reality. If you wait for a tram, the idea "tram" might slide into the background and you might entertain yourself by thinking, observing, reading or whatever pastime is at hand until the tram arrives. If, however, the tram remains a figure in your mind, then ¶ appears as impatience, you feel like running to meet the tram. "If the mountain does not come to Mohammed, Mohammed must go to the mountain." If you suppress the tendency to run towards the tram (and this self-control has become, with most of us, automatic and unconscious) you become restless, annoyed; if you are too inhibited to let off steam by swearing and becoming "nervous," and if you repress this impatience, you will probably transform it into anxiety, headache or some other symptom.

Someone was asked to explain Einstein's theory of relativity. He answered: "When you spend an hour with your girl, the time flies; an hour seems like a minute; but when you happen to sit on a hot stove, time crawls, seconds seem like hours." This does not conform to the psychological reality. In an hour of love, if the contact is perfect, the time factor does not enter the picture at all. Should the girl, however, become a nuisance, should contact with her be lost and boredom set in, then you might start counting the minutes until you can get rid of her. The time factor will also be experienced, if time is limited, when you want to cram as much as possible into the minutes at your disposal.

There are, however, exceptions to the rule. The repressed memories in our Unconscious are, according to Freud, timeless. This means that they are not subject to change as long as they remain in a system isolated from the rest of the personality. They are like sardines in a tin which apparently remain for ever six weeks old or whatever their age was, when they were caught. As long as they are isolated from the rest of the world very little change takes place until (by being eaten up or oxydized) they return to the world metabolism.

The time centre of ourselves as conscious human time-space events is the present. *There is no other reality than the present.* Our desire to retain more of the past or to anticipate the future might completely overgrow this sense of reality. Although we can isolate the present from the past (causes) and from the future (purpose), any giving up of the present as the centre of balance—as the lever of our life—must lead to an unbalanced personality. It does not matter if you sway over to the right (over-conscientiousness) or to the left (impulsiveness), if you over-balance forward (future) or backwards (past), you can lose your balance in any direction.

This applies to everything, and, of course, to the psycho-analytical treatment as well. Here the only existing reality is the analytical interview. Whatever we experience there, we experience in the present. This must be the basis for every attempt at "organismic reorganization." When we remember, we remember at that very second and to certain purposes; when we think of the future we anticipate things to come, but we do so at the present moment and from various causes. Predilection for either historical or futuristic thinking always destroys contact with reality.

Lack of contact with the present, lack of the actual "feel" of ourselves, leads to flight either into the past (historical thinking) or into the future (anticipatory thinking). Both "Epimetheus" Freud and "Prometheus" Adler, co-operating with the neurotic's desire to dig into the past or to safeguard the future, have missed the Archimedic point of readjustment. By giving up the present as a permanent referent the advantage of going back to the past in order to profit from our experiences and mistakes, changes into its opposite: it becomes detrimental to development. We become sentimental or acquire the habit of blaming parents or circumstances (resentment); often the past becomes a "consummation devoutly to be wished for." In short, we develop a retrospective character. The prospective character, in contrast, loses himself in the future. His impatience leads him to phantastic anticipations which—in contrast to planning—are eating up his interest in the present, his contact with reality.

Freud has the correct intuition in his belief that contact with the present is essential. He demands free-floating attention, which means awareness of all experiences; but what happens is that slowly but surely patient and analyst become conditioned to two things; firstly, to the technique of free associations, of the flight of ideas and, secondly, to a state in which analyst and patient form, as it were, a company fishing for memories, the free-floating attention floating away. Open-mindedness is in practice narrowed down to the almost exclusive interest in the past and the libido.

Freud is not exact about time. When he says the dream stands with one leg in the present, with the other in the past, he includes the past few days into the present. But what happened even only a minute ago is past, not present. The difference between Freud's conception and mine may seem irrelevant, yet actually it is not merely a matter of pedantry, but a principle involving practical applications. A fraction of a second might mean the difference between life and death, as we have seen in Chapter I, in the coincidence of the falling stone killing a man.

The disregard of the present necessitated the introduction of "transference." If we do not leave room for the spontaneous and creative attitude of the patient, then we have either to search for explanations in the past (to assume that he transfers every bit of his behaviour from remote times to the analytical situation) or, following up Adler's teleological thinking, we have to restrict ourselves to finding out what purposes, what arrangements the patient has in mind, what plans he has up his sleeve.

By no means do I deny that everything has its origin in the past and tends to further development, but what I want to bring home is, that past and future take their bearings continuously from the present and have to be related to it. Without the reference to the present they become meaningless. Consider such a concrete thing as a house built years ago, originating in the past and having a purpose, namely to be lived in. What happens to the house if one is satisfied with the historical fact alone of its having been built? Without being cared for, the house would fall into ruin, subjected, as it would be, to the influence of wind and weather, to dry and wet rot, and other decaying influences which, though small and sometimes invisible, have an accumulative effect.

Freud has shaken up our concepts of causality, morality and responsibility; but he stopped half-way: he has not driven the analysis to its ultimate conclusions. He said we are not as good or bad as we believe we are, but we are unconsciously mostly worse, sometimes better. Accordingly, he transferred responsibility from the Ego to the Id. Furthermore, he unmasked intellectual causes as rationalizations and decided that the Unconscious provides the causes for our actions.

How can we replace causal thinking? How do we overcome the difficulties of taking our bearings from the present and achieving a scientific understanding without asking for reasons? I have mentioned before the advantages that accrue from functional thinking. If we have the pluck to attempt to follow modern science in its decision that there are no ultimate answers to the "Why?" we come across a very comforting discovery: all relevant questions can be answered by asking: "How?" "Where?" and "When?" Detailed description is identical with concentration and increased knowledge. Research requires detailed descriptions, without neglecting the context. The rest is a matter of opinion or theory, faith or interpretation.

Past and Future

Although we do not know much more about time than that it is one of the four dimensions of our existence, we are able to define the present. The present is the ever-moving zero-point of the opposites past and future. A properly balanced personality takes into account past and future without abandoning the zero-point of the present, without seeing past or future as realities. All of us look both backward and forward, but a person who is unable to face an unpleasant present and lives mainly in the past or future, wrapped up in historic or futuristic thinking, is not adapted to reality. Thus reality—in addition to the figure-background-formation, as shown previously—gets a new aspect provided by the sense of actuality.

Day-dreaming is one of the few occupations which are generally recognized as flight from the zero-point of the present into the future, and in such a case it is customary to refer to this as escape from reality. On the other hand, there are people who come to the analyst, only too willing to comply with the popular idea of psycho-analysis—namely to unearth all possible infantile memories or traumata. With a retrospective character the analyst can waste years in following up this wild-goose chase. Being convinced that digging up the past is a panacea for neurosis he merely collaborates with the patient's resistance of facing the present.

The constant delving into the past has a further disadvantage, in that it neglects to take into account the opposite, the future, thereby missing the point in a whole group of neuroses. Let us consider a typical case of anticipatory neurosis: A man, on going to bed, worries about how he will sleep; in the morning he is full of resolutions as to the work he is going do in his office. On his arrival there he will not carry out his resolutions, but will prepare all the material he intends conveying to the analyst, although he will not bring forward this material in the analysis. When the time comes for him to use the facts he has prepared, his mind occupies itself instead with his expectation of having supper with his girl friend, but during the meal he will tell the girl all about the work he has to attend to before going to bed, and so on and on. This example is not an exaggeration, for there are quite a number of people always a few steps or miles ahead of the present. They never collect the fruits of their efforts, as their plans never make contact with the present—with reality.

What is the use of making a man, haunted by unconscious fear of starvation, realize that his fear originated in the poverty experienced in his childhood? It is much more important to demonstrate that by staring into the future and striving for security he spoils his *present* life; that his ideal of accumulating superfluous wealth is isolated and separated from the sense of life. It is essential that such a man should learn the "feel of himself," should restore all the urges and needs, all the pleasures and pains, all the emotions and sensations that make life worth living, and which have become background or have been repressed for the sake of his golden ideal. He must learn to make other contacts in life besides his business connections. He must learn to work *and* play.

Such people develop an open neurosis once they have lost their only contact with the world—the business contact. This is known as the neurosis of the retired business-man. Of what use is an historical analysis to him, except for providing a pastime to fill a few hours of his empty life? Sometimes a game of cards might serve the same purpose. At the seaside one often finds this type of man (having no contact with nature), who would refuse to leave the stuffy cardroom, to have a look at the beauty of a sunset. He would rather stick to his senseless occupation of exchanging cards, of holding on to his "dummy" than to face contact with nature.

Other types that look into the future are the worriers, the astrologists, the safety-first-never-take-a-chance fellows.

Historians, archaeologists, explanation seekers and complainers look in the other direction, and most attached to the past is the person who is unhappy in life, "because" his parents have not given him a proper education, or who is sexually impotent, "because" he acquired a castration complex, when his mother had threatened to cut off his penis as a punishment for masturbation.

Seldom is the discovery of such a "cause" in the past a decisive factor in the cure. The majority of people in our society have not had an "ideal" education, and most people have experienced castration threats in their childhood without becoming impotent. I know of a case in which all the possible details of such a castration complex came to the surface without essentially influencing the impotency. The analyst had interpreted the patient's disgust towards the female sex. The patient had accepted the interpretation, but never managed to feel, to experience nausea. So he could not change disgust into its opposite, appetite.

The retrospective person avoids taking the responsibility for his life and actions; he prefers placing the blame on something that happened in the past instead of taking steps to remedy the present situation. For manageable tasks one does not need scapegoats or explanations.

In the analysis of the retrospective character one always finds a distinct symptom: the suppression of *crying*. Mourning is a part of the resignation-process, necessary if one is to overcome the clinging to the past. This process called "mourning labour" is one of the most ingenious discoveries of Freud. The fact that resignation requires the work of the whole organism demonstrates how important the "feel of oneself" is, how the experience and expression of the deepest emotions is needed to adjust oneself after the loss of a valuable contact. In order to regain the possibility of making contact anew, the task of

mourning must be finished. Though the sad event is past, the dead is not dead—it is still present. The mourning labour is done in the present: it is not what the dead person meant to the mourner that is decisive, but what he still *means* to him. The loss of a crutch is of no importance if one was injured about five years ago and has since been cured; it matters only if one is still lame and needs the crutch.

Although I have tried to deprecate futuristic and historical thinking, I do not wish to give a wrong impression. We must not entirely neglect the future (e.g., planning) or the past (unfinished situations), but we must realize that the past has gone, leaving us with a number of unfinished situations and that *planning must be a guide to, not a sublimation of, or a substitute for, action.*

People often make "historical mistakes." By this expression I do not mean the confounding of historical data but the mistaking of past for actual situations. In the legal sphere laws are still valid which have long since lost their *raison d'être*. Religious people, too, dogmatically hold on to rites which once made sense but which are out of place in a different civilization. When the ancient Jew was not allowed to drive a vehicle on the Sabbath, it made sense, for the beast of burden should have a day's rest, but the pious Jew of our time submits to unnecessary inconvenience by refusing to use a tram which runs in any case. He changes sense into nonsense—at least so it appears to us. He looks at it from a different angle. Dogma could not retain its dynamic, could not even exist, if it were not supported by futuristic thinking. The believer holds up the religious law *in order to* be in "God's good books," to gain prestige as a religious man or to avoid unpleasant pricks of conscience. He must not feel the historical mistake he makes, otherwise his life-gestalt, the sense of his existence, would fall to pieces, and he would be thrown into utter confusion by the loss of his bearings.

Similar to the historical are the futuristic mistakes. We expect something, we hope for something, and we are disappointed, maybe very unhappy, if our hopes are not fulfilled. We are then very much inclined to blame either fate, other people, or our own inabilities, but we are not prepared to see the fundamental mistake of expecting that reality should coincide with our wishes. We avoid seeing that we are responsible for the disappointment which arises from our expectation, from our futuristic thinking, especially if we neglect the actuality of our limitations. Psycho-analysis has overlooked this essential factor, although it has dealt abundantly with disappointment "reactions."

The most important "historical mistake" of classical psycho-analysis is the indiscriminate application of the term "regression." The patient evinces a helplessness, a reliance on his mother, unbefitting an adult, becoming to a child of three. There is nothing to be said against an analysis of his childhood (if the patient's historical mistake is sufficiently emphasized), but in order to realize a mistake we must contrast it with its opposite, the correct behaviour. If you have spelt a word wrongly you cannot eliminate the mistake unless you know the correct spelling. The same applies to historical or futuristic mistakes.

The patient in question has perhaps never reached the maturity of an adult and does not know what it feels like to be independent of his mother, how to make contact with other people; and unless he is made to feel this independence, he cannot realize his historical mistake. We take it for granted that he has this "feel," and we are only too ready to assume that he has reached the adult position and has regressed to childhood only temporarily. We are inclined to overlook the question of situations. As his behaviour is normal in situations representing no difficulties or in matters requiring reactions similar to those expected of a child, we take it for granted that he is essentially grown-up. When more difficult situations arise, however, he proves that he has not developed a mature attitude. How can we expect him to know how to change if he does not realize the difference between infantile and mature behaviour? He would not have "regressed" if his "self" was already mature, if he had assimilated and not only copied (introjected) adult behaviour.

We may conclude then that the immediate future is contained in the present, especially in its unfinished situations (completion of the instinct cycle). Large parts of our organism are built for "purposes." Purposeless, e.g. senseless, movements can range from slight peculiarities to the inexplicable behaviour of the insane.

Conceiving the present as the result of the past we find as many schools of thought as we find causes. Most people believe in a "primary cause" like a creator, others fatalistically stick to the inherited constitution as the only recognizable and deciding factor, whilst for others, again, the environmental influence is the only cause of our behaviour. Some people have found economics to be the cause of all evil, others the repressed childhood. The present, in my opinion, is the coincidence of many "causes" leading to the ever changing, kaleidoscopic picture of situations which are never identical.

34 The Practice of Rational-Emotive Therapy

Albert Ellis

The practice of RET is almost always a complex and comprehensive process. The reason is that RET therapists don't view their clients as individuals who have just a specific symptom or disturbed behavior that can be effectively isolated from the rest of their personalities and lives. Instead, they see their clients as individuals who usually have a com-

bination of cognitive, emotive, and behavioral disturbances. Consequently, in order to help their clients, RET therapists employ many different kinds of rational, evocative-confrontational, and activity-oriented techniques to unravel some of the core problems. This means that RET makes use of a wide variety of psychological techniques and is never a monolithic and invariant treatment process. Some of the techniques that RET uses are those employed in regular behavior therapy (Lazarus, 1971, 1976), with which general, or inelegant, RET is practically synonymous.

Main Assumptions about Cognition and Emotional Disturbance

The core of RET, however, is its heavy cognitive emphasis. This emphasis follows directly from its main assumptions about cognition and emotional disturbance. A summary of these assumptions follows.

1. Human "thinking" and "emotion" do not constitute two disparate processes but significantly interrelate with each other. We tend to "cause" or "create" most of our feelings by our thinking, and we also "cause" some of our thinking by our emoting. Especially important from the point of view of psychotherapy and personality change is the fact that, if we experience disordered emotions (such as anxiety and depression), we can often significantly change such emotions by discovering and modifying the cognitions that underlie them. This kind of modification can be accomplished in many ways. One of the most elegant of these consists of vigorously and persistently disputing, debating, and reconstructing our self-defeating cognitions that directly underlie our emotional hang-ups.

2. When people come to therapy with neurotic symptoms or Consequences (C) after they have gone through some Activating Experiences or Events (A), the RET practitioner assumes that A may importantly *contribute to* C but doesn't directly *cause* it. People's Beliefs (B) about A are the more direct "cause" of C. If this is true—as scores of research studies now seem to indicate (see my article on research data supporting RET's hypotheses in Section 2 of this book)—it would seem that effective therapy will concern itself mainly with B, people's Belief systems, rather than primarily with A or C. And this is what the RET therapist does: he or she tries to help clients discover and understand, as clearly as they are able, the detailed Beliefs with which they *make themselves*—yes, do not *become* but *make themselves*—disturbed.

3. RET therapists also assume that, when people feel or act in a disturbed manner at point C after experiencing some undesirable Activating Event at point A, their Beliefs (at point B) are of two major varieties: rational Beliefs (rB's) and irrational Beliefs (iB's). Since people have a large variety of "rational" and "irrational" Beliefs, RET zeroes in on the main ones only—those that have to do with emotional health and disturbance. The irrational Beliefs that are at the root of unhealthy

and neurotic behaviors take the form of unrealistic or absolutistic expectations (or demands) about what is happening and about one's own and others' behaviors. The rational Beliefs that result in healthy behaviors take, instead, the form of realistic or relativistic desires, preferences, and wishes.

These same principles can be stated in terms of self-evaluation. We all have basic goals, purposes, and desires—particularly those of surviving and of being relatively happy with ourselves, with others, and with our surroundings. In order to fulfill these goals, we have the biological, as well as learned, tendency to ceaselessly evaluate our performances, those of others, and the surrounding conditions as "good" or "bad," "desirable" or "undesirable." Thus, we evaluate a caress as "good" and a toothache as "bad," because the former contributes to our happiness while the latter interferes with it.

I said that our tendency to evaluate, measure, or assess performances and events in the light of our goals of survival and happiness has a biological basis, because, if all of us suddenly stopped desiring and evaluating, human life would probably cease to exist. Therefore, we can call evaluation an intrinsically biological process. And, since men, women, and children do it in a rather different and far more complex way than other animals do it, evaluation is almost the essence of the human condition, as Frankl (1966) and many existentialist thinkers have claimed. Also, as Kelly (1955), Friedman (1975), and a good many other psychologists and philosophers have indicated, human evaluation is done in a uniquely creative, scientific, and predictive manner. Unlike other animals, humans act in a natural "rational" manner, in that they are self-conscious (they think about their thinking as well as merely think). They also have a pretty clear-cut notion that they have a future as well as a present and past life, and they use their thinking and evaluating abilities to plan for that future, thereby increasing their chances of surviving and being happy (Ellis, 1962, 1971, 1973, 1977c).

In RET terms, when people stick rigorously to desiring, wishing, and preferring, they remain rational; when they escalate their desires into absolutistic and often unrealizable demands or commands, they make themselves irrational. If they remain rational, they rarely, if ever, become what we call "emotionally disturbed." It is when they become irrational that they frequently make themselves "disturbed." Certain forms of disturbance—such as epilepsy, dyslexia, and some forms of psychosis—are basically neurological disorders that have little to do with desiring and commanding or with rationality and irrationality. But other forms of *emotional* disturbance, even though they have an important biological or neurological basis (as, of course, do *all* human processes), are very closely related to unrealistic expectations or demands.

The basic RET premise, then, is that, if humans had only or mostly desires and wishes and if they never or rarely evaluated their own, others', and the world's conditions in a commanding, absolutistic, and unrealistic way, they would have little or no "emotional" disturbance. They wouldn't be utterly happy or undisturbed, for they would still be heir to various "nonemotional" disorders. But they would be free of the vast majority of self-defeating thinking, feeling, and behavior that now frequently drive them to psychotherapy.

4. RET follows some of the teachings of Buddhism and the ancient Stoics, without, however, espousing many of the misleading overgeneralizations of these schools. RET assumes that, when people are emotionally disturbed and their disturbances can be tracked down to their crooked thinking, they can be helped to get rid of such disturbances. Helping them make a profound and deep-seated change in some of their values and encouraging them to replace absolutistic and overgeneralized demands with realistic wishes will make it possible for them to eliminate their disturbances and enable them to behave in a significantly less self-defeating manner in the future.

5. RET assumes that, when people view external situations, others' reactions, and their own behavior as out of their control and believe that they cannot cope "adequately" or "properly" with what is going on in their lives, they are likely to make themselves disturbed. When, instead, they see themselves as being in control of important aspects of their lives, they tend to be more relaxed and actually do more to help themselves live in accordance with their own basic goals.

6. People who feel emotionally disturbed tend to attribute motives, reasons, and causes to others and to outside events, thus distorting their own perceptions of reality. When these people come to see that they are making false attributions and assume responsibility for their own actions, they frequently feel and act better (that is, less self-defeatingly) in their relationships with others and in their responses to the environment.

These assumptions now have a large amount of research studies behind them and have been validated, at least partially, by controlled experimental studies. Other studies supporting the validity of RET's view of humans and of the possibility of bringing about personality changes keep appearing continually in the psychological literature (Murphy & Simon, in press; Ellis, 1980).

Other RET therapeutic hypotheses are validated by a great deal of supporting data in the form of clinical and case-study presentations (Ellis, 1980) but have not yet been sufficiently tested by controlled experiments. Here are some of them.

1. While it is highly desirable that we rate our deeds, feelings, and traits so we can see whether our behaviors and characteristics are helpful or self-defeating, it is undesirable that we rate our selves, our essences, our totality, and our personhoods. When we decide to live fully and enjoy ourselves, our goals are rational and sane. Rating and measuring are then helpful means of checking to see whether we are behaving in conformity to our goals. But as soon as we take what RET calls the "magical" or "illegitimate" jump from rating our traits and deeds to rating ourselves in our totality, we head toward psychological and emotional trouble. We become anxious or depressed and (ironically!) less able to change our goal-sabotaging characteristics.

2. Therapists had better give clients unconditional self-acceptance, carefully listen to their complaints, and see things from the clients' frames of reference. This kind of acceptance will help clients feel better, and so will warmth, support, encouragement, and approval by therapists. But *feeling better* is by no means equivalent to *getting better*, and in some ways the former interferes with the latter. Getting better means fully accepting ourselves under virtually *any* conditions, even when we do poorly at some tasks and even when others, including the therapist, don't particularly approve of us. Therapeutic support, therefore, may help "hook" clients on therapy and motivate them to work harder at it. But it also has potential drawbacks and limitations.

3. Intensive, depth-centered, or elegant

psychotherapy doesn't consist of mere symptom removal; it also consists of helping clients achieve higher frustration tolerance about their symptoms. Thus, when a female client comes to therapy with a great fear of failure and rejection and damns herself whenever she fails and gets rejected, a RET-oriented therapist tries to help her overcome her anxiety and self-downing. But the therapist also investigates her ego anxiety and her discomfort-anxiety about her original anxiety and self-downing. She is probably telling herself "I *must* not feel anxious, because that makes me an inept, rotten individual!" thereby creating ego anxiety. And she is also quite likely to tell herself "I *must* not feel anxious and self-downing, because I *can't stand* the pain of feeling that way. That makes the world too horrible to live in!" thus creating discomfort-anxiety. Unless the therapist sees and works with both levels of this woman's symptoms—the primary level of the symptoms themselves and the secondary level of her condemning herself for and whining about the primary symptoms—elegant therapy is not likely to be accomplished. One of RET's goals is to help people dispute and eliminate the secondary symptoms of anxiety about their anxiety, depression about their depression, and guilt about their hostility—as well as the primary feelings of anxiety, depression, and guilt in their own right.

4. Clients manifest their irrational Beliefs (iB's) in the form of unrealistic, antiempirical statements such as "If I fail this time, I will *never* be able to succeed in the future!" or "Since it is so horrible to die in a plane crash, there is a good chance that my plane will crash!" RET cognitive restructuring, or the Disputing of irrational Beliefs, includes debating and ripping up these kinds of antiempirical statements. But RET posits that behind such irrational Beliefs there almost invariably lie some basic *must*urbatory ideas and that these *musts* largely predetermine the antiempirical ideas. Thus, the full implicit philosophy behind the first irrational statement in this paragraph is "Since I *must* succeed every single time and I failed this time, I'll never be able to succeed in the future!" And the full philosophy behind the second irrational statement is "Because I *must* not die in the near future, it is horrible if I die in a plane crash; therefore there is a good chance that my plane will actually crash."

In other words, when people make outlandish antiempirical statements and believe devoutly in them, they generally have a tacit or implicit *must* that leads or encourages them to make such statements. Elegant therapy doesn't consist of merely combating such antiempirical observations but of getting at the fundamental *must*urbatory notions behind these observations and helping the clients to give them up. RET therapists, therefore, keep looking for the three basic *musts* that their clients hold—"I *must* do well!" "You *must* treat me beautifully!" and "The conditions I want *must* be easily available!"—and attempt to help their clients give up both the musts and the antiempirical statements that follow such musts.

5. Because people think largely in terms of language and can think much more precisely and clearly if they use the language properly, RET hypothesizes that semantic reeducation, which employs the principles of both general semantics and RET, can be an effective method of psychotherapy (Ellis, 1957a; Ellis & Harper, 1975; Moore, 1977).

6. RET, being a form of cognitive-emotive-behavioral therapy, employs activity homework assignments combined with a good deal of operant conditioning and self-management techniques. Skinner (1971) and other behaviorists usually favor reinforcement schedules rather than aversive conditioning or penalties for poor behavior. However, I have found that reinforcement works better for normally functioning children than for rather seriously disturbed adolescents and adults. I and other RET therapists, therefore, frequently use contingency management to help people change their dysfunctional behaviors, but we also use a good measure of self-enforced penalization. Thus, a male client who has trouble controlling his impulsive and compulsive sex behavior (such as compulsive exhibitionism) might be reinforced by allowing himself to eat favorite foods or engage in some sport after he has refrained from his compulsion for a certain period of time. He may also agree, however, to penalize himself by burning a 100-dollar bill (or a 1000-dollar bill, if necessary) every time he has given in to an exhibitory urge. RET holds that penalization, as well as reinforcement, is often desirable to help D.C.'s (difficult customers!) change their self-defeating behaviors.

7. The RET therapist frequently disputes the poor logic and the specious data that clients marshal to support their irrational Be-

liefs. And he or she gives relevant information—such as sex information to individuals with problems of sexual inadequacy—that helps people undermine their own crooked thinking and change it into more rational Beliefs. But in elegant RET we also try to teach clients some of the main elements of logic and scientific thinking and show them how to apply this kind of thinking to their own personal problems (Ellis, 1962, 1977c; Edelstein, 1976; Fulmer, 1975; Guinagh, 1976; Phadke, 1977). It is hypothesized that the straighter and more scientific people's thinking is, the less disturbed they will become and remain.

Cognitive Methods of RET

The principles set forth in the preceding pages, as well as in the previous article, serve as a framework for actual RET clinical practice. In the course of this practice, RET practitioners virtually always use a number of cognitive, emotive, and behavioral techniques. Under each of these modalities, several specific methods may be employed with each client—but not, of course, the same methods. Some techniques, such as the Disputing of irrational Beliefs, tend to be used with virtually all RET clients. But other procedures, such as the paradoxical intention or the reduction of some of the client's beliefs to absurdity, are used only with selected individuals and when the therapist thinks that the client will benefit from them.

RET, then, is highly eclectic, in that it employs a multimodal approach and tailors several different therapeutic techniques, selected from a wide variety of sources, to individual clients (Lazarus, 1971, 1976). It is also very pragmatic. With most clients, the therapist starts off with the basic methods—methods that have worked well with a majority of people for the last quarter of a century. But, as soon as these methods appear to be getting poor or even mediocre results, the therapist switches to other procedures that he or she thinks may work better for that particular client.

All told, RET therapists tend to use perhaps 40 or 50 regular techniques, many of which will be outlined in this chapter. But they may also employ any number of other "irregular" methods—including somewhat idiosyncratic ones like body massage or

psychodramatic abreaction—as long as these methods are used in a general RET philosophical framework and are not employed in a hit-or-miss manner because the therapist has some vague idea that they might work with certain clients.

RET, in other words, has a pronounced theoretical outlook; consequently, whatever techniques are employed are used in accordance with, and rarely against, this outlook. For example, since RET is based on the assumption that cognitive dogmatism, rigidity, and bigotry lead to *mus*turbation and thence to emotional disturbance, it would rarely employ devout suggestion as a therapeutic technique, as some hypnotherapists or other therapists do. I said "rarely" because the RET practitioner might occasionally use even such an "irrational" procedure, if nothing else seemed to work with a client and it looked as if this procedure might be of some help. The rational-emotive therapist would tend to use this kind of method only temporarily, hoping that the client would later be amenable to the use of more scientific and "rational" procedures.

As I have noted several times before, the RET therapist generally incorporates into the therapeutic process a pronounced and forceful amount of cognitive methodology. Some RET practitioners are very heavily cognitive and didactic and use relatively few of the emotive and behavioral methods outlined later in this article. Few are on the other side of the fence and stress feelings and behaviors, with little emphasis on cognition. If they were doing this, it could be questioned whether they were really doing RET.

In regard to cognitive methodology, RET is in the forefront of the therapies (such as transactional analysis and psychoanalytically oriented therapy) that rely heavily on thinking, interpreting, explaining, and teaching. Although its special methodology, as explained in detail below, includes the Disputing of irrational Beliefs, this is only *one* cognitive RET procedure (Ellis, 1978a; Ellis & Abrahms, 1978). Theoretically, cognitive-oriented therapists have a dozen or more major procedures at their disposal. Each of these major procedures includes from 10 to 20 subcategories. Therefore, we can safely assume that there are between 100 and 200 forms of psychological treatment that can be labeled primarily "cognitive." And more are being invented almost every day! Some of the psychoeducational techniques that are most often used in RET and that fit better under the rubric of "cognition" than under that of "emotion" or "behavior" will now be outlined.

Disputing of Irrational Beliefs

The most elegant and probably the most common cognitive method of RET consists of the therapist's actively-directively Disputing the client's irrational Beliefs. If there is any fundamental rational-emotive method, this is probably it. So much so, in fact, that some commentators on RET wrongly assume that the Disputing or debating process (sometimes called "antiawfulizing" or "anti*must*urbation") *is* RET (Mahoney, 1977; Meichenbaum, 1977). It definitely is not! But if RET were totally devoid of this kind of Disputing, it would be almost unrecognizable.

As noted in the previous articles, Disputing usually starts with the therapist showing the client that, in one way or another, the A-B-C's of RET. That is, the therapist shows the client that, after experiencing an Activating Event at point A, he or she experiences an emotional Consequence or disturbed symptom at point C not *because* of A but because of the set of Beliefs that he or she brings to A at point B. It is these Beliefs in general, and the irrational Beliefs (iB's) in particular, that more directly lead to or even "cause" the person's disordered emotional Consequences (C's). Once the therapist has demonstrated to the client that he or she is essentially causing his or her own disturbances by strongly and persistently maintaining certain irrational Beliefs, the next step is to teach the client how to Dispute these iB's at point D.

Behavioral Techniques of RET

When I began to do RET in early 1955, I realized that verbal therapy alone can be exceptionally useful in helping people see exactly what they are doing to disturb themselves and how they can stop indoctrinating themselves with irrational Beliefs (iB's) that lead to neurotic Consequences (C's). But I also realized that some form of active homework assignments is almost always necessary before the person actually changes his or her thinking, emoting, and behaving. I probably

saw this because, although behavior therapy at that time was almost unknown, I had read some of the early experiments of John B. Watson and his co-workers, which showed that *in vivo* desensitization can work very well with children and adults. I was also aware of the work of other pioneers in the field, such as Dunlap (1946), Herzberg (1945), and Salter (1949), who had actively sent clients out to do what they were afraid of doing in order to break their dysfunctional habits in practice as well as in theory.

The important thing, however, was the fact that I entered the field of psychotherapy with a specialization in marriage and family counseling and in sex therapy. In my field, I found that it was virtually always necessary to supplement the therapy sessions with specific instructions to the clients with regard to what they were supposed to do with themselves and others in between sessions (Ellis, 1954). Largely as a result of my experience with using active-directive methods of therapy in the course of my marriage and family counseling and sex therapy, I almost completely abandoned my psychoanalytic training and practice and began to develop RET.

Following my own lead with the techniques I had originated for my clients with marital and sex problems, I incorporated behavioral assignments into RET. Also, as I had done in my earlier practice, I used largely *in vivo* behavioral methods rather than the imaginal desensitization techniques that many other behavioral therapists, such as Cautela (1966) and Wolpe (1958, 1973), tend to favor. This doesn't mean that RET *has to* include *in vivo* homework assignments, since its behavioral components can be carried out in many different ways. But a full course of RET treatment with a person presenting fairly serious problems would rarely be effectuated without the inclusion of at least some *in vivo* retraining procedures.

Summary

In looking over the cognitive, emotive, and behavioral methods that are commonly employed in RET, as well as some of the popular therapeutic procedures that RET minimizes or avoids, we can see that rational-emotive therapists tend to emphasize a fairly rapid-fire, active-directive, persuasive-philosophic approach to psychological treatment. They continually challenge clients to validate their observations and ideas and show them how to do this kind of challenging or Disputing themselves. RET therapists logically parse some of the fundamental irrational Beliefs (iB's) that clients hold and demonstrate how and why these do not lead to desirable emotional and behavioral results. They also reduce some irrational Beliefs to absurdity, often in a highly humorous way. They teach clients how to think scientifically, so that they can subsequently incisively observe, logically parse, and effectively annihilate new self-defeating ideas and behaviors that they may experience in the future.

RET acknowledges that there are many kinds of psychological treatment and a number of techniques under each treatment modality. But an efficient system—such as RET strives to be—aims to save time and effort on the part of both therapists and clients; to help clients zero in on their major problems and start working to ameliorate them in a reasonably short period of time; to be effective with a large number of different kinds of clients; to offer an "elegant" or "deep" solution that deals with basic difficulties and encourages clients to continue the therapeutic process by themselves long after the sessions with the therapist have ended; and to produce relatively long-lasting results.

On most of these counts some amount of clinical and experimental evidence now exists that RET works as well as or better than other commonly used therapeutic procedures (DiGiuseppe, Miller, & Trexler, 1977; Ellis & Grieger, 1977; Ellis & Harper, 1975; Lembo, 1976; Morris & Kanitz, 1975; Murphy & Simon, in press). If RET does turn out to be an unusually effective means of therapy, this will probably be because of the depth and hardheadedness of its philosophic position. I am referring to the fact that it zeroes in on and combats absolutistic, dogmatic, and superstitious thinking more intensively than do other systems of therapy. Also, it is designed to be realistic and unindulgent, and it strives, incisively and determinedly, to get to the core of and to vigorously and actively undermine the childish demandingness that seems to be the main element of serious emotional disturbance.

REFERENCES

Cautela, J. R. Treatment of compulsive behavior by covert sensitization. *Psychological Record*, 1966, *16*, 33–41.

Dunlap, K. *Personal adjustment*. New York: McGraw-Hill, 1946.

Edelstein, M. The ABC's of rational-emotive therapy: Pitfalls in going from D to E. *Rational Living*, 1976, *11*(1), 28–30.

Ellis, A. *The American sexual tragedy*. New York: Twayne, 1954. (Revised edition: New York: Lyle Stuart & Grove Press, 1962.)

Ellis, A. *How to live a "neurotic."* New York: Crown, 1957. (a)

Ellis, A. *Reason and emotion in psychotherapy*. New York: Lyle Stuart, 1962. (Also, New York: Citadel, 1977.)

Ellis, A. *Growth through reason*. Palo Alto: Science and Behavior Books, 1971. (Also, Hollywood, Calif.: Wilshire Books, 1971.)

Ellis, A. *Humanistic psychotherapy: The rational-emotive approach*. New York: Julian Press and McGraw-Hill Paperbacks, 1973.

Ellis, A. *How to live with–and without–anger*. New York: Reader's Digest Press, 1977. (c)

Ellis, A. *Discomfort anxiety: A new cognitive-behavioral construct* (cassette recording). New York: BMA Audio Cassettes, 1978. (a)

Ellis, A., & Abrahms, E. *Brief psychotherapy in medical and health practice*. New York: Springer, 1978.

Ellis, A. *A comprehensive bibliography of articles and books on rational-emotive therapy and cognitive-behavior therapy*. New York: Institute for Rational Living, 1980.

Ellis, A., & Harper, R. A. *A new guide to rational living*. Englewood Cliffs, N.J.: Prentice-Hall, 1975. (Also, Hollywood, Calif.: Wilshire Books, 1975.)

Frankl, V. E. *Man's search for meaning*. New York: Washington Square Press, 1966.

Friedman, M. *Rational behavior*. Columbia: University of South Carolina Press, 1975.

Fulmer, G. Equality, toleration and truth. *Rational Living*, 1975, *10*(1), 38–40.

Guinagh, B. Disputing clients' logical fallacies. *Rational Living*, 1976, *11*(2), 15–18.

Herzberg, A. *Active psychotherapy*. New York: Grune & Stratton, 1945.

Kelly, G. *The psychology of personal constructs*. New York: Norton, 1955.

Lazarus, A. A. *Behavior therapy and beyond*. New York: McGraw-Hill, 1971.

Lazarus, A. A. *Multimodal therapy*. New York: Springer, 1976.

Mahoney, M. J. A critical analysis of rational-emotive theory and therapy. *The Counseling Psychologist*, 1977, *7*(1), 44–46.

Meichenbaum, D. Dr. Ellis, please stand up. *The Counseling Psychologist*, 1977, *7*(1), 43–44.

Moore, R. H. *Alienation in college students: A ra-*

tional and semantic analysis. Doctoral dissertation, Walden University, April 1977.

Murphy, R., & Simon, W. *An annotated bibliography of research on rational-emotive therapy and cognitive-behavior therapy.* New York: Institute for Rational Living, in press.

Phadke, K. M. *Bull fighting: A royal road to health and happiness.* Unpublished manuscript, Bombay, 1976.

Salter, A. *Conditioned reflex therapy.* New York: Creative Age, 1949.

Skinner, B. F. *Beyond freedom and dignity.* New York: Knopf, 1971.

Wolpe, J. *Psychotherapy by reciprocal inhibition.* Stanford, Calif.: Stanford University Press, 1958.

Wolpe, J. *The practice of behavior therapy.* New York: Pergamon Press, 1973.

PART IV
Behavioral Theories

Introduction

Taken in its strictest form, the behavioral approach requires that all concepts and propositions be anchored precisely to measurable properties in the empirical world. That behavioral concepts are, in fact, not always formulated as operational concepts is a concession to the limits of practicality. Nevertheless, empirically unanchored speculation is anathema to behaviorists; hypothetical constructs, which abound in intrapsychic and phenomenological theories, are rarely found in behavioral theories.

Behaviorism originated with the view that subjective introspection was "unscientific" and that it should be replaced by the use of objectively observable behavior. Further, all environmental influences upon behavior were likewise to be defined objectively. If unobservable processes were thought to exist within the individual, they were to be defined strictly in terms of observables which indicate their existence.

Recent theories of behavioral pathology have included concepts generated originally in experimental learning research. They are not simple translations of psychoanalytic concepts into behavioral terminology, as were earlier theories of behavioral pathology, but are based on the ostensible "empirical" laws of learning. Theorists using these concepts lay claim to the virtues of science since their heritage lies with the objective studies of systematic learning research and not with the dubious methods of clinical speculation.

That learning concepts are helpful in understanding pathology cannot be denied, but behavioral theorists take a stronger position. They state that pathological behavior is learned behavior that develops according to the same laws as those governing the development of normal behavior. Disturbed behavior differs from normal behavior only in magnitude, frequency, and social adaptiveness. Were these behavior patterns more adaptive, or less frequent and extreme, they would possess no other distinguishing features.

Orientation

〜〜〜〜〜

Early behavioral theories restricted their conception of pathology entirely to objective behavioral processes, eschewing all reference to internal phenomena such as the unconscious or conscious cognitive processes. According to strict behaviorism, it was unnecessary and misleading to posit the existence of unobservable states to account for behavior. Hence, all reference to hypothetical inner events or constructs was discarded. Guided by concepts derived from laboratory-based learning principles, all abnormal phenomena were conceived solely in terms of conditioning and reinforcement. In this paradigm, external reinforcements conditioned the behavioral repertoire of the individual; differences between adaptive and maladaptive behavior resulted, therefore, from differences in learning which, in turn, stemmed from differences in the reinforcement experience to which individuals were exposed.

The paper presented here by Albert Bandura goes beyond these early conceptions, providing a more contemporary formulation of behavior theory. In his social learning model, Bandura stresses the importance of cognitive processes in learning, especially those which derive from and relate to the "self."

35 Behavior Theory and the Models of Man

Albert Bandura

The views about the nature of man conveyed by behavior theory require critical examination on conceptual and social grounds. What we believe man to be affects which aspects of human functioning we study most thoroughly and which we disregard. Premises thus delimit research and are, in turn, shaped by it. As knowledge gained through study is put into practice, the images of man on which social technologies rest have even vaster implications. This is nowhere better illustrated than in growing public concern over manipulation and control by psychological methods. Some of these fears arise from expectations that improved means of influence will inevitably be misused. Other apprehensions are aroused by exaggerated claims of psychological power couched in the language of manipulation and authoritarian control. But most fears stem from views of behaviorism, articulated by popular writers and by theorists

From *American Psychologist*, *29*, 859–869, 1974. Copyright 1974 by the American Psychological Association. Reprinted by permission of the publisher and author.

themselves, that are disputed by the empirical facts of human behavior.

In the minds of the general public, and of many within our own discipline, behavior theory is equated with "conditioning." Over the years, the terms *behaviorism* and *conditioning* have come to be associated with odious imagery, including salivating dogs, puppetry, and animalistic manipulation. As a result, those who wish to disparage ideas or practices they hold in disfavor need only to label them as behavioristic or as Pavlovian precursors of a totalitarian state.

Contrary to popular belief, the fabled reflexive conditioning in humans is largely a myth. *Conditioning* is simply a descriptive term for learning through paired experiences, not an explanation of how the changes come about. Originally, conditioning was assumed to occur automatically. On closer examination it turned out to be cognitively mediated. People do not learn despite repetitive paired experiences unless they recognize that events are correlated (Dawson & Furedy, 1974; Grings, 1973). So-called conditioned reactions are largely self-activated on the basis of learned expectations rather than automatically evoked. The critical factor, therefore, is not that events occur together in time, but that people learn to predict them and to summon up appropriate anticipatory reactions.

The capacity to learn from correlated experiences reflects sensitivity, but because Pavlov first demonstrated the phenomenon with a dog, it has come to be regarded as a base animalistic process. Had he chosen to study physiological hyperactivity in humans to cues associated with stress, or the development of empathetic reactions to expressions of suffering, conditioning would have been treated in a more enlightened way. To expect people to remain unaffected by events that are frightening, humiliating, disgusting, sad, or pleasurable is to require that they be less than human. Although negative effects such as fears and dislikes can arise from paired experiences of a direct or vicarious sort, so do some of the enobling qualities of man. The pejorative accounts of learning principles, which appear with regularity in professional and lay publications, degrade both the science of psychology and the audiences that the offensive rhetoric is designed to sway.

It is well documented that behavior is influenced by its consequences much of the time. The image of man that this principle connotes depends on the types of consequences that are acknowledged and on an understanding of how they operate. In theories that recognize only the role of proximate external consequences and contend they shape behavior automatically, people appear as mechanical pawns of environmental forces. But external consequences, influential as they often are, are not the sole determinants of human behavior, nor do they operate automatically.

Response consequences serve several functions. First, they impart information. By observing the effects of their actions individuals eventually discern which behaviors are appropriate in which settings. The acquired information then serves as a guide for action. Contrary to the mechanistic metaphors, outcomes change behavior in humans through the intervening influence of thought.

Consequences motivate, through their incentive value, as well as inform. By representing foreseeable outcomes symbolically, future consequences can be converted into current motivators of behavior. Many of the things we do are designed to gain anticipated benefits and to avert future trouble. Our choices of action are largely under anticipatory control. The widely accepted dictum that man is ruled by response consequences thus fares better for anticipated than for actual consequences. Consider behavior on a fixed-ratio schedule (say, 50:1) in which only every fiftieth response is reinforced. Since 96% of the outcomes are extinctive and only 4% are reinforcing, behavior is maintained despite its dissuading consequences. As people are exposed to variations in frequency and predictability of reinforcement, they behave on the basis of the outcomes they expect to prevail on future occasions. When belief differs from actuality, which is not uncommon, behavior is weakly controlled by its actual consequences until repeated experience instills realistic expectations (Bandura, 1971b; Kaufman, Baron, & Kopp, 1966).

Had humans been ruled solely by instant consequences, they would have long become museum pieces among the extinct species. Not that our future is unquestionably secure. The immediate rewards of consumptive lifestyles vigorously promoted for short-term profit jeopardize man's long-term chances of survival. But immediate consequences, unless unusually powerful, do not necessarily outweigh deferred ones (Mischel, 1974). Our descendants shall continue to have a future only because those who foresee the aversive long-term consequences of current practices mobilize public support for contingencies that favor survival behavior. Hazardous pesticides, for example, are usually banned before populations suffer maladies from toxic residues. The information-processing capacities with which humans are endowed provide the basis for insightful behavior. Their capacity to bring remote consequences to bear on current behavior by anticipatory thought supports foresightful action.

Explanations of reinforcement originally assumed that consequences increase behavior without conscious involvement. The still prevalent notion that reinforcers can operate insidiously arouses fears that improved techniques of reinforcement will enable authorities to manipulate people without their knowledge or consent. Although the empirical issue is not yet completely resolved, there is little evidence that rewards function as automatic strengtheners of human conduct. Behavior is not much affected by its consequences without awareness of what is being reinforced (Bandura, 1969; Dulany, 1968). After individuals discern the instrumental relation between action and outcome, contingent rewards may produce accommodating or oppositional behavior depending on how they value the incentives, the influencers, and the behavior itself, and how others respond. Thus reinforcement, as it has become better understood, has changed from a mechanical strengthener of conduct to an informative and motivating influence.

People do not function in isolation. As social beings, they observe the conduct of others and the occasions on which it is rewarded, disregarded, or punished. They can therefore profit from observed consequences as well as from their own direct experiences (Bandura, 1971c). Acknowledgment of vicarious reinforcement introduces another human dimension—namely, evaluative capacities—into the operation of reinforcement influences. People weigh consequences to themselves against those accruing to others for similar behavior. The same outcome can thus become a reward or a punishment depending upon the referents used for social comparison.

Human conduct is better explained by the relational influence of observed and direct consequences than by either factor alone. However, behavior is not fully predictable from a relational coefficient because social justifications alter the impact of outcome disparities. Inequitable reinforcement is willingly accepted when people are graded by custom into social ranks and rewarded according to position rather than by performance. Arbitrary inequities are also likely to be tolerated if the underrewarded are led to believe they possess attributes that make them less deserving of equal treatment. Persuasively justified inequities have more detrimental personal effects than acknowledged unfairness because they foster self-devaluation in the maltreated. Negative reactions to inequitable reinforcement, which is acknowledged to be unwarranted, can likewise be diminished by temporizing. If people are led to expect that unfair treatment will be corrected within the foreseeable future, it becomes less aversive to them.

Theories that explain human behavior as the product of external rewards and punishments present a truncated image of man because people partly regulate their actions by self-produced consequences (Bandura, 1971c; Thoresen & Mahoney, 1973). Example and precept impart standards of conduct that serve as the basis for self-reinforcing reactions. The development of self-reactive functions gives humans a capacity for self-direction. They do things that give rise to self-satisfaction and self-worth, and they refrain from behaving in ways that evoke self-punishment.

After self-reinforcing functions are acquired, a given act produces two sets of consequences: self-evaluative reactions and external outcomes. Personal and external sources of reinforcement may operate as supplementary or as opposing influences on behavior. Thus, for example, individuals commonly experience conflicts when rewarded for conduct they personally devalue. When self-condemning consequences outweigh rewarding inducements, external influences are relatively ineffective. On the other hand, if certain courses of action produce stronger rewards than self-censure, the result is cheerless compliance. Losses in self-respect for devalued conduct can be abated, however, by self-exonerating justifications. I shall return to this issue shortly.

Another type of conflict between external and self-produced consequences arises when individuals are punished for behavior they regard highly. Principled dissenters and nonconformists often find themselves in this predicament. Personally valued conduct is expressed provided its costs are not too high. Should the threatened consequences be severe, one inhibits self-praiseworthy acts under high risk of penalty but readily performs them when the chances of punishment are reduced. There are individuals, however, whose sense of self-worth is so strongly invested in certain convictions that they will submit to prolonged maltreatment rather than accede to what they regard as unjust or immoral.

External consequences exert greatest influence on behavior when they are compatible with those that are self-produced. These conditions obtain when rewardable acts are a source of self-pride and punishable ones are self-censured. To enhance compatibility between personal and social influences, people select associates who share similar standards of conduct and thus ensure social support for their own system of self-reinforcement.

Individualistic theories of moral action assume that internalization of behavioral standards creates a permanent control mechanism within the person. Restraints of conscience thereafter operate as enduring controls over reprehensible conduct. The testimony of human behavior, however, contradicts this view. Much human maltreatment and suffering are, in fact, inflicted by otherwise decent moral people. And some of the most striking changes in moral conduct, as evidenced, for example, in political and military violence, are achieved without altering personality structures or moral standards. Personal control is clearly more complex and flexible than the theorizing implies.

Although self-reinforcing influences serve as regulators of conduct, they can be dissociated from censurable deeds by self-exonerating practices (Bandura, 1973). One device is to make inhumane behavior personally and socially acceptable by defining it in terms of high moral principle. People do not act in ways they ordinarily consider evil or destructive until such activities are construed as serving moral purposes. Over the years, much cruelty has been perpetrated in the name of religious principles, righteous ideologies, and regulatory sanctions. In the transactions of everyday life, euphemistic labeling serves as a handy linguistic device for masking reprehensible activities or according them a respectable status. Self-deplored conduct can also be made benign by contrasting it with more flagrant inhumanities. Moral justifications and palliative comparisons are especially effective because they not only eliminate self-generated deterrents but engage self-reward in the service of reprehensible conduct. What was morally unacceptable becomes a source of self-pride.

A common dissociative practice is to obscure or distort the relationship between one's actions and the effects they cause. People will perform behavior they normally repudiate if a legitimate authority sanctions it and acknowledges responsibility for its consequences. By displacing responsibility elsewhere, participants do not hold themselves accountable for what they do and are thus spared self-prohibiting reactions. Exemption from self-censure can be facilitated additionally by diffusing responsibility for culpable behavior. Through division of labor, division of decision making, and collective action, people can contribute to detrimental practices without feeling personal responsibility or self-disapproval.

Attribution of blame to the victim is still another exonerative expedient. Victims are faulted for bringing maltreatment on themselves, or extraordinary circumstances are invoked as justifications for questionable conduct. One need not engage in self-reproof for committing acts prescribed by circumstances. A further means of weakening self-punishment is to dehumanize the victim. Inflicting harm upon people who are regarded as subhuman or debased is less likely to arouse self-reproof than if they are looked upon as human beings with sensitivities.

There are other self-disinhibiting maneuvers that operate by misrepresenting the consequences of actions. As long as detrimental effects are ignored or minimized, there is little reason for self-censure. If consequences are not easily distortable, distress over conduct that conflicts with self-evaluative standards can be reduced by selectively remembering the benefits and forgetting the harm of one's acts.

Given the variety of self-disinhibiting devices, a society cannot rely on control by conscience to ensure moral and ethical conduct. Though personal control ordinarily serves as a self-directive force, it can be nullified by social sanctions conducive to destructiveness. Indoctrination and social justifications give meaning to events and create anticipations that determine one's actions. Control through information, which is rooted in cognitive processes, is more pervasive and powerful than conditioning through contiguity of events. Cultivation of humaneness therefore requires, in addition to benevolent personal codes, safeguards built into social systems that counteract detrimental sanctioning practices and uphold compassionate behavior.

A conceptual orientation not only prescribes what facets of man will be studied in depth but also how one goes about changing human behavior. Early applications of reinforcement principles, for example, were guided by the then prevalent belief that consequences alter behavior automatically and unconsciously. Since the process supposedly operated mechanically, the reinforcers had to occur instantly to be effective. Participants in change programs were, therefore, uninformed about why they were being reinforced, and, in an effort to ensure immediacy of effects, reinforcers were presented intrusively as soon as the requisite responses were emitted. The net effect was a tedious shaping process that produced, at best, mediocre results in an ethically questionable manner. In many public and professional circles, reinforcement still connotes furtive control even though reinforcement theory and practices have progressed well beyond this level.

Realization that reinforcement is an unarticulated way of designating appropriate conduct prompted the use of cognitive factors in the modification of behavior. Not surprisingly, people change more rapidly if told what behaviors are rewardable and punishable than if they have to discover it from observing the consequences of their actions. Competencies that are not already within their repertoires can be developed with greater ease through the aid of instruction and modeling than by relying solely on the successes and failures of unguided performance.

As further research revealed that reinforcers function as motivators, consequences were recognized as sources of motivation that depend heavily for their effectiveness upon the incentive preferences of those undergoing change. Hence, people do not indiscriminately absorb the influences that impinge upon them. Outcomes resulting from actions need not necessarily occur instantly. Humans can cognitively bridge delays between behavior and subsequent reinforcers without impairing the efficacy of incentive operations.

At this second evolutionary stage, reinforcement practices changed from unilateral control to social contracting. Positive arrangements affirm that if individuals do certain things they are entitled to certain rewards and privileges. In the case of negative sanctions, reprehensible conduct carries punishment costs. The process is portrayed in reinforcement terms, but the practice is that of social exchange. Most social interactions are, of course, governed by conditional agreements, though they usually are not couched in the language of reinforcement. Describing them differently does not change their nature, however.

Contingencies vary in the human qualities they embody and in the voice individuals have in decisions concerning the social arrangements that affect their lives. Reflecting the salient values of our society, reinforcement practices have traditionally favored utilitarian forms of behavior. But conditions are changing. With growing reservations about materialistic life-styles, reinforcement practices are being increasingly used to cultivate personal potentialities and humanistic qualities. These

emerging changes in value commitments will probably accelerate as people devote fewer hours to working for income and have more leisure time for self-development.

Another change of some consequence is the renewed concern for individual rights. People are seeking a collaborative role in the development of societal contingencies that affect the course and quality of their lives. As part of this social trend, even the actions taken in the name of psychotherapy are being examined for their ethics and social purposes. These concerns have provided the impetus for prescripts to ensure that reinforcement techniques are used in the service of human betterment rather than as instruments of social control.

A closely related issue is the relative attention devoted to changing individuals or to altering the institutions of society to enrich life. If psychologists are to have a significant impact on common problems of life, they must apply their corrective measures to detrimental societal practices rather than limit themselves to treating the casualties of these practices. This, of course, is easier said than done. Practitioners, whatever their specialty, are reinforced more powerfully for using their knowledge and skills in the service of existing operations than for changing them. Socially oriented efforts are hard to sustain under inadequate reinforcement supports.

The methods of change discussed thus far draw heavily upon external consequences of action. Evidence that people can exercise some control over their own behavior provided the impetus for further changes in reinforcement practices. Interest began to shift from managing conduct to developing skills in self-regulation. In the latter approach, control is vested to a large extent in the hands of individuals themselves: They arrange the environmental inducements for desired behavior; they evaluate their own performances; and they serve as their own reinforcing agents (Goldfried & Merbaum, 1973; Mahoney & Thoresen, 1974). To be sure, the self-reinforcing functions are created and occasionally supported by external influences. Having external origins, however, does not refute the fact that, once established, self-influence partly determines what actions one performs. Citing historical determinants of a generalizable function cannot substitute for contemporaneous influences arising through exercise of that function.

The recognition of self-directing capacities represents a substantial departure from exclusive reliance upon environmental control. But the emerging self-influence practices are still closely rooted in physical transactions—the self-administered consequences are, for the most part, material. Eventually changes in form, as well as source, of reinforcement will appear as the insufficiency of material outcomes is acknowledged. Most people value their self-respect above commodities. They rely extensively on their own self-demands and self-approval as guides for conduct. To ignore the influential role of covert self-reinforcement in the regulation of behavior is to disavow a uniquely human capacity of man.

Proponents who recognize only external consequences restrict their research and practice to such influences and thus generate evidence that reinforces their conceptions. Those who acknowledge personal influences as well tend to select methods that reveal and promote self-directing capabilities in man. The view of man embodied in behavioral technologies is therefore more than a philosophical issue. It affects which human potentialities will be cultivated and which will be underdeveloped.

The preceding remarks addressed the need to broaden the scope of research into the reinforcement processes regulating human behavior. Much the same might be said for the ways in which human learning is conceptualized and investigated. Our theories have been incredibly slow in acknowledging that man can learn by observation as well as by direct experience. This is another example of how steadfast adherence to orthodox paradigms makes it difficult to transcend the confines of conceptual commitment. Having renounced cognitive determinants, early proponents of behaviorism advanced the doctrine that learning can occur only by performing responses and experiencing their effects. This legacy is still very much with us. The rudimentary form of learning based on direct experience has been exhaustively studied, whereas the more pervasive and powerful mode of learning by observation is largely ignored. A shift of emphasis is needed.

The capacity to represent modeled activities symbolically enables man to acquire new patterns of behavior observationally without reinforced enactment. From observing others, one forms an idea of how certain behavior is performed, and on later occasions the coded information serves as a guide for action. Indeed, research conducted within the framework of social learning theory shows that virtually all learning phenomena resulting from direct experience can occur on a vicarious basis by observing other people's behavior and its consequences for them (Bandura, 1969). The abbreviation of the acquisition process through observational learning is, of course, vital for both development and survival. Modeling reduces the burden of time-consuming performance of inappropriate responses. Since errors can produce costly, if not fatal, consequences, the prospects of survival would be slim indeed if people had to rely solely on the effects of their actions to inform them about what to do.

In many instances the behavior being modeled must be learned in essentially the same form. Driving automobiles, skiing, and performing surgery, for example, permit little, if any, departure from essential practices. In addition to transmitting particular response patterns, however, modeling influences can create generative and innovative behavior. In the latter process, observers abstract common features from seemingly diverse responses and formulate generative rules of behavior that enable them to go beyond what they have seen or heard. By synthesizing features of different models into new amalgams, observers can achieve through modeling novel styles of thought and conduct. Once initiated, experiences with the new forms create further evolutionary changes. A partial departure from tradition eventually becomes a new direction.

Some of the limitations commonly ascribed to behavior theory are based on the mistaken belief that modeling can produce at best mimicry of specific acts. This view is disputed by growing evidence that abstract modeling is a highly effective means of inducing rule-governed cognitive behavior (Bandura, 1971a; Zimmerman & Rosenthal, 1974). On the basis of observationally derived rules, people alter their judgmental orientations, conceptual schemes, linguistic styles, information-processing strategies, as well as other forms of cognitive functioning. Nevertheless, faulty evaluations continue to be mistaken for weaknesses inherent in theory.

Observational learning has recently come to be accepted more widely, but some theorists are willing to grant it full scientific respectability only if it is reduced to performance terms. As a result, enactment paradigms are used which are rooted in the traditional assumption that responses must be performed before they can be learned. Instant reproduction of modeled responses is favored, thereby minimizing dependence upon cognitive functions which play an especially influential role when retention over time is required. The issue of whether reinforcement enhances modeling is pursued to the neglect of the more interesting question of whether one can keep people from learning what they have seen.

When learning is investigated through observational paradigms, a broader range of determinants and intervening mechanisms gains prominence. Learning by observation is governed by four component processes: (*a*) attentional functions regulate sensory input and perception of modeled actions; (*b*) through coding and symbolic rehearsal, transitory experiences are transformed for memory representation into enduring performance guides; (*c*) motor reproduction processes govern the integration of constituent acts into new response patterns; and (*d*) incentive or motivational processes determine whether observationally acquired responses will be performed. Studied from this perspective, observational learning emerges as an actively judgmental and constructive, rather than a mechanical copying, process.

Because observational learning entails several subfunctions that evolve with maturation and experience, it obviously depends upon prior development. Differences in theoretical perspectives prescribe different methodologies for studying how the capacity for observational learning itself is acquired. When modeling is conceptualized in terms of formation of stimulus–response linkages, efforts are aimed at increasing the probability of imitative responses through reinforcement. Modeling can be increased by rewarding matching behavior, but such demonstrations are not of much help in identifying what exactly is being acquired during the process, or in explaining imitation failures under favorable conditions of reinforcement. From a social learning view, the capability for observational learning is developed by acquiring skill in discriminative observation, in memory encoding, in coordinating ideomotor and sensorimotor systems, and in judging probable consequences for matching behavior. Understanding how people learn to imitate becomes a matter of understanding how the

requisite subfunctions develop and operate. Capacity for observational learning is restricted by deficits, and expanded by improvements, in its component functions.

Over the years, proponents of the more radical forms of behaviorism not only disclaimed interest in mentation but also marshaled numerous reasons why cognitive events are inadmissible in causal analyses. It was, and still is, argued that cognitions are inaccessible except through untrustworthy self-reports, they are inferences from effects, they are epiphenomenal, or they are simply fictional. Advances in experimental analysis of behavior, it was claimed, would eventually show them to be unnecessary. Empirical evidence, however, has shown the opposite to be true. A large body of research now exists in which cognition is activated instructionally with impressive results. People learn and retain much better by using cognitive aids that they generate than by repetitive reinforced performance (Anderson & Bower, 1973; Bandura, 1971a). With growing evidence that cognition has causal influence in behavior, the arguments against cognitive determinants are losing their force.

These recent developments have shifted emphasis from the study of response learning to analyses of memory and cognition. From this effort we have gained a better understanding of the mechanisms whereby information is acquired, stored, and retrieved. There is more to learning, however, than the acquisition and retention of information. Behavioristic theories addressed themselves to performance but deemphasized internal determinants, whereas the cognitive approaches remain immersed in thought but divorced from conduct. In a complete account of human behavior, internal processes must eventually be tied to action. Hence, explanations of how information eventuates in skilled performance must additionally be concerned with the organization and regulation of behavior. Social learning includes within its framework both the processes internal to the organism as well as performance-related determinants.

Speculations about man's nature inevitably raise the fundamental issues of determinism and human freedom. In examining these questions it is essential to distinguish between the metaphysical and the social aspects of freedom. Many of the heated disputes on this topic arise as much, if not more, from confusion over the dimensions of freedom being discussed as from disagreements over the doctrine of determinism.

Let us first consider freedom in the social sense. Whether freedom is an illusion, as some writers maintain, or a social reality of considerable importance depends upon the meaning given to it. Within the social learning framework, freedom is defined in terms of the number of options available to people and the right to exercise them. The more behavioral alternatives and social prerogatives people have, the greater is their freedom of action.

Personal freedom can be limited in many different ways. Behavioral deficits restrict possible choices and otherwise curtail opportunities to realize one's preferences. Freedom can therefore be expanded by cultivating competencies. Self-restraints arising from unwarranted fears and stringent self-censure restrict the effective range of activities that individuals can engage in or even contemplate. Here freedom is restored by eliminating dysfunctional self-restraints.

In maximizing freedom a society must place some limits on conduct because complete license for any individual is likely to encroach on the freedom of others. Societal prohibitions against behavior that is socially injurious create additional curbs on conduct. Conflicts often arise over behavioral restrictions when many members of society question conventional customs and when legal sanctions are used more to enforce a particular brand of morality than to prohibit socially detrimental conduct.

The issue of whether individuals should be allowed to engage in activities that are self-injurious but not detrimental to society has been debated vigorously over the years. Prohibitionists argue that it is difficult for a person, other than a recluse, to impair himself without inflicting secondary harm on others. Should self-injury produce incapacities, society usually ends up bearing the treatment and subsistence costs. Libertarians do not find such arguments sufficiently convincing to justify a specific prohibition because some of the self-injurious activities that society approves may be as bad or worse than those it outlaws. Normative changes over time regarding private conduct tend to favor an individualistic ethic. Consequently, many activities that were formerly prohibited by law have been exempted from legal sanctions.

Some groups have their freedom curtailed by socially condoned discrimination. Here, the alternatives available to a person are limited by skin color, sex, religion, ethnic background, or social class, regardless of capabilities. When self-determination is prejudicially restricted, those who are subordinated remove inequities by altering practices that compromise or temporize the professed values of society.

Freedom deals with rights as well as options and behavioral restraints. Man's struggle for freedom is principally aimed at structuring societal contingencies so that certain forms of behavior are exempted from aversive control. After protective laws are built into the system, there are certain things that a society may not do to an individual, however much it might like to. Legal prohibitions on societal control create freedoms that are realities, not simply feelings or states of mind. Societies differ in their institutions of freedom and in the number and types of behaviors that are officially exempted from punitive control. Social systems that protect journalists from punitive control, for example, are freer than those that allow authoritative power to be used to silence critics or their vehicles of expression. Societies that possess an independent judiciary ensure greater social freedom than those that do not.

In philosophical discourses, freedom is often considered antithetical to determinism. When defined in terms of options and rights, there is no incompatibility of freedom and determinism. From this perspective, freedom is not conceived negatively as the absence of influences or simply the lack of external constraints. Rather, it is defined positively in terms of the skills at one's command and the exercise of self-influence upon which choice of action depends.

Psychological analyses of freedom eventually lead to discourses on the metaphysics of determinism. Are people partial determiners of their own behavior, or are they ruled exclusively by forces beyond their control? The long-standing debate over this issue has been enlivened by Skinner's (1971) contention that, apart from genetic contributions, human behavior is controlled solely by environmental contingencies, for example, "A person does not act upon the world, the world acts upon him" (p. 211). A major problem with this type of analysis is that it depicts the environment as an autonomous force that automatically shapes and controls behavior. Environments have causes as do behaviors.

For the most part, the environment is only a potentiality until actualized and fashioned by appropriate actions. Books do not influence people unless someone writes them and others select and read them. Rewards and punishments remain in abeyance until prompted by appropriate performances.

It is true that behavior is regulated by its contingencies, but the contingencies are partly of a person's own making. By their actions, people play an active role in producing the reinforcing contingencies that impinge upon them. Thus, behavior partly creates the environment, and the environment influences the behavior in a reciprocal fashion. To the oft-repeated dictum, change contingencies and you change behavior, should be added the reciprocal side, change behavior and you change the contingencies.

The image of man's efficacy that emerges from psychological research depends upon which aspect of the reciprocal control system one selects for analysis. In the paradigm favoring environmental control, investigators analyze how environmental contingencies change behavior [B = f(E)]. The personal control paradigm, on the other hand, examines how behavior determines the environment [E = f(B)]. Behavior is the effect in the former case, and the cause in the latter. Although the reciprocal sources of influence are separable for experimental purposes, in everyday life two-way control operates concurrently. In ongoing interchanges, one and the same event can thus be a stimulus, a response, or an environmental reinforcer depending upon the place in the sequence at which the analysis arbitrarily begins.

A survey of the literature on reinforcement confirms the extent to which we have become captives of a one-sided paradigm to map a bidirectional process. Environmental control is overstudied, whereas personal control has been relatively neglected. To cite but one example, there exist countless demonstrations of how behavior varies under different schedules of reinforcement, but one looks in vain for studies of how people, either individually or by collective action, succeed in fashioning reinforcement schedules to their own liking. The dearth of research on personal control is not because people exert no influence on their environment or because such efforts are without effect. Quite the contrary. Behavior is one of the more influential determinants of future contingencies. As analyses of sequential interchanges reveal, aggressive individuals actualize through their conduct a hostile environment, whereas those who display friendly responsiveness produce an amicable social milieu within the same setting (Rausch, 1965). We are all acquainted with problem-prone individuals who, through their aversive conduct, predictably breed negative social climates wherever they go.

It should be noted that some of the doctrines ascribing preeminent control to the environment are ultimately qualified by acknowledgement that man can exercise some measure of countercontrol (Skinner, 1971). The notion of reciprocal interaction, however, goes considerably beyond the concept of countercontrol. Countercontrol portrays the environment as an instigating force to which individuals react. As we have already seen, people activate and create environments as well as rebut them.

People may be considered partially free insofar as they can influence future conditions by managing their own behavior. Granted that selection of particular courses of action from available alternatives is itself determined, individuals can nevertheless exert some control over the factors that govern their choices. In philosophical analyses all events can be submitted to an infinite regression of causes. Such discussions usually emphasize how man's actions are determined by prior conditions but neglect the reciprocal part of the process showing that the conditions themselves are partly determined by man's prior actions. Applications of self-control practices demonstrate that people are able to regulate their own behavior in preferred directions by arranging environmental conditions most likely to elicit it and administering self-reinforcing consequences to sustain it. They may be told how to do it and initially may be given some external support for their efforts, but self-produced influences contribute significantly to future goal attainment.

To contend, as environmental determinists often do, that people are controlled by external forces and then to advocate that they redesign their society by applying behavioral technology undermines the basic premise of the argument. If humans were in fact incapable of influencing their own actions, they could describe and predict environmental events but hardly exercise any intentional control over them. When it comes to advocacy of social change, however, thoroughgoing environmental determinists become ardent exponents of man's power to transform environments in pursuit of a better life.

In backward causal analyses, conditions are usually portrayed as ruling man, whereas forward deterministic analyses of goal setting and attainment reveal how people can shape conditions for their purposes. Some are better at it than others. The greater their foresight, proficiency, and self-influence, all of which are acquirable skills, the greater the progress toward their goals. Because of the capacity for reciprocal influence, people are at least partial architects of their own destinies. It is not determinism that is in dispute, but whether it is treated as a one-way or a two-way control process. Considering the interdependence of behavior and environmental conditions, determinism does not imply the fatalistic view that man is but a pawn of external influences.

Psychological perspectives on determinism, like other aspects of theorizing, influence the nature and scope of social practice. Environmental determinists are apt to use their methods primarily in the service of institutionally prescribed patterns of behavior. Personal determinists are more inclined to cultivate self-directing potentialities in man. The latter behavioral approach and humanism have much in common. Behavioral theorists, however, recognize that "self-actualization" is by no means confined to human virtues. People have numerous potentialities that can be actualized for good or ill. Over the years, man has suffered considerably at the hands of self-actualized tyrants. A self-centered ethic of self-realization must therefore be tempered by concern for the social consequences of one's conduct. Behaviorists generally emphasize environmental sources of control, whereas humanists tend to restrict their interest to personal control. Social learning encompasses both aspects of the bidirectional influence process.

When the environment is regarded as an autonomous rather than as an influenceable determinant of behavior, valuation of dignifying human qualities and accomplishments is diminished. If inventiveness emanates from external circumstances, it is environments that should be credited for people's achievements and chastised for their failings or inhumanities. Contrary to the unilateral view, human accomplishments result from reciprocal interaction of external circumstances with a host of personal determinants including endowed potentialities, acquired competencies, reflective thought, and a high level of self-initiative.

Musical composers, for example, help to shape tastes by their creative efforts, and the public in turn supports their performances until advocates of new styles generate new public preferences. Each succeeding form of artistry results from a similar two-way influence process for which neither artisans nor circumstances deserve sole credit.

Superior accomplishments, whatever the field, require considerable self-disciplined application. After individuals adopt evaluative standards, they expend large amounts of time, on their own, improving their performances to the point of self-satisfaction. At this level of functioning, persistence in an endeavor is extensively under self-reinforcement control. Skills are perfected as much, or more, to please oneself as to please the public.

Without self-generated influences most innovative efforts would be difficult to sustain. This is because the unconventional is initially resisted and gradually accepted only as it proves functionally valuable or wins prestigious advocates. As a result, the early efforts of innovators bring rebuffs rather than rewards or recognition. In the history of creative endeavors, it is not uncommon for artists or composers to be scorned when they depart markedly from convention. Some gain recognition later in their careers. Others are sufficiently convinced of the worth of their work that they labor indefatigably even though their productions are negatively received during their lifetimes. Ideological and, to a lesser extent, technological advances follow similar courses. Most innovative endeavors receive occasional support in early phases, but environmental conditions alone are not especially conducive to unconventional developments.

The operation of reciprocal influence also has bearing on the public concern that advances in psychological knowledge will produce an increase in human manipulation and control. A common response to such apprehensions is that all behavior is inevitably controlled. Social influence, therefore, is not a question of imposing controls where none existed before. This type of argument is valid in the sense that every act has a cause. But it is not the principle of causality that worries people. At the societal level, their misgivings center on the distribution of controlling power, the means and purposes for which it is used, and the availability of mechanisms for exercising reciprocal control over institutional practices. At the individual level, they are uneasy about the implications of psychotechnology in programming human relations.

Possible remedies for exploitative use of psychological techniques are usually discussed in terms of individual safeguards. Increased knowledge about modes of influence is prescribed as the best defense against manipulation. When people are informed about how behavior can be controlled, they tend to resist evident attempts at influence, thus making manipulation more difficult. Awareness alone, however, is a weak countervalence.

Exploitation was successfully thwarted long before there existed a discipline of psychology to formulate principles and practices of behavior change. The most reliable source of opposition to manipulative control resides in the reciprocal consequences of human interactions. People resist being taken advantage of, and will continue to do so in the future, because compliant behavior produces unfavorable consequences for them. Sophisticated efforts at influence in no way reduce the aversiveness of yielding that is personally disadvantageous. Because of reciprocal consequences, no one is able to manipulate others at will, and everyone experiences some feeling of powerlessness in getting what they want. This is true at all levels of functioning, individual and collective. Parents cannot get their children to follow all their wishes, while children feel constrained by their parents from doing what they desire. At universities, the administrators, faculty, students, and alumni all feel that the other constituencies are unduly influential in promoting their self-interests but that one's own group is granted insufficient power to alter the institutional practices. In the political arena, Congress feels that the executive branch possesses excessive power, and conversely the executive branch feels thwarted in implementing its policies by congressional counteraction.

If protection against exploitation relied solely upon individual safeguards, people would be continually subjected to coercive pressures. Accordingly, they create institutional sanctions which set limits on the control of human behavior. The integrity of individuals is largely secured by societal safeguards

that place constraints on improper means and foster reciprocity through balancing of interests.

Because individuals are conversant with psychological techniques does not grant them license to impose them on others. Industrialists, for example, know full well that productivity is higher when payment is made for amount of work completed rather than for length of time at work. Nevertheless, they cannot use the reinforcement system most advantageous to them. When industrialists commanded exclusive power, they paid workers at a piece-rate basis and hired and fired them at will. Reductions in power disparity between employers and employees resulted in a gradual weakening of performance requirements. As labor gained economic coercive strength through collective action, it was able to negotiate guaranteed wages on a daily, weekly, monthly, and eventually on an annual basis. At periodic intervals new contractual contingencies are adopted that are mutually acceptable. In the course of time, as better means of joint action are developed, other constituents will use their influence to modify arrangements that benefit certain segments of labor and industry but adversely affect the quality of life for other sectors of society.

As the previous example illustrates, improved knowledge of how to influence behavior does not necessarily raise the level of social control. If anything, the recent years have witnessed a diffusion of power, creating increased opportunities for reciprocal influence. This has enabled people to challenge social inequities, to effect changes in institutional practices, to counteract infringements on their rights, and to extend grievance procedures and due process of law to activities in social contexts that hitherto operated under unilateral control. The fact that more people wield power does not in and of itself ensure a humane society. In the final analysis, the important consideration is the purposes that power serves, however it might be distributed. Nor does knowledgeability about means of influence necessarily produce mechanical responsiveness in personal relations. Whatever their orientations, people model, expound, and reinforce what they value. Behavior arising out of purpose and commitment is no less genuine than improvised action.

The cliché of *1984*, and its more recent kin, diverts public attention from regulative influences that pose continual threats to human welfare. Most societies have instituted reciprocal systems that are protected by legal and social codes to prevent imperious control of human behavior. Although abuses of institutional power arise from time to time, it is not totalitarian rule that constitutes the impending peril. The hazards lie more in the intentional pursuit of personal gain, whether material or otherwise, than in control by coercion. Detrimental social practices arise and resist change, even within an open society, when many people benefit from them. To take a prevalent example, inequitable treatment of disadvantaged groups for private gain enjoys public support without requiring despotic rule.

Man, of course, has more to contend with than inhumanities toward one another. When the aversive consequences of otherwise rewarding life-styles are delayed and imperceptibly cumulative, people become willful agents of their own self-destruction. Thus, if enough people benefit from activities that progressively degrade their environment, then, barring contravening influences, they will eventually destroy their environment. Although individuals contributed differentially to the problem, the harmful consequences are borne by all. With growing populations and spread of lavish life-styles taxing finite resources, people will have to learn to cope with new realities of human existence.

Psychology cannot tell people how they ought to live their lives. It can, however, provide them with the means for effecting personal and social change. And it can aid them in making value choices by assessing the consequences of alternative life-styles and institutional arrangements. As a science concerned about the social consequences of its applications, psychology must also fulfill a broader obligation to society by bringing influence to bear on public policies to ensure that its findings are used in the service of human betterment.

REFERENCES

Anderson, J. R., & Bower, G. H. *Human associative memory.* New York: Wiley, 1973.

Bandura, A. *Principles of behavior modificaiton.* New York: Holt, Rinehart & Winston, 1969.

Bandura, A. (Ed.) *Psychological modeling: Conflicting theories.* Chicago: Aldine-Atherton, 1971. (a)

Bandura, A. *Social learning theory.* New York: General Learning Press, 1971. (b)

Bandura, A. Vicarious and self-reinforcement processes. In R. Glaser (Ed.), *The nature of reinforcement.* New York: Academic Press, 1971. (c)

Bandura, A. *Aggression: A social learning analysis.* Englewood Cliffs, N.J.: Prentice-Hall, 1973.

Dawson, M. E., & Furedy, J. J. The role of relational awareness in human autonomic discrimination classical conditioning. Unpublished manuscript, University of Toronto, 1974.

Dulany, D. E. Awareness, rules, and propositional control: A confrontation with S-R behavior theory. In T. R. Dixon & D. L. Horton (Eds.), *Verbal behavior and general behavior theory.* Englewood Cliffs, N.J.: Prentice-Hall, 1968.

Goldfried, M. R., & Merbaum, M. (Eds.) *Behavior change through self-control.* New York: Holt, Rinehart & Winston, 1973.

Grings, W. W. The role of consciousness and cognition in autonomic behavior change. In F. J. McGuigan & R. Schoonover (Eds.), *The psychophysiology of thinking.* New York: Academic Press, 1973.

Kaufman, A., Baron, A., & Kopp, R. E. Some effects of instructions on human operant behavior. *Psychonomic Monograph Supplements,* 1966, **1**, 243−250.

Mahoney, M. J., & Thoresen, C. E. *Self-control: Power to the person.* Monterey, Calif.: Brooks/Cole, 1974.

Mischel, W. Processes in delay of gratification. In L. Berkowitz (Ed.), *Advances in experimental social psychology.* Vol. 7. New York: Academic Press, 1974.

Rausch, H. L. Interaction sequences. *Journal of Personality and Social Psychology,* 1965, **2**, 487−499.

Skinner, B. F. *Beyond freedom and dignity.* New York: Knopf, 1971.

Thoresen, C. E., & Mahoney, M. J. *Behavioral self-control.* New York: Holt, Rinehart & Winston, 1973.

Zimmerman, B. J., & Rosenthal, T. L. Observational learning of rule-governed behavior by children. *Psychological Bulletin,* 1974, **81**, 29−42.

Etiology and Development

Behaviorists are concerned minimally with when and what is learned. The specific events which may be associated with the development of pathological behavior interest them little; what they have to say on this score usually is a rewording of the speculations of the intrapsychic theorists. Their distinction lies in proposing a limited number of rigorously derived principles which can account for a wide variety of learned pathological behavior patterns. Behaviorists are wary of the excessive number of empirically unanchored concepts included in intrapsychic theory, and propose that all behavior—normal or pathological—can be reduced to a few objective principles and concepts. Their focus on the process of learning in behavioral pathology, rather than on the content of what is learned, has added a precision and clarity to the study of psychopathology that has been sorely lacking.

John Watson was the founder of the behaviorist movement. In the paper reprinted here, perhaps the first designed to explicitly demonstrate the conditioning of an emotional response, Watson and Rayner established a model that was followed closely by most later behaviorists.

Joseph Wolpe, a major contemporary figure in behavioral thinking, describes his analysis of a number of traditional neurotic disorders in the excerpt printed here. Although he accepts the traditional schema of syndromes, it is evident that he reconstructs these disorders in terms consistent with behavioral theory.

36 Conditioned Emotional Reactions

John B. Watson and Rosalie Rayner

In recent literature various speculations have been entered into concerning the possibility of conditioning various types of emotional response, but direct experimental evidence in support of such a view has been lacking. If the theory advanced by Watson and Morgan[1] to the effect that in infancy the original emotional reaction patterns are few, consisting so far as observed of fear, rage and love, then there must be some simple method by means of which the range of stimuli which can call out these emotions and their compounds is greatly increased. Otherwise, complexity in adult response could not be accounted for. These authors without adequate experimental evidence advanced the view that this range was increased by means of conditioned reflex

From *F. Exp. Psychol.*, 3, 1–14, 1920. By permission of the American Psychological Association.

factors. It was suggested there that the early home life of the child furnishes a laboratory situation for establishing conditioned emotional responses. The present authors have recently put the whole matter to an experimental test.

Experimental work has been done so far on only one child, Albert B. This infant was reared almost from birth in a hospital environment; his mother was a wet nurse in the Harriet Lane Home for Invalid Children. Albert's life was normal: he was healthy from birth and one of the best developed youngsters ever brought to the hospital, weighing 21 lbs. at 9 months of age. He was on the whole stolid and unemotional. His stability was one of the principal reasons for using him as a subject in this test. We felt that we could do him relatively little harm by carrying out such experiments as those outlined below.

At approximately 9 months of age we ran

him through the emotional tests that have become a part of our regular routine in determining whether fear reactions can be called out by other stimuli than sharp noises and the sudden removal of support. Tests of this type have been described by the senior author in another place.[2] In brief, the infant was confronted suddenly and for the first time successively with a white rat, a rabbit, a dog, a monkey, with masks with and without hair, cotton wool, burning newspapers, etc. A permanent record of Albert's reactions to these objects and situations has been preserved in a motion picture study. Manipulation was the most usual reaction called out. *At no time did this infant ever show fear in any situation.* These experimental records were confirmed by the casual observations of the mother and hospital attendants. No one had ever seen him in a state of fear and rage. The infant practically never cried.

Up to approximately 9 months of age we had not tested him with loud sounds. The test to determine whether a fear reaction could be called out by a loud sound was made when he was 8 months, 26 days of age. The sound was that made by striking a hammer upon a suspended steel bar, 4 ft. in length and ¾ in. in diameter. The laboratory notes are as follows: "One of the 2 experimenters caused the child to turn its head and fixate her moving hand; the other, stationed back of the child, struck the steel bar a sharp blow. The child started violently, his breathing was checked and the arms were raised in a characteristic manner. On the 2nd stimulation the same thing occurred, and in addition the lips began to pucker and tremble. On the 3rd stimulation the child broke into a sudden crying fit. This is the first time an emotional situation in the laboratory has produced any fear or even crying in Albert."

We had expected just these results on account of our work with other infants brought up under similar conditions. It is worth while to call attention to the fact that removal of support (dropping and jerking the blanket upon which the infant was lying) was tried exhaustively upon this infant on the same occasion. It was not effective in producing the fear response. This stimulus is effective in younger children. At what age such stimuli lose their potency in producing fear is not known. Nor is it known whether less placid children ever lose their fear of them.

This probably depends upon the training the child gets. It is well known that children eagerly run to be tossed into the air and caught. On the other hand it is equally well known that in the adult fear responses are called out quite clearly by the sudden removal of support, if the individual is walking across a bridge, walking out upon a beam, etc. There is a wide field of study here which is aside from our present point.

The sound stimulus, thus, at 9 months of age, gives us the means of testing several important factors. (I) Can we condition fear of an animal, e.g., a white rat, by visually presenting it and simultaneously striking a steel bar? (II) If such a conditioned emotional response can be established, will there be a transfer to other animals or other objects? (III) What is the effect of time upon such conditioned emotional responses? (IV) If after a reasonable period such emotional responses have not died out, what laboratory methods can be devised for their removal?

The Establishment of Conditioned Emotional Responses

At first there was considerable hesitation upon our part in making the attempt to set up fear reactions experimentally. A certain responsibility attaches to such a procedure. We decided finally to make the attempt, comforting ourselves by the reflection that such attachments would arise anyway as soon as the child left the sheltered environment of the nursery for the rough and tumble of the home. We did not begin this work until Albert was 11 months, 3 days of age. Before attempting to set up a conditioned response we, as before, put him through all of the regular emotional tests. *Not the slightest sign of fear response was obtained in any situation.*

The steps taken to condition emotional response are shown in our laboratory notes.

11 months, 3 days—(1) White rat suddenly taken from the basket and presented to Albert. He began to reach for rat with left hand. Just as his hand touched the animal the bar was struck immediately behind his head. The infant jumped violently and fell forward, burying his face in the mattress. He did not cry, however.

(2) Just as the right hand touched the rat the bar was again struck. Again the infant

jumped violently, fell forward and began to whimper.

In order not to disturb the child too seriously no further tests were given for 1 week.

11 months, 10 days—(1) Rat presented suddenly without sound. There was steady fixation but no tendency at first to reach for it. The rat was then placed nearer, whereupon tentative reaching movements began with the right hand. When the rat nosed the infant's left hand, the hand was immediately withdrawn. He started to reach for the head of the animal with the forefinger of the left hand, but withdrew it suddenly before contact. It is thus seen that the two joint stimulations given the previous week were not without effect. He was tested with his blocks immediately afterwards to see if they shared in the process of conditioning. He began immediately to pick them up, dropping them, pounding them, etc. In the remainder of the tests the blocks were given frequently to quiet him and to test his general emotional state. They were always removed from sight when the process of conditioning was under way.

(2) Joint stimulation with rat and sound. Started, then fell over immediately to right side. No crying.

(3) Joint stimulation. Fell to right side and rested upon hands, with head turned away from rat. No crying.

(4) Joint stimulation. Same reaction.

(5) Rat suddenly presented alone. Puckered face, whimpered and withdrew body sharply to the left.

(6) Joint stimulation. Fell over immediately to right side and began to whimper.

(7) Joint stimulation. Started violently and cried, but did not fall over.

(8) Rat alone. *The instant the rat was shown the baby began to cry. Almost instantly he turned sharply to the left, fell over on left side, raised himself on all fours and began to crawl away so rapidly that he was caught with difficulty before reaching the edge of the table.*

This was as convincing a case of a completely conditioned fear response as could have been theoretically pictured. In all seven joint stimulations were given to bring about the complete reaction. It is not unlikely had the sound been of greater intensity or of a more complex clang character that the number of joint stimulations might have been materially reduced. Experiments designed to define the nature of the sounds that will serve best as emotional stimuli are under way.

When a Conditioned Emotional Response Has Been Established for One Object, Is There a Transfer?

Five days later Albert was again brought back into the laboratory and tested as follows:

11 months, 15 days—(1) Tested first with blocks. He reached readily for them, playing with them as usual. This shows that there has been no general transfer to the room, table, blocks, etc.

(2) Rat alone. Whimpered immediately, withdrew right hand and turned head and trunk away.

(3) Blocks again offered. Played readily with them, smiling and gurgling.

(4) Rat alone. Leaned over to the left side as far away from the rat as possible, then fell over, getting up on all fours and scurrying away as rapidly as possible.

(5) Blocks again offered. Reached immediately for them, smiling and laughing as before.

The above preliminary test shows that the conditioned response to the rat had carried over completely for the 5 days in which no tests were given. The question as to whether or not there is a transfer was next taken up.

(6) Rabbit alone. The rabbit was suddenly placed on the mattress in front of him. The reaction was pronounced. Negative responses began at once. He leaned as far away from the animal as possible, whimpered, then burst into tears. When the rabbit was placed in contact with him he buried his face in the mattress, then got up on all fours and crawled away, crying as he went. This was a most convincing test.

(7) The blocks were next given him, after an interval. He played with them as before. It was observed by 4 people that he played far more energetically with them than ever before. The blocks were raised high over his head and slammed down with a great deal of force.

(8) Dog alone. The dog did not produce as violent a reaction as the rabbit. The moment fixation occurred the child shrank back and as the animal came nearer he attempted to get on all fours but did not cry at first. As soon as the dog passed out of his range of vision he became quiet. The dog was then made to approach the infant's head (he was lying down at the moment). Albert straightened up immediately, fell over to the opposite side and turned his head away. He then began to cry.

(9) The blocks were again presented. He began immediately to play with them.

(10) Fur coat (seal). Withdrew immediately to the left side and began to fret. Coat put close to him on the left side, he turned immediately, began to cry and tried to crawl away on all fours.

(11) Cotton wool. The wool was presented in a paper package. At the end the cotton was not covered by the paper. It was placed first on his feet. He kicked it away but did not touch it with his hands. When his hand was laid on the wool he immediately withdrew it but did not show the shock that the animals or fur coat produced in him. He then began to play with the paper, avoiding contact with the wool itself. He finally, under the impulse of the manipulative instinct, lost some of his negativism to the wool.

(12) Just in play W. put his head down to see if Albert would play with his hair. Albert was completely negative. Two other observers did the same thing. He began immediately to play with their hair. W. then brought the Santa Claus mask and presented it to Albert. He was again pronouncedly negative.

11 months, 20 days—(1) Blocks alone. Played with them as usual.

(2) Rat alone. Withdrawal of the whole body, bending over to left side, no crying. Fixation and following with eyes. The response was much less marked than on first presentation the previous week. It was thought best to freshen up the reaction by another joint stimulation.

(3) Just as the rat was placed on his hand the rod was struck. Reaction violent.

(4) Rat alone. Fell over at once to left side. Reaction practically as strong as on former occasion but no crying.

(5) Rat alone. Fell over to left side, got up on all fours and started to crawl away. On this occasion there was no crying, but strange to say, as he started away he began to gurgle and coo, even while leaning far over to the left side to avoid the rat.

(6) Rabbit alone. Leaned over to left side as far as possible. Did not fall over. Began to whimper but reaction not so violent as on former occasions.

(7) Blocks again offered. He reached for them immediately and began to play.

All of the tests so far discussed were carried out upon a table supplied with a mattress, located in a small, well-lighted dark-room. We wished to test next whether conditioned fear responses so set up would appear if the situation were markedly altered. We thought it best before making this test to freshen the reaction both to the rabbit and to the dog by showing them at the moment the steel bar was struck. It will be recalled that this was the first time any effort had been made to directly condition response to the dog and rabbit. The experimental notes are as follows:

(8) The rabbit at first was given alone. The reaction was exactly as given in test (6) above. When the rabbit was left on Albert's knees for a long time he began tentatively to reach out and manipulate its fur with forefingers. While doing this the steel rod was struck. A violent fear reaction resulted.

(9) Rabbit alone. Reaction wholly similar to that on trial (6) above.

(10) Rabbit alone. Started immediately to whimper, holding hands far up, but did not cry. Conflicting tendency to manipulate very evident.

(11) Dog alone. Began to whimper, shaking head from side to side, holding hands as far away from the animal as possible.

(12) Dog and sound. The rod was struck just as the animal touched him. A violent negative reaction appeared. He began to whimper, turned to one side, fell over and started to get up on all fours.

(13) Blocks. Played with them immediately and readily.

On this same day and immediately after the above experiment Albert was taken into the large well-lighted lecture room belonging to the laboratory. He was placed on a table in the center of the room immediately under the skylight. Four people were present. The situation was thus very different from that which obtained in the small dark room.

(1) Rat alone. No sudden fear reaction appeared at first. The hands, however, were held up and away from the animal. No positive manipulatory reactions appeared.

(2) Rabbit alone. Fear reaction slight. Turned to left and kept face away from the animal but the reaction was never pronounced.

(3) Dog alone. Turned away but did not fall over. Cried. Hands moved as far away from the animal as possible. Whimpered as long as the dog was present.

(4) Rat alone. Slight negative reaction.

(5) Rat and sound. It was thought best to freshen the reaction to the rat. The sound was

given just as the rat was presented. Albert jumped violently but did not cry.

(6) Rat alone. At first he did not show any negative reaction. When rat was placed nearer he began to show negative reaction by drawing back his body, raising his hands, whimpering, etc.

(7) Blocks. Played with them immediately.

(8) Rat alone. Pronounced withdrawal of body and whimpering.

(9) Blocks. Played with them as before.

(10) Rabbit alone. Pronounced reaction. Whimpered with arms held high, fell over backward and had to be caught.

(11) Dog alone. At first the dog did not produce the pronounced reaction. The hands were held high over the head, breathing was checked, but there was no crying. Just at this moment the dog, which had not barked before, barked 3 times loudly when only about 6 in. from the baby's face. Albert immediately fell over and broke into a wail that continued until the dog was removed. The sudden barking of the hitherto quiet dog produced a marked fear response in the adult observers!

From the above results it would seem that emotional transfers do take place. Furthermore it would seem that the number of transfers resulting from an experimentally produced conditioned emotional reaction may be very large. In our observations we had no means of testing the complete number of transfers which may have resulted.

The Effect of Time upon Conditioned Emotional Responses

We have already shown that the conditioned emotional response will continue for a period of 1 week. It was desired to make the time test longer. In view of the imminence of Albert's departure from the hospital we could not make the interval longer than 1 month. Accordingly no further emotional experimentation was entered into for 31 days after the above test. During the month, however, Albert was brought weekly to the laboratory for tests upon right- and left-handedness, imitation, general development, etc. No emotional tests whatever were given and during the whole month his regular nursery routine was maintained in the Harriet Lane Home. The notes on the test given at the end of this period are as follows:

1 year, 21 days—(1) Santa Claus mask. Withdrawal, gurgling, then slapped at it without touching. When his hand was forced to touch it, he whimpered and cried. His hand was forced to touch it two more times. He whimpered and cried on both tests. He finally cried at the mere visual stimulus of the mask.

(2) Fur coat. Wrinkled his nose and withdrew both hands, drew back his whole body and began to whimper as the coat was put nearer. Again there was the strife between withdrawal and the tendency to manipulate. Reached tentatively with left hand but drew back before contact had been made. In moving his body to one side his hand accidentally touched the coat. He began to cry at once, nodding his head in a very peculiar manner (this reaction was an entirely new one). Both hands were withdrawn as far as possible from the coat. The coat was then laid on his lap and he continued nodding his head and whimpering, withdrawing his body as far as possible, pushing the while at the coat with his feet but never touching it with his hands.

(3) Fur coat. The coat was taken out of his sight and presented again at the end of a minute. He began immediately to fret, withdrawing his body and nodding his head as before.

(4) Blocks. He began to play with them as usual.

(5) The rat. He allowed the rat to crawl towards him without withdrawing. He sat very still and fixated it intently. Rat then touched his hand. Albert withdrew it immediately, then leaned back as far as possible but did not cry. When the rat was placed on his arm he withdrew his body and began to fret, nodding his head. The rat was then allowed to crawl against his chest. He first began to fret and then covered his eyes with both hands.

(6) Blocks. Reaction normal.

(7) The rabbit. The animal was placed directly in front of him. It was very quiet. Albert showed no avoiding reactions at first. After a few seconds he puckered up his face, began to nod his head and to look intently at the experimenter. He next began to push the rabbit away with his feet, withdrawing his body at the same time. Then as the rabbit came nearer he began pulling his feet away, nodding his head, and wailing "da da." After about a minute he reached out tentatively and slowly and touched the rabbit's ear with his right hand, finally manipulating it. The rabbit

was again placed in his lap. Again he began to fret and withdrew his hands. He reached out tentatively with his left hand and touched the animal, shuddered and withdrew the whole body. The experimenter then took hold of his left hand and laid it on the rabbit's back. Albert immediately withdrew his hand and began to suck his thumb. Again the rabbit was laid in his lap. He began to cry, covering his face with both hands.

(8) Dog. The dog was very active. Albert fixated it intensely for a few seconds, sitting very still. He began to cry but did not fall over backwards as on his last contact with the dog. When the dog was pushed closer to him he at first sat motionless, then began to cry, putting both hands over his face.

These experiments would seem to show conclusively that directly conditioned emotional responses as well as those conditioned by transfer persist, although with a certain loss in the intensity of the reaction, for a longer period than one month. Our view is that they persist and modify personality throughout life. It should be recalled again that Albert was of an extremely phlegmatic type. Had he been emotionally unstable probably both the directly conditioned response and those transferred would have persisted throughout the month unchanged in form.

"Detachment" or Removal of Conditioned Emotional Responses

Unfortunately Albert was taken from the hospital the day the above tests were made. Hence the opportunity of building up an experimental technique by means of which we could remove the conditioned emotional responses was denied us. Our own view, expressed above, which is possibly not very well grounded, is that these responses in the home environment are likely to persist indefinitely, unless an accidental method for removing them is hit upon. The importance of establishing some method must be apparent to all. Had the opportunity been at hand we should have tried out several methods, some of which we may mention. (1) Constantly confronting the child with those stimuli which called out the responses in the hopes that habituation would come in corresponding to "fatigue" of reflex when differential reactions are to be set up. (2) By trying to "recondition" by showing objects

calling out fear responses (visual) and simultaneously stimulating the erogenous zones (tactual). We should try first the lips, then the nipples and as a final resort the sex organs. (3) By trying to "recondition" by feeding the subject candy or other food just as the animal is shown. This method calls for the food control of the subject. (4) By building up "constructive" activities around the object by imitation and by putting the hand through the motions of manipulation. At this age imitation of overt motor activity is strong, as our present but unpublished experimentation has shown.

Incidental Observations

(a) *Thumb sucking as a compensatory device for blocking fear and noxious stimuli*—During the course of these experiments, especially in the final test, it was noticed that whenever Albert was on the verge of tears or emotionally upset generally he would continually thrust his thumb into his mouth. The moment the hand reached the mouth he became impervious to the stimuli producing fear. Again and again while the motion pictures were being made at the end of the 30-day rest period, we had to remove the thumb from his mouth before the conditioned response could be obtained. This method of blocking noxious and emotional stimuli (fear and rage) through erogenous stimulation seems to persist from birth onward. Very often in our experiments upon the work adders with infants under 10 days of age the same reaction appeared. When at work upon the adders both of the infants' arms are under slight restraint. Often rage appears. They begin to cry, thrashing their arms and legs about. If the finger gets into the mouth crying ceases at once. The organism, thus apparently from birth, when under the influence of love stimuli, is blocked to all others.* This resort to sex stimulation when under the influence of noxious and emotional situations,

---

*The stimulus to love in infants according to our view is stroking of the skin, lips, nipples and sex organs, patting and rocking, picking up, etc. Patting and rocking (when not conditoned) are probably equivalent to actual stimulation of the sex organs. In adults of course, as every lover knows, vision, audition and olfaction soon become conditioned by joint stimulation with contact and kinaesthetic stimuli.

or when the individual is restless and idle, persists throughout adolescent and adult life. Albert, at any rate, did not resort to thumb sucking except in the presence of such stimuli. Thumb sucking could immediately be checked by offering him his blocks. These invariably called out active manipulation instincts. It is worthwhile here to call attention to the fact that Freud's conception of the stimulation of erogenous zones as being the expression of an original "pleasure" seeking principle may be turned about and possibly better described as a compensatory (and often conditioned) device for the blockage of noxious and fear and rage producing stimuli.

(b) *Equal primacy of fear, love and possibly rage*—While in general the results of our experiment offer no particular points of conflict with Freudian concepts, one fact out of harmony with them should be emphasized. According to proper Freudians, sex (or in our terminology, love) is the principal emotion in which conditioned responses arise which later limit and distort personality. We wish to take sharp issue with this view on the basis of the experimental evidence we have gathered. Fear is as primal a factor as love in influencing personality. Fear does not gather its potency in any derived manner from love. It belongs to the original and inherited nature of man. Probably the same may be true of rage although at present we are not so sure of this.

The Freudians 20 years from now, unless their hypotheses change, when they come to analyze Albert's fear of a seal skin coat— assuming that he comes to analysis at that age—will probably tease from him the recital of a dream which upon their analysis will show that Albert at 3 years of age attempted to play with the pubic hair of the mother and was scolded violently for it. (We are by no means denying that this might in some other case condition it.) If the analyst has sufficiently prepared Albert to accept such a dream when found as an explanation of his avoiding tendencies, and if the analyst has the authority and personality to put it over, Albert may be fully convinced that the dream was a true revealer of the factors which brought about the fear.

It is probable that many of the phobias in psychopathology are true conditioned emotional reactions either of the direct or the transferred type. One may possibly have to believe that such persistence of early conditioned responses will be found only in persons who are constitutionally inferior. Our argument is meant to be constructive. Emotional disturbances cannot be traced back to sex alone. They must be retraced along at least three collateral lines—to conditioned and transferred responses set up in infancy and early youth in all three of the fundamental human emotions.

REFERENCES

1. Watson, J. B. and Morgan. (April, 1917). Emotional reactions and psychological experimentation. *Amer. J. Psychol.*, 28, 163–174.
2. Watson, J. B. *Psychology from the Standpoint of a Behaviorist*, p. 202.

37 Etiology of Human Neuroses

Joseph Wolpe

The Causal Relations of Pervasive ("Free-floating") Anxiety

Under certain circumstances it is not only to well-defined stimulus configurations that anxiety responses are conditioned, but also to more or less omnipresent properties of the

From *Psychotherapy by Reciprocal Inhibition* by Joseph Wolpe, pages 83–94, copyright 1958 by the Board of Trustees of the Leland Stanford Junior University. With the permission of the publishers, Stanford University Press.

environment, of which extreme examples would be light, light and shade contrasts, amorphous noise, spatiality, and the passage of time. Since each of these enters into most, if not all, possible experience, it is to be expected that if any of them becomes connected to anxiety responses the patient will be persistently, and apparently causelessly anxious. He will be suffering from what is erroneously called "free-floating" anxiety, and for which a more suitable label would be *pervasive anxiety.*

It must be unequivocally stated, in case it is not quite self-evident, that there is no sharp dividing line between specific anxiety-evoking stimuli and stimuli to pervasive anxiety. The pervasiveness of the latter is a function of the pervasiveness of the stimulus element conditioned; and there are degrees of pervasiveness ranging from the absolute omnipresence of time itself through very common elements like room walls to rarely encountered configurations like hunchbacks.

What reason is there for believing that pervasive anxiety has definable stimulus sources?

Questioning of patients with pervasive anxiety usually reveals that definable aspects of the environment are especially related to this anxiety. For example, one patient reported increased anxiety in the presence of any very large object; another an uncomfortable intrusiveness of all sharp contrasts in his visual field—even the printed words on a page, and particularly contrasts in the periphery of the field. A third felt overwhelmed by physical space. Frequently, patients with pervasive anxiety observe that noise causes a rise in the level of their anxiety. In some cases the noise need not be loud, and in some even music is disturbing.

Although pervasive anxiety is usually felt less when the patient lies down and closes his eyes, it does not disappear. To some extent this may be explained on the basis of perseveration due to prolonged reverberation of the effects of the stimulus in the nervous system. But this does not account for the fact that usually *some* anxiety is already felt at the moment of waking. An obvious explanation is that anxiety evocable by stimuli that enter into the very structure of experience is likely to be produced by the first contents of the awakening subject's imagination. Anxiety increases when the outside world makes its impact; and it is consonant with this that, very commonly, the level of pervasive anxiety gradually rises as the day goes on.

This diurnal rise in level is less likely to occur when the general level of pervasive anxiety is low; for then there is a greater likelihood of the arousal, during a normal day's experience, of other emotions which may be physiologically antagonistic to anxiety, so that the anxiety will be inhibited and its habit strength each time slightly diminished. On the other hand, invariably (in

my experience) the patient with pervasive anxiety also has unadaptive anxiety reactions to specific stimuli, and if he should encounter and react to any one of the latter during that day, the level of pervasive anxiety will promptly rise. In the normal course of events it is to be expected that level of pervasive anxiety will fluctuate because of "chance" occurrences which strengthen or weaken its habit strength.

Sometimes, when a patient is fortunate enough not to meet with any specific disturbing stimuli over an extended period, his pervasive anxiety may practically cease, but subsequent response to a relevant specific anxiety-evoking stimulus will condition it lastingly again. This reconditioning was beautifully demonstrated in one of my patients, who, in addition to pervasive anxiety, had a number of severe phobias on the general theme of illness. The pervasive anxiety responded extremely well to La Verne's carbon dioxide-oxygen inhalation therapy. The patient stopped coming for treatment until several months later when the pervasive anxiety was reinduced after he had witnessed an epileptic fit in the street. The pervasive anxiety was again speedily removed by carbon dioxide-oxygen and the patient again stopped treatment after a few more interviews. The essence of this sequence was repeated about ten times before the patient finally allowed desensitization to the phobic stimuli to be completed.

The question naturally arises: What factors determine whether or not pervasive anxiety will be part of a patient's neurosis? At the moment two possible factors may be suggested on the basis of clinical impressions. One seems to be the intensity of anxiety evocation at the time of the induction of the neurosis. It is hypothesized that the more intense the anxiety the more stimulus aspects are likely to acquire *some* measure of anxiety conditioning. Indirect support for this hypothesis comes from the observation that, on the whole, it is the patient who reacts more severely to specific stimuli who is also likely to suffer from pervasive anxiety.

The second possible factor is a lack of clearly defined environmental stimuli at the time of neurosis induction. For example, one patient's pervasive anxiety began after a night in a hotel during which he had attempted intercourse with a woman to whom he felt both sexual attraction and strong revulsion. He had felt a powerful and strange, predominantly nonsexual excitation, and ejaculation had occurred very prematurely without pleasure. The light had been switched off, and *only the dark outlines of objects could be seen.* After this, so great was his feeling of revulsion to the woman that he spent the remainder of the night on the carpet. This experience left him, as he subsequently found, with an anxiety toward a wide range of sexual objects, along with much pervasive anxiety, characterized by a special intrusiveness of all heavy dark objects.

The Causal Process in Hysteria

Hysterical reactions are clearly distinguishable from the rather diffuse discharges of the autonomic nervous system that characterize anxiety reactions. In most instances hysterical reactions do not find expression in the autonomic nervous system at all, but in the sensory system, the motor system, or groups of functional units involved in the production of imagery or of consciousness in general. Thus, they may take the form of anesthesias, paresthesias, hyperesthesias, or disturbances of vision or hearing; of paralyses, pareses, tics, tremors, disturbances of balance, contractures or fits; of amnesias, fugues, or "multiple personality" phenomena. Occasionally, hysterical reactions do appear to involve functions within the domain of the autonomic nervous system—in the form of vomiting (or nausea) or enuresis, but it is noteworthy that each of the two functions involved is to some extent within voluntary control.

Anxiety frequently accompanies hysterical reactions and then they occur side by side as two distinct forms of *primary* neurotic response. This state of affairs must be sharply distinguished from that in which sensory or motor phenomena are secondary effects of the normal components of anxiety, and as such do not qualify as hysterical. For example, a headache due to tension of the temporal muscles, backache due to tension of the longitudinal spinal muscles, or paresthesia due to hyperventilation are not to be regarded as hysterical.

It is necessary also to differentiate hysterical from obsessional reactions. Hysterical reactions are at a relatively low level of organization, affecting well-defined sensory areas and specific motor units, and causing changes in the general character of consciousness or the exclusion from consciousness of "blocks" of experience limited in terms of a time span or some other broad category. The details of the reactions tend to be fixed and unchanging. Obsessional reactions consist by contrast of highly organized movements or of elaborate and complex thinking, in either of which there is a great variety in the individual instances of expression of a specific constant theme.

Like other neurotic reactions, hysterical reactions are acquired by learning. It is intriguing to note that Freud's very early observations on hysterical subjects could easily have led him to this conclusion had he not been sidetracked by a spurious deduction from observations on therapeutic effects. In a paper published in 1893, speaking of the relation of the symptoms of hysteria to the patients' reactions at the time of the precipitating stress, he states:

> The connection is often so clear that it is quite evident how the exciting event has happened to produce just this and no other manifestation; the phenomenon is determined in a perfectly clear manner by the cause; to take the most ordinary example, a painful effect, which was originally excited while eating, but was suppressed, produces nausea and vomiting, and this continues for months, as hysterical vomiting. A child who is very ill at last falls asleep, and its mother tries her utmost to keep quiet and not to wake it; but just in consequence of this resolution (hysterical counterwill) she makes a clucking noise with her tongue. On another occasion when she wishes to keep absolutely quiet this happens again, and so a tic in the form of tongue-clicking develops which for a number of years accompanies every excitement. . . . A highly intelligent man assists while his brother's ankylosed hip is straightened under an anesthetic. At the instant when the joint gives way with a crack, he feels a violent pain in his own hip joint which lasts almost a year. . . . (pp. 25–26)

The attack then arises spontaneously as memories commonly do; but they may also be provoked, just as any memory may be aroused according to the laws of association. Provocation of an attack occurs either by stimulation of a hysterogenic zone or by a new experience resembling the pathogenic experience. We hope to be able to show that no essential difference exists between the two conditions, apparently so distinct; and in both cases a hyperaesthetic memory has been stirred. (p. 40)

Apart from the reference to the possibility of attacks arising "spontaneously" (which Freud later explicitly repudiated) we have here an account of the formation by learning of stimulus-response connections. That Freud did not *see* this was mainly because, having observed patients cured when they recalled and narrated the story of the precipitating experience, he concluded that the symptoms were due to the imprisonment of emotionally disturbing memories. He states ". . . we are of the opinion that the psychical trauma, or the memory of it acts as a kind of foreign body constituting an effective agent in the present, even long after it has penetrated. . . ." There can be little doubt that this statement would not have been made, and the mind-structure theory that is psychoanalytic theory would not have been born, if Freud could have known that memories do not exist in the form of thoughts or images in some kind of repository within us, but depend on the establishment, through the learning process, of specific neural interconnections that give *a potentiality* of evocation of particular thoughts and images when and only when certain stimulus conditions, external or internal, are present.

When a clear history of the onset of hysterical symptoms is obtained, it is usually found, as illustrated in Freud's cases quoted above, that the hysterical reaction displays a repetition of features that were present in response to the initiating disturbing experience. The stimulus to the reaction varies. Sometimes it is a fairly specific sensory stimulation. For example, a 33-year-old woman had as a hysterical reaction an intolerable sensation of "gooseflesh" in her calves in response to any rectal sensation such as a desire to defecate, ever since, three years previously, a surgeon had unceremoniously performed a rectal examination upon her, while, drowsy from premedication with morphia, she was awaiting the administration of an anesthetic for an abdominal operation.

In other cases it appears that the hysterical reaction is aroused by ubiquitous stimuli, being then the hysterical equivalent of pervasive ("free-floating") anxiety. An example of this is wryneck that is present throughout the working day and relaxes the moment the patient falls asleep. In yet others anxiety appears to *mediate* the hysterical reaction. The hysteria of one of my patients had both a pervasive component and an anxiety-mediated component. This was a 58-year-old woman

who 18 months earlier had encountered a deadly snake in a copse. She had been terrified and momentarily paralyzed; her ears were filled with the sound of waves and she had been unable to speak for two hours. The sound of waves had never left her, and any considerable anxiety such as might arise from tension in her home would intensify this sound and then lead to vertigo, loss of balance, and a feeling of great weakness in all her limbs, so that sometimes she fell.

The central feature of hysterical reactions is the conditioning, in situations of stress, of neurotic reactions other than anxiety, although anxiety is often also conditioned as well. It is necessary to ask what determines this. There are two possible answers. One is that these reactions are conditioned when they happen to be evoked in addition to anxiety. The other is that although such reactions may be evoked by stress in all subjects, they become the neurotic responses conditioned only in those in whom some special factor is present that gives preference to nonanxiety conditioning. Since, in fact, the immediate response to neurotigenic stimulation always seems to implicate all response systems, the latter possibility is the more likely to be relevant. And there is evidence that it is people with distinct personality features who usually develop hysterical reactions.

Jung (1923) long ago observed that hysterics tend to exhibit extravert character traits while other neurotic subjects tend to be introverted. In this partition of personalities, he was followed by other writers who, while differing in many ways, agreed, as Eysenck (1947, p. 58) concluded from a survey, in the following particulars: (*a*) the introvert has a more subjective, the extravert a more objective outlook; (*b*) the introvert shows a higher degree of cerebral activity, the extravert a higher degree of behavioral activity; (*c*) the introvert shows a tendency to self-control (inhibition), the extravert a tendency to lack of such control. Eysenck (1955*b*) has pointed out on the basis of experiments performed by Franks (1956) and himself (1955*a*) that extraverted subjects besides learning more poorly also generate reactive inhibition more readily than introverts do. He postulates (1955*b*, p. 35) that subjects in whom reactive inhibition is generated quickly and dissipated slowly "are predisposed thereby to develop extraverted patterns of behaviour and to develop hysterico-psychopathic disorders in cases of neurotic breakdown." Clearly what his facts actually demonstrate is that the hysterical type of breakdown is particularly likely in subjects in whom reactive inhibition has the feature stated. The *causal* role of reactive inhibition is not shown, nor is a possible mechanism suggested.

A possibility is this: that in addition to their easily generated and persistent reactive inhibition (and perhaps in some indirect way bound up with it) extraverted people have one or both of the following characteristics: *(a)* when exposed to anxiety-arousing stimuli they respond with relatively low degrees of anxiety so that other responses are unusually prominent; *(b)* when anxiety and other responses are simultaneously evoked in them, contiguous stimuli become conditioned to the other responses rather than to the anxiety—by contrast with introverts.

This hypothesis lends itself readily to direct experimentation. In the meantime a survey from my records of the 22 patients with hysterical symptoms has yielded some suggestive evidence. nine of them (41 per cent) had initial Willoughby scores below 30. This is in striking contrast to 273 nonhysterical neurotic patients, in only 50 (18 per cent) of whom were the initial scores below this level. The Kolmogorov-Smirnov test shows the difference to be significant at the .05 level. It is interesting to note that insofar as this supports our hypothesis it accords with the time-worn conception of the hysterical patient with little or no anxiety—*la belle indifference*. It is relevant to the same point that the hysterical patients with low Willoughby scores all benefited by procedures that varied greatly but did not obviously affect anxious sensitivity. By contrast, in the 13 patients whose hysterical reactions were accompanied by much anxiety there was a direct correlation between diminution of anxious sensitivity and decreased strength of hysterical reactions except in two cases where this consisted purely of amnesia, which was unaffected. (In one of these events the forgotten period were later retrieved under hypnosis, in the other they remained forgotten. It seemed to make no difference either way to the patient's recovery.)

Summarizing the above facts, it may be said that hysterical reactions may either accompany anxiety or occur on their own. In the former case their treatment is the treatment of anxiety, in the latter it is different in a way that will be discussed in the chapter on treatment. It is supposed that anxiety is a feature

when hysteria occurs in subjects relatively far from the extraverted extreme of Eysenck's introversion-extraversion dimension, just because the hypothetical preferential conditioning of responses other than anxiety to neurotigenic stimuli is less marked in these people. This supposition needs to be tested.

Meanwhile it may be noted that there is experimental evidence of a competitive relationship in certain contexts between autonomic and motor responses. Mowrer and Viek (1948), using two groups of rats, placed each animal after a period of starvation on the electrifiable floor of a rectangular cage and offered him food on a stick for ten seconds. Whether the animal ate or not, shock was applied ten seconds later. In the case of one group of ten rats, jumping into the air resulted in the experimenter switching off the shock (shock-controllable group). Each animal in this group had an experimental "twin" to which the shock was applied for the same length of time as it had taken its counterpart to jump into the air (shock-uncontrollable group). One trial a day was given to each animal. The animals in each group whose eating responses during the ten seconds were inhibited (by conditioned anxiety responses resulting from the shocks) were charted each day, and it was found that in the shock-controllable group the number of eating inhibitions was never high and declined to zero, whereas in the shock-uncontrollable group the number rose to a high level and remained there. Apparently, the constant evocation of jumping in the former group resulted in gradual development of conditioned inhibition of anxiety. By contrast with this, in the typical Cornell technique for producing experimental neuroses (p. 43) a very localized musculoskeletal conditioned response comes to be increasingly dominated by autonomic anxiety responses. The whole matter has been discussed in more detail elsewhere (Wolpe, 1953).

Obsessional Behavior

Sometimes, besides the autonomic discharges characteristic of anxiety, ideational, motor, and sensory responses are prominent in a neurosis. If simple and invariate in character, they are labeled *hysterical*. The term *obsessional* is applied to behavior that is more complex and variable in detail, consisting of well-defined and often elaborate thought sequences or relatively intricate acts which, though they may differ in outward form from one occasion to the next, lead or tend to lead to the same kind of result. The term is applicable even to those cases characterized by an obstinate impulse to behavior that rarely or never becomes manifest. Examples of obsessions predominantly of thought are a woman's insistent idea that she might throw her child from the balcony of her apartment, or a man's need to have one of a restricted class of "pleasant" thoughts in his mind before he can make any well-defined movement such as entering a doorway or sitting down. Exhibitionism and compulsive handwashing are characteristic examples of predominantly motor obsessional behavior.

Sometimes the word *compulsive* has been preferred to obsesssional for those cases in which motor activity predominates. However, as most cases display both elements, there is little practical value in the distinction. Furthermore, the term compulsive is open to the objection that *all* behavior is compulsive in a sense, for causal determinism implies that the response that occurs is always the only one that could have occurred in the circumstances. The feature of any example of obsessional behavior is not its inevitability but its *intrusiveness*. Its elicitation or the impulse toward it is an encumbrance and an embarrassment to the patient.

If hysterical and obsessional reactions involve similar elements, we may expect that borderline cases will be found. An example of this is a 47-year-old male nurse employed in an industrial first-aid room who for 17 years had an uncontrollable impulse to mimic any rhythmic movements performed before him, e.g., waving of arms or dancing, and to obey any command no matter from whom. In this was combined the basic simplicity of hysteria and the situationally determined variability of obsessional behavior.

It may be stated almost as dogma that the strength and frequency of evocation of obsessional behavior is directly related to the amount of anxiety being evoked in the patient. Pollitt (1957) in a study of 150 obsessional cases noted that obsessional symptoms became more severe and prominent "when anxiety and tension increased for whatever causes." However, it is not always that the source of the anxiety is irrelevant. Sometimes the obsessional behavior is evident only when anxiety arises from specific, usually neurotic sources. For example, an exhibitionist experienced impulses to expose himself when he felt inadequate and inferior among his friends but not when he was anxious about the results of a law examination.

Anxiety-Elevating Obsessions

Two types of obsessional behavior are clearly distinguishable in clinical practice. One type appears to be part and parcel of the immediate response to anxiety-evoking stimulation and has secondary effects entirely in the direction of increasing anxiety. When a motor mechanic of 45 had neurotic anxiety exceeding a certain fairly low level, he would have a terrifying though always controllable impulse to strike people. From the first moment of awareness of the impulse he would feel increased anxiety, and if at the time he was with an associate or even among strangers—for example, in a bus—he would thrust his hands firmly into his pockets "to keep them out of trouble." In the history of such patients one finds that behavior similar to that constituting the obsession was present during an earlier situation in which conditioning of anxiety took place. In 1942 this motor mechanic, on military service, had been sentenced to 30 days' imprisonment in circumstances which he had with some justice felt to be grossly unfair. Then, as he had resisted the military police rather violently in protest, he was taken to a psychiatrist who said there was nothing wrong with him and that the sentence should be carried out. At this his feeling of helpless rage had further increased and he was taken out by force. Then for the first time he had had "this queer feeling" in his abdomen and had struck a military policeman who tried to compel him to work. Horror at the implications of this act intensified his disturbed state. The obsession to strike people made its first appearance in 1953, eleven years later. He had been imprisoned overnight (for the first time since 1942) because, arriving home one night to find his house crowded with his wife's relatives, he had shouted and been violent until his wife had called the police. After emerging from jail, burning with a sense of injustice much like that experienced during his imprisonment in the army, he had felt the impulse to strike a stranger who was giving him a lift in an automobile, and then again, much more strongly, a few days later toward his wife at their first meeting since his night in jail. This time he had gone into a state of panic, and since then, for a period of five months, the obsession had recurred very frequently and in an increasing range of conditions, e.g., at work he would often have a fear-laden desire to hit fellow workmen with any tool he happened to be holding. (There was subsequently a secondary conditioning of anxiety to the *sight* of tools, including knives and forks.)

Anxiety-Reducing Obsessions

The second type of obsessional behavior occurs as a *reaction* to anxiety, and its performance *diminishes* anxiety to some extent, for at least a short time. It occurs in many forms—tidying, handwashing, eating, buying—activities which are of course "normal" when prompted by usual motivations and not by anxiety; rituals like touching poles, perversions like exhibitionism, and various thinking activities. In some of these cases secondary heightening of anxiety occurs as a response to some aspect of the obsessional behavior. For example, in a case of obsessional eating, the anxiety was at first reduced by the eating, and then its level would rise in response to the idea of getting fat.

Obsessional behavior of this kind owes its existence to the previous conditioning of anxiety-relieving responses. This has been strikingly demonstrated in a recent experiment by Fonberg (1956). This writer conditioned each of several dogs to perform a definite movement in response to several auditory and visual stimuli using food reinforcement. When these instrumental conditioned responses had been firmly established, she proceeded to elaborate defensive instrumental conditioned responses, employing stimuli and responses distinct from those of the alimentary training. The noxious stimulus used was either an electric shock to the right foreleg or a strong air puff to the ear. As a result of this conditioning, upon presentation of the conditioned stimulus an animal would be able to avert the noxious stimulus—for example, by lifting a particular foreleg. The dogs were then made neurotic by conditioning an excitatory alimentary response to a strong tone of 50 cycles and an inhibitory response to a very weak tone of the same frequency, and

then bringing the two differentiated tones nearer and nearer to each other from session to session either by progressive strengthening of the inhibitory tone or by both strengthening the inhibitory and weakening the excitatory. In all animals, as soon as neurotic behavior appeared it was accompanied by the previously elaborated defensive motor reaction. Besides this deliberately conditioned reaction, "shaking off" movements were observed in those dogs in whom the noxious stimulation had originally been air puffed into the ear. The more intense the general disturbance the more intense and frequent were the defensive movements. The alimentary conditioned reflexes disappeared completely. With the disappearance of general disturbed symptoms, the defensive movements subsided, reappearing with any new outburst of behavioral disturbance.

It appears clear from these observations that in elaborating the conditioned defensive reaction to the auditory stimulus, anxiety-response-produced stimuli were also conditioned to evoke the defensive reaction, and this reaction was consequently evocable *whenever* the animal had anxiety responses, no matter what the origin of these may have been.

Similarly, in the history of patients displaying this kind of obsessional behavior, it is found that at an earlier period, some important real threat was consistently removed by a single well-defined type of behavior, and this behavior later appears as a response to *any* similar anxiety. The behavior must owe its strength to its association with exceptionally strong reinforcement-favoring conditions—either very massive or very numerous anxiety-drive reductions or both. Its development is also, no doubt, greatly favored when from the outset no other significant anxiety-relieving activity has occurred to compete with it. Its maintenance depends upon the reduction of anxiety it is able to effect at each performance.

One patient was the youngest daughter of a man who despised females and would not forgive his wife for failing to bear him a son. She was very clever at school, and found that intellectual achievement, and that alone, could for brief periods abate her father's blatant hostility and therefore her own anxiety. Consequently, "thinking things out" became her automatic response to *any* anxiety. Since there are many objective fears for which careful thought is useful, there were no serious consequences for years. But when a series of experiences in early adult life led to a severe anxiety state in her, she automatically resorted to her characteristic "problem-solving" behavior. Because the anxiety responses now arose from such sources as imaginary social disapproval, and could not be removed by the solution of a well-defined problem, she began to set herself complex problems in which she usually had to decide whether given behavior was morally "good" or "bad." Partial and brief alleviation of anxiety followed both the formulation of a "suitable" problem and the solution thereof, while prolonged failure to solve a problem increased anxiety sometimes to terror. Although the anxiety soon returned in full force, its temporary decrements at the most appropriate times for reinforcement maintained the problem-finding and problem-solving obsessions, and could well have continued to do so indefinitely.

In other cases obsessional behavior is less episodically determined because everyday circumstances contain aspects of the special situation in which the obsessional mode of behavior alone brought relief from severe anxiety. A history of more than 100 undetected thefts of money by a 17-year-old university student began at the age of 5 when his mother joined the army and left him in the care of an elder sister who beat him severely or tied him to a tree for a few hours if he was slightly dirty or did anything "wrong." He feared and hated her and retaliated by stealing money from her. He was never caught and the possession of the stolen gains gave him a feeling of "munificence and security." The kleptomania continued all through the early home life and school life and was clearly connected with the chronic presence of punishment-empowered authority in the shape of parents or teachers.

It is not surprising, if obsessional behavior is so consistently followed by reduction of anxiety drive, that it is apt to become conditioned to other stimuli too, especially any that happen to be present on repeated occasions. Thus, after therapy had rendered the young woman with the problem-solving obsession mentioned above practically free from neurotic anxieties, mild problem-solving activity was still occasionally aroused by a trifling question, such as "Is it cloudy enough to rain?" The conditioned stimulus was apparently the mere awareness of doubt. Similarly an exhibitionist whose exhibiting had almost entirely disappeared with the overcoming of his anxious sensitivities, still had some measure of the impulse when he saw a girl dressed in a school ("gym") uniform, because he had in the past exhibited to schoolgirls particularly frequently and with special relish. Of course, in this instance sex-drive reduction may have played as important a role in the reinforcement as anxiety-drive reduction.

Amnesia and "Repression"

The amnesias that are usually encountered in the course of neurotic states can be conveniently divided into two classes, according to the emotional importance of the incidents forgotten. Patients who are in a chronic state of emotional disturbance frequently fail to register many trifling events that go on around them. For example, a patient may go into a room and conduct a brief conversation with his wife and an hour later have no recollection whatever that he went into that room at all. Here we seem to have a simple case of deficient registration of impressions (retrograde amnesia). Apparently, the patient's attention is so much taken up by his unpleasant anxious feelings that very little is left to be devoted to what goes on around him.

The forgetting of the contents of highly emotionally charged experiences has been given foremost importance by Freud and his followers as the cause of neurosis. It seems, however, that forgetting of this character is rather unusual, and when it does occur it appears to be merely one more of the conditionable occurrences in the neurotigenic situation. It does not appear that the repression as such plays any part in the maintenance of neurosis. It is quite possible for the patient to recover emotionally although the forgotten incidents remain entirely forgotten.

REFERENCES

Eysenck, H. J. (1947) Dimensions of Personality. London, Routledge.
———. (1955a) A dynamic theory of anxiety and hysteria. *J. Ment. Sci. 101:* 28.
———. (1955b) Cortical inhibition, figural aftereffect and theory of personality. *J. Abnorm. Soc. Psychol. 51:* 94.
Fonberg, E. (1956) On the manifestion of conditioned defensive reactions in stress. *Bull. Soc. Sci. Lettr. Lodz. Class III, Sci. Math. Natur. 7:* 1.

Franks, C. M. (1956) Conditioning and personality: A study of normal and neurotic subjects. *J. Abnorm. Soc. Psychol. 52:* 143.

Freud, S. (1893) On the psychical mechanism of hysterical phenomena. In Collected Works of Freud, Vol. I. London, Hogarth Press, 1949.

Jung, C. G. (1923) Psychological Types. New York, Harcourt, Brace.

Mowrer, O. H., and Viek, P. (1948) Experimental analogue of fear from a sense of helplessness. *J. Abnorm. Soc. Psychol. 43:* 193.

Pollitt, J. (1957) Natural history of obsessional states: A study of 150 cases. *Brit. Med. J. 1:* 194.

Wolpe, J. (1953) Learning theory and "abnormal fixations." *Psychol. Rev. 60:* 111.

Pathological Patterns

~~~~~~~~~~~~~

Pathology is defined by most behaviorists as socially maladaptive or deficient behavior. Since the varieties of such behavior are infinite, these theorists feel that the traditional classification system adopted by the psychiatric profession is a figment of Kraepelin's imagination. As evidence for this view they point to the fact that classification schemes are constantly revised and rarely hold up under research analysis. To them, whatever regularities are found can be accounted for by similarities in cultural patterns of conditioning.

The excerpt reprinted here by Frederick Kanfer and George Saslow illustrates a major new direction in diagnoses oriented toward a reformulation of traditional psychiatric classification. Anchored both to personal and situational elements, it derives its impetus and rationale from behavioral theory.

The chapter reprinted here by B.F. Skinner, the eminent learning theorist, provides a wide ranging view of how his operant conditioning model can be fruitfully applied to the analysis of psychological abnormalities. Skinner's formulations are excellent illustrations of what may be termed "pure" behaviorism. As is evident in other papers of this section, this classical behavioral approach has been broadened considerably in recent decades.

Charles Ferster's article provides a specific and in-depth application of the traditional behavioral approach. Drawing inspiration from the Skinnerian reinforcement model, Ferster presents a thorough and systematic "functional analysis" of the depressive syndrome.

38 Behavioral Analysis: An Alternative to Diagnostic Classification

Frederick H. Kanfer and George Saslow

During the past decade attacks on conventional psychiatric diagnosis have been so

From the *Archives of General Psychiatry 12:* 529–538, June 1965, copyright 1965 by the American Medical Association, by permission of the publisher and the authors.

widespread that many clinicians now use diagnostic labels sparingly and apologetically. The continued adherence to the nosological terms of the traditional classificatory scheme suggests some utility of the present categorization of behavior disorders, despite its apparently low reliability[1,21]; its limited prognostic value[7,26]; and its multiple feebly related assumptive supports. In a recent study of this problem, the symptom patterns of carefully diagnosed schizophrenics were compared. Katz et al[12] found considerable divergence among patients with the same diagnosis and concluded that "diagnostic systems which are more circumscribed in their intent, for example, based on manifest behavior alone, rather than systems which attempt to comprehend etiology, symptom patterns, and prognosis, may be more directly applicable to current problems in psychiatric research" (p 202).

We propose here to examine some sources of dissatisfaction with the present approach to diagnosis, to describe a framework for a behavioral analysis of individual patients which implies both suggestions for treatment and outcome criteria for the single case, and to indicate the conditions for collecting the data for such an analysis.

Problems in Current Diagnostic Systems

Numerous criticisms deal with the internal consistency, the explicitness, the precision, and the reliability of psychiatric classifications. It seems to us that the more important fault lies in our lack of sufficient knowledge to categorize behavior along those pertinent dimensions which permit prediction of responses to social stresses, life crises, or psychiatric treatment. This limitation obviates anything but a crude and tentative approximation to a taxonomy of effective individual behaviors.

Zigler and Phillips,[28] in discussing the requirement for an adequate system of classification, suggest that an etiologically-oriented closed system of diagnosis is premature. Instead, they believe that an empirical attack is needed, using "symptoms broadly defined as meaningful and discernable behaviors, as the basis of the classificatory system" (p 616). But symptoms as a class of responses are defined after all only by their nuisance value to the patient's social environment or to himself as a social being. They are also notoriously unreliable in predicting the patient's particular etiological history or his response to treatment. An alternate approach lies in an attempt to identify classes of dependent variables in human behavior which would allow inferences about the particular controlling factors, the social stimuli, the physiological stimuli, and the reinforcing stimuli, of which they are a function. In the present early stage of the art of psychological prognostication, it appears most reasonable to develop a program of analysis which is closely related to subsequent treatment. A classification scheme which implies a program of behavioral change is one which has not only utility but the potential for experimental validation.

The task of assessment and prognosis can therefore be reduced to efforts which answer the following three questions: (1) which specific behavior patterns require change in their frequency of occurrence, their intensity, their duration, or in the conditions under which they occur, (b) what are the best practical means which can produce the desired changes in this individual (manipulation of the environment, of the behavior, or the self-attitudes of the patient), and (c) what factors are currently maintaining it and what are the conditions under which this behavior was acquired. The investigation of the history of the problematic behavior is mainly of academic interest, except as it contributes information about the probable efficacy of a specific treatment method.

Expectations of Current Diagnostic Systems

In traditional medicine, a diagnostic statement about a patient has often been viewed as an essential prerequisite to treatment because a diagnosis suggests that the physician has some knowledge of the origin and future course of the illness. Further, in medicine diagnosis frequently brings together the accumulated knowledge about the pathological process which leads to the manifestation of the symptoms, and the experiences which others have had in the past in treating patients with such a disease process. Modern medicine recognizes that any particular disease need not have a single cause or even a small number of antecedent conditions. Nevertheless, the diagnostic label attempts to define at least the necessary conditions which are most relevant in considering a treatment program. Some diagnostic classification system is also invaluable as a basis for many social decisions involving entire populations. For example, planning for treatment facilities, research efforts, and educational programs take into account the distribution frequencies of specified syndromes in the general population.

Ledley and Lusted[14] give an excellent conception of the traditional model in medicine by their analysis of the reasoning underlying it. The authors differentiate between a disease complex and a symptom complex. While the former describes known pathological processes and their correlated signs, the latter represents particular signs present in a particular patient. The bridge between disease and symptom complexes is provided by available medicine knowledge and the final diagnosis is tantamount to labeling the disease complex. However, the current gaps in medical knowledge necessitate the use of probability statements when relating disease to symptoms, admitting that there is some possibility for error in the diagnosis. Once the diagnosis is established, decisions about treatment still depend on many other factors including social, moral, and economic conditions. Ledley and Lusted[14] thus separate the clinical diagnosis into a two-step process. A statistical procedure is suggested to facilitate the primary or diagnostic labeling process. However, the choice of treatment depends not only on the diagnosis proper. Treatment decisions are also influenced by the moral, ethical, social, and economic conditions of the individual patient, his family, and the society in which he lives. The proper assignment of the weight to be given to each of these values must in the last analysis be left to the physician's judgment (Ledley and Lusted[14]).

The Ledley and Lusted model presumes available methods for the observation of relevant behavior (the symptom complex), and some scientific knowledge relating it to known antecedents or correlates (the disease process). Contemporary theories of behavior pathology do not yet provide adequate guidelines for the observer to suggest what is to be observed. In fact, Szasz[25] has expressed the view that the medical model may be totally inadequate because psychiatry should be concerned with problems of living and not with diseases of the brain or other biological organs. Szasz[25] argues that "mental illness is a myth, whose function it is to disguise and thus render more potable the bitter pill of moral conflict in human relations" (p 118).

The attack against use of the medical model in psychiatry comes from many quarters. Scheflen[23] describes a model of somatic psychiatry which is very similar to the tradi-

tional medical model of disease. A pathological process results in onset of an illness; the symptoms are correlated with a pathological state and represent our evidence of "mental disease." Treatment consists of removal of the pathogen, and the state of health is restored. Scheflen suggests that this traditional medical model is used in psychiatry not on the basis of its adequacy but because of its emotional appeal.

The limitations of the somatic model have been discussed even in some areas of medicine for which the model seems most appropriate. For example, in the nomenclature for diagnosis of disease of the heart and blood vessels, the criteria committee of the New York Heart Association[17] suggests the use of multiple criteria for cardiovascular diseases, including a statement of the patient's functional capacity. The committee suggests that the functional capacity be ". . . estimated by appraising the patient's ability to perform physical activity" (p 80), and decided largely by inference from his history. Further,[17] ". . . (it) should not be influenced by the character of the structural lesion or by an opinion as to treatment or prognosis" (p 81). This approach makes it clear that a comprehensive assessment of a patient, regardless of the physical disease which he suffers, must also take into account his social effectiveness and the particular ways in which physiological, anatomical, and psychological factors interact to produce a particular behavior pattern in an individual patient.

Multiple Diagnosis

A widely used practical solution and circumvention of the difficulty inherent in the application of the medical model to psychiatric diagnosis is offered by Noyes and Kolb.[18] They suggest that the clinician construct a diagnostic formulation consisting of three parts: (1) A *genetic* diagnosis incorporating the constitutional, somatic, and historical-traumatic factors representing the primary sources or determinants of the mental illness; (2) A *dynamic* diagnosis which describes the mechanisms and techniques unconsciously used by the individual to manage anxiety, enhance self-esteem, ie, that traces the psychopathological processes; and (3) A *clinical* diagnosis which conveys useful connotations concerning the reaction syndrome, the probable course of the disorder, and the

methods of treatment which will most probably prove beneficial. Noyes' and Kolb's multiple criteria[18] can be arranged along three
simpler dimensions of diagnosis which may
have some practical value to the clinician: (1)
etiological, (2) behavioral, and (3) predictive.
The kind of information which is conveyed
by each type of diagnostic label is somewhat
different and specifically adapted to the purpose for which the diagnosis is used. The
triple-label approach attempts to counter the
criticism aimed at use of any single classificatory system. Confusion in a single system is due in part to the fact that a diagnostic
formulation intended to describe current behavior, for example, may be found useless in
an attempt to predict the response to specific
treatment, or to postdict the patient's personal history and development, or to permit
collection of frequency data on hospital populations.

Classification by Etiology

The Kraepelinian system and portions of
the 1952 APA classification emphasize etiological factors. They share the assumption that
common etiological factors lead to similar
symptoms and respond to similar treatment.
This dimension of diagnosis is considerably
more fruitful when dealing with behavior
disorders which are mainly under control of
some biological condition. When a patient is
known to suffer from excessive intake of
alcohol his hallucinatory behavior, lack of
motor coordination, poor judgment, and
other behavioral evidence disorganization can
often be related directly to some antecedent
condition such as the toxic effect of alcohol on
the central nervous system, liver, etc. For
these cases, classification by etiology also has
some implications for prognosis and treatment. Acute hallucinations and other disorganized behavior due to alcohol usually clear
up when the alcohol level in the blood stream
falls. Similar examples can be drawn from any
class of behavior disorders in which a change
in behavior is associated primarily or exclusively with a single, *particular* antecedent factor. Under these conditions this factor can be
called a pathogen and the situation closely
approximates the condition described by the
traditional medical model.

Utilization of this dimension as a basis for
psychiatric diagnosis, however, has many
problems apart from the rarity with which a

specified condition can be shown to have a
direct "causal" relationship to a pathogen.
Among the current areas of ignorance in the
fields of psychology and psychiatry, the etiology of most common disturbances probably
takes first place. No specific family environment, no dramatic traumatic experience, or
known constitutional abnormality has yet
been found which results in the same pattern
of disordered behavior. While current research efforts have aimed at investigating
family patterns of schizophrenic patients, and
several studies suggest a relationship between
the mother's behavior and a schizophrenic
process in the child,[10] it is not at all clear why
the presence of these same factors in other
families fails to yield a similar incidence of
schizophrenia. Further, patients may exhibit
behavior diagnosed as schizophrenic when
there is no evidence of the postulated
mother-child relationship.

In a recent paper Meehl[16] postulates schizophrenia as a neurological disease, with
learned content and a dispositional basis.
With this array of interactive etiological factors, it is clear that the etiological dimension
for classification would at best result in an
extremely cumbersome system, at worst in a
useless one.

Classification by Symptoms

A clinical diagnosis often is a summarizing
statement about the way in which a person
behaves. On the assumption that a variety of
behaviors are correlated and consistent in any
given individual, it becomes more economical
to assign the individual to a class of persons
than to list and categorize all of his behaviors.
The utility of such a system rests heavily on
the availability of empirical evidence concerning correlations among various behaviors
(response-response relationships), and the
further assumption that the frequency of occurrence of such behaviors is relatively independent of specific stimulus conditions and of
specific reinforcement. There are two major
limitations to such a system. The first is that
diagnosis by symptoms, as we have indicated
in an earlier section, is often misleading because it implies common etiological factors.
Freedman[7] gives an excellent illustration of
the differences both in probable antecedent
factors and subsequent treatment response
among three cases diagnosed as schizophrenics. Freedman's patients were diagnosed by

at least two psychiatrists, and one would expect that the traditional approach should result in whatever treatment of schizophrenia is practiced in the locale where the patients are seen. The first patient eventually gave increasing evidence of an endocrinopathy, and when this was recognized and treated, the psychotic episodes went into remission. The second case had a definite history of seizures and appropriate anticonvulsant medication was effective in relieving his symptoms. In the third case, treatment directed at an uncovering analysis of the patient's adaptive techniques resulted in considerable improvement in the patient's behavior and subsequent relief from psychotic episodes. Freedman[7] suggests that schizophrenia is not a disease entity in the sense that it has a unique etiology, pathogenesis, etc., but that it represents the evocation of a final common pathway in the same sense as do headache, epilepsy, sore throat, or indeed any other symptom complex. It is further suggested that the term "schizophrenia has outlived its usefulness and should be discarded" (p 5). Opler[19,20] has further shown the importance of cultural factors in the divergence of symptoms observed in patients collectively labeled as schizophrenic.

Descriptive classification is not always this deceptive, however. Assessment of intellectual performance sometimes results in a diagnostic statement which has predictive value for the patient's behavior in school or on a job. To date, there seem to be very few general statements about individual characteristics, which have as much predictive utility as the IQ.

A second limitation is that the current approach to diagnosis by symptoms tends to center on a group of behaviors which is often irrelevant with regard to the patient's total life pattern. These behaviors may be of interest only because they are popularly associated with deviancy and disorder. For example, occasional mild delusions interfere little or not at all with the social or occupational effectiveness of many ambulatory patients. Nevertheless, admission of their occurrence is often sufficient for a diagnosis of psychosis. Refinement of such an approach beyond current usage appears possible, as shown for example by Lorr et al[15] but this does not remove the above limitations.

Utilization of a symptom-descriptive approach frequently focuses attention on by-products of larger behavior patterns, and results in attempted treatment of behaviors (symptoms) which may be simple consequences of other important aspects of the patient's life. Emphasis on the patient's subjective complaints, moods, and feelings tends to encourage use of a syndrome-oriented classification. It also results frequently in efforts to change the feelings, anxieties, and moods (or at least the patient's report about them), rather than to investigate the life conditions, interpersonal reactions, and environmental factors which produce and maintain these habitual response patterns.

Classification by Prognosis

To date, the least effort has been devoted to construction of a classification system which assigns patients to the same category on the basis of their similar response to specific treatments. The proper question raised for such a classification system consists of the manner in which a patient will react to treatments, regardless of his current behavior, or his past history. The numerous studies attempting to establish prognostic signs from projective personality tests or somatic tests represent efforts to categorize the patients on this dimension.

Windle[26] has called attention to the low degree of predictability afforded by personality (projective) test scores, and has pointed out the difficulties encountered in evaluating research in this area due to the inadequate description of the population sampled and the improvement criteria. In a later review Fulkerson and Barry[8] came to the similar conclusion that psychological test performance is a poor predictor of outcome in mental illness. They suggest that demographic variables such as severity, duration, acuteness of onset, degree of precipitating stress, etc., appear to have stronger relationships to outcome than test data. The lack of reliable relationships between diagnostic categories, test data, demographic variables, or other measures taken on the patient on the one hand, and duration of illness, response to specific treatment, or degree of recovery, on the other hand, precludes the construction of a simple empiric framework for a diagnostic-prognostic classification system based only on an array of symptoms.

None of the currently used dimensions for diagnosis is directly related to methods of modification of a patient's behavior, attitudes, response patterns, and interpersonal actions. Since the etiological model clearly stresses causative factors, it is much more compatible with a personality theory which strongly emphasizes genetic-developmental factors. The classification by symptoms facilitates social-administrative decisions about patients by providing some basis for judging the degree of deviation from social and ethical norms. Such a classification is compatible with a personality theory founded on the normal curve hypothesis and concerned with characterization by comparison with a fictitious average. The prognostic-predictive approach appears to have the most direct practical applicability. If continued research were to support certain early findings, it would be indeed comforting to be able to predict outcome of mental illness from a patient's premorbid social competence score,[28] or from the patient's score on an ego strength scale,[4] or from many of the other signs and single variables which have been shown to have some predictive powers. It is unfortunate that these powers are frequently dissipated in cross validation. As Fulkerson and Barry[8] have indicated single predictors have not yet shown much success.

A Functional (Behavioral-Analytic) Approach

The growing literature on behavior modification procedures derived from learning theory[3,6,11,13,27] suggests that an effective diagnostic procedure would be one in which the eventual therapeutic methods can be directly related to the information obtained from a continuing assessment of the patient's current behaviors and their controlling stimuli. Ferster[6] has said ". . . a functional analysis of behavior has the advantage that it specifies the causes of behavior in the form of explicit environmental events, which can be objectively identified and which are potentially manipulable" (p 3). Such a diagnostic undertaking makes the assumption that a description of the problematic behavior, its controlling factors, and the means by which it can be changed are the most appropriate "explanations." It further makes the assumption that a diagnostic evaluation is never complete. It implies that additional informa-

tion about the circumstances of the patient's life pattern, relationships among his behaviors, and controlling stimuli in his social milieu and his private experience is obtained continuously until it proves sufficient to effect a noticeable change in the patient's behavior, thus resolving "the problem." In a functional approach it is necessary to continue evaluation of the patient's life pattern and its controlling factors, concurrent with attempted manipulation of these variables by reinforcement, direct intervention, or other means until the resultant change in the patient's behavior permits restoration of more efficient life experiences.

The present approach shares with some psychological theories the assumption that psychotherapy is *not* an effort aimed at removal of intrapsychic conflicts, nor at a change in the personality structure by therapeutic interactions of intense nonverbal nature, (eg, transference, self-actualization, etc.). We adopt the assumption instead that the job of psychological treatment involves the utilization of a variety of methods to devise a program which controls the patient's environment, his behavior, and the consequences of his behavior in such a way that the presenting problem is resolved. We hypothesize that the essential ingredients of a psychotherapeutic endeavor usually involve two separate stages: (1) a change in the perceptual discriminations of a patient, ie, in his approach to perceiving, classifying, and organizing sensory events, including perception of himself, and (2) changes in the response patterns which he has established in relation to social objects and to himself over the years.[11] In addition, the clinician's task may involve direct intervention in the patient's environmental circumstances, modification of the behavior of other people significant in his life, and control of reinforcing stimuli which are available either through self-administration, or by contingency upon the behavior of others. These latter procedures complement the verbal interactions of traditional psychotherapy. They require that the clinician, at the invitation of the patient or his family, participate more fully in planning the total life pattern of the patient outside the clinician's office.

It is necessary to indicate what the theoretical view here presented does *not* espouse in order to understand the differences from other procedures. It does *not* rest upon the assumption that (*a*) insight is a sine qua non of psychotherapy, (b) changes in thoughts or ideas inevitably lead to ultimate changes in actions, (c) verbal therapeutic sessions serve as replications of and equivalents for actual life situations, and (d) a symptom can be removed only by uprooting its cause or origin. In the absence of these assumptions it becomes unnecessary to conceptualize behavior disorder in etiological terms, in psychodynamic terms, or in terms of a specifiable disease process. While psychotherapy by verbal means may be sufficient in some instances, the combination of behavior modification in life situations as well as in verbal interactions serves to extend the armamentarium of the therapist. Therefore verbal psychotherapy is seen as an *adjunct* in the implementation of therapeutic behavior changes in the patient's total life pattern, not as an end in itself, nor as the sole vehicle for increasing psychological effectiveness.

In embracing this view of behavior modification, there is a further commitment to a constant interplay between assessment and therapeutic strategies. An initial diagnostic formulation seeks to ascertain the major variables which can be directly controlled or modified during treatment. During successive treatment stages additional information is collected about the patient's behavior repertoire, his reinforcement history, the pertinent controlling stimuli in his social and physical environment, and the sociological limitations within which both patient and therapist have to operate. Therefore, the initial formulation will constantly be enlarged or changed, resulting either in confirmation of the previous therapeutic strategy or in its change.

A Guide to a Functional Analysis of Individual Behavior

In order to help the clinician in the collection and organization of information for a behavioral analysis, we have constructed an outline which aims to provide a working model of the patient's behavior at a relatively low level of abstraction. A series of questions are so organized as to yield immediate implications for treatment. This outline has been found useful both in clinical practice and in teaching. Following is a brief summary of the categories in the outline.

1. Analysis of a Problem Situation:* The patient's major complaints are categorized into classes of behavioral excesses and deficits. For each excess or deficit the dimensions of frequency, intensity, duration, appropriateness of form, and stimulus conditions are described. In content, the response classes represent the major targets of the therapeutic intervention. As an additional indispensable feature, the behavioral assets of the patient are listed for utilization in a therapy program.

2. Clarification of the Problem Situation: Here we consider the people and circumstances which tend to maintain the problem behaviors, and the consequences of these behaviors to the patient and to others in his environment. Attention is given also to the consequences of changes in these behaviors which may result from psychiatric intervention.

3. Motivational Analysis: Since reinforcing stimuli are idiosyncratic and depend for their effect on a number of unique parameters for each person, a hierarchy of particular persons, events, and objects which serve as reinforcers is established for each patient. Included in this hierarchy are those reinforcing events which facilitate approach behaviors as well as those which, because of their aversiveness, prompt avoidance responses. This information has as its purpose to lay plans for utilization of various reinforcers in prescription of a specific behavior therapy program for the patient, and to permit utilization of appropriate reinforcing behaviors by the therapist and significant others in the patient's social environment.

4. Developmental Analysis: Questions are asked about the patient's biological equipment, his sociocultural experiences, and his charac-

*For each patient a detailed analysis is required. For example, a list of behavioral excesses may include specific aggressive acts, hallucinatory behaviors, crying, submission to others in social situations, etc. It is recognized that some behaviors can be viewed as excesses or deficits depending on the vantage point from which the imbalance is observed. For instance, excessive withdrawal and deficient social responsiveness, or excessive social autonomy (nonconformity) and deficient self-inhibitory behavior may be complementary. The particular view taken is of consequence because of its impact on a treatment plan. Regarding certain behavior as excessively aggressive, to be reduced by constraints, clearly differs from regarding the same behavior as a deficit in self-control, subject to increase by training and treatment.

teristic behavioral development. They are phrased in such a way as (a) to evoke descriptions of his habitual behavior at various chronological stages of his life, (b) to relate specific new stimulus conditions to noticeable changes from his habitual behavior, and (c) to relate such altered behavior and other residuals of biological and sociocultural events to the present problem.

5. Analysis of Self-Control: This section examines both the methods and the degree of self-control exercised by the patient in his daily life. Persons, events, or institutions which have successfully reinforced self-controlling behaviors are considered. The deficits or excesses of self-control are evaluated in relation to their importance as therapeutic targets and to their utilization in a therapeutic program.

6. Analysis of Social Relationships: Examination of the patient's social network is carried out to evaluate the significance of people in the patient's environment who have some influence over the problematic behaviors, or who in turn are influenced by the patient for his own satisfactions. These interpersonal relationships are reviewed in order to plan the potential participation of significant others in a treatment program, based on the principles of behavior modification. The review also helps the therapist to consider the range of actual social relationships in which the patient needs to function.

7. Analysis of the Social-Cultural-Physical Environment: In this section we add to the preceding analysis of the patient's behavior as an individual, consideration of the norms in his natural environment. Agreements and discrepancies between the patient's idiosyncratic life patterns and the norms in his environment are defined so that the importance of these factors can be decided in formulating treatment goals which allow as explicitly for the patient's needs as for the pressures of his social environment.

The preceding outline has as its purpose to achieve definition of a patient's problem in a manner which suggests specific treatment operations, or that none are feasible, and specific behaviors as targets for modification. Therefore, the formulation is *action oriented*. It can be used as a guide for the initial collection of information, as a device for organizing available data, or as a design for treatment.

The formulation of a treatment plan follows from this type of analysis because knowledge of the reinforcing conditions suggests the motivational controls at the disposal of the clinician for the modification of the patient's behavior. The analysis of specific problem behaviors also provides a series of goals for psychotherapy or other treatment, and for the evaluation of treatment progress. Knowledge of the patient's biological, social, and cultural conditions should help to determine what resources can be used, and what limitations must be considered in a treatment plan.

The various categories attempt to call attention to important variables affecting the patient's *current* behavior. Therefore, they aim to elicit descriptions of low-level abstraction. Answers to these specific questions are best phrased by describing classes of events reported by the patient, observed by others, or by critical incidents described by an informant. The analysis does not exclude description of the patient's habitual verbal-symbolic behaviors. However, in using verbal behaviors as the basis for this analysis, one should be cautious not to "explain" verbal processes in terms of postulated internal mechanisms without adequate supportive evidence, nor should inference be made about nonobserved processes or events without corroborative evidence. The analysis includes many items which are not known or not applicable for a given patient. Lack of information on some items does not necessarily indicate incompleteness of the analysis. These lacks must be noted nevertheless because they often contribute to the better understanding of what the patient needs to learn to become an autonomous person. Just as important is an inventory of his existing socially effective behavioral repertoire which can be put in the service of any treatment procedure.

This analysis is consistent with our earlier formulations of the principles of comprehensive medicine[9,22] which emphasized the joint operation of biological, social, and psychological factors in psychiatric disorders. The language and orientation of the proposed approach are rooted in contemporary learning theory. The conceptual framework is consonant with the view that the course of psychiatric disorders can be modified by systematic application of scientific principles from the fields of psychology and medicine to the patient's habitual mode of living.

This approach is not a substitute for assignment of the patient to traditional diagnostic categories. Such labeling may be desirable for statistical, administrative, or research purposes. But the current analysis is intended to replace other diagnostic formulations purporting to serve as a basis for making decisions about specific therapeutic interventions.

Methods of Data Collection for a Functional Analysis

Traditional diagnostic approaches have utilized as the main sources of information the patient's verbal report, his nonverbal behavior during an interview, and his performance on psychological tests. These observations are sufficient if one regards behavior problems only as a property of the patient's particular pattern of associations or his personality structure. A mental disorder would be expected to reveal itself by stylistic characteristics in the patient's behavior repertoire. However, if one views behavior disorders as sets of response patterns which are learned under particular conditions and maintained by definable environmental and internal stimuli, an assessment of the patient's behavior output is insufficient unless it also describes the conditions under which it occurs. This view requires an expansion of the clinician's sources of observations to include the stimulation fields in which the patient lives, and the variations of patient behavior as a function of exposure to these various stimulational variables. Therefore, the resourceful clinician need not limit himself to test findings, interview observations in the clinician's office, or referral histories alone in the formulation of the specific case. Nor need he regard himself as hopelessly handicapped when the patient has little observational or communicative skill in verbally reconstructing his life experiences for the clinician. Regardless of the patient's communicative skills the data must consist of a description of the patient's behavior *in relationship* to varying environmental conditions.

A behavioral analysis excludes no data relating to a patient's past or present experiences as irrelevant. However, the relative merit of any information (as, eg, growing up in a broken home or having had homosexual experiences) lies in its relation to the independent variables which can be identified as controlling the current problematic behavior. The observation that a patient has halluci-

nated on occasions may be important only if it has bearing on his present problem. If looked upon in isolation, a report about hallucinations may be misleading, resulting in emphasis on classification rather than treatment.

In the *psychiatric interview* a behavioral-analytic approach opposes acceptance of the content of the verbal self-report as equivalent to actual events or experiences. However, verbal reports provide information concerning the patient's verbal construction of his environment and of his person, his recall of past experiences, and his fantasies about them. While these self-descriptions do not represent data about events which actually occur internally, they do represent current behaviors of the patient and indicate the verbal chains and repertoires which the patient has built up. Therefore, the verbal behavior may be useful for description of a patient's thinking processes. To make the most of such an approach, variations on traditional interview procedures may be obtained by such techniques as role playing, discussion, and interpretation of current life events, or controlled free association. Since there is little experimental evidence of specific relationships between the patient's verbal statements and his nonverbal behavioral acts, the verbal report alone remains insufficient for a complete analysis and for prediction of his daily behavior. Further, it is well known that a person responds to environmental conditions and to internal cues which he cannot describe adequately. Therefore, any verbal report may miss or mask the most important aspects of a behavioral analysis, ie, the description of the relationship between antecedent conditions and subsequent behavior.

In addition to the use of the clinician's own person as a controlled stimulus object in interview situations, *observations of interaction with significant others* can be used for the analysis of variations in frequency of various behaviors as a function of the person with whom the patient interacts. For example, use of prescribed standard roles for nurses and attendants, utilization of members of the patient's family or his friends, may be made to obtain data relevant to the patient's habitual interpersonal response pattern. Such observations are especially useful if in a later interview the patient is asked to describe and discuss the observed sessions. Confrontations with tape recordings for comparisons between the patient's report and the actual session as witnessed by the observer may provide information about the patient's perception of himself and others as well as his habitual behavior toward peers, authority figures, and other significant people in his life.

Except in working with children or family units, insufficient use has been made of material obtained from *other informants* in interviews about the patient. These reports can aid the observer to recognize behavioral domains in which the patient's report deviates from or agrees with the descriptions provided by others. Such information is also useful for contrasting the patient's reports about his presumptive effects on another person with the stated effects by that person. If a patient's interpersonal problems extend to areas in which social contacts are not clearly defined, contributions by informants other than the patient are essential.

It must be noted that verbal reports by other informants may be no more congruent with actual events than the patient's own reports and need to be equally related to the informant's own credibility. If such crucial figures as parents, spouses, employers can be so interviewed, they also provide the clinician with some information about those people with whom the patient must interact repeatedly and with whom interpersonal problems may have developed.

Some observation of the patient's daily *work behavior* represents an excellent source of information, if it can be made available. Observation of the patient by the clinician or his staff may be preferable to descriptions by peers or supervisors. Work observations are especially important for patients whose complaints include difficulties in their daily work activity or who describe work situations as contributing factors to their problem. While freer use of this technique may be hampered by cultural attitudes toward psychiatric treatment in the marginally adjusted, such observations may be freely accessible in hospital situations or in sheltered work situations. With use of behavior rating scales or other simple measurement devices, brief samples of patient behaviors in work situations can be obtained by minimally trained observers.

The patient himself may be asked to provide samples of his own behavior by using tape recorders for the recording of segments of interactions in his family, at work, or in other situations during his everyday life. A television monitoring system for the patient's behavior is an excellent technique from a theoretical viewpoint but it is extremely cumbersome and expensive. Use of recordings for diagnostic and therapeutic purposes has been reported by some investigators.[2,5,24] Playback of the recordings and a recording of the patient's reactions to the playback can be used further in interviews to clarify the patient's behavior toward others and his reaction to himself as a social stimulus.

Psychological tests represent problems to be solved under specified interactional conditions. Between the highly standardized intelligence tests and the unstructured and ambiguous projective tests lies a dimension of structure along which more and more responsibility for providing appropriate responses falls on the patient. By comparison with interview procedures, most psychological tests provide a relatively greater standardization of stimulus conditions. But, in addition to the specific answers given on intelligence tests or on projective tests these tests also provide a behavioral sample of the patient's reaction to a problem situation in a relatively stressful interpersonal setting. Therefore, psychological tests can provide not only quantitative scores but they can also be treated as a miniature life experience, yielding information about the patient's interpersonal behavior and variations in his behavior as a function of the nature of the stimulus conditions.

In this section we have mentioned only some of the numerous life situations which can be evaluated in order to provide information about the patient. Criteria for their use lies in economy, accessibility to the clinician, and relevance to the patient's problem. While it is more convenient to gather data from a patient in an office, it may be necessary for the clinician to have first-hand information about the actual conditions under which the patient lives and works. Such familiarity may be obtained either by utilization of informants or by the clinician's entry into the home, the job situation, or the social environment in which the patient lives. Under all these conditions the clinician is effective only if it is possible for him to maintain a nonparticipating, objective, and observational role with no untoward consequences for the patient or the treatment relationship.

The methods of data collecting for a functional analysis described here differ from traditional psychiatric approaches only in that they require inclusion of the physical and social stimulus field in which the patient actually operates. Only a full appraisal of the patient's living and working conditions and his way of life allow a description of the actual problems which the patient faces and the specification of steps to be taken for altering the problematic situation.

Summary

Current psychiatric classification falls short of providing a satisfactory basis for the understanding and treatment of maladaptive behavior. Diagnostic schemas now in use are based on etiology, symptom description, or prognosis. While each of these approaches has a limited utility, no unified schema is available which permits prediction of response to treatment or future course of the disorder from the assignment of the patient to a specific category.

This paper suggests a behavior-analytic approach which is based on contemporary learning theory, as an alternative to assignment of the patient to a conventional diagnostic category. It includes the summary of an outline which can serve as a guide for the collection of information and formulation of the problem, including the biological, social, and behavioral conditions which are determining the patient's behavior. The outline aims toward integration of information about a patient for formulation of an action plan which would modify the patient's problematic behavior. Emphasis is given to the particular variables affecting the *individual* patient rather than determination of the similarity of the patient's history or his symptoms to known pathological groups.

The last section of the paper deals with methods useful for collection of information necessary to complete such a behavior analysis.

This paper was written in conjunction with Research grant MH 06921-03 from the National Institutes of Mental Health, United States Public Health Service.

REFERENCES

1. Ash, P. Reliability of Psychiatric Diagnosis, J Abnorm Soc Psychol 44:272–277, 1949.
2. Bach, G. In Alexander, S. Fight Promoter for Battle of Sexes, Life 54:102–108 (May 17) 1963.
3. Bandura, A. Psychotherapy as Learning Process, Psychol Bull 58:143–159, 1961.
4. Barron, F. Ego-Strength Scale Which Predicts Response to Psychotherapy, J Consult Psychol 17:235–241, 1953.
5. Cameron, D. E., et al. Automation of Psychotherapy, Compr Psychiat 5:1–14, 1964.
6. Ferster, C. B. Classification of Behavioral Pathology, in Ullman, L. P., and Krasner, L. (eds.). Behavior Modification Research, New York: Holt, Rinehart & Winston, 1965.
7. Freedman, D. A. Various Etiologies of Schizophrenic Syndrome, Dis Nerv Syst 19:1–6, 1958.
8. Fulkerson, S. E., and Barry, J. R. Methodology and Research on Prognostic Use of Psychological Tests, Psychol Bull 58:177–204, 1961.
9. Guze, S. B., Matarazzo, J. D., and Saslow, G. Formulation of Principles of Comprehensive Medicine With Special Reference to Learning Theory, J Clin Psychol 9:127–136, 1953.
10. Jackson, D. D. A. Etiology of Schizophrenia, New York: Basic Books Inc., 1960.
11. Kanfer, F. H. Comments on Learning in Psychotherapy, Psychol Rep 9:681–699, 1961.
12. Katz, M. M., Cole, J. O., and Lowery, H. A. Nonspecificity of Diagnosis of Paranoid Schizophrenia, Arch Gen Psychiat 11:197–202, 1964.
13. Krasner, L. Therapist as Social Reinforcement Machine, in Strupp, H., and Luborsky, L. (eds.). Research in Psychotherapy: Washington, D.C.: American Psychological Association, 1962.
14. Ledley, R. S., and Lusted, L. B. Reasoning Foundations of Medical Diagnosis, Science 130:9–21, 1959.
15. Lorr, M., Klett, C. J., and McNair, D. M. Syndromes of Psychosis. New York: Macmillan Co., 1963.
16. Meehl, P. E. Schizotaxia, Schizotypy, Schizophrenia, Amer Psychol 17:827–838, 1962.
17. New York Heart Association. Nomenclature and Criteria for Diagnosis of Diseases of the Heart and Blood Vessels, New York: New York Heart Association, 1953.
18. Noyes, A. P., and Kolb, L. C. Modern Clinical Psychiatry, Philadelphia: W. B. Saunders & Co., 1963.
19. Opler, M. K. Schizophrenia and Culture, Sci Amer 197:103–112, 1957.
20. Opler, M. K. Need for New Diagnostic Categories in Psychiatry, J Nat Med Assoc 55:133–137, 1963.

21. Rotter, J. B. Social Learning and Clinical Psychology, New York: Prentice-Hall, 1954.
22. Saslow, G. On Concept of Comprehensive Medicine, Bull Menninger Clin 16:57–65, 1952.
23. Scheflen, A. E. Analysis of Thought Model Which Persists in Psychiatry, Psychosom Med 20:235–241, 1958.
24. Slack, C.W. Experimenter-Subject Psychotherapy — A New Method of Introducing Intensive Office Treatment for Unreachable Cases, Ment Hyg 44:238–256, 1960.
25. Szasz, T. S. Myth of Mental Illness, Amer Psychol 15:113–118, 1960.
26. Windle, C. Psychological Tests in Psychopathological Prognosis, Psychol Bull 49:451–482, 1952.
27. Wolpe, J. Psychotherapy in Reciprocal Inhibition, Stanford, Calif.: Stanford University Press, 1958.
28. Zigler, E., and Phillips, L. Psychiatric Diagnosis: Critique, J Abnorm Soc Psychol 63:607–618, 1961.

39 What Is Psychotic Behavior?

B. F. Skinner

Since my field of specialization lies some distance from psychiatry, it may be well to begin with credentials. The first will be negative. In the sense in which my title is most likely to be understood, I am wholly unqualified to discuss the question before us. The number of hours I have spent in the presence of psychotic people (assuming that I am myself sane) is negligible compared with what many of you might claim, and the time I have spent in relevant reading and discussion would suffer equally from the same comparison. I am currently interested in some research on psychotic subjects, to which I shall refer again later, but my association with that program in no way qualifies me as a specialist.

Fortunately, I am not here to answer the question in that sense at all. A more accurate title would have been "What is *behavior?*— with an occasional reference to psychiatry." Here I will list such positive credentials as seem appropriate. I have spent a good share of my professional life in the experimental analysis of the behavior of organisms. Almost all my subjects have been below the human level (most of them rats or pigeons) and all, so far as I know, have been sane. My research

From *Theory and Treatment of the Psychoses*, pages 77–99, 1956, Washington University Studies, by permission of the Washington University Press and the author.

has not been designed to test any theory of behavior, and the results cannot be evaluated in terms of the statistical significance of such proofs. The object has been to discover the functional relations which prevail between measurable aspects of behavior and various conditions and events in the life of the organism. The success of such a venture is gauged by the extent to which behavior can, as a result of the relationships discovered, actually be predicted and controlled. Here we have, I think, been fortunate. Within a limited experimental arrangement, my colleagues and I have been able to demonstrate a lawfulness in behavior which seems to us quite remarkable. In more recent research it has been possible to maintain—actually, to sharpen—this degree of lawfulness while slowly increasing the complexity of the behavior studied. The extent of the prediction and control which has been achieved is evident not only in "smoothness of curves" and uniformity of results from individual to individual or even species to species, but in the practical uses which are already being made of the techniques—for example, in providing baselines for the study of pharmacological and neurological variables, or in converting a lower organism into a sensitive psychophysical observer.

Although research designed in this way has an immediate practical usefulness, it is not independent of one sort of theory. A primary concern has been to isolate a useful and expedient measure. Of all the myriad aspects of behavior which present themselves to observation, which are worth watching? Which will prove most useful in establishing functional relations? From time to time many different characteristics of behavior have seemed important. Students of the subject have asked how well organized behavior is, how well adapted it is to the environment, how sensitively it maintains a homeostatic equilibrium, how purposeful it is, or how successfully it solves practical problems or adjusts to daily life. Many have been especially interested in how an individual compares with others of the same species or with members of other species in some arbitrary measure of the scope, complexity, speed, consistency, or other property of behavior. All these aspects may be quantified, at least in a rough way, and any one may serve as a dependent variable in a scientific analysis. But they are not all equally productive. In research which emphasizes prediction and control, the topography of behavior must be carefully specified. Precisely what is the organism doing? The most important aspect of behavior so described is its probability of emission. How likely is it that an organism will engage in behavior of a given sort, and what conditions or events change this likelihood? Although probability of action has only recently been explicitly recognized in behavior theory, it is a key concept to which many classical notions, from reaction tendencies to the Freudian wish, may be reduced. Experimentally we deal with it as the *frequency* with which an organism behaves in a given way under specified circumstances, and our methods are designed to satisfy this requirement. Frequency of response has proved to be a remarkably sensitive variable, and with its aid the exploration of causal factors has been gratifyingly profitable.

One does not engage in work of this sort for the sheer love of rats or pigeons. As the medical sciences illustrate, the study of animals below the level of man is dictated mainly by convenience and safety. But the primary object of interest is always man. Such qualifications as I have to offer in approaching the present question spring about equally from the experimental work just mentioned and from a parallel preoccupation with human behavior, in which the principles emerging

from the experimental analysis have been tested and put to work in the interpretation of empirical facts. The formal disciplines of government, education, economics, religion, and psychotherapy, among others, together with our everyday experience with men, overwhelm us with a flood of facts. To interpret these facts with the formulation which emerges from an experimental analysis has proved to be strenuous but healthful exercise. In particular, the nature and function of *verbal* behavior have taken on surprisingly fresh and promising aspects when reformulated under the strictures of such a framework.

In the long run, of course, mere interpretation is not enough. If we have achieved a true scientific understanding of man, we should be able to prove this in the actual prediction and control of his behavior. The experimental practices and the concepts emerging from our research on lower organisms have already been extended in this direction, not only in the experiments on psychotic subjects already mentioned, but in other promising areas. The details would take us too far afield, but perhaps I can indicate my faith in the possibilities in a single instance by hazarding the prediction that we are on the threshold of a revolutionary change in methods of education, based not only upon a better understanding of learning processes, but upon a workable conception of knowledge itself.

Whether or not this brief personal history seems to you to qualify me to discuss the question before us, there is no doubt that it has created a high probability that I will do so, as shown by the fact that I am here. What I have to say is admittedly methodological. I can understand a certain impatience with such discussion particularly when, as in the field of psychiatry, many pressing problems call for action. The scientist who takes time out to consider human nature when so many practical things need to be done for human welfare is likely to be cast in the role of a Nero, fiddling while Rome burns. (It is quite possible that the fiddling referred to in this archetypal myth was a later invention of the historians, and that in actual fact Nero had called in his philosophers and scientists and was discussing "the fundamental nature of combustion" or "the epidemiology of conflagration.") But I should not be here if I believed that what I have to say is remote from practical consequences. If we are now entering an era of research in psychiatry which is to be as extensive and as productive as other types of medical research, then a certain detachment from immediate problems, a fresh look at human behavior in general, a survey of applicable formulations, and a consideration of relevant methods may prove to be effective practical steps with surprisingly immediate consequences.

The study of human behavior is, of course, still in its infancy, and it would be rash to suppose that anyone can foresee the structure of a well-developed and successful science. Certainly no current formulation will seem right fifty years hence. But although we cannot foresee the future clearly, it is not impossible to discover in what direction we are likely to change. There are obviously great deficiencies in our present ways of thinking about men; otherwise we should be more successful. What are they, and how are they to be remedied? What I have to say rests upon the assumption that the behavior of the psychotic is simply part and parcel of human behavior, and that certain considerations which have been emphasized by the experimental and theoretical analysis of behavior in general are worth discussing in this special application.

It is important to remember that I am speaking as an experimental scientist. A conception of human behavior based primarily on clinical information and practice will undoubtedly differ from a conception emanating from the laboratory. This does not mean that either is superior to the other, or that eventually a common formulation will not prove useful to both. It is possible that questions which have been suggested by the exigiencies of an experimental analysis may not seem of first importance to those of you who are primarily concerned with human behavior under therapy. But as psychiatry moves more rapidly into experimental research and as laboratory results take on a greater clinical significance, certain problems in the analysis of behavior should become common to researcher and therapist alike, and should eventually be given common and cooperative solutions.

The study of behavior, psychotic or otherwise, remains securely in the company of the natural sciences so long as we take as our subject matter the observable activity of the organism, as it moves about, stands still, seizes objects, pushes and pulls, makes sounds, gestures, and so on. Suitable instruments will permit us to amplify small-scale activities as part of the same subject matter. Watching a person behave in this way is like watching any physical or biological system. We also remain within the framework of the natural sciences in explaining these observations in terms of external forces and events which act upon the organism. Some of these are to be found in the hereditary history of the individual, including his membership in a given species as well as his personal endowment. Others arise from the physical environment, past or present. We may represent the situation as in Figure 1 (p. 364). Our organism emits the behavior we are to account for, as our dependent variable, at the right. To explain this, we appeal to certain external, generally observable, and possibly controllable hereditary and environmental conditions, as indicated at the left. These are the independent variables of which behavior is to be expressed as a function. Both input and output of such a system may be treated within the accepted dimensional systems of physics and biology. A complete set of such relations would permit us to predict and, insofar as the independent variables are under our control, to modify or generate behavior at will. It would also permit us to *interpret* given instances of behavior by inferring plausible variables of which we lack direct information. Admittedly the data are subtle and complex, and many relevant conditions are hard to get at, but the program as such is an acceptable one from the point of view of scientific method. We have no reason to suppose in advance that a complete account cannot be so given. We have only to try and see.

It is not, however, the subtlety or complexity of this subject matter which is responsible for the relatively undeveloped state of such a science. Behavior has seldom been analyzed in this manner. Instead, attention has been diverted to activities which are said to take place within the organism. All sciences tend to fill in causal relationships, especially when the related events are separated by time and space. If a magnet affects a compass needle some distance away, the scientist attributes this to a "field" set up by the magnet and reaching to the compass needle. If a brick falls from a chimney, releasing energy which was stored there, say, a hundred years ago when the chimney was built, the result is explained by saying that the brick has all this time

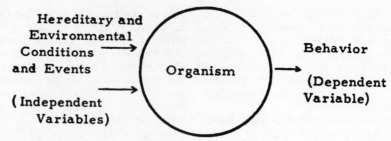

FIGURE 1

possessed a certain amount of "potential energy." In order to fill such spatial and temporal gaps between cause and effect, nature has from time to time been endowed with many weird properties, spirits, and essences. Some have proved helpful and have become part of the subject matter of science, especially when identified with events observed in other ways. Others have proved dangerous and damaging to scientific progress. Sophisticated scientists have usually been aware of the practice and alert to its dangers. Such inner forces were, indeed, the hypotheses which Newton refused to make.

Among the conditions which affect behavior, hereditary factors occupy a primary position, at least chronologically. Differences between members of different species are seldom, if ever, disputed, but differences between members of the same species, possibly due to similar hereditary factors, are so closely tied up with social and ethical problems that they have been the subject of seemingly endless debate. In any event, the newly conceived organism begins at once to be influenced by its environment; and when it comes into full

contact with the external world, environmental forces assume a major role. They are the only conditions which can be changed so far as the individual is concerned. Among these are the events we call "stimuli," the various interchanges between organism and environment such as occur in breathing or eating, the events which generate the changes in behavior we call emotional, and the coincidences between stimuli or between stimuli and behavior responsible for the changes we call learning. The effects may be felt immediately or only after the passage of time—perhaps of many years. Such are the "causes"—the independent variables—in terms of which we may hope to explain behavior within the framework of a natural science.

In many discussions of human behavior, however, these variables are seldom explicitly mentioned. Their place is taken by events or conditions within the organism for which they are said to be responsible (see Figure 2). Thus, the species status of the individual is dealt with as a set of instincts, not simply as patterns of behavior characteristic of the species, but as biological drives. As one text

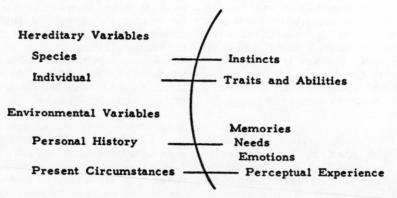

FIGURE 2

puts it, "instincts are innate biological forces, urges, or impulsions driving the organism to a certain end." The individual genetic endowment, if not carried by body-type or other observable physical characteristic, is represented in the form of inherited traits or abilities, such as temperament or intelligence. As to the environmental variables, episodes in the past history of the individual are dealt with as memories and habits, while certain conditions of interchange between organism and environment are represented as needs or wants. Certain inciting episodes are dealt with as emotions, again in the sense not of patterns but of active causes of behavior. Even the present environment as it affects the organism is transmuted into "experience," as we turn from what is the case to what "seems to be" the case to the individual.

The same centripetal movement may be observed on the other side of the diagram (see Figure 3). It is rare to find behavior dealt with as a subject matter in its own right. Instead it is regarded as evidence for a mental life, which is then taken as the primary object of inquiry. What the individual does—the topography of his behavior—is treated as the functioning of one or more personalities. It is clear, especially when personalities are multiple, that they cannot be identified with the biological organism as such, but are conceived of, rather, as inner behavers of doubtful status and dimensions. The act of behaving in a given instance is neglected in favor of an impulse or wish, while the probability of such an act is represented as an excitatory tendency

or in terms of psychic energy. Most important of all, the changes in behavior which represent the fundamental behavioral processes are characterized as mental activities—such as thinking, learning, discriminating, reasoning, symbolizing, projecting, identifying, and repressing.

The relatively simple scheme shown in the first figure does not, therefore, represent the conception of human behavior characteristic of most current theory. The great majority of students of human behavior assume that they are concerned with a series of events indicated in the expanded diagram of Figure 4. Here the hereditary and environmental conditions are assumed to generate instincts, needs, emotions, memories, habits, and so on, which in turn lead the personality to engage in various activities characteristic of the mental apparatus, and these in turn generate the observable behavior of the organism. All four stages in the diagram are accepted as proper objects of inquiry. Indeed, far from leaving the inner events to other specialists while confining themselves to the end terms, many psychologists and psychiatrists take the mental apparatus as their primary subject matter.

Perhaps the point of my title is now becoming clearer. Is the scientific study of behavior—whether normal or psychotic—concerned with the behavior of the observable organism under the control of hereditary and environmental factors, or with the functioning of one or more personalities engaged in a variety of mental processes under the promptings of instincts, needs, emotions, memories,

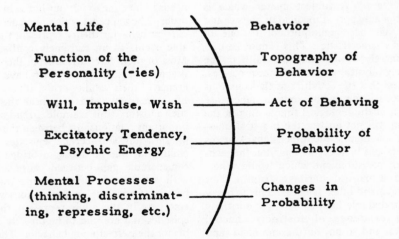

FIGURE 3

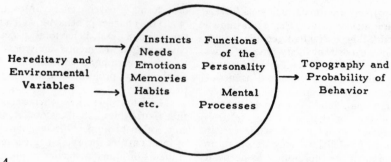

FIGURE 4

and habits? I do not want to raise the question of the supposed *nature* of these inner entities. A certain kinship between such an explanatory system and primitive animism can scarcely be missed, but whatever the historical sources of these concepts, we may assume that they have been purged of dualistic connotations. If this is not the case, if there are those who feel that psychiatry is concerned with a world beyond that of the psychobiological or biophysical organism, that conscious or unconscious mind lacks physical extent, and that mental processes do not affect the world according to the laws of physics, then the following arguments should be all the more cogent. But the issue is not one of the nature of these events, but of their usefulness and experience in a scientific description.

It can scarcely be denied that the expansion of subject matter represented by Figure 4 has the unfortunate effect of a loss of physical status. This is more than a question of prestige or "face." A subject matter which is unquestionably part of the field of physics and biology has been relinquished for one of doubtful characteristics. This cannot be corrected merely by asserting our faith in the ultimately physical nature of inner processes. To protest that the activities of the conscious and unconscious mind are only in some sense an aspect of the biological functioning of the organism will not answer the practical question. In abandoning the dimensional systems of physics and biology, we abandon the techniques of measurement which would otherwise be a natural heritage from earlier achievements in other sciences. This is possibly an irreparable loss. If we come out flatly for the existence of instincts, needs, memories, and so on, on the one hand, and

the mental processes and functions of the personality on the other, then we must accept the responsibility of devising methods of observing these inner events and of discovering dimensional systems according to which they can be measured. The loss of the opportunity to measure and manipulate in the manner characteristic of the physical sciences would be offset only by some extraordinary advantage gained by turning to inner states or conditions.

It is possible, however, to argue that these inner events are merely ways of representing the outer. Many theorists will contend that a habit is only a sort of notation useful in reporting a bit of the history of the individual, just as so-called "mental processes" are ways of talking about changes in behavior. This is a tempting position, for we may then insist that the only dimensional systems required are those appropriate to the terminal events. But if we are to take that line, a great deal still needs to be done to put our house in scientific order. The concepts which one encounters in current behavior theory represent the observable events in an extremely confusing way. Most of them have arisen from theoretical or practical considerations which have little reference to their validity or usefulness as scientific constructs, and they bear the scars of such a history. For example, Freud pointed to important relationships between the behavior of an adult and certain episodes in early childhood, but he chose to bridge the very considerable gap between cause and effect with activities or states of the mental apparatus. Conscious or unconscious wishes or emotions in the adult represent the earlier episodes and are said to be directly responsible for their effect upon behavior. The adult is said, for example, to be suffering from conscious or unconscious anxiety generated when as a child he was punished for aggressive behavior toward a sibling. But many details of the early episode are glossed over (and may, as a result, be neglected) in attributing the disturbances in his behavior to a current anxiety rather than to the earlier punishment. The number of references to anxiety in treatises on behavior must greatly exceed the number of references to punishing episodes, yet we must turn to the latter for full details. If the details are not available, nothing can take their place.

Other kinds of independent variables provide similar examples. Everyone is familiar with the fact that, in general, organisms eat or do not eat depending upon a recent history of deprivation or ingestion. If we can establish that a child does not eat his dinner because he has recently eaten other food, there may seem to be no harm in expressing this by saying that "he is not hungry," provided we explain this in turn by pointing to the history of ingestion. But the concept of hunger represents quite inadequately the many features of schedules of deprivation and other conditions and events which alter the behavior of eating. In the same way the inner surrogates of hereditary variables function beyond the line of duty. We often have no other explanation of a given bit of behavior than that, like other features of anatomy and physiology, it is characteristic of a species; but when we choose instead to attribute this behavior to a set of instincts, we obscure the negative nature of our knowledge and suggest more active causes than mere species status warrants. Similarly, we accept the fact that individuals differ in their behavior, and we may, in some instances, show a relation between aspects of the behavior of successive generations, but these differences and relationships are optimistically misrepresented when we speak of hereditary traits and abilities. Again, the term "experience" incorrectly represents our information about a stimulating field. It has often been observed, for example, that some trivial incident generates a reaction altogether out of proportion to its magnitude. A person seems to be reacting, not to the physical world as such, but to what the world "means to him." Eventually, of course, the effect must be explained—for example, by pointing to some earlier connection with more important events. But whatever the explanation, it is almost certainly not

adequately expressed by the notion of a momentary experience. There are obvious difficulties involved in representing a physical environment *plus a personal history* as a current psychological environment alone.

So far as our independent variables are concerned, then, the practice we are examining tends to gloss over many important details and complexities. The conceptual structure conceals from us the inadequacy of our present knowledge. Much the same difficulty is encountered with respect to the dependent variable, when observable behavior takes second place to mental functionings of a personality. Just as the physical environment is transmuted into experience, so physical behavior comes to be described in terms of its purpose or meaning. A man may walk down the street in precisely the same way upon two occasions, although in one instance he is out for exercise and in another he is going to mail a letter. And so it is thought necessary to consider, not the behavior itself, but "what it means" to the behaving individual. But the additional information we are trying to convey is not a property of behavior but of an independent variable. The behavior we observe in the two cases *is* the same. In reading meaning or intention into it, we are speculating about some of its causes. To take another example, it is commonly said that we can "see" aggression. But we "see" it in two steps: (1) we observe the behavior of an organism, and (2) we relate it to observed or inferred variables having to do with injurious consequences and with the kinds of circumstances which make such behavior probable. No behavior is itself aggressive by nature, although some forms of behavior are so often a function of variables which make them aggressive that we are inclined to overlook the inferences involved. Similarly, when we observe two or more behavioral systems in the same individual and attribute them to different personalities, we gain a considerable advantage for certain descriptive purposes. For example, we can then describe oppositions between such systems as we would between different persons. But we have almost certainly suggested a unity which is not justified by the observed systems of behavior, and we have probably made it more difficult to represent the actual extent of any conflict as well as to explain its origins. And when we observe that the behavior of a person is characterized by a certain responsiveness or probability of responding and speak instead of a given amount of psychic energy, we neglect many details of the actual facts and dodge the responsibility of finding a dimensional system. Lastly, mental processes are almost always conceived of as simpler and more orderly than the rather chaotic material from which they are inferred and which they are used to explain. The "learning process" in experimental psychology, for example, does not give us an accurate account of measured changes in behavior.

We look inside the organism for a *simpler* system, in which the causes of behavior are less complex than the actual hereditary and environmental events and in which the behavior of a personality is more meaningful and orderly than the day-to-day activity of the organism. All the variety and complexity of the input in our diagram seems to be reduced to a few relatively amorphous states, which in turn generate relatively amorphous functions of the personality, which then suddenly explode into the extraordinary variety and complexity of behavior. But the simplification achieved by such a practice is, of course, illusory, for it follows only from the fact that a one-to-one correspondence between inner and outer events has not been demanded. It is just this lack of correspondence which makes such an inner system unsuitable in the experimental analysis of behavior. If "hunger" is something which is produced by certain schedules of deprivation, certain drugs, certain states of health, and so on, and if in turn it produces changes in the probability of a great variety of responses, then it must have very complex properties. It cannot be any simpler than its causes or its effects. If the behavior we observe simply expresses the functioning of a personality, the personality cannot be any simpler than the behavior. If some common learning process is responsible for the changes observed in a number of different situations, then it cannot be any simpler than these changes. The apparent simplicity of the inner system explains the eagerness with which we turn to it, but from the point of view of scientific method it must be regarded as a spurious simplicity, which foreshadows ultimate failure of such an explanatory scheme.

There is another objection. Although speculation about what goes on within the organism seems to show a concern for completing a causal chain, in practice it tends to have the opposite effect. Chains are left incomplete. The layman commonly feels that he has explained behavior when he has attributed it to something in the organism—as in saying "He went *because* he wanted to go," or "He could not work *because* he was worried about his health." Such statements may have value in suggesting the relevance of one set of causes as against another, but they do not give a full explanation until it is explained *why* the person wanted to go, or *why* he was worried. Frequently this additional step is taken, but perhaps just as often these incomplete explanations bring inquiry to a dead stop.

No matter how we may wish to represent such a sequence of causal events, we cannot satisfy the requirements of interpretation, prediction, or control unless we go back to events acting upon the organism from without—events, moreover, which are observed as any event is observed in the physical and biological sciences. It is only common sense, therefore, as well as good scientific practice, to make sure that the concepts which enter into a theory of behavior are explicitly and carefully related to such events. What is needed is an operational definitions of terms. This means more than simple translation. The operational method is commonly misused to patch up and preserve concepts which are cherished for extraneous and irrelevant reasons. Thus it might be possible to set up acceptable definitions of instincts, needs, emotions, memories, psychic energy, and so on, in which each term would be carefully related to certain behavioral and environmental facts. But we have no guarantee that these concepts will be the most useful when the actual functional relationships are better understood. A more reasonable program at this stage is to attempt to account for behavior without appeal to inner explanatory entities. We can do this within the accepted framework of biology, gaining thereby not only a certain personal reassurance from the prestige of a well-developed science, but an extensive set of experimental practices and dimensional systems. We shall be prevented from oversimplifying and misrepresenting the available facts because we shall not transmute our descriptions into other terms. The practical criteria of prediction and control will force us to take into account the complete causal chain in every instance. Such a program is not concerned with establishing the existence of inferred events, but with assessing the state of our knowledge.

This does not mean, of course, that the organism is conceived of as actually empty, or that continuity between input and output will not eventually be established. The genetic development of the organism and the complex interchanges between organism and environment are the subject matters of appropriate disciplines. Some day we shall know, for example, what happens when a stimulus impinges upon the surface of an organism, and what happens inside the organism after that, in a series of stages the last of which is the point at which the organism acts upon the environment and possibly changes it. At that point we lose interest in this causal chain. Some day, too, we shall know how the ingestion of food sets up a series of events, the last of which to engage our attention is a reduction in the probability of all behavior previously reinforced with similar food. Some day we may even know how to bridge the gap between the behavioral characteristics common to parents and offspring. But all these inner events will be accounted for with techniques of observation and measurement appropriate to the physiology of the various parts of the organism, and the account will be expressed in terms appropriate to that subject matter. It would be a remarkable coincidence if the concepts now used to refer inferentially to inner events were to find a place in that account. The task of physiology is not to find hungers, fears, habits, instincts, personalities, psychic energy, or acts of willing, attending, repressing, and so on. Nor is that task to find entities or processes of which all these could be said to be other "aspects." Its task is to account for the causal relations between input and output which are the special concern of a science of behavior. Physiology should be left free to do this in its own way. Just to the extent that current conceptual systems fail to represent the relationships between terminal events correctly, they misrepresent the task of these other disciplines. A comprehensive set of causal relations stated with the greatest possible precision is the best contribution that we, as students of behavior, can make in the co-operative venture of giving a full account of the organism as a biological system.

But are we not overlooking one important source of knowledge? What about the direct observation of mental activity? The belief that the mental apparatus is available to direct inspection anticipated the scientific analysis of human behavior by many hundreds of years. It was refined by the introspective psychologists at the end of the nineteenth century into a special theory of knowledge which seemed to place the newly created science of consciousness on a par with natural science by arguing that all scientists necessarily begin and end with their own sensations and that the psychologist merely deals with these in a different way for different purposes. The notion has been revived in recent theories of perception, in which it has been suggested that the study of what used to be called "optical illusions," for example, will supply principles which help in understanding the limits of scientific knowledge. It has also been argued that the especially intimate empathic understanding which frequently occurs in psychotherapy supplies a kind of direct knowledge of the mental processes of other people. Franz Alexander and Lawrence Kubie have argued in this manner in defense of psychoanalytic practices. Among clinical psychologists Carl Rogers has actively defended a similar view. Something of the same notion may underlie the belief that the psychiatrist may better understand the psychotic if, through the use of lysergic acid, for example, he may temporarily experience similar mental conditions.

Whether the approach to human behavior which I have just outlined ignores some basic fact, whether it is unable to take into account the "stubborn fact of consciousness," is part of a venerable dispute which will not be settled here. Two points may be made, however, in evaluating the evidence from direct "introspection" of the mental apparatus. Knowledge is not to be identified with how things look to us, but rather with what we do about them. Knowledge is power because it is action. How the surrounding world soaks into the surface of our body is merely the first chapter of the story and would be meaningless were it not for the parts which follow. These are concerned with behavior. Astronomy is not how the heavens look to an astronomer. Atomic physics is not the physicist's perception of events within the atom, or even of the macroscopic events from which the atomic world is inferred. Scientific knowledge is what people *do* in predicting and controlling nature.

The second point is that knowledge depends upon a personal history. Philosophers have often insisted that we are not aware of a difference until it makes a difference, and experimental evidence is beginning to accumulate in support of the view that we should probably not know anything at all if we were not forced to do so. The discriminative behavior called knowledge arises only in the presence of certain reinforcing contingencies among the things known. Thus, we should probably remain blind if visual stimuli were never of any importance to us, just as we do not hear all the separate instruments in a symphony or see all the colors in a painting until it is worth while for us to do so.

Some interesting consequences follow when these two points are made with respect to our knowledge of events within ourselves. That a small part of the universe is enclosed within the skin of each of us, and that this constitutes a private world to which each of us has a special kind of access can scarcely be denied. But the world with which we are in contact does not for that reason have any special physical or metaphysical status. Now, it is presumably necessary to learn to observe or "know" external events, and our knowledge will consist of doing something about them. But the society from which we acquire such behavior is at a special disadvantage. It is easy to teach a child to distinguish between colors by presenting different colors and reinforcing his responses as right or wrong accordingly, but it is much more difficult to teach him to distinguish between different aches or pains, since the information as to whether his responses are right or wrong is much less reliable. It is this limited accessibility of the world within the skin, rather than its nature, which has been responsibile for so much metaphysical speculation.

Terms which refer to private events tend to be used inexactly. Most of them are borrowed in the first place from descriptions of external events. (Almost all the vocabulary of emotion, for example, has been shown to be metaphorical in origin.) The consequences are well known. The testimony of the individual regarding his mental processes, feeling, needs, and so on, is, as the psychiatrist above all others has insisted, unreliable. Technical sys-

tems of terms referring to private events seldom resemble each other. Different schools of introspective psychology have emphasized different features of experience, and the vocabulary of one may occasionally be unintelligible to another. This is also true of different dynamic theories of mental life. The exponent of a "system" may show extraordinary conviction in his use of terms and in his defense of a given set of explanatory entities, but it is usually easy to find someone else showing the same conviction and defending a different and possibly incompatible system. Just as experimental psychology once found it expedient to train observers in the use of terms referring to mental events, so the education of experimental psychologists, educators, applied psychologists, psychotherapists, and many others concerned with human behavior is not always free from a certain element of indoctrination. Only in this way has it been possible to make sure that mental processes will be described by two or more people with any consistency.

Psychiatry itself is responsible for the notion that one need not be aware of the feelings, thoughts, and so on, which are said to affect behavior. The individual often behaves *as if* he were thinking or feeling in a given way although he cannot himself say that he is doing so. Mental processes which do not have the support of the testimony supplied by introspection are necessarily defined in terms of, and measured as, the behavioral facts from which they are inferred. Unfortunately, the notion of mental activity was preserved in the face of such evidence with the help of the notion of an unconscious mind. It might have been better to dismiss the concept of mind altogether as an explanatory fiction which had not survived a crucial test. The modes of inference with which we arrive at knowledge of the unconscious need to be examined with respect to the conscious mind as well. Both are conceptual entities, the relations of which to observed data need to be carefully re-examined.

In the long run the point will not be established by argument, but by the effectiveness of a given formulation in the design of productive research. An example of research on psychotic subjects which emphasizes the end terms in our diagram is the project already mentioned. This is not the place for technical details, but the rationale of this research may be relevant.* In these experiments a patient spends one or more hours daily, alone, in a small pleasant room. He is never coerced into going there, and is free to leave at any time. The room is furnished with a chair, and contains a device similar to a vending machine, which can be operated by pushing a button or pulling a plunger. The machine delivers candies, cigarettes, or substantial food, or projects colored pictures on a translucent screen. Most patients eventually operate the machine, are "reinforced" by what it delivers, and then continue to operate it daily for long periods of time—possibly a year or more. During this time the behavior is reinforced on various "schedules"—for example, once every minute or once for every thirty responses—in relation to various stimuli. The behavior is recorded in another room in a continuous curve which is read somewhat in the manner of an electrocardiogram and which permits a ready inspection and measurement of the rate of responding.

The isolation of this small living space is, of course, not complete. The patient does not leave his personal history behind as he enters the room, and to some extent what he does there resembles what he does or has done elsewhere. Nevertheless, as time goes on, the conditions arranged by the experiment begin to compose, so to speak, a special personal history, the important details of which are known. Within this small and admittedly artificial life space, we can watch the patient's behavior change as we change conditions of reinforcement, motivation, and to some extent emotion. With respect to these variables the behavior becomes more and more predictable and controllable or—as characteristic of the psychotic subject—fails to do so in specific ways.

The behavior of the patient may resemble

*Dr. Harry Solomon of the Boston Psychopathic Hospital has served as co-director of the project, although the preceding arguments do not necessarily represent his views. Ogden R. Lindsley is in immediate charge and responsible for much of the overall experimental design as well as for the actual day-to-day conduct of the experiments. Support has been provided by the Office of Naval Research and by the National Institute of Mental Health. The work is being carried out at the Metropolitan State Hospital in Waltham, Massachusetts, with the co-operation of Dr. William McLaughlin, Superintendent, and Dr. Meyer Asakoff, Director of Research.

that of a normal human or infrahuman subject in response to similar experimental conditions, or it may differ in a simple quantitative way—for example, the record may be normal except for a lower over-all rate. On the other hand, a performance may be broken by brief psychotic episodes. The experimental control is interrupted momentarily by the intrusion of extraneous behavior. In some cases it has been possible to reduce or increase the time taken by these interruptions, and to determine where during the session they will occur. As in similar work with other organisms, this quantitative and continuous account of the behavior of the individual under experimental control provides a highly sensitive base line for the observation of the effects of drugs and of various forms of therapy. For our present purposes, however, the important thing is that it permits us to apply to the psychotic a fairly rigorous formulation of behavior based upon much more extensive work under the much more propitious control of conditions obtained with other species. This formulation is expressed in terms of input and output without reference to inner states.

The objection is sometimes raised that research of this sort reduces the human subject to the status of a research animal. Increasing evidence of the lawfulness of human behavior only seems to make the objection all the more cogent. Medical research has met this problem before and has found an answer which is available here. Thanks to the parallel work on animals, it has been possible, in some cases at least, to generate healthier behavior in men, even though at this stage we are not directly concerned with such a result.

Another common objection is that we obtain our results only through an oversimplification of conditions, and that they are therefore not applicable to daily life. But one always simplifies at the start of an experiment. We have already begun to make our conditions more complex and will proceed to do so as rapidly as the uniformity of results permits. It is possible to complicate the task of the patient without limit, and to construct not only complex intellectual tasks but such interactions between systems of behavior as are seen in the Freudian dynamisms.

One simplification sometimes complained of is the absence of other human beings in this small life space. This was, of course, a deliberate preliminary measure, for it is much more difficult to control social than mechanical stimulation and reinforcement. But we are now moving on to situations in which one patient observes the behavior of another working on a similar device, or observes that the other patient receives a reinforcement whenever he achieves one himself, and so on. In another case the patient is reinforced only when his behavior corresponds in some way to the behavior of another. Techniques for achieving extraordinarily precise competition and cooperation between two or more individuals have already been worked out with lower organisms, and are applicable to the present circumstances.

This project has, of course, barely scratched the surface of the subject of psychotic behavior. But so far as it has gone, it seems to us to have demonstrated the value of holding to the observable data. Whether or not you will find them all significant, the data we report have a special kind of simple objectivity. At least we can say: this is what a psychotic subject did under these circumstances, and this is what he failed to do under circumstances which would have had a different effect had he not been psychotic.

Although we have been able to describe and interpret the behavior observed in these experiments without reference to inner events, such references are, of course, not interdicted. Others may prefer to say that what we are actually doing is manipulating habits, needs, and so on, and observing changes in the structure of the personality, in the strength of the ego, in the amount of psychic energy available, and so on. But the advantage of this over a more parsimonious description becomes more difficult to demonstrate, as evidence of the effectiveness of an objective formulation accumulates. In that bright future to which research in psychiatry is now pointing, we must be prepared for the possibility that increasing emphasis will be placed on immediately observable data and that theories of human behavior will have to adjust themselves accordingly. It is not inconceivable that the mental apparatus and all that it implies will be forgotten. It will then be more than a mere working hypothesis to say—to return at long last to my title—that psychotic behavior, like all behavior, is part of the world of observable events to which the powerful methods of natural science apply and to the understanding of which they will prove adequate.

40 Behavioral Approaches to Depression

Charles B. Ferster

Probably the single most important experience that inclines behavioral psychologists toward clinical psychology and behavior modification is that of controlling the behavior of an animal by means of reinforcement. A dramatic illustration of this control is offered in every course in experimental psychology: the alteration of the conduct of the pigeon by operating a food dispenser with a hand switch. It is reliably found that predictable and immediate changes occur in the frequency of the bird's activity in close, point-to-point correspondence with the experimenter's acts. A person viewing such a demonstration gains the conviction that the behavior of the organism is plastic and unlimited if a properly reactive environment can be arranged. He frequently asks why the same approach could not be extended to resolve the pressing problems found in complex human situations.

The conviction which the experimentalist gains from his success in the laboratory—that human behavior is plastic and unlimited—appears to be as powerful a challenge for the experimental psychologist as it has been for mental health professionals from other fields. Skinner's (1948) *Walden Two* is an early statement of the conviction that human behavior is plastic, as is the following statement by this author (Ferster 1958):

Many psychiatric patients or potential psychiatric patients may be characterized as having

From *The Psychology of Depression*, edited by R.J. Friedman and M.M. Katz, pp. 29–44, by permission of the publisher, Hemisphere Corporation.

repertoires whose performances are not producing the reinforcements of the world: because too much behavior is being punished; because nearly all of the individual's behavior is maintained by avoiding aversive consequences rather than producing positive effects; because the projections of the environment are so distorted that the individual's performances are emitted inappropriately; or a combination of all of these. A potential reinforcing environment exists for every individual, however, if he will only emit the required performances on the proper occasion. One has merely to paint the picture, give affection artfully and the world will respond in kind with prestige, money, social response and love. Conversely, a repertoire which will make contact with the reinforcements of the world will be subsequently maintained because of the effect of the reinforcement on the performance.

Although such a statement does point to the environment and the details of a person's relation to it, it is basically a clarion call exclaiming that a psychological solution is possible for psychological problems. The task still remains to discover why individuals do not make effective contact with the positive and avoid the aversive aspects of their environment. We still need to know what events in a person's developmental history prevent appropriate interaction with the environment.

A second aspect of the behavioral psychologist's clinical work is the actual skills and procedures used to work with patients, as exemplified by the practitioners of behavior therapy and behavior modification (Ayllon & Azrin 1968; Franks 1969; Lieberman 1970; and Wolpe 1969). These psychologists are practitioners who, either from experience in behavioral animal research or by study of the behavioral literature, have developed a specific point of view on which to base their technique of interaction with the patient. The practices of some behavioral psychologists, like those of psychodynamic practitioners, are sometimes hard to describe because there may be a difference between the language and theory with which the practitioner describes his work and his actual activity with the patient. Presumably the behavioral orientation of the behavior therapist makes his practices more amenable to objective description than those of the psychodynamic therapist, but this is not necessarily the case (Ferster 1972). For some practitioners, the differences between behavioral and psychodynamic

therapy may be considerably less than appears from their own descriptions of their practices. The convergence of psychotherapeutic practice despite differences in theoretical approaches is greater when the therapist is controlled by the immediate evidence of his interaction with the patient rather than by a preconceived theory. Thus, the behavior of the therapist, if he is in effective contact with the patient, may come as much from his experience with the patient as from the theory that guides him. The relation between therapist and patient is reminiscent of the operant-conditioning cartoon which appeared in a student newspaper showing one rat in a Skinner Box saying to another, as he pressed the bar, "Boy, have I got this guy conditioned. Every time I press the bar he drops in a pellet."

A third aspect of the behaviorist's work in the clinical field is the use of a functional and experimental analysis of behavior as a language with which the data of clinical practice can be described objectively and communicably. Whatever the theoretical basis of the psychotherapist's activities, the actual interaction with the patient is a natural event. Clinical theory becomes complementary to behavior theory rather than contradictory to it when clinical theory is used to suggest the actual events the therapist is observing. When we see an experienced, dedicated practitioner trying to communicate something, we must assume that an important observable event prompts him to do so. Behavior theory is profitably used as a language and conceptual tool for making the events the therapist is observing objective and communicable without translating them into vague, theoretical terms. By paying attention to the observations that prompt the clinical theorist and his related epistemology, a behavior analyst may discover the critical dimensions of complex human situations which otherwise require long experience and sensitivity to observe. By focusing on objective material and scientific descriptions of normal behavioral process, a functional analysis of behavior may serve as a frame of reference for integrating the mass of clinical insights presently available about clinical depression and make them more communicable. For such an analysis, Skinner's (1957) account of verbal behavior is a crucial tool because so many of the phenomena of psychopathology and psychotherapy are verbal.

A Functional Analysis of Depression

Depression as Reduced Frequency of Adjustive Behavior

The most obvious aspect of depression is a marked reduction in the frequency of certain kinds of activity and an increase in the frequency of others, usually avoidance and escape. Such a specification of depression allows us to search for the kinds of behavioral processes that may potentially reduce the frequency of a performance. The clinical definition of depression as "an emotional state with retardation of psychomotor and thought processes, a depressive emotional reaction, feelings of guilt or criticism, and delusions of unworthiness" is a good starting place to uncover the actual forms of conduct that describe the way a depressed person interacts with his environment.

Reduced frequency of many normal activities is the major characteristic we observe in most depressed people. The depressed person may sit silently for long periods, or perhaps even stay in bed all day. The time taken to reply to a question may be longer than usual, and speaking, walking, or carrying out routine tasks will also occur at a slower pace. While he may at a particular time answer questions, ask for something, or even speak freely, his overall frequency of such actions is low. Certain kinds of verbal behavior may seldom occur, such as telling an amusing story, writing a report or a letter, or speaking freely without solicitation. The reduced frequency of activity is referred to clinically as a reduction in gratification (Beck 1967). There is usually a lack of interest in hobbies and sports, and a lack of concern for emotional attachments to other people. Even eating or sexual activity may no longer be rewarding and hence occur less frequently. The frequency of a performance and its reinforcement are obviously related aspects of the same event. When eating or sexual activity are less reinforcing (possibly because of a loss of the social and verbal components involved in them), the frequency of the performance is reduced.

The depressed person's perception of his own activities and those of people around him may be grossly distorted as indicated, for example, by extreme feelings of self-blame or incompetence and indifference to and rejection by those around him. The connection between these verbal distortions and the amount of normal activity requires extensive comment and will be taken up in a later section.

Despite its diagnostic usefulness, bizarre or irrational behavior confuses the objective description of the depressed person's repertoire because it is so prominent. The frequency of such behavior does not imply that it is a strongly maintained or motivated part of the depressed person's repertoire or even a causal factor of the psychosis or neurosis. Such simple, repetitive acts have at best no useful connection to the ordinary social environment, despite their prominence. Sometimes they serve to annoy a particular person or whomever may be in the vicinity. Despite an overall low rate of speech, a depressed person may talk excessively without regard to a listener, become incoherent, repeat hand gestures, adopt complex rituals, or spend a large part of the day in simple innocuous acts like hand wringing, pacing, doodling, playing with hair, genitals or other parts of the body, or compulsively carrying around some object. Despite the high frequency of these performances, we cannot assume that they have the same functional relationship to the environment or even the same persistence and durability as those in a normal repertoire. The frequency of such behaviors may be high because they operate without competition from other, more significant activities. A high frequency of such activities could occur by default of the rest of the repertoire. If the normal repertoire were better maintained, such trivial activities would occur less often.

Skinner has compared bizarre or irrational symptoms to the erratic patterns on the TV set when it is not working properly. The TV repairman deals with the malfunctioning components of the television set rather than with the details of the aberrant picture. Bizarre, irrational, or nonfunctional behaviors frequently occur with the same relation to the normal repertoire in both undepressed and depressed persons when they are in situations where normal activity is restricted. A conference participant, in the presence of a speaker who does not hold his interest but generates enough anxiety to command at least a nominal show of attention, may repetitively rub a spot on the table, doodle, repeatedly touch his body in a ritualistic way, or have bizarre, unconnected, or irrational thoughts. These performances are not significant in themselves but occur in the absence of performances in which a person might otherwise engage. No other activity is appropriate at the moment and the frequency of the irrational behavior is due to its prepotency over an essentially zero repertoire. Similar symptomatic prominence is common with schizophrenic or autistic children (Ferster 1961). The autistic child will often engage in simple repetitive acts and rituals because there are no other significant behaviors in his repertoire. Whenever the child learns to deal successfully with a normal environment we find that the new repertoire preempts nonfunctional activities.

The depressed person's complaints or requests for help are frequent and prominent almost to the exclusion of positively reinforced behavior. He repeatedly tells how bad he feels, talks about suicide, and complains of the inadequacy of his own conduct, external circumstances, fatigue, and illness. Complaints and other negatively reinforced components of the depressed person's repertoire are sometimes accompanied by high frequencies of agitated activities such as hand wringing, pacing, or compulsive talking. These activities serve a function similar to complaints because by prepotency they mask other aversive conditions such as silence, inactivity, or anxiety-producing activities.

All of these performances are, functionally speaking, avoidance and escape behaviors (technically, they are behaviors reinforced by the removal of an aversive stimulus). Suicide is, of course, the ultimate expression of the aversiveness of life's experiences. A complaint ("I can't sleep," for example) is a class of activity that has removed or ameliorated aversive conditions in the past, even though it is incapable of ending the current aversive stimulus. In more common forms, "Please turn down the volume of the radio," for example, is a performance which is commonly reinforced. The frequent reinforcements of complaints in ordinary life account for the extensions of similar but ineffective performances in the face of other aversive situations. In technical jargon (Skinner 1957, pp. 46–48) these are superstitious or extended demands akin to the declaration of a child inside on a rainy day who says, "I wish it would stop raining."

Besides their significance for indicating aversive aspects of the patient's life experiences, these negative reinforced activities also indicate a low frequency of positive reinforcement. The objective of the depressed person's therapy ultimately has to deal with those behaviors that are missing. The avoidance and "depressed behaviors" that do occur are important insofar as they preempt the normal repertoire or are symptomatic of deficits elsewhere. It is problematical whether a person whose repertoire consisted solely of negatively reinforced performances could survive.

The Repertoire of the Depressed Person Is a Passive One

A passive person can be described by the kind of reinforcers sustaining his activity. Magic, superstitious, or extended escape and avoidance behavior are one kind of passive response to the environment, in this case the internal one. The depressed person also responds to the other person's initiative in social interactions. In a two-person interaction, the behavior the active person emits is reinforced by the effect it has on the passive person. The passive person, on the other hand, in complying with the demands of the active one is largely escaping and avoiding aversive consequences. Thus, one connotation of a passive repertoire is that in which the behaviors that are emitted tend to be negatively reinforced by aversive stimuli applied by other people.

A second aspect of a passive repertoire related to depression is associated with the failure to deal with, avoid, or escape from aversive social consequences. Consider, for example, an event that frequently produces depression in a therapy group. A member of the group, who had been severely criticized during a previous session by a number of other members, fails to attend a particular meeting. The therapist has evidence that there is a depression of all of the members of the group because they assume the blame for having injured the person so much that he did not return. When the therapist prompts the group by noting that one member is missing, the conversation reveals evidence that is incompatible with their blame and the depression lifts. Without the prompting and cues from the therapist, however, the aversive stimuli derived from the sense of responsibility for injuring the missing member might prevail.

Passivity surrounds the nature of the control by the aversive stimulus. When it disrupts the ongoing repertoire its control is that of an emotional effect by an aversive stimulus. When the nature of the aversive stimulus is clarified, the control is that of negative reinforcement—the aversive stimulus increases the frequency of those performances that terminate it. The verbal activity that clarifies the actual events that occurred are negatively reinforced because they alter an aversive situation into one which is not.

Depression Needs to Be Defined Functionally, Rather Than Topographically

The missing performances are usually a part of a depressed person's potential repertoire. On many occasions in the past he probably dressed, traveled to work, completed his job, and engaged in many performances reinforced by their interpersonal effects. The problem is that the current conditions do not support the activities of which he is potentially capable. A topographic description of the depressed person's repertoire does not distinguish it from the normal one. Almost any item of conduct to be observed in a depressed person may be seen at one time or another in an undepressed person. The depressed person is distinguished from one who is not by the relative frequency of occurrence of these performances in the total repertoire. Most persons, at one time or another, sit looking quietly out a window, say, "That was a dumb thing for me to do." are sad, unhappy, or dejected, or lose interest in an activity. In any one of these instances it may not be possible to distinguish them from pathologically depressed persons.

Different Meanings of the Term "Behavior"

Contrary to the prejudices of many clinical writers, general behavior theory does not talk about a person's repertoire as a collection of response topographies. The phrase "functional analysis of behavior" implies a systematic description in which the significance of a person's activities is connected with the way it operates on the environment, on both sides of his skin. Thus, one person who talks compulsively and another who leaves the room as soon as an unfamiliar person enters may be acting in identical ways, even though the acts are very different topographically. Skinner (1959) notes that a man walking down the street to mail a letter is engaged in very different behaviors from those of a man walking for exercise, even though the topography of the two activities is virtually identical. Despite the identical topographies of the two performances, in no way could they be considered the same when analyzed functionally because their behavioral significance is intimately connected with the reinforcers maintaining them. A description is behavioral, not because it differs from a clinical interpretation but because the component events of the functional relation between performance and the environment are described objectively, as would be any other natural event.

The distinction is sometimes made clinically between behaviors such as muscular tension, reaction time, handwriting, performance on a pursuit rotor, or written personality tests, and the underlying psychological processes of which the behaviors are symptomatic. Besides the term "behavioral" has such explicit connotations to clinical practitioners it will be useful to distinguish between such symptomatic behavior and a functional analysis of behavior. Beck, for example, distinguishes between self-evaluation by a patient and behavioral tests of the patient (1967, p. 177). A functional analysis of behavior does not necessarily reject the patient's self-evaluation as nonbehavioral. The way a depressed patient talks about himself is an important class of factual information and it becomes nonbehavioral and unobjective only when it is taken as symptomatic of events elsewhere rather than as an activity of importance in itself. A behavioral analysis of the patient's self-evaluation stresses its functional relation to the person the patient is talking with or to whom he is complaining about himself.

The Basic Behavioral Process Which Contributes to or Reduces the Frequency of a Person's Conduct

Depressions, certainly these generally characterized as reactive, appear to be a functional rather than a topographically defined category. The common denominator among depressed persons is the decreased frequency of many different kinds of positively reinforced activity. We cannot therefore expect that one cause or a single psychological process will be responsible because the frequency of the items in the depressed person's repertoire is a product of so many different psychological processes. Every process that accounts for the frequency of a person's actions explains part of the pathology of depression.

Schedules of Reinforcement

The schedule of reinforcement of a performance is an important determinant of that performance's frequency, independently of the kind of reinforcer or the associated deprivation.

In general, reinforcement schedules requiring large amounts of behavior to produce the relevant change in the environment (e.g., fixed ratio schedules of reinforcement, Skinner 1938; Ferster & Skinner 1957) are those most susceptible to loss. The critical factor is a fixed and large amount of activity required for each reinforcement. The salesman who needs to call on a large number of persons before he consummates a sale, or the person engaged in studying all semester for a final examination, working on a term paper, writing a novel, persuading someone, carrying out an experiment which requires long and arduous procedures without indication of success before completion, or a difficult therapeutic encounter in which much thought and stress go into small indicators of progress, or a housewife's routine housework which may require a fixed and large amount of repetitive work—all exemplify a schedule of reinforcement that may potentially weaken the behavior severely. The result is frequently seen as an abulia in which the novelist, for example, is unable to work for considerable periods after completing his previous work. The effect of such schedules of reinforcement is hard to observe because they at times generate high, persistent rates of activity, even though the predominant result is long periods of inactivity. The parallel to the manic side of depression comes immediately to mind. The enormous influence of such schedules of reinforcement apart from the reinforcer or the associated deprivation is conveyed by animal experiments in which a pigeon pecking for food on a fixed-ratio schedule, for example, will starve to death because the frequency of the performance is so low. Yet the same bird, when exposed to a variable reinforcement schedule, requiring the same amount of activity per reinforcement, sustains its activity easily.

It is tempting to speculate that this particular schedule of reinforcement exemplifies the middle period of life when most individuals settle down to a routine in which there is a constant steady work requirement as opposed to the variability in quality and amount of work that occurs as one prepares for a career or enters into job experiences that change rapidly. Perhaps relevant here is the classical phenomenon of the highly successful professional who, on reaching the pinnacle of achievement, undergoes a profound depression. The upwardly striving person is one whose schedules of reinforcement are variable, sometimes requiring large amounts of activity for reinforcement and at other times requiring less. Such variable schedules of reinforcement are much less likely to produce strain and low frequencies than the schedules associated with a stable work situation in which day in and day out there is a constant amount of activity associated with the required accomplishment.

Changes in the Environment

Where is an organism's behavior when it is not engaging in it? Where is the patellar reflex when it is not being elicited? Where are the reminiscenses that occur with a close friend when the friend is absent? From a behavioral point of view they are "in the repertoire." There are potential performances that will occur when the necessary collateral circumstances are present. Behaviors, in a person's repertoire but not occurring because the current situation has reduced their frequency to zero, are as unavailable as if they had never occurred before. Most people's conduct occurs appropriately to the circumstances in which it has been and can be reinforced. When the circumstances change too drastically, the result may be depression—a loss of behavior.

The death of a close companion or other radical changes in the physical and social environment may reduce the frequency of significant items in a person's repertoire as markedly as schedules of reinforcement. It is even possible to conceive of sudden changes that may virtually denude an individual of his entire repertoire as, for example, the death of a close companion to a secluded spinster. The seclusion of her life produces a situation in which all her conduct is narrowly under the control of her companion. The companion's sudden death therefore removes the occasions that supported almost all her activity. A case history of an autistic child illustrates the same process. The nearly psychotic mother of a four-year-old girl hired a teenage babysitter to take care of her daughter for almost a year. Although the mother remained in the house during the whole year, during which the babysitter took care of the child, she completely abdicated control to the babysitter by having literally nothing to do with the child. If the child said, "Mom, can I have a cookie?", there would be no answer; if she said, "Janet [the babysitter], could I have a cookie?", Janet said, "Yes," and gave the child the cookie. If the child said, "Let's go outside," the mother did not answer. Janet, on the other hand, might reply, "Okay," and take the child outside.

Such interpersonal interactions are functionally identical to standard pigeon experiments in which the pigeon produces food by pecking a key. When reinforcement depends on the color of the light illuminating the key, the pigeon's pecking is brought under the control of the colors by withholding reinforcement on one occasion and allowing it to occur on the other. When the key is red, pecks do not produce food and hence decrease in frequency. Pecking continues in the green color because those pecks continue to produce food. Such control of the bird's behavior by the environment makes it possible to alter its repertoire rapidly by simply changing the color of the light behind the key. An analogy could be drawn between the mother and the babysitter, and the red and green keys in the pigeon experiment. The babysitter's presence (the red light) defined an occasion during which any kind of verbal request of nonverbal interaction had a normal effect. When the babysitter left the child alone with the mother at the end of the year there was a loss of almost all of the child's repertoire. She became incontinent, could not be kept in the nursery school, and lost speech. There is a similar functional parallel between the behavior of the spinster and its control by the presence of her companion.

The normal processes of growth and development, particularly during middle age, occur when similar important changes in life's circumstances take place which require corresponding changes in a person's repertoire. The physical changes associated with aging and normal development may have a major influence on the kinds of positive reinforcement that are possible. Hormonal changes, and the associated changes in amount of sexual activity including fantasy, are one important area of change. Another area of change lies in overall physical capacity for work and severe physical exertion. Even behaviors reinforced by ingesting food become less available as a rewarding activity because decreased physical activity reduces the metabolic requirements of most middle-aged people. Ironically, a person who can finally afford bountiful, rich, and tempting foods cannot eat them because they would produce obesity. Even important social interactions, which in so many cultures surround food and eating, become stressful or less frequent because of limitations on food ingestion or because of disease or decreased metabolic need.

Disease or other kinds of physical incapacity may reduce the change of performances that are possible for the middle-aged or older person. Retirement may impose a very drastic change in an older person's environment, opposite to the problem facing the adolescent. Just as the adolescent faces a complex world for which he does not yet have an adequate repertoire, the older person also encounters a new environment which needs for its reinforcement an entirely new repertoire. All of the activities previously reinforced by the work environment can no longer be emitted. A successful transition to retirement depends on whether the retired person has a sufficient repertoire to make contact with the environment of retirement. The problem is doubly complex because the repertoire available for the transition was shaped and formed in the work world that is no longer present.

The Relationship of Depression to a Limited Repertoire of Observation

One common characterization of a depressed person's repertoire is a distorted, incomplete, and misleading view of the environment which includes hallucinations and delusions, distortions of body image and phy-

sical appearance, distortions of his competence, exaggeration of errors, complete inability to evaluate the way other people see him, a
tendency to take blame for events for which
there is really no responsibility, and a limited
and unhopeful view of the world.

Even though our language and accustomed
patterns of thinking stress distortions of the
person's perceptions and his view of events, a
behavioral analysis requires that we talk about
how the environment prompts and otherwise
controls a person's activity, rather than the
way he perceives his own and the outside
world. The event that influences the person is
the same, no matter how we choose to talk
about it. The behavioral description is more
useful than the mentalistic one because we can
see the details of how a person comes to act
distinctively to the various features of his
inside and outside environment. When we can
describe the process in detail it will suggest
therapeutic procedures which can produce
performances that can then act successfully on
important environments.

Ideally, if a person's every act occurred
under circumstances in which it could be
effective, there would be a high frequency of
reinforcement. Conversely, if a person cannot
observe the environment around him accurately (the environment does not control the
performances appropriate to activating it), a
large proportion of his behavior will be unsuccessful and go unreinforced. The distortions
of the depressed person's perceptions may be
seen to reduce the possibility of positive reinforcement because the major component of
the distortion is the emission of performances
that cannot be reinforced. A failure of control
by the characteristics of the environment
could therefore cause or contribute substantially to a depression.

The low frequency of positively reinforced
behaviors in the depressed person's repertoire
might perpetuate the incomplete or distorted
perception of the environment because the
primary event responsible for acting on the
environment selectively is some tendency to
influence it. In general, the ability to observe
the environment depends on a high enough
frequency of interacting with it so that the
successful reinforcement of the performance
on one occasion and its unsuccessful reinforcement on another occasion eventually
tailors it to the environment in which it can be
reinforced.

An important way in which we learn to
observe the environment is to comment on it
and describe it verbally. The low frequency of
verbal activity, other than complaints, is a
serious impediment to an improvement of the
depressed person's view of the world. The
depressed person may not be able to emit
enough potentially reinforceable behavior to
discover the differential reaction of the environment, depending upon the kind of performance that is emitted.

The reader may ask, of course, which came
first, the depression in which the person
behaves without observing the consequences
or effectiveness of his performance, or a lack
of sufficient repertoire so that the person
could effectively discover the characteristics
of the environment in which he operates.
From a clinical point of view, three aspects of
the patient's repertoire bear on the technical
behavioral analysis. The patient has (1) a
limited view of the world, (2) a "lousy" view
of the world, and (3) an unchanging view of
the world.

A limited view of the world refers to the
differential control of the social and physical
environment. Patients' behaviors are not appropriate to the changing circumstances in the
external environment. Thus, for example, a
person may pout, complain, or sulk in circumstances in which he had but to interact
along the lines needed for assistance. We
cannot assume that the depressed person actually sees very many of the features of the
social world around him. William James'
"bloody, blooming confusion" might be the
most apt characterization of the depressed
person's view of the world.

The "lousy" view of the world describes
the aversive consequences of being unable to
see the environment clearly enough to avoid
aversive situations. Some of the aversive conditions are the inability to behave appropriately to the environment, and the lack of the
repertoire by which one can act effectively and
positively without engendering punishment
by acting in ways that are aversive to other
people.

The unchanging view of the world refers to
the processes, probably stemming from the
person's development history, that prevent
the normal exploration of the environment,
and the clarification and expansion of the
repertoire that comes from such exploration.
These developmental arrests seem to be the

same as the fixation of personality development described psychoanalytically. There still remains the task, however, of identifying the actual behaviors and the interactions that cause the developmental stoppages. The disparity between the person's repertoire and the environment he is in effective contact with also needs to be described. The circumstances are sufficiently complex so that a separate discussion is warranted.

Factors That Block the Cumulative Development of a Repertoire

Ideally, normal growth and development represent a continuous approximation of a complex repertoire. Should there be a hiatus in development in which the contingencies of reinforcement are not consistent with the person's currently emitted behavior, however, the process becomes negatively autocatalytic. Failure to make contact with the current environment reduces the frequency of behavior and prevents the further development of the repertoire. In the normal process of feeding, whether by breast or bottle, the infant engages in an active interplay with the mother. The child's activities are variously successful or unsuccessful from moment to moment as the child adjusts its conduct. Behavior that successfully meets the characteristics of the mother and the relevant features of the physical environment produces physical contact, food, and other rewarding reactions. The adjustment between the child and mother is a teaching device from which the child's view of the mother and the physical environment evolve. The sight of the approaching nipple, for example, becomes an occasion that prompts the child to open its mouth. It is problematical whether the child would in any case notice the mother or be influenced by her if there were not some activity whose outcome was not influenced by her. Even the simplest act, such as the child's moving its fingers across the mother's arm or touching its blanket, is subject to the same kind of differential reinforcement. The visual characteristics of the blanket or the mother's arm come to control the moment of contact between the hand and blanket or skin. The differential reaction of the mother, such as the way she acts in return, further distinguishes the occasions on which the child acts on the mother and serves to enlarge the child's perceptual capability.

Such normal development of the child's perceptual repertoire may be interrupted if there is a serious interference with or interruption of the reinforcers maintaining the child's activities. For example, a child may experience difficulties in feeding which prevent the "give and take" that normally makes eating a natural result of a continuous interaction with the mother. The mother may not be aware of the flow of milk from the bottle, so that the milk passively pours down the child's throat, or the flow might be so slow and require so much sucking that the movements are not reinforced. A mother who does not react to the tension and relaxation of the child's muscular posture will fail to reinforce the child's movements as it adjusts its posture to produce greater body contact with the mother or to escape discomfort when the mother shows physical strain because she is holding the child like a "sack of potatoes." Not only is there a loss of repertoire that would normally emerge from these interactions, but there is a corresponding lack of perceptual development. The child who does not interact in close correspondence with its mother as she holds him also does not learn to observe the nuances that prompt and cue interactions.

The large magnitudes of emotional reaction that not only preempt positively reinforced behavior but also become firmly established because they produce an effect on the parent which reinforces and increases their frequency are an equally serious consequence of the nonreinforcement of important (high frequency) activities. The child who does not receive food from its mother satisfactorily enough to satiate the underlying deprivation, or one who experiences collateral aversive effects such as choking or extreme physical constraint, may react emotionally. Such activities in turn generate a reaction in the parent, who may either remove the aversive situation by providing the food or react emotionally in direct response to the child's actions. The result is an increase in frequency of the child's rage and frustration because of their influence on the parent. Not only does a primitive, atavistic mode of dealing with the parent become a prominent part of the child's repertoire, but it blocks the child's perception of his world. The diffuse emotional reaction is prepotent over the smaller magnitude component activities of a normal interaction.

The behaviors involved in such disruptions

appear to be the same ones described psychodynamically along the dimensions of primary to secondary process. The shift from primary to secondary process appears to describe the adjustment between the child's current behavior and its progressive adjustment to the complex features of its social environment. The child whose interactions with its mother are primarily associated with its own deprivations, which are reinforced because of their aversiveness to her, is ultimately blocked from developing an adequate perception of other people and hence adequate ways of interacting with them (secondary process). The child who fails to come under the control of the nuances of the mother's behavior is progressively left behind in its development of interpersonal behaviors, and whole sectors of interpersonal reactivity are not available to it as a means of commerce with the external world, much along the lines of the classical connotations of the fixation of a personality at a particular stage of development.

Such failures in the perceptual area may at once suggest causes of some kinds of depression and a means of ameliorating them. Behaviorally, the most general way of increasing the perceptual repertoire is to begin with simple activities whose reinforcement is reliable but not so invariant that there are not some circumstances in which the performance is appropriate and others in which it is not. The reinforcement of the performance on the one occasion and its nonreinforcement on another teaches the person to observe the appropriate features. The most important element, however, is to find a way to increase the person's tendency to act positively on the environment rather than to react passively and emotionally. A useful reinforcement schedule applicable to such a problem is the differential reinforcement of other behavior. The increase in frequency of reinforcement behaviors other than primitive or atavistic activities eventually decreases their frequency by prepotency and nonreinforcement (Ferster and Perrott 1968).

Ideally, a therapeutic interaction with a psychotherapist stimulates just such a differential reinforcement of other behavior when the therapist observes and functionally analyzes the current verbal activity. By his reactions and questions he reinforces selected parts of the patient's current interaction. Many of these behaviors constitute the patient's talk about his activity. Although the ultimate goal of therapy is the patient's activity rather than his talk about his activity, this class of verbal behavior also serves an important function. First, it is an increase in general verbal activity which of itself could be of practical use. Second, it becomes a means for the patient to observe his own activity because his speech is a repertoire of performances differentially reinforced (by the therapist) according to its relation to the patient's activity. Third, the patient's descriptions of his own primitive reactions to aversive or thwarting situations may prompt more effective ways to escape or produce positive reinforcers, when he observes the incompatibility between what he is doing and what he can say about it rationally. Such talking about one's own behavior needs to be quite durable and of a high frequency before it can preempt more primitive, less effective forms of conduct.

Anger and Aggressive Acts as Factors in Depression

Clinicians speak of "problems of dealing with anger and aggressive impulses" as a prominent feature of psychopathology. It is obvious that such performances have a high frequency of occurrences in normal human activity and that parental and other communities often punish such activities severely. The pathology stemming from anger and aggression is generally agreed to be a by-product of their punishment and suppression when they affect others adversely.

Anger Turned Inward

To understand the suppression or repression of anger behaviorally we first need to describe anger as an operant performance and second to note the characteristics of punishment as a behavioral process. Aggressive or angry acts are generally those reinforced by the injury they produce to another person, by the actual removal of reinforcers, or by the creation of situations or events that are aversive because they indicate a loss of reinforcers. The class of performances is defined, not by its topography, but by the way the performances influence another person. Aggressive acts are frequently disguised or "softened" because a nakedly aggressive act will produce such a large aversive reaction. Sarcasm exemplifies one kind of softening; aggressive humor is another. Their form may be as unobtrusive as a tendency to comment on the unfavorable aspects of another person's conduct, either by criticism or by especially noting unfortunate lapses.

Since aggressive acts are aversive to others by design, their punishment is the rule rather than the exception. Experimental psychology contributes to our understanding of this problem by creating knowledge of the characteristics of the punishment process. There is some dispute in the psychological literature about whether punishment can directly reduce the frequency of the punished act, as in an algebraic subtraction (Azrin & Holz 1966), or whether the reduced frequency is *always* a temporary suppression. However this dispute is resolved, it is clear that the temporary suppression of punished acts is a frequently observed phenomenon. The process is illustrated by the child, facing a piece of bric-a-brac, who has been punished for playing with it. In the face of a tendency to play with the attractive toy, the child puts his hand behind his back. Or the child provoked to laughter in the classroom bites his lip to the point of pain because the teacher would punish laughter. Both of these performances prevent the punished act because they are incompatible with it. Thus, the smiling and the reaching for the piece of bric-a-brac may remain intact in the repertoire, but with a reduced frequency only because any incipient tendency creates an aversive situation whose removal reinforces and increases the frequency of the incompatible performances such as putting the hands behind the back or biting the lip.

The phenomenon of psychodynamic suppression is a close analogue, except that the performances tend to be verbal. As a word, a phrase, a thought, or an association comes into consciousness (its probability of emission increases), there is an automatic reinforcement of incompatible behavior. The repression, according to this process, is an actual activity or performance which will occur in a dynamic balance with the punished or anxiety-provoking performance. Such activity is in its own right a kind of behavior with a certain persistence and frequency which is a part of the person's repertoire. As a prominent and frequent activity, not serving any useful function in the person's commerce with the external environment, it may be a substantial part of the finite amount of activity of which a person is capable. The

metaphor of a fixed amount of energy, which may be apportioned to the repression activity or the external world, seems to convey the sense of the behavioral analysis. The repression of punished behavior appears to be a potentially serious contributor to depression because it commits such a large part of a person's repertoire to activities that do not produce positive reinforcement.

Aggressive Social Acts Imply a Loss of Important Social Reinforcers

A person who is angry at someone who can potentially or has in the past supplied important reinforcers creates the possibility that he may lose important reinforcers. There is an obvious incompatibility between acting to injure someone and continuing to expect him to interact socially and to provide positive events. For this reason, anger comes to serve what is behaviorally called a preaversive stimulus—a situation that precedes the loss of positive reinforcement. Such preaversive stimuli, in classical animal experiments, markedly reduce the frequency of the ongoing operant behavior in the sense of an emotional change—a state of the organism that has a global effect. It is easy to conjecture vignettes from a child's developmental history in which a parent significantly withdrew from a child, perhaps totally, in the face of its anger. The effect on the child is exacerbated because the withdrawal of reinforcers may increase the child's anger and emotionality, leading to further instances of loss of parental attention, affection, and ordinary items of daily support.

REFERENCES

Ayllon T., & Azrin, N. H. *Token economy; A motivational system for therapy and rehabilitation.* New York: Appleton-Century-Crofts, 1968.

Azrin, N. H., & Holz, W. C. *Punishment in operant behavior: Areas of research and application.* New York: Appleton-Century-Crofts, 1966.

Beck, A. T. *Depression.* Philadelphia: University of Pennsylvania Press, 1967.

Ferster, C. B. Reinforcement and punishment in the control of human behavior by social agencies. *Psychiatric Research Reports,* 1958, 101–118.

Ferster, C. B. Positive reinforcement and behavioral deficits of autistic children. *Child Development,* 1961, **32,** 437–456.

Ferster, C. B. The experimental analysis of clinical phenomena. *The Psychological Record*, 1972, **22**, 1–16.

Ferster, C. B. & Perrott, M. C. *Behavior principles.* New York: Appleton-Century-Crofts, 1968.

Ferster, C. B. & Skinner, B. F. *Schedules of reinforcement.* New York: Appleton-Century-Crofts, 1957.

Franks, C. M. (Ed.) *Behavior therapy: Appraisal and status.* New York: McGraw Hill, 1969.

Lieberman, R. P. A behavioral approach to group dynamics. *Behavior Therapy*, 1970, **1**, 141–175.

Skinner, B. F. *The behavior of organisms.* New York: Appleton-Century-Crofts, 1938.

Skinner, B. F. What is psychotic behavior? *Cumulative Record.* New York: Appleton-Century-Crofts, 1959.

Skinner, B. F. *Walden Two.* New York: MacMillan, 1948.

Skinner, B. F. *Verbal behavior.* New York: Appleton-Century-Crofts, 1957.

Wolpe, J. *The practice of behavior therapy.* New York: Pergamon Press, 1969.

Therapeutic Approaches

Behavioral therapy consists of the direct application of experimentally derived principles of learning to the treatment of pathological disorders. The therapist does not seek to remove the "underlying" causes of psychopathology, nor does he give the patient free rein to explore his attitudes and feelings. Instead, he arranges a program of conditioning and extinction in which the behavior patterns he wishes to alter are specified, the environmental elements which have reinforced the maladaptive behavior are eliminated, and a series of new reinforcements are instituted in order to condition new adaptive behaviors.

The British psychologist Hans Eysenck has been in the forefront as an exponent of behavioral therapy. In the paper presented here, he offers an illuminating commentary on the logic and rationale of the entire behavioral movement.

Limiting this section to British writers, the distinguished psychiatrist, Isaac Marks, provides a thoughtful assessment of the degree to which the behavioral approach to treatment has fulfilled its early aspirations.

41 Learning Theory and Behaviour Therapy*

H. J. Eysenck

It would probably be true to say that the present position in the psychiatric treatment of neurotic disorders is characterized by the following features. (1) With the exception of electroshock, the only method of treatment at all widely used is psychotherapy. (2) In prac-

*This paper was delivered on 3 July 1958 to a meeting of the R.M.P.A., and its style inevitably bears traces of the fact that it was orginally prepared for verbal presentation. It was followed by another paper, delivered by Mr. Gwynne Jones, giving concrete examples of the application of behaviour

From *J. Mental Science 105:* 61–75, 1959, by permission of the Royal Medico-Psychological Association and the author.

therapy from our own experience. Some of these are discussed in his article published in this Journal,[1] and it is suggested that readers interested in the theories here advanced may like to consult this article in order to obtain some notion of the practical methods emanating from these theories. A more detailed discussion of many theoretical points that arise may be found in *Dynamics of Anxiety and Hysteria*,[2] as well as several of my previous books.[3,4,5]

tically all its manifestations, psychotherapy is based on Freudian theories. (3) With the exception of intelligence testing, psychological contributions consist almost entirely in the administration and interpretation of projective tests, usually along psychoanalytic lines. I have argued in the past and quoted numerous experiments in support of these arguments, that there is little evidence for the practical efficacy of psychotherapy,* whether strictly Freudian or "eclectic"[7,8] that Freudian theories are outside the realm of science because of their failure to be consistent, or to generate testable deductions[9]; and that projective tests are so unreliable and lacking in validity that their use, except in research, cannot be defended.[10]† I shall not here argue these points again; the evidence on which these views are based is quite strong and is growing in strength every year. I shall, instead, try to make a somewhat more constructive contribution by discussing an alternative theory of neurosis, an alternative method of treatment and an alternative way of using the knowledge and competence of psychologists in the attempted curing of neurotic disorders. It need hardly be emphasized that the brief time at my disposal will make it inevitable that what I have to say will sound much more dogmatic than I would like it to be; I have to ask your indulgence in this respect, and request you to bear in mind all the obvious qualifying clauses which, if included in this paper, would swell it to three times its present size.

Few psychiatrists are likely to deny that all

---

*When I first suggested that the literature did not contain any kind of unequivocal proof of the efficacy of psychotherapeutic treatment, this conclusion was widely criticized. Since then however, Dr. Weinstock, Chairman of the Fact-Finding Committee of the Amer. Psychoanalyt. Assoc., has explicitly stated in a lecture delivered at the Maudsley Hospital that his Association made *no claims of therapeutic usefulness for psychoanalytic methods* and in this country Glover[6] has equally explicitly disavowed such claims. On this point, therefore, leading psychoanalysts appear to share my views to a considerable extent.

†This fact is also beginning to be more widely realized, and it is symptomatic that such well-known departments as that belonging to the New York Psychiatric Hospital, have followed the lead of the Institute of Psychiatry and discontinued the routine use of projective techniques like the Rorschach.

behaviour ultimately rests on an inherited basis, but even fewer would be prepared to assert that environmental influences played no part in the genesis and modification of behaviour. Once we are agreed that learning and conditioning are instrumental in determining the different kinds of reaction we may make to environmental stimulation, we will find it very difficult to deny that neurotic reactions, like all others, are *learned* reactions and must obey the laws of learning. Thus, I would like to make my first claim by saying that modern learning theory,[11] and the experimental studies of learning and conditioning carried out by psychologists in their laboratories are extremely relevant to the problems raised by neurotic disorders. If the laws which have been formulated are, not necessarily true, but at least partially correct, then it must follow that we can make deductions from them to cover the type of behaviour represented by neurotic patients, construct a model which will duplicate the important and relevant features of the patient and suggest new and possibly helpful methods of treatment along lines laid down by learning theory. Whether these methods are in fact an improvement over existing methods is, of course, an empirical problem; a few facts are available in this connection and will be mentioned later. It is unfortunate that insistence on empirical proof has not always accompanied the production of theories in the psychiatric field—much needless work, and many heartbreaking failures, could have been avoided if the simple medical practice of clinical trials with proper controls had always been followed in the consideration of such claims.

How, then, does modern learning theory look upon neurosis? In the first place, it would claim that neurotic symptoms are *learned patterns of behaviour* which for some reason or other are *unadaptive*. The paradigm of neurotic symptom formation would be Watson's famous experiment with little Albert, an eleven months old boy who was fond of animals.[14] By a simple process of classical Pavlovian conditioning, Watson created a phobia for white rats in this boy by standing behind him and making a very loud noise by banging an iron bar with a hammer whenever Albert reached for the animal. The rat was the conditioned stimulus in the experiment, the loud fear-producing noise was the unconditioned stimulus. As predicted, the unconditioned response (fear) became conditioned to the C.S. (the rat), and Albert developed a phobia for white rats, and indeed for all furry animals. This latter feature of the conditioning process is of course familiar to all students as the generalization gradient[12]; an animal or a person conditioned to one stimulus also responds, although less and less strongly, to other stimuli further and further removed from the original one along some continuum.

The fear of the rat thus conditioned is unadaptive (because white rats are not in fact dangerous) and hence is considered to be a neurotic symptom; a similarly conditioned fear of snakes would be regarded as adaptive, and hence not as neurotic. Yet the mechanism of acquisition is identical in both cases. This suggests that chance and environmental hazards are likely to play an important part in the acquisition of neurotic responses. If a rat happens to be present when the child hears a loud noise, a phobia results; when it is a snake that is present, a useful habit is built up!

The second claim which modern learning theory would make is this. People and animals differ in the speed and firmness with which conditioned responses are built up.[15] Those in whom they are built up particularly quickly and strongly are more likely to develop phobias and other anxiety and fear reactions than are people who are relatively difficult to condition.[2] Watson was lucky in his choice of subject; others have banged away with hammers on metal bars in an attempt to condition infants, but not always with the same success. Individual differences must be taken into account in considering the consequences of any course of attempted conditioning. Nor is the degree of conditionability the only kind of individual variability with which we are concerned. Learning theory tells us that the amount of reinforcement following any action determines in part the amount of conditioning that takes place.[16] Thus the louder the noise, the greater the fright of the infant, and the greater the fright, the stronger the phobia. But different children have different types of autonomic system, and the same amount of noise produces quite unequal amounts of autonomic upheaval in different children. Consequently, autonomic reactivity must also be considered; the more labile or reactive the child, the more likely he is to produce strongly conditioned fear reactions, anxieties and phobias. The individual differences in autonomic reactivity and in conditionability

have been conceptualized as giving rise to two dimensions of personality, namely neuroticism and introversion respectively.[5] The more autonomically reactive, the more prone will the individual be to neurotic disorders. The more easily he forms conditioned responses, the more introverted will his behaviour be. Combine introversion and neuroticism, and you get the dysthymic individual, the person almost predestined to suffer from anxieties, conditioned fears and phobias, compulsions and obsessions, reactive depressions and so forth.

But this is only part of the story. Many conditioned responses are unadaptive, and consequently may embarrass the individual and even drive him into a mental hospital if sufficiently intense. Yet other conditioned responses are obviously necessary and desirable; indeed, many of them are indispensable for survival. It has been argued very strongly that the whole process of socialization is built up on the principle of conditioning[17]; the overt display of aggressive and sexual tendencies is severely punished in the child, thus producing conditioned fear and pain responses (anxiety) to situations in which the individual is likely to display such tendencies. He consequently refrains from acting in the forbidden manner, not because of some conscious calculus of hedonic pleasure which attempts to equate the immediate pleasure to be gained from indulgence with the remote probability of later punishment, but because only by not indulging, and by physically removing himself can he relieve the very painful conditioned anxiety responses to the whole situation. Anxiety thus acts as a mediating drive, a drive which may be exceedingly powerful by virtue of its combination of central, autonomic, skeletal and hormonal reactions. This mediating role of anxiety, and its capacity to function as an acquired drive, have been subjected to many well conceived experimental studies, and the consensus of opinion appears to leave little doubt about the great value and predictive capacity of his conception.[18]

Let us now consider an individual who is deficient in his capacity to form quick and strong conditioned responses. He will be all the less likely to be subject to phobias and other anxieties, but he will also be less likely to form useful conditioned responses, or to become a thoroughly socialized individual. When this lack of socialization is combined with strong autonomic drive reactions (high neuroticism), such an individual is likely to show the neurotic symptomatology of the psychopath or the hysteric, and indeed, in our experimental work we have found that, as predicted, dysthymic patients, and normal introverts, are characterized by the quick and strong formation of conditioned responses, while psychopaths and normal extraverts are characterized by the weak and slow formation of conditioned responses.[19,20,2] Thus the deviation from the average in either direction may prove disastrous—too strong conditioning easily leads to dysthymic reactions, too weak conditioning easily leads to psychopathic and hysterical reactions. The logic of this whole approach leads me to postulate two great classes of neurotic symptoms which between them exhaust in principle all the possible abnormal reactions with which you are all familiar. On the one hand we have *surplus conditioned reactions*, i.e., reactions acquired along the lines I have adumbrated, and where the reaction is unadaptive, even though orginally it may have been well suited to circumstances. On the other hand we have *deficient conditioned reactions*, i.e., reactions normally acquired by most individuals in society which are adaptive, but which because of defective conditioning powers have not been acquired by a particular person. It is necessary to emphasize that surplus conditioned reactions and deficient conditioned reactions are due to an interplay between such individual factors as conditionability and autonomic lability, on the one hand, and environmental conditions on the other. There will be no socialization for an individual who cannot form conditioned responses at all, but conversely, there will be no socialization for a person growing up on a desert island, however powerful his conditioning mechanism may happen to be. In this paper I have no time to deal with differences in the conditioning forces of the environment, and their relation to such factors as social class, but they should certainly not be forgotten.

Many other testable deductions, apart from the differential conditionability of dysthymics and hysterics, follow from such a formulation. Some of these deductions can be tested in the laboratory, and examples have been given in my book, *Dynamics of Anxiety and Hysteria*.[2] But others can be tested clinically, and for the sake of an example I shall give just one of these. I have shown how psychopathic reactions originate because of the inability of the psychopath, due to his low level of conditionability, to acquire the proper socialized responses. But this failure is not absolute; he conditions much less quickly and strongly than others, but he does condition. Thus, where the normal person may need 50 pairings of the conditioned and the unconditioned stimulus and where the dysthymic may need 10, the psychopath may require 100. But presumably in due course the 100 pairings will be forthcoming, although probably much later in life than the 10 of the dysthymic or the 50 of the normal person, and then he will finally achieve a reasonable level of socialization. If this chain of reasoning is correct, it would lead us to expect that the diagnosis "psychopath" would by and large be confined to relatively young people, say under thirty years of age; after thirty the course of life should have brought forth the required 100 pairings and thus produced the needed amount of socialization. As far as I can ascertain, clinical psychiatric opinion is in agreement with this prediction.

How does our theory compare with the psychoanalytic one? In the formation of neurotic symptoms, Freud emphasizes the traumatic nature of the events leading up to the neurosis, as well as their roots in early childhood. Learning theory can accommodate with equal ease traumatic single-trial learning, for which there is good experimental evidence,[21] but it can also deal with repeated subtraumatic pain and fear responses which build up the conditioned reaction rather more gradually.[22] As regards the importance of childhood, the Freudian stress appears to be rather misplaced in allocating the origins of *all* neurosis to this period. It is possible that many neurotic symptoms find their origin in this period, but there is no reason at all to assume that neurotic symptoms cannot equally easily be generated at a later period provided conditions are arranged so as to favour their emergence.

The point, however, on which the theory here advocated breaks decisively with psychoanalytic thought of any description is in this. Freudian theory regards neurotic symptoms as adaptive mechanisms which are evidence of repression; they are "the visible upshot of unconscious causes."[23] Learning theory does not postulate any such "unconscious causes," but regards neurotic symptoms as simple learned habits; there is no neurosis underlying the symptom, but merely the symptom itself. *Get rid of the symptom and you have eliminated the neurosis.* This notion of purely symptomatic treatment is so alien to psychoanalysis that it may be considered the crucial part of the theory here proposed. I would like to explore its implications a little further later on.

From the point of view of learning theory, treatment is in essence a very simple process. In the case of surplus conditioned responses, treatment should consist in the extinction of these responses; in the case of deficient conditioned responses, treatment should consist in the building up of the missing stimulus-response connections. Yet this apparent simplicity should not mislead us into thinking that the treatment of neurotic disorders offers no further problems. It is often found in scientific research that the solution of the problems posed by applied science is as complex and difficult as is the solution of the problems posed by pure science; even after Faraday and Maxwell had successfully laid the foundations of modern theories of electricity it needed fifty years and the genius of Edison to make possible the actual application of these advances to the solution of practical problems. Similarly here: a solution in principle, even if correct, still needs much concentrated and high-powered research in the field of application before it can be used practically in the fields of cure, amelioration, and prophylaxis.

What are the methods of cure suggested by learning theory? I shall give two brief examples only, to illustrate certain principles; others have been given by G. Jones.[1] One method of extinguishing the neurotic response X to a given stimulus S is to condition another response R to S, provided that R and X are mutually incompatible. This method, called "reciprocal inhibition" by Wolpe,[24] harks back to Sherrington[25] of course, and may be illustrated by returning to our rat-phobic little boy. Essentially, what Watson had done was to condition a strong sympathetic reaction to the sight of the rat. If we could now succeed in establishing a strong parasympathetic reaction to the sight of the rat, this might succeed in overcoming and eliminating the sympathetic response. The practical difficulty arises that, to begin with at least, the already established conditioned response is of necessity stronger

than the to-be-conditioned parasympathetic response. To overcome this difficulty, we make use of the concept of stimulus gradient already mentioned. The rat close by produces a strong conditioned fear reaction; the rat way out in the distance produces a much weaker reaction. If we now feed the infant chocolate while the rat is being introduced in the far distance the strong parasympathetic response produced by the chocolate-munching extinguishes the weak sympathetic response produced by the rat. As the conditioned parasympathetic response grows in strength, so we can bring the rat nearer and nearer, until finally even close proximity does not produce sympathetic reactions. The sympathetic reaction has been extinguished; the phobia has been cured. This is in fact the method which was used experimentally to get rid of the experimentally induced fear,[26] and it has been used successfully by several workers in the field of child psychiatry. More recently Herzberg[27] in his system of active psychotherapy, and more particularly, Wolpe[24] in his psychotherapy by reciprocal inhibition, have shown that these principles can be applied with equal success to the severe neuroses of adult men and women—substituting other methods, of course, for the chocolate-munching, which is more effective with children than with adults.

As an example of the cure of deficient conditioned responses, let me merely mention *enuresis nocturna*, where clearly the usual conditioned response of waking to the conditioned stimulus of bladder extension has not been properly built up. A simple course of training, in which a bell rings loudly whenever the child begins to urinate, thus activating an electric circuit embedded in his bedclothes, soon establishes the previously missing connection, and the extremely impressive list of successes achieved with this method, as compared with the very modest success of psychotherapeutic methods, speaks strongly for the correctness of the theoretical point of view which gave rise to this conception.[28]

We thus have here, I would suggest, an alternative theory to the Freudian, a theory which claims to account for the facts at least as satisfactorily as does psychoanalysis, and which in addition puts forward quite specific suggestions about methods of treatment. I have called these methods "behaviour therapy" to contrast them with methods of psychotherapy.* This contrast of terms is meant to indicate two things. According to psychoanalytic doctrine, there is a psychological complex, situated in the unconscious mind, underlying all the manifest symptoms of neurotic disorder. Hence the necessity of therapy for the psyche. According to learning theory, we are dealing with unadaptive behaviour conditioned to certain classes of stimuli; no reference is made to any underlying disorders or complexes in the psyche. Following on this analysis, it is not surprising that psychoanalysts show a preoccupation with psychological methods involving mainly *speech*, while behaviour therapy concentrates on actual *behaviour* as most likely to lead to the extinction of the unadaptive conditioned responses. The two terms express rather concisely the opposing viewpoints of the two schools. [Table 1] is a tabulation of the most important differences between psychotherapy and behaviour therapy.

What kind of answer would we expect from the Freudians? I think their main points would be these. They would claim, in the first place, that conditioning therapy has frequently been tried, but with very poor results; aversion therapies of alcoholism are often mentioned in this connection. They would go on to say that even where symptomatic treatments of this kind are appar-

*The growth of the theoretical concepts and practical methods of treatment subsumed in the term "behaviour therapy" owes much to a large number of people. Apart from Pavlov and Hull, who originated the main tenets of modern learning theory, most credit is probably due to Watson, who was among the first to see the usefulness of the conditioned paradigm for the explanation of neurotic disorders; to Miller and Mowrer, who have done so much to bring together learning theory and abnormal human behaviour; to Spence, whose important contributions include the detailed analysis of the relation between anxiety and learning; and to Wolpe, who was the first to apply explicitly some of the laws of learning theory to the large-scale treatment of severe neurotics. If there is any novelty in my own treatment of these issues it lies primarily: (1) in the pulling together of numerous original contributions into a general theory and (2) in the introduction into this system of the concepts of neuroticism and extraversion-introversion as essential parameters in the description and prediction of behaviour. I would like to emphasize, however, that this contribution could not have been made had the groundwork not been well and truly laid by the writers quoted above and by many more, only some of whom are quoted in the bibliography.

ently successful, as in enuresis, the symptom is likely to return, or be supplanted by some other symptom, or by an increase in anxiety. Finally, they would claim that even if in some cases the therapies suggested might be successful, yet in the great majority of cases psychoanalysis would be the only method to produce lasting cures. Let me deal with these points one by one.

There is no doubt that conditioning treatment of alcoholism has often been tried, and that it has often failed. I have no wish to take refuge in a *tu quoque* argument by pointing out that alcoholism has been particularly difficult to treat by any method whatever, and that psychoanalytic methods also have been largely unsuccessful. I would rather point out that learning theory is an exact science, which has elaborated quite definite rules about the establishment of conditioned reflexes; it is only when these rules are properly applied by psychologists with knowledge and experience in this field that the question of success or failure arises. Thus it is quite elementary knowledge that the conditioned stimulus must precede the unconditioned stimulus if conditioning is to take place; backward conditioning, if it occurs at all, is at best very weak. Yet some workers in the field of alcoholism have used a method in which the unconditioned stimulus regularly preceded the conditioned stimulus; under these conditions learning theory would in fact predict the complete failure of the experiment actually reported! Again, the time relation between the application of the conditioned stimulus and the unconditioned stimulus is a very important one; it is controlled to very fine limits of hundredths of a sec. in psychological experimentation and it has been universally reported that conditioning in which any but the optimal time relation is chosen is relatively ineffective. Taking eye-blink conditioning as an example: it is found that a time interval of about ½ sec. is optimal and that with intervals of 2½ sec. no conditioning at all takes place.[29,30] No attention seems to have been paid to these points by most workers on alcoholism, who apply the conditioned and unconditioned stimuli in such a vague way that it is often impossible to find out what the actual time relations were. This lack of rigour makes it quite impossible to adduce these so-called experiments as evidence either in favour or against conditioning therapy.[31]

How about the return of symptoms? I have made a thorough search of the literature deal-

TABLE 1

Psychotherapy	Behaviour Therapy
1. Based on inconsistent theory never properly formulated in postulate form.	Based on consistent, properly formulated theory leading to testable deductions.
2. Derived from clinical observations made without necessary control observations or experiments.	Derived from experimental studies specifically designed to test basic theory and deductions made therefrom.
3. Considers symptoms the visible upshot of unconscious causes ("complexes").	Considers symptoms as unadaptive conditioned responses.
4. Regards symptoms as evidence of *repression*.	Regards symptoms as evidence of faulty learning.
5. Believes that symptomatology is determined by defence mechanisms.	Believes that symptomatology is determined by individual differences in conditionability and autonomic lability, as well as accidental environmental circumstances.
6. All treatment of neurotic disorders must be *historically* based.	All treatment of neurotic disorders is concerned with habits existing at *present;* their historical development is largely irrelevant.
7. Cures are achieved by handling the underlying (unconcious) dynamics, not by treating the symptom itself.	Cures are achieved by treating the symptom itself, i.e. by extinguishing unadaptive C.Rs and establishing desirable C.Rs.
8. Interpretation of symptoms, dreams, acts, etc. is an important element of treatment.	Interpretation, even if not completely subjective and erroneous, is irrelevant.
9. Symptomatic treatment leads to the elaboration of new symptoms.	Symptomatic treatment leads to permanent recovery provided autonomic as well as skeletal surplus C.Rs are extinguished.
10. Transference relations are essential for cures of neurotic disorders.	Personal relations are not essential for cures of neurotic disorder, although they may be useful in certain circumstances.

ing with behaviour therapy with this particular point in view. Many psychoanalytically trained therapists using these methods have been specially on the outlook for the return of symptoms, or the emergence of alternative ones; yet neither they nor any of the other practitioners have found anything of this kind to happen except in the most rare and unusual cases.[17] Enuresis, once cured by conditioning therapy, remains cured as a general rule; relapses occur, as indeed one would expect in terms of learning theory under certain circumstances, but they quickly yield to repeat treatment. So certain of success are the commercial operators of this method that they work on a "money back if unsuccessful" policy; their financial solvency is an adequate answer to the psychoanalytic claim. Nor would it be true that alternative symptoms emerge; quite the contrary happens. The disappearance of the very annoying symptom promotes

peace in the home, allays anxieties, and leads to an all-round improvement in character and behaviour. Similar results are reported in the case of major applications of behaviour therapy to adults suffering from severe neurotic disorders; abolition of the symptom does not leave behind some mysterious complex seeking outlet in alternative symptoms.[17] Once the symptom is removed, the patient is cured; when there are multiple symptoms, as there usually are, removal of one symptom facilitates removal of the others, and removal of all the symptoms completes the cure.[24]

There is one apparent exception to this rule which should be carefully noted because it may be responsible for some of the beliefs so widely held. Surplus conditioned reactions may themselves be divided into two kinds, autonomic and motor. Anxiety reactions are typical of the autonomic type of surplus conditioned reactions, whereas tics, compulsive movements, etc. are typical of motor conditioned reactions. What has been said about the complete disappearance of the symptom producing a complete disappearance of the neurosis is true only as far as the autonomic conditioned reactions are concerned. Motor reactions are frequently activated by their drive reducing properties *vis-à-vis* the historically earlier conditioned autonomic responses[17]; the extinction of the motor response without the simultaneous extinction of the conditioned autonomic response would only be a very partial cure and could not be recommended as being sufficient. As pointed out at the end of the previous paragraph, "removal of *all* the symptoms completes the cure," and clearly removal of the motor conditioned response by itself, without the removal of the autonomic conditioned response is only a very partial kind of treatment. Behaviour therapy requires the extinction of all nonadaptive conditioned responses complained of by the patient, or causally related to these symptoms.

But how frequently does this type of treatment result in cures? Again I have made a thorough search of the literature, with the following outcome. GP treatment, not making use of psychotherapy in any of its usual forms, results in a recovery of about two seriously ill neurotics out of three.[32] Eclectic psychotherapy results in a recovery of about two seriously ill neurotics out of three.[7] Psychotherapy by means of psychoanalysis fares slightly worse, but results are at a comparable level.[8] Results of behaviour therapy of seriously ill neurotics, as reported by Wolpe, are distinctly superior to this, over 90 per cent recovering.[24] This difference is highly significant statistically and it should be borne in mind that the number of sessions required by behaviour therapy is distinctly smaller than that required by psychotherapy, whether eclectic or psychoanalytic. (Wolpe reports an average of about 30 sittings for his cases.)

These results are encouraging, but of course, they must not be taken too seriously. Actuarial comparisons of this kind suffer severely from the difficulty of equating the seriousness of disorders treated by different practitioners, the equally obvious difficulty of arriving at an agreed scale for the measurement of "recovery," and the impossibility of excluding the myriad chance factors which may affect gross behaviour changes of the kind we are here considering. I would not like to be understood as saying that behaviour therapy has been *proved* superior to psychotherapy; nothing could be further from my intention. What I am claiming is simply that as far as they go—which is not very far—available *data* do not support in any sense the Freudian belief that behaviour therapy is doomed to failure, and that only psychoanalysis or some kindred type of treatment is adequate to relieve neurotic disorders. This Freudian belief is precisely this—a belief; it has no empirical or rational foundation. I have no wish to set up a counter-belief, equally unsupported, to the effect that psychotherapy is doomed to failure and that only behaviour therapy is adequate to relieve neurotic disorders. What I would like to suggest is simply that a good case can be made out, both on the theoretical and the empirical level, for the proposition that behaviour therapy is an effective, relatively quick, and probably lasting method of cure of some neurotic disorders. This case is so strong that clinical trials would appear to be in order now to establish the relative value of this method as compared with other available methods, such as psychoanalysis, or electroshock treatment. Even more important, I think the evidence would justify psychiatrists in experimenting with the method, or rather set of methods, involved, in order to come to some preliminary estimate of their efficiency. I have noted with some surprise that many psychotherapists have refused to use such methods as conditioning therapy in enuresis, not on empirical grounds, but on *a priori* grounds, claiming that such mechanical methods simply could not work, and disregarding the large body of evidence available. Even in long established sciences *a priori* considerations carry little weight; in such a young discipline as psychology they are quite out of place. Only actual use can show the value of one method of treatment as opposed to another.

There is one point I would like to emphasize. Freud developed his psychological theories on the basis of his study of neurotic disorders and their treatment. Behaviour therapy, on the contrary, began with the thorough experimental study of the laws of learning and conditioning in normal people and in animals; these well-established principles were then applied to neurotic disorders. It seems to me that this latter method is in principle superior to the former; scientific advance has nearly always taken the form of making fundamental discoveries and then applying these in practice, and I can see no valid reason why this process should be inverted in connection with neurosis. It may be objected that learning theorists are not always in agreement with each other[11] and that it is difficult to apply principles about which there is still so much argument. This is only very partially true; those points about which argument rages are usually of academic interest rather than of practical importance. Thus, reinforcement theorists and contiguity theorists have strong differences of view about the necessity of reinforcement during learning and different reinforcement theorists have different theories about the nature of reinforcement. Yet there would be general agreement in any particular case about the optimum methods of achieving a quick rate of conditioning, or extinction; these are questions of fact and it is only with the interpretation of some of these facts that disagreements arise. Even when the disputes about the corpuscular or wavular nature of light were at their height, there was sufficient common ground between contestants regarding the facts of the case to make possible the practical application of available knowledge; the same is true of learning theory. The 10 per cent which is in dispute should not blind us to the 90 per cent which is not—disagreements and disputes naturally attract more attention, but agreements on facts and principles are actually much more common. Greater familiarity with the large and rapidly growing literature will quickly substantiate this statement.[12]

It is sometimes said that the model offered here differs from the psychoanalytic model only in the terminology used and that in fact the two models are very similar. Such a statement would be both true and untrue. There undoubtedly are certain similarities, as Mowrer[17] and Miller and Dollard[33] have been at pains to point out. The motivating role of anxiety in the Freudian system is obviously very similar in conception to the drive-producing conditioned autonomic responses of learning theory, and the relief from anxiety produced by hysterical and obsessional symptoms in Freudian terminology is very similar to the conditioned drive-reducing properties of motor movements. Similarly, a case could be made out in favour of regarding the undersocialized, non-conditionable psychopathic individual as being Id-dominated, and the dysthymic, over-conditionable individual as being Super-Ego dominated. Many other similarities will occur to the reader in going

through these pages and indeed the writer would be the first to acknowledge the tremendous service that Freud has done in elucidating for the first time some of these dynamic relationships and in particular in stressing the motivating role of anxiety.

Nevertheless, there are two main reasons for not regarding the present formulation as simply an alternative differing from the psychoanalytic one only in the terminology used. In the first place, the formulation here given differs from the Freudian in several essential features, as can be seen most clearly by studying Table 1. Perhaps these differences are most apparent with respect to the deductions made from the two theories as to treatment. Psychoanalytic theory distrusts purely symptomatic treatment and insists on the removal of the underlying complexes. Behaviour theory on the other hand stresses the purely symptomatological side of treatment and is unconvinced of the very existence of "complexes." It might, of course, be suggested that there is some similarity between the Freudian "complex" and the "conditioned surplus autonomic reaction" posited by behaviour theory. That there is some similarity cannot be denied, but no one familar with psychoanalytic writings would agree that the Freudian complex was not in essence a very different conception from the conditioned autonomic response, both from the point of view of its origins, as well as from the point of view of the appropriate method of extinction.

This brings me to the second great difference between the two models. What the Freudian model lacks above all, is an intelligible objectively testable *modus operandi* which can be experimentally studied in the laboratory, which can be precisely quantified and which can then be subjected to the formulation of strict scientific laws. The stress on such a mechanism, namely that of conditioning, is the most noteworthy feature of the model here advocated. It is entirely due to the great body of research which has been done in connection with the elaboration of laws of modern learning theory, that we are enabled to make fairly precise deductions resulting in different methods of treatment for patients suffering from neurotic disorders and it is with respect to this feature of the model that the relevant case histories and accounts of treatment should be read.[34,35,36]

It has sometimes been suggested that the criticisms which I have levelled against the psychotherapeutic schools because of their failure to provide adequate control groups to validate their claims regarding the curative properties of their methods, could justifiably be levelled against the accounts given by those who have used behaviour therapy and reported upon the effects achieved. Such a criticism would not be justified for two reasons. In the first place, the cases quoted are *illustrative of methods,* not *proofs of psychotherapeutic efficacy;* the only case in which claims regarding the relative efficacy have been made contains a statistical comparison with the effects of psychoanalytic treatment of similar cases.[24] In the second place, the concept of "control" in scientific experiments is somewhat more than simply the provision of a control *group;* the control in an experiment may be *internal.* As an example, consider the experiment reported by Yates[36] on the extinction of 4 tics in a female patient by means of a rather novel and unusual method, namely that of repeated voluntary repetition of the tic by massed practice. Precise predictions were made as to the effects that should follow and these predictions were studied by using the fate of some of the tics as compared to the fate of other tics submitted to dissimilar treatment. Thus, practice for 2 tics might be discontinued for a fortnight, while practice on the other two would go on. By showing that the predictions made could thus be verified and the *rate of extinction* of the tics varied at will—in accordance with the experimental manipulation for such variables as massing of practice—a degree of control was achieved far superior to the simple assessment of significance produced in the comparison of two random groups submitted to different treatments. It is by its insistence on such experimental precision and the incorporation of experimental tests of the hypotheses employed, even during the treatment, that behaviour theory differs from psychotherapy.

There is one further method of pointing up the differences between the two theories and of deciding between them; I mention this matter with some hesitation because to many psychiatrists it seems almost sacrilegious to use animal experimentation in the consideration of human neurosis. However, Fenichel himself,[37] p. 19, has quoted "experimental neuroses" as support for the Freudian conception of neurotic disorders and it is with respect to these experiments that the contrast

between the psychoanalytic and our own model may be worked out most explicitly. Fenichel maintains that the model of psychoneurosis "is represented by the artificial neuroses that have been inflicted upon animals by experimental psychologists. Some stimulus which had represented pleasant instinctual experiences or which has served as a signal that some action would now procure gratification is suddenly connected by the experimenter with frustrating or threatening experiences, or the experimenter decreases the difference between stimuli which the animal had been trained to associate with instinct gratification and threat respectively; the animal then gets into a state of irritation which is very similar to that of a traumatic neurosis. He feels contradictory impulses; the conflict makes it impossible for him to give in to the impulses in the accustomed way; the discharge is blocked, and this decrease in discharge works in the same way as an increase in influx: it brings the organism into a state of tension and calls for emergency discharges.

"In psychoneuroses some impulses have been blocked; the consequence is a state of tension and eventually some 'emergency discharges.' These consist partly in unspecific restlessness and its elaborations and partly in much more specific phenomena which represent the distorted involuntary discharges of those very instinctual drives for which a normal discharge has been interdicted. Thus we have in psychoneuroses, first a defense of the ego against an instinct, then a conflict between the instinct striving for discharge and the defensive forces of the ego, then a state of damming up and finally the neurotic symptoms which are distorted discharges as a consequence of the state of damming up—a compromise between the opposing forces. The symptom is the only step in this development that becomes manifest; the conflict, its history, and the significance of the symptoms are unconscious."

Hebb[38] has laid down certain requirements for attempting to demonstrate that experimental neurosis occurs in animals and Broadhurst[39,40] has examined the literature, and particularly that referred to by Fenichel, from this point of view. Here is his summary. "How does the large body of American work stand up to such an assessment? For the purposes of a recent review,[40] the available literature was examined in the light of

Hebb's criteria. Noteworthy among this is the work of the group headed by Liddell,[41] one of the pioneers of conditioning methodology in the United States, who has used principally the sheep as his experimental subject; of Gantt,[42] whose long term study of the dog 'Nick' is well known; and of Masserman,[43] who has done extensive work using cats. This is not the place to enter into the details of this evaluation, which is reported elsewhere,[40] but the overall conclusion which was reached was that there are few instances in all this work of any cases of experimentally induced abnormalities of animal behaviour which meet all of Hebb's criteria. Let us take, for example, the work of Masserman, whose theoretical interpretation of abnormal behaviour need not concern us here except to note that it was the basis upon which he designed his experiments to produce 'conflict' between one drive and another. What he did was this. He trained hungry cats to respond to a sensory signal by opening a food box to obtain food. Then he subjected them to a noxious stimulus, a blast of air, or electric shock, just at the moment of feeding. The resulting changes in behaviour—the animals showed fear of the situation and of the experimenter, and refused to feed further—he identified as experimental neurosis. But the behaviour observed fails to fulfill more than one or two of Hebb's criteria and, moreover, certain deficiencies in the design of his experiments make it impossible to draw any satisfactory conclusions from them. Thus Wolpe[44] repeated part of Masserman's work using the essential control group which Masserman had omitted—that is, he gave the cats the noxious stimulus alone, without any 'conflict' between the fear motivation thus induced, and the hunger which, in Masserman's animals, operated as well—and found that the same behaviour occurred. It hardly needs to be said that a fear response to a threatening stimulus is not abnormal and cannot be regarded as an experimental neurosis."

It is clear from the studies cited that Fenichel is quite wrong in claiming that "experimental neurosis" is in any way analogous to the Freudian model of human neurosis. It appears, therefore, that insofar as these studies are relevant at all they can be regarded as demonstrating nothing but simple conditioned fear responses of the kind called for by our theory. It is perhaps worthy of note that the failure of psychoanalysis to use control groups in the human field has extended to their work with animals, as in the case of Masserman quoted above. Fenichel's easy acceptance of data congruent with his hypothesis is paralleled by his failure to mention data contrary to the psychoanalytic viewpoint. By taking into account all the data it seems more likely that a correct conclusion will be reached.

I would now like to return to some of the points which I raised at the beginning of this paper. I argued then, that the special knowledge and competence of psychologists in mental hospitals was largely wasted because of concentration on and preoccupation with Freudian theories and projective types of test. I would now like to make a more positive suggestion and maintain that by virtue of their training and experience psychologists are (or should be) experts in the fields of conditioning and learning theory, laboratory procedures and research design. In suitable cases, surely their help would be invaluable in diagnostic problems, such as ascertaining a given patient's speed of conditioning, in the theoretical problem of constructing a model of his personality dynamics and in the practical problem of designing a suitable course of behaviour therapy which would take into account all the available information about the case.* I am not suggesting that psychologists should themselves necessarily carry out this course of treatment; it would appear relatively immaterial whether the therapy is carried out by one person or another, by

*It will be clear that the function here sketched out for the psychologist demands that he be furnished with the necessary tools of his trade, such as soundproof rooms, conditioning apparatus and all the other techniques for delivering stimuli and measuring responses on a strictly quantified basis.[45] It is equally clear that such facilities do not exist in the majority of our mental hospitals. Until they do, the handicaps under which the clinical psychologists work at such institutions will be all but insurmountable, and no reasonable estimate of their potential usefulness can be formed. One might just as well employ an electroencephalographer and refuse to pay for the machine which he has been trained to use! It would be better to have a few, properly equipped departments than a large number of small, ill-equipped ones as at present. Even in the United States the position is bad; in this country it is worse. A relatively small capital investment would be likely to bear considerable fruit.

psychologist or psychiatrist. Both types of procedure have been experimented with and both have shown equally promising results. Indeed, certain aspects of the therapy can obviously be carried out by less senior and experienced personnel, provided the course of treatment is reviewed periodically by the person in charge. Psychoanalysis lays much stress on what is sometimes called "transference," a devil conjured up only to be sent back to his usual habitat with much expenditure of time and energy.[37] Behaviour therapy has no need of this adjunct, nor does it admit that the evidence for its existence is remotely adequate at the present time. However that may be, relinquishing the personal relationship supposed to be indispensable for the "transference" relation allows us to use relatively unqualified help in many of the more time-consuming and routine parts of behaviour therapy. In certain cases, of course, personal relationships may be required in order to provide a necessary step on the generalization gradient; but this is not always true.†

From a limited experience with this kind of work, carried out by various members of my department, I can with confidence say two things. The direct application of psychological theories to the practical problem of effecting a cure in a particular person, here and now, acts as a very powerful challenge to the psychologist concerned, and makes him more aware than almost anything else of the strengths and weaknesses of the formulations of modern learning theory. And the successful discharge of this self-chosen duty serves more than almost anything else to convince his psychiatric colleagues that psychology can successfully emerge from its academic retreat and take a hand in the day-to-day struggle with the hundred-and-one problems facing the psychiatrist. It seems to me that the tragic fratricidal struggle between psychiatrists and psychologists, which has so exacerbated relations between them in the United

†As an example of this we may quote a case reported by Graham White. This concerns a child who became anorexic after the death of her father. The therapist adopted the father's role in a variety of circumstances, ranging in order from play with dolls' teasets to the actual eating situation, and reinforcing those reactions which were considered desirable. The theoretical rationale was that the father had become a conditioned stimulus on which eating depended.

States, could easily be avoided here by recognizing the special competence of the psychologist in this particular corner of the field, while acknowledging the necessity of keeping the general medical care of the patient in the hands of the psychiatrist. I believe that most psychiatrists are too well aware of the precarious state of our knowledge in the field of neurotic disorders to do anything but welcome the help which the application of learning theory in the hands of a competent psychologist may be able to bring.

REFERENCES

1. Jones, H. G. (1958). Neurosis and experimental psychology. *J. Ment. Sci.*, *104*, 55–62.
2. Eysenck, H. J. (1957). *Dynamics of Anxiety and Hysteria*. Routledge & Kegan Paul, London.
3. Eysenck, H. J. (1947). *Dimensions of Personality*. Routledge & Kegan Paul, London.
4. Eysenck, H. J. (1952). *The Scientific Study of Personality*. Routledge & Kegan Paul, London.
5. Eysenck, H. J. (1953). *The Structure of Human Personality*. Methuen, London.
6. Glover, E. (1955). *The Technique of Psychoanalysis*. Bailliere, London.
7. Eysenck, H. J. (1952). The effects of psychotherapy: an evaluation. *J. Cons. Psychol.*, *16*. 319–324.
8. Eysenck, H. J. (1960). The effects of psychotherapy. In *Handbook of Abnormal Psychology*. Ed. by H. J. Eysenck. Pitman, London.
9. Eysenck, H. J. (1953). *Uses and Abuses of Psychology*. Pelican, London.
10. Eysenck, H. J. (1958). Personality tests: 1950–1955. In *Recent Progress in Psychiatry*. Ed. by G. W. T. W. Fleming, J. & A. Churchill, London.
11. Hilgard, G. A. (1956). *Theories of Learning*. Appleton-Century, New York.
12. Osgood, C. E. (1953). *Method and Theory in Experimental Psychology*. Oxford Univ. Press, London.
13. Shoben, E. J. (1949). Psychotherapy as a problem in learning theory. *Psychol. Bull.*, *46*, 366–392.
14. Watson, J. B., and Rayner, R. (1920). Conditioned emotional reaction. *J. Exp. Psychol.*, *3*, 1–4.
15. Pavlov, I. P. (1927). *Conditioned Reflexes*. Oxford Univ. Press, London.

16. Spence, K. G., Haggard, P. F., and Ross, L. G. (1958). UCS intensity and the associated (habit) strength of the eyelid CR. *J. Exp. Psychol.*, 95, 404−411.

17. Mowrer, O. H. (1950). *Learning Theory and Personality Dynamics.* Ronald Press, New York.

18. Miller, V. G. (1951). Learnable drives and rewards. *Handbook of Experimental Psychology.* Ed. by S. S. Spencer. Wiley, New York.

19. Eysenck, H. J. (1954). Zur Theorie der Personlichkeitsmessung. *Z. Diag. Psychol. Personlichkeitsforsch.*, 2, 87−101, 171−187.

20. Eysenck, H. J. (1957). Los principios del condicionamiento y la teorias de la personalidad. *Riv. Psicol.*, 12, 655−667.

21. Hudson, B. B. (1950). One-trial learning in the domestic rat. *Genet. Psychol. Monogr., 41,* 94−146.

22. Solomon, R. L., Kamin, L. J., and Wynne, L. C. (1953). Traumatic avoidance learning. *J. Abnorm. (Soc.) Psychol.*, 48, 291−302.

23. Munroe, R. L. (1955). *Schools of Psychoanalytic Thought.* Dryden Press, New York.

24. Wolpe, J. (1958). *Psychotherapy by Reciprocal Inhibition.* Stanford Univ. Press.

25. Sherrington, C. S. (1926). *The Integrative Action of the Central Nervous System.* Oxford Univ. Press, London.

26. Jersild, A. T., and Holmes, F. B. (1935). Methods of overcoming children's fears. *J. Psychol.*, 1, 25−83.

27. Herzberg, A. (1941). Short treatment of neuroses by graduated tasks. *Brit. J. Med. Psychol.*, 19, 36−51.

28. Mowrer, O. H., and Morer, W. A. (1938). Enuresis. A method for its study and treatment. *Amer. J. Orthopsychiat.*, 8, 436−447.

29. McAllister, W. R. (1953). Eyelid conditioning as a function of the CS-UCS interval. *J. Exp. Psychol.*, 45, 412−422.

30. McAllister, W. R. (1953). The effect on eyelid conditioning of shifting the CS-UCS interval. *J. Exp. Psychol.*, 45, 423−428.

31. Frank, C. M. (1958). Alcohol, alcoholics and conditioning: a review of the literature and some theoretical considerations. *J. Ment. Sci., 104,* 14−33.

32. Denker, P. G. (1946). Results of treatment of psychoneuroses by the general practitioner. A follow-up study of 500 cases. *N.Y. State J. Med., 46,* 2164−2166.

33. Dollard, J., and Miller, V. G. (1950). *Personality and Psychotherapy.* McGraw-Hill. New York.

34. Jones, H. G. (1956). The application of conditioning and learning techniques to the treatment of a psychiatric patient. *J. Abnorm. (Soc.) Psychol., 52,* 414−420.

35. Meyer, V. (1957). The treatment of two phobic patients on the basis of learning principles. *J. Abnorm. (Soc.) Psychol., 55,* 261−266.

36. Yates, A. (1958). The application of learning theory to the treatment of tics. *J. Abnorm. (Soc.) Psychol., 56,* 175−182.

37. Fenichel, O. (1945). *The Psychoanalytic Theory of Neurosis.* Kegan Paul, London.

38. Hebb, D. O. (1947). Spontaneous neurosis in chimpanzees: theoretical relations with clinical and experimental phenomena. *Psychosom. Med., 9,* 3−16.

39. Broadhurst, P. L. (1958). The contribution of animal psychology to the concept of psychological normality-abnormality. *Proc. XII Internat. Congr. Appl. Psychol.*

40. Broadhurst, P. L. (1960). Abnormal animal behaviour. In *Handbook of Abnormal Psychology.* Ed. by H. J. Eysenck. Pitman, London.

41. Anderson, O. P., and Parmenter, A. (1941). A long-term study of the experimental neurosis in the sheep and dog. *Psychosom. Med. Monogr., 2,* Nos. 3 and 4, 1−150.

42. Gantt, W. H. (1944). Experimental basis for neurotic behaviour. *Psychosom. Med. Monogr., 3,* 1−211.

43. Masserman, J. K. (1943). *Behavior and Neurosis.* Univ. Press, Chicago.

44. Wolpe, J. (1952). Experimental neurosis as learned behaviour. *Brit. J. Psychol., 43,* 243−268.

45. Eysenck, H. J. (1955). *Psychology and the Foundation of Psychiatry.* H. K. Lewis, London.

46. Estes, W. K. *et al* (1954). *Modern Learning Theory.* Appleton-Century, New York.

47. Hilgard, E. A., and Marquis, D. G. (1940). *Conditioning and Learning.* Appleton-Century. New York.

42 Behavioral Psychotherapy: Theory and Practice

Isaac M. Marks

The principles of behavioral psychotherapy reach back over the centuries. The ideas that govern the behavioral treatment of anxiety were enunciated clearly in the 1650s by John Locke. He recommended that if "your child shrieks and runs away at the sight of a frog, let another catch it, and lay it down at a good distance from him: at first accustom him to look upon it; when he can do that to come nearer to it, and see it leap without emotion; then to touch it lightly, when it is held fast in another's hand; and so on until he can come to handle it as confidently as a butterfly or a sparrow" (1, pp. 481–482). Today this principle is called exposure in vivo, and we could thus say that behavioral theory is Lockean in origin. It could also be said to be Freudian if one goes by Freud's comment in 1919: "One can hardly master a phobia if one waits till the patient lets the analysis influence him to give it up . . . one succeeds only when one can induce them by the influence of the analysis to . . . go [about alone] . . . and to struggle with their anxiety while they make the attempt" (2, pp. 165–166).

Another behavioral principle, that of satiation, is described in Shakespeare's opening lines of *Twelfth Night:* "If music be the food of love, play on; . . . that, surfeiting, the appetite may sicken, and so die." The concept of contingent reward dates back to the first parent who gave his child a candy or a kiss for good behavior.

The fact that the principles of behavioral treatment have been around so widely for so long indicates that they are rooted in common sense, which is as old as the human species. What, then, is new? The answer is that these commonsense principles have been welded together over the past two decades into a potent therapeutic technology that can now relieve several formerly untreatable conditions and holds promise for further advances. This development hinges on combining an experimental and a clinical approach. It enables treatment to be tested and refined so that redundant elements are gradually eliminated

From *Amer. J. Psychiat.*, 133, 253–261, 1976, by permission of the American Psychiatric Association.

while effective ingredients are retained and extended.

This pragmatic approach reminds one of a legendary South African millionaire who was confronted with some awkward facts about his policies at an annual meeting of the board of his company. He faced his inquisitors squarely, thumped his fist on the table, and declared, "Gentlemen, those are my principles, and if you don't like them, I have many more."

Critics might call this theoretical promiscuity or gutless eclecticism. Progress, however, depends on keeping track of the main question facing clinicians: "What methods of treatment produce reliable improvements in problem X, and what principles govern such successful methods?" In short, what works and why? Advances can be rapid if we keep this question in mind and maintain a willingness to submit our ideas to experimental destruction. Inert therapeutic practices can thus be discarded and more potent methods introduced.

It is true that the behavioral field, like any other, has had its fill of dogmas. There has been no shortage of all-explanatory schools, each trimming the richness of clinical experience to its own Procrustean formula in the name of ideological purity. But the clash of rival parties becomes more muted as the area of tested knowledge expands. Behavioral treatment is beginning to take its place as one of several forms of psychotherapy available to the clinician for the relief of psychiatric suffering. Behavioral psychotherapy is not a panacea or an all-embracing theory or method. Like psychopharmacology, it is a therapeutic technology that can aid general clinical management and has its indications and contraindications.

Indications for Behavioral Psychotherapy

There is no danger of a takeover bid by behaviorists for the whole of psychiatric practice. At the present time behavioral psychotherapy can help perhaps 10% of all *adult* psychiatric patients when used as the chief instrument of change. This means that 90% of all adult cases require other approaches as the main form of treatment. Behavioral psychotherapy is probably the *approach of choice* in phobic disorders, including social anxieties, and in obsessive-compulsive rituals. It is also helpful in sexual dysfunctions such as impotence and frigidity and in sexual deviations such as exhibitionism. In these areas behavioral methods have been found to be more useful than contrasting approaches.

In other adult disorders behavioral psychotherapy may be useful, but more controlled data about efficacy are needed. Examples include obsessive thoughts (as opposed to rituals); deficits and problems in social skills; disorders of habit or of impulse control such as stammering, hair pulling, self-mutilation, and compulsive gambling; appetitive disorders including obesity and anorexia; conversion hysteria; and some personality disorders. An operant approach can be helpful for the social rehabilitation of persons with certain chronic disorders such as schizophrenia and personality and organic deficits. In such cases the behavioral approach can be a worthwhile adjuvant to other treatment methods.

In several important adult disorders behavioral psychotherapy is *not of value*. Examples are acute schizophrenia, severe depression, and hypomania. This approach is also not useful in adult neurotic patients for whom clearly definable goals cannot be worked out.

In children behavioral psychotherapy might be the treatment of choice for nocturnal enuresis and phobias. It is also helpful for the educational rehabilitation of children with subnormal intelligence or learning problems. It has also been useful in institutional settings for the rehabilitation of delinquents, although backup facilities are a problem. Anecdotal reports suggest that behavioral therapies are sometimes useful in treating conduct disorders in children.

Until recently much of the evidence for behavioral psychotherapy fell far short of the ideal, i.e., controlled studies of groups of patients with clearly definable characteristics who were treated by either a behavioral or a contrasting method. Data were originally based primarily on uncontrolled case histories or on controlled trials of volunteers (3, 4), who may differ from patients in important ways. However, an increasing number of controlled trials of clinical patients is beginning to support the value of some behavioral methods.

Behavioral approaches are being applied increasingly not only for the relief of psychopathology, but also in educational, social, and other nonclinical settings. At certain points interventions with patients can be said to lie more in the domain of the educationalist and social psychologist than that of the clinician. However, this report is concerned only with behavioral psychotherapy in the field of clinical psychiatry and will not go into wider areas of behavior change.

Principal Forms of Behavioral Psychotherapy

Behavioral methods assume diverse forms, some which bear little resemblance to one another. A cynic might argue that those methods which are found to be effective tend to be called behavioral and those which are not are disowned and given some other name. Often the same technique is practiced by adherents of different schools. A case in point comes from Viktor Frankl (5, 6), who attributed his ideas to existentialist logotherapy. In the treatment of an obsessive-compulsive ritualizer he described how he demonstrated to the patient that he could dirty his own hands by touching the floor and refrain from washing thereafter; then he asked the patient to imitate the same action. Behaviorists might call this modeling with exposure in vivo and response prevention. But we need not quibble about theoretical pedigrees. It is more important to describe our methods so that others can test and use them in a similar way.

Behavioral treatments can be administered to patients individually or in groups, depending on what is practical and desirable in a given case. Behavioral treatments can be arbitrarily divided into those which 1) reduce anxiety-linked behavior (e.g., phobias or compulsive rituals), 2) reduce appetitive behaviors (e.g., exhibitionism or obesity), and 3) develop new behavior (e.g., teaching social skills to the socially incompetent).

Anxiety reduction is usually effected by some variant of exposure treatment such as desensitization or flooding; self-regulation and modeling can also be useful. Appetitive behavior can be reduced by self-regulation, satiation, and aversive methods such as covert sensitization. In covert sensitization, for example, an exhibitionist might be asked to imagine exposing his genitals to a pretty young girl in the street and then to imagine a policeman at his side arresting him. The fantasy of the policeman acts as an aversive stimulus. Equally, the exhibitionist could be asked to wear an elastic band on his wrist wherever he went, and when he felt an urge to expose himself, simply to snap the elastic band sharply against his wrist, repeatedly if necessary, until the temptation disappeared. This can be construed as a form of self-regulation as well as aversion. It could also be called thought-stopping. One patient I saw had morbidly jealous thoughts about his wife. After a few trials with the elastic band, he found it sufficient simply to stare at the band on his wrist and imagine the sensation of a sting on his wrist without actually snapping the band. Anticipation of the sting dispelled the jealous thoughts. He remained well at 6 months' follow-up after only 3 sessions of treatment.

These examples illustrate how the same technique can be described and used in several different ways. The elastic band can be an aversive stimulus, a thought-stopper, a self-regulator, or a response-disruptor.

A variety of methods is employed for the development of new behavior, including social skills training, educational programs, modeling, shaping, prompting, pacing, fading, self-regulation, contracting, and contingent reward. In social skills groups there is a great deal of overlap with techniques also found in psychodrama and encounter groups, e.g., warm-up games, role rehearsal, role reversal, and doubling. The same can occur in groups for family and marital therapy. These approaches are strictly behavioral only to the extent that they are directive and involve clearly specified goals of treatment and measurements of change.

General Issues

Certain general principles run across the arbitrary subdivision of behavioral methods. *Clear delineation of treatment goals* is essential. Often these are called target problems. If the behaviors to be changed by the end of successful treatment cannot be identified, then the patient is untreatable by behavioral means. Clear targets need to be set toward which treatment is directed. "Self-actualization" would be too vague to be a suitable target; so would "increased self-confidence." Examples of clear

targets are "being able to ask a girl for a date without trembling" and "being able to shop in a crowded supermarket." Several targets are commonly needed for each patient. Targets must be specific and useful for a patient in terms of his life handicap.

Cooperation of the Patient

Behavioral treatment can only be given to adult neurotics if they are cooperative; successful treatment cannot be forced on patients against their will. Treatment often involves the patient in detailed, complex programs that require his daily cooperation for completion.

Family Involvement

Significant family members must participate in therapy when the patient's psychopathology is hindering family functioning. Treatment often needs to be continued away from the psychiatrist's office in the natural setting of the problem, which frequently includes the patient's home. Patients with social phobias may need to accompany a behavioral psychotherapist into a crowded restaurant and have a meal with him several times in order to overcome their anxiety. A compulsive handwasher may need to visit her home with her therapist and jointly contaminate the home with "dirty" material and refrain from washing thereafter. These unconventional roles may require some relearning experiences by therapists.

Backup Facilities in the Community

Backup facilities in the community are often required. Patients may need to be discharged to a residential treatment facility or other accommodation where treatment and supervision can gradually be "faded out." When the patient lives far from the treatment center, local personnel may be essential to provide necessary follow-up treatment after discharge.

Homework by the Patient Between Sessions

Another important issue concerns homework assignments and practice in self-regulation. Patients may be given set tasks to perform between sessions, and, indeed, the sessions may be contingent upon patients completing their homework first; e.g., a person with a social phobia may need to take his girlfriend out to a restaurant three times between two given sessions. Self-regulation may take the form of keeping a diary, monitoring and rating one's anxiety in phobic situations, practicing deep-breathing exercises during them, and learning to remain in the same spot until the anxiety has abated, which might take an hour or more.

It is usual practice to combine more than one therapeutic principle in the treatment of a given patient, as the occasion demands. The following example illustrates this.

Case 1. Jill was an 18-year-old girl with borderline intelligence and mild cerebral palsy. She had complicating chronic agoraphobia, compulsive handwashing, and frequent temper tantrums at home. The nurse-therapist treated Jill by first escorting her on walks outside the outpatient department for increasingly long distances, fading himself out of the situation, and persuading Jill to do the same exercises herself both during the session and at home between sessions. Between sessions Jill was asked to undertake increasingly long bus trips and to enter her achievements in a diary. The agoraphobia rapidly improved.

At the beginning the nurse-therapist had told Jill and her mother that he would leave the compulsive rituals for treatment at a later date when the agoraphobia had improved. The mother inquired about the nature of that treatment, and the nurse-therapist explained the principles of exposure in vivo. By the time the agoraphobia had improved, the mother reported that she had spontaneously carried out the expo-

sure in vivo treatment of her daughter's compulsions. She contaminated the house with dreaded material and asked Jill to do the same and refrain from washing thereafter. The patient's ritualistic behavior ceased when the mother acted as a cotherapist without the therapist's assistance.

The temper tantrums were dealt with by family contracting. The therapist jointly interviewed Jill, her mother, and her father and arranged an exchange of contracts whereby the parents agreed to lavishly praise their daughter for such behavior as helping at mealtimes to set and clear the table and wash the dishes. Jill promised to carry out such activities and not to engage in temper tantrums. Soon the temper tantrums ceased and the parents rewarded their daughter more often. At one-year follow-up Jill's improvement in her phobias, rituals, and temper tantrums continued and she was attending a special training course to develop work skills.

An Operational Framework for Therapeutic Influences

The many influences that bear on treatment can be viewed within a dual-process operational framework (see figure 1). First, a patient needs to be *motivated* to seek and complete treatment. Many influences will affect this process, including the patient's own commitment to change, social pressure on him to improve, that vague element called suggestion, and the credibility of the therapist. Of several hundred patients in my unit who were offered behavioral treatment, 23% refused it. This refusal rate is similar to

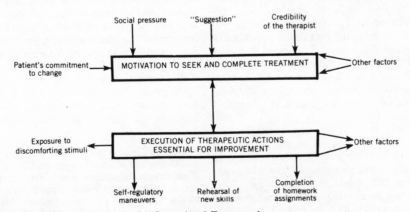

FIGURE 1 Therapeutic Influences: An Operational Framework

that with many other treatments. In such cases treatment fails at the motivational stage because the patient fails to swallow his psychological pill, so to speak. Most behavioral treatments are, in fact, readily acceptable to patients.

The second process involves the patient's *execution* of therapeutic actions essential for improvement, e.g., a few hours' exposure to a phobic stimulus or a complicated set of interactions with other people in a social training program. When execution of these actions is satisfactory, the failure rate is very low in phobic and obsessive-compulsive patients.

Approach to Phobic and Obsessive-Compulsive Disorders

Let us examine the principles and results of behavioral psychotherapy in two extensively studied syndromes—phobic disorders and compulsive rituals. Most behavioral approaches to their treatment employ a common principle called *exposure*. The concept of exposure holds that relief from phobias and compulsions comes from the individual's continued contact with the situations that evoke his discomfort. Clinicians need to search for those cues which trigger phobias and rituals and to confront the patient, given his agreement, with these cues. The principle of exposure does not explain why improvement occurs under these conditions.

Several controlled trials with phobic and obsessive-compulsive patients have shown that exposure treatments produce significant improvement in phobias or compulsions up to the latest 2- to 4-year follow-ups that are available. These results can be obtained with real-life exposure after 1 to 30 sessions. The last 100 patients treated in my unit required a mean of 11 treatment sessions. The more complex problems with wider ramifications require longer treatment. Chronicity of illness, however, is not important; even long-standing problems can be relieved in a few hours of treatment.

An early form of exposure treatment was Wolpe's (7) desensitization in fantasy, in which the patient is relaxed and asked to repeatedly imagine himself gradually approaching the object that causes him fear. Phobic images are visualized only for a few seconds at a time, and the subject is asked to relax between images. In an early series of

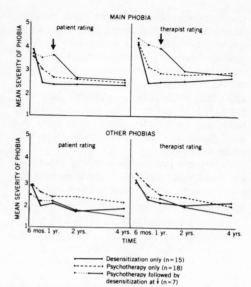

FIGURE 2 Improvement in Phobic Patients with Desensitization and Psychotherapy*

trials by Gelder, Marks, and Wolff (8–10), desensitization in fantasy reduced phobias more than dynamic psychotherapy (see figure 2). Patients who did not improve with psychotherapy were given desensitization in fantasy, which reduced their phobias. The superiority of desensitization was gradually eroded as other patients similarly improved over the years, but subjects receiving desensitization improved earlier and with less treatment and maintained their improvement at 4-year follow-up (11) (see figure 2).

These results were replicated by Gillan and Rachman (12) in a similar group of phobic patients. They found that desensitization in fantasy was superior to dynamic psychotherapy for the relief of phobias and that improvement continued to 3 months' follow-up. The amount of improvement with each treatment was comparable to that obtained in the earlier investigation.

More recently, emphasis has been on exposure in vivo. This gives quicker results by bringing the patient into contact with his

*Based on material from Gelder and associates (8) and Gelder and Marks (9). Reprinted by permission from "Phobic Disorders Four Years After Treatment: A Prospective Follow-Up," by I.M. Marks, *British Journal of Psychiatry*, volume 118, pages 683–688. Copyright 1971, the Royal College of Psychiatrists.

discomforting situation without the relaxation exercises. A partially controlled experiment (13) showed that exposure in vivo improved obsessive-compulsive rituals significantly more than did relaxation treatment (see figure 3). In a subexperiment, patients who had exposure in vivo without preceding relaxation did just as well as those whose exposure followed relaxation. Improvement with exposure in vivo thus occurred whether it was given as the first or second treatment block (14). Improvement continued to 2-year follow-up (see figure 3).

Exposure Treatment

Varieties

Exposure treatments come in many forms. To illustrate these, let the reader imagine a man with a height phobia quivering at the foot of a 20-foot ladder. His aim is to climb to the top of the ladder to retrieve a book titled *How To Overcome Your Fear of Heights*. In this therapy many options are open. We can ask him to close his eyes, relax, and imagine himself slowly putting his foot on the first rung of the ladder and then relaxing again, and to imagine this several times until that

inspires no anxiety, after which he can imagine himself on the second rung of the ladder, etc. That is *desensitization in fantasy.* If we asked the patient to carry out the same maneuvers in real life rather than in fantasy, that would be *desensitization in vivo.*

An alternative strategy would be to ask the patient to close his eyes and imagine himself standing right at the top of the ladder looking down, swaying, and feeling dizzy and scared at the same time, and to continue to imagine this until he feels better. This is *implosion* or *flooding in fantasy.* The *real-life flooding* variant would be (with his permission) to grab him by the scruff of his neck and thrust him to the top of the ladder and keep him there, sweating out his fear, until he becomes used to the situation. If for any of these procedures we first demonstrate to the patient what to do, e.g., if we precede him up the ladder, we would call this *modeling.* If we praise the patient each time he takes a step up the ladder this is *operant conditioning* or *shaping.* If we ask the patient to close his eyes and imagine himself persuading another patient with a height phobia that it is good for him to go up the ladder, this would be *cognitive rehearsal.* If the patient is asked to say to himself, "This is not so bad, I can really tolerate this fear"— that is *self-regulation.*

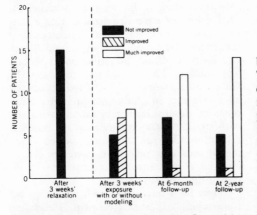

FIGURE 3 Improvement in Obsessive-Compulsive Patients with Exposure in Vivo and Relaxation*

*Reprinted by permission from "Treatment of Chronic Obsessive-Compulsive Neurosis by *in-vivo* Exposure: A Two-Year Follow-Up and Issues in Treatment," by I.M. Marks and associates, *British Journal of Psychiatry*, volume 127, pages 349–364, 1975. Copyright 1975, the Royal College of Psychiatrists.

The Exposure Principle

These and many other techniques are called by a bewildering array of confusing terms. There is a natural tendency to seek a single explanatory principle behind diverse treatments, although reality is usually more complex than our constructs. A therapeutic element more pervasive than most in all the methods described for getting the height phobic up the ladder is that of exposure to a noxious stimulus until he becomes used to it. Alternative terms for "becomes used to it" are habituates, extinguishes, or adapts, each of these terms having overlapping implications. The noxious stimulus may be a troublesome fantasy, a feeling of uncertainty about the future, an airplane flight, or sexual intercourse. It is not my brief to discuss how such stimuli come to be perceived as noxious in the first place. However, once situations repeatedly produce discomfort, as in phobias and obsessions, then sufferers usually lose this discomfort by agreeing to remain exposed to those situations until they feel better about them.

Exposure is a similar concept to extinction. "Extinction" simply means that the response ceases to occur, without explaining why. Similarly, the concept of exposure simply holds that given enough contact with the provoking situation, the phobic or obsessive person ceases to respond with avoidance, distress, or rituals. Patients rarely become sensitized to a situation through clinical exposure. Unfortunately, we do not know what causes such sensitization, a reaction that has important theoretical implications. The problem is why 3% fail to improve at all, rather than a problem of relapse, which is a different but not a serious issue. The question is why exposure to a trauma sometimes produces phobias and at other times cures them. Which sets of conditions predict a traumatic or a curative outcome must still be delineated, but systematic research has begun to chart some dimensions of this problem.

Low Anxiety

Wolpe has suggested that relaxation or other procedures are necessary to "reciprocally inhibit" anxiety during contact with the phobic stimulus, in order that improvement can follow. Many experimenters since then have found that the outcome to desensitization in fantasy is not impaired by omitting relaxation; the evidence points strongly to relaxation's being a redundant element in the therapeutic package (4). An example of an experiment that disconfirms the idea of reciprocal inhibition comes from Benjamin and associates' work (15) with chronic phobic patients. In a controlled study these patients imagined phobic images up a hierarchy while they were either relaxed or in a neutral affective state. The hypothesis of reciprocal inhibition predicts that relaxed subjects will show less anxiety to phobic images during treatment and have a superior outcome in reduction of fear.

The experimental manipulation was successful in producing two significantly differentiable treatment conditions. During treatment sessions relaxed patients had significantly less skin conductance activity between phobic images than did patients who had not been relaxed, i.e., they were less aroused. However, contrary to prediction from our reciprocal inhibition model, arousal between images during treatment did not correlate with decreased anxiety either during or after

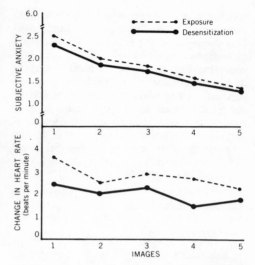

FIGURE 4 Change in Heart Rate and Subjective Anxiety With Successive Presentations of Images During Desensitization in Fantasy With and Without Relaxation*

treatment. Relaxation did not increase the speed with which patients lost their fears during sessions and did not increase the extent of improvement at the end of treatment. During sessions, subjective anxiety and heart rate diminished at the same rate whether the phobic images were visualized during a state of relaxation (desensitization) or neutral affect (exposure) (see figure 4). After the end of each treatment condition the reduction in phobias was similar. This result was replicated by Gillan and Rachman (12), who found comparable outcomes in phobic patients after treatment by desensitization in fantasy with and without accompanying training in muscular relaxation. One can thus conclude that training in muscular relaxation exercises can be omitted from exposure treatment without impairing results.

Thus far I have dealt with relaxation accompanying exposure treatment. Relaxation without exposure is also not helpful. Rachman and associates (13, 14) found that compulsive rituals did not improve after 15 sessions with muscular relaxation but were reduced significantly after 15 sessions of exposure in vivo (see figure 3). These findings were subsequently replicated in a study by Roper and associates (16). In fact, relaxation is such an inert factor in the treatment of phobias, compulsions, and even sexual deviations that it can safely be used as a control to contrast with more active treatments under investigation (17).

High Anxiety

A view opposite to that of reciprocal inhibition is the notion of implosion (18). The concept of implosion holds that for improvement to occur, anxiety must be maximally aroused during exposure until the patient is so exhausted that he cannot experience any more emotion. The evidence for this concept is based on uncontrolled clinical experience and can be paraphrased from Stampfl's comment about one obsessive-compulsive handwasher: "He who has lived in a cesspool for a few days [in his mind] will not worry later about a bit of dirt on his hands" (18).

The question is whether the deliberate evocation of anxiety adds to the therapeutic effect of exposure. Mathews and associates (19) found that high anxiety yielded no better results than low anxiety during fantasy exposure with phobics.

Whether high arousal facilitates in vivo exposure was tested by Hafner and Marks (20). Chronic agoraphobic patients were exposed continuously for 3 hours a day over 4 days to their real phobic situations, e.g., they were asked to shop in crowded supermarkets or to ride in subway trains until they felt better about being in these situations. In a high-anxiety condition the therapist commented on how bad the patients looked and mentioned all the catastrophes that might befall them in these situations. In a low-anxiety condition the therapist was reassuring, although he could not eliminate all anxiety. The experimental manipulation produced two significantly differentiable treatment conditions, with patients experiencing significantly more discomfort during exposure in the high-anxiety condition. However, this produced no difference in outcome on any measure. Low-anxiety patients improved at the same speed and to the same extent as high-anxiety patients. Thus anxiety did not facilitate improvement during exposure.

Further evidence that higher arousal is not especially helpful comes from a second controlled experiment by Hafner and Marks (20). In a double-blind study chronic agoraphobics were exposed as groups to their real phobic situations. Two groups of patients receiving diazepam reported less discomfort during exposure than patients receiving placebo, and they improved at the same rate as the placebo patients. Results from these studies of phobics are in line with findings from 3 earlier experiments that anxiety during exposure does not predict subsequent outcome in phobic patients (21–23).

In summary, phobias and obsessions improve with exposure treatment, but it does not matter whether patients are relaxed, neutral, or anxious during such exposure.

A more important variable is *duration of exposure*. In a Latin-square design, Stern and Marks (23) exposed chronic agoraphobics to flooding for long or short periods in fantasy and in vivo. Exposure in vivo gave significantly better results when carried out for 2 continuous hours rather than for 4 interrupted half-hour periods in one afternoon. Long, continuous exposure was more effective in reducing hear rate during treatment sessions and in decreasing phobias at the end of treatment. Boulougouris and Rabavilas (24) replicated these results in obsessive-compulsive patients.

These experiments involved chronic patients, and the optimum time of exposure might well be less for those whose phobias are of more recent duration. Duration of exposure is presumably important because it gives certain unidentified processes more time to work while exposure is going on. For example, it might give people time to develop self-regulatory strategies to control their own emotions or to reach critical levels of habituation that may be necessary for lasting change to occur. The latter is implied in the question, "Is it best to end on a good note?" We have no answer as yet.

Fantasy versus in Vivo Exposure

Another important variable is whether exposure is to the real or merely the fantasied situation. Recent studies of volunteer phobics (4), agoraphobic patients (4), and obsessive-compulsives (24) have shown that phobias and rituals are reduced more efficiently by in vivo exposure. However, another study (25) failed to confirm this finding. The optimal strategy is probably to opt for in vivo exposure, using fantasy exposure only in special situations such as an unobtainable real phobic situation or a physical danger contraindicating marked anxiety, e.g., angina or severe asthma.

I have shown that what at first sight seem to be widely different forms of fear reduction—e.g., desensitization in fantasy, flooding in vivo, cognitive rehearsal, modeling, and operant conditioning—can all be subsumed under the rubric of exposure. The different names simply describe variations on the theme of exposure. The current treatment of choice for obsessive-compulsive and phobic disorders seems to be prolonged in vivo exposure of the patient to the noxious stimulus (with his consent). Response prevention may be yet another example of a treatment that finally works through exposure. In compulsive ritualizers, active prevention of the ritualistic behavior during exposure may be unnecessary except as a way of prolonging exposure, an idea supported in a pilot experiment by Lipsedge (26).

The principle of exposure to the stressful situation is important not only for phobias and obsessions but also for social deficits and sexual problems, although here it is bound up with training in interpersonal and other skills. In social skills training and in sexual retraining programs, of which Masters and Johnson pioneered one form, patients are required to rehearse appropriate behavior repeatedly in their problem situations until they lose their discomfort and acquire the requisite fluency of performance. In a controlled study of sexually dysfunctional patients, Mathews and Bancroft (27) found that one therapist was not significantly less therapeutic for a couple than a dual sex therapist team.

Shortcomings of the Exposure Model

The exposure hypothesis of fear reduction leaves several important facts unexplained:

1. A small minority of patients do not habituate during exposure despite their fulfillment of all criteria for predicted success, i.e., adequate motivation, absence of serious depression, no attempts to escape in fantasy or reality during exposure, and adequate duration of treatment. This is not a problem of relapse after improvement but rather the failure of any improvement at all. In these patients some crucial unknown factor for success is missing.

2. Some phobic, obsessive-compulsive, and other forms of anxiety improve with antidepressant drugs, without the need for any exposure.

3. Without any exposure to the specific phobic stimulus, anxiety sometimes remits after the abreaction of intense emotion, e.g., fear that is irrelevant to the phobic stimulus (22), anger (28), or other feelings.

A tempting explanation for the value of irrelevant fear might be that it teaches the patient a form of coping. This is a widening of the exposure hypothesis. It states that the patient benefits from exposure to irrelevant fear as he would to unpleasant emotions in general. This notion leads into muddy theoretical waters that are capable of experimental clarification.

The concept of coping with unpleasant emotions is related to that of stress immunization. It raises the possibility of preventing disorders by appropriate procedures in childhood and later periods. The idea was not new in ancient Sparta and amounts to the teaching of stoicism. Experiments with children (29) and students (30) indicate that this form of coping can be used in specific situations like visits to the dentist or pain in the forearm from ischemia induced by a pressure cuff on the arm. The question is to what extent stress immunization can be generalized, when it should be applied, in what way, for how long, and at what ages. We are only at the start of a long road of research into adaptive behavior.

Delivery of Behavioral Services

As behavioral treatments have been found to be effective for certain conditions, the demand for this therapy has greatly outstripped the supply of trained personnel. One possible solution is to produce new classes of therapists with shorter training that that required of doctors or psychologists. Operational research in this area has been successfully conducted in Britain. Given special training, psychiatric nurses working with patients with phobic, obsessive-compulsive, and sexual disorders achieved results as good as those of doctors and psychologists using comparable methods with similar patients (31).

The outcome of this work has been the development of an 18-month course, recognized throughout England and Wales, for the training of nurses in behavioral psychotherapy. These nurse-therapists act as the primary therapist in a therapeutic team while working with doctors or psychologists. This development greatly extends the number of patients who can be treated by a given team led by a doctor or psychologist. This is as true for private practice as for the public sector.

Many other classes of personnel have been involved in the administration of behavioral treatments for a wide variety of problems. More research is needed into possible models for the delivery of behavioral services in different countries. Such operational research might indicate improved ways of getting effective treatment to as many people as possible at a reasonable cost.

Conclusions

Behaviorial psychotherapy is a vigorous growing point in psychiatric treatment. Several hitherto untreatable conditions now respond to behavioral treatment, and it is at times a useful adjuvant for other problems as well. Behavioral psychotherapy is taking its place among the definitive treatments available for the relief of psychiatric suffering, and further advances in the field are appearing regularly. Although useful molecular theories are emerging to guide the discipline, no global theory is likely to be satisfactory in the foreseeable future. As always, as we learn to understand any area, the dialectic dance moves on to fresh ground.

REFERENCES

1. Locke J: Some Thoughts Concerning Education (1693). London, Ward Lock & Co (no date)
2. Freud S: Lines of advance in psycho-analytic therapy (1919), in Complete Psychological Works, standard ed, vol 17. Translated and edited by Strachey J. London, Hogarth Press, 1955, pp 157−168
3. Marks IM: Fears and Phobias. New York, Academic Press, 1969
4. Marks IM: Behavioral treatments of phobic and obsessive-compulsive disorders: a critical appraisal, in Progress in Behavior Modification, vol 1. Edited by Herson M. Eisler M, Miller PM. New York, Academic Press, 1975, pp 65−168
5. Frankl V: The Doctor and the Soul. London, Souvenir Press, 1955
6. Frankl V: Psychotherapy and Existentialism.

Selected Papers on Logotherapy. New York, Washington Square Press, 1967
7. Wolpe J: Psychotherapy by Reciprocal Inhibition. Stanford, Calif, Stanford University Press, 1958
8. Gelder MG, Marks IM, Wolff H: Desensitization and psychotherapy in the treatment of phobic states: a controlled inquiry. Br J Psychiatry 113:53−73, 1967
9. Gelder MG, Marks IM: Desensitization and phobias: a crossover study. Br J Psychiatry 114:323−328, 1968
10. Marks IM: Fears and Phobias. New York, Academic Press, 1969
11. Marks IM: Phobic disorders four years after treatment: a prospective follow-up. Br J Psychiatry 118:683−688, 1971
12. Gillan P, Rachman S: An experimental investigation of desensitization in phobic patients. Br J Psychiatry 124:392−401, 1974
13. Marks IM, Hodgson R, Rachman S: Treatment of chronic obsessive-compulsive neurosis by *in-vivo* exposure: a two-year follow-up and issues in treatment. Br J Psychiatry 127:349−364, 1975
14. Rachman S, Marks IM, Hodgson R: The treatment of obsessive-compulsive neurotics by modeling and flooding in vivo. Behav Res Ther 11:463−471, 1973
15. Benjamin S, Marks IM, Huson J: Active muscular relaxation in desensitization of phobic patients. Psychol Med 2:381−390, 1972
16. Roper G, Marks IM, Rachman S: Passive and participant modelling in exposure treatment of obsessive-compulsive neurotics. Behav Res Ther 13:271−279, 1975
17. Rooth FG, Marks IM: Persistent exhibitionism: short-term response to aversion, self-regulation, and relaxation treatments. Arch Sex Behav 3:227−248, 1974
18. Stampfl TG: Implosive therapy: the theory, the subhuman analogue, the strategy and the technique: part 1. The theory, in Behavior Modification Techniques in the Treatment of Emotional Disorders. Edited by Armitage SG. Battle Creek, Mich, Veterans Administration, 1967, pp 22−37
19. Mathews AM, Johnston DW, Shaw PM, et al: Process variables and the prediction of outcome in behaviour therapy. Br J Psychiatry 125:256−264, 1974
20. Hafner J, Marks IM: Exposure in vivo of agoraphobics: the contributions of diazepam, group exposure and anxiety evocation. Psychol Med (in press)

21. Marks IM, Boulougouris J, Marset P: Flooding versus desensitization in the treatment of phobic disorders: a crossover study. Br J Psychiatry 119:353–375, 1971

22. Watson JP, Marks IM: Relevant vs irrelevant flooding in the treatment of phobias. Behavior Therapy 2:275–293, 1971

23. Stern RS, Marks IM: A comparison of brief and prolonged flooding in agoraphobics. Arch Gen Psychiatry 28:270–276, 1973

24. Boulougouris J, Rabavilas J: Prognosis after exposure in vivo of obsessive-compulsive neurosis. Behav Res Ther (in press)

25. Johnston DW, Gelder MG, Lancashire M, et al: Comparison of imaginal and in vivo procedures in the treatment of agoraphobia. Presented at the third annual meeting of the British Association for Behavioural Psychotherapy, York, England, July 11–13, 1975

26. Lipsedge MS: Therapeutic approaches to compulsive rituals: a pilot study. London, Institute of Psychiatry, University of London (unpublished master's dissertation), 1974

27. Mathews AM, Bancroft JHJ: A comparison of different procedures for the treatment of sexual dysfunction. Presented at the third annual meeting of the British Association for Behavioural Psychotherapy, York, England, July 11–13, 1975

28. Marks IM: Patterns of Meaning in Psychiatric Patients, Maudsley Monograph number 13. New York, Oxford University Press, 1965

29. Surwit R: The anticipatory modification of the conditioning of a fear response in humans. Montreal, Department of Psychology, McGill University (unpublished doctoral dissertation), 1974

30. Meichenbaum D: Cognitive Behavior Modification. University Programs Modular Studies. Morristown, NJ, General Learning Press, 1974

31. Marks IM, Hallam RS, Philpott R, et al: Nurse therapists in behavioural psychotherapy. Br Med J 3:144–148, 1975

Critical Evaluation

Behavioral theorists of psychopathology borrow their concepts from experimental learning research; consequently, one would expect their work to be subject to little scientific faulting. The failure to live up to this expectation, according to some critics, points up the difficulty of transferring concepts from one field to another. Borrowing the rigorously derived concepts of laboratory research may be no more than a specious ennoblement of one's meagre accomplishments, a cloak of falsely appropriated prestige which duly impresses the naïve.

Breger and McGaugh's penetrating critique of the logical and empirical foundations of the behavioral approach raises the question of whether the laboratory based concepts borrowed from the prestigious field of learning are genuinely useful in psychopathology or whether they are merely bandied about in an allegorical and superficial manner. They note further that the "basic" laws of learning are not so basic after all; much dissent exists among learning theorists as to which concepts and laws are "basic." They ask whether laws of learning should be applied to highly complex clinical processes when the existence of these laws in simple situations remains a matter of dispute.

43   Critique and Reformulation of "Learning-Theory" Approaches to Psychotherapy and Neurosis

Louis Breger and James L. McGaugh

A careful look at the heterogeneous problems that are brought to psychotherapy points up the urgent need for new and varied theories and techniques. While some new methods have been developed in recent years, the field is still characterized by "schools"—groups who adhere to a particular set of ideas and techniques to the exclusion of others. Thus, there are dogmatic psychoanalysts, Adlerians, Rogerians, and, most recently, dogmatic behaviorists.

It is unfortunate that the techniques used by the behavior-therapy group (Bandura, 1961; Eysenck, 1960; Grossberg, 1964; Wolpe, 1958) have so quickly become encapsulated in a dogmatic "school," but this seems to be the case. Before examining the theory and practice of behavior therapy, let us first distinguish three different positions, all of which are associated with the behaviorism or "learning-theory" label. These are: (*a*) Dollard and Miller (1950) as represented in their book, (*b*) the Wolpe-Eysenck position as represented in Wolpe's work (1958; Wolpe, Salter, & Reyna, 1964) and in the volume edited by Eysenck (1960), and (*c*) the Skinnerian position as seen in Krasner (1961) and the work that appears in the *Journal of the Experimental Analysis of Behavior*.

Dollard and Miller present an attempt to translate psychoanalytic concepts into the terminology of Hullian learning theory. While many recent behavior therapists reject Dollard and Miller because of their identification with psychoanalysis and their failure to provide techniques distinct from psychoanalytic therapy, the Dollard-Miller explanation of neurotic symptoms in terms of conditioning and secondary anxiety drive is utilized extensively by Wolpe and his followers. Wolpe's position seems to be a combination of early Hullian learning theory and various active therapy techniques. He relies heavily on the idea of reciprocal inhibition, which is best exemplified by the technique of countercondi-

tioning. In line with this Hullian background, Wolpe, Eysenck, and others in this group use explanations based on Pavlovian conditioning. They define neurosis as "persistent unadaptive habits that have been conditioned (that is, learned)" (Wolpe et al., 1964, p. 96), and their explanation of neurosis stresses the persistence of "maladaptive habits" which are anxiety reducing.

The Skinnerian group (see Bachrach in Wolpe et al., 1964) have no special theory of neurosis; in fact, following Skinner, they tend to disavow the necessity of theory. Their approach rests heavily on *techniques* of operant conditioning, on the use of "reinforcement" to control and shape behavior, and on the related notion that "symptoms," like all other "behaviors," are maintained by their effects.

Our discussion will be directed to the Wolpe-Eysenck group and the Skinnerians, keeping in mind that some of the points we will raise are not equally applicable to both. Insofar as the Skinnerians disavow a theory of neurosis, for example, they are not open to criticism in this area.

It is our opinion that the current arguments supporting a learning-theory approach to psychotherapy and neurosis are deficient on a number of grounds. First, we question whether the broad claims they make rest on a foundation of accurate and complete description of the basic data of neurosis and psychotherapy. The process of selecting from among the data for those examples fitting the theory and techniques while ignoring a large amount of relevant data seriously undermines the strength and generality of the position. Second, claims for the efficacy of methods should be based on adequately controlled and accurately described evidence. And, finally, when overall claims for the superiority of behavioral therapies are based on alleged similarity to laboratory experiments and alleged derivation from "well-established laws of learning," the relevance of the laboratory experimental findings for psychotherapy data should be justified and the laws of learning should be shown to be both relevant and valid.

In what follows we will consider these

From *Psychol. Bull.* 63: 338–358, 1965, by permission of the American Psychological Association and the authors.

issues in detail, beginning with the frequently voiced claim that behavior therapy rests on a solid "scientific" base. Next, we will examine the nature and adequacy of the learning-theory principles which they advocate. We will point out how their learning theory is unable to account for the evidence from laboratory studies of learning. That is to say, the laws or principles of conditioning and reinforcement which form the basis of their learning theory are insufficient explanations for the findings from laboratory experiments, let alone the complex learning phenomena that are encountered in psychotherapy. Then we will discuss how the inadequate conception of learning phenomena in terms of conditioned responses is paralleled by an equally inadequate conception of neurosis in terms of discrete symptoms. Within learning theory, conceptions of habit and response have been shown to be inadequate and are giving away to conceptions emphasizing "strategies," "plans," "programs," "schemata," or other complex central mediators. A central point of this paper is that conceptions of habit and response are also inadequate to account for neuroses and the learning that goes on in psychotherapy and must here too be replaced with conceptions analogous to strategies. Next we will turn our attention to an evaluation of the claims of success put forth by the proponents of behavior therapy. Regardless of the adequacy of their theory, the claims that the methods work are deserving of careful scrutiny. Here we shall raise a number of questions centering around the issue of adequate controls. Finally, we shall attempt a reformulation in terms of more recent developments within learning, emphasizing the role of central processes.

Science Issue

Claims of scientific respectability are made with great frequency by the behavior therapists. Terms such as laboratory based, experimental, behavioral, systematic, and control are continually used to support their position. The validity of a theory or method must rest on empirical evidence, however. Thus, their use of scientific sounding terminology does not make their approach scientific, but rather seems to obscure an examination of the evidence on which their claims are based.

Let us examine some of this evidence. Bandura (1961) provides the following account of a typical behavior-therapy method (Wolpe's counterconditioning):

> On the basis of historical information, interview data, and psychological test responses, the therapist constructs an anxiety hierarchy, a ranked list of stimuli to which the patient reacts with anxiety. In the case of desensitization based on relaxation, the patient is hypnotized, and is given relaxation suggestions. He is then asked to imagine a scene representing the weakest item on the anxiety hierarchy and, if the relaxation is unimpaired, this is followed by having the patient imagine the next item on the list, and so on. Thus, the anxiety cues are gradually increased from session to session until the last phobic stimulus can be presented without impairing the relaxed state. Through this procedure, relaxation responses eventually come to be attached to the anxiety evoking stimuli (p. 144).

Without going into great detail, it should be clear from this example that the use of the terms stimulus and response are only remotely allegorical to the traditional use of these terms in psychology. The "imagination of a scene" is hardly an objectively defined stimulus, nor is something as general as "relaxation" a specifiable or clearly observable response. What the example shows is that counterconditioning is no more objective, no more controlled, and no more scientific than classical psychoanalysis, hypnotherapy, or treatment with tranquilizers. The claim to scientific respectability rests on the misleading use of terms such as stimulus, response, and conditioning, which have become associated with some of the methods of science because of their place in experimental psychology. But this implied association rests on the use of the same *words* and on the use of the same *methods*.

We should stress that our quarrel is not with the techniques themselves but with the attempt to tie these techniques to principles and concepts from the field of learning. The techniques go back at least as far as Bagby (1928), indicating their independence from "modern learning theory." Although techniques such as these have received little attention in recent years (except from the behavior therapists) they are certainly worth further consideration as potentially useful techniques.[1]

The use of the term conditioning brings us to a second point, that the claims to scientific respectability rest heavily on the attempts of these writers to associate their work with the prestigious field of learning. They speak of something called modern learning theory, implying that psychologists in the area of learning have generally agreed upon a large number of basic principles and laws which can be taken as the foundation for a "scientific" approach to psychotherapy. For example, Eysenck (1960) states:

> Behavior therapy . . . began with the thorough experimental study of the laws of learning and conditioning in normal people and animals; these well-established principles were then applied to neurotic disorders. . . . It may be objected that learning theorists are not always in agreement with each other and that it is difficult to apply principles about which there is still so much argument. This is only very partially true; those points about which argument rages are usually of academic interest rather than of practical importance. . . . The 10% which is in dispute should not blind us to the 90% which is not— disagreements and disputes naturally attract more attention, but agreements on facts and principles are actually much more common. Greater familiarity with the large and rapidly growing literature will quickly substantiate this statement (pp. 14–15).

As we shall show in the next section, this assertion is untenable. "Greater familiarity with the large and rapidly growing literature" shows that the very core of "modern learning theory," as Eysenck describes it, has been seriously questioned or abandoned in favor of alternative conceptualizations. For example, the notion that the discrete response provides an adequate unit of analysis or that reinforcement can be widely used as an explanation of both learning and performance, or that mediational processes can be ignored are being or have been rejected. Eysenck's picture of the field as one

[1]Another early application of behavioral techniques has recently been brought to our attention: Stevenson Smith's use of the Guthrie approach to learning in his work at the children's clinic at the University of Washington. Guthrie's interpretation of reinforcement avoids the pitfalls we discuss shortly, and contemporary behaviorists might learn something from a review of his work (see Guthrie, 1935).

with 90% agreement about basic principles is quite simply untrue. The references that Eysenck himself gives for this statement (Hilgard, 1956; Osgood, 1953) do not support the claim. Hilgard presented many theories, not one "modern learning theory," some of which (Gestalt, Tolman, Lewin) might just as easily be said to be in 90% disagreement with behavioristic conditioning approaches. In the same vein, Osgood's text was one of the first to give heavy emphasis to the role of mediation, in an attempt to compensate for the inadequacies of a simple conditioning or one-stage S-R approach. Eysenck seems largely unaware of the very problems within the field of learning which necessitated the introduction of mediational concepts, even by S-R theorists such as Osgood.

These inadequacies center, in part, around the problem of generalization. The problem of generalizing from the level of conditioning to the level of complex human behavior has been recognized for a long time (Lewin, 1951; Tolman, 1933). It is a problem that is crucial in simple laboratory phenomena such as maze learning where it has resulted in the introduction of a variety of mediational concepts, and it is certainly a problem when complex human behavior is being dealt with. For example, Dollard and Miller (1950) began their book with an attempt to explain neurosis with simple conditioning principles. A careful reading of the book reveals, however, that as the behavior to be explained became more and more complex, their explanations relied more and more on mediational concepts, including language. The necessity for these mediators arises from the inadequacy of a simple *peripheral* S-R model to account for the generality of learning, the equivalence of responses, and the adaptive application of behavior in novel situations. We shall return to these points shortly; here we just wish to emphasize that the field of learning is not "one big happy family" whose problems have been solved by the widespread acceptance of a simple conditioning model. The claim to scientific respectability by reference back to established laws of learning is, thus, illusory.

Learning and Learning Theories

We have already noted the differences between the Wolpe-Eysenck and the Skinnerian approaches; let us now examine the similarities. Three things stand out: the focus on the overt response, the reliance on a conditioning model, and the notion of reinforcement. First, there is the belief that the response, consisting of some discrete aspect of overt behavior, is the most meaningful unit of human behavior. While this should ideally refer to a specific contraction of muscles or secretion of glands, with the possible exception of Guthrie (1935), traditional S-R theorists have tended to define response in terms of an effect on the environment rather than as a specific movement of the organism. The problems raised by the use of the response as a basic unit, both in traditional learning phenomena and in the areas of neuroses and psychotherapy will be discussed in the section entitled, What is Learned? A second common assumption is that the concepts taken from conditioning, either as described by Pavlov or the operant conditioning of Skinner, can be used as explanatory principles. The assumption in question here is that conditioning phenomena are the simplest kinds of learning and that all other behavior can be explained in terms of these "simple" principles. We shall deal with the problems that arise from this source in a second section. The third assumption is that rewards play an essential role in the learning phenomena. We shall consider the problems that stem from this assumption in a third section.

What Is Learned?

Since its inception in the early twentieth century, behaviorism has taken overt stimuli and responses as its core units of analysis. Learning, as the behaviorist views it, is defined as the tendency to make a *particular response* in the presence of a *particular stimulus;* what is learned is a discrete response. Almost from its inception, however, this view has been plagued by a number of problems.

First, findings from studies of perception, particularly the fact of perceptual constancy, provide embarrassment for a peripheral S-R theory. Perceptual constancy findings show, for example, that the stimulus is much more than peripheral receptor stimulation. For example, once we have learned a song in a particular key (i.e., particular stimulus elements), we can readily recognize it or sing it in other keys. We are amazingly accurate in recognizing objects and events as being "the same" or equivalent, even though the particular stimulation they provide varies considerably on different occasions (Gibson, 1950). Although the bases of perceptual constancies (size, shapes, brightness, etc.) are not yet well understood, the facts of perceptual constancy—invariance in percept with variation in perceptual stimulation—are not in question. The related phenomenon of transposition has received considerable attention in animal experimentation. Animals, infrahuman as well as human, respond to relations among stimuli (Köhler, 1929). For a number of years, transposition was not considered to pose a serious problem for a peripheral S-R theory since it was thought that it could be adequately handled by principles of conditioning and stimulus generalization (Spence, 1937). This view has not been supported by later experiments, however (Lawrence & DeRivera, 1954; Riley, 1958). It now appears more likely that stimulus generalization is but a special case of the more general complex phenomenon of stimulus equivalence. The absolute theory of transposition was important and instructive because it revealed in clear relief the nature and limitations of a peripheral S-R approach to behavior. The effective stimulus is clearly more "central" than receptor excitation. The chapters on learning in the recent Koch series make it clear that workers in this area have seen the need for coming to terms with the facts of perception (Guttman, 1963; Lawrence, 1963; Leeper, 1963; Postman, 1963).

Second, the facts of response equivalence or response transfer posed the same kind of problem for a peripheral S-R view. A learned response does not consist merely of a stereotyped pattern of muscular contraction or glandular secretion. Even within the S-R tradition (e.g., Hull, Skinner) there has been a tendency to define responses in terms of environmental achievements. Anyone who has trained animals has recognized that animals can achieve the same general response, that is, make the same environmental change, in a variety of different ways once the response is learned. "What is learned," then, is not a mechanical sequence of responses but rather, *what needs to be done in order to achieve some final event.* This notion is not new; Tolman stressed it as early as 1932 when he wrote of "purposive behavior," and it has been strongly supported by a variety of experimental findings (e.g., Beach, Hebb, Morgan, &

Nissen, 1960; Ritchie, Aeschliman, & Peirce, 1950). As this work shows, animals somehow seem to be able to bypass the execution of specific responses in reaching an environmental achievement. They can learn to go to particular places in the environment in spite of the fact that to do so requires them to make different responses from trial to trial. The learning of relatively specific responses to specific stimuli appears to be a special case which might be called steroterotyped learning (canalization) rather than a basic prototype on the basis of which all other learning may be explained.

It should be noted further that even the stereotyped learning that forms the basic model of S-R conditioning does not hold up under closer scrutiny. First, once a subject has learned a stereotyped movement or response, he is still capable of achieving a goal in other ways when the situation requires it. Thus, while we have all learned to write our names with a particular hand in a relatively stereotyped fashion, we can switch to the other hand, or even write our name with a pencil gripped in our teeth if we have to, in spite of the fact that we may not have made this specific response in this way before. Second, even a response that is grossly defined as constant, stable, or stereotyped does not appear as such a stereotyped pattern of muscular contractions when it is closely observed.[2] These findings in the area of response transfer indicate that a response seems to be highly variable and equipotential. This notion is, of course, quite old in the history of psychology, and it has been stressed repeatedly by numerous investigators including Lashley (see Beach et al., 1960), Osgood (1953), Tolman (1932), and Woodworth (1958).

The facts of both response transfer and stimulus equivalence seem much more adequately handled if we assume that what is learned is a *strategy* (alternatively called cognitive maps, programs, plans, schemata, hypotheses, e.g., Krechevsky, 1932) for obtaining environmental achievements. When we take this view, habits, in the traditional behaviorist sense, become a later stage of response learning rather than a basic explanation (building block) for later, more complex learning.

Perhaps this whole problem can be

clarified if we look at a specific example such as language learning. As Chomsky (1959) has demonstrated in his excellent critique of Skinner's *Verbal Behavior* (1957), the basic facts of language learning and usage simply cannot be handled within an S-R approach. It seems clear that an adequate view of language must account for the fact that humans, at a rather early age, internalize a complex set of rules (grammar) which enable them to both recognize and generate meaningful sentences involving patterns of words that they may never have used before. Thus, in language learning, what is learned are not only sets of responses (words and sentences) but, in addition, some form of internal strategies or plans (grammar). We learn a grammar which enables us to generate a variety of English sentences. We do not merely learn specific English sentence habits. How this grammar or set of strategies is acquired, retained, and used in language comprehension and generation is a matter for serious research effort; but, it is clear that attempts to understand language learning on the basis of analogies from bar-pressing experiments are doomed before they start. To anticipate, we will argue shortly that if we are to make an attempt to understand the phenomena of neurosis, using analogies from the area of learning, it will be much more appropriate to take these analogies from the area of psycholinguistics and language learning rather than, as has typically been done, from studies of classical and operant conditioning. That is, the focus will have to be on response transfer, equipotentiality, and the learning of plans and strategies rather than on stereotyped response learning or habituation.

Use of a Conditioning Model

As we indicated earlier, when writers in the behaviorist tradition say "learning theory," they probably mean a conditioning theory; most of the interpretations of clinical phenomena are reinterpretations in terms of the principles of conditioning. Thus, a phobic symptom is viewed as a conditioned response, maintained by the reinforcement of a secondary fear drive or by a Skinnerian as a single operant maintained by reinforcement. Two types of conditioning are involved in these explanations by reduction. The first is Pavlo-

[2]G. Hoyle, personal communication, 1963.

vian or classical conditioning, frequently used in conjunction with later Hullian concepts such as secondary drive; the second is operant conditioning of the kind proposed by Skinner. The use of both of these models to explain more complex phenomena such as transposition, response transfer, problem solving, language learning, or neurosis and psychotherapy poses a number of difficulties.

The basic assumption that underlies the use of either kind of conditioning as an explanation for more complex phenomena is that basic laws of behavior have been established in the highly controlled laboratory situation and may thus be applied to behavior of a more complex variety. When we look at the way conditioning principles are applied in the explanation of more complex phenomena, we see that only a rather flimsy analogy bridges the gap between such laboratory defined terms as stimulus, response, and reinforcement and their referents in the case of complex behavior. Thus, while a stimulus may be defined as an electric shock or a light of a certain intensity in a classical conditioning experiment, Bandura (1961) speaks of the "imagination of a scene"; or, while a response may consist of salivation or a barpress in a conditioning experiment, behavior therapists speak of anxiety as a response. As Chomsky (1959) puts it, with regard to this same problem in the area of language:

> He [Skinner in *Verbal Behavior*] utilizes the experimental results as evidence for the scientific character of his system of behavior, and analogic guesses (formulated in terms of a metaphoric extension of the technical vocabulary of the laboratory) as evidence for its scope. This creates the illusion of a rigorous scientific theory with a very broad scope, although in fact the terms used in the description of real-life and laboratory behavior may be mere homonyms, with at most a vague similarity of meaning (p. 30).

A second and related problem stems from the fact that the behavior-therapy workers accept the findings of conditioning experiments as basic principles or laws of learning. Unfortunately, there is now good reason to believe that classical conditioning is no more simple or basic than other forms of learning. Rather, it seems to be a form of learning that is in itself in need of explanation in terms of more general principles. For example, a popular but naive view of conditioning is that of

stimulus substitution—the view that conditioning consists merely of the substitution of a conditioned stimulus for an unconditioned stimulus. Close examination of conditioning experiments reveals that this is not the case, however, for the conditioned response is typically *unlike* the unconditioned response (Zener, 1937). Apparently, in conditioning, a new response is learned. Most of the major learning theorists have taken this fact into account in abandoning the notion of conditioning as mere stimulus substitution.

More than this, the most important theoretical developments using essentially Pavlovian conditioning principles have not even stressed overt behavior (Osgood, 1953). Hull and the neo-Hullians, for example, have relied quite heavily on Tolman's (1932) distinction between learning and performance, performance being what is observed while learning (conditioning) is but one essential ingredient contributing to any instance of observed performance. The most important, and perhaps the most sophisticated, developments in Hullian and neo-Hullian theory concern the attempts to explain complicated goal-directed behavior in terms of the conditioning of fractional responses. Unobserved, fractional responses (already we see the drift away from the overt behavior criteria of response) are assumed to serve a mediating role in behavior. Once a fractional response is conditioned in a particular situation, it is assumed to occur to the stimuli in that situation when those stimuli recur. The stimulus consequences of the fractional response referred to as the r_g are assumed to serve as guides to behavior either by serving as a cue or by activating responses or by serving to reinforce other responses by secondary reinforcement. The latter-day proponents of a conditioning point of view (Bugelski, 1956; Osgood, 1953) have come to rely more and more heavily on concepts like the fractional response to bridge the gap between stimulus and overt behavior and to account for the facts of response transfer, environmental achievements, and equipotentiality. What this indicates is that a simple conditioning paradigm which rests solely on observable stimuli and responses has proved inadequate even to the task of encompassing simple conditioning and maze-learning phenomena, and the workers within this tradition have come to rely more and more heavily on mediational (central, cognitive, etc.) concepts, although they still attempt to clothe these concepts in traditional conditioning garb. To add to the problem, a number of recent papers (Deutsch, 1956; Gonzales & Diamond, 1960) have indicated that the r_g interpretations of complex behavior are neither simple nor adequate.

When we look again at the way conditioning principles have been applied to clinical phenomena, we see an amazing unawareness of these problems that have been so salient to experimental and animal psychologists working with conditioning.

While the above discussion has been oriented primarily to classical conditioning, the general argument would apply equally well to those attempts to make the principles of learning derived from operant conditioning the basis of an explanation of neurosis and psychotherapy (as in Krasner, 1961). The Skinnerians have been particularly oblivious to the wide variety of problems that are entailed when one attempts to apply concepts and findings from laboratory learning experiments to other, and particularly more complex, phenomena. While we will deal more directly with their point of view shortly, a few comments might be in order now concerning their use of the operant-conditioning paradigm as a basis for the handling of more complex data. When Skinnerians speak of laws of learning, they have reference to the curves representing rate of responding of rats pressing bars (Skinner, 1938), and pigeons pecking (Ferster & Skinner, 1957) which are, in fact, a function of certain highly controlled contingencies such as the schedule of reinforcement, the amount of deprivation, the experimental situation itself (there is very little else to do in a Skinner box), and the species of animals involved. These experiments are of some interest, both as exercises in animal training under highly restricted conditions, and for what light they may shed on the more general question of partial reinforcement. It is dubious that these findings constitute laws of learning that can be applied across species (see Breland & Breland, 1961) or even to situations that differ in any significant way from the Skinner box.

Use of Reinforcement

Advocates of the application of learning theory to clinical phenomena have relied heavily on the "law of effect" as perhaps their foremost established principle of learning. We shall attempt to point out that a good deal of evidence from experimental animal studies argues strongly that, at the most, the law of effect is a weak law of performance.

Essentially, the controversy can be reduced to the question of whether or not reward is necessary for learning. The initial source of evidence indicating that it was not came from the findings of latent learning studies (Blodgett, 1929; Tolman & Honzik, 1930) in which it was found, for example, that rats who were allowed to explore a maze without reward made fewer errors when learning the maze than controls who had no opportunity for exploration. Thus, these early latent learning studies, as well as a variety of more recent ones (Thistlethwaite, 1951) indicate that learning can take place without reward but may not be revealed until a reward situation makes it appropriate to do so (or to put it another way, the reward elicits the performance but plays little role during learning). Other sources which point to learning without reward come from studies of perceptual learning (Hebb, 1949), imitation (Herbert & Harsh, 1944), language learning (Chomsky, 1959), and imprinting (Moltz, 1960).

Defenders of the point of view that reinforcement is necessary for learning have attempted to handle results such as these in a variety of ways. One has been by appealing to the concept of secondary reinforcement (e.g., a maze has secondary reinforcing properties which account for the learning during exploration). When this sort of thing is done, even with respect to experiments where attempts were made to minimize secondary reinforcements (Thistlethwaite, 1951), it seems clear that this particular notion of reinforcement has become incapable of disproof. Another way of handling these potentially embarrassing results has been by the invention of a new set of drives (curiosity drive, exploratory drive, etc.) but this too has a post hoc flavor to it, and one wonders what kind of explanation is achieved by postulating an "exploratory drive" to account for the fact that animals and humans engage in exploration. In fact, the assumption that exploration reduces an exploratory drive makes it difficult to explain why a rat's tendency to enter an alley of a maze *decreases* after he has explored the alley (Watson, 1961). Finally, there are those (particularly the Skinnerians) who tend to define reinforcement so broadly that neither the findings from latent learning nor any other source can prove embarrassing, since whenever learning has taken place this "proves" that there has been reinforcement. To better understand this problem, however, we had best look for a moment at the general problem of defining reinforcement in a meaningful way.

Obviously, if the view that reinforcement is necessary for learning is to have any meaning, what constitutes a reinforcement must be defined independently from the learning situation itself. There has been a great deal of difficulty in getting around a circular definition of the law of effect, and it might be worthwhile to examine some of the attempts that have been made in the past.

One of the best known was the attempt to relate the reinforcing properties of stimuli to their drive-reducing characteristics (Hull, 1951). The drive-reduction model has had to be abandoned, however, because of evidence from a variety of areas including latent learning, sensory preconditioning (Brogden, 1939), and novelty and curiosity (Berlyne, 1960). Other evidence such as that of Olds and Milner (1954) on the effect of direct brain stimulation have strengthened the conviction that the drive-reduction interpretation of reinforcement is inadequate; and, in fact, original adherents of this view have begun to abandon it (e.g., Miller, 1959).

The other most frequent solution to the circularity problem has been by way of the "empirical law of effect," an approach typified by Skinner's definition of reinforcement as any stimulus that can be demonstrated to produce a change in response strength. Skinner argues that this is not circular since some stimuli are found to produce changes and others are not, and they can subsequently be classified on that basis. This seems to be a reasonable position if it is adhered to; that is, if care is taken to define reinforcement in terms of class membership *independently* of the observations that show that learning has taken place. When we examine the actual use of the term reinforcement by Skinner (see especially *Verbal Behavior,* 1957) and by other Skinnerians (Lundin, 1961), we find that care is only taken in this regard within the context of animal experiments, but that when the jumps are made to other phenomena, such as language and psychotherapy, care is usually *not* taken to define reinforcement independently from learning as indicated by response strength. This leads to a

state of affairs where any observed change in behavior is said to occur *because of* reinforcement, when, in fact, the change in behavior is itself the only indicator of what the reinforcement has been. Chomsky (1959) reviews the use of the concept of reinforcement by Skinner with regard to language and reaches the following conclusion:

> From this sample, it can be seen that the notion of reinforcement has totally lost whatever objective meaning it may ever have had. Running through these examples, we see that a person can be reinforced though he emits no response at all, and the reinforcing "stimulus" need not impinge on the reinforced person or need not even exist (it is sufficient that it be imagined or hoped for). When we read that a person plays what music he likes (165), says what he likes (165), thinks what he likes (438–9), reads what books he likes (163), etc., *because* he finds it reinforcing to do so, or that we write books or inform others of facts *because* we are reinforced by what we hope will be the ultimate behavior of reader or listener, we can only conclude that the term "reinforcement" has a purely ritual function. The phrase "X is reinforced by Y (stimulus, state of affairs, event, etc.)" is being used as a cover term for "X wants Y," "X likes Y," "X wishes that Y were the case," etc. Invoking the term "reinforcement" has no explanatory force, and any idea that this paraphrase introduces any new clarity or objectivity into the description of wishing, liking, etc., is a serious delusion [pp. 37–38].

This problem is exemplified in the area of psychotherapy by the attempts to use the studies of verbal conditioning (Krasner, 1958) as analogues to psychotherapy. First we should note that if these studies are taken at face value (i.e., if subjects are conditioned to increase the emission of certain responses because of reinforcement, without their awareness of this fact) it appears that a simple conditioning model is inadequate since subjects are presumably responding in terms of a class of responses (e.g., plural nouns, etc.) rather than in terms of a specific response (e.g., bar press), such classes implying response transfer and mediation. Second, and more to the point, a number of recent investigators (Eriksen, 1962) have begun to question whether verbal conditioning does occur without the subject's awareness. If it does not, the whole phenomenon begins to look like nothing more than a rather inefficient way to get subjects to figure out what the experimenter wants them to do (telling them directly to emit plural nouns would probably be much more efficient) after which they can decide whether they want to do it or not. In any case, there seems to be enough question about what goes on in verbal conditioning itself to indicate that it cannot be utilized as a more basic explanation for complex phenomena such as psychotherapy. Psychotherapists of many persuasions would agree that rewards of some kind are important in work with patients. Thus, the view that the psychotherapist is a "reinforcement machine" is trivial. The difficult problems are in specifying just what therapist activities are rewarding, in what ways, to what sorts of patients, and with what effects.

The above discussion should make clear that the use of the concept of reinforcement is only of explanatory usefulness when it is specified in some delimited fashion. As an empirical law of performance almost everyone in and out of psychology would accept it, including Lewin, Freud, Tolman, and others outside the traditional S-R movement. But this amounts to saying nothing more than that some events, when presented, tend to increase the probability of responses that they have followed. The hard job, but the only one that will lead to any meaningful use of the concept of reinforcement, is specifying what the various events called reinforcers have in common. Some have argued that since this is such a difficult task, we should restrict ourselves to listing and cataloging so-called reinforcers. But this is nearly impossible, in a general way, because reinforcers differ from individual to individual, from species to species, from situation to situation, and from time to time (the saying "one man's meat is another man's poison" is trite but true). Meaningful analysis must stem from a comprehensive study of the particular learning phenomena in question, whether it is language learning, the development of perceptual and perceptual-motor skills (Fitts, 1964; Hebb, 1949), the acquisition of particular species behavior patterns during critical periods of development (Scott, 1962), the learning of a neurosis, or the learning that takes place during psychotherapy. Experience with all of these phenomena has revealed that different kinds of events seem to be involved and that these can only be understood in the context of the phenomena in question. Lumping all these events together under the single term reinforcement serves to muddle rather than to clarify understanding.

The staunch reinforcement adherent might respond that all these complicated arguments may be true but we can ignore them, since all we are really interested in is predicting what the organism will do, and we can do this when we know the organism's reinforcement history. The answer to this is that the experimental literature does not support such a claim; rather, it shows that, in many instances, performance *cannot* be predicted on the basis of a knowledge of the history of reinforcement.

Latent learning studies indicate this quite clearly. Perhaps of more interest are the findings of discrimination-reversal learning studies (Goodwin & Lawrence, 1955; Mackintosh, 1963). Here, we find that subjects that have been trained on a series of discrimination reversals learn to select the correct stimulus with very few errors even though they may have been rewarded *much more frequently and more recently for responding to another stimulus*. Similarly, in the double drive discrimination studies (Thistlethwaite, 1951) animals chose alleys leading to food when they were hungry and water when they were thirsty, even though they have been rewarded equally frequently on the alleys on previous trials. In other words, "what is learned" was not equivalent with "reinforcement history." The law of effect is not disproved by these studies; it is merely shown to be irrelevant.

To summarize: The "law of effect," or reinforcement, conceived as a *"law of learning,"* occupies a very dubious status. Like the principles of conditioning, it appears to be an unlikely candidate as an explanatory principle of learning. As a strong law of learning it has already been rejected by many of the theorists who previously relied on it. As an empirical "law of *performance*" it is noncontroversial, but usually so generally stated as to be of little explanatory value.

Conception of Neurosis

In this section we will explicate the conception of neurosis that forms the basis of the behavior-therapy approach (particularly of the Wolpe-Eysenck group) and attempt to demonstrate its inadequacies both in terms of learning theory and as a way of accounting for the observed facts of neurosis. Our argument in the first instance will be that the conception of neurosis in terms of symptoms and anxiety parallels the general conception of learning in terms of overt responses, conditioning, and secondary drives, and suffers from the same inadequacies that we have outlined in the preceding section. With regard to the facts of neurosis, we will argue that the behavior-therapy position is inadequate at a descriptive level as well as being conceptually incorrect. It should be pointed out again that we are discussing the explanation or theory of neurosis here and not the techniques used by the behavior therapists. The strict Skinnerian may excuse himself at this point if he adheres to a "no-theory" position and is only concerned with the effects of environmental manipulation. Furthermore, certain techniques themselves may be useful and have some of the effects attributed to them regardless of the theory.

In its essence, the conception of neurosis put forth by the behavior therapists is that neuroses are conditioned responses or habits (including conditioned anxiety) and *nothing else*, though it should be noted that they do not adhere to this argument when they describe the success of their methods. Wolpe, for example, while ostensibly treating overt symptoms, describes his patients as becoming more productive, having improved adjustment and pleasure in sex, improved interpersonal relationships, and so forth. The argument that removal of a troublesome symptom somehow "generalizes" to all of these other areas begs the question. Their conception is typically put forth as an alternative to a psychodynamic viewpoint, which they characterize as resting on a distinction between symptoms and underlying causes (unconscious conflicts, impulses, defenses, etc.). They stress the point that inferences about underlying factors of this sort are unnecessary and misleading and that a more parsimonious explanation treats symptoms (which are typically equated with behavior or that which can be objectively observed) as the neurosis per se. They argue that by equating neurosis with symptoms, and symptoms, in turn, with habits (conditioned responses), they are able to bring "modern learning theory" with its "well-established laws" to bear on the understanding and treatment of neurosis.

As we have labored to show in the preceding section, the well-established laws of learning to which they refer have considerable difficulty within the area of simple animal behavior. More specifically, it seems clear that a wide variety of behaviors (from maze learning to more complex forms) cannot be adequately dealt with when the overt response and conditioned habit are the units of analysis. Furthermore, their learning position leads the behavior therapists into postulating an isomorphic relationship between antecedent learning and present behavior in which observed differences are accounted for in terms of principles of generalization. This is a key issue, and we shall explore it a little further at this time.

Much of the behaviorist conception of neurosis rests on a rejection of the distinction between symptoms and underlying causes (Eysenck, 1960) as typified by Yates' (1958) argument against "symptom substitution." By focusing attention on overt symptoms and banishing all underlying causes, however, the behavior therapists are faced with the same problem that has long confronted behaviorism; namely, the difficulty of explaining how *generality* of behavior results from specific learning experiences. The problem of *generality* (i.e., as exemplified by the facts of transposition and response transfer) has, in fact, brought about the downfall of peripheral S-R learning, of the conditioned habit as a basic unit, and tangentially, is leading to the dethroning of the law of effect. With regard to neurosis, this view has led the behavior therapists into the position where they must posit a specific learning experience for each symptom of a neurosis. They have partly avoided this problem by focusing their attention on those neuroses that can be described in terms of specific symptoms (bedwetting, if this is a neurosis, tics, specific phobias, etc.) and have tended to ignore those conditions which do not fit their model, such as neurotic depressions, general unhappiness, obsessional disorders, and the kinds of persistent interpersonal entanglements that characterize so many neurotics. This leaves them free to explain the specific symptoms in terms of a specific learning experience, as, for example, when a fear of going outdoors is explained in terms of some previous experience in which the stimulus (outdoors) has been associated with (conditioned to) something unpleasant or painful and has now, through generalization, spread to any response of going outdoors. As our previous analysis should make clear, however, even a simple conceptualization such as this, in terms of stimuli, responses, and conditioning is extremely cumbersome and begs the important questions. Within an S-R framework, in which generalization occurs along the dimension of physical stimulus similarity, it is difficult, if not impossible, to show how a previous experience such as being frightened in the country as a child could generalize to the "stimulus" outdoors without a great deal of *mediation* in which the concept of "outdoors" carried most of the burden of generalization. As we have pointed out, most workers in the field of learning recognize this and rely heavily on mediational concepts in their explanations of complex behavior. Dollard and Miller (1950), for example, return again and again to mediational explanations once they move beyond the "combat neuroses" which lend themselves more readily to a simple isomorphic explanation.

A second important facet of the behaviorist conception of neurosis is the use of the concept of anxiety as a secondary drive. Here, Wolpe and Eysenck and some others seem to follow the explanatory model laid down by Dollard and Miller. Anxiety is viewed as the main motivating force for symptoms and, in general, occupies a central place in their thinking. Briefly, it is worth pointing out that the concept of drive reduction, the distinction between primary drives and secondary drives, as well as the early thinking about the uniquely persistent qualities of fear-motivated behavior have had serious difficulty within learning theory (Watson, 1961; Solomon, 1964). The use of these concepts to explain clinical phenomena thus rests on an exceedingly shaky foundation.

Let us turn our attention now to the phenomena of neuroses. We shall try to point out that underlying the dispute over symptoms versus underlying causes is the real difference in definition that arises at the descriptive level, which, in a sense, antedates disagreements at the level of theory and explanation.

To keep the presentation simple, we will adopt the terms psychodynamic to refer too all those theorists and therapists, following Freud, whose view of neurosis and its treatment deals with motives (conscious and unconscious), conflict, etc. This covers a wide variety of workers, in addition to the more or less traditional followers of Freud, including Sullivan and his adherents (Fromm-Reichman, 1950), other neo-Freudians, and that broad group of psychiatrists and clinical psychologists who have been strongly influenced by the Freudian and neo-Freudian viewpoints even though they may not claim allegiance to any of the formal schools.

The point we wish to make here is that disagreement between the behaviorist and psychodynamic viewpoints seems to rest on a very real difference at the purely descriptive or observational level. The behaviorist looks at a neurotic and sees specific symptoms and anxiety. The psychodynamicist looks at the same individual and sees a complex intra- and interpersonal mode of functioning which may or may not contain certain observable fears[3] or certain behavioral symptoms such as compulsive motor acts. When the psychodynamicist describes a neurosis, his referent is a cohering component of the individual's functioning, including his characteristic ways of interacting with other people (e.g., sweet and self-effacing on the surface but hostile in covert ways), his characteristic modes of thinking and perceiving (e.g., the hysteric who never "remembers" anything unpleasant, the obsessive whose memories are over-elaborated and circumstantial, etc.), characteristic modes of fantasy and dreaming, a variety of secondary gain features, and the like. Specific or isolatable symptoms may sometimes be a part of such an integrated neurotic pattern, but, even viewed descriptively, they in no sense constitute the neurosis per se.

So far, we have considered the behavior therapists' position at face value. In actuality, a good case can be made that they *behave* in a way which is quite inconsistent with their own position. A specific example, taken from one of Wolpe's own case descriptions, will illustrate this point, and, at the same time, show what the psychodynamicist sees when he looks at a neurotic. Wolpe (1960) presents the following case:

Case 5—An attracive woman of 28 came for treatment because she was in acute distress as a result of her lovers' casual treatment of her. Every one of very numerous love affairs had followed a similar pattern—first she would attract the man, then she would offer herself on a platter. He would soon treat her with contempt and after a time leave her. In general she lacked

---

[3]The term anxiety is frequently used as a theoretical inference, i.e., a patient deals with personal material in an overly intellectual fashion, and this is described as a defense mechanism — intellectualization — whose purpose is to ward off anxiety.

assurance, was very dependent, and was practically never free from feelings of tension and anxiety.

What is described here is a complex pattern of interpersonal relationships, psychological strategies and misunderstandings (such as the way she became involved with men, the way she communicated her availability to them, her dependency, etc.), expectations that she had (presumably that men would not react with contempt to her generosity, that being dependent might lead to being taken care of, etc.), and thoughts and feelings about herself (lack of assurance, acute distress, etc.). Many of the statements about her (e.g., the description of the course of her love affairs) are abbreviations for very complex and involved processes involving two people interacting over a period of time. It is this, the psychodynamicist would argue, that *is* the neurosis. The tension and anxiety may be a part of it in this particular case (though there might be other cases in which there is no complaint of anxiety but, rather, its reverse—seeming inability to "feel" anything)—but it is secondary and can be understood only in relation to the other aspects of the patient's functioning. Wolpe's case histories are classic testaments to the fact that he cannot, and does not, apply the symptom approach when working with actual data. As a further example, consider the argument against a symptom-substitution point of view (Yates, 1958) in which it is implied that anything other than symptoms is some sort of metaphysical inference. While it may be true that theories such as psychoanalysis deal with a number of inferential and higher-order constructs in their attempts to integrate the complex mass of data that constitutes a neurosis, it is also true that much more than symptoms exist at the level of observation. Secondary-gain features of a neurosis, in which it is apparent that a variety of goals may be served by a set of interchangeable symptoms are the rule in most neurotic individuals. We are not defending the view (attributed to psychoanalysis by Yates) that if one symptom is removed another pops up to take its place; rather, we are arguing that the empirical phenomena of neurosis does not fit the symptom or response theory, but is much more compatible with a theory built around central mediators. Whether unconscious conflicts and defense mechanisms are adequate

ways of conceptualizing the problem is an entirely separate question. What is clear is that a view stressing central mediators in which specific responses are seen as equipotential means of reaching certain goals is necessary to encompass the data of neurosis just as it has proven necessary to encompass the phenomena of animal learning.

To sum up, it would seem that the behaviorists have reached a position where an inadequate conceptual framework forces them to adopt an inadequate and superficial view of the very data that they are concerned with. They are then forced to slip many of the key facts in the back door, so to speak, for example, when all sorts of fantasy, imaginary, and thought processes are blithely called responses. This process is, of course, parallel to what has gone on within S-R learning theory where all sorts of central and mediational processes have been cumbersomely handled with S-R terminology (e.g., Deutsch, 1956). Thus, we have a situation where the behavior therapists argue strongly against a dynamic interpretation of neurosis at some points and at other points behave as if they had adopted such a point of view. This inconsistency should be kept in mind in reading the next section in which we evaluate the claims of success put forth by the behaviorist group. Insofar as there is disagreement as to what constitutes the descriptive facts of neurosis, it makes little sense to compare the effectiveness of different methods. However, since the behaviorist group adopts very broad (or psychodynamic, if you will) criteria for improvement, and since their *techniques* may have some effectiveness, in spite of theoretical and conceptual inadequacies, it is crucial that we look carefully at the empirical results that they lay claim to.

Claims of Success

While much of the writing of the behavior therapists consists of arguments and appeals to principles of science and learning, the claims that are made for the success of the methods seem open to empirical analysis. No doubt a great deal of the appeal of behavior therapy lies right here. Here seem to be methods whose application can be clearly described (unlike such messy psychodynamic methods as "handling countertransference" or "interpreting resistance"), whose course is relatively short, and which seem to achieve a large number of practical results in the form of removal of symptoms. Wolpe (1960), for example, presents the following data: of 122 cases treated with behavioral techniques, 44% were "apparently cured," 46% were "much improved," 7% were "slightly or moderately improved," and 3% were "unimproved." Combining categories, he claims 90% "apparently cured or much improved," and 10% "improvement moderate, slight or nil." (Criteria of improvement consists of "symptomatic improvement, increased productiveness, improved adjustment and pleasure in sex, improved interpersonal relationships and ability to handle ordinary psychological conflicts and reasonable reality stresses.")

He compares this with data from the Berlin Psychoanalytic Institute (Knight, 1941) which shows 62—40.5% in the first category and 38—59.5% in the second. Wolpe concludes, as have others (Bandura, 1961; Eysenck, 1960; Lazarus, 1963), that this demonstrates the superiority of the behavior therapy methods. The fact that the psychoanalytic method showed as much as 62% improvement is explained as being due to whatever accidental "reciprocal inhibition" occurred during the therapy. (There is, however, no analysis or description of how this might have happened.) The behavioral methods achieve superior results presumably because of the more explicit application of these techniques.

It is fair to say that if these results can be substantiated they present a very strong argument in favor of behavioral *techniques*— even granting the theoretical and empirical inconsistencies we have discussed. However, we must ask if these claims are any better substantiated than those made by the practitioners of other methods of psychotherapy. Insofar as claims such as Wolpe's are based on uncontrolled case histories, they may reflect the enthusiasm of the practitioner as much as the effect of the method. History shows that new methods of therapy (ECS, tranquilizing drugs, as well as various schools of psychotherapy) have been oversold by their original proponents. Thus, a careful look at what lies behind the claims of the behavior-therapy group is in order.

The following does not purport to be a comprehensive review of the behavior-therapy literature. Rather, it is based on a survey of all the studies reported in the two reviews that

have appeared (Bandura, 1961; Grossberg, 1964). The most striking thing about this large body of studies is that they are almost all case studies. A careful reading of the original sources reveals that only one study (Lang & Lazovik, 1963) is a controlled experiment, and here the subjects were not neurotics but normal college students. Thus, most of the claims (including those of Wolpe which have been widely quoted) must be regarded as no better substantiated than those of any other enthusiastic school of psychotherapy whose practitioners claim that their patients get better. Behavior therapy has appeared to differ on this score because of its identification with experimental psychology and with "well-established laws of learning." We have already dealt with this issue, so let us now turn to some problems in evaluating psychotherapy as a technique.

The problems here are essentially those of control, and they may be broken down into three areas: (*a*) sampling biases, (*b*) observer bias, and (*c*) problems of experimental control. While research in psychotherapy presents particular difficulties in controlling "experimental input," more sophisticated workers (Frank, 1959) have attempted to deal with at least the sampling and observer problems. It thus comes as somewhat of a surprise that the behavior-therapy workers, despite their identification with experimental psychology, base their claims on evidence which is almost totally lacking in any form of control. Let us examine these issues in greater detail.

Sampling Biases

Obviously a claim such as Wolpe's of 90% success has meaning only when we know the population from which the sample of patients was drawn and the way in which they were selected. Ideally, a comparison of treatment techniques would involve the random assignment of patient from a common population pool to alternative treatments. Since, in practice, this is rarely feasible, it is essential for anyone making comparisons of different treatment methods to, at the very least, examine the comparability of the populations *and* of the methods used in selecting from these populations. Neither Wolpe's data nor that of Lazarus (1963) contains this evidence. Wolpe reports, for example, that:

Both series (70 patients reported on in 1952 and 52 patients reported on in 1954 on which the

90% figure is based) include only patients whose treatment has ceased after they have been afforded a reasonable opportunity for the application of the available methods; i.e., they have had as a minimum both a course of instruction on the changing of behavior in the life situation and a proper initiation of a course of relaxation-desensitization. This minimum takes up to about 15 interviews, including anamestic interviews and *no patient who has had 15 or more interviews has been omitted from the series* [emphasis added].

We may conclude from this that some patients (how many we do not know) having up to 14 interviews have been excluded from the sample—a procedure highly favorable to the success of the method but which violates the simplest canons of sampling. Wolpe's final sample of 122 consists of those patients most likely to show improvement, since both they and he were satisfied enough with the first 14 (or less) interviews to warrant proceeding further. Those patients least likely to improve are those most likely to drop out early (14 sessions or less) and not be included in the computation of success rate. The fact that a large number of poor-prognosis patients would very likely be eliminated during these early sessions is supported by a variety of research findings (Strickland & Crowne, 1963), which show that most dropping-out of untreatable or unsuccessful cases occurs during the first 10 sessions. This serious sampling bias would be expected to spuriously inflate the percent showing improvement.

When we add this to whatever unknown factors operate to delimit the original population (presumably there is some self-selection of patients who seek out this form of treatment), it becomes apparent that little confidence can be given to the reports of success.

Observer Bias

Psychologists have long been aware that human beings are fallible observers, particularly when they have predispositions or vested interests to protect. In controlled studies, we try to protect judges from their own biases by not acquainting them with the hypotheses, or with the nature of the groups they are judging, or by using blind and double-blind designs. This problem is particularly acute with regard to psychotherapy because both therapist and patient have investments of time, involvement, competence,

and reputation to protect. For these reasons, workers in the area have become extremely skeptical of claims put forth for any method which rests on the uncontrolled observation of the person administering the treatment. At a minimum we expect some sort of external evidence. Beyond this minimum we hope for an independent judge who can compare differentially treated groups without knowing which is which.

In addition, there is the problem of the patient's freedom to report effects which may be seriously curtailed when all his reports go directly to the person who has treated him. It seems reasonable to assume that some patients are prevented from expressing dissatisfaction with treatment when they must report directly to the therapist, either because they do not want to hurt his feelings, or are afraid, or are just saying what they think is being demanded of them, or are being polite, or for some other reason. Again, it would be highly appropriate to provide the patients with the opportunity of reporting results in a situation as free from such pressure as possible.

Examination of the 26 studies reviewed by Bandura reveals a surprising lack of concern with these problems. Of the 26 studies sampled, only 12 report evaluation of results by persons other than the treating therapist; four of these use ratings of the hospital staff (who may be acquainted with the treatment), four use mothers or parents reporting on their children to the treating therapist, one is a wife reporting on her husband to the therapist, and three use a second observer. Obviously, whatever factors enter in to cause observer and reporter biases are allowed full reign in most cases. While we cannot conclude from this that the reported results are *due to* observer and reporter biases (as is clearly indicated with the sampling biases), it is impossible to rule them out. Furthermore, a great deal of evidence from many areas of psychology leads us to be very skeptical of claims in which biases of this sort go uncontrolled.

Experimental Control

While control of sampling and observer effects are basic to a wide variety of research activities, including field and clinical research, more exacting control over experimental conditions has long been the sine qua non of the laboratory methods of experimental psychology. The power of the experimental method stems, in part, from keeping careful control over all but a few conditions, which are experimentally varied, with the subsequent effects of these variations being observed. Since psychotherapy is not a controlled experiment, it is probably unfair to expect this type of control. However, there are more and less accurate descriptions of what goes on during any form of therapy, and we can demand as accurate a description as possible in lieu of experimental control. Thus, while we are led to believe that methods such as counterconditioning, extinction of maladaptive responses, methods of reward, and the like, are applied in a manner analogous to their laboratory counterparts—examination of what is *actually done* reveals that the application of the learning techniques is embedded in a wide variety of activities (including many of the traditional therapy and interview techniques) which make any attribution of effect to the specific learning techniques impossible. Let us consider a few examples. From Wolpe (1960):

> Case 4—the patient had 65 therapeutic interviews, unevenly distributed over 27 months. The greater part of the time was devoted to discussions of how to gain control of her interpersonal relationships and stand up for herself. She had considerable difficulty with this at first, even though it had early become emotionally important to her to please the therapist. But she gradually mastered the assertive behavior required of her, overcame her anxieties and became exceedingly self-reliant in all interpersonal dealings, including those with her mother-in-law.

From Lazarus and Rachman (1957) on systematic desensitization:

> Case 1—The patient was instructed in the use of assertive responses and deep (nonhypnotic) relaxation. The first anxiety hierarchy dealt with was that of dull weather. Starting from "a bright sunny day" it was possible for the subject to visualize "damp overcast weather" without anxiety after 21 desensitization sessions, and 10 days after the completion of this hierarchy, she was able to report that, "the weather is much better, it doesn't even bother me to look at the weather when I wake up in the morning" (previously depressing). . . . During the course of therapy, part of the reason for the development of the anxiety state in this patient was unearthed. When she was 17 years old she had

become involved in a love affair with a married man 12 years her senior. The affair had been conducted in an extremely discreet manner for 4 years, during which time she had suffered from recurrent guilt feelings and shame—so much so, that on one occasion she had attempted suicide by throwing herself into a river. It was her custom to meet her lover after work *in the late afternoon*. The dull weather can be accounted for, as this affair took place in London.

From Rachman (1959):

> *Interview No. 12.* The patient having received a jolt in her love relationship, this session was restricted to a sort of nondirective, cathartic discussion. No desensitizing was undertaken because of A.G.'s depressed mood and obvious desire to "just talk."

These excerpts have been presented because they seem representative of the practices of behavioral therapists. As can be seen, the number and variety of activities that go on during these treatment sessions is great, including, in these few examples, discussions, explanations of techniques and principles, explanations of the unadaptiveness of anxiety and symptoms, hypnosis of various sorts, relaxation practice and training with and without hypnosis, "nondirective cathartic discussions," "obtaining an understanding of the patient's personality and background," and the "unearthing" of a 17-year-old memory of an illicit affair. The case reports are brief and presented anecdotally so that it is really impossible to know what else went on in addition to those things described. What should be abundantly clear from these examples is that there is no attempt to restrict what goes on to learning techniques. Since it seems clear that a great variety of things do go on, any attribution of behavior change to specific learning techniques is entirely unwarranted.

In summary, there are several important issues that must be differentiated. First, a review of both learning theory and of the empirical results of behavior therapy demonstrates that they can claim no special scientific status for their work on either ground. Second, there are important differences of opinion concerning the type of patient likely to be affected by behavior therapy. Grossberg (1964), for example, states that: "Behavior therapies have been most successful when applied to neurotic disorders with specific behavioral manifestations (p. 81)." He goes

on to point out that the results with alcoholism and sexual disorders have been disappointing and that the best results are
achieved with phobias and enuresis. He later
states that "desensitization only alleviates
those phobias that are being treated, but other
coexisting phobias remain at high strength,
indicating a specific treatment effect (p. 83)."
Wolpe et al. (1964), on the other hand, argue
that: "The conditioning therapist differs from
his colleagues in that he *seeks out* the precise
stimuli to anxiety, and finds himself able to
break down almost every neurosis into what
are essentially *phobic systems* (p. 11)." The
best controlled study (Lang & Lazovik, 1963)
indicates that "desensitization is very effective
in reducing the intense fear of snakes held by
normal subjects, though it can be questioned
whether this is a phobia in the clinical sense."

Thus, there seems to be some evidence
that these *techniques* (as techniques and not as
learning theory) are effective with certain
conditions.[4] We feel that this bears stressing
because psychotherapy has come to be narrowly defined in terms of dynamic, evocative,
and nondirective methods, placing unnecessary limitations on the kind of patient suitable
for psychotherapy. First, we must note that
behavior techniques are not new (as Murray,
1964, points out in a recent article). Freud
and Breuer used similar techniques prior to
the development of psychoanalysis. Bagby
described a number of these methods in 1928,
and therapy based on techniques designed to
eliminate undesirable responses was used for
many years by Stevenson Smith at the University of Washington Clinic. While most of
these techniques have been superseded by the
various forms of dynamic psychotherapy, recent work (Frank, 1961) suggests that the
time may be ripe for taking a fresh look at a
variety of methods such as hypnosis, suggestion, relaxation, and other approaches of a
more *structured nature* in which the therapist
takes a *more active role*. Needless to say, this
fresh look would best proceed unencumbered
by an inadequate learning theory and with
some minimal concern for control. As an

example of a nondynamic approach to patient
management, we refer to the work of Fairweather (1964) and his colleagues.

Reformulation

Up to this point our analysis has been primarily
critical. We have tried to show that many of the
so-called principles of learning employed by
workers with a behaviorist orientation are inadequate and are not likely to provide useful
explanations for clinical phenomena. In this
section we will examine the potential value of
ideas from different learning conceptions. Before proceeding, however, we would like to
discuss briefly the issue of the application of
"laws," principles, and findings from one area
(such as animal experimentation) to another
(such as neurosis and psychotherapy). The behaviorists have traditionally assumed that
principles established under highly controlled
conditions, usually with animal subjects, form
a scientific foundation for a psychology of
learning. Yet when they come to apply these
principles to human learning situations, the
transition is typically bridged by rather flimsy
analogies which ignore crucial differences between the situations, the species, etc. Recently, Underwood (1964) has made the following comments concerning this problem:

> Learning theories as developed in the animal-
> learning laboratory, have never seemed . . . to
> have relevance to the behavior of a subject in
> learning a list of paired associates. The emphasis
> upon the role of a pellet of food or a sip of water in
> the white rat's acquiring a response somehow
> never seemed to make contact with the human *S*
> learning to say VXK when the stimulus DOF
> was presented [p. 74].

We would add that the relevance is at least
equally obscure in applications of traditional
S-R reinforcement theory to clinical
phenomena.

We do *not* wish, however, to damn any and
all attempts to conceptualize clinical
phenomena in terms of principles of learning
developed outside the clinic. On the contrary,
recent work in learning may suggest certain
theoretical models which may prove useful in
conceptualizing the learning processes involved in psychotherapy and the development
of neuroses. Whether these notions can form
the basis for a useful learning conceptualization of clinical phenomena will depend upon

---

[4]Just how many neurotics fit the phobia and/or
specific symptom model is a complicated question,
the answer to which depends in part on what one's
own point of view leads one to look for. For example,
an informal census of the first 81 admissions to the
University of Oregon Psychology Clinic in 1964 revealed only 2 patients who could be so classified.

the ingenuity with which they are sub-sequently developed and upon their adequacy in encompassing the facts of neurosis and psychotherapy. Further, we would like to stress that their association with experimental work in the field of learning does not give them any a priori scientific status. Their status as explanatory principles in the clinical area must be empirically established within that area. In what follows, then, we will outline some ideas about learning and make some suggestions concerning their relevance to clinical problems.

Our view of learning centers around the concepts of information storage and retrieval. Learning is viewed as the process by which information about the environment is ac-quired, stored, and categorized. This cognitive view is, of course, quite contrary to the view that learning consists of the acquisition of specific responses; responses, according to our view, are mediated by the nature of the stored information, which may consist of facts or of strategies or programs analogous to the grammar that is acquired in the learning of a language. Thus, "what is learned" may be a system for generating responses as a conse-quence of the specific information that is stored. This general point of view has been emphasized by Lashley (see Beach et al., 1960), by Miller, Galanter, and Pribram (1960), in the form of the TOTE hypothesis, and by a number of workers in the cognitive learning tradition (Tolman, 1951; Wood-worth, 1958). Recently it has even been suggested as a necessary formulation for deal-ing with that eminently S-R area, motor skills (Adams, 1964; Fitts, 1964).

This conception of learning may be useful in the clinical area in two ways; one, in formulating a theoretical explanation for the acquisition or development of neurosis, symptoms, behavior pathology, and the like, and, two, in conceptualizing psychotherapy as a learning process, and suggesting new methods stemming from this learning model.

A conceptualization of the problem of neurosis in terms of information storage and retrieval is based on the fundamental idea that what is learned in a neurosis is a set of central strategies (or a program) which guide the indi-vidual's adaptation to his environment. Neuroses are not symptoms (responses) but are strategies of a particular kind which lead to certain observable (tics, compulsive acts, etc.) and certain other less observable, phenomena

(fears, feelings of depression, etc.). The whole problem of symptom substitution is thus seen as an instance of response substitution or response equipotentiality, concepts which are supported by abundant laboratory evidence.

Similarly, the problem of a learning con-ceptualization of unconscious phenomena may be reopened. Traditional S-R approaches have equated the unconscious with some kind of avoidance of a verbalization response. From our point of view, there is no reason to assume that people can give accurate descrip-tions of the central strategies mediating much of their behavior any more than a child can give a description of the grammatical rules which govern the understanding and produc-tion of his language. As a matter of fact, consciousness may very well be a special or extraordinary case—the rule being "unaware-ness" of the mediating strategies—which is in need of special explanation, rather than the reverse. This view avoids the cumbersome necessity of having to postulate specific fear experiences or the persistence of anxiety-motivated behavior, as has typically been done by S-R theorists with regard to uncon-scious phenomena. It also avoids equating the unconscious with the neurotic, which is a virtue since there is so much that goes on within "normal" individuals that they are unaware of. It further avoids the trap of attributing especially persistent and maladap-tive consequences to painful experiences. As Solomon (1964) points out, the existing evi-dence does not support the view that punish-ment and pain lead unequivocally to anxiety and maladaptive consequences.

The view of learning we have outlined does not supply a set of ready-made answers to clinical problems that can be applied from the laboratory, but it indicates what sort of ques-tions will have to be answered to achieve a meaningful learning conceptualization of neurosis and symptoms. Questions such as "What are the conditions under which strategies are acquired or developed?" stress the fact that these conditions may be quite different from the final observed behavior. That is to say, a particular symptom is not necessarily acquired because of some learning experience in which its stimulus components were associated with pain or fear-producing stimuli. Rather, a symptom may function as an equipotential response, mediated by a cen-tral strategy acquired under different cir-cumstances. As an example, consider Harlow's (1958, 1962) monkeys who developed a number of symptoms, the most striking being sexual impotence (a much better animal analogue of human neurosis than those typically cited as experimental neuroses [Liddell, 1944]). Their longitudinal record, or "learning history," indicates that the development of this abnormal "affectional system," as Harlow terms it, is dependent on a variety of nonisomorphic experiences, including the lack of a mother-infant relationship and the lack of a variety of peer-play experiences.

These brief examples are only meant to give a flavor of where a learning conception of neurosis which stresses the acquisition of strategies will lead. A chief advantage of this view is that it has *generality* built in at the core, rather than imported secondarily, as is the case with S-R concepts of stimulus and response generalization.

Let us now turn our attention to the very difficult problem of applying learning concepts to psychotherapy. Basically, we would argue that the development of methods and techniques is largely a function of the empirical skill and ingenuity of the individual-craftsman-therapist. Even a carefully worked-out and well-established set of learning principles (which we do not have at this time) would not necessarily tell us how to modify acquired strategies in the individual case—just as the generally agreed-upon idea that rewards affect performance does not tell us what will be an effective reward in any specific instance.

Bearing these cautions in mind, we might still address ourselves to the question of what applications are suggested by the learning approach we have presented. As a first suggestion, we might consider the analogy of learning a new language. Here we see a process that parallels psychotherapy insofar as it involves modifying or developing a new set of strategies of a pervasive nature. A careful study of the most effective techniques for the learning of a new language might yield some interesting suggestions for psychotherapy. Learning a new language involves the development of a new set of strategies for responding—new syntax as well as new vocabulary. Language learning *may or may not* be facilitated by an intensive attempt to make the individual *aware* of the strategies used, as is done in traditional language instruction which teaches old-fashioned grammar, and as is done, analogously, in those psychotherapies which stress insight. Alternatively, language learning sometimes seems

most rapid when the individual is immersed in surroundings (such as foreign country) where he hears nothing but the new language and where his old strategies and responses are totally ineffective.

Using this as a model for psychotherapy, we might suggest something like the following process: First, a careful study should be done to delineate the "neurotic language," both its vocabulary and its grammar, of the individual. Then a situation might be constructed (e.g., a group therapy situation) in which the individual's existing neurotic language is not understood and in which the individual must develop a new "language," a new set of central strategies, in order to be understood. The detailed working out of such a procedure might very well utilize a number of the techniques that have been found effective in existing therapies, both group and individual, and in addition draw on some new techniques from the fields of psycholinguistics and language learning.

These are, of course, but initial fragmentary guesses, and they may be wrong ones. But we believe that the conceptions on which these guesses are based are sufficiently supported by recent learning research to warrant serious attention. Although this reconceptualization may not lead immediately to the development of effective psychotherapeutic techniques, it may at least provide a first step in that direction.

REFERENCES

Adams, J. A. Motor skills. In P. R. Farnsworth (Ed.), *Annual Review of Psychology*, 1964, *15*, 181–202.

Bagby, E. *The psychology of personality*. New York: Holt, 1928.

Bandura, A. Psychotherapy as a learning process. *Psychological Bulletin*, 1961, *58*, 143–159.

Beach, F. A., Hebb, D. O., Morgan, C. T., and Nissen, H. *The neuropsychology of Lashley*. New York: McGraw-Hill, 1960.

Berlyne, D. E. *Conflict, arousal, and curiosity*. New York: McGraw-Hill, 1960.

Blodgett, H. C. The effect of introduction of reward upon the maze performance of rats. *University of California Publications in Psychology*, 1929, *4*, 113–134.

Breland, K., and Breland, M. The misbehavior of organisms. *American Psychologist*, 1961, *16*, 681–684.

Brogden, W. J. Sensory preconditioning. *Journal of Experimental Psychology,* 1939, *25,* 323–332.

Bugelski, B. R. *The psychology of learning.* New York: Holt, 1956.

Chomsky, N. Review of B. F. Skinner, *Verbal Behavior. Language,* 1959, *35,* 26–58.

Deutsch, J. A. The inadequacy of Hullian derivations of reasoning and latent learning. *Psychological Review,* 1956, *63,* 389–399.

Dollard J., and Miller, N. E. *Personality and psychotherapy.* New York: McGraw-Hill, 1950.

Eriksen, C. W. (Ed.) *Behavior and awareness.* Durham, N.C.: Duke Univer. Press, 1962.

Eysenck, H. J. (Ed.) *Behaviour therapy and the neuroses.* New York: Pergamon Press, 1960.

Fairweather, G. W. *Social psychology in treating mental illness: An experimental approach.* New York: Wiley, 1964.

Ferster, C. B., and Skinner, B. F. *Schedules of reinforcement.* New York: Appleton-Century-Crofts, 1957.

Fitts, P. M. Perceptual-motor skill learning. In A. W. Melton (Ed.), *Categories of human learning.* New York: Academic Press, 1964, pp. 244–285.

Frank, J. D. Problems of control in psychotherapy as exemplified by the psychotherapy research project of the Phipps Psychiatric Clinic. In E. A. Rubenstein and M. B. Parloff (Eds.), *Research in psychotherapy.* Washington, D.C.: American Psychological Association, 1959.

Frank, J. D. *Persuasion and healing: A comparative study of psychotherapy.* Baltimore: Johns Hopkins Press, 1961.

Fromm-Reichmann, Frieda. *Principles of intensive psychotherapy.* Chicago: Univer. Chicago Press, 1950.

Gibson, J. J. *The perception of the visual world.* Boston: Houghton Mifflin, 1950.

Gonzales, R. C., and Diamond, L. A test of Spence's theory of incentive motivation. *American Journal of Psychology,* 1960, *73,* 396–403.

Goodwin, W. R., and Lawrence, D. H. The functional independence of two discrimination habits associated with a constant stimulus situation. *Journal of Comparative and Physiological Psychology,* 1955, *48,* 437–443.

Grossberg, J. M. Behavior therapy: A review. *Psychological Bulletin,* 1964, *62,* 73–88.

Guthrie, E. R. *The psychology of learning.* New York: Harper, 1935.

Guttman, N. Laws of behavior and facts of perception. In S. Koch (Ed.), *Psychology: A study of a science.* Vol. 5. New York: McGraw-Hill, 1963, pp. 114–179.

Harlow, H. F. The nature of love. *American Psychologist,* 1958, *13,* 673–685.

Harlow, H. F. The heterosexual affectional system in monkeys. *American Psychologist,* 1962, *17,* 1–9.

Hebb, D. O. *The organization of behavior: A neurophysiological theory.* New York: Wiley, 1949.

Herbert, M. J., and Harsh, C. M. Observational learning by cats. *Journal of Comparative Psychology,* 1944, *37,* 81–95.

Hilgard, E. R. *Theories of learning.* New York: Appleton-Century-Crofts, 1956.

Hull, C. L. *Essentials of behavior.* New Haven: Yale Univer. Press, 1951.

Knight, R. P. Evaluation of the results of psychoanalytic therapy. *American Journal of Psychiatry,* 1941, *98,* 434.

Kohler, W. *Gestalt psychology.* New York: Liveright, 1929.

Krasner, L. Studies of the conditioning of verbal behavior. *Psychological Bulletin,* 1958, *55,* 148–170.

Krasner, L. The therapist as a social reinforcement machine. In H. H. Strupp (Ed.), *Second research conference on psychotherapy.* Chapel Hill, N.C.: American Psychological Association, 1961.

Krechevsky, I. The genesis of "hypotheses" in rats. *University of California Publications in Psychology,* 1932, *6,* 45–64.

Lang, P. J., and Lazovik, A. D. Experimental desensitization of a phobia. *Journal of Abnormal and Social Psychology,* 1963, *66,* 519–525.

Lawrence, D. H. The nature of a stimulus: Some relationships between learning and perception. In S. Koch (Ed.), *Psychology: A study of a science.* Vol. 5. New York: McGraw-Hill, 1963, pp. 179–212.

Lawrence, D. H., and DeRivera, J. Evidence for relational transposition. *Journal of Comparative and Physiological Psychology,* 1954, *47,* 465–471.

Lazarus, A. A. The results of behaviour therapy in 126 cases of severe neurosis. *Behaviour Research and Therapy,* 1963, *1,* 69–80.

Lazarus, A. A., and Rachman, S. The use of systematic desensitization in psychotherapy. *South African Medical Journal,* 1957, *32,* 934–937.

Leeper, R. L. Learning and the fields of perception, motivation and personality. In S. Koch (Ed.), *Psychology: A study of a science.* Vol. 5. New York: McGraw-Hill, 1963. pp. 365–487.

Lewin, K. *Field theory in social science.* New York: Harper, 1951. Ch. 4, pp. 60–86.

Liddell, H. S. Conditioned reflex method and experimental neurosis. In J. McV. Hunt (Ed.), *Personality and the behavior disorders.* New York: Ronald Press, 1944. Ch. 12.

Lundin, R. W. *Personality: An experimental approach.* New York: Macmillan, 1961.

Mackintosh, N. J. Extinction of a discrimination habit as a function of overtraining. *Journal of Comparative and Physiological Psychology,* 1963, *56,* 842–847.

Miller, G. A., Galanter, E. H., and Pribram, K. H. *Plans and the structure of behavior.* New York: Holt, Rinehart & Winston, 1960.

Miller, N. E. Liberalization of basic S-R concepts: Extension to conflict behavior, motivation, and social learning. In S. Koch (Ed.), *Psychology: A study of a science. Vol. 2.* New York: McGraw-Hill, 1959, pp. 196–292.

Moltz, H. Imprinting, empirical basis, and theoretical significance. *Psychological Bulletin,* 1960, *57,* 291–314.

Murray, E. J. Sociotropic learning approach to psychotherapy. In P. Worchel and D. Byrne (Eds.), *Personality change.* New York: Wiley, 1964, pp. 249–288.

Olds, J., and Milner, P. Positive reinforcement produced by electrical stimulation of septal area and other regions of rat brain. *Journal of Comparative and Physiological Psychology,* 1954, *47,* 419–427.

Osgood, C. E. *Method and theory in experimental psychology.* New York: Oxford Univer. Press, 1953.

Postman, L. Perception and learning. In S. Koch (Ed.), *Psychology: A study of a science. Vol. 5.* New York: McGraw-Hill, 1963, pp. 30–113.

Rachman, S. The treatment of anxiety and phobic reactions by systematic desensitization psychotherapy. *Journal of Abnormal and Social Psychology,* 1959, *58,* 259–263.

Riley, D. A. The nature of the effective stimulus in animal discrimination learning: Transposition reconsidered. *Psychological Review,* 1958, *65,* 1–7.

Ritchie, B. F., Aeschliman, B., and Peirce, P. Studies in spatial learning. VIII. Place performance and the acquisition of place dispositions. *Journal of Comparative and Physiological Psychology,* 1950, *43,* 73–85.

Rotter, J. B. *Social learning and clinical psychology.* New York: Prentice-Hall, 1954.

Scott, J. P. Critical periods in behavioral development. *Science,* 1962, *138,* 949–958.

Skinner, B. F. *The behavior of organisms: An experimental analysis.* New York: Appleton-Century-Crofts, 1938.

Skinner, B. F. *Verbal behavior.* New York: Appleton-Century-Crofts, 1957.

Solomon, R. L. Punishment. *American Psychologist,* 1964, *19,* 239–253.

Spence, K. W. The differential response in animals to stimuli varying within a single dimension. *Psychological Bulletin,* 1937, *44,* 430–440.

Strickland, Bonnie R., and Crowne, D. P. The need for approval and the premature termination of psychotherapy. *Journal of Consulting Psychology,* 1963, *27,* 95–101.

Thistlethwaite, D. A critical review of latent learning and related experiments. *Psychological Bulletin,* 1951, *48,* 97–129.

Tolman, E. C. *Purposive behavior in animals and men.* New York: Appleton-Century, 1932.

Tolman, E. C. Sign gestalt or conditioned reflex? *Psychological Review,* 1933, *40,* 391–411.

Tolman, E. C. *Collected papers in psychology.* Berkeley: Univer. California Press, 1951.

Tolman, E. C., and Honzik, C. H. Introduction and removal of reward and maze performance in rats. *University of California Publications in Psychology,* 1930, *4,* 257–275.

Underwood, B. J. The representativeness of rote verbal learning. In A. W. Melton (Ed.), *Categories of human learning.* New York: Academic Press, 1964, pp. 47–78.

Watson, A. J. The place of reinforcement in the explanation of behavior. In W. H. Thorpe and O. L. Zangwill, *Current problems in animal behavior.* Cambridge, Cambridge Univer. Press, 1961.

Wolpe, J. *Psychotherapy by reciprocal inhibition.* Palo Alto, Calif.: Stanford Univer. Press. 1958.

Wolpe, J. Reciprocal inhibition as the main basis of psychotherapeutic effects. In H. J. Eysenck (Ed.), *Behaviour therapy and the neuroses.* New York: Pergamon Press, 1960, pp. 88–113.

Wolpe, J., Salter, A., and Reyna, L. J. (Eds.) *The conditioning therapies.* New York: Holt, Rinehart & Winston, 1964.

Woodworth, R. S. *Dynamics of behavior.* New York: Holt, 1958.

Yates, A. J. Symptoms and symptom substitution. *Psychological Review,* 1958, *65,* 371–374.

Zener, K. The significance of behavior accompanying conditioned salivary secretion for theories of the conditioned response. *American Journal of Psychology,* 1937, *50,* 384–403.

Integrative Directions

The task of bridging concepts drawn from one theoretical orientation to those of another is not only a feat of no mean proportions intellectually, but is often one met with dismay, if not derogation, by doctrinaire loyalists who stand on one or another side of the attempted synthesis.

Such was the fate that befell John Dollard and Neal Miller in response to their epoch-making book, *Personality and Psychotherapy*. To psychoanalysts it was seen as a simplification, if not perversion, of their fundamental thesis, a series of flimsy analogies to analytic theory, offering no new explanatory powers or insights. To behaviorists, it was old wine in new bottles. As they saw it, a proper application of behavior-learning principles would lead, not to mere translations of analytic notions, but to the formulation of an entirely new conception of psychopathology and therapy.

A more recent effort, more broad-ranging in scope, yet also derived and informed from a behavioral perspective, is to be found in the work of Arnold Lazarus. That his integration has also been subject to dismissal, if not denunciation, by proponents of more doctrinaire views, should not be surprising either.

44 New Conditions of Therapeutic Learning

John Dollard and Neal E. Miller

Repression interferes with the neurotic's higher mental precesses and prevents him from using these effectively in solving his emotional problems. This repression was learned in a social situation in which fear, shame, or guilt were attached to certain spoken words and generalized from them to thoughts. In therapy a new type of social situation is created, the opposite of that responsible for the learning of repression. In this new type of social situation the patient is urged to say whatever comes into his mind and to be especially sure to resist suppressing those words that he finds himself afraid, ashamed, or reluctant to say. As the patient says words that provoke fear or shame, the therapist does not punish him or show any signs of disapproval; he remains warm and accepting. In this way, the fear, shame, and

From *Personality and Psychotherapy* by John Dollard and Neal E. Miller, copyright 1950, and used by permission of McGraw-Hill Book Company and the authors.

guilt attached to talking about tabooed topics are extinguished. This extinction generalizes from speaking to thinking. It also generalizes from the painful but not completely repressed topics that are discussed to similar topics that could not be discussed because they were repressed. As the drives motivating repression are weakened by such generalization, it becomes possible to talk about those additional topics that had been weakly repressed, and another cycle of extinction and generalization is initiated. Thus repression is gradually unlearned under permissive social conditions that are the opposite to the punitive ones under which it was learned. This is the general outline of the procedure; the specific steps will now be discussed in more detail.

New conditions permit new learning. We may ask why does the patient not unlearn repression for himself and shake off its hampering effects alone? The answer seems to be that the ordinary conditions of social life favor the learning of repression and favor maintaining it in those who have already learned it.

Unless some new circumstances can be brought to bear on the problem, the patient will continue to live his distorted life until its end without relief from neurotic tension.

The therapeutic situation which Freud hit upon after considerable trial and error is arranged so that anxiety can be steadily weakened by extinction. As anxiety is reduced, the repressed sentences gradually become articulate. This situation is different from that of childhood in that it is vastly more permissive of free speech and free naming of emotional factors. The constricting conditions of childhood learning are reversed.

Free Association: The Compulsion to Utter

The first of the new conditions of learning imposed on the patient is that of free association. Under the rule of free association the patient is required to say everything that comes to mind immediately, to resist and abandon the etiquette of the ordinary conversation. He is not to reject any thought whatever, be it trivial, personal, embarrassing, obscene, aggressive, or fanciful. The patient is to try hardest to say that which is most difficult. He is to resist the ordinary constraints of logic, and he is not to try for a connected narrative account. If imageal responses occur, he is to describe them since they may be the cues to which emotional responses are attached by primitive mechanisms. In short he is to say immediately what comes to his mind, using his voice to describe what occurs on the stage of the mind much as a radio announcer might give a play-by-play account of a game to his unseeing audience.

The rule of free association is not a mere invitation to speak freely. It is an absolute obligation which is the foundation of the therapeutic situation. It is a compulsion which has some of the rigor of any compulsion. This rule defines the "patient's work" which is to drive ruthlessly through to the pronouncement of sentences which may evoke sickening anxiety. The rule is a force which is applied against the force of neurotic fear. Without it, and unless he follows it, the patient will remain fixed in his neurotic habits and cannot recover the free use of his mind.

Even if he wished to, the therapist could not elicit the relevant information by questioning because he does not know what questions to ask. At the outset the therapist is baffled himself. Furthermore, the patient must *volunteer* information, *i.e.*, he must take the risk of saying what he must say in the face of whatever hampering forces there are. Only thus can extinction of fear occur.

The effect of the rule is to motivate the patient to talk. The intense energy of the neurotic conflict must be put *behind* the work of the therapy. The therapist must discover what the patient's difficulties are and must surmise how the neurotic responses are motivated and rewarded. Looking to the future, he must estimate what motivations and rewards are available for establishing new habits and what conflicting responses stand in the way of these habits. The information needed to form these judgments can come only from the patient.

The patient invariably finds the therapeutic situation surprising—"different" from what he thought it would be. This is natural since the patient inevitably thought it would be like the suppressive situations of his past. It is different in another respect also. The patient has not realized how much of the burden of therapy would be placed upon him. He does not understand the nature of psychological treatment and has little belief in it. He had hoped for a quick, and often passive, cure. He learns, not always with pleasure, that no drugs, surgery, or other physical measure will be helpful.

Free association is not free and easy. Free association is in some respects not aptly named. Certainly it is far from "free and easy." At times and recurrently, the patient finds it very hard work. As he loyally follows the rule he finds mysterious opposition arising within him. He finds that same fear arising which was present when he last tried to talk freely to himself, that is, in childhood. Anxiety reappears at the slightest cues of the forbidden sentences. Habits of suppression also tend to be activated and the patient is inclined to dodge the rule by "private assumptions" that such-and-such matter surely could not be relevant.

Such was the case in the first four hours of the treatment of Mrs. A. These hours were marked by reiteration of her symptoms, by pleadings for advice, and by silent periods. Each of these manifestations prevented her from getting ahead with her task. On the fifth day it appeared that Mrs. A was limiting herself to a narrow area, *i.e.*, "things connected with my illness as I define them." Mrs. A rehearsed her litany of symptoms and then came again to the end of her line of thought, saying, "I've told you everything that happened in the last four months." The therapist again explained the rule of free association and asked her to make no exceptions to it: nothing was to be left out because it referred to events before the last four months (when the neurosis became evident), because it seemed to her unconnected to the illness, or for any other reason. In short, Mrs. A was to exercise no censorship and to say what came to her mind. Although Mrs. A followed the rule with ever better success, she showed the expected tendencies to repression and suppression whenever a new fundamental theme was hit upon.

We must not conclude from this discussion that the course of psychotherapy is one continuous anxiety attack provoked by the effort to state the forbidden. The rule of free association, though rigorously stated, is gently and gradually taught. Though therapy is bound to bring some discomfort, the patient will pause for many a breather. He will hit on some lines of association of a highly hopeful and encouraging character. He will find comfort in seeing some of the dread memories of the past in the proportionate light of adult reason. The situation is so arranged that, despite stormy moments, the patient does not dread every hour. Anxiety reduction is intended to be gradual and the amount of anxiety which the patient is asked to bear, bearable.

New Benign Conditions: Permissiveness

We now turn from the rules of the psychotherapeutic situation to the nature of the situation itself. From the patient's standpoint, the novelty of the therapeutic situation lies in its permissiveness. He is allowed a good turn to talk. His statements are received by the therapist with an even, warm attention. The therapist is understanding and friendly. He is willing, so far as he can, to look at matters from the patient's side and make the best case for the patient's view of things. The therapist is not shocked by what he hears and does not criticize. The frightened patient learns that here is a person he can really talk to—perhaps the first such person in his life. These permissive circumstances are genuinely new, and they have their great effect. The fears evoked by free communication are gradually extinguished through lack of punishment. If the situation were not so designed, if acid comments and horrified surprise greeted the patient's statements, no extinction of fear, and therefore no therapy, could occur.

Generalization to the therapist. Therapy occurs as part of a relation to another human being. The therapist acts as a focusing stimulus in the therapeutic situation. He is similar to real-world persons whom the patient has known and yet some of his behavior is markedly different from that displayed by other persons in the patient's past. The therapist attempts to define himself as a stimulus as little as possible. Nevertheless, he immediately evokes two types of reaction from his patient which indicate that he is a very important stimulus. Since he is a human being, similar to those who have punished the patient in the past, a great deal of anxiety is immediately and automatically generalized to him. Were this not so, psychotherapy could not occur. On the other hand, the patient views the therapist as a specialist and accords him the prestige of his specialist's role. To the therapist as a specialist, the patient generalizes responses of trust, confidence, optimism. In this role the therapist acquires immediately the capacity to reassure the patient. This capacity to be reassured is generalized from other authoritarian figures and specialists who have, in the past, aided the patient to solve difficult problems.

Therapist not prude, judge, or gossip. Freedom from fear of punishment is a highly permissive circumstance. Thus, the therapist discriminates himself from a variety of frightening human beings, such as the prude, the judge, or the gossip. If necessary, the therapist will indicate that the patient need have no fear of "shocking" him. He is accustomed to viewing the trials, strivings, and failings of others with compassionate neutrality.

The therapist may need to discriminate himself from the judge who listens, evaluates, and condemns. As Hanns Sachs put it in a lecture at the Berlin Psychoanalytic Institute (in 1932), the therapist does *not* act like the bailiff who must warn his prisoner, "What you say may be used against you." The wisdom of this aspect of the therapist's role is evident when we consider how hard it is to get at the truth, say in a court of law, when the defendant resists through fear of punishment.

The patient usually comes to the therapeutic situation with a lively fear of gossip. The therapist may reduce this fear by assuring him that information given will not be passed on.

Then the therapist must make good on this assertion—a matter of considerable delicacy in hospitals and clinics where records must be kept. Despite these assurances of reversal of conventional attitudes, the patient will have to "learn" to trust the therapist in the actual situation. Such trust is not automatic but is slowly built up as the patient risks confidences and finds they are not punished.

How the Therapist Rewards Talking

Talking despite anxiety, talking while anxious is "the patient's work." He must be kept at this work if therapeutic results are to occur. Like any other habit, talking while anxious must be rewarded strongly enough so that the net balance of reward is in favor of talking, else the patient will remain silent or will hit upon lines of sentences which do not produce anxiety. This behavior often occurs for shorter or longer periods of time.

The most obvious reward for talking is the full, free, and exclusive attention of the therapist. The therapist is a good listener—sometimes, the patient feels, too good a listener. Usually the patient has a strong need for such attention. He has complained about his difficulties until he has exhausted the patience of his environment, and others have become tired of listening. To such a starved person, the permissive attention of the therapist comes as a new and striking reward. To have others give real thought to one's problems is a frequent precondition of help; the therapist's attention, therefore, makes the patient more hopeful and reduces anxiety at being isolated.

Therapist's acceptance of past. As noted above, the therapist listens, accepts, does not condemn. The patient has been used to being interrupted, judged, and often condemned. The therapist takes the view that what is past had to happen. The patient understands this acceptance as forgiveness which, in a sense, it is. But it is no routine forgiveness based on the supposition that the patient, once forgiven, will go forth and make the same mistake again. The therapist accepts the past because he must do so in order to understand it. Without understanding the past, the future cannot be changed.

Mere catharsis not effective. In this connection we state that we do not accept the "catharsis doctrine" of psychotherapy. This doctrine seems to say that merely telling someone else of one's sins or mistakes will have a therapeutic effect. We would not expect such therapeutic effect from mere recital. If the recital is followed by condemnation and punishment we would not expect the effect of confession to be therapeutic. The patient is not relieved by a confession if he is told at the end "What an awful thing to do!" Catharsis should work, according to our hypothesis, only under permissive conditions. Its essential features seem to be two: confession followed by nonpunishment may lower guilt or anxiety; being forgiven reduces a sense of isolation and indicates acceptance into the circle of cooperative human beings. Being forgiven also makes it possible for the patient to hope for reward if he tries a new solution.

Therapist's understanding and remembering a reward. Another powerful reward for the patient's work is that the therapist *understands* what the patient is saying. He understands the communications in their literal, obvious sense and often much more deeply, seeing relations between apparently separate acts. In the past the patient has had much trouble in getting his points across; neither he nor anyone else had understood his behavior very well. The patient shows a justifiable annoyance if the therapist is stupid or unable to understand the patient's native tongue.[1]

In this connection, having the therapist remember what the patient has said in the past is one of the most effective guarantees of good listening. Mr. Earl F. Zinn, one of our finest therapists, remarked on the great importance of having the patient feel himself to be "in the therapist's thoughts" even when the interview is not occurring. Zinn mentioned a case where such an indication on the part of the therapist had converted an apathetic patient into one zealously doing the patient's work.

Therapist's calmness and sympathy rewards talking. To have the therapist speak in a calm manner about matters of intense importance to the patient gives marked reward. The therapist is not frightened or appalled by the patient's problems; his manner indicates that he has seen such, perhaps worse, before. The patient's shame or anxiety will be greatly

---

[1] Dollard remembers his first control at the Berlin Psychoanalytic Institute. Dr. Max Eitingon had secured for him a German patient. Dollard's German, though deemed sufficient for the purpose, was far from overlearned to the point where easy communication was possible. The German patient was correspondingly annoyed whenever the therapist failed to grasp the fine points of a statement.

reduced if he is able to assume the therapist's attitude toward his own problems.

The therapist may occasionally reward by direct expressions of sympathy or approval if the patient has had an especially trying time or endured unusual suffering in the effort to carry out his part of the work. But the therapist is careful and niggardly with his approval. He gives no loose sympathy. He tries to place his rewards directly after those actions of the patient which have the best chance of forwarding the therapeutic work. He knows that, to a degree at least, the patient must suffer to learn and that there is no way in which this suffering can be entirely abolished.

Therapist speaks tentatively, does not cross-question. The patient comes to therapy with justified fears that he will be asked to bear more than he can stand. The life situations which have precipitated his symptoms have usually done just this. The therapist therefore does well not to justify any such fears. For example, if he must label unconscious drives or point out unseen connections, he does so tentatively, thus permitting the patient to feel free rather than trapped. He suggests that such-and-such is possible, may be the case, etc. If the patient is alarmed, the therapist does not press.

Furthermore, the therapist does not cross-question his patient. The patient doses himself with the amount of anxiety he can stand at that time. He is not exposed by cross-questioning. Such questioning might punish free association by evoking unbearable embarrassment or fear. In therapy, the patient is able to push his thinking up to his limit without granting himself the margin of safety which he would soon find he needed if he were exposed to interrogation.

The therapist, on his part, must learn to wait and hear his patient out, letting him say what he must say when he is able to do so. The therapist must therefore learn to endure stopping on many a hot trail and failing to complete a factual picture that seemed almost obvious. The patient likes a man who takes his time.

How the Therapist Recognizes What Is Repressed

The patient frequently needs help in identifying distortions of his mental life and the therapist must be able to give this help. But before he can do so he must construct a rational account for himself. The technique is this. He is trained to listen attentively to the patient, noting all evenly, and failing to impose *a priori* hypotheses. His goal is to have a complete and rational verbal account of the patient's life. In the ideal case the therapist has no tendency to repress any of the elements of the patient's verbal account nor the emotions which may be evoked by these. He has within himself the learned drives to give a complete account, to be logical, to judge appropriateness of response. These drives are aroused by the cues of incompleteness or inappropriateness in the patient's account; he will sense that the stimuli alleged should not provoke a certain kind of response or that there is "something missing" in the account. He will then ask himself what response would be appropriate or what the missing link of thought could be. The therapist may suddenly feel that a given anecdote does not "make sense" and will ask himself what would have to be true if it were to be sensible.

As he tries to answer these questions for himself he hits on hypotheses about the patient's motivation and behavior. Frequently these hypotheses refer to what is repressed, those motives which are present and active but inexpressible. Summed up and taken together these queries and hunches constitute a theory of the patient's life; they become part of the therapist's plan of campaign of conducting the therapy. The therapist, so to say, plays the patient's tune softly on his own piano and listens for gaps, disharmonies, sour notes, and failures to end the music. The therapist listens at once to the patient and to the sentences that dart into his own mind concerning the patient's account of his behavior. In the best case these sentences which the therapist can make, but which the patient cannot make, describe that which is repressed in the patient's mental life.

Blocked associations as pointers. Although the foregoing is the most fundamental activity, there are many additional aids and helps. For instance, blocked lines of association act as pointers. The therapist notes the places where the blocking occurs and asks himself what "should" have come next. Such blocking can occur through a fearful withholding or through repression. In the case of the former, the patient must overcome his fear and speak what he knows; repression can best be attacked by following to the letter the rule of free association.

Significance of the blank mind. "Nothing

coming to mind" indicates repressive activity. The patient who has been starved for years for a chance to speak and who has his whole life behind him suddenly cannot think of anything else to say. Since the therapist knows that this is impossible in a free mind, he assumes that repression is at work, *i.e.*, that the patient has something to say but unconsciously dares not say it. In this case, the therapist may merely insist that the patient can talk and urge him to proceed, or he may attempt to stimulate the patient by interpretation. In the latter case, he might ask, "Have you had any thoughts about me, my office, or our association?" Frequently this move on the therapist's part will bring the patient to state that he had personal or critical thoughts regarding the therapist which were the reason for his reluctance to talk. The patient fears particularly to alienate the therapist by criticism and thus run the risk of losing his help and support in dealing with the neurosis. However, any strong motive of which the patient is deeply ashamed can cause silence. Repression falls alike on the description of the motive and on all other sentences lest they might lead to it.

Patient B spent almost a month in therapy during which nothing important happened and the treatment was at a standstill. Considerable parts of every session were spent in resistant silence. The patient insisted that he had no thoughts at all. At the end of this difficult period of waiting, he finally brought out some sentences which indicated strong fear of homosexual motivation within himself and some real evidence for the existence of such motivation. Thereafter his ability to communicate was remarkably freed for a time. The silent "spots" dropped out and much new information was brought forward.

Failure to deal with common areas of response. If the patient fails to talk about a common area of response, the therapist may infer that there is some conflict in connection with this area. If a married person, for instance, is in the therapeutic situation for three months and does not mention his sexual life, the therapist will sense something "peculiar" about this omission. The therapist argues that the matter of sex response would be bound to come to mind in a free discussion during this period of time. If this did not occur, it was because the discussion was not free and repression or withholding was somehow operating.

Dreams. Dreams also may point to re-pressed material; in fact, they have been called by Freud the "straight road" to unconscious mental life. As already noted, dreams are private, imageal responses which produce cues. These cues are what are "seen" as the dream. Since they are private responses they are less likely to have strong anxiety attached to them and are likely to be "franker." For example, early in Mrs. A's treatment, she had a dream which portrayed her as being married to her foster brother. This dream pointed to an incestuous wish which Mrs. A could not express in a more direct way at that time. Later it was learned that she had had sex relations with this brother.

Slips of the tongue. Slips of the tongue and other errors sometimes attract attention to repressed material. Mrs. A said that her husband had once agreed to meet her in downtown New York and then failed to appear at the agreed-upon time and place. "He left me *strangled* there," she said. Her intent was to say "stranded" but her strong feelings of anger and fear entered and caused the slip. At the time this slip occurred, however, she was not able to express resentment of her husband directly. It seemed to the therapist that the slip condensed the following thought: "He neglected me, left me stranded; I could have strangled him for this; had I tried he would have strangled me."

Steretyped failures may point to repressed. Steretyped outcomes of life dilemmas may also indicate a conflict area. Repeated divorces, for instance, may point to severe sexual anxieties which become attached to each wife in turn and ultimately drive the husband away. Once out of the committed sex situation, anxiety is reduced and sex approach tendencies become dominant, thus leading to another marriage. The girl who would like to marry but always finds some serious fault with the actual man who presents himself is suspect by the man in the street as well as by the psychiatrist who asks, "Is she perhaps afraid to marry?" The man whose friendships with other men always begin with great intimacy and run through an inevitable course to neglect and termination shows another type of "stereotyped outcome." The therapist would like to know, "Does he perhaps discover that he likes his new friend too well and does he fear that the relationship might become more than friendship?" With some such hypothesis the repeated breaking off may become intelligible.

In the case of Mrs. A, repeated seductions

pointed to an area of conflict. In speaking of these seductions Mrs. A always said, "He *took advantage* of me." This might have been a mere fashion of phrasing the matter but proved not to be so. Mrs. A was stating that she had had sex relations but denying that she had had any responsibility for such relations. There was a hint in this disclaimer, which proved to be a

fact, that Mrs. A's "conditions of love" included the condition that she should not be responsible herself for sexual activity but should have it forced upon her. It turned out that the problem of assuming responsibility for her own sexual feelings was central in Mrs. A's life.

45 Multimodal Behavior Therapy: Treating the BASIC ID

Arnold A. Lazarus

Progress in the field of psychotherapy is hindered by a factor that is endemic in our society: an item is considered newsworthy, and accolades are accorded when claims run counter to the dictates of common sense. Thus everything from megavitamins to anal lavages and primal screams gains staunch adherents who, in their frenetic search for a panacea, often breed confusion worse confounded. The present paper emphasizes that patients are usually troubled by a multitude of *specific* problems which should be dealt with by a similar multitude of *specific* treatments. The approach advocated herein is very different from those systems which cluster presenting problems into ill-defined constructs and then direct one or two treatment procedures at these constructs. The basic assumption is that durable (long-lasting) therapeutic results depend upon the amount of effort expended by patient and therapist across at least six or seven parameters.

Research into the interaction between technique and relationship variables in therapy has shown that an effective therapist "must be more than a 'nice guy' who can exude prescribed interpersonal conditions— he must have an armamentarium of scientifically derived skills and techniques to supplement his effective interpersonal relations" (Woody, 1971, p. 8). Deliberately excluded

From *The Journal of Nervous and Mental Disease*, *156*, 404–411. Copyright 1973, The Williams & Wilkins Company. Reprinted by permission.

Several colleagues made incisive criticisms of the initial draft. I am especially grateful to Bob Karlin, Bill Mulligan, Carole Pearl, and Terry Wilson.

from the present formulation is the empathic, nonjudgmental warmth, wit, and wisdom which characterize those therapists who help rather than harm their clients (Bergin, 1971). If this were an article on surgical techniques and procedures, we would presuppose that individuals who apply the prescribed methods are free from pronounced tremors and possess more than a modicum of manual dexterity. Thus, it is hoped that multimodal behavioral procedures will attract nonmechanistic therapists who are flexible, empathic, and genuinely concerned about the welfare of their clients.

The main impetus for all forms of treatment probably stems from the general urgency of human problems and the need for practical assistance. This has lent acceptance to technically faulty work that would not pass muster in other fields, and every informed practitioner is all too aware of the fragmentary and contradictory theories that hold sway in the absence of experimental evidence. Apart from the plethora of different techniques, systems, and theories, we have conflicting models and paradigm clashes as exemplified by the differences between radical behaviorists and devout phenomenologists. Attempts to blend divergent models into integrative or eclectic harmony may often result in no more than syncretistic muddles (Reisman, 1971; Woody, 1971). And yet without general guiding principles that cut across all systems of therapy, we are left with cabalistic vignettes in place of experimental data or even clinical evidence. Multimodal behavior therapy encompasses: (1) specification of goals and problems; (2) specification of treatment techniques to achieve these goals and remedy these problems; and (3) systematic measurement of the relative success of these techniques.

Since all patients are influenced by processes that lie beyond the therapist's control and comprehension, the field of psychological treatment and intervention is likely to foster superstitious fallacies as readily as well-established facts. The tendency to ascribe causative properties to the *last* event in any sequence is all too well known (e.g., her stomach pains must be due to the sausage she just ate for lunch). Thus a patient, after grappling with a problem for years, starts massaging his left kneecap while plucking his right ear lobe and experiences immediate and lasting relief from tenacious symptoms. If a therapist happens to be close at hand, a new technique is likely to be born and placed alongside the parade of other "break-throughs" with the screamers, confronters, disclosers, relaxers, dreamers, and desensitizers. And if the therapist happens to be sufficiently naive, enthusiastic, and charismatic, we will probably never convince him, his students, or his successful patients that the knee-and-ear technique per se is not the significant agent of change. To guard against this penchant, we must insist upon the precise specification of the operations by which systematic assessment of the efficacy of a treatment for a specific problem is made on a regular basis.

The foregoing variables plus the power struggle between psychiatrists and psychologists and the various schools therein tend to hamper progress. The field, over the span of the past eight years, is described by two leading research clinicians as "chaotic" (Colby, 1964; Frank, 1971). Part of the confusion may also be ascribed to the fact that there is a human (but unscientific) penchant to search for unitary treatments and cures. How nice if insight alone or a soul-searing scream could pave the way to mental health. How simple and convenient for countless addicts if aversion therapy afforded long-lasting results. And what a boon to phobic sufferers if their morbid fears were enduringly assuaged by systematic desensitization and assertive training methods. But while short-lived relief is available to most, we must concur with Lesse that for most syndromes "there is very little proof at this time that any one given technique is superior to another in the long-range therapy of a particular type of psychogenic problem" (1972, p. 330).

Notwithstanding the biases that lead to theoretical befuddlement, most clinicians would probably agree with the pragmatic assumption that the more a patient learns in therapy, the less likely he is to relapse afterwards. Thus, an alcoholic treated only by aversion therapy would be more likely to relapse than his counterpart who had also received relaxation therapy (Blake, 1965). The benefits that accrue from aversion therapy plus relaxation training would be further potentiated by the addition of assertive training, family therapy, and vocational guidance (Lazarus, 1965). This general statement implies that *lasting change* is at the very least a function of combined *techniques, strategies,* and *modalities.* This vitiates the search for a panacea, or a single therapeutic modality. But a point of diminishing returns obviously exists. If two aspirins are good for you, ten are not five times better. When and why should we stop pushing everything from transcendental meditation to hot and cold sitz baths at our clients? Conversely, how, when, where, and why do we infer that in a given instance, meditation plus sensitivity training is preferable to psychodrama and contingency contracting? Above all, how can we wield Occam's razor to dissect the chaos of these diverse psychotherapeutic enterprises into meaningful and congruent components?

Seven Modalities

An arbitrary division created *sui generis* would simply turn back the clock on the composite theories and facts that psychologists have amassed to date. It is no accident that ever since the publication of Brentano's *Psychologie vom empirischen Standpunkte* in 1874, acts like ideation, together with feeling states and sensory judgments, have constituted the main subject matter of general psychology. In other words, psychology as the scientific study of behavior has long been concerned with sensation, imagery, cognition, emotion, and interpersonal relationships. If we examine psychotherapeutic processes in the light of each of these basic modalities, seemingly disparate systems are brought into clearer focus, and the necessary and sufficient conditions for long-lasting therapeutic change might readily be discerned.

Every patient-therapist interaction involves *behavior* (be it lying down on a couch and free associating, or actively role-playing a significant encounter), *affect* (be it the silent joy of nonjudgmental acceptance, or the sobbing release of pent-up anger), *sensation* (which covers a wide range of sensory stimuli from the spontaneous awareness of bodily discomfort to the deliberate cultivation of specific sensual delights), *imagery* (be it the fleeting glimpse of a childhood memory, or the contrived perception of a calm-producing scene), and *cognition* (the insights, philosophies, ideas, and judgments that constitute our fundamental values, attitudes, and beliefs). All of these take place within the context of an *interpersonal* relationship, or various interpersonal relationships. An added dimension with many patients is their need for medication or *drugs* (e.g., phenothiazine derivatives and various antidepressants and mood regulators). Taking the first letter of each of the foregoing italicized words, we have the acronym BASIC ID. Obviously, the proposed seven modalities are interdependent and interactive.

If we approach a patient *de novo* and inquire in detail about his salient behaviors, affective responses, sensations, images, cognitions, interpersonal relationships, and his need for drugs or medication, we will probably know more about him than we can hope to obtain from routine history taking and psychological tests. Whether or not these general guidelines can provide all that we need to know in order to be of therapeutic service is an empirical question.*

Other Systems

While it is important to determine whether the BASIC ID and the various combinations thereof are sufficiently exhaustive to encompass most vagaries of human conduct, it is perhaps more compelling first to view, very briefly, a few existing systems of therapy in the light of these modalities. Most systems touch lightly on the majority of modalities; very few pay specific and direct attention to each particular zone. Psychoanalysis deals almost exclusively with cognitive-affective interchanges. The neo-Reichian school of bioenergetics (Lowen, 1967) focuses upon behavior (in the form of "body language"), and the sensory-affective dimension. Encounter

*Some may argue that the absence of a "spiritual" dimension is an obvious hiatus, although in the interests of parsimony, it can be shown that cognitive-affective interchanges readily provide the necessary vinculum.

groups and Gestalt therapy display a similar suspicion of the "head" and are inclined to neglect cognitive material for the sake of affective and sensory responses. Gestalt therapists also employ role-playing and imagery techniques. The Masters and Johnson (1970) sex-training regimen deals explicitly with sexual behavior, affective processes, the "sensate focus," various re-educative features, and the correction of misconceptions, all within a dyadic context, preceded by routine medical and laboratory examinations. They do not avail themselves of imagery techniques (e.g., desensitization, self-hypnosis, or fantasy projection), a fact which may limit their overall success rate. (See the final chapter of this book for further elaboration on this point.)

Perhaps it is worth stressing at this point that the major hypothesis, backed by the writer's clinical data, is that *durable results are in direct proportion to the number of specific modalities deliberately invoked by any therapeutic system.* Psychoanalysis, for instance, is grossly limited because penetrating insights can hardly be expected to restore effective functioning in people with deficient response repertoires—they need explicit training, modeling, and shaping for the acquisition of adaptive social patterns. Conversely, nothing short of coercive manipulation is likely to develop new response patterns that are at variance with people's fundamental belief systems. Indeed, insight, self-understanding, and the correction of irrational beliefs must usually precede behavior change whenever faulty assumptions govern the channels of manifest behavior. In other instances, behavior change must occur before "insight" can develop (Lazarus, 1971a). Thus, cognitive restructuring and overt behavior training are often reciprocal. This should not be misconstrued as implying that a judicious blend of psychoanalysis and behavior therapy is being advocated. Psychoanalytic therapy is unscientific and needlessly complex; behavioristic therapy is often mechanistic and needlessly simplistic. The points being emphasized transcend any given system or school of therapy. However, adherence to social learning theory (Bandura, 1969) as the most elegant theoretical system to explain our therapeutic sorties places the writer's identification within the province of behavior therapy—hence "multimodal behavior therapy." Perhaps the plainest way of expressing our major thesis is to stress that comprehensive treatment at the very least calls for the correction of irrational beliefs, deviant behaviors, unpleasant feelings, intrusive images, stressful relationships, negative sensations, and possible biochemical imbalance. To the extent that problem identification (diagnosis) systematically explores each of these modalities, whereupon therapeutic intervention remedies whatever deficits and maladaptive patterns emerge, treatment outcomes will be positive and long-lasting. To ignore any of these modalities is to practice a brand of therapy that is incomplete. Of course, not every case requires attention to each modality, but this conclusion can only be reached after each area has been carefully investigated during problem identification (i.e., diagnosis). A similar position stressing comprehensive assessment and therapy has been advocated by Kanfer and Saslow (1968).

Problem Identification

Faulty problem identification (inadequate assessment) is probably the greatest impediment to successful therapy. The major advantage of a multimodal orientation is that it provides a systematic framework for conceptualizing presenting complaints within a meaningful context. A young man with the seemingly monosymptomatic complaint of "claustrophobia" was seen to be troubled by much more than "confined or crowded spaces" as soon as the basic modalities had been scanned. The main impact upon his *behavior* was his inability to attend social gatherings, plus the inconvenience of avoiding elevators, public transportation, and locked doors. The *affective* concomitants of his avoidance behavior were high levels of general anxiety and frequent panic attacks (e.g., when a barber shop became crowded, and at the check-out counter of a supermarket). The *sensory* modality revealed that he was constantly tense and suffered from muscle spasms. His *imagery* seemed to focus on death, burials, and other morbid themes. The *cognitive* area revealed a tendency to catastrophize and to demean himself. At the *interpersonal* level, his wife was inclined to mother him and to reinforce his avoidance behavior. This information, *obtained after a cursory 10- to 15-minute inquiry*, immediately underscored crucial antecedent and maintaining factors that warranted more detailed exploration as a prelude to meaningful therapeutic intervention.

In contrast with the foregoing case, little

more than *sensory unawareness* in a 22-year-old woman seemed to be the basis for complaints of pervasive anxiety, existential panic, and generalized depression. She was so preoccupied with lofty thoughts and abstract ideation that she remained impervious to most visual, auditory, tactile, and other sensory stimuli. Treatment was simply a matter of instructing her to attend to a wide range of specific sensations. "I want you to relax in a bath of warm water and to examine exact temperature contrasts in various parts of your body and study all the accompanying sensations." "When you walk into a room I want you to pay special attention to every object, and afterwards, write down a description from memory." "Spend the next ten minutes listening to all the sounds that you can hear and observe their effects upon you." "Pick up that orange. Look at it. Feel its weight, its texture, its temperature. Now start peeling it with that knife. Stop peeling and smell the orange. Run your tongue over the outside of the peel. Now feel the difference between the outside and the inside of the peel. . . ." These simple exercises in sensory awareness were extraordinarily effective in bringing her in touch with her environment and in diminishing her panic, anxiety, and depression. She was then amenable to more basic therapy beyond her presenting complaints.

The multimodal approach to therapy is similar to what is called "the problem-oriented record approach." This emphasis upon problem specification is just coming into its own in psychiatry as evidenced in an article by Hayes-Roth, Longabaugh, and Ryback (1972). In medicine this approach to record keeping and treatment is slightly older, being best illustrated by Weed's work (1968). Multimodal behavior therapy not only underscores the value of this new approach, but also provides a conceptual framework for its psychiatric implementation. Let us now turn to a case illustration of its use.

Case Illustration

A case presentation should lend substance to the string of assertions outlined on the foregoing pages.

Mary Ann, aged 24, was diagnosed as a chronic undifferentiated schizophrenic. Shortly after her third admission to a mental hospital, her parents referred her to the writer for treatment. According to the hospital reports, her prognosis was poor. She was overweight, apathetic, and withdrawn, but against a background of lethargic indifference, one would detect an ephemeral smile, a sparkle of humor, a sudden glow of warmth, a witty remark, an apposite comment, a poignant revelation. She was heavily medicated (Trilafon 8 mg. t.i.d., Vivactil 10 mg. t.i.d., Cogentin 2 mg. b.d.), and throughout the course of therapy she continued seeing a psychiatrist once a month who adjusted her intake of drugs.

A life history questionnaire, followed by an initial interview, revealed that well-intentioned but misguided parents had created a breeding ground for guilty attitudes, especially in matters pertaining to sex. Moreover, an older sister, five years her senior, had aggravated the situation "by tormenting me from the day I was born." Her vulnerability to peer pressure during puberty had rendered her prone to "everything but heroin." Nevertheless, she had excelled at school, and her first noticeable breakdown occurred at age 18, shortly after graduating from high school. "I was on a religious kick and kept hearing voices." Her second hospital admission followed a suicidal gesture at age 21, and her third admission was heralded by her sister's sudden demise soon after the patient turned 24.

Since she was a mine of sexual misinformation, her uncertainties and conflicts with regard to sex became an obvious area for therapeutic intervention. The book *Sex Without Guilt* by Albert Ellis (1965 Grove Press edition) served as a useful springboard toward the correction of more basic areas of sexual uncertainty and anxiety. Meanwhile, careful questioning revealed the Modality Profile given below.

The Modality Profile may strike the reader as a fragmented or mechanistic barrage of techniques that would call for a disjointed array of therapeutic maneuvers. In actual practice, the procedures follow logically and blend smoothly into meaningful interventions.

During the course of therapy, as more data emerged and as a clearer picture of the patient became apparent, the Modality Profile was constantly revised. Therapy was mainly a process of devising ways and means to remedy Mary Ann's shortcomings and problem areas throughout the basic modalities. The concept of "technical eclecticism" came into its own (Lazarus, 1967). In other words, a wide array of therapeutic methods drawn from numerous

disciplines was applied, but to remain theoretically consistent, the active ingredients of every technique were sought within the province of social learning theory.

In Mary Ann's case, the array of therapeutic methods selected to restructure her life included familiar behavior therapy techniques such as desensitization, assertive training, role-playing, and modeling, but many additional procedures were employed such as time projection, cognitive restructuring, eidetic imagery, and exaggerated role-taking as described in some of the writer's recent publications (1971a, 1972). The empty chair technique (Perls, 1969) and other methods borrowed from Gestalt therapy and encounter group procedures were added to the treatment regimen. Mary Ann was also seen with her parents for eight sessions, and was in a group for 30 weeks.

During the course of therapy she became engaged and was seen with her fiancé for premarital counseling for several sessions.

The treatment period covered the span of 13 months at the end of which time she was coping admirably without medication and has continued to do so now for more than a year. This case was chosen for illustrative purposes because so often, people diagnosed as "psychotic" receive little more than chemotherapy and emotional support. Yet, in the writer's experience once the florid symptoms are controlled by medication, many people are amenable to multimodal behavior therapy. It is tragic that large numbers of people who can be reached and helped by multimodal behavior therapy are often left to vegetate.

Conclusions

Those who favor working with one or two specific modalities may inquire what evidence there is to support the contention that multimodal treatment is necessary. At present, the writer's follow-up studies have shown that relapse all too commonly ensues after the usual behavior therapy programs, despite the fact that behavioral treatments usually cover more modalities than most other forms of therapy. Of course, the run-of-the-mill behavior therapist does not devote as much attention to imagery techniques as we are advocating (even when using covert reinforcement procedures and imaginal desensitization), nor

Modality	Problem	Proposed Treatment
Behavior	Inappropriate withdrawal responses	Assertive training
	Frequent crying	Nonreinforcement
	Unkempt appearance	Grooming instructions
	Excessive eating	Low calorie regimen
	Negative self-statements	Positive self-talk assignments
	Poor eye contact	Rehearsal techniques
	Mumbling of words with poor voice projection	Verbal projection exercises
	Avoidance of heterosexual situations.	Re-education and desensitization
Affect	Unable to express overt anger	Role playing
	Frequent anxiety	Relaxation training and reassurance
	Absence of enthusiasm and spontaneous joy	Positive imagery procedures
	Panic attacks (Usually precipitated by criticism from authority figures)	Desensitization and assertive training
	Suicidal feelings	Time projection techniques
	Emptiness and aloneness	General relationship building
Sensation	Stomach spasms	Abdominal breathing and relaxing
	Out of touch with most sensual pleasures	Sensate focus method
	Tension in jaw and neck	Differential relaxation
	Frequent lower back pains	Orthopedic exercises
	Inner tremors	Gendlin's focusing method (Lazarus, 1971a, p.232)
Imagery	Distressing scenes of sister's funeral	Desensitization
	Mother's angry face shouting "You fool!"	Empty chair technique
	Performing fellatio on God	Blow up technique (implosion)
	Recurring dreams about airplane bombings	Eidetic imagery invoking feelings of being safe
Cognition	Irrational self-talk: "I am evil." "I must suffer." "Sex is dirty." "I am inferior."	Deliberate rational disputation and corrective self-talk
	Syllogistic reasoning, overgeneralization	Parsing of irrational sentences
	Sexual misinformation	Sexual education
Interpersonal relationships	Characterized by childlike dependence	Specific self-sufficiency assignments
	Easily exploited /submissive	Assertive training
	Overly suspicious	Exaggerated role taking
	Secondary gains from parental concern	Explain reinforcement principles to parents and try to enlist their help
	Manipulative tendencies	Training in direct and confrontative behaviors

does he delve meticulously enough into cognitive material, being especially neglectful of various philosophical values and their bearing on self-worth.

Another fact worth emphasizing is that in order to offset "future shock," multimodal therapy attempts to anticipate areas of stress that the client is likely to experience in time to come. Thus, one may use imaginal rehearsal to prepare people to cope with the marriage of a child, a possible change in occupation, the purchase of a new home, the process of aging, and so forth. In my experience, these psychological "fire drills" can serve an important preventive function.

As one investigates each modality, a clear understanding of the individual and his interpersonal context emerges. Even with a "simple phobia," new light is shed, and unexpected information is often gleaned when examining the behavioral, affective, sensory, imaginal, cognitive, and interpersonal consequences of the avoidance responses. Whenever a plateau is reached in therapy and progress falters, the writer has found it enormously productive to examine each modality in turn in order to determine a possibly neglected area of concern. More often than not, new material emerges and therapy proceeds apace.

REFERENCES

Bandura, A. *Principles of behavior modification.* New York: Holt, Rinehart and Winston, 1969.

Bergin, A. E. The evaluation of therapeutic outcomes. In Bergin, A.E., & Garfield, S.L., Eds. *Handbook of psychotherapy and behavior change,* pp. 217–270. New York: Wiley, 1971.

Blake, B. G. The application of behavior therapy to the treatment of alcoholism. *Behavior Research and Therapy,* 1965, *3,* 75–85.

Colby, K. M. Psychotherapeutic processes. *Annual Review of Psychology,* 1964, *15,* 347–370.

Frank, J. D. Therapeutic factors in psychotherapy. *American Journal of Psychotherapy,* 1971, *25,* 350–361.

Hayes-Roth, F., Longabaugh, R., & Ryback, R. The problem-oriented medical record and psychiatry. *British Journal of Psychiatry,* 1972, *121,* 27–34.

Kanfer, F.H., & Saslow, G. Behavioral diagnosis. In C. M. Franks, Ed. *Behavior therapy: Appraisal and status,* pp. 417–444. New York: McGraw-Hill, 1969.

Lazarus, A. A. Towards the understanding and effective treatment of alcoholism. *South African Medical Journal,* 1965, *39,* 736–741.

Lazarus, A. A. In support of technical eclecticism. *Psychological Reports,* 1967, *21,* 415–416.

Lazarus, A. A. *Behavior therapy and beyond.* New York: McGraw-Hill, 1971.(a)

Lazarus, A. A. Notes on behavior therapy, the problem of relapse and some tentative solutions. *Psychotherapy: Theory, Research & Practice,* 1971, *8,* 192–196.(b)

Lazarus, A. A., Ed. *Clinical behavior therapy.* New York: Brunner/Mazel, 1972.

Lesse, S. Anxiety—Its relationship to the development and amelioration of obsessive-compulsive disorders. *American Journal of Psychotherapy,* 1972, *26,* 330–337.

Lowen, A. *The betrayal of the body.* New York: Macmillan, 1967.

Masters, W. H., & Johnson, V. E. *Human sexual inadequacy.* Boston: Little Brown, 1970.

Perls, F. S. *Gesalt therapy verbatim.* Lafayette, California: Real People Press, 1969.

Reisman, J. M. *Toward the integration of psychotherapy.* New York: Wiley, 1971.

Weed, L. L. Medical records that guide and teach. *New England Journal of Medicine,* 1968, *278,* 593–600.

Woody, R. H. *Psychobehavioral counseling and therapy.* New York: Appleton-Century-Crofts, 1971.

Conclusion

∽

46 An Integrative Theory of Personality and Psychopathology

Theodore Millon

Introduction

There are those who contend that the major traditions of psychology and psychiatry have, for too long now, been doctrinaire in their assumptions. These critics claim that theories which focus their attention on only one level of data cannot help but generate formulations that are limited by their narrow preconceptions; moreover, their findings must, inevitably, be incompatible with the simple fact that psychological processes are multidetermined and multidimensional in expression. In rebuttal, those who endorse a single-level approach assert that theories which seek to encompass this totality will sink in a sea of data that can be neither charted conceptually nor navigated methodologically. Clearly, those who undertake to propose "integrative theories" are faced with the formidable task, not only of exposing the inadequacies of single-level theories, but of providing a convincing alternative that is both comprehensive and systematic. It is for the reader to judge whether integrative theorists possess the intellectual skills and analytic powers necessary, not only to penetrate the vast labyrinths of man's mind and behavior, but to chart these intricate pathways in a manner that is both conceptually clear and methodologically testable.

As the title of this paper suggests, an attempt will be made to formulate a schema that is neither doctrinaire nor loosely eclectic in its approach; rather, the theory presented is intended to be both broad in scope and sufficiently systematic in its application of principles to enable the major varieties of psychopathology to be derived logically and

Abridged from T. Millon, *Disorders of Personality, DSM-III, Axis II*, Wiley-Interscience, 1981.

coherently. In the following sections a few of the major themes of the model will be provided in condensed form.

Biosocial Development

A. For pedagogical purposes, it is often necessary to separate biogenic from psychogenic factors as influences in personality development; this bifurcation does not exist in reality. Biological and experiential determinants combine and interact in a reciprocal interplay throughout life. This sequence of biogenic—psychogenic interaction evolves through a never-ending spiral; each step in the interplay builds upon prior interactions and creates, in turn, new potentialities for future reactivity and experience. *Etiology in psychopathology may be viewed, then, as a developmental process in which intraorganismic and environmental forces display not only a reciprocity and circularity of influence but an orderly and sequential continuity throughout the life of the individual.*

The circular feedback and serially unfolding character of the developmental process defy simplification, and must constantly be kept in mind when analyzing the etiological background of personality. There are few unidirectional effects in development; it is a multideterminant transaction in which a unique pattern of biogenic potentials and a distinctive constellation of psychogenic influences mold each other in a reciprocal and successively more intricate fashion.

B. Each individual is endowed at conception with a unique set of chromosomes that shapes the course of his physical maturation and psychological development. The physical and psychological characteristics of children are in large measure similar to their parents because they possess many of the same genetic units. Children are genetically disposed to be similar to their parents not only physically but also in stamina, energy, emotional sensitivity, and intelligence.

Each infant displays a distinctive pattern of behaviors from the first moments after birth. These characteristics are attributed usually to the infant's "nature," that is, his constitutional makeup, since it is displayed prior to the effects of postnatal influences.

It is erroneous to assume that children of the same chronological age are comparable with respect to the level and character of their biological capacities. Not only does each infant start life with a distinctive pattern of neurological, physiochemical, and sensory equipment, but he progresses at his own maturational rate toward some ultimate but unknown level of potential. Thus, above and beyond initial differences and their not insignificant consequences are differences in the rate with which the typical sequence of maturation unfolds. Furthermore, different regions in the complex nervous system within a single child may mature at different rates. To top it all, the potential or ultimate level of development of each of these neurological capacities will vary widely, not only among children but within each child.

C. The maturation of the biological substrate for psychological capacities is anchored initially to genetic processes, but its development is substantially dependent on environmental stimulation. The concept of *stimulus nutriment* may be introduced to represent the belief that the quantity of environmental experience activates chemical processes requisite to the maturation of neural collaterals. Stimulus impoverishment may lead to irrevocable deficiencies in neural development and their associated psychological functions; stimulus enrichment may prove equally deleterious by producing pathological overdevelopments or imbalances among these functions.

D. The notion of sensitive developmental periods may be proposed to convey the belief that stimuli produce different effects at different ages, that is, there are limited time periods during maturation when particular stimuli have pronounced effects which they do not have either before or after these periods. It may be suggested, further, that these peak periods occur at points in maturation when the potential is greatest for growth and expansion

of neural collaterals and other psychologically relevant structures.

Three neuropsychological stages of development, representing peak periods in neurological maturation, may be proposed. Each developmental stage reflects transactions between constitutional and experiential influences which combine to set a foundation for subsequent stages; if the interactions at one stage are deficient or distorted, all subsequent stages will be affected since they rest on a defective base.

1. The first stage, termed *sensory-attachment* in the theory, predominates from birth to approximately 18 months of age. This period is characterized by a rapid maturation of neurological substrates for sensory processes, and by the infant's attachment and dependency on others.

2. The second stage, referred to as *sensorimotor-autonomy*, begins roughly at 12 months and extends in its peak development through the sixth year. It is characterized by a rapid differentiation of motor capacities which coordinate with established sensory functions; this coalescence enables the young child to locomote, manipulate, and verbalize in increasingly skillful ways.

3. The third stage, called the period of *intracortical-initiative*, is primary from about the fourth year through adolescence. There is a rapid growth potential among the higher cortical centers during this stage, enabling the child to reflect, plan, and act independent of parental supervision. Integrations developed during earlier phases of this period undergo substantial reorganization as a product of the biological and social effects of puberty.

E. Maladaptive consequences can arise as a result of either stimulus impoverishment or stimulus enrichment at each of the three stages.

1. From experimental animal research and naturalistic studies with human infants, it appears that marked stimulus impoverishment during the sensory-attachment period will produce deficiencies in sensory capacities and a marked diminution of interpersonal sensitivity and behavior. There is little evidence available with regard to the effects of stimulus enrichment during this stage; it may be proposed, however, that excessive stimulation results in hypersensitivities, stimulus seeking behaviors, and abnormal interpersonal dependencies.

2. Deprived of adequate stimulation during the sensorimotor stage, the child will be deficient in skills for behavioral autonomy, will

display a lack of exploratory and competitive activity, and be characterized by timidity and submissiveness. In contrast, excessive enrichment and indulgence of sensorimotor capacities may result in uncontrolled self-expression, narcissism and, social irresponsibility.

3. Among the consequences of understimulation during the intracortical-initiative stage is an identity diffusion, an inability to fashion an integrated and consistent purpose for one's existence, and an inefficiency in channeling and directing one's energies, capacities and impulses. Excessive stimulation, in the form of overtraining and overguidance, results in the loss of several functions, notably spontaneity, flexibility, and creativity.

F. There has been little systematic attention to the child's own contribution to the course of his development. Environmental theorists of psychopathology have viewed disorders to be the result of detrimental experiences that the individual has had no part of producing himself. This is a gross simplification. Each infant possesses a biologically based pattern of reaction sensitivities and behavioral dispositions which shape the nature of his experiences and may contribute directly to the creation of environmental difficulties.

The biological dispositions of the maturing child are important because they strengthen the probability that certain kinds of behavior will be learned.

Highly active and responsive children relate to and learn about their environment quickly. Their liveliness, zest, and power may lead them to a high measure of personal gratification. Conversely, their energy and exploratory behavior may result in excess frustration if they overaspire or run into insuperable barriers; unable to gratify their activity needs effectively, they may grope and strike out in erratic and maladaptive ways.

Adaptive learning in constitutionally passive children also is shaped by their biological equipment. Ill-disposed to deal with their environment assertively and little inclined to discharge their tensions physically, they may learn to avoid conflicts and step aside when difficulties arise. They are less likely to develop guilt feelings about misbehavior than active youngsters who more frequently get into trouble, receive more punishment, and are therefore inclined to develop aggressive feelings toward others. But in their passivity, these youngsters may deprive themselves of rewarding experiences and relationships; they may

feel "left out of things" and become dependent on others to fight their battles and to protect them from experiences they are ill-equipped to handle on their own.

It appears clear from studies of early patterns of reactivity that *constitutional tendencies evoke counterreactions from others which accentuate these initial dispositions.* The child's biological endowment shapes not only his behavior but that of his parents as well.

If the child's primary disposition is cheerful and adaptable and has made his care easy, the mother will tend quickly to display a positive reciprocal attitude; conversely, if the child is tense and wound up, or if his care is difficult and time consuming, the mother will react with dismay, fatigue, or hostility. Through his own behavioral disposition then, the child elicits a series of parental behaviors which reinforce his initial pattern.

Unfortunately, the reciprocal interplay of primary patterns and parental reactions has not been sufficiently explored. It may prove to be one of the most fruitful spheres of research concerning the etiology of psychopathology and merits the serious attention of investigators. The *biosocial-learning approach* presented in this paper stems largely from the thesis that the child's constitutional pattern shapes and interacts with his social reinforcement experiences.

G. The fact that early experiences are likely to contribute a disproportionate share to learned behavior is attributable in part to the fact that their effects are difficult to extinguish. This resistance to extinction stems largely from the fact that learning in early life is presymbolic, random, and highly generalized.

Additional factors which contribute to the persistence and continuity of early learnings are social factors such as the repetitive nature of experience, the tendency for interpersonal relations to be reciprocally reinforcing, and the perseverance of early character stereotypes.

Beyond these are a number of self-perpetuating processes which derive from the individual's own actions. Among them are protective efforts which constrict the person's awareness and experience, the tendency to perceptually and cognitively distort events in line with expectancies, the inappropriate generalization to new events of old behavior patterns, and the repetitive compulsion to create conditions which parallel the past.

Children learn complicated sequences of attitudes, reactions, and expectancies in response to the experiences to which they were exposed.

Initially, these responses are specific to the particular events which prompted them; they are piecemeal, scattered, and changeable. Over the course of time, however, through learning what responses are successful in obtaining rewards and avoiding punishments, the child begins to crystallize a stable pattern of instrumental behaviors for handling the events of everyday life. These coping and adaptive strategies come to characterize his way of relating to others, and comprise one of the most important facets of what we may term his personality pattern.

On the Nature of Personality Patterns

A. As noted above, in the first years of life children engage in a wide variety of spontaneous behaviors. Although they display certain characteristics consonant with their innate or constitutional dispositions, their way of reacting to others and coping with their environment tends, at first, to be capricious and unpredictable; flexibility and changeability characterize their moods, attitudes, and behaviors. This seemingly random behavior serves an exploratory function; each child is "trying out" and testing during this period alternative modes for coping with his environment. As time progresses, the child learns which techniques "work," that is, which of these varied behaviors enable him to achieve his desires and avoid discomforts. Endowed with a distinctive pattern of capacities, energies, and temperaments, which serve as base, he learns specific preferences among activities and goals and, perhaps of greater importance, learns that certain types of behaviors and strategies are especially successful for him in obtaining these goals. In his interaction with parents, siblings, and peers, he learns to discriminate which goals are permissible, which are rewarded, and which are not.

Throughout these years, then, a shaping process has taken place in which the range of initially diverse behaviors becomes narrowed, selective and, finally, crystallized into particular preferred modes of seeking and achieving. In time, these behaviors persist and become accentuated; not only are they highly resistant to extinction but they are reinforced by the restrictions and repetitions of a limited social environment, and are perpetuated and intensified by the child's own perceptions, needs and actions. Thus, given a continuity in basic biological equipment, and a narrow band of

experiences for learning behavioral alternatives, the child develops a distinctive pattern of characteristics that are deeply etched, cannot be eradicated easily, and pervade every facet of his functioning. In short, these characteristics *are* the essence and sum of his personality, his automatic way of perceiving, feeling, thinking, and behaving.

When we speak of a personality pattern, then, we are referring to those intrinsic and pervasive modes of functioning which emerge from the entire matrix of the individual's developmental history, and which now characterize his perceptions and ways of dealing with his environment. We have chosen the term pattern for two reasons: first, to focus on the fact that these behaviors and attitudes derive from the constant and pervasive interaction of both biological dispositions and learned experience; and second, to denote the fact that these personality characteristics are not just a potpourri of unrelated behavior tendencies, but a tightly knit organization of needs, attitudes, and behaviors. People may start out in life with random and diverse reactions, but the repetitive sequence of reinforcing experiences to which they are exposed gradually narrows their repertoire to certain habitual strategies, perceptions, and behaviors which become prepotent, and come to characterize their distinctive way of relating to the world.

B. We stress the centrality of personality patterns in our formulations in order to break the long entrenched habit of thinking that all forms of psychopathology are diseases, that is, identifiable foreign entities or intruders which attach themselves insidiously to the person, and destroy his "normal functions." The archaic notion that all forms of illness are a product of external intruders can be traced back to such prescientific ideas as demons, spirits, and witches, which ostensibly "possessed" the person and cast spells upon him. The recognition in modern medicine of the role of infectious agents has reawakened this archaic view; no longer do we see "demons," but we still think, using current medical jargon, that alien, malevolent, and insidious forces undermine the patient's otherwise healthy status. This view is a comforting and appealing simplification to the layman; he can attribute his discomforts, pains, and irrationalities to the intrusive influence of some external agent, something he ate or caught or some foreign object he can blame that has assaulted his normal and "true" self. This simplification of "alien disease bodies" has its appeal to the physician as well; it enables him to believe that he can find a malevolent intruder, some tangible factor he can hunt down and destroy.

The disease model carries little weight among informed and sophisticated psychiatrists and psychologists today. Increasingly, both in medicine and psychiatry, disorders and disturbances are conceptualized in terms of the patient's *total capacity to cope* with the stress he faces. In medicine, it is the patient's overall constitution—his vitality and stamina—which determine his proclivity to, or resistance against, ill health. Likewise, in psychology, it is the patient's personality pattern, his coping skills, outlook, and objectivity, which determines whether or not he will be characterized as mentally ill. Physical ill health, then, is less a matter of some alien disease than it is an imbalance or dysfunction in the overall capacity to deal effectively with one's physical environment. In the same manner, psychological ill health is less the product of an intrusive psychic strain or problem than it is an imbalance or dysfunction in the overall capacity to deal effectively with one's psychological environment. Viewed this way, the individual's personality pattern becomes the foundation for his capacity to function in a mentally healthy or ill way.

C. Normality and pathology are relative concepts; they represent arbitrary points on a continuum or gradient. Psychopathology is shaped according to the same processes and principles as those involved in normal development and learning; however, because of differences in the character, timing, intensity, or persistence of certain influences, some individuals acquire maladaptive habits and attitudes whereas others do not.

When an individual displays an ability to cope with his environment in a flexible and adaptive manner and when his characteristic perceptions and behaviors foster increments in personal gratification, then he may be said to possess a normal and healthy personality pattern. Conversely, when average responsibilities and everyday relationships are responded to inflexibly or defectively, or when the individual's characteristic perceptions and behaviors foster increments in personal discomfort or curtail his opportunities to learn and grow, then a pathological personality pattern may be said to exist. Of course, no sharp line divides normality and pathology; not only are personality patterns so complex that certain spheres of functioning may operate "normally" while others do not, but environmental

circumstances may change such that certain behaviors aand strategies prove "healthy" one time but not another.

Despite the tenuous and fluctuating nature of the normality–pathology distinction, it may be useful to note three criteria by which it may be made: *adaptive inflexibility*, that is, the rigid use of a limited repertoire of strategies for coping with different and varied experiences; *vicious circles*, that is, possessing attitudes and behaviors which intensify old difficulties, and which set into motion new self-defeating consequences; and *tenuous stability*, that is, a susceptibility and lack of resilience to conditions of stress. Together, these three features perpetuate problems and make life increasingly difficult for the unfortunate individual.

Personality Patterns, Symptom Disorders, and Behavior Reactions

A. A classification system will go awry if its major categories encompass too diverse a range of clinical conditions; there is need to subdivide psychopathology in terms of certain fundamental criteria. In this regard, particular attention must be paid to drawing distinctions among patients who appear overtly similar but differ in ways that have significant prognostic consequences. It is for this reason that an attempt is made here to differentiate among personality *patterns*, symptom *disorders*, and behavior *reactions*.

The essential criterion for making these distinctions is the extent to which the observed pathology reflects ingrained personal traits versus transient situational difficulties. Thus, personality patterns are defined as clinical syndromes composed of intrinsic, deeply embedded, and pervasive ways of functioning. At the opposite end of a continuum are the behavior reactions, defined as highly specific pathological responses that are precipitated by and largely attributable to circumscribed external events. Between these two extremes lie the symptom disorders, categories of psychopathology that are anchored simultaneously to ingrained personal traits and transient stimulus events. Conceived as intensifications or disruptions in a patient's characteristic style of functioning, symptom disorders are viewed as a reaction to a situation for which the individual's personality is notably vulnerable.

B. Personality patterns are deeply embedded and pervasive, and are likely to persist, essentially unmodified, over long periods of time. In contrast, behavior reactions are expressed in a narrow range of situations or are weakly anchored to the person's characteristic way of functioning; for these reasons, they can be uprooted readily by proper environmental manipulations. Symptom disorders possess well-delineated clinical features that are less difficult to modify than the ingrained personal traits from which they arise, but are more difficult to extinguish than the situationally manipulable behavior reactions.

Viewed from a different perspective, the traits that comprise personality patterns have an inner momentum and autonomy; they are expressed with or without inducement or external precipitation. In contrast, the responses comprising behavior reactions are stimulus-specific; that is, they are linked to external conditions in that they operate independent of the individual's personality and are elicited by events that are "objectively" troublesome. Symptom disorders are similar to behavior reactions in that they are prompted also by external events, but their close connection to personality results in the intrusion of traits and behaviors that complicate what might otherwise be a simple reaction to the environment.

C. Symptom disorders occur in response to situations that appear rather trivial or innocuous when viewed objectively. Nevertheless, disordered patients feel and respond in a manner similar to that of persons who face realistically distressing situations. As a consequence, symptom disorders fail to "make sense" and often appear irrational and strangely complicated. To the experienced clinician, however, the response signifies the presence of an unusual vulnerability on the part of the patient; in effect, a seemingly neutral stimulus apparently has touched a painful hidden memory or emotion. Viewed in this manner, symptom disorders arise among individuals encumbered with adverse past experiences. They reflect the upsurge of deeply rooted feelings that press to the surface, override present realities, and become the prime stimulus to which the individual responds. It is this flooding into the present of the reactivated past that gives symptom disorders much of their symbolic, bizarre, and hidden meaning.

D. In contrast to symptom disorders, behavior reactions are simple and straightforward. They do not "pass through" a chain of complicated and circuitous transformations before emerging in manifest form. Uncontaminated by the intrusion of distant memories and intrapsychic processes, behavior reactions tend to be rational and understandable in terms of the precipitating stimulus. Isolated from past emotions and from defensive manipulations, they are expressed in an uncomplicated and consistent fashion—unlike symptom disorders, whose features are highly fluid, wax and wane, and take different forms at different times.

E. The terminology and categories of the DSM-III are not differentiated in accord with the preceding discussion; the term *disorder* is applied to all clinical syndromes, including those of "personality disorders." Nevertheless, there is reason to reflect further on these distinctions. For the present, we note once more that personality is a concept that represents a network of deeply embedded and broadly exhibited traits that persist over extended periods of time and characterize the individual's distinctive manner of relating to the environment. Pathological personalities are distinguished from their normal counterparts by their adaptive inflexibility, their tendency to foster vicious circles, and their tenuous stability under stressful conditions.

F. The consistency-specificity issue in personality theory and research corresponds closely to distinctions made in differentiating personality patterns, behavioral reactions, and symptom disorders. Personality patterns are conceived as enduring (stable) and pervasive (consistent) characteristics of behavior, that is, pathological traits that persist over time and are displayed across situations. At the other end of the continuum are the behavior reactions, described as situationally specific pathological responses induced by the conditions of the environment. Symptom disorders lie between these two and are formulated as pathological phenomena that reflect the interaction of personality vulnerabilities and situational stimuli. In essence, symptom disorders represent the interactionist view concerning the origin of pathological symptoms; behavior reactions reflect the situationist position; and personality patterns correspond to the personological perspective. By differentiating the major categories of pathology in accord with the three-fold schema of patterns, reactions, and disorders, a small step will be taken toward distinguishing syndromes in a manner that parallels the three primary sources of pathogenesis, the individual (personological), the environment (situational), and their interaction.

G. Empirical research shows that individuals differ in the degree to which their behaviors exhibit consistency. Moreover, each individual displays consistency only in certain characteristics; that is, each of us possesses particular traits that are resistant to situational influence and others that can be readily modified. Stated differently, the several characteristics comprised in our personality do not display equal degrees of consistency and stability. Furthermore, the traits that exhibit consistency in one person may not exhibit consistency in others. In general, consistency is found only in traits that are central to the individual's style of functioning. For some, what is of significance is being compliant and agreeable, never differing or having conflict; for another, it may be crucial to keep one's distance from people so as to avoid rejection or the feeling of being humiliated; and for a third, the influential characteristic may be that of asserting one's will and dominating others. Thus, each individual possesses a small and distinct group of primary traits that persist and endure, and exhibit a high degree of consistency across situations. These enduring (stable) and pervasive (consistent) characteristics are what we mean when we speak of personality. Going one step further, personality pathology comprises those stable and consistent traits that persist inflexibly, are exhibited inappropriately, and foster vicious circles that perpetuate and intensify already present difficulties.

H. Our attention turns next to specifying the eleven stable and persistent pathological personality patterns that comprise Axis II of DSM-III. Each personality exhibits a distinctive interpersonal coping strategy that persists inflexibly, is exhibited inappropriately, and fosters vicious circles that perpetuate and intensify the individual's prior difficulties. These eleven patterns will be deduced theoretically in the paragraphs that follow.

Interpersonal Coping Strategies That Underlie Personality Patterns

A. This section turns to a formulation that employs a set of theoretical concepts for deducing and coordinating personality syndromes. The full scope of this schema has been published by the author in earlier texts. Identified as a *biosocial-learning theory*, it attempts to generate the established and recognized personality categories through formal deduction and to

show their covariation with other mental disorders.

In reviewing the many theories that have been formulated through the centuries, a reader cannot help but be impressed by both the number and diversity of concepts and types proposed. In fact, one might well be inclined to ask, first, where the catalog of possibilities will end and, second, whether these different frameworks overlap sufficiently to enable the identification of common trends or themes. In response to this second question, we find that theorists, going back to the turn of this century, began to propose a threefold group of dimensions that were used time and again as the raw materials for personality construction. Thus, Freud's "three polarities that govern all of mental life" were "discovered" by theorists both earlier and later than he—in France, Germany, Russia, and other European nations, as well as in the United States. The three dimensions of *active-passive*, *subject-object*, and *pleasure-pain* were identified either in part or in all their components by Heymans and Wiersma, McDougall, Meumann, Kollarits, Kahn, Fiske and Maddi, and others. For example, the subject-object distinction parallels Jung's introversive-extroversive dichotomy; active-passive is the same polarity utilized by Adler and is traceable directly to a major distinction drawn by Aristotle. Clearly, then, a review of the basic ingredients selected for building personality typologies since the turn of the century uncovers an unusual consensus. It is these very three dimensions that were "discovered" once more by the author.

B. When theorists speak of the *active-passive* dimension they usually mean that the vast range of behaviors engaged in by a person may be fundamentally grouped in terms of whether the individual takes the initiative in shaping surrounding events or whether behavior is largely reactive to those events. The distinction of *pleasure-pain* recognizes that motivations are ultimately aimed in one of two directions, toward events which are attractive or positively reinforcing versus away from those which are aversive or negatively reinforcing. Similarly, the distinction of subject-object, or *self-other*, recognizes that among all objects and things in our environment there are two that stand out above all others in their power to affect us: our own selves and others. Using this threefold framework as a foundation, the author derived a series of personality "coping strategies" that correspond in close detail to each of the "official" personality disorders in the DSM-III.

Coping strategies may be viewed as complex forms of instrumental behavior, that is, ways of achieving positive reinforcements and avoiding negative reinforcements. These strategies reflect what kinds of reinforcements individuals have learned to seek or avoid (pleasure-pain), where individuals look to obtain them (self-others), and how individuals have learned to behave in order to elicit or escape them (active-passive). Eight basic coping patterns and three severe variants were derived by combining the *nature* (positive or pleasure versus negative or pain), the *source* (self versus others), and the *instrumental behaviors* (active versus passive) engaged in to achieve various reinforcements. Describing pathological strategies of behavior in reinforcement terms merely casts them in a somewhat different language than that utilized in the past.

C. A major distinction derived from the theoretical model is that people may be differentiated in terms of whether their primary *source of reinforcement* is within themselves or within others. This distinction corresponds to the dependent and independent patterns.

Dependent personalities have learned that feeling good, secure, confident, and so on—that is, those feelings associated with pleasure or the avoidance of pain—are best provided by *others*. Behaviorally, these personalities display a strong need for external support and attention; should they be deprived of affection and nurturance they will experience marked discomfort, if not sadness and anxiety.

Independent personality patterns, in contrast, are characterized by a reliance on the *self*. These individuals have learned that they obtain maximum pleasure and minimum pain if they depend on themselves rather than others. In both dependent and independent patterns, individuals demonstrate a distinct preference as to whether to turn to others or to themselves to gain security and comfort.

Such clear-cut commitments are not made by all personalities. Some, those whom we speak of as *ambivalent*, remain unsure as to which way to turn; that is, they are in conflict regarding whether to depend on themselves for reinforcement or on others. Some of these patients vacillate between turning to others in an agreeable conformity one time, and turning to themselves in efforts at independence, the next. Other ambivalent personalities display

overt dependence and compliance; beneath these outwardly conforming behaviors, however, are strong desires to assert independent and often hostile feelings and impulses.

Finally, certain patients are characterized by their diminished ability to experience both pain and pleasure; they have neither a normal need for pleasure nor a normal need to avoid punishment. Another group of patients are also distinguished by a diminished ability to feel pleasurable reinforcers, but they are notably sensitive to pain; life is experienced as possessing few gratifications but much anguish. Both groups share a deficit capacity to sense pleasurable reinforcers, although one is hyperreactive to pain. We describe both of these as *detached* patterns; unable to experience rewards from themselves or from others, they drift increasingly into socially isolated and self-alienated behaviors.

D. Another theory-derived distinction reflects the fact that we instrumentally elicit the reinforcements we seek in essentially one of two ways: *actively* or *passively*.

Descriptively, those who are typically *active* tend to be characterized by their alertness, vigilance, persistence, decisiveness, and ambitiousness in a goal-directed behavior. They plan strategies, scan alternatives, manipulate events, and circumvent obstacles, all to the end of eliciting pleasures and rewards, or avoiding the distress of punishment, rejection, and anxiety. Although their goals may differ from time to time, they initiate events and are enterprising and energetically intent on controlling the circumstances of their environment.

By contrast, *passive* personalities engage in few overtly manipulative strategies to gain their ends. They often display a seeming inertness, a lack of ambition and persistence, an acquiescence, and a resigned attitude in which they initiate little to shape events and wait for the circumstances of their environment to take their course.

E. Using these polarities as a basis, the author derived a classification that combined in a four-by-two matrix the dependent, independent, ambivalent, and detached styles with the activity-passivity dimension. This produced eight basic types, with three severe variants, for a total of 11 theory-derived personality patterns. Despite their close correspondence to the official DSM-III personality disorders, these coping patterns are conceived as heuristic, and not as reified diagnostic entities. In the following paragraphs the eight milder pathological patterns are described first, followed by the three more severe variants. The labels assigned by the author and the DSM-III are noted in parentheses.

1. The *passive-dependent* coping strategy (Millon Submissive personality; DSM-III Dependent disorder) is characterized by a search for relationships in which one can lean upon others for affection, security, and leadership. This personality's lack of both initiative and autonomy is often a consequence of parental overprotection. As a function of these early experiences, these individuals have simply learned the comforts of assuming a passive role in interpersonal relations, accepting whatever kindness and support they may find, and willingly submitting to the wishes of others in order to maintain their affection.

2. The *active-dependent* coping strategy (Millon Gregarious personality; DSM-III Histrionic disorder) shows an insatiable and indiscriminate search for stimulation and affection. This personality's sociable and capricious behaviors give the appearance of considerable independence of others, but beneath this guise lies a fear of autonomy and an intense need for signs of social approval and attention. Affection must be replenished constantly and must be obtained from every source of interpersonal contact.

3. The *passive-independent* coping strategy (Millon Narcissistic personality; DSM-III Narcissistic disorder) is noted by an egotistic self-involvement. As a function of early experience these persons have learned to overvalue their self-worth; their confidence in their superiority may, however, be based on false premises. Nevertheless, they assume that others will recognize their specialness, maintain an air of arrogant self-assurance, and, without much thought or even conscious intent, benignly exploit others to their own advantage.

4. The *active-independent* coping strategy (Millon Aggressive personality; DSM-III Antisocial disorder) reflects a learned mistrust of others and a desire for autonomy and retribution for what are felt as past injustices. There is an indiscriminate striving for power and a disposition to be rejecting of others; these actions are seen as justified because people are unreliable and duplicitous. Autonomy and hostility are claimed to be the only means to head off deceit and betrayal.

5. The *passive-ambivalent* coping strategy (Millon Conforming personality; DSM-III

Compulsive disorder) is based on a conflict between hostility toward others and a fear of social disapproval. These persons resolve their ambivalence not only by suppressing resentment but by overconforming and overcomplying, at least on the surface. Lurking behind this front of propriety and restraint, however, are anger and intense oppositional feelings that, on occasion, break through their controls.

6. The *active-ambivalent* coping strategy (Millon Negativistic personality; DSM-III Passive-aggressive disorder) represents an inability to resolve conflicts similar to those of the passive-ambivalent; however, this ambivalence remains close to consciousness and intrudes into everyday life. These individuals get themselves into endless wrangles and disappointments as they vacillate between deference and conformity, at one time, and aggressive negativism, the next. Their behavior displays an erratic pattern of explosive anger or stubbornness intermingled with moments of guilt and shame.

7. The *passive-detached* coping strategy (Millon Asocial personality; DSM-III Schizoid disorder) is characterized by social impassivity. Affectionate needs and emotional feelings are minimal, and the individual functions as a passive observer detached from the rewards and affections, as well as from the demands, of human relationships.

8. The *active-detached* coping strategy (Millon Avoidant personality; DSM-III Avoidant disorder) represents a fear and mistrust of others. These individuals maintain a constant vigil lest their impulses and longing for affection result in a repetition of the pain and anguish they have experienced with others previously. Only by active withdrawal can they protect themselves. Despite desires to relate, they have learned that it is best to deny these feelings and keep an interpersonal distance.

Three additional personality coping strategies are identified at a moderately dysfunctional level of pathology. They are differentiated from the first eight by several criteria, notably deficits in social competence and periodic (but reversible) psychotic episodes. Less integrated and effective in coping than their milder personality counterparts, they appear especially vulnerable to the strains of everyday life. Their major features and similarities to DSM-III personality disorders are briefly summarized.

9. The author's *cycloid personality* corre-

sponds to the DSM-III "borderline personality disorder" and represents a moderately dysfunctional dependent or ambivalent orientation. These personalities experience intense endogeneous moods, with recurring periods of dejection and apathy interspersed with spells of anger, anxiety, or euphoria. Many reveal recurring self-mutilating and suicidal thoughts, appear preoccupied with securing affection, have difficulty maintaining a clear sense of identity, and display a cognitive-affective ambivalence evident in simultaneous feelings of rage, love, and guilt toward others.

10. The *paranoid* personality is described in a similar fashion by both the author and the DSM-III. It represents a dysfunctional independent coping strategy. Here are seen a vigilant mistrust of others and an edgy defensiveness against anticipated criticism and deception. There is an abrasive irritability and a tendency to precipitate exasperation and anger in others. Expressed often is a fear of losing independence, leading this personality to vigorously resist external influence and control.

11. The DSM-III schizotypal disorder and the author's *schizoid* personality both display a constellation of behaviors that reflect a poorly integrated or dysfunctional detached personality pattern. These persons prefer isolation with minimal personal attachments and obligations. Behavioral eccentricities are notable, and the individual is often perceived by others as strange or different. Depending on whether the pattern is passive or active, there will be either an anxious wariness and hypersensitivity, or an emotional flattening and deficiency of affect.

On the Severity of the Personality Disorders

In presenting the syndromes of personality, we sequenced them in terms of their level of severity. However, a question must be asked: How are severity levels gauged; that is, what criteria are employed to determine whether one personality disorder is typically more severe than another?

Two classification systems in current use pay special attention to criteria differentiating personality disorders along the dimension of severity, those of Kernberg and of the author.

Direct comparison is not feasible since the character types presented by Kernberg do not correspond to the DSM-III personality disorders. Nevertheless, it will be useful to put aside DSM-III comparability and consider the conceptual distinctions that differentiate Kernberg's views from those of the author.

The major distinction between Kernberg and the author is not found in the clinical signs they include to gauge severity but rather in the ones they choose to emphasize. For Kernberg, primary attention is given to the *internal* structural characteristics of the personality, whereas for the author the *external* social system and interpersonal dynamics are given a status equal that of internal organization.

Kernberg focuses on "nonspecific manifestations of ego weakness," as illustrated in shifts toward primary process thinking, defensive operations characterized as "splitting," increasingly primitive idealizations, and early forms of projection and omnipotence. Though differences do exist, both Kernberg and the author identify the following similar features: loss of impulse control, disturbed psychological cohesion, rigid versus diffused ego functions, adaptive inflexibility, ambivalent or conflict-ridden defenses, blurrings of self and nonself, and so on. My own view goes beyond these, however, by stressing a systems perspective that interprets the internal structure as being functional or dysfunctional depending on its efficacy and stability within the context of interpersonal, familial, and other social dynamics. Thus, I speak additionally of such severity criteria as deficits in social competence, checkered personal relationships, digressions from early aspirations, and repetitive interpersonal quandries and disappointments. From this view, severity is conceived as a person—field interaction that includes not only intrapsychic dynamics but interpersonal dynamics as well. Although Kernberg recognizes the importance of internalized object relations, the author assigns them a major role by stressing both "internalized" past and contemporary "real" social relationships. In this way, the boundaries of both structure and dynamics are expanded such that internal structural features are placed within a context or system of external social dynamics.

A positive consequence of broadening the criteria of severity is that personality pathology need no longer be traced exclusively to intrapsychic origins in conflict and defense. By enlarging our vista so as to include interpersonal efficacy within a social context, our reference base for conceptualizing disordered personality has been expanded. A shift from the view that all pathogenic sources derive from internal conflicts is consistent with Fenichel's notion of "sublimation" character types and reinforces the ego analysts' assertion of conflict-free spheres of development and learning. No longer restricted by the limiting intrapsychic outlook, personality disorders can now be conceived best as any behavior pattern that is consistently inappropriate, maladaptive, or deficient in the social and familial system within which the individual operates. And, in accord with this broader systems perspective, several personality syndromes described by the author and formulated for the DSM-III are recognized as having developed "conflict-free"—that is, they are products of inadequate or misguided learning; others, of course, are conceived more traditionally as primarily "reactive"—that is, they are consequences of conflict resolutions. For example, some dependent personalities unfold in large measure as a result of simple parental overprotection and insufficiently learned autonomous behaviors, and not from instinctual conflicts and regressive adaptations.

The logic for broadening the criteria of severity to include the interplay of both individual and social systems seems especially appropriate when considering personality syndromes. Not only do personality traits express themselves primarily within group and familial environments, but the patient's style of communication, interpersonal competency and social skill will, in great measure, elicit reactions that feed back to shape the future course of whatever impairments the person may already have. Thus, the behavior and attitudes that individuals exhibit with others will evoke reciprocal reactions that influence whether their problems will improve, stabilize or intensify. Internal organization or structure is significant, of course, but the character or style of relating interpersonally may have as much to do with whether the sequence of social dynamics will prove rewarding or destructive. It is not only the structural ego capacity, therefore, but also the particular features of social and familial be-havior that will dispose the patient to relate to others in a manner that will prove increasingly adaptive or maladaptive.

B. Utilizing a systems perspective that includes the interplay of both internal and external dynamics groups the eleven personality disorders of the DSM-III into three broad categories.

1. The *first* includes the dependent, histrionic, narcissistic, and antisocial personality disorders. These four personality patterns are *either* dependent or independent in their style of interpersonal functioning. Their intrapsychic structures enable them to conceive of themselves and to deal with others in a relatively coherent, "nonsplit," or nonconflictful manner—that is, in a reasonably consistent and focused rather than a diffused or divided way. Moreover, because the needs and traits that underlie their coping style dispose them to seek out others and to relate socially, they are able either to adapt to or to control their interpersonal environment so as to be sustained and nourished emotionally, and thereby maintain their psychic cohesion.

2. The *second* group, that viewed at a mid-level of personality severity, includes the compulsive, passive-aggressive, schizoid, and avoidant personality disorders. These represent a lower level of functioning than the first group for several reasons. In the two ambivalent types, the compulsive and passive-aggressive personalities, there is a split within both their interpersonal and their intrapsychic orientations; they are unable to find a coherent or consistent direction to focus either their personal relationships or their defensive operations. They are in conflict, split between assuming an independent or dependent stance; hence, they often undo or reverse their social behaviors and frequently feel internally divided. The second pair of this foursome, the two detached types, labeled the schizoid and avoidant personalities in the DSM-III, are judged at a mid-level of severity because they are characteristically isolated or estranged from external support systems. As a consequence, they are likely to have few subliminatory channels and fewer still interpersonal sources of nurturance and stability, the lack of which will dispose them to increasingly autistic preoccupations and regressions.

3. The *third* set, reflecting still lower levels of personality functioning, includes the DSM-III borderline, paranoid, and

schizotypal disorders. All three are socially "incompetent," difficult to relate to, and often isolated, hostile, or confused; hence, they are not likely to elicit the interpersonal support that could bolster their flagging defenses and orient them to a more effective and satisfying life-style. Moreover, a clear breakdown in the cohesion of personality organization is seen in both schizotypal and borderline disorders. The converse is evident in the paranoid, where there is an overly rigid and narrow focus to the personality structure. In the former pair there has been a dissolution or diffusion of ego capacities; in the latter, the paranoid pattern, there is an inelasticity and constriction of personality, giving rise to a fragility and inadaptability of functions.